FINANCIAL MANAGEMENT AND DECISION MAKING

D0898681

FINANCIAL MANAGEMENT AND DECISION MAKING

John Samuels
Michael Wilkes
and
Robin Brayshaw

INTERNATIONAL THOMSON BUSINESS PRESS
I Ⓣ P® An International Thomson Publishing Company

London • Bonn • Boston • Johannesburg • Madrid • Melbourne • Mexico City • New York • Paris
Singapore • Tokyo • Toronto • Albany, NY • Belmont, CA • Cincinnati, OH • Detroit, MI

Financial Management and Decision Making

Copyright © 1999 International Thomson Business Press

I (T) P®   A division of International Thomson Publishing Inc.
The ITP logo is a trademark under licence

British Library Cataloguing-in-Publication Data
A catalogue record for this book is available from the British Library

First published 1999 by International Thomson Business Press

Typeset by Columns Design Limited, Reading, UK
Printed in Italy by L.E.G.O. Spa, Vicenza

ISBN 1–86152–101–4

International Thomson Business Press
Berkshire House
168–173 High Holborn
London WC1V 7AA
UK

http://www.itbp.com

CONTENTS

PREFACE

Financial Management and Decision Making is designed for use both by the academic student and the practising manager. MBA and undergraduate students who need to be aware of the workings of financial markets and of the techniques for decision making on financial issues within companies will each find this book useful. It is also designed to be used by those studying for the financial management examinations of the professional accounting bodies.

This book is written by the authors of the larger volume: *Management of Company Finance* which was first published in 1971. By 1995, *MCF* had reached its sixth edition. In its near 30 year life to date it has so far sold around 150,000 copies. It has proved its value to students and professionals. The sixth edition of *Management of Company Finance* had grown to over 1,000 pages.

It was decided, therefore, to produce a related text with a sharper focus on key issues and which contained less mathematics and fewer theoretical technicalities. Moreover, unlike most books on financial management, *Financial Management and Decision Making* is not based on the situation in the United States. It is firmly grounded on the situation in the UK, in Europe.

The book emphasises the importance of the links between company financial management and the financial community. The reactions of the stock market and the financial institutions to a company's decisions are especially important to the company, and the future of the management of a company can depend upon the stock market. A text on financial management should, therefore, attach considerable importance to the workings of the financial community.

The 1990s have seen the rapid growth in the global financial markets, with a resulting increase in risks. The movement of funds around the world can cause problems for national governments, as has been seen directly in Asian economies such as Indonesia, Thailand, Korea and Japan, and in other parts of the world such as Mexico. Repercussions can be global and the volatility in foreign exchange rates and in interest rates increase the financial risks faced by companies. There is, therefore, an emphasis in *Financial Management and Decision Making* on risk management. Another change over recent years has been the increasing importance of financial derivatives. This topic is also thoroughly covered in the book.

It is surprising how rapidly the subject of company finance alters, what is appropriate at the time of one economic situation becomes outdated by new circumstances. The theory of the subject does not, of course change so quickly, but tends to evolve as new ideas and techniques are developed over time. It is in the day-to-day problems faced by financial managers that most changes occur and for which the perspective provided by *Financial Management and Decision Making* should be valuable.

We would like to express our thanks for help we hav received in the preparation both of this book and the editions of *MCF*, in particular to Scott Goddard, whose imaginative questions have often been used to enliven a particular section. We would also like to thank the Institute of Chartered Accountants in England and Wales and the Association of Chartered Certified Accountants for permission to reproduce a number of their examination questions. And special thanks to Margaret Watson and Karen Hanson for valuable assistance in the preparation of *Financial Management and Decision Making*.

John Samuels
Michael Wilkes
and
Robin Brayshaw

1 THE FINANCIAL ENVIRONMENT

LEARNING OUTCOMES

By the time the reader has finished studying this chapter he or she should:

- understand the issues involved in ascertaining the objectives of the company
- appreciate the complexity of the relationship between the owners of the company and those who manage the company
- understand the significance of institutional investors
- have a basic knowledge of how taxation issues influence company decision making
- have a basic knowledge of the alternative measures of company performance

1.1 INTRODUCTION

In this chapter we shall examine the objectives of the firm. Are the decisions made by those who manage the firm designed to maximize the wealth of the owners of the firm? How are the interests of the other parties involved in a firm taken into account?

We then introduce the theory of business finance. We consider the shareholders, the interest group who are legally the owners of the company, and examine the financial aspects of the relationship between shareholders and managers. By focusing on this relationship we are not suggesting that it is more or less important than that between any of the other interested parties and the company, but these other relationships are subjects for other primarily non-financial books. We consider some of the problems that exist in the relationship between the investment community and companies, problems in the financial environment in which companies have to operate.

Finally we introduce the subject of corporate taxation, an important aspect of the financial environment, and a factor influencing the decision in most areas of finance.

A company has a responsibility towards employees, customers, shareholders, creditors and society. Each of these interest groups sees the role of that company in a slightly different way. This book is concerned with the financial aspects of companies, with the optimal use of their financial resources. Sound financial management is necessary for a company's survival and for its growth. All interest groups benefit from good financial management.

The types of questions that financial management seeks to answer are as follows.

1 What percentage of funds needed by a business should be obtained from borrowing and what percentage from the owners?
2 What percentage of the annual profits should be paid out to shareholders as dividends?

3 Is it worthwhile for the company to replace its existing manufacturing machines with a new computer-integrated system?

4 The earnings per share figure for the company is falling, despite the fact that the manufacturing facilities have been recently modernized. Should a shareholder be concerned?

5 A potential customer has enquired whether the company will sell goods to him or her now, and allow the customer six months to pay. Is it profitable to do so?

6 The bank keeps offering me new types of business loans, but I like the traditional overdraft arrangement. Should I, as financial manager, change my policy?

1.2 OBJECTIVES OF THE COMPANY

One of the long-term objectives of a company must be to make money for its owners, and its future is guaranteed or jeopardized according to the satisfaction, or lack of it, that the shareholders exhibit regarding its performance on their behalf. There are of course many other stakeholders in a company, for example, employees, directors and customers, whose interests must be considered, but it is not possible to compromise on the financial objective.

During particular periods of time it may seem rather optimistic to think in terms of making money for the owners, and in the short term all efforts may have to be devoted to keeping the company liquid and to maintaining the value of the owners' investment. These are, however, only short-term situations, and in the long run the owners of capital must be encouraged to invest in companies by the prospect of gains which are at least as great as those they can obtain from investing elsewhere.

The last century and a half has seen the rise and fall of more than one business philosophy dedicated to the problem of a company's rationale. When enlightened self-interest was a notion dear to the hearts of nineteenth-century capitalists, it was fashionable to justify the company almost exclusively as a quasi-benevolent institution satisfying a yawning social need by generously providing employment and other opportunities. Today, cynicism permits us to recognize this as a half-truth inspired by some real benevolence and more real guilt. The fact is, and was, that a company must make sufficient money to be able to offer the providers of its capital an attractive return. This is not to deny that it should also attempt to provide all its employees, from directors down, with the means to enjoy an attractive life and to consider the interests of other stakeholders.

All who agree with some form of the capitalist system should not find anything contentious in the preceding paragraphs. However, when we start to consider whether the owners' position should be maximized and the employees' position satisfied or the shareholders' position satisfied and the employees' position maximized, we immediately enter into the political arena – as we do when we start to consider whether the employees of the firm should receive a 2% annual pay rise and the directors of the firm a 20% increase.

The classical view of the firm is that it should be operated so as to maximize profits. Hayek states: 'the only specific purpose which corporations ought to serve is to secure the highest long-term return on their capital' [1]. Milton Friedman states: 'there is one and only one social responsibility of business – to use its resources and to engage in activities designed to increase its profits as long as it stays within the rules of the game [2].

According to this classical approach the objective of the firm should be to maximize the shareholders' wealth, subject to a number of constraints. However, in certain periods of time this approach might not be satisfactory to the values of society. There are many interests represented in a company, and the importance attached to each interest depends on the political system, the attitudes of the community at a particular time, and the bargaining power of the interests at the time. The 1980s and 1990s have been a period where shareholders interests dominate.

The theory of business finance is based on the assumption that the company should seek to maximize the wealth of the shareholder. The shareholders own the company and there is therefore some logic in the idea that it should be run in their interests. Although this is the theory, it is recognized that in practice companies do not always make decisions based on this assumption.

Stakeholders' interests

In recent years much has been written about the fact that companies exist within society and have responsibilities to that society.

We now refer to the stakeholders in a business. These are not only the shareholders and managers, but all employees, customers, suppliers, the local community, and the environment. It is argued that the interests of no one group should prevail to the extent that it excludes the interest of others.

Although much is written about stakeholders' interests, such interests are often only seen as relevant to the extent that they help create shareholder values. Although there is discussion on stakeholders' interests, there is also increasing emphasis on economic values and the creation of shareholder value. There is also increasing concern with making managers more accountable to shareholders.

Do managers or directors really run the business in the shareholders' interests or their own? Managers have considerable discretion. Managers have more information about the opportunities available to a company than do shareholders. Managers do on occasions have different interests from those of shareholders. For example, in some circumstances managers might be less willing to become involved in a risky investment than would a shareholder. If a project fails the manager's career might be ruined, but to a diversified shareholder, it is just a loss in one part of a portfolio.

In many situations it is difficult for the shareholders of a company to know whether or not a manager is doing a good job. Without knowing the opportunities available to managers, outsiders tend to compare the performance of a company 'relative' to the performance of similar companies. This provides an incentive for managers in different companies to pursue similar strategies: for them not to stick their head out.

Even some compensation schemes which are designed to encourage goal congruence are based on relative performance. For example, executive share-option schemes reward directors for movements in the company's share price which are influenced by the overall level of stock-market prices, rather than offering rewards for extraordinary performance.

A commonly assumed objective of business is to maximize profits. The theory of finance refined this concept and for a long period of time it was assumed that the objective of a business was to maximize the owners' wealth. With the separation of ownership and control of many businesses, it became appreciated that widely dispersed shareholders often only exercise a limited control over managers.

Managers, the so-called agents of the owners, have in many companies a considerable amount of freedom. It is in managers' interests to produce corporate plans and mission statements written in terms of creating 'shareholder value', but in reality we have to appreciate that certain decisions taken within a company will be of greater benefit to managers than to shareholders.

The difficulty arises because in large and medium-sized companies control and investment are usually in different hands. The shareholders have to leave the decision making to the top management of the company, who may well be looking for rewards other than through returns on the small number of shares that they own. Top management is concerned with salaries, pensions, executive life style and security. Top management is in a good position to look after its own interests.

The top managers are acting as agents of the shareholders. Shareholders may attempt to bring about 'goal congruence' through share-option schemes. But with other rewards to take into account there is no reason to believe that top management will always be seeking to maximize shareholders' wealth. It is not easy for the owners to monitor the actions of the top managers, and it is expensive to try to do so. In using the funds they manage, to look after their own position and/or that of the shareholders, it is often said that in the UK this leads to 'short-termism'. The environment in which they manage gives greater rewards for short-term performance than for long-term performance. They are motivated to take advantage of any short-term opportunities that arise.

Whether the directors maximize or satisfy the shareholders' interests, at least they must be aware of the share price, for it is through capital gains, i.e. increases in share price, that the shareholders receive much of their return. They must be aware of how the decisions they take will influence the share price.

Not only must a company earn a return on its shareholders' funds, it must ensure that its earning power is reflected in its share price. It is possible to have two companies with identical profit performance and potential, and yet for one to have a higher stock-market value than the other simply because one group of directors is more concerned than the other group about their stock-market image.

The stock-market price is possibly the most important single criterion by which the company is judged. An increasing share price, or one that is falling less quickly than the market index, will keep the shareholders content, and the management will have little reason to worry about survival or a takeover. If the company is prospering nicely but failing to reflect the fact in its share price, it becomes of course an ideal candidate for a takeover, and in the event of being swallowed up – or fired – the management would have no one to blame but themselves for neglecting the shareholders' interests by failing to ensure that the company's true future earning ability was reflected in its share price.

1.3 THE SHAREHOLDERS

The importance ascribed to the role of the shareholders has changed in recent years. It was once common to play down their influence; though legally the owners of the business, it was assumed that they did not much concern themselves with the way that the company was run. Some of them might make their opinions known at the annual general meeting, but usually few of them attend, and in any case the directors could well have obtained enough proxy votes to overcome any opposition.

This position has changed, partly because of a change in the type of shareholder, partly as a result of takeover activity and partly because of social pressure.

The characteristics of the typical shareholder have changed. No longer can he or she be regarded as an individual afflicted with a comforting inability to read a balance sheet. The growth of shareholding by institutions has been dramatic, and these institutions employ experts to advise on the investment of their funds. The financial performance of a company is thus judged by a knowledgeable body of people who may be either existing or potential shareholders. The company must accordingly be run in a way that guarantees the satisfaction of the shareholder – an increasingly sophisticated shareholder, who will be both competent and keen to assess the truth behind any optimistic statements.

Table 1.1 *Beneficial ownership of UK equities (in percentages) 1963–93*

	1963	1969	1975	1981	1990	1993
Pension funds	6.4	9.0	16.8	26.7	31.6	34.2
Insurance companies	10.0	12.2	15.9	20.5	20.4	17.3
Unit trusts	1.3	2.9	4.1	3.6	6.1	6.6
Banks	1.3	1.7	0.7	0.3	0.7	0.6
Investment trusts, and other financial institutions	11.3	10.1	10.5	6.8	2.3	3.1
Individuals	54.0	47.4	37.5	28.2	20.3	17.7
Other personal sector	2.1	2.1	2.3	2.2	1.9	1.6
Public sector	1.5	2.6	3.6	3.0	2.0	1.3
Industrial and commercial sector	5.1	5.4	3.0	5.1	2.8	1.5
Overseas	7.0	6.6	5.6	3.6	11.8	16.3
Total	100	100	100	100	100	100

Source: Central Statistical Office.

In the UK, as in many other countries with a developed financial system, institutions now own the vast majority of shares. In the UK they now own nearly 85% of the value of listed equity shares. The main institutional holders are the insurance companies, the pension funds, the investment trusts and the unit trusts. This ownership pattern results from the savings of individuals flowing to pension funds and insurance companies partly because of the tax advantages arising from contractual savings schemes. The unit trusts have also been successful in attracting the savings of private investors.

Table 1.1 shows the estimated ownership of UK equity shares by different categories up to 1993. The points to observe are:

1 The dramatic increase in the percentage of total shares held by the pension funds and to a lesser extent by the insurance companies. Although these institutions only account for a small percentage of the total bargains conducted on the Stock Exchange, the average bargain size with which they are involved makes them the major players in the markets.

2 The growth of overseas ownership of UK equities. The increase has been particularly fast in recent years; it increased from 11.8% in 1990 to 13.1% in 1992 and then to 16.3% in 1993. This growth reflects the globalization of financial markets with portfolio funds moving around the world seeking high returns.

   It should be appreciated that most of this investment is by institutional investors. The US accounted for 41.8% of the known origin of this investment, with European Union countries responsible for only 15%.

3 The considerable decline in the percentage of shares held by individuals. The importance of the individual investor declined, but not the number of investors.

4 The banks in the UK only own a very small percentage of the equity of companies. This contrasts with the position in many other countries, and reflects a deliberate policy on the part of UK banks. By way of contrast, in Japan banks own 19% of the equity shares of listed companies, and in Germany banks own 10%.

5 Other companies (non-financial) only own a small percentage of outstanding shares. This again contrasts with the situation in certain other countries that have a different system of corporate governance. What is called 'interlocking shareownership' is common in Germany, where non-financial companies own 42% of the listed equity shares, and in Japan, where they own 25%.

This trend in institutional holdings has caused concern because of the increasing levels of concentration of ownership. It has also caused problems because, as a result of the channelling of the funds available for investment into a few hands, certain classes of business have found it difficult to obtain finance. The institutions have shown a preference for listed shares and, in particular, for the shares of the very large companies.

The reasons are perfectly understandable. The institutions wish to hold investments that are easily marketable, and it can be difficult to dispose of shares in unquoted companies. It is easy for them to obtain information on the large publicly quoted companies. The administrative costs are reduced if an institution invests in a few large shareholdings rather than holding a few shares in many companies. It is not necessary to hold shares of a large number of companies in order to spread risk. It has been shown that most of the advantages of diversification can be obtained from holding the shares of 30–40 companies. Yet another reason, if another is needed, is that the institutions wish to be in a position to unload a large number of shares on the stock market quickly without moving the share price by more than a few pence, and this would not be possible if the shares were those of a smaller company where the one holding would be a large proportion of the total company shares.

The attitude towards investing in smaller and medium-sized companies has changed over recent years. Partly because of political pressure, partly because of changes in the capital markets and partly because of tax changes, the equity shares of smaller companies have become attractive to investors. The Alternative Investment Market (AIM), like its predecessor, the Unlisted Securities Market (USM), attracts both new smaller and medium-sized companies seeking funds and financial institutions with funds to invest. There is even a market in the shares of unquoted companies.

1.4 CORPORATE GOVERNANCE

This topic, which became of increasing interest in the late 1980s, is concerned with who governs a company and in whose interest it is run. In small private companies there is usually no conflict of interest. The owners of the company are the same people who make the key management decisions and who control the company. But with larger companies there has been for a long time a 'divorce' of ownership and control. Those who provide the funds are not the same people as those who control the company.

The various Companies Acts are explicit, in that the directors of a company are supposed to run the company in the interests of the shareholders. However, when ownership and control become separated there are situations in which there is a potential conflict of interest between shareholders and managers. Managers may be motivated to behave in a way which from the shareholders' point of view is sub-optimal. In 1989 Charkham, in a Bank of England discussion paper, raised the question of whether there is the possibility that our system (the UK system), 'so excellent when viewed in isolation, may put us at a disadvantage in international competition by those who have superior linkages and lines of accountability within it, and a greater sense of patience?' [3].

The governance debate centres on whether the relationship between the owners and the controllers of a business that exists in the UK puts us at a disadvantage to our European and Japanese competitors. A similar concern exists in the USA. The UK and US Systems are similar in that they rely on the market to exercise control (an external control system). This contrasts with the more flexible relationship between providers of finance and managers to be found with many of our major competitors, who have stronger internal control systems.

Internal control means that within the structure of the company through committees and boards, the top management of the company is subject to control. Top management is accountable. External control means that investors in the market place control top management. If they do not like decisions being made by the directors of a company or are dissatisfied with the performance of the company they let their feelings be known. They can do this either by voting at annual general meetings (using their voice) or they can take an 'exit' route by selling their shares (voting with their feet). With external control top management might not be strongly controlled within the company, but they are aware they are ultimately accountable in the market place. We will briefly examine (a) problems with the system in the UK, (b) how the system of corporate governance in the UK differs from that in our 'competitor' countries and (c) what is being done to change the position in the UK.

The ideal model for accountability in the UK is:

Shareholders	←	Market for corporate control
↑	←	Efficient capital market
↑	←	AGM
	←	Accounting reports true and fair view
Board of directors		
↑	←	Board controls executives
Executive management		

Some of the things that are alleged to have gone wrong with the system in the UK are:

- shareholders pursue own short-term goals (portfolio investors);
- directors act in own interests;
- boards dominated by executive directors;
- non-executive directors in weak position/not independent;
- AGMs do not work (shareholders keep arm's-length relationship);
- market for corporate control (takeovers and mergers):
  – expensive;
  – it is not always the good company that acquires the bad company;
- poor accounting standards (poor monitoring);
- stock market not always efficient.

These failings in the UK system have allegedly resulted in what is known as 'short-termism'. The owners of the company, the vast majority in the UK being institutional shareholders, have been accused of avoiding a long-term involvement with a company. The institutions are themselves under pressure to show good financial performance, so they need to be able to buy and sell the shares of a company as the opportunity for profits arises. They are portfolio investors rather than long-term stakeholders in a company.

There are pressures on institutional investment managers to show good relative returns each quarter in the funds they manage. If they find the performance on their portfolios amongst the lower rankings of the performance league tables they themselves will be removed.

Similar criticisms have been made about the system in the USA. Donaldson [4] and Jensen [5] have pointed to a number of possible areas of conflict which arise in the financial field. One problem is that shareholders and managers have different attitudes towards risk. Shareholders can spread their risks by investing their money in a number of companies; one company may go into liquidation but a diversified shareholders' financial security is not threatened. A manager's financial security, however, usually depends on what happens to the one company that employs him or her. The manager could therefore be less inclined than the shareholder to invest the company's funds in a risky investment. The manager is interested in the total risk position of the company, whereas a diversified shareholder is interested in the systematic risk. These terms will be explained later in the book.

A further situation in which conflict can arise is when a company is the subject of a takeover bid. It has been shown in many studies that the shareholders of acquired firms very often receive above normal gains in share price. However, shareholders of companies that have been the subject of unsuccessful takeover bids do not receive such gains. It can therefore be argued that it is not always in the shareholders' interests for the managers of sought-after companies to put up such a defence as to drive the bidder away. Yet many managers lose either their jobs or their status if the company that employs them is taken over. In whose interests, therefore, do the managers act when their company is the subject of a takeover bid?

Jensen wrote an article entitled 'The eclipse of the public corporation' [6]. He expressed the view that in certain industries for a variety of reasons the present relationship between owners and managers is out of date. He believes it is changing and needs further change. He argues that the clear separation of ownership and control has worked against efficiency and growth. His views are representative of those who want fundamental change. He makes the point that many investors are dissatisfied, and that managers have been putting their own interests first over the last 10–20 years. Golden parachute-type contracts and other perks have shown that managers are not taking the interest of the investor seriously enough.

Rappaport, disagreeing with Jensen, argues against fundamental change. He believes that the existing system will be improved when the USA (and UK) moves to a 'governance system that provides effective monitoring of and checks on managerial authority' [7]. It seems to be agreed that the present system in the UK and USA, with a strong emphasis on external control, is not an effective monitoring system.

There are significant differences between countries within the EU in the form of ownership and control of companies. The UK system is based on the promotion of free markets, and close links between investors and managers, are discouraged by law and stock exchange rules. A major concern is the prevention of insider dealing and the protection of minority-interest shareholders. One result is that with an arm's-length relationship between owners and managers the annual financial reports take on a greater significance. Also there is less opportunity for owners to monitor the decisions and policies of managers.

In France and Germany, traditionally far less emphasis has been placed on the operations of the stock markets. There are therefore less restrictions on the closeness of the relationship between owners and managers. More information is exchanged informally. The financial reports are therefore of less significance, with a more established informal communication system.

Another important difference between countries within the European Union arises because of the different structure of financing by companies. As is well known, UK companies have traditionally worked with lower levels of gearing than companies in other European countries. Debt and equity lead to different forms of corporate governance. Debt governance works mainly through rules, with covenants and other legal restraints restricting the actions of those who manage companies. Equity governance, on the other hand, allows much greater discretion. With a greater proportion of funds being provided through equity, those who run UK companies are more concerned than management in other European countries in creating a favourable impression in the stock market. With an over-active market in corporate control (takeovers and mergers) the short-term survival of the UK manager depends on it.

In Germany, companies have a two-tier board structure. The supervisory board consists of representatives of many interest groups, with far more outside directors involved than is found in a UK company. Most countries have some criticisms of their own system. In Germany the minority shareholders feel their interests are not represented. It is the power and influence of the large banks – through (a) their direct share-holdings in companies, (b) the loans advanced to companies and (c) the votes they can control through the proxy system – that worries many people.

The Cadbury Report and after

In the UK in response to increasing concern about the system of corporate governance, a committee was set up to examine the financial aspects of corporate governance (known as the Cadbury Committee) [8]. They concluded that the basic system of corporate governance in the UK was sound, but did recommend a number of changes.

Two key areas where they thought that changes were necessary were in connection with making the board of directors more effective and increasing the long-term commitment to a company of its institutional shareholders.

They were concerned to prevent a board of directors being dominated by a powerful person, who was both the chairman and chief executive. They wished to ensure that the views of non-executive directors (NEDs) carry weight in board decisions. They recommend that there will be at least three NEDs on a board, and that the people appointed to such positions be of independent minds who could represent the shareholders' interests.

They wished the NEDs to take a leading role in the remuneration committee and audit committees to be set up within companies. They wished to improve the system of internal control that existed in some companies.

The recommendations of the Cadbury Committee were accepted by the Stock Exchange.

The Cadbury Committee was intended to be only the first step towards improved corporate governance in the UK. Following the initial report and recommendations there have been two further committees looking at the problems.

The Greenbury Report on directors' remuneration suggested that institutional investors use their power to influence the way company directors behaved [9]. This was followed by the Hampel Committee [10] which supported the conclusion of the other two committees. It found little fundamentally wrong with the UK system of corporate governance, it endorsed the unitary board structure and rejected the idea of introducing the dual board structure (a supervisory board and a management board) which is prevalent in other European countries.

1.5 PERFORMANCE MEASUREMENT

Shareholders of a company need to be able to monitor the past performance of a company so as to be able to judge the performance of managers. They also need information to enable them to assess the future prospects of a company.

Managers also need performance indicators to enable them to make decisions on some rational basis, and to enable them to control present activities.

What measures should be used to assess performance?

How can we determine whether or not a company is performing well? This of course depends on who is judging the company and what is their relationship to the company. A shareholder wishes to see his or her wealth increase. They wish to see increases in the share price. An employee wants a high income and security. A customer wants a product that is good value for the price paid. An environmentalist has other expectations.

As this book is about finance we are mainly concerned with financial measures.

We have a choice of measures. There are the traditional accounting numbers, such as earnings per share and return on capital employed, and a vast number of new 'trendier' measures.

The managers of companies, or at least some of them, seem surprisingly gullible. They are susceptible to the latest fashionable concept (fad) which is being marketed by business gurus and/or management consultants. In recent years we have been introduced to a number of new ideas or techniques, which, it is suggested, if followed will lead to success for companies. These include:

- mission statements;
- total quality management;
- balanced scorecards;
- financial re-engineering;
- downsizing;
- focus;
- shareholder value added;
- economic value added.

Each of the ideas has been promoted by some management 'guru'. For a while the guru and the supporters of the fad claim that they have discovered an approach which, if followed, will lead to business success. The guru who thinks of the idea and the consulting company that is willing to help with the introduction of the approach of course benefit. The with-it management that follow the latest idea have been referred to as 'fad surfers'. They ride 'the crest of the latest management panacea then paddle out in time for the next one' [11].

Each of these ideas has a life of about five to ten years. Roach, one of the gurus who in the 1980s coined the phrase 'downsizing' (a euphemism for redundancies) was in the 1990s admitting his earlier ideas were wrong. He is reported to have said in the 1990s that if a company competes by building it has a future, but if it competes by cutting it does not.

One interesting anecdote on the subject relates to the stock market's reaction to a Marks and Spencers announcement. In 1996 the chairman of the company announced a 12% increase in annual profits over the previous year's level. He also announced that the company was to create 2000 new jobs. He explained that the company could in the short run make more money by cutting out jobs, but explained that he was 'not interested in the short term. I'm interested in where we are going to be four years from now'. He pointed out that the company 'offer quality products and quality service', and that the new jobs were necessary to maintain standards.

What happened to the share price following this announcement? The shares fell in value: the largest fall in that day of any of the FTSE top 100 companies.

At the time the downsizing ideas were being criticized, a new literature began to appear on 'intellectual capital'. This pointed out that in many businesses investing in fixed assets was becoming of less relevance to success, and it was the intellectual ability of employees that determined business success. It is argued that companies should measure the value of the 'intellectual capital' of their business, and should invest in this. This is what Marks and Spencers are doing.

The financial environment

Of course there are stakeholders who benefit from short term performance.

The problem is that each of the new concepts or ideas referred to above has a use. But none of them provides an answer in all situations. Too many managers seem to be looking for the one management technique that is perfect. Managers and analysts want one performance indicator that can be used to judge success. There is not one. Life and business are not that simple. We will return to this topic in Chapter 2.

1.6 REGULATION OF THE CITY

The control and regulation of the financial sector of the economy is the key to the contribution that sector makes to the growth of the economy and to the distribution of wealth. The two major issues are:

1 Should the regulations be set at a level which will not discourage the inward flow of international finance and so will allow the rapid growth of the 'City' and its institutions or set at a level which keeps 'hot' money out of the City and offers a high degree of protection to investors?
2 Whether supervision should be exercised by those who manage the financial institutions (what is called 'self-regulation') or by those who are more concerned with the interests of the savers and the investors.

Until 1997 the UK relied on self-regulation, the Bank of England regulated the banks and money markets. A number of what were known as self-regulating organizations (SROs) were responsible for controlling different sectors of the investment industry. There were, for example, separate SROs for building societies, for life insurance companies, for the Stock Exchange, for dealers in securities and futures (SFA), for investment managers (IMRO) and for independent personal financial advisers (PIA).

There is a danger that self-regulating bodies can become anti-competitive in nature. An SRO can become more concerned with protecting the interests of its members than with looking after the interests of companies and investors. There is always a danger that bodies representing the interests of one group begin to believe that what is good for their members is good for everyone.

A further problem that emerged was that at the very time when large financial conglomerates were being formed that could deal with all aspects of finance, the regulatory bodies were fragmented. The Department of Trade and Industry does not have the time or experience to be able to handle detailed consideration of the competing interests of the different SROs and to monitor the changes taking place within each aspect of the securities and investment industry.

The self-regulation system in the UK became expensive and not particularly effective. In 1997 the position changed with a move against self-regulation. There were at least three reasons for the change:

1 A number of financial scandals (e.g. BCCI, Barings, Barlow Clowes and the £2 billion involved in the misleading selling of private pension schemes) had indicated that not all was working well with the existing system, investors' interests were on many occasions not being protected.
2 The distinction between the different types of financial institution was becoming increasingly blurred. Building societies becoming banks. Barings, a bank, collapsed as a result of its securities trading activities.
3 A change in government, from Conservative to Labour, meant a different belief in the effectiveness of self-regulators.

Financial Services Authority

The Financial Services Act of 1986 set up a central controlling body (an umbrella organization) called the Securities and Investment Board (SIB) to oversee the regulation of investment business in the UK. One problem was that it had to operate through the numerous SROs. For example, the Bank of England continued to control the banking system, the wholesale money market and the foreign exchange market.

In 1997 the government announced that this was to change: the role of the SIB would pass to a new Financial Services Authority (FSA) which would have increased power. A number of SROs would be merged into the FSA. The new 'super' SIB was to be a statutory authority with sweeping powers over banks, stock exchanges, financial services, financial institutions and companies.

With the change in government in 1997 had come a change in attitude towards the level of regulation required in the City. In the 1980s and early 1990s the belief had been that the best results, in terms of the financial sector's international competitiveness and growth could be achieved by leaving the market place to itself and minimizing regulations. Undoubtedly this policy did lead to rapid growth, but also as has been mentioned, to a number of major scandals. These affected the image of the City of London in international circles. At an international conference in London in April 1997, lawyers from the USA expressed the opinion that a loose enforcement of regulations resulted in too many UK financial institutions turning a blind eye to dollar money-laundering.

With a change in attitude to self-regulating bodies there is planned to be stricter enforcement of the regulations, and a greater involvement of the government as guarantors of the financial system. The FSA, when finding individuals or institutions guilty of breaking the regulatory rules, will on most occasions punish by using civil penalties such as fines or banishing individuals from working in the City. On occasions, however, all the information relating to a case will be passed to the Serious Fraud Office for possible criminal prosecution.

One worry in any stock exchange is the extent of insider dealing. This is trading by certain individuals who are in possession of what is known as 'price-sensitive information'. It means that the person possessing this information is able to gain from trading with an individual who is not aware of the significant information. In the UK such practice is against the law, but it is hard to detect. It is not new: the practice and attempts to stop it have been going on for over 200 years.

In London there is a Stock Exchange surveillance department. This monitors all deals and attempts to detect unusual and suspicious trading. The department looks for large volumes of trading, and unexpected price movements. The Exchange has the power to question the people taking part in any deal to try to ascertain on what basis the investment decisions were made. It is possible that such questioning can lead to prosecution. Unfortunately in the vast majority of the suspicious cases the surveillance department finds there is insufficient evidence to make a prosecution.

The surveillance department identifies between 500 and 2000 deals a day that are unusual, but fortunately well over 99% of these turn out to be innocent.

The Serious Fraud Office

A key aspect of the system of regulation in the UK is the Serious Fraud Office (SFO). It is this office that is responsible for bringing cases of fraud to court. They have to build up the evidence against the likes of BCCI. It was they who made the case against Blue Arrow, a case in which the legal fees were in excess of £50 million.

The SFO is a very large operation. Unfortunately it has been criticized as being too slow, too expensive and not particularly effective. Its biggest enquiry, against BCCI, employed more than 60 people. The amount of fraud is increasing: fraud cases are extremely complex, requiring many accounting, legal and banking experts. In the Blue Arrow case a number of defendants were acquitted because the judge believed the evidence brought to the court by the SFO was too flimsy. Changes have been proposed in the way the SFO operates and whether or not changes are introduced, more money is required to support this office. Fraud in the City and financial community is a serious problem.

1.7 GOVERNMENTS AND GLOBAL FINANCIAL MARKETS

During the 1990s, as the global financial markets grew in size and influence, there was much discussion as to whether real power now lay with those who made decisions that moved financial resources around the world or whether it remained with national governments.

Certainly in the foreign exchange markets, where the daily turnover often exceeds the global stock of official foreign exchange reserves, central banks and governments may well have lost the power to control exchange rates. The cases of the UK, Mexico and Thailand have all shown that governments cannot prevent devaluations taking place when those involved in the foreign exchange markets believe that on the basis of economic fundamentals a currency is overvalued. It might well be men (and women) in grey suits that have more influence on exchange rates than elected politicians.

Governments still have, however, tremendous power over the financial system. Apart from regulations which have already been mentioned, governments are responsible for a major part of a nation's expenditure and for taxation policies.

Government spending as a percentage of GNP in the more advanced industrial nations averaged 47% in 1996 (in the UK it was 42%). This gives governments power to influence which areas of an economy grow and which companies benefit. The money is spent on such items as transfers to the household sector, subsidies, education, health, defence, investment and payment of interest on government borrowing.

Governments also decide on the level of taxation in an economy. They might use taxation to try to influence the flow of finance in and out of an economy. Some tax havens have zero levels of tax. Some countries offer generous capital expenditure allowances in an attempt to encourage inward investment.

Although governments talk about reducing the levels of taxation, and despite the growth of global market forces, the aggregate tax burden has continued to rise. In the European Union taxes were 41% of GNP in 1980, 44% in 1990, and 45% in 1996: governments therefore still have considerable power to influence the flow of funds between countries. What has happened in taxation is that although corporation tax rates and income tax rates have fallen indirect taxes have increased.

1.8 TAXATION POLICY

The problems of corporate taxation have reached proportions of Olympian grandeur and it would be unwise to pretend that anything but the barest outline could be offered adequately within the scope of this chapter. The object of this section is to explain a little of the system as it operates at present and to indicate some of the effects that fiscal policy is having on firms. It must be remembered, however, that the taxation system is one of almost continual change.

Taxation results in a transfer of funds away from the individual or company that has earned the income into the hands of the government. At times this transfer has been justified in that it is the opinion of some that decisions made by the government on the use of these funds are made in the so-called national interest. This leads to a 'better' society than if the decisions are left in private hands. At other times this transfer has been criticized in that it is a disincentive to individuals and companies to work and earn money when it is to be taken away from them. Many people believe that greater prosperity results if decisions on how money is spent are left in the hands of individuals, rather than if made by governments or economic planners.

The government may itself spend the revenue it raises from taxation on consumption or investment. The level of national income of a country largely depends upon the volume of investment undertaken and investment is a function of a number of variables, two of which are the rate of interest and the marginal efficiency of capital. Governments or central banks can adjust the interest rates and governments through fiscal policy can affect the marginal efficiency of capital. If the profits on investment earned by companies are reduced through taxation, the marginal efficiency of capital will decline and this will mean a fall in investment. However, it can be argued that through negative taxation (i.e. by way of grants, subsidies and other transfers from the public sector to the private sector) the government may be able to stimulate investment in the private sector.

A brief description follows of the taxes and allowances under the corporation tax system. The system was introduced in 1966. However, an important change took place in 1973 in the method of applying corporation tax; the UK moved to what is known as 'the imputation system'. Table 1.2 shows the rates of corporation tax that have been in operation from 1966 to 1997.

With the imputation system, a company pays corporation tax at a certain rate on the profits it earns, and the shareholders do not necessarily have to pay any further tax on the dividends received by them. The shareholder is allowed to have part of the tax that the company paid 'imputed' to him or her to offset against tax that would otherwise have to be paid on any dividends received. If the shareholder pays income tax at a rate above the basic rate, the amount he or she is allowed to 'impute' will not be sufficient to discharge all his or her tax liability on the income received. If he or she is paying tax at the basic rate then, after taking credit for the 'imputed' amount, there will be no further tax to pay on the dividends received.

There are shareholders who do not have to pay any income tax – in the past the most significant group being pension funds. Until 1997, pension funds received a refund of the tax deducted from the dividend received. The Budget of 1997 changed this position in that they no longer receive a refund; the dividends they receive are now taxed in a similar way to those of other investors.

Table 1.2 *Rates of corporation tax (%)*

1966–8	42.5	1984–5	45.0
1968–70	45.0	1985–6	40.0
1970–1	42.5	1986–90	35.0
1971–3	40.0	1990–1	34.0
1973–83	52.0	1991–7	33.0
1983–4	50.0	1997 →	31.0

Advanced corporation tax

One aspect of the UK tax system that has existed for many years, but disappears in 1999 is that, near the time dividends have been distributed to the shareholders, the company has had to make an advance payment of corporation tax (ACT). The amount of ACT that has had to be paid depends upon the amount of dividends being distributed and the rates of income tax. This method of tax collection which brings forward the time when companies have to pay tax has its critics. That is why it has been stopped.

We will use an example to illustrate the way the imputation system and ACT has worked.

Meriden PLC has for the year ending 31 March 1996 profits chargeable to UK tax of £2 000 000. The corporation tax rate is 33%. The rate of ACT is 25% of the net dividend. This means that for a dividend paid out of the 1995/96 profits the ACT that has to be paid to the tax authorities is $^{20}/_{80}$ of the amount distributed. The lower rate of income tax is 20%.

The company wishes to pay a dividend to shareholders (net of income tax) of £800 000. The ACT paid by the company would be £200 000 (i.e. ($^{20}/_{80}$) × £800 000). It can be seen that this $^{20}/_{80}$ fraction used in calculating the ACT payment gives the same result as if the gross dividend (£1 000 000) were being taxed in the shareholder's hands at the lower tax rate (£200 000).

(If the lower income tax rate was 25%, the fraction used to calculate ACT would be $^{25}/_{75}$ of the net dividend distributed.)

Taxation of dividends

Dividends are taxed at source. The company is acting as a tax collector for the government. In the Meriden example the shareholders receive £800 000 cash and a tax credit for the £200 000 that has been paid on their behalf. Depending on their individual tax status shareholders may have to pay additional tax, pay no further tax, or receive a refund of the tax paid. If the shareholders are charities, or individuals not eligible to pay tax they will receive refunds.

In some countries dividends paid are not taxed at source, and in many countries interest paid to bondholders is not taxed at source. Most Eurobonds are sold by companies through their financial subsidiaries which are located in countries (referred to as 'tax havens') that allow interest to be paid gross to the bondholder. In theory the interest paid on such bonds is taxed in the country in which the bondholder resides. In fact in most cases no tax is ever paid on such interest payments: neither at source nor in the bondholder's country of residence. The reason is that the tax authorities do not know who owns a large percentage of the vast amount of Eurobonds that have been issued. Eurobonds are bearer bonds, which means there is no register maintained of who owns them. In theory the holder of a bearer bond should declare the receipt of untaxed interest to the tax authority in the country in which he or she resides. In practice very few do this. This avoidance of tax is one reason why the issuing of Eurobonds is more attractive to companies than issuing bonds in a national stock exchange. It reduces the cost of capital to the company. It is also one reason why it is attractive to investors.

Mainstream corporation tax

This was the name given to that part of a company's corporation tax liability that remained to be paid in excess of ACT. Normally it would have been paid approximately nine months after the end of the company's financial year.

In the above example of Meriden PLC the tax bill would be:

Taxable profits	£2 000 000
Total tax payable (33%)	660 000
Advance corporation tax	200 000
Mainstream tax	460 000

From the company's point of view the division of profits would be

Total taxation	£660 000
Cash paid to shareholders	800 000
Retained earnings	540 000

1.9 REFERENCES

1 Hayek, F. (1960) The corporation in a democratic society – in whose interests ought it and should it be run? In *Management and Corporations* (eds M. Asher and C.L. Bach), McGraw-Hill, New York.
2 Freidman, M. (1970) The social responsibility of business is to increase its profits. *New York Magazine*, 30 September.
3 Charkham, J. (1989) *Corporate Governance and the Market for Companies: Aspects of the Shareholder's Role*, Bank of England Discussion Paper, London.
4 Donaldson, G. (1963) Financial goals: management v stockholders, *Harvard Business Review*, May–June.
5 Jensen, M.C. (1976) Theory of the firm: managerial behaviour, agency costs and ownership structure, *Journal of Financial Economics*, **3**.
6 Jensen, M.C. (1989) The eclipse of the public corporation, *Harvard Business Review*, Sept.–Oct.
7 Rappaport, A. (1990) The staying power of the public corporation, *Harvard Business Review*, Jan.–Feb.
8 *Report of the Committee on the Financial Aspects of Corporate Governance*, (1992) Gee, London.
9 Greenbury, R. (1995) *Directors' Remuneration: Report of a Study Group*, Gee, London.
10 Hampel, R. (1997) Committee on Corporate Governance. Preliminary Report.
11 Spariro, E.C. (1996) *Fad Surfing in the Boardroom*, Capstone, Oxford.

1.10 FURTHER READING

Charkham, J. (1994) *Keeping Good Company*, Clarendon Press, Oxford.
Clarke, M. 1986) *Regulating the City*, Open University Press, Milton Keynes.
Economist, (1997) Valuing shares: a star to sail by, 2 August, 61–3.
Miles, D. (1992) Testing for short-termism in the UK Stock Market, Bank of England Working Paper Series, Oct.
Pozen, R.C. (1994) Institutional investors: the reluctant activist, *Harvard Business Review*, Jan.–Feb., 140–9.
Sheridan, T. and Kendall, N. (1992) *Corporate Governance*, Financial Times/Pitman, London.
Tricker, R. (1984) *Corporate Governance around the World*, Gower, Aldershot.
Shleifer, A. and Vishny, R. (1997) A survey of corporate governance, *Journal of Finance*, June, 737–84

Books on taxation include:

Hancock, P.J. *An Introduction to Taxation: Policy and Practice*, Chapman and Hall, London.

James, S. and Nobes, C. (1992) *The Economics of Taxation*, 4th edn, Prentice-Hall, Hemel Hempstead.

Kay, J.A. and King, M.A. (1990) *The British Tax System*, Oxford University Press, Oxford.

1.11 PROBLEMS

1 To what extent is it in the interests of the shareholders of publicly quoted companies to link the rewards of managers to the financial performance of the company?

2 One of the most important elements of any decision is the specification of goals or objectives which the decision-maker seeks to achieve. The capital budgeting literature generally assumes the goal of the firm to be maximization of owner's welfare'. Discuss the rationale for this assumption, highlighting the disadvantages of alternative proposals.

3 Discuss how managers' objectives might differ from those of shareholders, especially if managers are not closely monitored by shareholders and are not subject to constraints and/or incentives imposed by shareholders. Illustrate for these differing objectives the policies that managers might adopt that are likely to be sub-optimal.

4 (a) Explain what is meant by corporate governance.
(b) Briefly discuss the major differences that exist between corporate governance practice in the UK, the USA and Japan.

5 Critically examine the view that *'voice'*-based corporate governance mechanisms are likely to have a greater positive impact on enterprise efficiency than mechanisms which rely on *'exit'*.

6 What are the arguments for and against self-regulation in City institutions?

2 FINANCE AND ACCOUNTING

LEARNING OUTCOMES

By the end of this chapter the reader should be able to:

- calculate and interpret a number of financial ratios
- understand the limitations of such ratios
- understand how they can be used to assess company performance
- appreciate the ways in which 'earnings disclosure' can be managed
- calculate financial ratios based on value added figures and cash-flow figures
- appreciate accounting principles and policies

2.1 INTRODUCTION

There is a close link between finance and accounting, a link that should often be closer than it is. The theories and concepts in the subject of finance are usually developed by economists who have an inadequate knowledge of the technical details of accounting, whilst accountants are often not sufficiently aware of the theories of finance and the economic consequences of accounting reports. In this chapter we try to bring the subjects closer together.

It is important to clarify the relationship between accounting and finance. One role of accounting is what is referred to as the 'stewardship' role. This involves the record-keeping activity and the internal and external audit function with the object of ensuring that the financial resources of the business are spent on legitimate purposes. This is part of the 'accountability' process; those who run the business, the directors and managers, are accountable to the owners of the business, and in fact to a wider social constituency.

An important part of the accountability process is the production of financial reports. These are of particular concern to those who provide finance as the reports enable an analysis to be made of a firm's past actions to assess its current standing and possibly to form opinions about its likely future performance. The fundamental object of financial reports, of the financial statements, is to communicate economic measurements of, and information about, resources and performance of the reporting entity useful to those having reasonable rights to such information. Shareholders, creditors, financial analysts and providers of debt finance are clearly groups with a right to such information.

It is not easy to be able to assess the performance and value of a company on the basis of its published financial reports. There is more to it than just looking at the earnings-per-share figures. The annual report usually contains an optimistic statement from the Chairman, some spectacular photographs of the company operations, photographs of an acceptable group of people who are the directors and what appear to be a boring looking set of numbers.

The standard technique used to analyse financial reports is what is known as 'ratio analysis'. But to do this meaningfully it is necessary to understand a few things about accounting practices and conventions. We shall deal with a few of the difficulties before moving on to ratio analysis.

Undoubtedly the complexity of, and amount of disclosure in, accounting statements has increased as bodies which set accounting standards have tried to improve the communication process between the users and the preparers of accounts.

The Finance Director of BAT Industries in the company's 1995 accounts stated that 'it has to be acknowledged that the various new accounting regulations which came into force during 1995 have made our full Report of Accounts even harder to understand than hitherto'.

Interpreting the information in a company's annual report and accounts is not easy. Professional accountants are paid very large salaries; they would not be if the subject was simple. There is a problem in that many business students think that if they understand a few ratios they will be able to 'read' a set of accounts. A little knowledge in accounting is a dangerous thing. The ratios can only really be understood if the footnotes that accompany the accounts are understood.

But first we need to consider how useful financial accounts are. There is no point in analysing accounts if the results we obtain are of no value. We shall consider the question from four points of view:

1   Are accounting numbers a good measure of company performance? (Section 2.2)
2   What is the impact on share price of the announcement by a company of its annual or interim earnings figure? (Section 2.3)
3   Can knowledge of the past financial performance of a company be used as a guide to future performance? (Section 2.4)
4   Are users of accounts able to 'detect' the correct signal from a set of accounts that have been prepared to 'create' a favourable impression? (Section 2.5)

2.2 PERFORMANCE MEASUREMENT

There are financial and non-financial measures of performance. The latter include market share, customer satisfaction and output in units per worker.

The non-financial measures can be divided into those concerned with production, marketing and administration. These non-financial performance indicators are very important: they are concerned with the factors that contribute to the financial success or failure of a business. They are the drivers of profitability.

Accounting numbers indicate what has happened in the past, and if used wisely can be useful. It is necessary to monitor the past performance of managers. An investor is also interested in the future success of a company, as is a manager. There are indicators other than financial that can be used as a guide to future success or failure. Such performance measures relate to factors on which the future success or failure is based.

The drivers of success in a business include quality, customer satisfaction and investment in intellectual capital. The 1980s and 1990s have seen the development of a number of new approaches to management, many of which rely on a number of performance measures, other than financial.

We will briefly look at two of these approaches.

Balanced scorecard

This refers to a technique that can be used to guide the management of a company and measure the overall performance of a company. It seeks to balance the short-term financial performance goals with the long-term drivers of growth and financial performance.

Companies are often urged to focus on the quality of their products and on the education and training of employees. These are clearly desirable pursuits. They help generate growth and long-term economic value. It is possible to produce non-financial performance measures which indicate how a company is performing against quality and investment in training targets. The problem is: how does a company balance these long-term goals against the short-term need to produce profits? Quality and customer satisfaction can result in good financial results in the long run but do not necessarily improve short-term financial results.

The balanced scorecard seeks to balance the short-run and long-run goals. Kaplan and Norton [1] identified corporate performance measures from four perspectives:

Financial:	Profits
Customers:	What do customers value from a company?
Internal:	In what processes must the company excel?
Innovation and learning:	How can a company create future value?

This approach is comparatively new and is being used in some companies to translate strategic objectives into operational measures. Performance indicators are identified for the many different factors that determine success. These are monitored against targets.

Tableau de bord

The scorecard is a similar idea to one developed in France in the 1950s – the 'tableau de bord'. This again is based on judging performance by observing a range of indicators, some financial and some non-financial. It has been suggested that there is a similarity between controlling a successful business and controlling the flight of an aeroplane. In the latter the pilot sits in front of many dials each indicating something about how well the plane is performing. All the dials need to be observed. When controlling a business, again a number of indicators need to be monitored. 'Tableau de bord' literally means dashboard. The manager monitors key variables, such as orders received, order lead time, process time, quality costs and the lead time to launch a new product. The manager compares actual figures with budgeted figures. People are assigned a responsibility for key variables. The technique is attempting to control the factors that drive profitability.

Every measure is ultimately tied to financial results. For example, employee satisfaction leads to a more sympathetic understanding of customer needs, it leads to developing the products offered, and to better cross-selling of the product line. These three results of employee satisfaction lead to an improvement in the confidence of customers in advice being given. This leads to a broader revenue base, which leads to improved financial results.

Financial performance measures

This book is concerned with finance, and so our emphasis will be on financial indicators of performance. Such performance measures can be divided into four categories, those concerned with:

1 market-based performance;
2 earnings (profits) figures;
3 cash-flow figures;
4 value-added measures.

Market-based performance
Such measures include

- growth in share price;
- dividend yield;
- earnings yield.

These are obviously the measures that are of most concern to shareholders as it is the growth in share price and dividends received that directly affects their wealth.

Earnings (profits) measures
Such measures include

- earnings per share;
- return on capital employed;
- dividend cover;
- growth in capital employed, or in turnover.

All these measures depend on accounting numbers. They depend on assumptions, policies and practices. Even turnover (sales) figures depend on the accounting policies concerned with the timing of income recognition.

Growth in earnings per share is the most popular measure used to measure performance, but as Terry Smith points out, 'A company can generate earnings per share growth without creating any real value for shareholders. There is no relationship between the two numbers' [2].

One problem is that too many of those professionally interested in measuring company performance are looking for a simple solution. There is a long history of the pursuit of 'the one number' that will enable the reader of financial accounts to determine the financial health of a company. There is no such number; there are not even a magic four or five numbers that give an easy solution.

The hope of finding a simple solution can lead to:

1 An 'earnings fixation'. This is simply looking at the bottom line in the financial accounts – the earnings per share.
2 Ignoring the actual published annual financial report and accounts of companies and relying on information from specialized companies supplying summarized information via a computer network. The so-called user of accounts does not even look at the accounts, but relies on a 'potted version' that appears on a computer screen, the 'user' being supplied with all the ratios that can be thought of, but with little detail on the footnotes that need to be read before the numbers used in the ratios can be understood.
3 Looking at a drawing of a face which is supposed to represent the financial health of a company. If the face is smiling the 'analyst' knows the company is performing well; a down-turned mouth indicates concern. This visual approach to presenting performance is not new: it tends to be rediscovered every decade and then quickly forgotten.

Cash-flow measures
Companies now produce cash-flow statements in their annual report and accounts. These provide alternative measures to profits which can be used to judge performance.

Profits are based on accrual accounting. This is a technique for matching events to accounting periods. When measuring profit the revenues of a period are not always the receipts of that period and the expenses are not always the outlays. Sales are recognized in the period in which they are invoiced; payments made in one period that produce benefits in another are treated as expenses of the period in which the benefits are derived. When capital equipment is purchased, the cash flow usually leaves the business immediately, but the cost is spread over the life of the asset by means of a depreciation charge to the profit-and-loss account. Accruals accounting involves a large amount of estimation and judgement. Cash-flow figures do not. It is for this reason that some analysts prefer cash-flow figures to earnings figures.

One cash-flow ratio is

$$\frac{\text{market price per share}}{\text{free cash flow per share}}$$

This is sometimes used as an alternative to the well-known price/earnings ratio when valuing a company. Sometimes in the press reference is made to the fact that one company is acquiring another at a price of say 15 times the free cash flow figure. Table 2.4 shows the cash-flow statement of Guinness for the year 1996. If we take the figure referred to as 'free cash flow before dividends' and calculate this per share, we have a value of £0.21. The share price at the end of June 1997 was £5.70.

This gives a market price/free cash flow ratio of

$$\frac{£5.70}{£0.21} = 27 \text{ to } 1$$

At the time the price/earnings ratio was 16 to 1.

The free cash flow figure before dividends gives the cash generated during the year that would be free to distribute to each shareholder if the company should choose to do so. Cash figures can be very volatile from year to year, because unlike the earnings of the company there is no attempt to smooth cash-flow receipts and payments. There may, for example, in one year be a large investment in fixed assets, whereas in another year there might be large receipts from a rights issue. With cash-flow ratios it is often useful to monitor the moving-average figure over a three-year period.

We return to the subject of cash-flow ratios later in this chapter.

Value added
This is equal to sales less bought-in costs (i.e. materials, components and outside services). As the name implies, it is the amount that is added by a company to the value of a product. It is equal to the sum of wages, salaries, tax paid and financing costs. It is not a new concept. Many companies produced a value-added statement in their annual report and accounts during the 1960s and 1970s. It did not add to the information provided elsewhere in the profit-and-loss account and notes to the accounts. It just presented the information in a different way. In the 1980s it became a requirement in the UK to publish cash-flow statements and these replaced value-added statements in company annual report and accounts.

There are, however, a number of ratios that make use of the value-added concept, and one particular measure has been heavily promoted during the 1990s. Simple ratios include:

- value added/capital employed;
- working capital/value added;
- value added/employment costs;
- stock/value added.

As can be seen in these ratios, value added is being substituted for sales or cost of sales figures usually used in the traditional financial ratios.

Economic value added (EVA)

This value-added figure has become a well-publicized measure of performance. It is a single figure that can be produced for each company and is said by its promoters to be a new way of evaluating past performance. The *Sunday Times* and *Fortune Business Magazine* have produced annual league tables in which they rank the performance of companies based on their EVA.

In fact, the letters 'EVA' have been trade-marked. The rights to use them belong to a US consulting company, Stern Stewart and Co. The EVA of a company is calculated by deducting from the 'true' operating profits, both taxes and the cost of debt and equity capital [3]. Equity capital has a cost, as does debt capital. The cost of debt is always deducted in the profit-and-loss account in arriving at an earnings figure. With EVA the cost of equity is also deducted. The resulting figure indicates how much the company has really added in terms of value to the products it produces and services it delivers when 'all' costs are taken into account. It should be pointed out that there is more to calculating the cost of equity than simple deduction of the dividends paid.

To arrive at the true profit figure for most companies it will be necessary to adjust the figure shown in the profit-and-loss account. In fact, up to 164 adjustments may have to be made to arrive at the trade-marked EVA figure.

The supporters of EVA as a useful performance measure claim that it can be used as a tool in decision making within a company. It can be used to integrate customer satisfaction, operating efficiency asset management and financial policies into a single measure in a way that other measures cannot. It is claimed it enables trade-offs to be assessed. For example, a decision which might result in an increase in the level of investment in a company would in the short run reduce the asset turnover ratio but it might be good for the company because the higher level of investment could in the long run boost sales.

The arguments used to justify EVA are sometimes based on an incorrect approach to the use of alternative measures. Nobody suggests that accounting ratios such as asset turnover should be used as a guide to investment decision. Most accounting ratios are minor indicators of performance – they just help explain what has been happening within a company.

EVA is a reasonable measure; it was 30 years ago when a close 'relation' to it was referred to by accountants and economists as 'residual income'. It is, however, not a panacea. Nobody can measure the cost of equity capital accurately, and yet this is crucial to measuring EVA. The technique also relies on manipulating accounting numbers in an attempt to establish the 'true' operating profit of a company. It is very difficult for those outside a company to be able to make such adjustments. The adjustments depend on many assumptions.

EVA is based on the performance in one year, and does not allow for increases in the economic value of a company that may result from investing in such items as brands, investing in people, or investing in new assets that have not yet had time to show improved results.

MVA (market value added) is another system developed by the US consultants, Stern Stewart. It is determined by measuring the total amount of funds that have been invested in the company (based on cash flow) and comparing it with the current market value of the securities of the company. The funds invested include equity, retained earnings and borrowings. The market value of the debt and securities is compared with the cash that has been invested. If the market value of the company exceeds funds invested, value has been created.

The concepts of EVA and MVA have been of benefit to some companies. No performance measure is perfect, each method has its advantages and disadvantages. The search continues for 'the best' measure.

It has been shown that the actual publication of the annual financial report by a company and prior to that the announcement of its annual earnings figures do not (on most occasions) have any great impact on the share price of the company.

Movement before announcement

Ball and Brown and other researchers have found that for most companies the information contained in the annual financial report has already been anticipated before its release; the anticipation is very accurate, and the drift upwards or downwards in share price has begun 12 months before the report was released [4]. With regard to the value of the information contained in the final report, no more than 10–15% has not been anticipated by the month of the report. The value of the information conveyed by the report at the time of its release constitutes on average only 20% of the value of all information coming to the market in that month. About 70% of all information appears to be offsetting, which means that it is of no lasting use for decision making, although it may cause investors to act in the short run. Therefore only 30% of all information coming to the market at the time of the final report has a continuing value.

Investors build up expectations about earnings, and when actual results are announced some portion of these will have been anticipated already. Therefore this expected part should already have been reflected in the share price. If the market is efficient, only the unexpected part of the total information would be relevant to the market. The price of securities should react quickly to the unexpected news and in the appropriate direction.

If the actual change in earnings is greater than that forecast this is termed 'good news', while 'bad news' is when the actual unexpected income change was less than that expected. Research has shown that the share prices of the 'good news' companies gradually rose throughout the 12 months prior to the announcement date. Conversely, 'bad news' companies found their share price gradually declining prior to the announcement date. In other words, the market anticipated the direction of the movement in a company's earnings figures.

Over time the market receives a large amount of information that is relevant to a particular company. In addition to the annual report of the company, there might be press releases put out by the company, interim financial statements and reports on the prospects for the economy and the industry in which the company is engaged. There are also meetings between investment analysts and directors of the company and of course rumours.

At one level, therefore, it could be said that the annual financial report is just one piece of information that will enable the market to form opinions on the financial strength of a company and its potential for taking advantage of future opportunities. Investors value shares on the basis of the expected future position of a firm. When the financial accounts are produced, investors can ascertain whether or not their expectations relating to the year just completed have been realized. The annual accounting report can confirm or refute the expectations of investors. It provides an opportunity to reassess future expectations.

During the course of a year the large financial institutions will be considering the purchase and sale of many companies' shares. They will evaluate their equity portfolio on a continuous basis. The timing of the decision on whether to buy or sell any particular share could be influenced by:

- the liquidity position of the institution (have they recently received a large inflow of cash?);
- the release of non-financial data about the company;
- new information on the state of the economy, or developments in an industry;
- the time needed to analyse and digest the information given in the annual report and accounts.

One can therefore expect adjustments to the price of a company's shares to take place at any time during a year. It is not surprising that much movement in price appears not to be connected with the publication of accounting numbers. This does not mean accounting information is not useful. It is only if the actual profit figures announced by a company are different from those expected that one would expect a significant adjustment to price at the time of the announcement.

Accounting reports can be said to be useful in that they either confirm or refute the expectations of investors relating to the financial performance of a company.

Movement after announcements

Studies (see Bernard and Thomas [5]) on the movement in share price following the release of earnings figures find that the price does not adjust instantaneously to its new 'true value'. There is movement over a period of time following the announcement of results.

This continuing movement after the announcement of earnings is referred to as 'post-announcement drift'. It can be explained by the fact that it can take time for the financial reports to be properly analysed. The preliminary announcement of a company's annual results is followed later by the publication of the annual report and accounts, and still later by the annual general meeting. New information with more detail is being brought to the attention of the analysts in the period following the announcement.

This release of more detailed information which may clarify certain concerns plus the time needed to digest the implications of the figures can explain post-announcement movement. This issue is returned to in Chapter 8 on stock market efficiency, in which the 'good news, bad news' phenomenon is discussed in the context of a possible anomaly. It has been shown to be possible for investors to obtain above-normal returns during this period of 'drift' of a company's share price.

2.4 FORECASTING FUTURE EARNINGS

Over time the movement in a firm's earnings is a major determinant of the movement in share price. It would be helpful, therefore, when making decisions on whether or not to purchase a company's shares if it was possible to forecast the company's future earnings. There are a number of forecasting methods available, some much more successful (and expensive) than others.

Particularly involved in forecasting the future earnings of companies are financial analysts, banks and other institutions that lend funds to companies, and of course the management of companies. Management forecasts are, not surprisingly, usually the most accurate, but are not generally available. Managers have access to inside information.

Financial analysts' forecasts can be good. Usually they look at a company in detail. They consider segmental information on a company; they divide it into its many parts on a geographical and industrial basis. They then obtain relevant information, qualitative and quantitative, on factors affecting the future of the different countries in which the company operates and in changes in technology, costs and prices in the different industries in which the company is engaged.

The analysts form opinions on the relative strengths and weaknesses of the management of a company. They are often in contact with the management of the company. How much weight they attach to the different sources of information they have available will vary from one group of analysts to another. They will revise their forecasts during a year as new information becomes available.

Time-series analysis of earnings

One approach to forecasting is to use a statistical technique. There are many techniques available, ranging from simple moving-average techniques to advanced econometric models. Some of the techniques just look at the movement in a single variable, such as past earnings; others might analyse the movement in many variables such as national income data and industrial output figures as well as company-specific figures.

This chapter is concerned with the usefulness of financial statement information. The most important question on this issue is whether knowledge of past earnings figures helps in the prediction of future earnings figures.

Obviously, for the vast majority of companies, earnings increase over time. This, however, does not mean that it is possible to forecast annual changes in earnings. Indeed, the empirical studies on the subject show convincingly that for the vast majority of companies the change in the level of annual earnings and in the earnings per share follow a path which can be described as a 'random walk'. Unfortunately, like the daily changes in equity share price, corporate earnings figures appear, on average, to behave as if generated by a random process (martingale process) so that successive earnings changes are largely independent over time, and so cannot be forecast with any accuracy.

Little and Raynor's works showed this randomness applied to the typical or average firm [6]. The research of others has, however, shown that for the atypical firm, including those firms with the least erratic record, there is some persistence in the relative growth rate. It may be thought that the recent past can be used as a guide to the future, but the findings of Little and Raynor and others dispose of that supposition. They find that in the short run it is virtually impossible to find any consistent earnings growth, and the name 'higgledy-piggledy growth' was used to describe the observed patterns of company earnings growth.

One implication of these findings is that even those companies that are generally thought to be well managed cannot be expected to continue to produce an above-average growth of earnings for the company for period after period. It has been shown in particular that a company with a large relative increase in earnings in one period is generally likely to produce results in the next two or more periods of below-average growth performance. Alternatively, a firm with a large relative decrease in earnings in one period generally outperforms the average or most likely outcome for the next two or more periods. Only a small number of the best-performing companies in 1997 will be in the best-performing group in 1998, and even fewer in 1999.

The so-called random walk in the growth rate of company earnings should not worry investors or managers. It is the rate of change in earnings that is random, not the absolute earnings figure. If, for example, Marks and Spencers make a profit of £11 million in 1995 the random walk finding does not mean that we cannot say anything useful about its expected profits in the next year.

Let us say the profits in 1994 were £10 million; then the rate of change in earnings between 1994 and 1995 is plus 10%. Higgledy-piggledy growth means that we cannot say whether the rate of change in earnings in Marks and Spencers profits over 1996 is more likely to be + 10%, than say +15% or +5%. If we plot the rate of change, the line follows a random path. Each year the change in annual profits might be positive but some years will show a lower rate of increase than others.

Our best estimate is that the rate of change will be the same as in the previous year, not that there will be no change. But this should not worry an investor too much. On the basis of past information the investor's best estimate of the profits of Marks and Spencers in 1996 will be that of 1995, namely £11 million plus the same rate of growth as in the previous year. This is not bad – a profit of £12.1 million. The random walk finding is not saying the best estimate is that the company will not show an increase in profits. It is saying that we cannot predict whether the increase will be higher or lower than in the past year.

If an investor wants a better estimate than that based on the above, then additional information needs to be obtained. That is what investment analysts are seeking to do – obtain new relevant information. Performance in any period depends partly on what is happening in the economy, global as well as national. It depends on what is happening in the industry as well as in the company. One cannot logically expect to obtain good forecasts based on just extrapolating past figures.

There are reasons why one might not find consistency in the short run. One cannot, for instance, expect management to be able to readjust themselves or their plant in the short run to changes in the overall level of economic activity. Many short-run changes are beyond the control of management, and so one would expect the return on capital to fluctuate over time, depending on such factors as capacity utilization.

This does not mean past earnings figures are not useful. An individual company's past profit levels cannot be relied upon as a guide to its future profits. Past profits may, however, be used to give an indication of above- or below-average management ability. Accordingly, the forecasting of economy and industry factors together with knowledge of the quality of a particular company's management may give some guidance as to the future company profit level.

2.5 CAN THE MARKET BE FOOLED BY CREATIVE ACCOUNTING?

The fact that the major stock markets of the world – London, New York and Tokyo – were efficient was for a long time accepted as an act of faith. To suggest otherwise was to imply that one did not really understand the concept and did not know how to follow the vast empirical evidence on the topic. Recently, however, the evidence has been re-examined. The current position is that there is strong consistent evidence that markets such as London and New York are efficient, but there are some anomalies. These anomalies have shaken the faith of a few.

If the market is efficient, it should not on the whole be fooled by creative accounting techniques. The evidence is that in most cases it is not fooled.

However, the directors of companies do still continue to manipulate earnings-per-share figures. They know of the existence of the efficient market hypothesis (EMH), but they still act as if they believe that the 'adjustment' or 'window dressing' of the financial accounts is worthwhile. Perhaps the fact that it has only been found that manipulation does not mislead the market in most cases encourages them. It has not been found that it does not work in *all* cases. The directors hope that their company accounts might be one of the few that the market does not 'read' properly in the short term.

The management of earnings disclosure

Creative accounting has now been given a respectable name, 'the management of earnings disclosure'. Production people and sales people feel that it is they who are responsible for earning the profits of a company. Engineers often claim that it is they who are responsible for creating the wealth of a company or a country. This may be true. But it is the accountants who decide when shareholders and other investors will be told about the profits. It is possible to delay the disclosure of profits that have been earned, and to speed up the recognition of profits that will be earned.

Davidson, Stickney and Weil, in discussing what they refer to as 'accounting magic', define the managing of earnings disclosure as a 'process of taking deliberate steps within the constraints of generally accepted accounting principles to bring about a desired level of earnings' [7].

Holmes and Sugden refer to the fact that financial analysts expect some companies to 'try to show continuous growth year after year and to pull out all the stops to avoid reporting a downturn' [8].

Evidence of manipulation

Lev, in his survey article on the usefulness of earnings research, concludes that 'prima facie evidence on manipulation of financial information is widespread' [9]. He quotes from Scholes *et al.* (1988) who found evidence of income smoothing [10]. Even banks have been found to manage their earnings disclosure. Allen and Saunders found 'almost 85% of banks in the sample window dressing their balance sheet upwards' [11].

McNichols and Wilson (1988) found evidence that firms manage their earnings 'by choosing income-decreasing accruals when income is extreme' [12]. This means that they adopt a policy of income smoothing. It is quite easy for banks to do this through varying their policy on bad-debt provision. The reason a firm might wish to reveal lower income is of course to avoid criticism from regulatory agencies. The researchers believe, however, that whereas managers are able to alter some accruals the discretionary component of total accruals is only a small portion. A small portion of the debtors figure can, however, be a large portion of the profits figure.

A question that has worried investors and analysts for some time is what percentage of companies engage in the management of earnings disclosure. There are high-profile cases that hit the headlines, such as Asil Nadir and Polly Peck, and Robert Maxwell and his group of companies. But the impression that those who are engaged in finance like to give is that these are just isolated cases, and that 99% of companies do not engage in deliberate manipulation in order to mislead.

It came as somewhat of a shock, therefore, when in the UK in 1992, Smith wrote his book entitled *Accounting for Growth* [13]. The contents of the book were greeted by many with surprise, as was the fact that the author was an insider. The contents should not, however, have been a surprise to anyone engaged in the actual analysis of company accounts.

The results he reported were based on an analysis of the actual reporting practices of the major UK companies. Smith's research received widespread publicity as at the time of undertaking the research he was a banking analyst for UBS Phillips & Drew, one of the major UK brokers. He examined 12 areas in which dubious accounting methods were possible, and found that one company adopted as many as 9 of these manipulation techniques. Two companies used 8, four used 7, fifteen used 6. To be fair, there were a number of companies that only adopted managing disclosure practices in one of the 12 areas, and a few companies that had no dubious practices.

An interesting case study is that prepared by Brink that examines changes over a long period of time; it illustrates the problems. Brink analyses the actual changes in Philips's accounting policies from 1912 to the present time [14]. Brink points out that the company has with 'increasing frequency changed the principles used in determining its results'. With respect to recent changes Brink believes the reasons given in the financial report to explain the changes have not always been convincing. 'The figures leave the strong suspicion that an improvement in the company result was a motive. Every important change in accounting occurred in a period of decreasing results, and each change led to a higher result.'

It should be pointed out that what can appear to be manipulation can in fact be a genuine reflection of changed circumstances. For example, reducing the depreciation charge by lengthening the useful life of an asset could just be recognizing new knowledge. It would have been difficult for an airline company to appreciate the useful life of a Boeing 747 when it was first introduced.

Problems can arise, not because of any attempt to manipulate the reported figures, but just because of the fact that accounts have to be prepared every 12 months. At the end of an accounting period, many transactions will be incomplete, and in order to estimate profits many assumptions have to be made.

Why earnings management occurs

The reason why the earnings figures that are disclosed might be managed include:

1 Directors' remuneration schemes can create an incentive to manage earnings figures. Directors' bonus schemes are on occasions linked in some way to earnings per share. Directors often have only short-term contracts, sometimes one year or less. Why not speed up the recognition of profit so as to benefit from it as early as possible? The director may not be in office when profits on long-term ventures would normally pass through the accounts.
2 Asymmetry in information – managers have 'private' information that they can use when determining compensation or profit-sharing rules among interested parties in the company.
3 Directors or one shareholder group may want to impress a 'prospective' shareholder group with the firm's past performance (inviting/encouraging takeover bid/buy-out).
4 Following a takeover bid, management wishes to impress its existing shareholders with its own performance.
5 Firms will smooth income to create an impression of a low variability in income to give the impression to lenders of low risk, therefore low interest rates.
6 Earnings fixation. In the UK (and in the USA) the users of accounts and consequently the preparers of accounts have become obsessed with the earnings figures – with what is sometimes called 'the bottom line'. Whereas at one time in the UK, and still in some other countries accounts had a stewardship role, now the emphasis has shifted to earnings performance. It is the earnings per share, and the associated price–earnings ratio, that dominate analysis of a company's performance and consequently investment prospects.

Tinic refers to the 'functional fixation hypothesis' which in the stock market context means that 'decision makers who are unfamiliar with different methods of producing accounting outputs rely on bottom line accounting numbers without paying attention to the procedures used in generating them' [15]. If this hypothesis were proven it would mean that the efficient market hypothesis was incorrect, and that share prices do not reflect all available information. Tinic was not able to resolve the issue as to which hypothesis best explained stock market prices. The hypothesis does, however, illustrate the danger in users of accounts relying on the 'bottom line'.

2.6 ACCOUNTING POLICIES AND PRACTICES

Ratio analysis is useless unless it is combined with a sense of understanding of accounting policies and practices. Companies can and do adopt different accounting policies and practices. For example, one airline can assume a different life for a particular type of aeroplane than another airline. In 1994, Singapore Airlines were depreciating the Airbus over 10 years; assuming a residual value of 20%, Delta Airlines were assuming a 20-year life.

The assumed life of a plane will affect the depreciation charge, the depreciation charge will affect the profit figure, the profit figure affects many ratios including the popular profit/capital-employed ratio. How is it possible to meaningfully compare the profit/capital-employed of Singapore Airlines with that of Delta Airlines unless one knows of the different assumption about asset life.

The financial analyst should begin by understanding the few fundamental concepts that do, or should, underlie all company accounts.

When a company produces a profit figure it is based on hundreds of assumptions similar to the asset life assumption referred to above. By reading the statement on account policies in a company's accounts and the notes to the accounts, it should be possible to ascertain the major assumptions being made. The analyst is then in a position to compare the financial performance of one company with that of another. Not to read the detailed explanations given in the accounts is naive, and the resulting dividing of one accounting number by another is a waste of time. There is much more to financial ratio analysis than using a calculator. Simple books with titles such as 'How to read company accounts' are almost as dangerous as a book entitled 'How to be a brain surgeon'.

Fundamental concepts are working assumptions having general acceptance at a point in time. In no way are accounting concepts the same as accounting theory; they are just broad assumptions. They are practical rules which are adopted generally but can be varied and possibly changed over time.

The UK Accounting Standard on the Principles for Financial Reporting singles out four particular concepts for special mention: the going concern concept, the consistency concept, the prudence concept and the accruals concept. The standard requires that any material differences from the four fundamental concepts as well as the critical accounting policies must be disclosed in the annual accounts of a company and suitably explained.

The four concepts are as follows.

1 *Going concern*. This postulate is introduced to cope with the problem of periodic reporting for an entity having a life extending beyond the current period. It represents the assumption that, provided that there is no significant evidence to the contrary, the entity will be assumed to continue in existence long enough to carry out its commitments, sell its stock in trade in an orderly manner and derive the use from its assets not purchased for resale.

2 *Consistency*. Reflecting the user need of comparability, this principle requires the accounting treatment to be consistent both within a particular period and between different periods. Where changes occur, there is a need to provide information to help the user understand the effects.

3 *Prudence*. It is often recommended that, in accounting, pessimism should be adopted in preference to optimism, given the uncertainty that necessarily exists in the reporting of financial results. This conservative approach implies that revenue and profit should not be anticipated, but provision should be made for any expected liabilities. Assets should be valued at the lowest of several possible values, while liabilities and expenses should be valued at their highest. This approach is justified by assuming that overstatement is more dangerous than understatement, and that a businessman's optimism needs to be tempered with the accountant's pessimism.

4 *Accrual accounting*. This is a process whereby for a particular period an attempt is made to charge only those costs that have been incurred in generating the revenue of the period. If some costs have been incurred but they are to produce products or to deliver services in the next accounting period, these costs will be deferred. This means matching events to periods.

It is necessary to mention a feature of income reporting that stems from the accruals approach but is not always explicitly recognized. This is income smoothing. To the extent that accrual allows the reporting of receipts and outlays to be spread or allocated to 'appropriate' periods, it permits smoothing. Some would argue that this is desirable if it produces an income figure that projects the general trend of progress, rather than fluctuations caused by uneven cash flows. Smoothing is given effect in many accounting practices: depreciation and amortization spread expenditure of a capital or unusually 'lumpy' nature, the treatment of taxation involves smoothing, and extraordinary items are separated in an attempt to remove distortions from a smooth recurring trend of reported income.

Another concept is substance over form. This supports the idea of reporting to reflect financial reality, in preference to the legal position. There are many examples of this, including the reporting of assets acquired on a long-term lease as if they were, in fact, owned, and the treatment of associated (related) companies where the group's share of the earnings of the associate are reflected in group accounts and not merely the dividends to which there is a legal right.

2.7 FINANCIAL TERMINOLOGY

Certain basic financial terms will now be explained. The terms are used many times in the book and their usefulness is discussed; at this point they are being defined.

Dividend yield

Dividend yield is a simple enough concept. It is

$$\frac{\text{dividend per share}}{\text{price per share}} \times 100$$

This is a measure of the annual percentage return a shareholder receives from dividends, based on the current share price. It is not the total actual return earned by a shareholder for a company because it ignores the annual capital gains. It is also based on the current price of the share which is not necessarily the price the shareholder paid for the share.

A company pays dividends to shareholders net of a taxation deduction. The amount deducted is remitted to the Inland Revenue. The amount to be deducted has varied from time to time. As from April 1994, the amount became a reduced basic income tax rate of 20%. This means that if the gross dividend to be paid is 100p per share, the tax deduction is 20p (i.e. 20% of gross). This is the same as a rate of 25% on the net dividend (80p × 25%).

The result of this deduction at source is that if an individual shareholder pays income tax at this 20% rate, they will have no further liability to tax in respect of the dividend. If, however, an individual shareholder is liable to income tax at a higher rate (say 40%), he/she will be liable to the difference between the tax payable on the dividend at the higher rate (40p) and the tax that has been deducted at source (20p).

If a shareholder is not liable to income tax, they can reclaim the tax that has been deducted from the dividends. Until 1998 pension funds could reclaim this tax payment, but this position has changed and pension funds are now similar to other shareholders who have to pay tax.

When calculating dividend yields, should the calculation be based on the net dividend paid or on the gross dividend? An individual can calculate his or her own net dividend. An outsider can determine the gross yield or the yield net of the basic or the reduced rate of tax. The net yield equals

$$\frac{\text{dividend per share net of tax deducted}}{\text{share price}} \times 100$$

If a company pays a net dividend of 5p for the year ended 31 December 1994 and its share price is 100p, the net dividend yield is:

$$\frac{5}{100} \times 100 = 5\%$$

The gross yield to reflect the 20% tax credit is:

$$1.25 \, (5\%) = 6.25\%$$

The gross dividend yield is regarded by many as being a more useful measure than the net dividend yield. This is because not all shareholders pay the same rate of income tax and so the net yield is not the net of tax yield to all shareholders. The gross yield, i.e. before any income tax is deducted, is the same for all shareholders. The *Financial Times* quotes the gross dividend yield in its daily share price statistics (see Table 2.1, penultimate columns). In the share price statistics a number of signs and symbols appear, the meaning of which can be extremely complex. The only way to understand these is by reading the explanation given in the newspaper.

The tax payment deducted from dividends and handed over to the Inland Revenue is an advance payment of the company's annual corporation tax bill. This advance payment can be offset against the total annual tax bill.

If a company happens to be in a loss-making situation in a year it will not be liable to pay corporation tax. However, if it has paid dividends during the year it will have made an advance payment. It will not be in a position to offset this payment.

Earnings per share

With the corporation tax system the calculation of earnings per share (EPS) can be somewhat complicated. The two most common methods of calculating earnings per share are the nil method and the net method.

Nil method
This method is based on earnings available for distribution. It ignores the effect of the dividend policy on the level of tax paid. Those who support earnings-per-share calculations based on the nil method argue that it provides the best indication of one company's performance relative to another company.

Net method

In the net method earnings are effectively the net dividend, plus any retained earnings. For most companies the two methods give the same result. It is those companies with substantial overseas earnings that show a significant difference.

Reference is often made to 'fully diluted earnings per share', which takes into account not just the number of shares that have currently been issued but also the numbers that would need to be issued if all those on offer in the various share-option schemes of the company needed to be issued. The options which give an opportunity to purchase equity, as well as options on convertible loan stock issues, include those that have been issued to directors and employers.

Dividend cover

One way of determining whether or not the shares of a particular company are a good investment is to look at the dividend cover. This is one indication of the riskiness of the investment. It is the number of times by which available profits after tax cover the dividend payment. It indicates how far earnings could fall before dividends need to be cut. Because of the alternative measures of EPS the calculation can be complicated. The calculation is basically either

$$\frac{\text{EPS}}{\text{dividends per share}}$$

or

$$\frac{\text{total profits available for distribution to ordinary shareholders}}{\text{dividends paid to ordinary shareholders}}$$

We have to decide, however, which earnings figure to use and whether to take dividends gross or net.

Earnings yield and price-to-earnings ratio

The earnings yield is simply

$$\frac{\text{EPS}}{\text{share price}} \times 100$$

This particular yield is not often used. The much more common way of expressing earnings in relation to price is by the price-to-earnings ratio. This is simply the share price expressed as a multiple of EPS. It indicates how many times the current level of earnings investors are paying for a company's shares. Once again, however, we are faced with the problem of deciding which EPS figure to use.

The *Financial Times* in its daily Share Information Service quotes a price-to-earnings ratio for a large number of companies. This ratio is based on the relationship between the daily share price and the net EPS figure.

The meaning and interpretation of the price-to-earnings ratio will be returned to many times in this book. The above outline will serve as an introduction.

The price-to-earnings ratio is seen by many analysts as being the best single method of comparing the market value of one share with that of other shares in a similar risk class. The higher the price-to-earnings ratio the 'better' the company is thought to be – it indicates the market has growth expectations. The ratio is therefore very important when it comes to determining the price at which new shares should be offered to investors.

Financial Times statistics

The *Financial Times* lists the prices of about 3000 equity-based securities, including many which have their primary listing outside the UK. It is not always appreciated that companies pay the newspaper to have their names and share prices published. Companies are listed by industry sectors. With some companies the price of any warrants and 'A' or 'B' class shares are listed.

We show in Table 2.1, the details given for companies classified as being in the chemical sector. This is an extract from the paper for one day in October 1997.

Table 2.1 Extract from *Financial Times*, 10 October 1997

	Notes	Price	+or −	52 week high	low	Mkt Cap£m	Yld Gr's	P/E
AGA SKr		£$9\frac{19}{32}$	$-\frac{1}{4}$	£$10\frac{3}{16}$	£$7\frac{15}{16}$	1,247	2.3	20.7
Akzo Fl		£$114\frac{15}{16}$	$-1\frac{13}{32}$	£$117\frac{1}{16}$	£$76\frac{1}{32}$	8,185	2.0	19.5
Albright & Wilson	♣N	$163\frac{1}{2}$xd	−4	200	142	512.6	5.0	17.0
Allied Colloids	♣♣	$117\frac{1}{2}$	$-3\frac{1}{2}$	*$146\frac{3}{4}$	$108\frac{1}{2}$	809.6	3.4	17.4
Amber ind	♣	116	......	*150	115	18.2	6.2	10.6
Amberley	♣♣	$111\frac{1}{2}$	......	$117\frac{1}{2}$	$88\frac{1}{2}$	68.7	1.8	20.5
Anglo Utd		$1\frac{3}{4}$	......	3	$0\frac{1}{2}$	16.1	−	Φ
BASF DM		£$22\frac{23}{32}$	$-\frac{19}{32}$	*£$25\frac{5}{16}$	£$19\frac{7}{16}$	14,034	2.6	−
BOC	♣u	$1104\frac{1}{2}$	+6	1195	819	5,378	3.2	18.9
BTP	♣♣	358	+13	$365\frac{1}{2}$	248	602.5	4.1	17.7
Bayer DM		£$25\frac{3}{16}$	$-\frac{25}{32}$	*£$28\frac{19}{32}$	£$22\frac{15}{32}$	18,237	2.4	−
Brent	♣♣†	99	$-\frac{1}{2}$	$118\frac{1}{2}$	$68\frac{1}{2}$	66.9	4.2	10.5
British Vita	♣†	$246\frac{1}{2}$xd	−3	263	$185\frac{1}{2}$	545.3	4.3	13.2
Brunner Mond		$157\frac{1}{2}$xd	−1	$192\frac{1}{2}$	$132\frac{1}{2}$	119.9	6.9	8.6
Canning (W)	♣♣†	$243\frac{1}{2}$	+1	$315\frac{1}{2}$	$241\frac{1}{2}$	71.1	4.6	11.5
Cementone		$67\frac{1}{2}$#	......	$71\frac{1}{2}$	$24\frac{1}{2}$	14.8	2.8	35.7
Warrants		$27\frac{1}{2}$	......	$27\frac{1}{2}$	$41\frac{1}{2}$	0.24	−	−
Courtaulds	♣	$332\frac{1}{2}$	+1	466	288	1,352	6.2	16.1
Croda	♣N	380xd	$-2\frac{1}{2}$	408	246	514.1	3.1	16.0
Doeflex	♣♣†	$244\frac{1}{2}$	......	$305\frac{1}{2}$	$204\frac{1}{2}$	42.5	4.1	10.4
Ellis & Everard	♣♣	304	......	$320\frac{1}{2}$	$238\frac{1}{2}$	273.0	4.1	13.5
Engelhard US$		£12	$-\frac{1}{4}$	£$14\frac{31}{32}$	£$10\frac{13}{16}$	1,765	1.8	−
European Colour	♣♣	$61\frac{1}{2}$	−1	$84\frac{1}{2}$	$49\frac{1}{2}$	28.2	4.9	11.0
Gibbon		$119\frac{1}{2}$	......	$123\frac{1}{2}$	$81\frac{1}{2}$	12.7	7.3	10.8
Hickson	♣♣	$71\frac{1}{2}$	......	$82\frac{1}{2}$	52	125.8	−	13.7
Hoechst DM		£$27\frac{27}{32}$	$-\frac{5}{32}$	*£$29\frac{3}{16}$	£$20\frac{7}{16}$	16,374	1.8	−
Holliday Chemical	♣♣†	$191\frac{1}{2}$	......	$192\frac{1}{2}$	$118\frac{1}{2}$	201.3	3.7	13.8
ICI	♣N	985	$-8\frac{1}{2}$	1110	$681\frac{1}{2}$	7,151	3.7	33.8
Inspec	♣†	$247\frac{1}{2}$xd	......	$247\frac{1}{2}$	$163\frac{1}{2}$	431.9	3.3	12.3
Kalon	♣♣†	$167\frac{1}{2}$	......	$180\frac{1}{2}$	$108\frac{1}{2}$	594.6	4.1	25.1
Laporte	♣♣N	$761\frac{1}{2}$xd	−1	779	$592\frac{1}{2}$	1,478	3.8	15.3

It will be seen that in addition to well-known British chemical companies such as ICI and Courtaulds, the main leading foreign companies such as Bayer and BASF from Germany, and Akzo from the Netherlands also appear. By the side of the names of these foreign companies the currencies in which the shares are denominated is given. A number of symbols also appear.

The price is the closing price of the previous day. It does not mean shares can be bought at this price. The price is the mid-price of the best bid and offer price at the end of the day. If an investor is buying he or she will pay more than this price; if selling they will receive a lower price. For the less liquid shares, those with less trading, the spread between the bid and offer price can be wide and so the price paid or received may be significantly different from the price as listed.

It should also be appreciated that the price given in the newspaper is the one at which a market maker is ready to deal in small volumes. For a large transaction the prices might well be different.

The high and low price for the last 52 weeks is self-explanatory. The layout shown in the table is the traditional way in which the FT indicates the extremes in price that have occurred over a period of time.

The market capitalization is the number of shares in issue times the share prices. The *Financial Times* quotes the gross dividend yield, which as explained above is the net yield adjusted to reflect a 20% tax credit. The yield is based on the most recent twelve-month dividend per share, divided by the latest closing share price expressed as a percentage.

The price–earnings ratio is the share price divided by the most recent 12 months' earnings per share. Unfortunately, as explained, there is more than one way of calculating the EPS of a company. There is a taxation issue which has already been discussed and an accounting issue.

We will now briefly deal with the accounting issues involved. The earnings figure should be net of minority interests and extraordinary items. Extraordinary items are defined as 'material items possessing a high degree of abnormality'. They arise from events or transactions that fall outside the normal activities of the company concerned. In order to obtain an impression of the success or failure of the 'core' business it is better they are excluded from the earnings-per-share calculation.

We take as an example the Annual Report and Accounts of Guinness PLC for 1996 (see Tables 2.2–4). Guinness in their 1996 profit-and-loss account (Table 2.2),

Table 2.2 *Group profit and loss account*

For the year ended 31 December 1996	Notes	1996 £m	1995 £m
Turnover (continuing operations)	1	4,730	4,681
Net trading costs	2	(3,769)	(3,738)
Net reorganisation costs	3	–	(64)
Total operating costs		(3,769)	(3,802)
Profit before interest and taxation (excluding Moët Hennessy (MH)) (continuing operations)	1	961	879
Share of profit before taxation of MH	4	113	111
Profit before interest and taxation		1,074	990
Net interest charge	6	(99)	(114)
Profit on ordinary activities before taxation		975	876
Taxation on profit on ordinary activities	7	(259)	(251)
Profit on ordinary activities after taxation		716	625
Minority interests (equity)		(31)	(30)
Profit for the financial year		685	595
Dividends	8	(295)	(302)
Retained earnings		390	293
EARNINGS PER SHARE	9		
Basic earnings per share		35.1p	29.4p
Diluted – before exceptional items		34.8p	32.9p
Net reorganisation costs		–p	(3.6)p
Diluted earnings per share		34.8p	29.3p
DIVIDENDS PER SHARE	8		
Paid or payable		16.10p	14.90p
Gross equivalent		20.13p	18.63p
Interest cover (times, before exceptional items)		10.8	9.2
Interest cover (times, after exceptional items)		10.8	8.7
Dividend cover (times, before exceptional items)		2.2	2.2
Dividend cover (times, after exceptional items)		2.2	2.0

Table 2.3 *Group balance sheet*

At 31 December 1996	Notes	1996 £m	1996 £m	1995 £m	1995 £m
NET ASSETS					
Fixed assets					
Acquired brands at cost	11		1,395		1,395
Tangible assets	12		1,750		1,811
Investment in MH	13	902		1,026	
Other long term investments	14	179		157	
			1,081		1,183
			4,226		4,389
Current assets					
Stocks	15	1,867		1,899	
Debtors – due within one year	16(A)	1,245		1,097	
Debtors – due after more than one year	16(B)	148		164	
Cash at bank and in hand		327		694	
		3,587		3,854	
Creditors (amounts falling due within one year)					
Short term borrowings	17	(1,136)		(1,149)	
Other creditors	18	(1,436)		(1,478)	
		(2,572)		(2,627)	
Net current assets			1,015		1,227
Total assets less current liabilities			5,241		5,616
Creditors (amounts falling due after more than one year)					
Long term borrowings	17	(622)		(776)	
Other creditors	19	(161)		(152)	
			(783)		(928)
Provisions for liabilities and charges	20		(211)		(291)
Total net assets	10		4,247		4,397
EQUITY					
Capital and reserves					
Called up share capital	21(B)		483		506
Share premium account	21(B)		590		569
			1,073		1,075
Other reserves	22(A)		2,141		2,069
Profit and loss account	22(A)		2,236		2,440
Goodwill	22(B)		(1,298)		(1,298)
Shareholders' funds			4,152		4,286
Minority interests (equity)			95		111
Total equity			4,247		4,397

Approved by the Board on 19 March 1997.

A A Greener, Chairman
P E Yea, Finance Director

Finance and accounting

Table 2.4 *Group cash flow statement*

For the year ended 31 December 1996	Notes	1996 £m	1995 £m
Cash flow from operating activities	23(A)	1,020	989
Interest received		25	33
Interest paid		(178)	(153)
Dividends paid to minority shareholders in subsidiary undertakings		(34)	(22)
Returns on investments and servicing of finance		(187)	(142)
United Kingdom corporation tax paid		(194)	(127)
Overseas tax paid		(61)	(81)
Taxation		(255)	(208)
Purchase of tangible fixed assets			
Spirits		(50)	(56)
Brewing		(134)	(123)
Sale of tangible fixed assets		22	24
Capital expenditure and financial investment		(170)	(155)
Free cash flow before dividends		408	484
Purchase of subsidiary undertakings	23(E)	(38)	(15)
Purchase of long term investments		(4)	(16)
Disposals	23(F)	5	90
Acquisitions and disposals		(37)	59
Equity dividends paid		(294)	(285)
Cash inflow before use of liquid resources and financing		77	258
Decrease/(increase) in liquid resources	23(D)	390	(231)
Financing:			
Issue of ordinary share capital (employee share schemes)		23	26
Repurchase of shares	21(B)	(466)	–
Increase/(decrease) in debt	23(C	32	(40)
Increase in cash in the period	23(D)	56	13
Reconciliation of net cash flow to movement in net debt			
Increase in cash in the period		56	13
Cash (inflow)/outflow from (increase)/decrease in debt financing		(32)	40
Cash (inflow)/outflow from increase/(decrease) in liquid resources		(390)	231
Changes in net debt resulting from cash flows	23(D)	(366)	284
Effect of foreign exchange rate changes	23(D)	166	(100)
Movement in net debt in the period		(200)	184
Net debt at 1 January	23(D)	(1,231)	(1,415)
Net debt at 31 December	23(D)	(1,431)	(1,231)

The Group cash flow statement and notes thereto for the current and prior year are prepared in accordance with Financial Reporting Standard 1 (Revised).

when disclosing the interest cover and dividend cover, refer to exceptional items. These are different from extraordinary items. They arise from events or transactions that fall within the ordinary activities of the company. If they are income they are credited above the line, if expenses they are debited above the line. They do therefore affect the earnings-per-share figure. The dividing line between exceptional and extraordinary has been controversial for a long time.

2.8 FINANCIAL RATIOS

It is necessary to be able to assess whether or not a company has performed well over a period of time. From its profit and loss account we can observe the profits it has made, but are these as high as they should be when considering the amount of money that has been invested in the business? Are they equivalent to the level earned by major competitors? We need to know whether the company is in a healthy short-term financial position, and whether it is in a good financial position for long-term expansion.

We need to know the answers to these and many other questions. The most common method of analysing accounts is by use of financial ratios. These ratios are used by analysts outside the company when making investment decisions and by managers within the company when comparing the performance of one division with another. They can be used by management for interpreting the performance of the past or for setting targets against which future performance will be measured.

A ratio by itself is not particularly useful: it has to be compared with something. The basis for comparison can be with any one or all of the following:

- a predetermined target, with the ratio being used within a firm for planning and management control purposes;
- the level of the ratio in the past, with the trend being observed to see whether or not it is favourable;
- the level of the ratio in similar firms, perhaps either in the same industry or the same risk class;
- a norm, i.e. a standard that experts, bankers or analysts consider to be acceptable or, in other words, normal.

Ratios can be divided into at least four categories: those measuring profitability, those measuring liquidity, those measuring overall financial strength, and those involving stock market data.

Definitions

An early problem we face is that we have different measures of profits. These include profit before interest and taxation (PBIT), profit on ordinary activities after taxation (PAT), and profit attributable to shareholders shown in the accounts as profit for the financial year. The exact profit figure we use in any ratio needs to be appropriate to which capital invested figure we are interested in. Some of the profits are distributed to the providers of loan capital as interest. Some of the profits belong to shareholders. It is essential to relate the correct profit figure to the appropriate source of finance.

Table 2.5 illustrates how the distribution of profit (earnings) is related to the sources of finance. Basically, interest is the return paid to the providers of loan capital, and any profits remaining after the deduction of interest and after deduction of tax on profits belongs to the providers of the equity finance (the shareholders). As can be seen from the profit and loss account, interest is deducted in arriving at the profits subject to tax. The taxation rules of most countries recognize interest as a tax-deductible expense. In addition interest has to be paid whether or not the company makes a profit.

The funds to purchase fixed and current assets typically come from sources such as those listed in Table 2.5. One item needs explanation: provisions. This item represents funds that have been set aside out of profits to meet future commitments. The funds do not need to be paid to outsiders, or spent on a specific need in the near future, so they can be used to acquire liquid assets which can be realized when the anticipated payments need to be made. In the case of Guinness this item mainly comprises deferred taxation and provisions made on acquisitions. Technically as at 31 December 1996 these funds belong to the shareholders, but they have been put aside for special purposes. As mentioned they will, most likely, have been invested in short-term assets.

An important point to appreciate is that there are no agreed definitions for each

Table 2.5 *Distribution of returns to sources of finance, Guinness 1996 (£m)*

			Taxation £259
Profit before interest and tax = £1074 (as per P&L a/c)	Total assets	Other creditors £1436	
		Other long-term creditors £161	
		Provisions £211	
Interest received £32	£(4226 + 3587 = £7813)	Short-term borrowings £1136	Interest paid £131
		Long-term borrowings £622	
		Ordinary shareholders' funds £4152	Profits attributable to ordinary shareholders £685
		Minority interests £95	Minority interests £31
↓	↓	↓	↓
Total returns before tax £1106	Total uses of funds £7813	= Total sources of funds £7813	Returns to individual sources of funds £1106

ratio. There are certainly no accounting or stock market standards on the subject. One company can, in its annual report, refer to its profits-to-assets ratio and use a different definition of profits and/or assets to another company using the same title to illustrate its performance. One textbook can use a different definition to another textbook. This is unfortunate for the student of the subject, who would like a precise definition. The important thing is for the user of the ratios to ensure that he or she is comparing like with like. The important thing is to be consistent. No one definition is right and the other wrong. But it is certainly wrong to compare two ratios, each prepared with a slightly different definition.

Financial ratios can be based on the numbers appearing in the accounting statements, i.e. the balance sheet and profit and loss account, the projection of cash flows and stock market statistics.

We shall illustrate the most important financial ratios with the figures taken from the 1996 Annual Report and Accounts of Guinness PLC. A summary of the balance sheet and profit and loss account is given in Tables 2.2 and 2.3. As with other companies not all the useful relevant information is shown on the face of these two statements, but some is hidden away in the notes to the accounts. It is not possible to perform a meaningful analysis of the performance of any company without considering the details given in the notes to the accounts.

Profitability

We shall begin with the ratios that attempt to analyse profitability. Basically a company's profitability can be measured in relationship to its level of sales, its level of assets and/or the level of capital invested. The more popular profitability ratios are given below. There are others, and there are variations on each of the ratios given.

Table 2.5 illustrates that total assets are financed from a variety of sources. If we wish to produce a ratio to show the pre-tax profits earned on the total assets under the management's control, the appropriate numerator is the PBIT:

(a) $$\frac{\text{PBIT}}{\text{total assets}} \times 100 = \frac{1074}{7813} \times 100 = 13.75\%$$

This reflects the profits earned before tax on all the assets employed, however they are financed.

A variation on this ratio is to use trading profits as the numerator. If this is done in the Guinness case it would exclude the share of results of related company MH (Moët Hennessy). To exclude these profits means that the investment in the related company must be excluded from the denominator. An investment is made to earn a return; if the return figure is excluded, the investment must be also. The accounts reveal that the investment in MH equals £902 million. The ratio therefore becomes

(b) $$\frac{\text{trading profits}}{\text{total assets less investment in LVMH}} = £\frac{961}{6911} \times 100 = 13.90\%$$

A further variation on this ratio is to use as the denominator total assets less creditors falling due within one year. This asset measure is referred to in the Guinness accounts as 'total assets less current liabilities', and is sometimes called 'capital employed'. It reflects the long-term capital investment in the business, and therefore those assets financed by 'creditors – amounts falling due within one year' are excluded.

It must be remembered that some of the total interest-payable figure relates to short-term borrowings which are included in this 'creditors falling due within one year' figure. If the denominator in the ratio excludes short-term borrowings, the numerator must be the figure obtained before deducting interest paid on long-term loans but after interest paid on short-term borrowings. With this alternative approach, if this is not done, one is ignoring the cost of some of the short-term funds being used and exaggerating what is available to pay for long-term funds.

In the case of Guinness the profit and loss account shows a net interest charge of £99 million. This is the net charge, i.e. the difference between interest paid and interest received. The total payable is £131 million, and the interest received is £32 million. The appropriate note to the accounts only divides the interest figure between that paid on 'bank loans and overdrafts' and that paid on 'other loans'. Therefore it is not possible to ascertain the interest paid on the borrowings that have to be repaid within one year.

The alternative ratio is

(c) $$\frac{\text{profit before tax and interest on bank loans and loan stock repayable after longer than one year}}{\text{total net assets (capital employed)}}$$

The above ratios have been calculated based on the total assets at the close of the accounting period. Yet another variation of this approach would be to use the average level of total assets employed over the accounting year as a denominator. The profits were in fact not necessarily earned on the level of assets on the last day of the accounting year. This point could be particularly important if a major acquisition of assets had been made near the year end.

A popular ratio is

(d) $$\frac{\text{profit on ordinary activities after taxation}}{\text{total equity}} = \frac{716}{4247} \times 100 = 16.86\%$$

It is measuring the return on the equity funds employed in the business, including those associated with minority interests. Because assets financed from current liabilities and longer-term loans are excluded from the denominator, the interest paid to the providers of loan funds has to be excluded from the numerator. This ratio could be based on profits before or after tax. Similarly, the total equity figure could include or exclude the minority interest figure. If it is excluded in the denominator, then of course the return belonging to minority interests (shown in the profit and loss account) has to be deducted from the numerator.

Another profit ratio is

(e) $$\frac{\text{profit attributable to ordinary shareholders}}{\text{ordinary shareholders' funds}} = \frac{685}{4152} \times 100 = 16.50\%$$

The numerator shows the after-tax profit figure attributable to the shareholders of Guinness PLC.

One issue that in the past made financial statement analysis comparisons difficult was the treatment of extraordinary items. These items which might have been unusual or non-recurring items were often treated differently by similar companies or even by the same company in successive years. Following the issue of Financial Reporting Standard 3 extraordinary items have effectively been outlawed; financial statements now contain references to few such items. However, this process has produced its own problems in that, by proposing an all-inclusive approach to profit disclosure, comparisons are still difficult where companies have unusual income or costs arising. Many companies now show more than one earnings-per-share figure which is what Guinness has done. The basic earnings-per-share is 35.1 pence. Some companies adjust the basic figure to allow for extraordinary items and alternative tax treatments. The analysts association, the IIMR, have themselves issued recommendations on this and databases are now tending to use 'headline earnings per share' figures.

A further important profit ratio is

(f) $$\frac{\text{PBIT}}{\text{sales}} \times 100 = \frac{1074}{4730} \times 100 = 22.70\%$$

This gives the profit margin on sales. It can be calculated on profit before or after tax, depending again on what one wishes to show.

The activity ratio

Asset turnover
The asset turnover indicates the number of times in a year that the firm's assets are being turned over; it shows how the assets are being used. The level of the ratio will of course vary from one industry to another. With a retailing company, for example, where the level of investment in assets does not need to be high, the asset turnover ratio will be much higher than in a heavy engineering or petrochemical company. For Guinness it is

$$\frac{\text{sales}}{\text{total assets}} = \frac{4730}{7813} = 0.605$$

In fact this ratio is one of the key ratios which indicates how a company is able (or is unable) to generate profits. Three key ratios, this one and (a) and (f) above, are linked by the following formula:

$$\frac{\text{PBIT}}{\text{total assets}} \times 100 = \frac{\text{PBIT} \times 100}{\text{total assets}} \times \frac{\text{sales}}{\text{sales}} \quad \frac{}{\text{total assets}}$$

$$= 13.75\% = 22.70 \times 0.605$$

Investors want a level of profit-to-total-assets commensurate with the level of risk. If the risks are the same in retailing as in heavy engineering then they will expect the same level of profitability. The fact that the asset turnover in heavy engineering is relatively low means that they need to obtain a higher profit margin on sales to give the same profit on assets as in retailing. In retailing they can get away with a low profit margin on sales, relying on their fast turnover of assets. If the retailer pushes up their profit margin, lowering the level of sales, they will reduce their asset turnover. Of course, these points are generalizations. But they indicate the way in which ratio analysis can be used.

This type of ratio analysis enables relevant questions to be asked. They focus attention on points where differences from expectations occur, and they indicate possible problem areas.

Problems with financial ratio analysis

Three points should be emphasized. One is that all ratios are imperfect and imprecise, and should only be treated as guidelines. Whilst users of financial statements should take account of these ratios, they ought not to regard them as providing the final word on all aspects of financial management and performance. For example, it can be dangerous to judge the liquidity and gearing position of a company on the basis of the balance sheet information, which relates to only one day in the year. The impression can be misleading, particularly if the company is engaged in a business subject to cyclical variations.

A second problem relates to comparisons. What are the targets for these ratios? No two companies are identical. Care has to be exercised when comparing the performance and financial position of one company with that of another. Of course, this is an even more difficult problem when comparing companies in different countries. Accounting conventions and practices differ from one country to another.

A third weakness is that the ratios are only as reliable as the accounting numbers on which they are based. The accounts of a company are prepared on the basis of a number of accounting conventions and assumptions. The users of ratios must be aware of what lies behind the accounting numbers.

Liquidity ratios

Perhaps the most important short-term ratio is the current ratio, i.e. the ratio of current assets to current liabilities, where current liabilities are creditors' amounts falling due within one year. A second working capital ratio, referred to as the 'acid test', is the ratio of quick assets (cash plus money at short call plus debtors) to current liabilities. Other ratios include debtors to net sales, which shows the average speed of collection, and inventory to sales, which shows the number of days' sales held in inventory.

The financial manager must watch these ratios because any noticeable movement from one annual report to the next can encourage observers to draw conclusions about the liquidity position and creditworthiness of the company. Whether ratios such as these actually merit the practical importance ascribed to them as guides in financial decision making is, of course, a debatable point.

While the theoreticians occupy themselves with the debate, the financial manager must be aware of the ratios and ensure that they do not move too far from the line of acceptable standards. The company does not exist in a vacuum, it coexists in a financial community, and while the 'arbitrary' standards of outsiders may have a low rating in company opinion, these constraints must nevertheless be acknowledged in the shaping of internal financial policy. In assessing the liquidity position of a company, outsiders use the current ratio and the liquidity ratio as two of their key indicators, and few companies can afford to ignore this fact entirely.

The current ratio

The current ratio is the ratio of current assets to current liabilities. The ratio for Guinness PLC, as at 31 December 1996 was

$$3587/2572 = 1.39\text{:}1$$

Traditionally the satisfactory norm accepted for the current ratio was 2:1 which was taken to indicate that the company's short-term financial position was healthy. With the financial problems of the 1970s and 1980s coupled with improved cash management techniques the acceptable level for this ratio has been reduced.

The current assets of a manufacturing company need to be well in excess of the current liabilities for a company to be classified as safe by anyone furnishing it with credit or a short-term loan. The reason for this cover is that one of the current assets – usually the largest – is the inventory. This is far from being the safest form of asset since the money it represents is not necessarily realizable in the short term, and even if it is, the actual returns from a hurried sale may amount to considerably less than valuation (cost or market value, whichever is lower) would suggest. Furthermore, inventory can deteriorate or become obsolete. Hence cover is required on the current assets over current liabilities.

The 'quick' ratio

The 'quick' ratio is the ratio of current assets less inventory to current liabilities. For Guinness the ratio was

$$1720/2572 = 0.67\text{:}1$$

Inventory is excluded because it is not usually regarded as an asset that can quickly be turned into cash. There are of course items of inventory to which this does not apply, e.g. commodity stocks. The 'rule of thumb' for this ratio used to be 1:1, but again in the more difficult liquidity conditions of the 1970s and 1980s a lower ratio was found to be acceptable. The typical ratio declined from 0.9:1 in the early 1970s to 0.8:1 in the mid-1980s, and lower levels are now regarded as acceptable.

This reduction in the ratio can be achieved partly as a result of tighter credit control. If some companies reduce their net trade credit (debtors − creditors) it means that somebody else has to provide more. Often it is the smaller companies that lose, for they lack the financial power and bargaining strength of the largest companies. The financial manager has to steer the ratios along a route determined partly by the accepted lower limit below which suppliers may be unwilling to grant credit and banks to lend. It is not, of course, a matter of a single absolute level inviting approval or disapproval: there exists a range of values, certain regions of which are considered less desirable than others. It is considered bad financial management to allow the ratio to become too high. For example, a current ratio of 2.5:1 would make a company a very sound client for anyone thinking of giving it credit – but the company's shareholders might reasonably be less happy with the situation. It could mean that the company has not made the best use of its borrowing possibilities. It could mean that too many resources are tied up in current assets.

Liquidity ratios such as the two referred to above have two important limitations. First, any thorough assessment of a company's working capital position should take into account the bank overdraft ceiling. This is not usually shown in the annual accounts, but the freedom to borrow from the bank can put a remarkably different complexion on the recorded liquidity position. It could be perfectly safe to supply goods on credit to a company whose quick ratio is far below 1:1, if it had adequate overdraft facilities to call on. It is, of course, difficult to find out about these standby arrangements.

Secondly, these liquidity ratios are all static; they do not reflect the flux or potentially rapid changeability of a company's financial situation. If the current liabilities of the company exceed its liquid assets (i.e. if the quick ratio is less than 1:1), it is relevant to know how quickly the situation could be remedied without drastic measures. Earnings would be the important factor here.

As with many accounting ratios, acceptable levels of ratios will be linked to the type of industry or business being analysed. With Guinness we are dealing with a company which manufactures products and also keeps long-term inventories of maturing liquor. Its sales will be made on credit to customers who will pay at the end of their account period. Guinness is likely to have a high profit mark-up but slow turnover of stock. We can contrast this with a retailer where nearly all sales will be for cash, inventories will be turned over quickly (particularly fresh foods) and credit will be taken from suppliers who will often be paid after the cash has been received for the sale of their product. These businesses may at first sight appear to be hopelessly insolvent as short-term liabilities may exceed short-term assets; however, because of the nature of the business they are able to operate successfully with these very low levels of liquidity. This emphasizes the point made earlier that comparisons need to be made with companies in similar industries or with industry-based norms or averages.

Financial efficiency ratios

The collection period is a well-used ratio. It indicates the period of time from when a sale is made to when the cash is received. In the Guinness example it equals

$$\frac{\text{trade debtors}}{\text{sales}} \times 365 = \frac{852}{4730} \times 365 = 66 \text{ days}$$

This period of time is not out of line with other manufacturing companies in the UK. Clearly it should be much lower for companies such as retail stores, for whom most of the sales are for cash and not on credit terms. The debtors figure used was obtained from the notes to the accounts and represents trade debtors. The balance sheet figure includes other debts not directly related to trading.

The other side of the coin to the collection period is the payments period. How long does it take a company to pay its creditors? If it takes longer to pay them than it does to collect from debtors it is on balance taking credit from other businesses. If it is the other way round it is supplying credit. Unfortunately very often it is the smaller company that ends up supplying credit because of its weak bargaining position.

The ratio that we need to ascertain the average payment period in days is

$$\frac{\text{trade creditors (relating to the supply of materials and goods)}}{\text{purchases of materials and goods}} \times 365$$

$$= \frac{333}{3121} \times 365 = 39 \text{ days}$$

Unfortunately we cannot calculate a ratio from an analysis of the published accounts in which one can have any confidence. The denominator includes three items Raw Materials and Consumables (866) Excise Duties (1168) and Other Operating Charges (1087). It is not certain whether Trade Creditors relate to all three items.

There are three principal financial ratios that management can employ to indicate when questions should be asked about the level of stocks. There may be perfectly good reasons why a high level of inventory is being maintained. Nevertheless, at a broad-brush level the financial ratios can provide a starting point for enquiry.

The inventory-to-sales ratio estimates the number of days' stock that the company has on hand:

$$\frac{\text{inventory}}{\text{cost of sales}} \times 365$$

Management can observe the movement of the ratio over time to see if any dangerous trends develop that cannot be explained by justifiable causes. It should be noted that it is the cost of sales figure which should be used as the denominator, rather than the sales revenue figure. This is because inventory is valued at cost price, as is the cost of sales. The sales revenue, however, includes profits.

In the Guinness example, if we take total operating costs as the denominator, the number of days' stock on hand becomes

$$\frac{1867}{3769} \times 365 = 180 \text{ days}$$

This is a particular high level of stock because of the large quantities of maturing spirits. For most manufacturing companies the stock on hand is in the region of 90 days. The ratio is obviously more useful if separate values are obtained for the different categories of inventory. This can easily be determined by management, but again the information is not available to an outsider as companies in the UK are not required to show the breakdown of inventories in their accounts.

Instead of expressing the inventory figure as the number of days' sales on hand, it is sometimes shown in the following form:

$$\frac{\text{cost of sales}}{\text{inventory}}$$

This is the turnover-to-inventory ratio, and is again intended to indicate whether a company's inventories are justifiable in relation to its sales. In this case a high ratio indicates that management can move its inventory quickly. However, caution is necessary in the use of these ratios, for in many businesses the inventory figure can vary considerably with the date of the balance sheet. It might be satisfactory for a company to consider the movement of its own ratio over time, but if it starts to compare this ratio with that of other companies in the same industry, it must ensure that the balance sheets are for comparable dates. Another danger is to read too much into the expression 'number of days' inventory on hand'. As mentioned above, for the typical company this figure is about 90 days, but this does not mean that there is sufficient inventory to be able to meet 90 days' sales if no more production takes place. This conclusion could only be drawn if the inventory was all finished goods, but the aggregate figure includes inventory not in a saleable form.

The third ratio that is concerned with inventory expresses inventory as a percentage of total assets, namely the inventory-to-assets ratio:

$$\frac{\text{inventory}}{\text{total assets}} \times 100$$

This ratio can also be affected by the closing date of the company's financial year, and is dependent upon the way that assets are valued.

In summary, the ratios at a highly aggregated level can point to the need for enquiry into how well the company's stock control policy is functioning.

Gearing (leverage) ratios

The guides or rules for determining the amount of funds that can be raised from loans are somewhat confusing. Perhaps the best-known rule of thumb is the ratio of total debt to total assets:

$$\text{debt ratio} = \frac{\text{total debt}}{\text{total assets}} \times 100$$

where total debt includes all the current liabilities plus long- and medium-term loans, leasing obligations and tax liabilities. 'Total assets' is self-explanatory: it includes all fixed and current assets. Sometimes it is suggested that only tangible assets should be included in the calculations. This means excluding assets such as goodwill, brands patents and any capitalized expenses. Very often the goodwill arises because upon the purchase of a company more was paid for the acquired assets than their book value; in such a case it could be argued that their real value was the price paid. Therefore a more realistic valuation of the assets of a company would include intangibles.

The rule of thumb in the UK for an acceptable ratio of total debt to total assets is 50% (or 1:2). This implies that it is reasonable to finance half the assets of the company by debt. Total debt always includes tax payments due in the next accounting period, and sometimes deferred tax. The justification for including these last two items is that the amounts represent somebody else's money which is being used to finance the business and in time these liabilities will have to be paid.

The ratio for Guinness PLC as at 31 December 1996 was

$$\frac{2572 + 622 + 161}{7813} = 42.9\%$$

The provisions for liabilities and charges (£211 million) have not been included as part of the total debt as at 31 December 1996. In this company's case it comprises a provision for deferred taxation and provision made on acquisitions.

We have not yet considered in detail the composition of Guinness's fixed assets. If this is done it will be seen that the major asset is 'Acquired brands at cost' which amounts to £1395 million. This is about 30% of the total of fixed assets. The recognition and valuation of brand names is a controversial subject in accounting. There is a large problem in valuing a brand name. To be fair to Guinness the value that they show in their balance sheet is the price that they paid to purchase their brand names. Guinness were engaged in a controversial takeover of Distillers PLC in 1986 and did have to pay a 'high' price to acquire many brand names.

The brands the company owns are well-known whisky names like Bells, Johnnie Walker and White Horse and also include well-known gin and brandy names. In fact, when we consult the notes to the accounts we find that the 'investments' figure is mainly represented by an investment in MH, the French company which itself owns many famous brands, some of which are capitalized on the MH balance sheet.

Two lessons can be learned from this for those engaged in analysing the accounts of companies:

- the importance of footnotes and the statement of accounting policies given with the accounts;
- the difficulty of comparison. If one were comparing Guinness's debt ratio with that of another company in the same industry one would need to ensure that the other company included the value of its brand names as an asset.

A slightly different way of looking at the borrowing position of a company is by means of the borrowing ratio:

$$= \frac{\text{long- and short-term borrowing}}{\text{capital employed (including short-term borrowing)}}$$

The calculation of this ratio needs some explanation. Bank overdrafts have traditionally been regarded as short-term debt and so have been included in the balance sheet under the heading of current liabilities. Certainly a bank has the legal right to recall an overdraft at comparatively short notice, and so it may be thought prudent always to treat the item as if it were a short-term liability. However, a number of companies tend to use overdrafts as if they were a continuing source of finance.

To obtain the total level of borrowing it is clearly necessary to add together overdrafts and longer-term loans. To obtain the figure of capital employed is a little more contentious. Traditionally, capital employed (total net assets) was taken to be total assets minus current liabilities, where, as explained, current liabilities included overdrafts. However, to obtain comparable statistics for capital employed in different companies, it is necessary not to deduct the assets financed by overdrafts.

It should be emphasized that this approach to determining borrowing potential is dependent on the correct valuation of assets. It is not possible to compare the ratio for a company that has recently revalued its assets, and one that has a historical valuation. Often the comparatively simple act of revaluing assets can reveal increased borrowing possibilities.

The debt ratio is sometimes expressed in a slightly different form, namely total debt to shareholders' funds, where shareholders' funds are the sum of ordinary capital, preference capital and all reserves. The rule of thumb for the total-debt-to-total-asset ratio implied that half the assets could be financed by debt. The other half of the assets must be financed from the sum of ordinary capital, preference capital and reserves, namely shareholders' funds. Therefore the rule of thumb for this total debt to shareholders' funds ratio is 1:1. This means that the assets could decline in value or be reduced in value by up to 50% before threatening the security of the funds provided from loans. If the debt to shareholders' funds ratio is higher than the norm, say 2:1, the claims of the debtholders and the creditors are not so safe: assets need to fall in value by only a third before their claims are threatened.

Debt capacity is here being expressed as the relationship between the balance sheet assets financed by debt and those financed by equity. The ratio for Guinness is as follows:

$$\text{total debt} : \text{equity} = 3355:4241 = 0.79:1$$

A problem with the use of such ratios as a guide to levels of debt is that the measure is static. Risk levels change over time, with the risk being the possible inability of the company to pay the interest or repay the debt. The balance sheet data on which the gearing ratios are based relate to one point of time, and do not reflect the cash flow and funds flow which can affect the level of risk.

A further problem arises because of new types of financial security that have been developed. These are called 'complex capital instruments'. It is not always clear whether they should be treated as debt or equity. One such instrument is a 'convertible redeemable preference share'. Under certain conditions it is equity, under other conditions debt.

The method of valuing assets, and depreciation policy, will affect the debt-to-asset ratio. These accounting policies should have no bearing on the ability to repay debt.

A better measure of risk might be the interest cover, namely the number of times by which earnings exceed interest payments. Interest cover shows whether a company is capable of servicing a level of debt. The ratio that shows interest cover is

$$\frac{\text{profits available to pay interest}}{\text{interest payable}}$$

For Guinness in 1996 this was

$$\frac{1074}{131} = 8.2$$

The interest payable figure is obtained from the notes to the accounts. The profit and loss account often only shows net interest, i.e. the difference between interest paid and interest received.

Of course, the amount of cover that is required depends on the economic conditions of the time. If the level of economic activity is expected to grow or at least remain stable, then less cover would be required than if the economy was expected to decline. On an unsecured loan, at the present time, interest cover of about five times would be required. It is obviously possible to obtain a loan with less cover, but the risks are greater, and it would be more difficult and probably more expensive. The measure shows how much earnings can fluctuate before the interest payments are threatened. It is a good measure, but it does have limitations. The earnings figure is not the same as cash flow. The ability to make payments depends upon cash flow. Also one can ask what guide past earnings are to future earnings, with the risk depending on future earnings. A meaningful attempt to determine risk should study the cash-flow patterns of the company, particularly during recession periods. It is these data that would give some guide to the possibilities of default, i.e. the possibility that the company will not be able to meet its fixed cash commitments.

Cash-flow ratios

With companies producing and publishing cash-flow statements it is now possible for the financial analyst to calculate a number of useful ratios based on cash figures rather than earnings figures.

(a) $$\frac{\text{Price per share}}{\text{Free cash flow per share}}$$

This ratio has already been discussed. For Guinness at mid-1996, this ratio equalled 27 to 1.

(b) $$\frac{\text{Operating cash flow}}{\text{Operating profit}} = \frac{1020}{961} = 1.06$$

This ratio should normally be around one. This shows that the accrual adjustments are not having too severe an affect on reported profits. If this ratio were significantly less than one, for a number of years, it could be worrying, suggesting that the profits figure was being 'managed' and that the cash was not really being generated.

(c) $\dfrac{\text{Capital expenditure (tangible fixed assets)}}{\text{Depreciation}} = \dfrac{170}{159} = 1.07$

This ratio indicates how much of the capital expenditure is on new developments and how much is replacement of existing activities. All measures have their own pitfalls, including this one. Capital expenditure levels tend to vary year by year, and depreciation is really just a way of enabling funds to be retained in the business so that management can decide how they are used. There is no real need to spend funds retained in the business, through a provision for depreciation, on replacing existing assets.

(d) Self-financing investment ratio is defined as:

$$\frac{\text{internal funding}}{\text{investment activities (net)}}$$

The company can obtain finance from internal or external sources. It uses the funds to increase assets (invest), reduce liabilities (repay loans), or change its cash liabilities. The above ratio indicates how much of the funds generated by the business are reinvested in assets. Internal funds are retained earnings plus depreciation.

The position can change from one year to the next; it is the movement over time in the ratio that needs to be observed. For example, BP have shown a steady increase over time in the amount of internal finance that they have generated, but the use to which such funds is put varies from year to year. In 1995 a considerable proportion of the internal funds generated was being used to repay borrowings, whereas in 1991 external funds were being raised through borrowing to help finance investment activities.

For Guinness in 1996 the ratio equalled

$$\frac{390 + 159}{170 + 37} = 2.65$$

The numerator consists of retained earnings plus depreciation. Retained earnings is not of course a true cash-flow figure. The denominator is capital expenditure, financial investment and acquisitions less disposals. In fact the cash inflow generated in excess of investment needs was used to re-purchase the company's shares; there was also a decrease in liquid resources.

The self-financing investment ratio clearly has to be exercised with care. As both the BP and Guinness examples show, cash inflows are used for financial restructuring purposes and repaying loans, not just to fund investment.

(e) Self-financing ratio is defined as:

$$\frac{\text{internal funding}}{\text{total funding}}$$

$$= \frac{\text{(net cash flow from operations + returns on investment and servicing of finance } - \text{ taxation)}}{\text{(internal funding + outside financing + changes in liquid resources)}}$$

The amounts required to calculate this ratio are all shown in published group cash-flow statements. The ratio indicates how much of the finance needed to fund investment activities and changes in the cash balances is obtained from the company's own activities.

For Guinness the ratio is.

$$\frac{1020 - 187 - 255}{578 + 56} = \frac{578}{634} = 0.91$$

In Guinness's case in 1996 their increase in cash from changes in liquid resources and new longer-term financing was very small (£56 million). Most of the funds they needed were generated internally, and these were partly used to reduce long-term finance.

Projected cash flows

Occasionally projected cash flows also be used to ascertain the creditworthiness of a borrower. A bank will want statements of expected future cash flows provided by independent experts (for example, mining engineers) rather than the in-house 'experts' of the potential borrower. Most project financing (e.g. North Sea oil and Eurotunnel) is based on projected cash-flow estimates.

Usually the banks will have their own rule of thumb as to the ratios based on cash flow that they consider desirable. One is a 'loan collateral value'. This could be written in a form such that the outstanding loans at any one time are always to be less than 50% of the discounted present value of the net cash flows from proven developed reserves. This is similar to the total debt cover ratio referred to in the Eurotunnel prospectus (see below). It can be used to determine at the outset how much borrowing will be allowed, and to monitor during the life of the investment whether adequate security is being provided.

A second common ratio is the debt service cover ratio. The typical wording of this ensures that the borrower will not allow the ratio of annual historic and projected cash flows (whichever is appropriate) to annual fixed charges to be less than say 1.3 to 1.0 at any time.

These ratios would be monitored. They would normally be written into what is referred to as the 'borrower's negative covenants' which accompany any loan agreements. The banks are of course still taking risks when lending on the security of proven oil and mineral reserves. The cash flow depends not just on quantity but also on price. Commodity prices are very volatile over time.

An interesting use of financial ratios based not on accounting estimates of profits or asset values but on estimates of cash-flow figures was shown in the original Eurotunnel prospectus. The tunnel is financed mainly by funds obtained from a syndicate of banks. The level of drawings obtained from this syndicate was in the form of cash or letters of credit issued to secure loans from third parties including the European Investment Bank and the Crédit National. Under the original credit agreement the funds made available could be drawn over a period of approximately seven years. A 'regular repayment schedule is designed to ensure repayment in full by 15th November 2005'.

The credit agreement contained a number of warranties and covenants by Eurotunnel in favour of the banks. The agreement listed a number of events, the occurrence of which would entitle the banks to take various actions, for example preventing further borrowing and going as far as allowing the banks to assume management of the project. These events included failing to achieve certain agreed target financial ratios.

The terms of the credit agreement provided for the banks to monitor the progress and expected cash flows of the project. Unfortunately, Eurotunnel encountered many financial difficulties, and the loans had to be restructured a number of times. The banks had little option but to accept a deal which swapped their loans into equity.

Value-added ratios

As explained earlier in the chapter some company analysts believe that value-added figures are useful. There are various measures of value added. One approach to estimating this figure is to deduct bought-in costs from turnover. Bought-in costs cover raw materials, components and use of outside services.

The value-added figure represents value a company has added to a product. An alternative way of measuring the figure is to add together wages, salaries, interest paid, dividend and tax. This represents the sum the firm has added to the cost of the bought-in components.

Having measured value added (VA) the following ratios can be calculated and monitored:

$$\text{Capital efficiency} = \frac{\text{VA}}{\text{Capital employed}}$$

$$\text{Total factor productivity} = \frac{\text{VA}}{\text{Employment costs} + \text{capital usage (depreciation)}}$$

$$\text{Use of liquid funds} = \frac{\text{VA}}{\text{Working capital}}$$

Tobin's *Q* ratio

This ratio relates the market value of a company's securities to the replacement cost of its assets:

$$Q = \frac{\text{Market value of debt} + \text{Market value of equity}}{\text{Replacement cost of net assets}}$$

It can be argued that if this ratio is less than one, the firm should cease trading, sell its assets and return the net funds to the holder of debt and equity securities. The value of the equity and debit reflects the market's expectations of a company's future returns; if these are less than the value of the net assets why should the business remain in existence?

It is difficult in practice to calculate this ratio. The replacement cost of assets is not the same as the book value. Very few companies disclose the replacement cost of their assets in their accounts.

Another problem with this ratio is that the value of many businesses depends not on tangible assets which are easy to value, but on intangible assets, such as brands and intellectual capital. Most businesses do not include brand values on their balance sheet and hardly any include the value of the creative people they employ. But in modern businesses it is the value of brands and people that are the value drivers. The value of equity depends on future profits which are a function of these intangible assets, not just on the value of machinery and buildings.

Lev has shown that for companies taken over the 'acquisition price to book value ratios' in the USA varies from 9 to 1 in the software industry and 7 to 1 in the communications industry to approximately 2 to 1 in the banking, public utilities, oil and motor industries. This is not exactly the same as the Q ratio, but it is similar. Acquisition price represents the market value of securities acquired; the book value of net assets is a rough approximation to replacement values.

The Q ratio has taken on a significance in the analysis of levels of share prices in stock markets. When there is debate on whether share price levels are too high, and whether or not the level of prices can be expected to fall in the future, the Q ratio is sometimes quoted. In 1997 it was being pointed out that the overall Q ratio in the market was 1:3, which meant security values were 130% of underlying company net assets. This level, it was stated, was higher than it had been for a considerable time.

Financial ratios are an indication of the financial strength of a company. However, they are only an indication; they do not prove anything. They are a trigger mechanism; if a ratio is out of the ordinary, questions need to be asked. There might be perfectly satisfactory explanations for the particular size of the ratio, but the ratio does need an explanation.

A number of researchers have attempted to forecast company failure based on the levels of the company's financial ratios. One distinguished writer on this topic in the USA is Altman [16]. In one of his studies he examined characteristics of a number of companies that became bankrupt over a period, and the characteristics of a sample of companies that remained solvent over the period. He used a statistical technique known as multiple discriminant analysis in an attempt to differentiate between the two groups. Initially he considered 22 potentially helpful variables (ratios), but from this list 5 variables were selected 'as doing the best overall job together in the prediction of corporate bankruptcy'. Of these 5, the liquidity variable which was found to be more useful for discrimination purposes than either the current ratio or the liquidity ratio was:

$$\frac{\text{working capital}}{\text{total assets}}$$

where working capital equals current assets minus current liabilities. The other four useful ratios were

$$\frac{\text{retained earnings}}{\text{total assets}}$$

$$\frac{\text{earnings before interest and taxes}}{\text{total assets}}$$

$$\frac{\text{market equity value}}{\text{book value of total debts}}$$

$$\frac{\text{sales}}{\text{total assets}}$$

The discriminant ratio model proved to have some success, with correct predictions in 94% of the bankrupt cases. Altman claims that 'investigation of the individual ratio movements prior to bankruptcy corroborated the model's findings that bankruptcy can be accurately predicted up to two years prior to actual failure'.

The one ratio that made the largest contribution to differentiating between the two groups was the current profitability ratio: earnings to total assets. In fact, there was no evidence of bankruptcy in companies earning profits. This may seem an undramatic observation, but it does underline the importance of considering liquidity ratios in a dynamic context. A company may have a current liquidity problem, but if it is profitable, the flow of funds should be able to remedy the liquidity position. This explains the importance of considering the ratios in conjunction with the current flow of funds.

Altman found that the so-called Z-score model was a good forecaster of failure two years prior to bankruptcy. The model was able to predict with 95% accuracy one year prior to bankruptcy and with 72% accuracy two years prior to bankruptcy. The accuracy diminished substantially as the lead time to bankruptcy extended beyond two years. The model was not used to examine its usefulness in predicting the failure of small firms.

Following Altman, numerous studies attempted to improve and extend the bankruptcy classification process. One was a zeta model, which is claimed to be quite accurate at predicting bankruptcy up to five years prior to failure. This model used seven financial variables, covering return on assets, stability of earnings, interest cover, cumulative profitability, the current ratio, size and a gearing ratio. The most significant variable was found to be cumulative profitability, which is measured by the ratio of retained earnings to total assets.

There are two types of error that can arise with such predictions. One is that the model will fail to identify a company that is in financial distress, and the other is that the model will identify a company as having a high probability of failure when in fact it is sound.

It should be appreciated that all accounting numbers can do is indicate something has gone wrong within a company. The cause of the financial distress is usually bad management, and the mistakes have already been made before that fact is revealed in the financial accounts. Those investing in companies and those making credit available may well have left it too late if they wait for the publication of the annual accounts in order to assess the company's strengths and weaknesses. Analysts should look for the symptoms of failure. Such issues are discussed in Chapter 23.

A number of other researchers have used a similar technique to that of Altman. Multiple discriminant analysis attempts to find the combination of variables which best discriminates between two or more groups. This involves attributing weights to each variable such that the distribution of scores obtained for each group has the least overlap. In the application of this technique in the financial distress area one group consists of those companies that became bankrupt during the period of study, and the other group consists of those companies that survived. The variables used to discriminate are of course the financial ratios. Having determined the relative importance of each ratio, these weights can then be used to predict the chance of failure for any company.

Research in the UK in this area has been led by Taffler [17]. In his 1982 paper he reports that as a result of testing the usefulness of 50 ratios the five most significant from a discrimination point of view were

$$\frac{\text{earnings before interest and tax}}{\text{total assets}}$$

$$\frac{\text{total liabilities}}{\text{net capital employed}}$$

$$\frac{\text{quick assets}}{\text{total assets}}$$

$$\frac{\text{working capital}}{\text{net worth}}$$

$$\frac{\text{cost of sales}}{\text{stock}}$$

The first two of these five ratios were found to be the most significant. The first ratio is a measure of the flow of funds into the business resulting from the company's own operations. It was also found to be important in Altman's study. The second ratio shows the outside claims on the resources of the business. The fifth ratio indicates stock turnover.

The Bank of England has looked at the potential of this technique [18]. Their model did not show results that were particularly encouraging. The Bank concluded that 'careful analysis of accounts over a long period together with scrutiny of other published information is likely to provide the best, indeed the only basis for any adequate assessment by an outsider of the financial position of a company'.

The discriminant approach is still used, however, to indicate companies at financial risk. A financial data service is available in which figures are produced that indicate the chance of a particular company failing.

There are many theoretical problems with this type of statistical analysis. There are also problems with the accounting data. Nevertheless, the results of these studies and other similar types of work are used by financial analysts and bankers.

Many of the studies have only used financial ratios. A few studies used mixed models (with some cash-flow variables and some financial ratios). The cash-flow ratio most often used in such studies is cash flow to total debt. Other cash-flow statistics used in the prediction of failure are cash to sales, cash to current liabilities and cash flow from operations.

It is hoped that there is more to the use of this approach than just 'self-fulfilling prophecies'. If bankers and analysts use the technique and believe in it, then any company that ranks badly as a result of the analysis might well find its funds cut off. As a result the company will fail and the technique will be said to have worked!

2.10 CONCLUSIONS

A very popular way of analysing the performance of a business is through the use of financial ratio analysis. Impressions formed on the basis of this analysis can affect decisions as to whether to supply the business with goods on credit, whether bank loans will be made available, whether a company will be given a stock market listing, and whether or not to buy the company's shares.

Accounting by its nature has to be an inexact subject. It is necessary to make many assumptions in preparing a set of financial accounts. All attempts to value a company must be estimated, whether based on measuring asset values or based on expected future cash flows. Nevertheless, those operating in the stock market must make decisions every day on what they believe should be the value of a company's shares.

There is a major debate as to whether those who operate in the stock market are or are not fooled by attempts to manipulate accounting earnings figures. There is much literature on how capital markets respond to accounting numbers. There is also concern as to how the system of rewarding managers affects reported earnings. These issues will be returned to later in the book.

2.11 REFERENCES

1 Kaplan, R.S. and Norton, D.P. (1992) The balanced scorecard: measures that drive performance, *Harvard Business Review*, Jan.–Feb.
2 Smith, T. (1996) *Accounting for Growth*, 2nd edn, Century Books, London.
3 Stewart, G.B. (1994) EVA, fact and fantasy, *Journal of Applied Corporate Finance*, **7**(2): 71–87.
4 Ball, R. and Brown, P. (1968) An empirical evaluation of accounting income numbers, *Journal of Accounting Research*, Autumn, 159–78.
5 Bernard, V.L. and Thomas, J. (1990) Evidence that stock prices do not fully reflect the implications of current earnings', *Journal of Accounting and Economics*, **13**, 305–40.
6 Little, I. and Raynor, A. (1966) *Higgledy Piggledy Growth Again*, Blackwell, Oxford.

7 Davidson, S., Stickney, C. and Weil, R. (1987) *Accounting: the Language of Business*, 7th edn, Horton, Arizona.

8 Holmes, G. and Sugden, A. (1990) *Interpreting Company Reports and Accounts*, 4th edn, Woodhead-Faulkner, Cambridge.

9 Lev, B. (1989) On the usefulness of earnings and earnings research: lessons and directions from two decades of empirical research, *Journal of Accounting Research*, Supplement, 153–92.

10 Scholes, M.S., Wilson, P. and Wolfson, M.A. (1988) Tax planning, regulatory capital planning and financial reporting strategy for commercial banks, *Review of Financial Studies*, **3**(4): 625–50.

11 Allen, L. and Saunders, A. (1988) Incentives to engage in bank window dressing: manager vs stockholder conflicts', working paper, Hofstra University.

12 McNichols, M. and Wilson, P. (1988) Evidence of earnings management from the provision for bad debts, *Journal of Accounting Research*, **26**, Supplement, 1–31.

13 Smith, T. – see [2].

14 Brink, H.L. (1992) A history of Philips' accounting policies on the basis of its annual reports, *European Accounting Review*, **1**: 255–75.

15 Tinic, S.H. (1990) A perspective on the market's fixation on accounting numbers, *Accounting Review*, **65**(4): 781–96, Oct.

16 Altman, E.I. (1968) Financial ratios, discriminant analysis and the prediction of corporate bankruptcy, *Journal of Finance*, September.
Altman, E.I. (1974) Evaluation of a company as a going concern, *Journal of Accounting*, December.

17 Taffler, R.J. (1982) Forecasting company failure in the UK using discriminant analysis and financial ratio data, *Journal of the Royal Statistical Society*, Series A, **146**(3): 342–58.
Taffler, R.J. (1983) The Z-score approach to measuring company solvency, *Accountants Magazine*, 91–6, March.
Taffler, R.J. and Tisshaw, H. (1977) Going, going, gone – four factors which predict, *Accountancy*, 50–4, March.

18 Techniques for assessing corporate financial strength (1982) *Bank of England Quarterly Bulletin*, 221–3, June.

2.12 FURTHER READING

There are many textbooks on financial accounting and some on financial statement analysis. Those below are the main texts dealing with the latter topic. The Altman book shows what can happen when things go wrong.

Altman, E.I. (1992) *Corporate Financial Distress: A Complete Guide to Predicting, Avoiding and Dealing with Bankruptcy*, John Wiley, New York.

Foster, G. (1986) *Financial Statement Analysis*, 2nd edn, Prentice-Hall, Englewood Cliffs, NJ.

Holmes, G. and Sugden, A. (1997) *Interpreting Company Reports and Accounts*, 7th edn, Woodhead-Faulkner, London.

ICAEW (1995) Developing comprehensive performance predictors, Institute of Chartered Accounts in England and Wales, London.

Lebas, M. (1994) Managerial accounting in France: overview of past tradition and current practice, *The European Accounting Review*, 3.3: 471–87.

Parker, R.H. (1994) *Understanding Company Financial Statements*, 4th edn, Penguin, London.

Rees, W. (1996) *Financial Analysis*, 2nd edn, Prentice-Hall, Hemel Hempstead.

Samuels, J.M., Brayshaw, R.E. and Craner, J.M. (1994) *Financial Statement Analysis in Europe*, Chapman and Hall, London.

Note: Certain of the following problems are concerned with dividend yields and price earnings ratios. These topics are dealt with again in Chapter 6.

1 (a) Complete the balance sheet and sales information shown for Jones Software Company using the following financial data:

Quick assets ratio, 0.8:1
Total assets turnover, 1.5×
Average collection period, 36.5 days
Inventory turnover, 5×
Net return on shareholders' funds, 20%

Balance sheet and sales data

	£		£
Equity shares	–	Fixed assets	–
Retained earnings	65 000	Inventories	–
Long-terrn debt	40 000	Amounts receivable	–
		Cash	–
Creditors	–		
		Total assets	200 000
		Profit after interest	
Sales	–	and tax	20 000

(b) C. Barngrover and Company had earnings per share of £4 last year, and it paid a £2 dividend. The book value per share at year-end was £40, while the total retained earnings increased by £12 million during the year. Barngrover has no preferred stock, and no new equity shares were issued during the year. If Barngrover's year-end debt (which equals its total liabilities) was £120 million, what was the company's year-end debt-to-assets ratio?

(c) What are the limitations of ratio analysis?

2 A friend of yours who has invested in the equity shares of Baxter PLC has recently received a copy of its annual report. He enjoys looking at the pictures in the early part of the report, but finds the financial accounts confusing. This is the first time that he has seen a set of published accounts. He seeks your advice and asks the following questions.

(a) How, if at all, can these accounts give him any guidance as to the future profitability of the company?

(b) In the ten year summary, many financial ratios are shown; these look impressive. Are there any dangers in relying on the numbers shown in these ratios?

(c) From the profit and loss account he can see that the company has made a profit but, given the circumstances in which the firm operates, how can he tell if this profit is satisfactory?

(d) He has read in the newspaper that although Baxter PLC is profitable it is experiencing liquidity problems. He asks how this can be – the company is either doing well or it is not – and you are asked to explain.

(e) Finally, he asks what figures in the accounts he should look at in order to see whether the company has liquidity problems, and at what figures he should look to see whether there could be long-term financing problems.

You are required to answer your friend's questions.

3 The trading and profit and loss accounts and the balance sheets for X Ltd and Y Ltd for the year ended 31 March 1998 are as shown below.

Trading and profit and loss accounts for the year ended 31 March 1998

	X Ltd £	Y Ltd £		X Ltd £	Y Ltd £
Opening stock	15 000	5 000	Sales	100 000	100 000
Purchases	80 000	86 000	Closing stock	25 000	11 000
Gross profit	30 000	20 000			
	125 000	111 000		125 000	111 000
Overheads	10 900	800			
Interest	2 000	7 000			
Dividends	3 000	5 000			
Taxation	6 000	–			
Net profit before extraordinary items	8 100	7 200	Gross profit	30 000	20 000
	30 000	20 000		30 000	20 000
Extraordinary items	2 000	(5 000)			

Balance sheets as at 31 March 1998

	X Ltd £	Y Ltd £		X Ltd £	Y Ltd £
Share capital (£1 shares)	50 000	50 000	Fixed assets	80 000	99 000
Profit and loss account	40 000	10 000	Current assets		
			Stocks	25 000	11 000
Shareholders' capital			Debtors	10 000	7 500
employed	90 000	60 000	Cash at bank	5 000	3 500
Loans	20 000	50 000			
Current liabilities	10 000	11 000			
	120 000	121 000		120 000	121 000

Both companies are quoted on the Stock Exchange. At 30 June 1998 the share price of X Ltd was £3.24 and the share price of Y Ltd was £2.16.

You are required (a) to calculate the liquidity, profit and gearing ratios of the two companies that would be of interest to investors, and (b) to calculate the price-to-earnings ratios of the two companies and give the reasons that might explain the difference in the market's evaluation of them.

3 INVESTMENT APPRAISAL

LEARNING OUTCOMES

By the end of this chapter the reader should:

- have seen the importance of the discounted cash flow approach to investment appraisal
- be able to use discounting to assess investment proposals in a variety of ways
- understand annuities and be able to take account of complicating factors
- be able to make judgements between competing capital investment projects and strategies

3.1 INTRODUCTION

An investment can be thought of as an action which changes the cash flow of the decision maker. Corporate investment can take the form of expenditures on buildings, equipment, land, research and development, changes in stock level, shares, deposits at financial institutions and the extension of credit. Major public-sector investments include economic development projects, schools, highways and other components of essential infrastructure. Private individuals make investment decisions when purchasing a house and major durable goods such as cars. Making such investments requires the outlay of funds at certain times, usually including the present, while income (or less tangible benefits) are produced at other times (usually in the future). Income benefits from private-sector investments are usually more readily identifiable than those from within the public sector. In the corporate realm, major investments not only change a company's cash flow, they also affect its financial position measured by key financial ratios and other statistics (changes in several measures of performance may need to be taken into account). These changes occur when the investment is made (or even when it is being considered in public) and during the lifetime of the investment.

Here we appraise investment possibilities in terms of the *cash flow* alterations that they bring about. This involves both the timing of returns and costs and an appropriate rate or rates of interest. Cash flow items are *discounted* (multiplied by a factor less than one) according to their distance from the present and the rate of discount used. All increases or decreases in revenues and costs (including tax payments) brought about by a project are *relevant* to the calculations and care is necessary to ensure that the right information is included. For example, while depreciation does not itself change the project's cash flow and so should not be included, depreciation allowances can affect cash flow through taxation payments. Calculations can sometimes be simplified through use of formulae – as in the case of annuities – and the use of tables, financial calculators, spreadsheets and other software can be helpful as circumstances justify. *Discounted cash flow*

(DCF) methods of investment appraisal include net present value and internal rate of return and imply familiarity with compound interest.

In the broader picture, corporate investment decision-making is set in the context of the company's capital budgeting process and its overall aims, culture and environment. Larger investment decisions will include wider considerations to be taken into account by senior management – who will need accurate and appropriate investment appraisals on which to ground the final decision.

3.2 COMPOUND INTEREST

The concept of compound interest underlies all financial transactions involving time-delayed receipts and payments. For commercial reasons some loans are quoted in terms of simple interest, but the packages are constructed following calculations in compound terms.

Consider an account paying interest at 10% annually compounded. Suppose that the sum deposited initially, the *principal*, is £1. At the end of one year the investor has £1.10 in the account. If this amount is left on deposit there is no reason to treat this investor less well than a new customer making a deposit of £1.10 at this time. So the entire £1.10 (made up of the principal of £1 and the first year's interest of £0.10) is available to earn interest in the second year. This is the key point of compounding – *interest itself gains interest*.

Interest in the second year is 10% of £1.10 (£0.11) so the total in the account after two years is £1.21. The 'pound's progress' is shown in Table 3.1. At 10% compound interest, after n years the principal of £1 becomes £$(1 + 0.1)^n$. Generalizing, £1 invested for n years at $100r\%$ becomes £$(1 + r)^n$. Table 1, at the back of the book, gives these *future* or *terminal values* for various r and n. So £1 invested at 10% for seven years grows to £1.9487 while £1 invested for 15 years at 25% becomes £28.4217.

Table 3.1

Principal	After one year	After two years	After three years
1	1 + 0.1(1) = 1.1	1.1 + 0.1(1.1) = 1.1(1 + 0.1) = $(1 + 0.1)^2$ = 1.21	1.21 + 0.1(1.21) = 1.21(1 + 0.1) = $(1 + 0.1)^3$ = 1.331

From Table 1 we can see the substantial consequences of quite small changes in interest rates when long periods of time are involved. For example, at 20% compound £1 becomes £38.3376 after 20 years, but at 21% the original £1 produces £45.2593 after 20 years. A 5% increase in the rate of interest (which has risen one percentage point from 20 to 21) has produced a much larger proportional increase in the end result – over 18%. If the horizon alters when high rates of interest are applied there will be large changes in the terminal sum. For example, at 30%, £1 becomes £190 after 20 years or £705 after 25 years. This highlights future dangers in debt rescheduling under high rates of interest.

If the principal sum is more than £1, the future value is found by multiplication of the principal by the appropriate factor from Table 1 as illustrated in the following problem.

Example 3.1

Find the future value of £75 invested for 12 years at 8%.

Answer

For $r = 0.08$ and $n = 12$ the compound interest factor given in Table 1 is 2.5182. Thus the original £75 would accumulate to £75(2.5182) = £188.87.

Compound interest

59

It can on occasion be necessary to find the principal required to generate a particular future value. An illustration is given in the following problem.

Example 3.2

How much would have to be invested originally in order to produce £250 after 16 years at 14%?

Answer

For $r = 0.14$ and $n = 16$ the compound interest factor is 8.1372. If the initial sum invested is £S, it is required that £$S(8.1372) = £250$. So:

$$S = \frac{250}{8.1372} = 30.72$$

This problem leads to consideration of present values.

3.3 DISCOUNTING AND PRESENT VALUES

The initial sum in Example 3.2 is the discounted present value or simply the *present value* of the future sum. The present value of £1 depends on the number of years (or compounding periods) and the rate of discount. The relationship is:

$$PV = \frac{1}{(1 + r)^n}$$

for if PV is invested now, its future value after n years' compound interest at $100r\%$ will be $PV(1 + r)^n = 1$. Table 2 gives present-value or *discount factors* for various values of r and n. For instance, £1 due after 16 years at 14% has a present value of £0.1229 and £250 due at this time has a present value of $250 \times 0.1229 = £30.72$. All the entries in this table are the reciprocals of the corresponding entries in Table 1, hence 0.1229 is the reciprocal of 8.1372. The present value of a stream of receipts or payments is found by adding the present values of individual items. So if receipts of £100, £150 and £200 occur at the end of each of three consecutive years, then the present value of this income stream at 10% interest will be:

$$PV = \frac{100}{(1 + 0.1)} + \frac{150}{(1 + 0.1)^2} + \frac{200}{(1 + 0.1)^3}$$

or, more conveniently, using the discount factor table:

$$PV = 100 \times 0.9091 + 150 \times 0.8264 + 200 \times 0.7513$$

$$= 364.93$$

Example 3.3

Find the present value of £450 to be received four years from the present at an interest rate of 8%.

Answer

The discount factor (Table 2) for $r = 0.08$ and $n = 4$ is 0.7350. So present value is:

$$£450 \times 0.7350 = £330.75$$

Example 3.4

Using a 15% discount rate find the present value of the cash flow:

$t = 0$	$t = 1$	$t = 2$	$t = 3$
−600	750	−150	1050

A convenient layout for the workings is:

Year	Sum	Discount factor	PV
0	−600	1	−600
1	750	0.8696	652.20
2	−150	0.7561	−113.42
3	1050	0.6575	690.38
		Total	629.16

3.4 THE NET PRESENT VALUE DECISION RULE

Investment projects typically generate a series of returns S_t where the subscript t is the timing of the return. If there are n returns in all, they could be written out in full as S_1, S_2, S_3, S_4, ..., where S_1 is the return after one year, S_2 is the return after two years, and so on. It is assumed that cash flow components arise at equally spaced intervals (adjustment can be made in cases where this is not so). The present value of the entire n-year stream is:

$$PV = \frac{S_1}{(1+r)} + \frac{S_2}{(1+r)^2} + \frac{S_3}{(1+r)^3} + \ldots + \frac{S_n}{(1+r)^n}$$

which can be made more concise in *summation* or *sigma notation* as:

$$PV = \sum_{t=1}^{n} S_t (1+r)^{-t}$$

in which the symbol Σ (*sigma*) tells us to add all following terms over the range of values of t from 1 up to n. Some of the S_t may be negative since in order to get the returns it will be necessary to invest money in one or more years. If an investment of £K now is required to secure the returns S_t then the present value obtained is the *gross present value* (GPV) of the investment, and GPV minus K (initial outlay) gives the formula for *net present value* (NPV) as:

$$NPV = \sum_{t=1}^{n} S_t (1+r)^{-t} - K$$

The *NPV decision rule* for a single project is:

Invest in the project if its NPV is positive. Do not invest if NPV is negative.

If NPV = 0 the rule is inconclusive, it makes no difference to the investor in terms of present value whether the project is accepted or rejected. The rule can be summarized in tabular form:

Outcome	Decision
NPV > 0	Accept
NPV < 0	Reject
NPV = 0	Inconclusive

A rationale for the rule is that GPV is an amount equivalent to all the returns. If it was invested now at $100r\%$ it would just generate the returns. That is, it would allow amounts S_t to be withdrawn in each year t. The amount £K is the sum of money which has to be paid now to secure the returns S_t, so if this price, K, is less than GPV then the deal is good. To illustrate this point consider the returns:

$t = 1$	$t = 2$
220	363

At a 10% rate of discount GPV is 500. Now consider an investment of 500 at $t = 0$. By $t = 1$ this becomes $500(1.1) = 550$, so if 220 is then withdrawn, 330 remains on deposit and becomes 330(1.1) = 363 by $t = 2$. So if GPV > K (and therefore NPV > 0) this means that the present value of the stream of returns exceeds the present value of the money required to secure them. But if GPV < K, initial outlay exceeds the value now of the returns that the outlay brings. So the proposed investment is rejected. GPV is a single-figure equivalent of the stream of net returns and the NPV decision rule compares like with like. The reason that NPV gives the correct decision for investors is that when one rate of interest applies to all financial transfers, the greater is NPV the greater are the cash sums that can be spent in *every* time period. This is because returns can be redistributed through time at the uniform rate of interest to suit the requirements of the investor. Financial markets allow consumption decisions to be made separately from the choice of investment, subject only to limits given by the value of NPV (the present value of consumption expenditures must not exceed NPV). To illustrate the NPV rule, consider the investment in the following problem.

Example 3.5

A company can buy a machine for £2200. The machine has a productive life of three years and net additions to cash flow (after tax and including scrap value at the end of year three) at the end of the three years are £770, £968 and £1331. The firm can buy the machine without having to borrow and the best alternative is investment elsewhere at an interest rate of 10%. Should the machine be bought?

Year	Sum	Discount factor	PV
0	−2200	1	−2200
1	770	0.9091	700
2	968	0.8264	800
3	1331	0.7513	1000
		NPV =	+300

The discount rate is important in the NPV rule. For example, if the discount rate used to evaluate the machine had been 20% ($r = 0.2$) instead of 10% ($r = 0.1$) then the NPV of the project would have been negative. Workings in this case are:

Answer

If the company chooses the investment it loses the chance to earn 10% compound. This gives the rate (in this context) to be used in the discount calculations. Putting the data into the formula for net present value gives NPV as:

$$NPV = \frac{770}{(1.1)} + \frac{968}{(1.1)^2} + \frac{1331}{(1.1)^3} - 2200 = 300$$

The investment is worthwhile and the machine should be bought. It can be convenient to put the workings into a table:

Year	Sum	Discount factor	PV
0	−2200	1	−2200.00
1	770	0.8333	641.64
2	968	0.6944	672.18
3	1331	0.5787	770.25
		NPV =	−115.93

and the project should be rejected. Although the investment in the machine is profitable in the sense that the undiscounted sum of the returns exceeds the outlay, *it is not profitable enough* when there is the chance to earn 20% on the money needed to buy the machine. The discount rate is the *opportunity cost* of the investment.

3.5 TERMINAL VALUE

Net terminal value (NTV) (also called net *future* value) can be a convenient yardstick for projects and it gives the same accept-or-reject decision as NPV. NTV is what the investor will end up with over and above the sum if the project was rejected. NTV is the *end-of-project excess*. The NTV decision rule for a single investment is:

Outcome	Decision
NTV > 0	Accept
NTV < 0	Reject
NTV = 0	Inconclusive

Suppose the firm in Example 3.5 had £3000 capital. If the machine is bought, £800 remains and can be invested at 10%, becoming £880 after one year when it is added to the first receipt from the project, £770, and carried forward at 10%. After three years of this reinvestment process, at the end of the project the investor has:

$$\{[(3000 - 2200) \times 1.1 + 770] \times 1.1 + 968\} \times 1.1 + 1331 = 4392.3$$

Take from this sum the amount that would have been obtained if the machine had not been bought:

$$3000 \times (1.1)^3 = 3993$$

the result is the NTV of the project:

$$NTV = 4392.3 - 3993 = 399.3$$

Recall that NPV was 300 and note that NTV is $300 \times (1.1)^3$ which shows the link between NTV and NPV. For an n-period project:

$$NTV = NPV(1 + r)^n$$

$$= \sum_{t=1}^{n} S_t (1+r)^{n-t} - K(1+r)^n$$

which illustrates an important point about NPV. For the formula to be appropriate, money coming in should be reinvested at the rate of discount. This also applies to the case of finance by borrowing, with returns being used to repay capital and interest on the borrowed sum. In NTV the reinvestment process is clear, and NPV is obtainable from NTV by dividing by $(1 + r)^n$.

3.6 THE INTERNAL RATE OF RETURN

Net present value represents the financial outcome of a project as an *amount* of return. The performance of an investment can also be measured as a *rate* of return. The *internal rate of return* (IRR) or DCF rate of return or *yield* of a project, is the discount rate required to make the present value of the returns equal to the initial outlay. So IRR is the rate of discount for which NPV is zero. This is $100i\%$ where i is given by:

$$\sum_{t=1}^{n} S_t (1+i)^{-t} - K = 0$$

The project's IRR is the maximum interest rate the investor can afford calculated in the declining balance manner (as in overdrafts). The returns to the investment, paid in as they occur, would just be enough to eliminate all liability. If project evaluation is based on IRR, the IRR is compared with a threshold or hurdle rate which will usually be the cost of capital. The single-project *IRR decision rule* is:

If the project's IRR exceeds the comparison rate (cost of capital) accept the investment; if IRR is less than the comparison rate, reject the investment.

That is, with a comparison rate of $100r\%$:

Outcome	Decision
$i > r$	Accept
$i < r$	Reject
$i = r$	Inconclusive

The inconclusive case, where the IRR is equal to the comparison rate, is of little practical importance. It is not usually easy to find the IRR of an investment by hand, but most spreadsheets and a number of other software packages will provide the yield for a straightforward cash flow. For manual work a method of approximation is used which gives answers accurate to one decimal place – usually sufficient. Consider the project in Example 3.5 (with cash flow: −2200, 770, 968, 1331) and plot the NPV of this investment against the discount rate used. As the rate rises, the NPV of a project with all positive returns will fall. This relationship is shown in Figure 3.1.

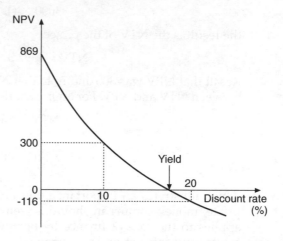

Figure 3.1

The point where NPV crosses the horizontal axis is the project's IRR. At a zero discount rate NPV is the sum of the undiscounted returns less the outlay: 869. At 10% we saw that NPV was +300 and at 20% it was −116. So zero NPV is at a discount rate between 10% and 20%. Greater accuracy can be achieved by a process of trial and error in which the whole-number rates of discount either side of the yield are determined, followed by *interpolation* between these values. Workings are shown in Table 3.2.

Table 3.2

Year	Sum	15% Discount factor	PV
0	−2200	1	−2200.00
1	770	0.8696	669.59
2	968	0.7561	731.90
3	1331	0.6575	875.13
		NPV =	+76.62

Year	Sum	16% Discount factor	PV
0	−2200	1	−2200.00
1	770	0.8621	663.83
2	968	0.7432	719.42
3	1331	0.6407	852.77
		NPV =	+36.01

Year	Sum	17% Discount factor	PV
0	−2200	1	−2200.00
1	770	0.8475	652.58
2	968	0.7305	711.48
3	1331	0.6244	831.08
		NPV =	−4.86

An initial guess of 15% gives an NPV of +76.62 and since the NPV graph still lies above the horizontal axis 15% is too low. We then try 16%, which gives NPV = +36.01, still too low. A rate of 17% gives NPV = −4.86, from which it is clear that the IRR is between 16% and 17% but nearer to 17%. The linear interpolation proceeds as follows. A straight line is drawn between the point on the NPV graph above 16% and the point on the NPV graph below 17%. Where this line crosses the axis is the estimated yield – as shown in Figure 3.2.

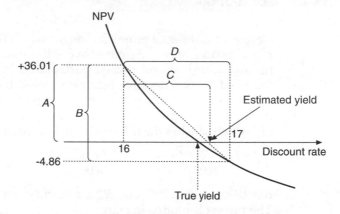

Figure 3.2

The approximation will be a slight overestimate – but not so much as might appear from the figure (in which the curvature of the NPV graph is exaggerated). For the calculations, note that the ratio of distance C to D is the same as the ratio of A to B so the straight line cuts the discount axis a proportion 36.01/(36.01 + 4.86) of the way along the 1% interval from 16% to 17%, so the estimated IRR is:

$$\left[16 + \frac{36.01}{40.87}\right]\% = 16.88\%$$

in which 16.88% might well be rounded to 16.9%.

Where there is a uniform discount rate, the yield and NPV rules give the same accept/reject decision for a single project. In Figure 3.3 the NPV of a project with a unique IRR is plotted against the discount rate.

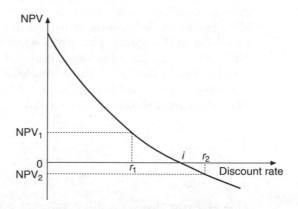

Figure 3.3

The figure shows that the IRR and NPV (and NTV) rules are consistent in the single-project case. If the cost of capital was $100r_1\%$ the project's NPV is NPV_1 which is positive, indicating acceptance. The IRR of the project, $100i\%$, exceeds the cost of capital, so the IRR rule also indicates acceptance. If the cost of capital was $100r_2\%$, NPV would be NPV_2 which, being negative, signals rejection. Since the project's IRR is less than $100r_2\%$ the project is also rejected by the IRR rule.

Care is required in using the IRR rule when the cash flow does not take the form of an initial outlay (negative cash flow) followed by positive returns. Other cash flow patterns can cause technical problems in the form of more than one value for IRR, but such difficulties can be overcome and conclusions about the use of IRR still apply.

3.7 THE EXTENDED YIELD METHOD

Define a *well-behaved* project as one for which the graph of NPV cuts the discount-rate axis once only and from above. All projects which make an accounting profit (undiscounted returns exceed outlay) and in which an initial cash flow out is followed by non-negative returns are well behaved. But if a project has a cash flow which includes more than one negative and positive return, there *may* be a multiple yield problem: the IRR is ambiguous, there may be more than one value of i which satisfies the IRR equation. For instance the project:

$t = 0$	$t = 1$	$t = 2$	$t = 3$
-1000	3600	-4310	1716

has IRRs of 10%, 20% and 30%, as can be verified by discounting at these rates. The project is plotted in Figure 3.4.

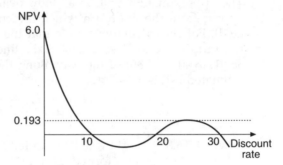

Figure 3.4

To use an IRR approach here, the cash flow must be modified to give a single IRR figure but without changing the project's NPV. The *extended yield method* brings negative returns towards the present, discounted appropriately, to be absorbed by earlier positive returns or, if a negative value still remains at $t = 1$, to be added to the outlay. This process produces a cash flow with an unchanged NPV but which has only one figure for IRR. Consider the application of the extended yield method to the multiple-IRR project above. Suppose that the cost of capital is 15%. First bring the year-2 figure back to year 1 discounted at 15%. The following cash-flow pattern results:

$t = 0$	$t = 1$	$t = 2$	$t = 3$
-1000	$3600 - \dfrac{4310}{1.15}$	0	1716
= -1000	-147.83	0	1716

This still contains a negative value at $t = 1$, which is now moved at the 15% discount rate to $t = 0$. This produces the cash flow:

$t = 0$	$t = 1$	$t = 2$	$t = 3$
$-1000 - \dfrac{147.83}{1.15}$	0	0	1716
= -1128.54	0	0	1716

which can only have one IRR. Since the negative return was redistributed using the cost of capital, the modified cash flow $-1128.54, 0, 0, 1716$ will have the same NPV as the original cash flow, which is slightly negative. IRR on the modified project is just under 15% (a fact disguised by rounding if four-figure tables of discount factors are used), so both NPV and IRR rules reject the project.

Projects giving cash flows with multiple IRRs are uncommon, since very large fluctuations in cash flow either side of zero are required. The phenomenon is more likely to arise when separate cash flows are being combined, as in the *incremental yield method* to be discussed in the following section. A further point is that the NPV of the projects *between* the multiple yield rates is usually trivial as a proportion of the outlay. So practical significance is small, and the NPV of multiple-IRR projects can usually be approximated to zero over the range of the multiple IRRs.

3.8 COMPARING ALTERNATIVE INVESTMENTS

The NPV and IRR rules give the same accept/reject decision for a single project. But where several investments are involved there can appear to be conflict and IRR should be used in a particular way to give decisions consistent with NPV. Two distinct situations will be distinguished:

- selection of all worthwhile projects;
- selection between mutually exclusive projects.

In both cases it is assumed that there are no financial or other constraints on choice. When NPV is used in case 1 all projects with positive NPV are selected. In case 2 the projects with the greater NPVs are preferred, so long as these are positive. In case 1 the IRR approach selects (correctly) all projects with IRRs above the NPV discount rate. But in situation 2 it is *not* correct to select those projects with the greatest IRRs. Decisions taken on this basis may conflict with NPV decisions which are formally correct. Where cost is to be minimized, the options producing the least present value of costs should be selected. If the revenue stream is the same in each case, the problem can be expressed in maximization terms by subtracting the cost alternatives from the revenues and selecting the option producing the greatest NPV.

Consider the four projects shown in Table 3.3. In case 1, with a 10% discount rate projects A, C and D should be accepted and project B should be rejected, as indicated by NPV. In situation 2, if only two projects were to be chosen these should be the two with greatest NPV, namely A and C.

Table 3.3

Project	Cash flow			NPV (10%)	NPV (25%)	NPV (30%)	NPV (35%)
A	−100	80	60	22.3	2.4	−3.1	−7.8
B	−120	40	100	−1.0	−24.0	−30.1	−35.5
C	−60	40	50	17.7	4.0	0.4	−2.9
D	−30	30	20	13.8	6.8	4.9	3.2

If the 25% discount rate is appropriate, the NPV rule would still identify A, C and D as being worthwhile, but if only two projects were required these should now be C and D. The fact that NPV gives different decisions at 25% and 10% in the latter case reflects the altered conditions. A change in the discount rate has different effects across the projects. Projects which produce their best returns in the distant future will be more severely affected by a rise in interest rates than those with their larger returns nearer to the present.

Now suppose that a straight choice between A and C is required. The projects may be a mutually exclusive pair – perhaps different ways of doing the same thing. The NPV rule selects project A if the discount rate is 10%. Figure 3.5 illustrates the choice.

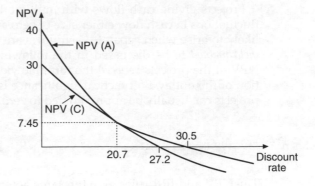

Figure 3.5

The present-value graphs cross at 20.7%. At costs of capital below this figure, project A is preferable, and for costs of capital above 20.7%, project C is superior. The IRRs of the two projects are 27.2% for A and 30.5% for C. A naive extension of the single-project IRR rule would prefer C to A on grounds of greater IRR. In comparing the IRR figures no account is taken of the cost of capital and this fact alone should arouse suspicions about the process. Consider the case where the NPV decision and the naive IRR approach clash directly – when the cost of capital is less than 20.7%. NPV then selects A and IRR would select C. The NPV decision is correct and the IRR rule has to be modified. Why?

One weakness of the IRR rule is that it considers only the *rate* of return on projects and not the *scale* of the benefit to be obtained. For instance, the projects −6, 4, 5 and −600, 400, 500 have equal IRRs, although the second project gives much greater total value. But scale is not the whole story; the naive IRR rule can be shown to contradict itself. Consider the choice between A and C with a discount rate of 10%. Suppose that a decision maker chooses C in preference to A simply because C has the greater IRR. Now offer an additional choice of C *plus* a further project E with cash flow:

E:	−40	40	10

Would C alone be preferred or C plus E? Since E has an IRR of 20.7% – well above the cost of capital – this IRR-oriented decision maker would presumably accept E in addition to C and consider themselves better off as a result. But now add up the outlay and returns on C and E:

C + E:	−100	80	60
=	project A		

So this decision maker should be happier with project A rather than C, contradicting the original choice. The point is that the extra outlay required for project A is money well spent since it gives an IRR greater than the cost of capital. The project E: −40, 40, 10 (the difference between A and C) is called the *incremental project*. To make a decision between two mutually exclusive projects using IRR, the incremental project should be formed by subtracting the cash flows of the project with the lower initial outlay from the other project. If the IRR on the incremental project exceeds the cost of capital the project with greater outlay should be selected. If the IRR on the incremental project is less than the cost of capital then the project with lower outlay should be selected. This is the *incremental yield method*. The incremental project A − B is plotted in Figure 3.6.

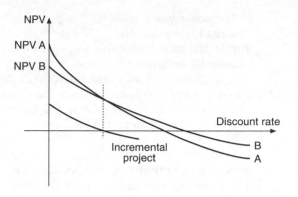

Figure 3.6

The IRR of the incremental project is the rate of discount at which the NPV graphs cross. More complicated pictures than Figure 3.6 can arise, for example the incremental project could have multiple IRR even if A and B individually did not.

Consider a further example. Project A has a constant return of 100 for ten years and costs 502 initially. B has a constant return of 144 also for ten years but costing 780 initially. The IRR of A is 15% and B's IRR is 13%. With an 8% cost of capital the NPV of A is 169 and the NPV of B is 185, indicating preference for B. The incremental project here costs 278 and gives a return of 44 in each of ten years. The IRR of this project is 9.6% which is greater than the cost of capital, so B is the better investment.

The incremental yield method is impractical in multi-project cases since many incremental projects may need to be evaluated. For example, suppose that two projects were to be chosen from the four in Table 3.3. Not only would the incremental yields of A, B and C over D be required, but we would also need to find the incremental yields of A − B and A − C, the result being a decision obtained much faster using NPV. Outside the two-project case, if a statement in terms of IRR is required, the choice should be made using NPV, and the results can then be presented in terms of IRR.

3.9 THE MODIFIED INTERNAL RATE OF RETURN

One of the points advanced in favour of the IRR approach is that IRR is expressed as a percentage and decision makers may prefer to think in percentage terms. This, to the extent that it is true, is fair enough; decision-making tools are made to fit people and not the other way about. But IRR has also been *criticized* on the grounds that it is a percentage: that it contains the implicit assumption that returns are invested at a rate equal to the IRR.

There has been much discussion about this point. If the existence of investment opportunities themselves having yields equal to any and every project that the company might consider was an essential precondition for the use of IRR, then the method would indeed be fatally flawed. But the argument is a red herring.

For decision-making purposes IRR can be seen as one number to be compared with another – the discount rate. In this context the discount rate can be regarded as a hurdle that must be cleared for project viability. A project accepted on the basis of IRR does *not* require the decision maker to find other projects with identical IRRs to absorb surpluses. An infinite regress would be created: if such projects did exist, they should themselves be accepted since their IRRs exceed the discount rate, but from the reinvestment argument acceptance would call for yet further projects with the same yield.

For consistency with NPV a project accepted on an IRR basis should have its returns invested at the NPV rate of discount. This is the opportunity cost of the funds, the most effective non-project use of money and the rate at which returns should be invested regardless of the decision rule used to select the investment. The reinvestment may take the form of deposits with financial institutions or the repayment of borrowing as circumstances dictate.

However, analysts favouring the use of IRR but concerned about the impact of the reinvestment debate have provided a modified device, also consistent with NPV, which circumvents any reinvestment worries. This is called the *modified internal rate of return* (MIRR) or the terminal rate of return. The MIRR of an investment is that rate of compounding which if applied to the initial outlay produces the terminal value of the project returns. For example, consider again the project with cash flow:

$t = 0$	$t = 1$	$t = 2$	$t = 3$
-2200	770	968	1331

The terminal value of the returns at 10% will be:

$$770(1.1)^2 + 968(1.1) + 1331 = 3327.5$$

The MIRR is $100m\%$ from

$$2200(1 + m)^3 = 3327.5$$

The value of m can be obtained by use of a scientific calculator or computer software. Linear interpolation can also be used. Writing

$$(1 + m)^3 = \frac{3327.5}{2200} = 1.5125$$

and using the future values in Table 1 we see that at 14% for three years, £1 becomes 1.4815, while at 15% for three years, £1 becomes 1.5208. So using linear interpolation over the 1% interval, the MIRR is

$$\text{MIRR} \approx 14 + \frac{1.5125 - 1.4815}{1.5208 - 1.4815} = 14.79\%$$

which is accurate to the two decimal places given. The project is acceptable on grounds of MIRR since MIRR > 10% (the discount rate in this case). In the single-project case, MIRR will always give a decision consistent with NPV or NTV. There are significant differences between MIRR and IRR although, as we shall see later on, they are similar in one important respect. Multiple values of MIRR will not arise so there is no need for an equivalent of the extended yield method. Unlike IRR, for projects lasting more than one period, the value of MIRR for a project depends on the discount rate used in compounding. In the example above, if a rate of 30% had been appropriate, the terminal value of the returns would be

$$770(1.3)^2 + 968(1.3) + 1331 = 3890.7$$

and MIRR as given by

$$(1 + m)^3 = \frac{3890.7}{2200} = 1.7685$$

is 20.93%. Note that in this case the project would, correctly, be rejected since MIRR < 30%.

An important similarity between MIRR and IRR concerns mutually exclusive projects. The project with the greater MIRR will not always have the greater NPV or NTV. This can be shown by example. For the mutually exclusive projects:

	$t = 0$	$t = 1$
A:	-1000	1331
B:	-10	110

With a discount rate of 10% results are as follows:

	NPV(10%)	NTV(10%)	IRR(%)	MIRR(%)
A:	210	231	33.1	33.1
B:	90	99	1100	1100

In this case the project with the greater NPV has the lesser MIRR. In other cases NPV and MIRR might have given consistent rankings. Use of MIRR for selection between mutually exclusive projects to guarantee consistency with NPV would involve the formation of incremental projects as for IRR. These complexities are quite unnecessary and it is better to select on an NPV basis and if desired give MIRRs for the selected projects as additional management information.

3.10 ANNUITIES

An annuity is a cash flow, either income or outgoings, involving the same sum in each period. There are many examples of annuities at governmental, corporate and personal finance levels. For example, when a company sets aside a fixed sum each year to meet a future obligation, it is using an annuity. A personal loan from a bank is a familiar fixed-term annuity. Other examples include mortgages (assuming a steady interest rate), leasing arrangements and fixed-interest coupons. We shall find the present values of annuities and the redemption yield on loan stock with a fixed maturity date.

The present value of an annuity *could* be found by discounting each return individually, but there is a better method. Consider an annuity of £100 for four years at 10% interest. Assume that the first payment will be made after one year. Using the discount factor table the PV is:

$$100(0.9091) + 100(0.8264) + 100(0.7513) + 100(0.6830)$$
$$= 100(0.9091 + 0.8264 + 0.7513 + 0.6830)$$
$$= 100(3.1699)$$
$$= 316.99$$

The most significant line in the workings above is the second, in which the annual amount of £100 is multiplied by the sum of the first four discount factors (3.1699 rather than the sum of the rounded values 3.1688). Table 3 is the annuity table and shows the sum of the discount factors up to n years – the present values of annuities of £1. These are given by:

$$\sum_{t=1}^{n}(1+r)^{-t} = \frac{1-(1+r)^{-n}}{r}$$

An annuity where the first payment is made after one year (as assumed in the formula above) is an *immediate annuity*. Where the first payment occurs at once this is an *annuity due* – for this the entries of Table 3 must be increased by one to obtain the present value. Where the first payment is delayed beyond one year, the annuity is called a *deferred annuity*. Consider an example:

Example 3.6

(a) Find the present value of an immediate annuity of £125 running for six years at 11%.

(b) Use Table 3 to find the present value at 12% of the cash flow:

$t = 1$	$t = 2$	$t = 3$	$t = 4$	$t = 5$	$t = 6$
1400	1400	1400	600	600	600

Now consider a company which leases a building for ten years for £10 000 a year, the first payment to be made after one year. At a 16% rate of interest, what is the present cost of the contract? This is £10 000(4.8332) = £48 332. The present cost of under £50000 shows the impact of discount factors on distant payments.

3.10 PERPETUITIES

A special case of an annuity is where a contract runs indefinitely, there being no end to the payments. This is called a *perpetuity*. Consols and War Loan are perpetuities and it is unlikely that the principal on these undated Government securities will ever be repaid. There is a simple formula for the present value of a perpetuity. If ever in the annuity formula we let n go to infinity, $(1 + r)^{-n}$ goes to zero and the present value of a perpetuity of £1 is simply:

$$PV = \frac{1}{r}$$

i.e. the annual sum divided by the interest rate as a decimal. If the annual sum is £S and the interest rate is $100r\%$, then:

$$PV = \frac{S}{r}$$

So at a 10% rate of interest a perpetuity of £50 has a present value of:

$$PV = \frac{50}{0.1} = 500$$

and if it can be sold, £500 should be its approximate price. For instance, what should be the price of a unit of $3\frac{1}{2}\%$ War Loan stock if the market rate of interest for this very low-risk security is $5\frac{1}{2}\%$? War Loan is quoted in units of £100 nominal value and the annual interest payment is $3\frac{1}{2}\%$ of this figure, i.e. £3.50. If for simplicity a single annual payment is assumed, the price should be the present value:

$$PV = \frac{3.5}{0.055} = £63.64$$

Figure 3.7 shows the graph of the present value of an annuity of £1 as the duration of the annuity increases.

The higher the rate of interest, the more rapidly the value of $1/r$ is approached. For example, in the case of a 25% rate of interest, a 20-year annuity has almost 99% of the value of a perpetuity at the same rate, whereas at 1% interest, a 20-year annuity has less than 19% of the value of a perpetuity. When interest rates are changing, there can be significant effects on the value of perpetuities – a point further developed in the following section.

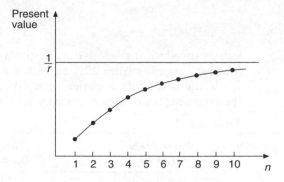

Figure 3.7

3.12 YIELD TO MATURITY

Here we consider securities giving a constant return for a fixed number of years, but such that in the final year the bond is redeemed. So, in addition to the fixed annual payment, the nominal issue price of the bond is refunded. The nearer is the redemption date to the present, the greater will be the effect on the yield and the price of the bond. As the redemption date nears the price of the bond rises to bring the yield on the bond: the *yield to maturity* or *redemption yield*, to a level appropriate to the terms of the bond. Special tables can be prepared, but yield to maturity can also be found by interpolation using the annuity table (Table 3) and the present value table (Table 2).

Consider a security currently priced at £900 (ex interest) which gives an annual interest payment of £100 with a redemption value of £1000 after five years. The cash flow on the investment is then:

$t = 0$	$t = 1$	$t = 2$	$t = 3$	$t = 4$	$t = 5$
−900	100	100	100	100	100 + 1000

Using the factors in the tables, the workings are:

	At 12%	At 13%
PV of interest:	360.48	351.72
PV of lump sum:	567.4	542.8
	927.88	894.52

and the yield to maturity is estimated as:

$$\left[12 + \frac{27.88}{33.36}\right]\% = 12.84\%$$

in which 27.88 = 927.88 − 900 and 33.36 = 927.88 − 894.52.

An important difference between long-dated and short-dated stock is sensitivity to interest rate changes. The price of short-dated stock is much less variable when interest rates are changing than is the price of long-dated stock. This exposure to price changes (and so to possible capital losses or gains) is called *interest rate risk*. To illustrate interest rate risk, consider two sharply contrasting securities – a two-year bond and a perpetuity. Suppose that each is priced at £100 at a 10% rate of interest. The cash flows are:

	$t = 1$	$t = 2$	$t \geq 3$
Two-year bond:	10	10 + 100	0
Perpetuity:	10	10	10

The value of the perpetuity is $10/r$ and the value of the two-year bond is:

$$PV = \frac{10}{(1+r)} + \frac{10+100}{(1+r)^2}$$

values of which for selected r are given in Table 3.4. It is evident that when the interest rate rises from 10% to 15% the two-year bond falls in price by 8.13% while the perpetuity experiences a $33\frac{1}{3}$% price fall. If the interest rate falls to 5% the two-year bond rises in price by 9.3% while the perpetuity doubles in value.

Table 3.4

Interest rate (100r%)	Two-year bond price	Perpetuity price
1	117.73	1000.00
5	109.30	200.00
10	100.00	100.00
15	91.87	66.67
20	84.72	50.00

3.13 SINKING FUNDS

Where an constant annual sum is saved – possibly to provide for payment of a future debt – it is useful to know the *terminal* value of the annuity. If £1 is set aside at the end of each of four years, how much will be on hand after four years, with interest at $100r$% per annum? The first pound attracts interest for three years and becomes $(1 + r)^3$, the second pound is interest-earning for two years and so becomes $(1 + r)^2$, the third pound becomes $(1 + r)$ and the fourth pound is placed in the account at the day of reckoning so that the terminal value at $t = 4$ is:

$$(1 + r)^3 + (1 + r)^2 + (1 + r) + 1$$

At a 10% rate of interest this is:

$$1.331 + 1.21 + 1.1 + 1 = 4.641$$

Table 4 gives these terminal values of an annuity of £1 for various interest rates and number of years. Consider an example.

Example 3.7

(a) Find the terminal value at eight years of £375 placed annually into an account starting after one year with interest at 6%.

(b) A company sets aside the following sum at the stated times:

$t = 0$	$t = 1$	$t = 2$	$t = 3$
10 000	5000	5000	20 000

Using Tables 1 and 4 and an interest rate of 9% find how much the company would have at $t = 3$.

Answer

(a) £375 × 9.8975 = £3711.56.

(b) The payments can be separated out as follows:

	$t = 0$	$t = 1$	$t = 2$	$t = 3$
Stream 1	10 000	–	–	–
Stream 2	–	5000	5000	5 000
Stream 3	–	–	–	15 000
Total	10 000	5000	5000	20 000

Using Table 1 the terminal value of stream 1 at $t = 3$ is £10 000 × 1.2950 = £12 950; using Table 4 the terminal value of stream 2 is £5000 × 3.2781 = £16 390.50 to which is added the £15 000 deposited at $t = 3$. The total is £44 340.50.

The related idea of a *sinking fund* is useful. Table 5 shows how much must be set aside each year to get a terminal value of £1. These numbers are the reciprocals of corresponding entries in Table 4. With a 12% rate of interest £0.0813 would need to be saved annually to produce £1 after eight years. Consider an example.

Example 3.8	Answer
A company has loan stock of £750 000 due to mature in seven years. The company wishes to pay off the debt rather than make another issue at this time. At an interest rate of 10% how much is needed annually to meet the liability?	To give a terminal value of £1 after seven years at 10%, £0.1054 must be saved each year; so to finish with £750 000 the annual sum required is: £750 000(0.1054) = £79 050

This process of *amortization* is one example of the conversion of a one-off charge to a recurrent sum. In the next section we consider another use for a capital-to-revenue transformation.

3.14 ANNUAL EQUIVALENT ANNUITIES

The conversion of a capital sum to an annuity with the same present value is helpful in many financial problems. It is useful to know what annuity results in a present value of £1, given the length of time the annuity would run and the rate of discount. The *annual equivalent annuity* table (Table 6), shows the annuity required to give a present value of £1 for various rates of interest and numbers of years. Thus a lump sum of £1 is equivalent to an immediate annuity for two years at 10% of £0.5762.

Suppose that the capital cost of a machine tool is £25 000 and that the expected life of the equipment is ten years. At an interest rate of 8% the capital cost is equivalent in present-value terms to an annual charge of £25 000(0.1490) = £3725. The £3725 could be compared with the annual cost of alternative financing arrangements and also represents the gross amount of the depreciation charged on the equipment using the annuity method of depreciation. Entries in Table 6 are the reciprocals of corresponding entries in Table 3. Annual equivalents can be used in project appraisal and are useful in repair-or-replace problems. Consider an exercise converting an irregular cash flow to annuity form.

Example 3.9

Using Tables 2 and 6 find the annual equivalent annuity for two years at 10% for a project with the cash flow:

$t = 0$	$t = 1$	$t = 2$
−700	650	800

Answer

First find the project's net present value in the usual manner:

Year	Sum	Discount factor	Present value
0	−700	1	−700
1	650	0.9091	590.92
2	800	0.8264	661.12
		NPV =	552.04

Next convert the lump-sum NPV to the two-year annual equivalent at 10%. This is £552.04(0.5762) = £318.09. This two-stage process – the capitalization of an irregular cash flow and amortization of the resulting capital sum over a standard term – forms the basis of a method for finding the best strategy for equipment replacement.

3.15 REPAIR OR REPLACE?

When should an asset be scrapped and with what, if anything, should it be replaced? As an asset ages operating and maintenance costs are likely to rise, and in some cases quality of output may fall, causing reduced revenues. But the longer an asset is kept the more the capital outlay on replacement is put off. When machinery is to be replaced by equipment generating similar cash flows, the problem is to determine the best interval between the installation of new machinery – the length of the replacement cycle. Data requirements are considerable because, not only do future cash flows need to be estimated, inter-dependencies must be untangled. For instance, some of the costs may be joint costs, machines may compete for resources, or may be complementary or competitive on the revenue side. Data required are:

- The net residual values of the asset;
- The capital cost of the new asset;
- Operating and maintenance costs (O and M);
- Revenues produced in each period.

The objective is a maximum of present value of net revenues (or a minimum of the present value of costs). The cost formulation is more convenient and any differences in revenue produced by machines of different ages can be included in operating costs as *opportunity costs*. Given the cost-based formulation there still remain several ways of expressing the problem:

- the annual equivalent annuity (AE) method;
- the lowest common multiple (LCM) method;
- the finite horizon (FH) method.

First consider the *annual equivalent annuity method* – also known as the equivalent annual cost method. Suppose that a firm operates one machine of a certain type and that all such machines (existing asset and replacements) have a maximum life of four years with the financial data shown in Table 3.5. The cost of capital is 10% and the objective is to choose the length of replacement cycle which minimizes the present value of costs.

Table 3.5

Time t (years)	0	1	2	3	4
Initial outlay (£)	10 000				
O and M (£)		3000	4000	5000	6000
Residual value (£)		6000	4500	3000	1000

First find the total present values of costs (some will be negative) associated with keeping the first machine for different lengths of time. Workings are shown in Table 3.6.

Table 3.6

t	1 year	2 years	3 years	4 years
0	10000	10000	10000	10000
1	−3000	3000	3000	3000
2		−500	4000	4000
3			2000	5000
4				5000
PV at 10%	7272.72	12314.05	17535.69	23204.70

The one-year column in Table 3.6 contains the cash flows associated with keeping the initial asset for one year. An outlay of £10 000 is required at $t = 0$ but at $t = 1$ the machine is scrapped for £6000 and only incurs O and M costs of £3000. Thus the net figure for costs is −£3000. Similarly, in the two-year column at $t = 2$, O and M costs are £4000, but scrapping at this point produces £4500, a net inflow of £500 (hence the 'cost' of −£500). Other entries are found in the same way and the present value of each cash flow is then calculated. Numbers in the last row of Table 3.6 represent the costs to the firm for different periods of time. Where the machine is retained for just one year, a new machine is required at $t = 1$, which will again (if kept for one year) produce a stream of costs giving a value at $t = 1$ of 7272.72.

One way to compare these different-length cycles is to find the constant annual sum (annual equivalent annuity) which would give a present value at $t = 0$ equal to indefinitely repeated cycles of the given lengths. For instance, in the case of a cycle length of one year, a payment of £8000 at $t = 1$ has a present value of 7272.72, and an annual payment of £8000 is equivalent in present value to the cash flow produced by a one-year cycle as shown in Table 3.7.

Table 3.7

	$t = 0$	$t = 1$	$t = 2$	$t = 3$	$t = 4$	$t = 5$
Machine 1	10000	3000				
Machine 2		10000	−3000			
Machine 3			10000	−3000		
Machine 4				10000	−3000	
Machine 5					10000	−3000
Machine 6						10000
etc.						
Net cash flow:	10000	7000	7000	7000	7000	7000

In the case of a two-year cycle, the AE for two years at 10% giving a present value of 12 314.05 is 7095.24. In each case the AE is found by multiplying the present-value entry in Table 3.6 by the AE factor for £1 at $100r\%$ for n years, which is obtained from Table 6. Results are shown in Table 3.8.

Table 3.8

Cycle length	PV of one cycle	AE factor	AE annuity
1	7272.72	1.1000	8000.00
2	12314.05	0.5762	7095.36
3	17535.69	0.4021	7051.10
4	23204.70	0.3155	7321.08

So a three-year cycle length is optimal: each machine is scrapped and replaced by a financially identical machine after three years.

The calculations as a whole can be summarized as in Table 3.9.

Table 3.9

Cycle length	$t = 0$	$t = 1$	Net cash flow $t = 2$	$t = 3$	$t = 4$	NPV	AE fac.	AE ann.
1 yr	10000	−3000				7273	1.10000	8000
2 yr	10000	3000	−500			12314	0.57619	7095
3 yr	10000	3000	4000	2000		17536	0.40211	7051
4 yr	10000	3000	4000	5000	5000	23205	0.31547	7320

Over an infinite horizon the total present value of costs with the optimal option is £70 511 which is the lowest figure achievable. The actual costs produced by the three-year cycle are:

$$10\,000 \quad 3000 \quad 4000 \quad 12\,000 \quad 3000 \quad 4000 \quad 12\,000 \quad \text{etc.}$$

and the figure of 70 511 is the present value of this cash flow.

If an existing machine is to be replaced by a new and different type of machine generating significantly different cash flows, there is the additional problem of when to break into the cycle for the existing type of equipment and introduce the *optimal* cycle (as calculated above) with the new machine. An enumerative approach (considering all possible alternatives) can be used.

The AE method assumes that the time horizon is long enough for each cycle length to complete a whole number of times. This allows a valid comparison of costs for the alternatives and is made explicit in the *lowest common multiple (LCM) method*. In the LCM method, the cycle lengths are compared by the present value of the costs they produce over a horizon equal to the LCM of the cycle lengths. In the example the horizon is twelve years. The AE method is preferable in almost all cases, although with careful use of tables the LCM method is not as bad as may appear from a case with eight-, nine-, and ten-year cycle alternatives and an LCM of 360 years!

Even if there is not a whole number of all cycles, in practice it is legitimate to use the AE approach whenever a long view is being taken. With a 10% discount rate, a cost or return is discounted by over 95% of its value at 32 years from the present – 17 years at 20% and 12 years at 30%. The *finite horizon (FH) method* compares the present values of the cash flows produced by the alternatives over a predetermined, long horizon in the knowledge that any inaccuracy through not having whole numbers of cycles is slight. The FH method has been used to assess cycles of road maintenance and upgrading in the USA. Other US public-utility investments have been appraised using a 50-year horizon.

An issue with the FH method is the treatment of post-horizon cash flows. In practice these are usually consolidated into a single figure at the horizon date. This issue becomes more significant the shorter is the horizon, and it may be necessary to work with a time horizon that is neither very long nor the LCM of the cycle lengths. This situation, which from the decision maker's point of view is just a *fact*, could occur with plant and equipment specific to a major project to be completed in a set length of time. In this case the finite horizon, although undesirably short, is imposed and the NPVs of the costs over this period are found inclusive of any residual value of the plant and equipment at the horizon date which may have worth in other uses or as scrap.

The AE method can be modified to take into account inflation at a uniform rate as long as the underlying structure of costs (to which the inflation applies) is unchanged. When the underlying structure of costs does change – as is normally the case under conditions of technical progress – the AE method cannot give exact answers unless the technical progress alters the original costs at a constant percentage rate. Things are rarely this convenient and either the AE method can be used to give approximate answers (usually more than sufficient for practical purposes) or the LCM or FH approach must be used.

3.16 MAKE OR BUY?

A classic problem in the application of discounted cash flow (DCF) methods is the *make-or-buy* problem which arises when a company has the choice of making an item it needs or buying in supplies made elsewhere. Costs in each case usually have a different structure. The make-or-buy decision can often be formulated as an investment appraisal problem, though some important factors may not readily be quantifiable – for instance, the benefits of any extra security of supply if the make decision is taken. The make-or-buy problem is a particular example of sourcing problems seen as investments.

Consider the case where the make decision requires an outlay of K now for equipment lasting n years; where $M_1, M_2, ..., M_n$ represent the costs of producing the required quantities of the item in each year and where $B_1, B_2, ..., B_n$ are the costs of buying. The cash flow to be evaluated is:

$$-K \quad B_1 - M_1 \quad B_2 - M_2 \quad B_3 - M_3 \quad \dots \quad B_n - M_n + S_n$$

where S_n is the scrap value of equipment at n. If the make decision displaces other projects, the returns to the forgone opportunities should be deducted. In terms of taxation, the effects of any allowances should also be taken into account.

Suppose that a firm is considering making a component for an assembly operation. This would require equipment costing £400 000 lasting four years with a residual value of £200 000. Manufacturing costs in each year would be £500 000, £700 000, £800 000 and £900 000 respectively. If the firm buys the components from a supplier the yearly costs are £900 000 £1 000 000, £1 100 000 and £1 400 000. However, the equipment would occupy floor space which could have been put to other uses generating £200 000 net in each of the four years. This opportunity is lost if the make option is adopted. If the cost of capital is 13%, should the company make or buy the component? The cost cash flow from manufacture (net of the residual value) is:

$t = 0$	$t = 1$	$t = 2$	$t = 3$	$t = 4$
400 000	500 000	700 000	800 000	700 000

while the costs associated with buying in the components are

$t = 0$	$t = 1$	$t = 2$	$t = 3$	$t = 4$
0	900 000	1 000 000	1 100 000	1 400 000

So *gross* cost savings if the component is made rather than bought are:

$t = 0$	$t = 1$	$t = 2$	$t = 3$	$t = 4$
−400 000	400 000	300 000	300 000	700 000

The income forgone in the make option is now deducted from these savings. This leaves the cash flow changes from making as:

$t = 0$	$t = 1$	$t = 2$	$t = 3$	$t = 4$
−400 000	200 000	100 000	100 000	500 000

The net present value of this stream is now found. Workings are:

Year	Cash flow	Discount factor	Present value
0	−400 000	1	−400 000
1	200 000	0.8550	177 000
2	100 000	0.7831	78 310
3	100 000	0.6931	69 310
4	500 000	0.6133	306 650
		Total	231 270

Since NPV is positive, the decision to make is confirmed.

3.17 DCF AND TAX PAYMENTS

The tax environment in which capital budgeting decisions are taken varies over time for a given country and also between nations. This section shows in general terms how, with a given tax structure, tax payments should be taken into account. We are not concerned with the finer points of corporate tax law or methods of tax assessment and for illustration will use a simple and adaptable framework.

Ideally, post-tax figures should be used in discounted cash flow calculations, but netting data of tax can be difficult. For instance, consider one of the returns to an investment – say the return R_3 in the third year. If the company is in profit, R_3 is added to taxable earnings. There is then a cash outflow of $t(R_3)$ (where t is tax rate) when the tax is payable. If R_3 is negative (a loss) then if the company is earning a profit on other activities the tax bill in total will be reduced by $t(R_3)$. But if the company was not making taxable profits and if R_3 was not large enough to change this, then the project adds the full R_3 to earnings with no offsetting additions to tax.

A further complication is that tax liability depends on how a project is financed – for example, tax relief on debt interest should be taken into account if debt is included in the financing mix. Tax payments represent cash out and should be treated in the same way as other cash flows. So project NPV is calculated after tax in the case of companies with shareholders, private firms or individuals. Apart from financing, the following example shows how tax can be taken into account in a DCF calculation.

A firm can buy a machine for £10 000. Net returns are £5000 in each of the next four years. The question is whether the investment is worthwhile after tax and after allowing for working capital. The rate of discount is 12% and £500 cash is set aside as working capital for its day-to-day contingencies. This sum is taken from other uses in year zero and replaced at the end of the final year. Suppose that the tax regime is that tax payable is 35% of net return less a writing-down allowance (WDA) on a straight line basis of 20% of the initial capital expenditure for five years. Depreciation is relevant to DCF financial appraisals only in so far as it affects tax payments (assumed here to be lagged by one year). Workings for this example are then as shown in Table 3.10.

Table 3.10

	Year						
	0	1	2	3	4	5	6
1 Outlay/returns	−10000	5000	5000	5000	5000	0	0
2 Working capital	−500	0	0	0	500	0	0
3 WDA*		2000	2000	2000	2000	2000	0
4 Taxable profit*		3000	3000	3000	3000	−2000	0
5 Taxation at 35%			−1050	−1050	−1050	−1050	700
6 Net cash flow	−10500	5000	3950	3950	4450	−1050	700
7 Discount factor	1.0000	0.8929	0.7972	0.7118	0.6355	0.5674	0.5066
8 Present value	−10500	4464	3149	2812	2828	−596	355
9 Net present value	2512						
10 IRR	23.4%						

* Not cash flow items

Note how the data in line 6 used for the DCF calculations differ from the original outlay and return figures both in respect of the figure in any given year and in the number of years over which project-related cash flow changes occur. Project IRR is 23.4% and at 12% NPV is £2512, so the investment should be made.

Alternative schemes (such as free depreciation or the use of declining balances) and the associated tax and cash flow consequences could be accommodated within a similar framework; the principle of determining post-tax cash flows is unchanged.

3.18 FURTHER READING

Drury, C. (1992) *Management and Cost Accounting*, 3rd edn, Chapman and Hall, London.

Drury, C., Braund, S., Osborne, P. and Tayles, M. (1992) *A Survey of Management Accounting Practices in UK Manufacturing Companies*, ACCA Research Occasional Paper, Chartered Association of Certified Accountants.

Emery, G.M. (1982) Some guidelines for evaluating capital investment alternatives with unequal lives, *Financial Management*, Spring.

Kay, J.A. and King, M.A. (1990) *The British Tax System*, 5th edn, Oxford University Press, Oxford.

Samuels, J.M., Wilkes, F.M. and Brayshaw, R.E. (1995) *Management of Company Finance*, 6th edn, International Thomson Business Press, London.

Wilkes, F.M. (1980) On multiple rates of return, *Journal of Business Finance and Accounting*, **7**(4).

3.19 PROBLEMS

1 Using a 12% rate of discount, find the net present value of the project with cash flow:

$t = 0$	$t = 1$	$t = 2$	$t = 3$
-400	500	-100	700

2 The net receipts and outlays (including tax payments) for a project are:

				Year		
	0	1	2	3	4	5
Outlay	500					
Net receipts		100	150	250	200	150

The receipt in year 5 includes the residual value of the project at that time. Show that while the project is acceptable at a 10% discount rate on the basis of the net present value criterion, it should be rejected at a discount rate of 20%.

3 Find the net *terminal* value of the investment in question 1.

4 Find the IRR of the project:

$t = 0$	$t = 1$	$t = 2$	$t = 3$
-1400	600	700	400

5 (a) Verify that the project with cash flow:

$t = 0$	$t = 1$	$t = 2$
$-10\,000$	24 000	$-14\,375$

  has yields of 15% and 25%.

  (b) Apply the extended yield method with a cost of capital of 20%.

  (c) Sketch the graph of NPV for this project against the discount rate. Would the owner of such an investment wish to see a rapid decline in interest rates?

6 With no restriction on expenditure, and with the following projects available:

	$t = 0$	$t = 1$	$t = 2$
A	-60	60	40
B	-120	80	100
C	-200	160	120

  (a) Which project would be chosen on the basis of NPV at:
    (i) 10%   (ii) 25%

  (b) Which project has the greatest IRR?

  (c) Use the incremental yield method to select one of projects B and C when the interest rate is 10%.

7 (a) With a 15% cost of capital, find the modified internal rate of return (MIRR) for the investment with the cash flow:

$t = 0$	$t = 1$	$t = 2$	$t = 3$	$t = 4$
−1000	360	330	300	270

would the project be acceptable on the basis of the MIRR criterion?

(b) Would the project have been accepted on the basis of its *unmodified* internal rate of return?

8 Use the appropriate formula to find the present value of an immediate annuity of £100 for six years at 10% compound interest.

9 What is the present value of a perpetuity of £200 p.a. with a discount rate of 4%?

10 A security is currently priced at £1200 (ex interest) and pays annual interest of £150. It has a redemption value of £1500 five years in the future. Estimate the yield to maturity on the security.

11 Find the terminal value achieved at ten years if £700 is placed annually into an account starting after one year. Interest is compounded at 10%.

12 A company has loan stock of £5 000 000 due to mature in nine years' time. At an interest rate of 15% how much should be set aside annually in order to meet the liability when it falls due?

13 (a) Determine the net present value of the cash flow:

$t = 1$	$t = 2$	$t = 3$	$t = 4$	$t = 5$
1500	1500	1500	500	500

at a discount rate of 12%.

(b) How might the calculations be carried out using only a table of annuity factors (Table 3)?

14 Making use of Tables 2 and 6 find the annual equivalent annuity (for 2 years) at 15% of the cash flow:

$t = 0$	$t = 1$	$t = 2$
1200	350	500

15 A company puts the following sums into an account at the stated times:

$t = 0$	$t = 1$	$t = 2$	$t = 3$
24 000	12 000	12 000	35 000

Using Tables 1 and 4 and an interest rate of 10% find the sum of money that the company would have at $t = 3$.

16 For a machine with the financial data given below, find the optimal length of replacement cycle with a 12% discount rate.

Time	$t = 0$	$t = 1$	$t = 2$	$t = 3$	$t = 4$
Outlay	5000				
Operating costs		1400	1500	1600	1700
Maintenance costs			300	400	500
Scrap value		3400	2000	800	600

17 A firm has to decide whether to make a component itself or buy it in. In the make option, the capital cost of the equipment is £1 000 000 incurred immediately. The equipment would last for four years with no residual value. Manufacturing costs would be £1 300 000 in year one, £1 400 000 in year two, £1 700 000 in year three and £1 800 000 in year four. These costs cover everything and no other opportunities are lost if the decision to manufacture is taken. If the component is bought in, there would be no immediate outlay and the costs would be £1 700 000 in years one and two and £2 200 000 in years three and four. The discount rate is 15% and apart from the outlay all costs occur at year-end. Should the component be made in-house or bought in?

4 RATIONING, UNCERTAINTY AND CORPORATE STRATEGY

LEARNING OUTCOMES

By the end of this chapter the reader should:

- understand and recognize situations of capital rationing
- be able to approach capital rationing problems by NPV-consistent means
- have the ability critically to assess traditional approaches to uncertainty and risk
- be able to conduct sensitivity analysis on project cash flows
- be able to use a range of 'what if' approaches to risk and uncertainty
- understand capital investment aspects of corporate strategy

4.1 INTRODUCTION

So far we have considered investment appraisal methods when the decision maker's success in achieving their objective was limited only by the range of opportunities available and where outcomes were assured. For practical purposes the cash flow and discount rate were certain and capital availability was limited only by ability to repay.

In this chapter a range of methods are introduced that can be useful to management when the ability to undertake possible projects is restricted by limits on financial or other resources and where there is appreciable uncertainty concerning important data.

Capital rationing and uncertainty not transmitted to yield rates can be considered as departures from a perfect market in capital assets. If managers seeking funds and the market itself function sufficiently well, it is arguable that no absolute shortage of capital should occur; it should always be available – at a price. Where this is so, all well and good. Where it is not so, useful analytical tools are available.

Appropriate treatment of risk also depends on how the market functions. Some parts of the market may work better than others and it is as well to have available methods relevant to either case. So we consider uncertainty and risk in two stages. Here we present some widely used, long-standing methods for cases where the ownership of the company is not fully diversified. The techniques apply when the impact of investments on the total risk of the enterprise is a consideration and where managerial judgement can play a decisive role.

Capital rationing – or the shortage of any other key resource – may arise in several ways. Funds for investment may not be unlimited at all points in time and there may be limitations on the availability of resources such as skilled labour, raw materials or machinery. Constraints also arise where projects are contingent and where there are limits on the investment levels themselves. There may also be acceptable limits to values taken by key financial ratios and management may try to avoid cash-flow patterns producing large fluctuations in year-to-year profits or which would inhibit the firm's ability to declare an adequate dividend. We shall use problems in which constraints are financial, but the same principles apply whatever the scarce resource or constraint.

Capital rationing exists when there are insufficient funds to finance all apparently profitable projects. Where wider considerations are incorporated, a *financial planning model* is produced. A distinction can be made between *hard* and *soft* capital rationing. *Hard capital rationing* arises when constraints are *externally* determined. *Soft capital rationing* arises with *internal*, management-imposed, limits on investment expenditure. In a perfect market hard capital rationing would not occur while soft capital rationing would be irrational.

In the real world both situations do arise – often with good reason. Borrowing limits are imposed by banks particularly in relation to smaller firms and individuals. Self-imposed restrictions are often prudential in character and can relate to questions of control within, and of, an organization. For example, there may be a reluctance to issue further equity by management fearful of losing control of the company. Public-sector organizations operate with cash-limited budgets with likely limits stated for future years and with spending restrictions on both capital and revenue programmes.

The distinction between hard and soft capital rationing is in some cases one of perspective. From the point of view of a department, cost centre or wholly owned subsidiary, the budgetary constraints determined by senior management or head office are effectively external, while from the boardroom they will be seen as internal. In both hard and soft rationing the limits are usually negotiated (in the first instance at least) and to an extent may be renegotiable, and the solution methodology should provide valuable input to such processes.

Either form of capital rationing could be said to signal a managerial failure to convince suppliers of funds of the value of available projects. Although there may be something in this argument, in practice it is not a well-informed judgement. Surveys suggest that a minimum of three out of five companies experience capital rationing. Furthermore, even if there were no limits on the total *amounts* of available finance, in reality the price may vary with the size as well as the term of the loan. If this variation takes the form of discrete tranches a rationing formulation is appropriate since finance *at each price* is rationed.

Capital rationing problems may involve one or several restrictions. Those with a single constraint can take a variety of forms. We shall consider those problems in which the limit is on initial capital expenditure rather than outlay in a subsequent time period or a resource other than capital. A simple solution procedure can be applied and the method is best explained through an example.

A company is considering investment in up to six projects and has £215 000 for the total initial outlay. The cost of capital is 10%, no other opportunities are available and there are no other constraints. Investments can be accepted in full or in part (indivisibility is considered later). No investment is repeatable. The company has the objective of maximizing present value overall. Details of the investments are as given in Table 4.1.

Table 4.1

Time	Investment number					
	1	2	3	4	5	6
0	−25000	−60000	−90000	−100000	−120000	−35000
1	7500	17500	25000	0	75000	40000
2	7500	17500	25000	0	75000	0
3	7500	17500	25000	50000	0	0
4	7500	17500	25000	50000	0	0
5	7500	17500	25000	50000	0	0
NPV	3431	6339	4770	2759	10163	1364
IRR	15.2	14.1	12.1	11.6	16.3	14.3

Table 4.2

Project	NPV	Outlay	Total outlay
5	10163	120000	120000
2	6339	60000	180000
7/18 of 3	1855	35000	215000
1			
4			
6			
Total NPV =	18357		

Table 4.3

Project	Yield	NPV	Outlay	Total outlay
5	16.3	10163	120000	120000
1	15.2	3431	25000	145000
6	14.3	1364	35000	180000
7/12 of 2	14.1	3698	35000	215000
3	12.1			
4	11.6			
	Total NPV =	18656		

It is evident from Table 4.1 that *all* projects would be accepted by NPV or IRR *if it were not for the capital rationing*. But which projects should be selected, given the constraint on outlay? First, consider what would seem to be the obvious extension of the NPV rule to the rationing case: namely, *rank projects by size of NPV and accept them in this order until the budget is exhausted*. The results of this process are shown in Table 4.2.

An NPV of £18 357 results from the selection of projects 5 and 2 in full and 38.89% of project 3. Now consider the projects selected and the NPV that results if the investments are ranked by IRR. The outcome is shown in Table 4.3.

In this case the total of £18 656 from the IRR ranking is better than that produced by NPV. So the NPV decision rule does not generalize to the rationing case. But the better result produced by IRR is just a feature of this particular problem. The outcome could have been better or worse than the NPV ranking. *Neither* process produces the optimal selection of investments. The correct procedure is to rank the alternatives according to *the ratio of NPV to initial outlay*. This ratio is sometimes called the *benefit–cost ratio*. First consider the results shown in Table 4.4.

There has been a substantial improvement from ranking by benefit–cost ratio. The total NPV is 9.7% higher than from the IRR ranking and 11.5% greater than ranking by NPV itself. The optimal group of projects produces the cash flow:

Table 4.4

Project	Ratio	NPV	Outlay	Total outlay
1	0.137	3431	25000	25000
2	0.106	6339	60000	85000
5	0.085	10163	120000	205000
1/9 of 3	0.053	530	10000	215000
6	0.039			
4	0.028			
	Total NPV =	20463		

$t = 0$	$t = 1$	$t = 2$	$t = 3$	$t = 4$	$t = 5$
−215 000	102 778	102 778	27 778	27 778	27 778

which gives an IRR of just over 15%. This is achieved because the project at the top of the benefit–cost ratio list has the *highest achievement of objective per unit of scarce resource*. Once project 1 has been accepted in full, the maximum gain in the objective for the next unit of resource spent is achieved through investment in project 2. When project 2 is fully accepted, project 5 produces the best increase in NPV per pound spent – and so on.

We've assumed that projects can't be repeated. It is worth examining the full impact of this restriction. If it was possible to repeat project 1, no other project would have been selected and the outcome would have been as shown in Table 4.5.

Table 4.5

Project	Ratio	NPV	Outlay	Total outlay
1	0.137	3431	25000	25000
1	0.137	3431	25000	50000
1	0.137	3431	25000	75000
1	0.137	3431	25000	100000
1	0.137	3431	25000	125000
1	0.137	3431	25000	150000
1	0.137	3431	25000	175000
1	0.137	3431	25000	200000
6/10 of 1	0.137	2059	15000	215000
	Total NPV =	29507		

£29,507 would have resulted from 8.6 units of project 1 – an increase of 44.2% on the total when projects can't be repeated. If project 1 was not repeatable, but project 2 was repeatable, the outcome would have been as shown in Table 4.6.

Table 4.6

Project	Ratio	NPV	Outlay	Total outlay
1	0.137	3431	25000	25000
2	0.106	6339	60000	85000
2	0.106	6339	60000	145000
2	0.106	6339	60000	205000
1/6 of 2	0.106	1057	10000	215000
	Total NPV =	23505		

The non-repeatability of project 1 results in a drop of £6002 in NPV if project 2 is repeatable. The present-value impact of the non-repeatability of projects 2 and 5 can be found in a similar way. The use of benefit–cost ratios can be illustrated graphically. Figure 4.1 plots the total NPV achievable against the total availability of funds.

In Figure 4.1, the benefit–cost ratios are the slopes of the line segments of the NPV graph. As available funds expand, the successive investments taken show a

Rationing, uncertainty and corporate strategy

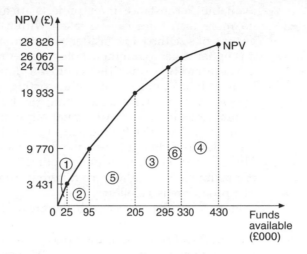

Figure 4.1

decreasing rate of increase of NPV per pound spent. This continues until project 4, the last project that could be undertaken, is completed. An overall NPV of £28 826 could be achieved if £430 000 was available for outlay and no project was repeatable. The ratio of *gross* present value (GPV) to outlay can also be used to obtain the optimum. This ratio, the *profitability index* (PI), always gives the same ranking as the benefit–cost ratio.

Now consider the marginal value of funds in the rationing problem with unrepeatable projects. If finance beyond the original £215 000 was available, what rate of interest would it be worth paying to get the funds? Consider the uncompleted marginal project 3 and its IRR of 12.1%. If money was available at a rate of interest between 10% and 12.1% the remaining 8/9 of project 3 would have a positive present value and increase the NPV achieved overall. But care must be exercised. It is not correct to say that 12.1% is the maximum rate worth paying for extra funds nor is it correct to say that if extra funds are obtainable below 12.1% project 3 should be completed.

Suppose that a further £35 000 was available at 12%. If this was used to take a further 7/18 of project 3, discounting at 12% gives an additional present value of £46.7. However, if the £35 000 was used in project 6 the increase in NPV would be £714.3. What has occurred is that the benefit–cost ratios of projects 3 and 6 now have different relative sizes. At 12% the ratio for project 6 is 1.0204 and for project 3 it is 1.0013. So if further funds are available the ratios for unused or uncompleted projects should be recalculated at the higher rate and, in effect, a separate problem must be solved. The maximum rate of interest worth paying for extra funds will be the highest IRR on any of the projects or part-projects which are still available. In the present case this is given by project 6 which has an IRR of 14.3%.

If some investments are mutually exclusive, care will be needed in using the ratio method. Sub-problems have to be solved for each possible combination of mutually exclusive projects. If many sub-problems were needed, this procedure would become rather complicated.

So far we have assumed that a fractional share in an investment is a practical possibility, as is often the case. But what of the problem where this is not so, and projects must be accepted or rejected in their entirety? A combinatorial element is introduced and a large number of different combinations of investments may arise. For instance, in a case with 20 all-or-nothing investments 184 756 different combinations of ten projects could be made up.

But the number of different combinations to evaluate will be nothing like this level if the size of initial outlay on a typical project is large relative to the budget available. For instance, if ten projects are available and the outlays are such that no more than three can be taken within budget, there is a maximum of 120 groups of size three to consider. Solution procedures for such problems exist but it is better to get round the whole-number requirement if possible.

There are two ways this could be done. It may be possible to stretch the budget. If this can be done at the existing cost of capital it is optimal to *round off the project at the margin*. Stretching the budget may be more likely under soft capital rationing than hard capital rationing. If the budget can be stretched, but at an increased price for the extra funds, this leads to complications as we have seen. But if the budget does not change an approximation method can be used. This method often produces an optimal result and is likely to be within 1 or 2% of maximum NPV although a different combination of projects may be involved. The procedure is as follows.

First, select the project with the greatest PI (if its outlay does not exceed the limit), then take the project with next greatest PI (if the two outlays do not exceed the limit) and so on until the project with the next greatest PI would exceed the budget. Projects with lower PIs are then examined and the one with the greatest PI *that can be afforded* is chosen. The list is then searched for the project with the greatest PI that can be afforded from the funds which then remain. Selection is completed when the cheapest project (of those remaining) cannot be financed from remaining funds. Let us apply this method to the six-project example. Projects 1, 2 and 5 are selected, giving an NPV of £19 933. This is the optimal solution in whole projects (verifiable in this case by listing all feasible combinations of projects – of which there are nine). Results are shown in Table 4.7.

Table 4.7

Project combinations	Net present value
5, 3	14933
5, 2, 6	17866
5, 2, 1	29933
5, 6, 1	14958
4, 3, 1	10960
4, 2, 6	10462
4, 2, 1	12529
4, 6, 1	7554
3, 2, 6, 1	15904

With each combination in Table 4.7 insufficient funds remain for acceptance of another complete project. Seven are three-project combinations, and there is one example each of a two-project and a four-project combination. The combination of projects 5, 2 and 1 turns out to be optimal (and is identified by the approximation procedure) for budget levels between £205 000 and £240 000. When the budget available reaches £240 000 the optimal combination of projects is 5, 2, 1 and 6. This too is identified by the approximation procedure.

Multi-constraint capital-rationing problems can be expressed in linear programming (LP) form and normally require LP methods for solution. But advanced methods are not always needed and we shall look at a simplified stock market investment problem in which a number of institutional constraints are included as well as an expenditure constraint. A financial manager has to decide on the percentages of a given sum to invest in various companies. The yields per pound invested in each company are as follows:

	Unit trusts		Chemicals		Stores		Mines	
Company no.	1	2	3	4	5	6	7	8
IRR (%)	4.8	5.4	7.5	8.5	9	10	15	18

Company policy does not give the investment manager a free hand. At least 30% of any portfolio must be in unit trusts, no more than 25% may be invested in mining, at least 10% must be in chemicals and no more than 20% of the portfolio may be invested in any one company. Given these constraints, the aim is to maximize overall yield (IRR). How should available capital be divided among the companies? It is worth a brief look at the LP model here. Let x_j represent the percentage of the portfolio invested in company j. IRR on the total sum is a weighted average of the individual IRRs. The problem is:

Maximize $F = 4.8x_1 + 5.4x_2 + 7.5x_3 + 8.5x_4 + 9x_5 + 10x_6 + 15x_7 + 18x_8$

Subject to:
$$
\begin{aligned}
x_1 + x_2 + x_3 + x_4 + x_5 + x_6 + x_7 + x_8 &= 100 \\
x_1 + x_2 &\geq 30 \\
x_7 + x_8 &\leq 25 \\
x_3 + x_4 &\geq 10 \\
x_1 &\leq 20 \\
x_2 &\leq 20 \\
x_3 &\leq 20 \\
x_4 &\leq 20 \\
x_5 &\leq 20 \\
x_6 &\leq 20 \\
x_7 &\leq 20 \\
x_8 &\leq 20
\end{aligned}
$$

and where:

$$x_1, x_2, x_3, x_4, x_5, x_6, x_7, x_8 \geq 0$$

The structure of this problem allows informal solution. Company 8 is the most lucrative investment and x_8 is set at 20. Company 7 is next most attractive, but x_7 may not exceed 5 because of constraint 3. The best way of satisfying constraint 2 is to set x_2 equal to 20 and x_1 equal to 10. Constraint 3 is met by setting x_4 equal to 10. Constraint 1 then allows x_6 to be set at 20 and x_5 at 15. The solution in full is:

$$x_1 = 10 \quad x_2 = 20 \quad x_3 = 0 \quad x_4 = 10 \quad x_5 = 15 \quad x_6 = 20 \quad x_7 = 5 \quad x_8 = 20$$

Overall IRR is 10.11%. Analysis on the predetermined policy elements reveals the effects of relaxing the constraints. For example, if the policy was changed so that 35% of the portfolio could be in mining, the new optimal levels of x_5 and x_7 would be 5 and 15 respectively and the average yield would increase to 10.71%.

There are many possible objectives for investing companies if finance is limited in more than one period. We shall consider a standard case where the objective is the maximization of equity value. In the *discounted dividend model* equity is measured by the present value of future dividend payments with discounting at the cost of equity capital. Undertaking an investment programme means changes in the stream of dividends. These changes are of two kinds. There may be years in which dividend is reduced because of higher retentions to help finance the investments. But there will be years in which increased dividends can be paid because of the returns from the investments. The present value of the set of dividend changes must be positive for an investment programme to be worthwhile. The requirement is:

$$\Delta D_0 + \frac{\Delta D_1}{(1+e)} + \frac{\Delta D_2}{(1+e)^2} + \ldots + \frac{\Delta D_n}{(1+e)^n} > 0$$

where the ΔD_t are the dividend changes over an n-year horizon and $100e\%$ is the cost of equity. The objective is to choose a set of investments, affordable in all years, to maximize this present value. Suppose that a company is settling its capital budget for 2000 and 2001 against a background which suggests a likely shortage of cash during the period. The company's existing activity will generate a cash surplus of £250 000 on 1 January 2000 ($t = 0$) and £240 000 on 1 January 2001 ($t = 1$). These sums are available for dividend payment and for financing new investments. Market conditions effectively rule out raising additional capital from external sources during the period, but things are expected to improve by 2002 and it is expected that the company will from that point no longer experience capital rationing. Six continuously divisible but not repeatable investments are available. Financial data are:

			Project number			
	1	2	3	4	5	6
Outlay at:						
$t = 0$	30	40	20	40	60	0
$t = 1$	0	0	40	40	40	80
Return at:						
$t = 2$	72	72	96	132	168	144

The objective is to maximize equity value $t = 0$, equity value being determined by the discounted dividend model. The cost of equity capital is 20%. The company can invest unused funds elsewhere at 15%. The previously determined dividends of £100 000 at $t = 0$ and £105 000 at $t = 1$ can be added to but not decreased. There is no restriction on dividend at $t = 2$ nor are the relative sizes of dividend payments restricted. The resulting increase in current value of equity is:

$$\Delta V = \Delta D_0 + \frac{\Delta D_1}{1.2} + \frac{\Delta D_2}{(1.2)^2}$$

and it is desired to maximize ΔV. Initial expenditure on the investments must not exceed £150 000. This is because while £250 000 is available at this time £100 000 has already been earmarked for dividend. So:

$$30x_1 + 40x_2 + 20x_3 + 40x_4 + 60x_5 + 0x_6 + \Delta D_0 + S_0 = 150$$

where x_1 to x_6 are the numbers of units taken of each investment and S_0 is unused funds, if any, at $t = 0$ which will be carried forward at 15%. At $t = 1$, funds outlaid on the projects must not exceed £135 000 (i.e. £240 000 − £105 000) plus any unused funds from $t = 0$ invested at 15%. The constraint is then:

$$0x_1 + 0x_2 + 40x_3 + 40x_4 + 40x_5 + 80x_6 + \Delta D_1 \leq 135 + S_0(1.15)$$

Which can be re-expressed as:

$$0x_1 + 0x_2 + 40x_3 + 40x_4 + 40x_5 + 80x_6 - 1.15S_0 + \Delta D_1 + S_1 = 135$$

in which S_1 is carried forward at 15% to $t = 2$. The increase in dividend possible at $t = 2$ depends on the investment returns and any surplus from $t = 1$ invested at 15%. This means that ΔD_2 is limited by:

$$-72x_1 - 72x_2 - 96x_3 - 132x_4 - 168x_5 - 144x_6 - 1.15S_1 + \Delta D_2 = 0$$

Subject to these requirements, the aim is to maximize the present value of dividends. We shall not be concerned with the mechanics of the solution here, but will give results and some interpretation to illustrate what is possible in models of this sort. The optimal policy would be to take five units of the first investment, nothing of the second to fifth investments, take 1.6875 units of investment 6, transfer no money from 1 January 2000 to 1 January 2001, pay the minimum dividends of £100 000 in 2000 and £105 000 in 2001 and increase dividend by £603 000 in 2002. If this is an unacceptable dividend policy, further constraints on ΔD_0, ΔD_1 and ΔD_2 should be included. The value of the firm's equity will rise by £418 750. So $\Delta D_3 = 603$, $\Delta D_0 = 0$, $\Delta D_1 = 0$ and $\Delta V = 418.75$ from:

$$\Delta V = 0 + \frac{0}{1.2} + \frac{603}{(1.2)^2} = 418.75$$

With a maximum of one unit of each investment, the optimal solution is:

$$x_1 = 1 \quad x_2 = 1 \quad x_3 = 0 \quad x_4 = 0.44 \quad x_5 = 1 \quad x_6 = 1 \quad S_0 = 2.33$$
$$\Delta D_0 = 0 \quad \Delta D_1 = 0 \quad \Delta D_2 = 514.33 \quad \Delta V = 357.17$$

So there is full acceptance of investments 1, 2, 5 and 6, an approximate 44% share in investment 4 and no investment in project 3. A sum of £2330 is transferred from 1 January 2000 to 1 January 2001. No dividend increases are scheduled for January 2000 or January 2001, the entire impact of the investments is to increase dividend in January 2002 by £514 330, producing an increase in the value of equity of £357 170. The upper bounds cut the equity value increase by £61 580.

In the optimal solution, a 'loan' is made for one period (S_0 = 2.33) which *apparently* yields less than the cost of capital. This can happen in capital rationing. The *nominal* yield on £1 invested at 15% in these conditions is 15%, but the IRR in effect is greater than the cost of equity due to the improved combination of investments and dividends it allows. Investing at 15% at $t = 0$ makes money available at $t = 1$ when it is more valuable. This enables a better investment programme with larger returns and $t = 2$ dividend. An inter-period transfer of funds would *not* be made if this implied yield was less than the objective-function discount rate.

The programming solution gives still more information. Maximum period-to-period borrowing interest between $t = 0$ and $t = 1$ and between $t = 1$ and $t = 2$ can be found. In this example it turns out that it would be worth paying up to 53.49% to obtain a further £1 from outside sources at $t = 1$ repayable at $t = 2$. So a project with the cash flow:

$t = 1$	$t = 2$
1	-1.3

would bring an improvement in the present value of divided payments despite its apparently negative 'NPV' at either the 15% or 20% external rate. The cash inflow at $t = 1$ enables lucrative opportunities to be taken which repay more than the 1.3 liability at $t = 2$. In fact, there is no figure that can be said to be the present or terminal value of a project in a multi-project context with multi-period constraints. The effect of a given stream of costs and returns on present or terminal value depends on the cash flow of other projects and the capital constraints. Any 'present value' for a project deduced at some rate or rates of discount will change if the project is added to a different set of other projects and/or constraints. A consequence of this is that under capital rationing an asset cannot be valued in isolation from other assets to which it may be joined or from the capital or other constraints which may apply.

Further information that could be obtained includes the value of relaxing the upper-bound constraints. It is also interesting to work out the overall rate of return obtained on the total sums invested. With the upper bounds imposed it is as if, using the x's as intermediaries, we had invested in a project with the cash flow:

$t = 0$	$t = 1$	$t = 2$
-150	-135	514.33

which has an internal rate of return of 45.56%.

Linear programming methods can also be used in short-term financial management. A model developed by Srinivasan [1] applied a transportation algorithm to the problem of the management of cash and short-term investments. The model optimizes investment of cash inflows and optimal financing for outflows, simultaneously producing payment schedules for the incurred liabilities. The model allows distinction between four decision variables: securities transactions, payment schedules, short-term financing and cash balance.

One approach to the interrelated (sub-)problems of capital investment, financing and short-term management of funds is through a comprehensive *financial planning model*. A *normative model* looks for an ideal set of consistent decisions in all sub-problems. Financial planning models can be vast even though uncertainties are dealt with indirectly. They can be used in several ways: for example, financial modelling could be tested in a restricted area and on a well-specified problem. *Simulating models* are based on accounting practices. Simulating models project the results from given courses of action and assumptions about the future. The models use as inputs forecasts and decisions from company departments and produce the consequent financial statements. The relative emphasis placed on the financial statistics produced and the final investment and financing decisions are then made by the company.

We shall not develop a full-scale financial planning model here. Rather, we shall give illustrations of the type of constraint that a financial planning context adds on to the capital rationing framework. Typically, management will wish to take account of the way that the use of investment funds affects other published financial results as well as cash flows. The changes that potential investments can cause in financial statistics based on accounts rather than cash flow cannot always be neglected. What are seen by the ownership as reasonable bounds for key financial ratios can be built into a model that represents the actual situation of a company. When the model is run, data will be produced which show the effects of the chosen bounds on achievement of corporate objectives. This information can provide powerful arguments for change. As an example of a constraint related to the value of a financial statistic consider the *current ratio* defined as:

$$\frac{\text{current assets}}{\text{current liabilities}}$$

Management decides an acceptable minimum for the ratio. To include the constraint in the model, current assets and current liabilities are expressed as functions of the investment levels.

Other requirements in financial planning models may include a minimum value for return on gross assets, minimum requirements for earnings net of tax and depreciation, and requirements relating to minimum values for dividend payments in each year. For example, it may be required that dividends in any year are a given proportion of earnings net of tax and depreciation. All these provisions, and other similar ones, can be handled in ways similar to the current ratio, and they result in further linear constraints to be added to the model. The objective function may be of discounted dividend form and, since a definite horizon will need to be employed, must include some assessment of wealth at the horizon. This will usually be the discounted value at the horizon of post-horizon cash flow from both new and existing investments.

When the financial planning model is run, solution values for the investment levels (the x_j) will result. Because the required constraints are built into the model, the optimal investment programme will produce acceptable values of the selected balance-sheet measures. Information is given in the solution as to the effects of varying key parameters (such as the size of the current ratio, M). The model could be run with different sets of values of the parameters for different possible *states of the world* or hypothetical *scenarios* and there may be a core of projects that would be accepted in all scenarios. These could be implemented, while more detailed studies of the likelihood of the different states of the world are carried out. Further possibilities for the use of the models include assessment of the effects of alternative dividend policies on the optimal investment programme and examination of alternatives that would make published results more consistent from year to year if this was not already included as a requirement within the model.

4.3 TRADITIONAL APPROACHES TO UNCERTAINTY AND RISK

Many investment decisions are made with some uncertainty about the outcome. Revenues may be lower or higher than initial estimates. Costs, although usually estimated with more confidence, can also be variable. Even if costs and revenues were guaranteed in amount, if relative *timings* are altered this may cause cash-flow problems. Although in practice relatively few methods are used, there are many possible approaches to risk. Traditional methods such as *payback* are widely used and there is no single approach to risk that is best for all companies or individuals in all circumstances.

Sometimes a distinction is drawn between *risk* and *uncertainty* – 'risk' meaning that cash-flow values have known probability distributions. 'Uncertainty' is said to exist when various outcomes are possible but probability information is incomplete or does not exist. We shall use the words interchangeably here. After capital rationing it is fitting that the first traditional method we consider is *payback*. This is because apologists for payback justify the method on the grounds that it is supposed to generate cash quickly in periods of shortage. In the following section we consider whether this view can be sustained.

Payback period for an investment is the number of years required for the undiscounted sum of returns to equal or exceed initial outlay – in other words to pay it back. To appraise an individual investment by this means, the project's payback period is found and compared with a pre-set threshold. If the project's payback is less than or equal to the pre-set value the project is accepted – otherwise it is rejected. Amongst several projects, those with shorter payback periods would be preferred. Suppose that company policy states that acceptable projects should pay back within six years. The project (no. 1):

$t = 0$	$t = 1$	$t = 2$	$t = 3$	$t = 4$	$t = 5$	$t = 6$	$t = 7$
-20000	11000	5000	2000	1000	2000	7000	9000

would be acceptable since the total of returns after five years is 21 000 and the outlay has been more than repaid in the pre-set period. If project 1 is compared with an alternative project, 2, with cash flow:

$t = 0$	$t = 1$	$t = 2$	$t = 3$	$t = 4$	$t = 5$	$t = 6$	$t = 7$
-20000	1000	3000	5000	11000	5000	3000	1000

then if the payback rule is rigidly applied, project 2, which returns its outlay in four years, would be preferred as it has the shorter payback period. A convenient layout for the workings is shown in Table 4.8.

Table 4.8

Year	Project 1 cash flow	Cumulative cash flow	Project 2 cash flow	Cumulative cash flow
0	-20000	-20000	-20000	-20000
1	11000	-9000	1000	-19000
2	5000	-4000	3000	-16000
3	2000	-2000	5000	-11000
4	1000	-1000	11000	0
5	2000	1000	5000	5000
6	7000	8000	3000	8000
7	9000	17000	1000	9000

The disadvantages of payback are obvious. It takes no account of the cost of capital; cash flows outside the payback period are ignored, as is the distribution of cash flow within the payback period. However, companies using payback may apply a degree of discretion so that the post-payback returns are somehow 'taken into account'. Consider the question of the distribution of returns within the payback period. Project 1 pays back a large proportion of the outlay (55%) in the first year whereas project 2 pays back only 5% at this point. The percentages of outlay returned (undiscounted) are shown in Table 4.9.

Table 4.9

Year	Project 1	Project 2
1	55	5
2	80	20
3	90	45
4	95	100
5	105	125
6	140	140
7	185	145

It is only around years 4 and 5 that project 2 has any advantage in the proportion of outlay returned. Figure 4.2 shows the advantage of project 1 in the early and later years.

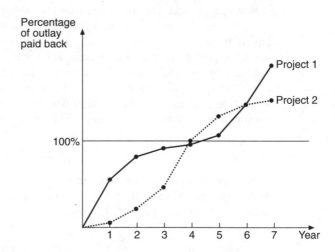

Figure 4.2

While the S-shaped track of project 2 in Figure 4.2 is more common than the early take-off, flat period and pick-up of project 1, a blinkered approach focusing exclusively on the 100% proportion clearly has its costs. Payback will tend to be less wide of the mark in cases where returns to competing projects always tail off over time in comparable fashions, and the rule can be made more sophisticated in a number of ways. For example, minimum payback percentages can be set at various points in time or discounted returns can be used. With discounting, payback can at least decide whether or not a project will become profitable in its own right, but it still cannot say *how* profitable nor make decisions between mutually exclusive projects. Such adaptations go some way towards meeting the criticisms of payback, but also remove some of the grounds on which payback is said to be preferred. There are three main justifications offered in its defence:

1 It is simple to use and easy to understand.
2 Projects which return their outlay quickly leave the investor less exposed to risk and uncertainty.

3 Under capital rationing, the sooner the money is returned the sooner can other profitable investments be undertaken.

It is tempting to argue that reason 1 ought not to carry much weight but in practice it often does. Reason 1 is less vulnerable to rational attack when, as under uncertainty, the theoretical underpinning of more sophisticated methods is often less than perfect. The more that uncertainty increases with time, the more force there is in reason 2. In industries where the pace of technological change is fast, the use of arbitrary and quite short horizons can be made more convincing. But the criticisms of lack of discounting or allowance for interest charges and lack of consideration for the cash-flow pattern within the payback period remain. Reason 3 also has something in it, but this does not justify ignoring more precise methods for dealing with capital rationing. For example, if year 1 was the point of most acute capital shortage, it is likely that project 1 would be preferred.

As regards NPVs for the projects of Table 4.9, project 1 has a greater NPV than project 2 at *any* discount rate. This suggests that if a large part of the uncertainty related to interest rates rather than cash-flow components there would be a strong case for project 1. Where the projects being compared have more or less constant returns, decision by payback can be shown to approximate to decision by IRR.

On balance, the greater the uncertainty, the more the uncertainty increases with time and the poorer the quality of information available to the decision makers, the less there is to be said against the use of payback. But is the use of payback ever fully justified? The answer can only be yes if the need for simplicity overrides all other considerations. The more information exists on probabilities, cash-flow data, times of capital shortage, etc., the more there is to be said for a DCF-based approach.

A method of investment appraisal with similarities to payback but which uses discounting is the *finite horizon* method (FHM) in which cash flows after a pre-set time are ignored. For long horizons and/or high interest rates, returns beyond a reasonable cut-off point are unlikely to make much difference to present values. Where uncertainty and risk increase with time, weight is added to the argument for not counting on (or counting in) the distant cash flow. But there is also the danger of ignoring a problematic legacy for future generations. If in the use of FHM a short horizon was selected, some assessment would have to be made of the value of post-horizon returns at the horizon date. This can be done (for example, by finding the discounted value of post-horizon cash flow at the horizon) but if this is done with sufficient accuracy the method ceases to have a meaningful finite horizon.

There are traditional appraisal methods based on return on capital. These begin with the disadvantage that the number of possible meanings for this concept is the product of the number of definitions of 'return' and the number of definitions of 'capital'. Usually a measure of capital associated with a project is divided into a measure of return or profit and the result is expressed as a percentage. Consider projects 1 and 2 of Table 4.8 if the 'rate' of return on capital is expressed as the ratio of average return to 'average' capital. If average capital is taken to be half of initial capital (initial outlay) in each case, and the average return is taken as the total of undiscounted cash-flow returns divided by project duration, then this measure of return on (average) capital for the two projects gives:

$$\frac{100(5286)}{10000}\% = 52.9\%$$

for project 1 and:

$$\frac{100(4143)}{10000}\% = 41.4\%$$

for project 2.

Accounting rate of return (ARR) divides a measure of annual *profit* (rather than net cash flow) defined as net returns less depreciation by the average investment defined as:

$$0.5(\text{initial outlay + residual value})$$

if straight-line depreciation is used. For example, with the assumption of zero residual value, for project 1 in Table 4.8, the average net return is the total of returns, 37 000, divided by the number of years, 7, with the result of 5286. From this is subtracted one-seventh of the cost of the investment, i.e. 20 000/7 = 2857, to give an annual profit figure of

$$5286 - 2857 = 2429$$

and an ARR of

$$100 \frac{2429}{10\,000}\% = 24.3\%$$

Similar calculations for project 2 give an ARR of

$$100 \frac{29\,000/7 - 20\,000/7}{10\,000}\% = 12.9\%$$

Decision rules based on ARR would accept an individual project if its return exceeded the target figure, and for a mutually exclusive pair would select the project with the greater ARR. So project 1 would be selected here. Arguments advanced in favour of return on capital measures are similar to those made in support of payback period. As with payback there is no theoretical underpinning.

In a comparison between projects of unequal duration giving similar total returns for similar outlay, ARR and other measures of return on capital will favour the shorter project. Although these measures do at least consider returns over the whole life of projects, the timing of returns, as with payback, is ignored. Equal value is effectively given to a return of £100 after one year and the same return after ten years. The measures are conservative if the larger returns come near the start of the project, when the averaging of returns understates the value of the project and thus provides a margin of safety. But, on the whole, the averaging of undiscounted returns obscures important differences between otherwise similar projects in the timing of larger returns. This is important if, as is usually the case, uncertainty increases with distance from the present. Consider, for example, the projects:

	$t = 0$	$t = 1$	$t = 2$	$t = 3$	$t = 4$
A	−1400	800	600	400	200
B	−1400	500	500	500	500
C	−1400	200	400	600	800

for which the following measures may be confirmed:

	A	B	C
Accounting rate of return	21.43	21.43	21.43
Return on capital (average)	71.43	71.43	71.43
Payback period	2	3	4
Internal rate of return	20.53	15.97	12.91
Net present value (15%)	126.70	27.49	−71.72

Rationing, uncertainty and corporate strategy

The three projects appear identical in terms of accounting rate of return and return on capital, but are clearly distinguished by all the other methods including, in this case, payback. A is preferred to B, which is preferred to C. There can be little doubt which is the most attractive project. In practice ARR may be one of a number of criteria the values of which are taken into account, though this does not mean that the decision maker can trust to the deficiencies of one approach being compensated by other methods. Most UK firms use several methods – around three typically. About nine out of ten use payback but upwards of eight out of ten use a DCF method (IRR somewhat more than NPV). Only around four out of ten use accounting rate of return. See Wilkes *et al.* [2], Pike [3] or Sangster [4] for further details.

In the *risk premium* approach a number of percentage points (a premium) is added to the discount rate to allow for the uncertainty. Although this very old pragmatic response to risk in banking and money lending can draw some support from the capital-asset pricing model if appropriate project-specific risk premia are used, in practice premia tend to be judgemental and can be lacking in consistency. The risk-discounted present value can be written as:

$$NPV = \sum_{t=1}^{n} R_t (1 + r + p)^{-t} - K$$

where the risk premium is $100p\%$ and where r is an estimate of the risk-free discount rate (for example, the yield to maturity on long-term government bonds). Historically the average extra return demanded from equities in the UK has been around 8% or 9% above the risk-free rate. The risk-adjusted discount rate is $100(r + p)\%$. For example, the project:

$t = 0$	$t = 1$	$t = 2$	$t = 3$	$t = 4$
-100	40	50	60	70

has an NPV of 70.6 at a discount rate of 10% ($r = 0.1$). The use of a 5% risk premium ($p = 0.05$) produces an NPV figure of 52.1. The use of the risk-adjusted discount rate causes a higher discount factor to be applied to all returns, but the further away a return is from the present, the larger is the increase in the discount factor. This increasing impact is shown in Table 4.10 where, for the data above, the 15% adjusted rate cuts the contribution to present value of the year-one return by 4.35% but the present value of the year-four return is reduced by 16.29%. Larger impacts would be made on the present values of more distant returns in longer-running projects.

Table 4.10

Time	Return	10%PV	15%PV	Reduction %
1	40	36.36	34.78	4.35
2	50	41.32	37.81	8.51
3	60	45.08	39.45	12.48
4	70	47.81	40.02	16.29

A variant of the basic risk-premium approach makes a distinction between investments with different perceived levels of risk by applying banded premia according to the risk category of a project. A typical categorization is a three-tier split into low-risk, medium-risk and high-risk classes, with a different risk premium applying within each class. For example, against the background of a 7% risk-free rate, management may determine risk premiums of 4, 9 and 15 percentage points as shown in Table 4.11.

Table 4.11

Risk class	Premium	Risk-adjusted discount rate
Low	4	11
Medium	9	16
High	15	22

Management then assesses the various factors involved in a project and places the project in one of the categories. An extension of this approach determines an individual risk premium for each project. Each investment then has its own risk-adjusted discount rate. At this level the risk-premium approach begins to gain theoretical support from the capital-asset pricing model. In this case the risk considered must be that component of project specific risk that cannot be diversified away (*systematic risk*). A more ambitious approach can be applied to large-scale complex projects if the components of the cash flow can be disentangled and different risk premia applied to the distinguishable types of income. Empirical support should be provided for the differential premia, the logical basis for which would be the capital-asset pricing model described in Chapter 11.

4.4 SENSITIVITY ANALYSIS

In sensitivity analysis, the viability of an investment is examined in relation to key parameters. A range of variation or *tolerance interval* is found for parameters individually or jointly. Consider an example. A company is considering a project that would involve the production of a commodity for six years. The initial estimates of the parameter values are as shown in Table 4.12

Table 4.12

Initial outlay (K)	40000
Selling price (p)	20
Unit cost (c)	15
Discount rate (r)	10
Lifetime (L)	6
Sales volumes: Year one	2000
Year two	2000
Year three	3000
Year four	3000
Year five	1500
Year six	1500

The return received in any year will be the unit profit $p - c$ multiplied by the sales volume, v. Thus, on the basis of the initial estimates the cash flow would be:

$t = 0$	$t = 1$	$t = 2$	$t = 3$	$t = 4$	$t = 5$	$t = 6$
$-40\,000$	$10\,000$	$10\,000$	$15\,000$	$15\,000$	7500	7500

At 10%:

$$\text{GPV} = 47761 \text{ and NPV} = 7761$$

The threshold for acceptability of the project is non-negative NPV. Single-parameter sensitivity analysis now determines the individual percentage variation in each parameter (p, c, v, K, r and L) that would produce zero NPV. First, consider the unit profit on the product. This is $p - c$ and is currently £5. Any variation in this figure would have equal proportionate effect on each return and hence on GPV as a whole, so that as long as unit profit is not less than

$$£5\frac{40\,000}{47\,761} = £4.19$$

with the other data unchanged, NPV will not become negative. So on the income side with unchanged unit costs, as long as the selling price is not less than £19.19, the project will still be viable. In other words, the price must not drop by more than 4.05%. On the cost side, with unchanged selling price, if unit costs remain below £15.81 then NPV will be positive, so that any increase must not exceed 5.40%. On the sales-volume front, if unit profits are unchanged but sales are:

$$100\frac{40\,000}{47\,761}\% = 83.75\%$$

of the original estimates in each year the project remains viable. Put another way, with other things equal, sales volume figures must not fall by more than 16.25%.

For the remaining parameters, again considered individually, NPV will become zero for an initial outlay of £47 761 or 19.40% above the original figure. As regards the discount rate, the yield of the project turns out to be 16.57%, so that a 65.7% increase over the original value for the discount rate is tolerable. Sensitivity to changes in lifetime is more difficult to assess as an approximation is needed if reductions of fractions of a year are involved. If the project's life is four years, i.e. if the last two returns of £7500 are ignored, the GPV would be £38 870, a decrease of £8891. To make GPV exactly £40 000 the contribution to present value of returns in the fifth year needs to be £1130. Suppose that if the project runs for a fraction f of the fifth year then the return that arises is $7500f$ received at time $t = 4 + f$. So, if the truncated fifth year is to produce a return giving a present value of £1130, then f must be such as to satisfy:

$$\frac{7500f}{(1.1)^{4+f}} = 1130$$

that is:

$$750f = 113(1.1)^{4+f}$$

The value of f satisfying this equation is $f = 0.2254$ with workings shown in Table 4.13.

Table 4.13

f	$750f$	$113(1.1)^{4+f}$
0.2000	150.00	168.63
0.2200	165.00	168.95
0.2250	168.75	169.03
0.2251	168.82	169.03
0.2252	168.90	169.03
0.2253	168.98	169.03
0.2254	169.05	169.04
0.2255	169.13	169.04

Thus with $f = 0.2254$, the breakeven lifetime is 4.2254 years, a reduction of 1.7746 years or 29.58% on the original value. The full results of the single-parameter breakeven exercise are shown in Table 4.14.

Table 4.14

Datum	Percentage change
Selling price	4.05
Unit cost	5.40
Sales volume	16.25
Initial outlay	19.40
Discount rate	65.70
Project lifetime	29.58

Entries in the percentage change column of Table 4.14 are the unfavourable changes (decrease or increase) which, if occurring individually, would reduce NPV to zero. It is evident that NPV is more sensitive to changes in sales price and unit costs than to any other datum and it is this area that would receive management attention if uncertainty is to be reduced. Calculations of sales-volume sensitivity could have been performed for each year individually. For example, consider the year-3 figure. With all else unchanged, the level of sales in year 3 necessary to produce an NPV of zero is V_3 where:

$$-40\,000 + 10\,000(0.9091) + 10\,000(0.8264) + 5V_3(0.7513)$$
$$+ 15\,000(0.6830) + 7500(0.6209) + 7500(0.5645)$$
$$= 0$$

So:

$$V_3 = 934.1$$

which is a percentage reduction of up to 68.9% in this individual figure.

The full results for sales volumes figures stated individually are shown in Table 4.15.

Table 4.15

Year	Original sales	Minimum for year	Percentage variation
1	2000	292.63	85.37
2	2000	121.90	93.91
3	3000	934.09	68.86
4	3000	727.49	75.75
5	1500	−999.76	166.65
6	1500	−1249.73	183.32

Some of the figures in Table 4.15 may seem surprising. The negative values for sales volume in years five and six simply indicate that if there were no sales at all in either of those years there would, with other data unchanged, still be a positive NPV – an outcome consistent with our findings for minimum length of life. The required minimum falls between years one and two and years three and four because the greater discount applied to the second of each pair of figures reduces its significance to present value.

As regards the initial outlay, a variation of almost 20% would be somewhat unusual in a one-off cost at a given time. However, had these costs been spread over a period, more variability might be expected. While the tolerable adverse variation in discount rate is the largest of any parameter in percentage terms, rates of interest are typically more volatile than are finished goods prices or manufacturing costs. So despite the apparent robustness of NPV to this parameter due caution should still be exercised. Similar caveats apply to interpretation of the tolerable change in project lifetime – the second largest percentage figure. Should demand for the end product be overtaken by technological progress or change in taste, then a variation in anticipated lifetime of around one-third is not that unlikely.

Multi-parameter analysis considers simultaneous changes in a number of values. For example, correlated movements in prices are likely if many are affected by common factors such as exchange rates or inflation. Another approach when several parameters change is to specify sets of changes and find the consequences for present value. The changes might correspond to states of the world or *scenarios*, and could represent government choices of economic goals or means of regulation. Consider some inflation scenarios. In scenario 1 suppose that market conditions and exchange-rate variations mean that selling price would rise by 10% per annum while unit costs would rise at 15% – both sets of rises based on $t = 0$. We shall need selling price and unit costs at the end of each year; then the difference – unit profit – is multiplied by sales volume and discounted. The results, with price in year t, p_t, given by

$$p_t = 20(1.1)^t$$

and costs in year c, c_t, given by

$$c_t = 15(1.15)^t$$

are shown in Table 4.16.

Table 4.16

Year	Price	Cost	Unit profit	Sales	Revenue	PV
1	22.00	17.25	4.75	2000	9500.00	8636.36
2	24.20	19.84	4.36	2000	8725.00	7210.75
3	26.62	22.81	3.81	3000	11420.63	8580.49
4	29.28	26.24	3.05	3000	9140.72	6243.23
5	32.21	30.17	2.04	1500	3059.76	1899.87
6	35.43	34.70	0.74	1500	1102.96	622.59
					GPV =	33193.29
					NPV =	−6806.71

The different rates of inflation have turned a positive NPV of £7761 into a loss of £6807. Note that the major impact of the different rates of inflation is in the later years. In the first two years there are relatively small reductions in unit profit, but profit is rapidly approaching zero by $t = 6$.

Now consider inflation scenario 2. In this case severe inflation at 23% in selling price and 28% of unit cost is expected. With a similar layout to Table 4.16, the results are displayed in Table 4.17.

Table 4.17

Year	Price	Cost	Unit profit	Sales	Revenue	PV
1	24.60	19.20	5.40	2000	10800.00	9818.18
2	30.26	24.58	5.68	2000	11364.00	9391.73
3	37.22	31.46	5.76	3000	17280.18	12982.85
4	45.78	40.27	5.51	3000	16536.03	11294.33
5	56.31	51.54	4.77	1500	7149.76	4439.44
6	69.26	65.97	3.29	1500	4928.74	2782.15
					GPV =	50708.68
					NPV =	10708.68

In this case the result is an *increase* of 38% in NPV. This is due to the increase in unit profit in money terms in the earlier years. This illusion of prosperity is due to the fact that although the escalation of selling price is slower than that of unit cost it works from a larger base. This is sufficient (at first) to more than counteract the difference of five percentage points in the inflation rates. However, as is seen from Table 4.17, the chickens are coming home to roost in the later years of the project with unit profit falling rapidly (it would have become negative by year eight). The example suggests that differences in inflation rates between prices and costs can be got away with for a while, provided that the project is profitable to begin with. The corrosive effect of the inflation becomes evident at a later stage.

So far we have used the original discount rate of 10%. However, where other prices are moving upwards the price of money will not usually remain constant for long. In inflation scenario 3 suppose that costs rise by 8% while product prices increase at 5% and where interest rates rise such that the discount rate becomes 12.5%. The results are shown in Table 4.18.

Table 4.18

Year	Price	Cost	Unit profit	Sales	Revenue	PV
1	21.00	16.20	4.80	2000	9600.00	8533.33
2	22.05	17.50	4.55	2000	9108.00	7196.44
3	23.15	18.90	4.26	3000	12770.46	8969.10
4	24.31	20.41	3.90	3000	11708.38	7309.48
5	25.53	22.04	3.49	1500	5228.57	2901.48
6	26.80	23.80	3.00	1500	4498.20	2218.83
					GPV =	37128.67
					NPV =	−2871.33

Here the apparently modest difference between the cost and price inflation rates, three percentage points, eats into unit profits from the outset. This is not surprising because the rate of cost inflation is 60% greater than the rise in selling prices. The rise in discount rate adds to the damage and the investment would not be undertaken if this scenario were assured.

Now consider scenario 4 in which inflation of both revenues and costs has been constrained to 3% in each case. The policies that achieved this have also produced low interest rates, reflected in a 7% discount rate. The downside is that the level of activity has fallen and sales volumes are down 10% in each year. Table 4.19 gives the results.

Table 4.19

Year	Price	Cost	Unit profit	Sales	Revenue	PV
1	20.60	15.45	5.15	1800	9270.00	8663.55
2	21.22	15.91	5.30	1800	9548.10	8339.68
3	21.85	16.39	5.46	2700	14751.81	12041.87
4	22.51	16.88	5.63	2700	15194.37	11591.71
5	23.19	17.39	5.80	1350	7825.10	5579.19
6	23.88	17.91	5.97	1350	8059.85	5370.62
					GPV =	51586.63
					NPV =	11586.63

Despite the fact that the level of economic activity has fallen, NPV in cash terms is greater than the original value. The increase in money values of unit profit combined with the lower rate of discount in this case more than offset the depressed state of sales and produce the financial improvement. Things are, however, rather delicately balanced in scenario 4.

In scenario 5, sales are still assumed to be 10% down, but the inflation and discount rate figures are also off their previous values by an adverse 1 percentage point in each case. So sales prices increase by 2%, costs rise by 4% and the discount rate is 8%. The outcome for the project is shown in Table 4.20.

Table 4.20

Year	Price	Cost	Unit profit	Sales	Revenue	PV
1	20.40	15.60	4.80	1800	8640.00	8000.00
2	20.81	16.22	4.58	1800	8251.20	7074.08
3	21.22	16.87	4.35	2700	11748.24	9326.13
4	21.65	17.55	4.10	2700	11072.07	8138.30
5	22.08	18.25	3.83	1350	5172.96	3520.63
6	22.52	18.98	3.54	1350	4783.67	3014.53
					GPV =	39073.66
					NPV =	−926.34

Here the picture is very different from scenario 4. Overall NPV is now negative and the decline in physical activity represented by the depressed sales volumes is now matched by a financial loss. There are many other possible futures that could be projected. For example, with inflation first rising and then falling, varying interest rates, different patterns of initial cash flow and more subtle differences in sales volumes.

Sensitivity analysis could be used in all these cases to project the outcome for NPV. There are three main uses to which management can put the results of a sensitivity analysis:

1   As derived information to be taken into account in an initial assessment of the project;
2   As a pointer to where more detailed data and estimates would be most valuable;
3   As an aid in the preparation of contingency plans should key parameters show unfavourable variation *ex post*.

Sensitivity analysis is not a *decision rule*. Management must weigh the information from the analysis and decide if investments are worthwhile. Sensitivity analysis is most valuable in uncertainty where probability information is inadequate. Hard-and-fast decision rules proposed for such circumstances would rightly be treated with reserve. The use of managerial judgement is most important. In other approaches, numerical values are attached to subjective elements and included in calculations with objective data. There may be some merit in this, but there is a strong case for keeping judgemental elements separate and avoiding what may be seen as spurious quantification.

In the second use, obtaining data takes time and costs money. If, on the basis of relatively inexpensive initial estimates, it is found that the project is sensitive to selling price, a more detailed investigation of demand conditions can be carried out on this parameter. Conversely, if a project is relatively insensitive to discount-rate changes, the costs of more detailed work in this area can be escaped.

Regarding use three, it is important to remember that with investments which are more than paper securities, the managerial function does not stop once the decision to go ahead with the project has been made. Management will not be passive if unfavourable variation in parameters seems likely. If unit costs are working out at a higher level than at first anticipated, it helps to know that the project is sensitive to this parameter and to have contingency plans ready.

4.5 SIMULATION

Where there is probabilistic information on variables in a project's cash flow, then *simulation* can be useful. The procedure involves taking samples from these distributions and computing present values. This process is repeated often enough for a reliable spread of present value to be obtained. The mean and variance of the distribution of NPV or IRR can be estimated in this way. Decisions are then taken on the basis of the simulated results. Simulation models are usually computer-based.

There is no clear dividing line between where sensitivity analysis ends and simulation begins. For example, *scenario* sensitivity analysis has been called *deterministic simulation*. Balance-sheet projections, giving values of financial statistics if particular projects were undertaken are an example of deterministic simulation or projective sensitivity analysis. However, simulation is usually taken to mean that random variables are involved.

Simulation is not usually used as an optimizing technique. It *can* be used in an accept-or-reject manner, for example accepting a project only if it has a given chance of having a positive NPV. Simulation provides a convenient representation of reality and, in some cases, can be used to *improve* performance by adjusting variables under the decision maker's control. The art of the process is at two levels: the construction of the model and the judgement of changes to be made to controllable variables.

Consider a simple exercise. Suppose that it is known with certainty that outlay on a project will be £65 000, the discount rate is 10% and the project will run for five years. Only the returns in each year are subject to random variability as described in Table 4.21.

Table 4.21

Probability	Return
0.1	10 000
0.2	15 000
0.4	20 000
0.2	25 000
0.1	30 000

Returns are assumed to be independent between years. The first step allocates single-digit numbers to each value of return with the numbers of digits allocated corresponding to the probabilities. The ten numbers used will be 0, 1, 2, 3, ..., 9. For the 10 000 return, having probability 0.1, we assign one of the numbers (a proportion 0.1 of the total of ten numbers) to this outcome. In principle *any* one of the numbers would do, but for convenience we shall select 0. The 15 000 return has probability 0.2, so 20% of the numbers are assigned to this outcome. Again, these 2 could be any of the remaining 9 numbers, but we shall use 1 and 2. The procedure is applied in a similar way to the remaining returns with the results shown in Table 4.22.

Table 4.22

Numbers allocated	Corresponding return
0	10 000
1,2	15 000
3,4,5,6	20 000
7,8	25 000
9	30 000

The next step is to obtain a series of random digits – for example by use of a computer program, a scientific calculator or a table of random numbers. Suppose that the sequence of digits is:

18756 34097 93214 44920 60340 29266

A digit is selected and for convenience let this be the first one: 1. This number is used to generate a value for the first-year return in run 1 of the exercise. The number falls in the group 1,2 so that the first return is 15 000. The second return is then given by the next digit. This is 8 and as it is in the group 7,8 it gives a value of 25 000 for the return in year 2. In a similar way the third-, fourth- and fifth-year returns, 25 000, 20 000 and 20 000, result from using the numbers 7, 5 and 6. This completes the data generation for the first run, the simulated cash flow being:

$t = 0$	$t = 1$	$t = 2$	$t = 3$	$t = 4$	$t = 5$
$-65\,000$	15 000	25 000	25 000	20 000	20 000

for which NPV at 10% is 14 159. It is important to note that this cash flow is *not* a prediction of what would happen if the project was accepted. It is a simulated sample drawn according to the appropriate probabilities. Continuing to use the random numbers in the same way, with a total of six runs the results are as shown in Table 4.23.

Table 4.23

	Run number					
	1	*2*	*3*	*4*	*5*	*6*
1	15000	20000	30000	20000	20000	15000
2	25000	20000	20000	20000	10000	30000
3	25000	10000	15000	30000	20000	15000
4	20000	30000	15000	15000	20000	20000
5	20000	25000	20000	10000	10000	20000
GPV	79159	78237	77735	73705	61342	75778
NPV	14159	13237	12735	8705	−3658	10778

In practice many more runs would be carried out, but for this illustration we shall restrict ourselves to six. The important row of Table 4.23 is the last one, with six values of NPV. From these numbers we obtain a simulation estimate of the *expected net present value*, ENPV, as the arithmetic mean of the NPV figures. So:

$$\Sigma\,\text{NPV} = 14\,159 + 13\,237 + 12\,735 + 8705 - 3658 + 10\,778$$
$$= 55\,956$$

so the six-run simulation estimate of expected net present value for the project is:

$$\text{ENPV} = \frac{55\,956}{6} = 9326$$

Of course, this figure is an *estimate* of ENPV and a different value would have been obtained if different random digits had been drawn to start with. The important point is that the larger is the number of runs, the smaller will these differences tend to be. To illustrate this point, ten trials of 1000 runs each were carried out and the results were as in Table 4.24.

From Table 4.24 it is reasonable to conclude that the true ENPV is between ten and eleven thousand pounds, so the estimate from our six-run case, 9326, looks rather low.

Other useful information could be obtained from an exercise like this. For example, the decision maker may wish to find the chance of achieving at least some minimal level of NPV – for example, zero. This can be done by setting up the simulation to count the occasions as a proportion of the total when the given level of NPV is reached. Simulation output can be presented graphically – for example, as a plot of the distribution of NPV or as a *risk profile* in which the chance that NPV will be above (or alternatively below) given figures is plotted.

Table 4.24

Run number	Average NPV
1	10 239
2	10 775
3	10 679
4	11 124
5	10 716
6	10 482
7	10 644
8	10 552
9	10 987
10	10 536

Data in a simulation should be the best available estimates of the distributions of the actual values of variable factors influencing present value. However, it has been argued that the discount rate values used in the simulation should be estimates of the risk-free rate, as the discount rate should already include an allowance for risk. This argument carries more force the nearer the company is to operating within a perfect capital market and less force the further away it is from this situation. In the framework of the capital-asset pricing model, one example of the use of simulation would be to give estimates of net returns from simulated sampling of the components of cash flow in any period. The net return data are then discounted at a rate determined by the model. Another use would be to examine the effects of possible initiatives to improve financial performance in a similar way to the following section.

4.6 SPREADSHEETS AND 'WHAT IF' ANALYSIS

Spreadsheets such as Excel or Lotus 1-2-3 are well suited to present-value, yield and financial calculations in general. The effects of changed values of parameters can be worked through in a 'what if we did this' manner. Most spreadsheets include financial functions, while third-party suppliers provide add-on templates. For example, Gazeley's *Spreadsheet Applications Manual* [5] introduces the techniques and describes investment and management accounting spreadsheet models. Here we illustrate the use of spreadsheets in the context of a simulation exercise to calculate the net present value of a project under a variety of possible futures. Table 4.25 shows initial projected cash flow and NPV for a project assuming stable prices, costs and sales and using a discount rate of 15%. The project, which involves the manufacture and sale of a product, runs for twelve years with the net cash flow, R_t, in any year t given by:

$$R_t = (P_t - C_t)Q_t$$

where P_t is the sales price of the product, C_t is the unit cost and Q_t is sales volume, all in year t. The returns R_t are discounted in the usual way. The initial outlay for the project is £50 000.

In Table 4.25, the numbers at the heads of the P_t and C_t columns (1.00) are rates of annual increase in prices and costs shown as $1 + r$, where $100r$ is the percentage rate of change – here zero. Column D gives the value of $(1 + i)^t$ where i is the discount rate as a decimal. E is the sales column (zero growth here) and G is the product of numbers in F ($P_t - C_t$ values) and E (the values of Q_t). The final column, giving the ratio of G and D values, is the present value of each year's cash flow. Apart from the initial outlay, the cash flow starts at $t = 1$ (the $t = 0$ row shows the base values of parameters) and the initial outlay is shown at the head

Table 4.25

Time	Price inflation 1.00	Cost inflation 1.00	Discount rate 1.15	Sales growth 1.00	[Outlay 50000.00]		
A	B	C	D	E	F	G	H
t	P_t	C_t	$(1 + i)^t$	Q_t	$P_t - C_t$	$F \times E$	G/D
0	50.00	30.00	1.00	1000.00	20.00	20000.00	20000.00
1	50.00	30.00	1.15	1000.00	20.00	20000.00	17391.30
2	50.00	30.00	1.32	1000.00	20.00	20000.00	15122.87
3	50.00	30.00	1.52	1000.00	20.00	20000.00	13150.33
4	50.00	30.00	1.75	1000.00	20.00	20000.00	11435.07
5	50.00	30.00	2.01	1000.00	20.00	20000.00	9943.54
6	50.00	30.00	2.31	1000.00	20.00	20000.00	8646.55
7	50.00	30.00	2.66	1000.00	20.00	20000.00	7518.74
8	50.00	30.00	3.06	1000.00	20.00	20000.00	6538.04
9	50.00	30.00	3.52	1000.00	20.00	20000.00	5685.25
10	50.00	30.00	4.05	1000.00	20.00	20000.00	4943.69
11	50.00	30.00	4.65	1000.00	20.00	20000.00	4298.87
12	50.00	30.00	5.35	1000.00	20.00	20000.00	3738.14
						GPV =	108412.40
						NPV =	58412.40

of column F. GPV is the sum of the entries in the final column and NPV is GPV less £50 000. With these initial projections, the investment is worthwhile with NPV = £58 412.

Table 4.26 makes the first of several changes to the original scenario. It shows the substantial improvement in NPV that could be achieved if a policy of finding annual cost savings of 2% was implemented.

Table 4.26

Time	Price inflation 1.00	Cost inflation 0.98	Discount rate 1.15	Sales growth 1.00	[Outlay 50000.00]		
A	B	C	D	E	F	G	H
t	P_t	C_t	$(1 + i)^t$	Q_t	$P_t - C_t$	$F \times E$	G/D
0	50.00	30.00	1.00	1000.00	20.00	20000.00	20000.00
1	50.00	29.40	1.15	1000.00	20.60	20600.00	17913.04
2	50.00	28.81	1.32	1000.00	21.19	21188.00	16021.17
3	50.00	28.24	1.52	1000.00	21.76	21764.24	14310.34
4	50.00	27.67	1.75	1000.00	22.33	22328.95	12766.65
5	50.00	27.12	2.01	1000.00	22.88	22882.37	11376.58
6	50.00	26.58	2.31	1000.00	23.42	23424.72	10127.16
7	50.00	26.04	2.66	1000.00	23.96	23956.23	9006.04
8	50.00	25.52	3.06	1000.00	24.48	24477.11	8001.61
9	50.00	25.01	3.52	1000.00	24.99	24987.56	7103.03
10	50.00	24.51	4.05	1000.00	25.49	25487.81	6300.20
11	50.00	24.02	4.65	1000.00	25.98	25978.05	5583.81
12	50.00	23.54	5.35	1000.00	26.46	26458.49	4945.28
						GPV =	123454.90
						NPV =	73454.90

NPV rises to £73 455. The increase is the maximum present price worth paying for the unit cost improvements. Table 4.27 shows the improvement to the original project from a drive to increase annual sales by 2%. Note that (in this project) sales growth brings less of an improvement in NPV than cost reduction. This was not obvious beforehand and may be useful in priority setting.

Table 4.27

Time A t	Price inflation 1.00 B P_t	Cost inflation 1.00 C C_t	Discount rate 1.15 D $(1 + i)^t$	Sales growth 1.02 E Q_t	[Outlay 50000.00] F $P_t - C_t$	G F × E	H G/D
0	50.00	30.00	1.00	1000.00	20.00	20000.00	20000.00
1	50.00	30.00	1.15	1020.00	20.00	20400.00	17739.13
2	50.00	30.00	1.32	1040.40	20.00	20808.00	15733.84
3	50.00	30.00	1.52	1061.21	20.00	21224.16	13955.23
4	50.00	30.00	1.75	1082.43	20.00	21648.64	12377.68
5	50.00	30.00	2.01	1104.08	20.00	22081.61	10978.46
6	50.00	30.00	2.31	1126.16	20.00	22523.25	9737.42
7	50.00	30.00	2.66	1148.69	20.00	22973.71	8636.67
8	50.00	30.00	3.06	1171.66	20.00	23433.18	7660.35
9	50.00	30.00	3.52	1195.09	20.00	23901.85	6794.40
10	50.00	30.00	4.05	1218.99	20.00	24379.88	6026.34
11	50.00	30.00	4.65	1243.37	20.00	24867.48	5345.10
12	50.00	30.00	5.35	1268.24	20.00	25364.83	4740.87
						GPV =	119725.49
						NPV =	69725.49

Selecting which initiative to implement is fine if circumstances allow. But management may need to take parallel action on all fronts, so Table 4.28 shows the effects of simultaneous cost-reduction and sales-increase programmes.

Table 4.28

Time A t	Price inflation 1.00 B P_t	Cost inflation 0.98 C C_t	Discount rate 1.15 D $(1 + i)^t$	Sales growth 1.02 E Q_t	[Outlay 50000.00] F $P_t - C_t$	G F × E	H G/D
0	50.00	30.00	1.00	1000.00	20.00	20000.00	20000.00
1	50.00	29.40	1.15	1020.00	20.60	21012.00	18271.30
2	50.00	28.81	1.32	1040.40	21.19	22043.99	16668.43
3	50.00	28.24	1.52	1061.21	21.76	23096.38	15186.25
4	50.00	27.67	1.75	1082.43	22.33	24169.58	13819.03
5	50.00	27.12	2.01	1104.08	22.88	25263.99	12560.67
6	50.00	26.58	2.31	1126.16	23.42	26380.04	11404.82
7	50.00	26.04	2.66	1148.69	23.96	27518.18	10345.10
8	50.00	25.52	3.06	1171.66	24.48	28678.83	9375.16
9	50.00	25.01	3.52	1195.09	24.99	29862.45	8488.77
10	50.00	24.51	4.05	1218.99	25.49	31069.49	7679.90
11	50.00	24.02	4.65	1243.37	25.98	32300.44	6942.76
12	50.00	23.54	5.35	1268.24	26.46	33555.76	6271.81
						GPV =	137014.00
						NPV =	87014.00

Note that the combined effect on NPV (an increase of £28 602) exceeds the sum of the individual effects (£26 356). This useful synergy would not have been obvious without the simulation.

Table 4.29 shows the effect on net present value of a scenario in which both sales price and unit costs rise by 5% p.a.; sales volumes are expected to grow at 2% while the discount rate increases to 20%. The outcome is NPV showing an increase in cash terms.

Table 4.29

Time A t	Price inflation 1.05 B P_t	Cost inflation 1.05 C C_t	Discount rate 1.20 D $(1 + i)^t$	Sales growth 1.02 E Q_t	[Outlay 50000.00] F $P_t - C_t$	G F × E	H G/D
0	50.00	30.00	1.00	1000.00	20.00	20000.00	20000.00
1	52.50	31.50	1.20	1020.00	21.00	21420.00	17850.00
2	55.12	33.07	1.44	1040.40	22.05	22940.81	15931.12
3	57.88	34.73	1.73	1061.21	23.15	24569.61	14218.52
4	60.78	36.47	2.07	1082.43	24.31	26314.06	12690.03
5	63.81	38.29	2.49	1104.08	25.53	28182.35	11325.85
6	67.00	40.20	2.99	1126.16	26.80	30183.30	10108.32
7	70.35	42.21	3.58	1148.69	28.14	32326.31	9021.68
8	73.87	44.32	4.30	1171.66	29.55	34621.47	8051.85
9	77.57	46.54	5.16	1195.09	31.03	37079.60	7186.27
10	81.44	48.87	6.19	1218.99	32.58	39712.24	6413.75
11	85.52	51.31	7.43	1243.37	34.21	42531.81	5724.27
12	89.79	53.88	8.92	1268.24	35.92	45551.56	5108.91
						GPV =	123630.56
						NPV =	73630.56

Many more variations on this theme would be possible. The ease with which such variations on DCF can be carried out using spreadsheets is hard to exaggerate, and the return in management information from 'what if' exercises can be considerable. The initial model does not take long to build (making good use of the spreadsheet's *copy* facility for both data and formulae) and each scenario is computed almost instantly.

4.7 STRATEGIC PLANNING

Capital budgeting methods enable management to make rational decisions based on investment cash flows. But for some types of investment the full cash flow may be difficult to establish and a positive decision may be made on strategic grounds even if a financial appraisal seems negative. Alternatively, a particular investment may appear to be profitable, and yet on strategic grounds a decision will be made not to proceed. To be acceptable, an investment not only has to be profitable, but it has to fit the strategic plan of the company.

Strategic planning is concerned with the allocation of resources to achieve a company's objectives. Financial planning is one part of the process. Strategic planning takes into account factors other than the directly financial, some of which are non-quantifiable and some of which are judgemental in nature. The strategic plan has to be based on more than access to and control of financial resources. Personnel, supplies, market opportunities and technological change all have to be considered. The company may have broader objectives – social, psychological, regional or national – that have to be taken into account. The plan is based on a careful analysis of the relative strengths and weaknesses of the company, and an assessment of the opportunities in the markets open to it. This means that the strategic plan has to deal with intangibles. Strategic management and capital budgeting complement one another.

Strategic planning usually starts with determining the *mission* of the business. This grand title is another name for long-range goals and targets. In the majority of businesses the primary objective is to continue in existence. This can be combined with certain growth targets, some of which can be expressed in financial terms. The next stage is to analyse the competitive strengths and weaknesses of the company. This involves analysing the structure of the industry or industries in which the company competes and the nature of the competition which it faces. This in turn determines the position of the business with respect to five competitive forces:

1 Competition from other businesses in the market. This depends on factors such as market share and product differentiation;
2 The threat of competition from potential market entrants;
3 The power of the buyers;
4 The power of suppliers;
5 Threats from substitute products.

In appraising its strengths and weaknesses, the business has now to take into account factors such as:

1 The global market place. The company might be strong in the home market, but on a global scale it could be weak;
2 The rapid speed of technological change, which means shortening product life cycles and an emphasis on quality;
3 Improvements in information technology.

In this appraisal of corporate strengths and weaknesses, it is usual to divide the business into *strategic business units* (SBUs). Each such unit produces a distinct product (or group of products) for an identifiable group of customers. It is, as far as possible within a group, a discrete unit. The strategic planners evaluate each unit and on the basis of this come up with a strategy for the SBUs. It is to these units that the headquarters of the company will allocate investment funds. The SBUs are analysed and placed into categories on the basis of their market attractiveness and their competitive strengths in these markets.

On the basis of the analysis of the relative strengths of the SBUs and an analysis of the opportunities in the market in which they operate, a strategy will be formulated for each SBU. A number of alternative strategies will be considered, each will be evaluated and the strategy that best meets the objectives (the mission) of the business will be selected. If the objectives were seen purely in terms of capital market theory, the goal would be simply to maximize shareholders' wealth. But there are several agents with an interest in a company, and so there might be a number of goals to consider, some of which may conflict. So the strategy formulation may be quite complex, with political pressures from different interest groups coming into the evaluation process. The strategic planning process can be divided into five stages:

Stage 1: Determine corporate objectives;
Stage 2: Evaluate the strengths and weaknesses of the strategic business units;
Stage 3: Determine the potential of each of the markets in which the SBUs operate;
Stage 4: Evaluate the alternative strategies in terms of the objectives;
Stage 5: Select an appropriate strategy for each strategic business unit.

Once a strategy is decided, it is possible to develop an appropriate business plan for each SBU. There will be several interlocking aspects to the business plan, including: a marketing plan, a production plan, a human resource plan, a research and development plan, and of course a capital investment plan. Since the overall performance of the business is ultimately measured in financial terms, all these plans need to be brought together in projected financial statements. Each aspect of the plan needs to be feasible within the total funds available. This means, for example, that in deciding on a human resource plan, finance is ultimately the yardstick that has to be used. It would be no good meeting agreed staffing targets in terms of numbers of people, if achieving this target resulted in financial distress for the business. A proposal to invest in any strategic business unit has then to be considered both in terms of the overall strategy to be followed for that SBU and in terms of its financial viability.

4.8 MODELS OF STRATEGIC MANAGEMENT

The typical strategic plan sets out where it sees the company going over the next ten years or so. In which industries will it expand, and in which will it contract? What growth target has it set itself? Will it rely on internal growth or will it resort to growth through acquisition? Which parts of the company will be sold off? The plan has to satisfy the financial objectives of those making the decisions on behalf of the company. Many models have been designed to help firms with strategic planning. One of the earliest of these was developed and marketed by the Boston Consulting Group in 1981 [6]. Their approach was to classify each SBU on the basis of its relative market share and its potential growth rate. Relative market share was defined as the sales by the SBU of a particular product divided by the sales of that product by the largest competitor. A colourful nomenclature was developed in which each area of the business – each segment – was classified as a *star*, a *dog*, a *cash cow* or a *problem child* as illustrated in Figure 4.3.

These classifications would be important if it came to making investment decisions. An investment proposal from a division classified as a *dog* would be most unlikely to receive approval, as this would be an area of the business in competitive disadvantage and with little or no market growth possibilities. However, an investment proposed by a division in the *star* category would stand a good chance of being approved. The investment would have satisfied the question: does it fit in with the strategic plan? Of course it would still be necessary for the investment to satisfy the relevant financial requirements.

In the case of minor schemes, and those in which all major cash flows are well quantified, the relevant financial requirements would be positive NPV. However, there are high-technology investments where a large proportion of the known (or strongly suspected) benefits cannot be adequately quantified. In such a case, management must make a judgement as to the wider, possibly strategic, value of the investment in the light of any shortfall of the quantified benefits in relation to costs.

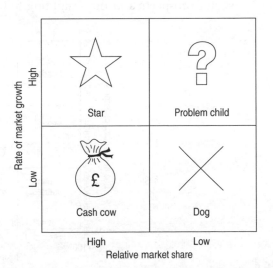

Figure 4.3

The Boston Consulting Group model, based on developing a product-market portfolio, was popular for a number of years, but it was subject to criticism. The matrix relies on just two variables: relative market share and the rate of market growth. These two factors are important, but there are other factors that influence the success (or lack of success) of an SBU and these were ignored. As a result of these criticisms of the product-market portfolio approach, other matrices were developed. A more general model, referred to as the *directional policy matrix*, has the competitive strength of the SBU on the horizontal axis. This would take into account factors other than market share. The matrix display for this model is shown in Figure 4.4.

The strategic policy implications of being located in each square are also shown. The investment implications are easy to deduce. Clearly, with a weak business position and unattractive business prospects, from a strategic point of view there is little reason to invest. With a strong business position in an unattractive business sector, one would be willing to invest minor amounts to maintain the cash-generating potential but not to invest large sums as there are no prospects in the market. For the central square, representing an average business position with average prospects for the market, careful appraisal would be required before large sums are invested. The product has no particular niche in the market, and it might not be worth trying to obtain one.

A problem with this type of analysis is in achieving consistency when scoring each business unit. Subjective judgement must be an important element in deciding whether a particular unit is in an average or weak business position. In attempting to minimize the differences that would arise if it was left to different individuals to make such judgements, it is usually agreed before the exercise what factors are to be considered when deciding on a unit's business position. Similarly, a list of factors that will be taken into account when deciding business prospects is agreed upon.

Not only are the factors themselves agreed, but so is the *weighting* given to each factor. Weighting is necessary if some factors are considered more important than others. For example, when assessing the future prospects in a particular business sector, it might be thought that technology changes are more important than prospects for economic growth. Different weightings would therefore be used. Unfortunately, of course, the appropriate weightings are a matter of judgement, although in principle a sensitivity analysis could be carried out on the values of the weights.

Having decided on the factors influencing the business position, the business sector prospects and the weighting to be assigned to each factor, the next step is

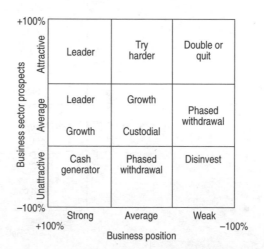

Figure 4.4

to analyse each SBU and give it a score for each of the factors. For example, product quality is an important factor influencing the relative strength or weakness – the business position of any SBU. We decide that its importance warrants a weighting of 5. In analysing a particular SBU within our company, say a unit manufacturing washing machines, we may give it a score of only 2 for its product quality. We multiply the score by the weighting for each factor to obtain an overall score. With this overall score for the business position and with the overall score for the business sector prospects, we are able to plot the position of the strategic business unit in the matrix.

4.9 PROFIT IMPACT OF MARKET STRATEGY

In plotting a business unit in the directional policy matrix a company takes into account the factors that it believes will influence its business position in the sector in which it operates. These will include its marketing strengths, its technological capability, its human resources, its financial position and its production strengths. The factors and the relevant weightings will vary from one business sector to another.

In the United States one approach to strategic management has been developed which attempts to be less subjective than those described above and which can lead to specific proposals. This is the *profit impact of market strategy* (PIMS) and is the result of a large and continuing study which brings together the experiences of the many businesses taking part in the programme. It is US-based, and over 250 companies operating over 3000 separate business units are involved. They have concluded that there are nine major strategic influences on the profitability of the cash-flow position of a business. They estimate that these nine factors account for about 80% of the reasons for business success or failure. They believe that there are regular and predictable ways in which situations develop, and that business situations are basically alike in obeying the same laws of the market place. Knowledge of these nine major influences therefore assists in formulating a strategy for each business unit. The nine strategic influences in order of importance are given below.

1 *Investment intensity* as measured by investment as a percentage of sales and of value added.

The higher the level of investment intensity the lower is the return on investment. This may seem surprising, but it is argued that this arises because increased investment can lead to higher wages and lower prices but also to improvements in quality. This last point is important and gives rise to the question: does quality lead to benefits for the business? It might not lead to higher returns in the short run but it can be essential for long-term survival. It must be remembered that the PIMS study is concerned with strategic influences on profitability. This finding is not an argument against increasing the levels of investment in a business; it points to a possible danger. The problem can be overcome by such policies as concentrating the investments in a particular segment of a market, increasing productivity and investing in equipment which is flexible in terms of its purpose.

The other eight main strategic influences are:

2 *Productivity*: an obvious influence on profitability.
3 *Market position*: a high relative market share helps profits and cash flow.
4 *Growth* in the market in which the product is being sold.
5 *Quality* of the product: the PIMS study shows that quality and profitability are strongly linked. A business offering a high level of service and a quality product is more profitable over time than one offering less service with poorer quality. The study finds that quality is important in almost all businesses.

6 *Innovation*: investment in research and development has a positive effect on the profit position of businesses with a strong market position.
7 *Vertical integration*: businesses in stable mature markets benefit from vertical integration.
8 *Cost push*: the influence of increased wages and raw material costs on profitability is complex. Few useful generalizations are possible.
9 *Strategic efforts*: attempting to change things can have adverse short-term effects on cash flow. For example, having a high market share is good for cash flow, but the commitment to obtain a higher market share will reduce cash flows while the efforts are being made.

Most of these points have strong intuitive appeal and indeed some are fairly obvious. Each of the points does give some guidance in the strategic planning process, however. The results are based on the position in the United States, but there is no reason to believe that they are not applicable in the UK. The results are also more relevant to larger companies than to small companies.

Although strategic planning is usually implemented as a top-down exercise, it should be a process which takes into account relevant information, feedback and the views of the units being planned. The overall capital budget of a company must be based on strategic considerations: it cannot just be a selection of individual investment proposals that have come forward in an uncoordinated way from the bottom up. The capital investment plan of a company is part of a larger planning exercise.

Strategic planning provides broad indications of the direction in which the business should be moving. In which areas is it worth considering proposals for expansion, and in which areas should the company be divesting? It is against this strategic background that investment proposals are sought and financial appraisals (and any associated judgemental exercises) carried out. Judgement comes in because quantitative investment appraisal techniques are not best suited to dealing with intangibles. Major decisions with a strategic dimension have to take into account intangible factors, and hence it is necessary to know the strategic position with regard to the business unit bringing forward the proposal.

4.10 APPRAISING STRATEGIC INVESTMENTS

In the use of quantitative methods it is good practice to separate out as far as possible the objective and judgemental elements. Judgemental factors can then be given due weight against the background of an agreed database. The alternative mix of facts and guesswork is unlikely to lead to good decisions. The approach recommended here tries to balance strategic and numerical considerations and has three stages.

The *first stage* is for management to consider the proposed investment in relation to the company's strategic plan. At this stage the proposal may be judged to be inconsistent with the strategic plan and management may rule against the investment on these grounds. So at this stage a proposal may be ruled out, but definite acceptance cannot be given. If the project fits the strategic plan, the proposal moves to the next stage.

The *second stage* consists of the following three steps:

1 *Model construction*: a DCF model of the company's decision problem is constructed. This should not be too complex, but might range from a simple NPV framework to a model with capital constraints.
2 *Data estimation*: obtaining estimates of cash-flow data is the most difficult part of the numerical stage. Estimates are required of all quantifiable cash-flow components along with the discount rate to be used in the NPV

Rationing, uncertainty and corporate strategy

calculation. While there is no sharp dividing line where intangibility ends and tangibility begins, it should be noted that finance and accounting frequently involve a degree of estimation. Selection of the most appropriate discount rate involves judgement as well as estimation.

3 *Calculation*: this is a straightforward step once the model has been constructed and the data estimated. If NPV is positive, the proposal is definitely worthwhile (the NPV is calculated using estimates of *tangible* benefits only). So if NPV is positive on this basis, the existence of intangible benefits would reinforce the decision and the process terminates. But if NPV is negative, the third stage of the process is entered.

The *third stage* is a justification analysis based on the sensitivity approach to uncertainty introduced earlier. If the tangible benefits do not exceeded tangible costs, in this third stage management must weigh the intangible elements against the shortfall in net present value. The question is: do the benefits from factors such as increased flexibility, greater product attractiveness in the market place, and improved employee skills and attitudes justify the cost not covered by the tangible benefits?

In addressing this question each intangible benefit should be analysed in depth. One way of doing this is to assign a points score to each item of benefit. Another approach used by one UK company is to lower the discount rate for the DCF calculations if intangible benefit can be demonstrated. The point scores are not translated directly into cash values. The points are generally regarded as ordinal numbers not to be added, so scores of 5 and 5 on each of two attributes of one system do not equal scores of 8 and 2 on the same attributes in another system. The use of scoring systems is often recommended in the strategic management literature. However, in the public sector *additive* points scoring systems are used to prioritize some public works projects for which most benefits, though undeniable, are intangible.

It is not suggested that the three-stage procedure should be a straitjacket. The nature of competitive business is such that there will be situations in which it is at least arguable that the decision should be taken on strategic grounds alone. For example, the question of the nature of the company's manufacturing processes may arise not in the form of a relatively detailed proposal but as a general question of policy – and possibly an urgent question at that. In these circumstances, in the absence of cash-flow data the second stage of the process could not be carried out, and any early decision would have to be made on purely strategic grounds.

There may also be cases in which the strategic dimension can be seen by management as overwhelming – the *need to have* argument. If the company's competitors were adopting a particular strategy and if their decision was correct and the company itself did not go ahead along similar lines, it would lose its market position. If the competitors were wrong and the company also adopted the same strategy, then at least it would still be in business. But it should be noted that when a decision has been taken on purely strategic grounds, where there are tangible costs and benefits involved, any strategic decision implies a bound on the valuation of the intangibles. The issue of evaluating intangible benefits cannot be circumvented altogether. So while there are occasions where a purely strategic judgement is warranted, the three-stage procedure should be adopted where possible.

4.11 REFERENCES

1 Srinivasan, V. (1974) A transhipment model for cash management decisions, *Management Science*, Ser. B, 20.

2 Wilkes, F.M., Samuels, J.M. and Greenfield, S.M. (1995) Investment decision making in UK manufacturing industry, *Management Decision*, **34**(4).

3 Pike, R.H. and Neal, C.W. (1993) *Corporate Finance and Investment: Decisions and Strategies*, Prentice-Hall.

4 Sangster, A. (1993) Capital investment appraisal techniques: a survey of current usage, *Journal of Business Finance and Accounting*, **20**(3).

5 Gazeley, A. (1992) *Spreadsheets Applications Manual*, Chapman and Hall, London.

6 Boston Consulting Group (1981) *Annual Perspective*.

4.12 FURTHER READING

Bromwich, M. and Bhimani, A. (1991) Strategic investment appraisal, *Management Accounting*, March.

Bryant, J.W. (ed.) (1987) *Financial Modelling in Corporate Management*, 2nd edn, Wiley.

Drury, C. (1992) *Management and Cost Accounting*, 3rd edn, Chapman and Hall, London.

Grinyer, P.H. (1982) The historical development and current practice of corporate modelling in the UK, In *Financial Modelling in Corporate Management* (ed. J.W. Bryant), Wiley.

Kemper, R.E. (1989) *Experiencing Strategic Management*, Dryden Press.

Kenny, B., Lea, E., Sanderson, S. and Luffman, G. (1987) *Business Policy: An Analytical Introduction*, Blackwell, Oxford.

Levy, H. and Sarnat, M. (1982) *Capital Investment and Financial Decisions*, 2nd edn, Prentice-Hall.

Pike, R.H. (1989) Do sophisticated capital budgeting approaches improve decision making effectiveness?, *The Engineering Economist*, **35**(2), Winter.

Samuels, J.M., Wilkes, F.M. and Brayshaw, R.E. (1995) *Management of Company Finance*, 6th edn, International Thomson Business Press, London.

Strategic Planning Institute (1981) *Basic Principles of Business Strategy, The PIMS Program*, Cambridge, Mass.

Thompson, J.L. (1990) *Strategic Management: Awareness and Change*, Chapman and Hall, London.

Wilkes, F.M. (1993) The interest in interest: interest rates and investment appraisal, *Business Studies*, **6**(2), December.

Wilkes, F.M. and Samuels, J.M. (1991) Financial appraisal to support technological investment, *Long Range Planning*, **24**(6), December.

4.13 PROBLEMS

1 A firm's cost of capital is 10%. It has £4300 available for outlay on five investments:

	Investment				
Year	1	2	3	4	5
0	−2400	−2000	−1800	−1200	−500
1	1500	0	500	350	150
2	1500	0	500	350	150
3	0	1000	500	350	150
4	0	1000	500	350	150
5	0	1000	500	350	150

Rationing, uncertainty and corporate strategy

No investment may be repeated but a fractional share may be taken.
(a) Which investments should be selected to maximize NPV?
(b) What would NPV have been if all investments were repeatable?
(c) Estimate the IRR on the marginal project under (a).
(d) Calculate the overall IRR on the total sum invested.
(e) Do you think the cash flow from the investments is acceptable?

2 A small trust company has to decide on the percentage of its total funds to invest in seven possible shares. The shares are classified into three sectors with the following details:

	Agriculture		Manufacturing			Retailing	
Share no:	1	2	3	4	5	6	7
Yield (%)	16	12	8	10	7	15	13

No more than 45% of the total may be in any one sector and no more than 25% can be invested in any one share. At least 20% must be invested in manufacturing. The objective is to maximize IRR overall.
(a) What proportion of the total should be invested in each share?
(b) What is the IRR achieved?
(c) Suppose that there was no longer a requirement to invest in manufacturing, what would be the effect on overall IRR?
(d) Suppose (as an alternative to (c)) the maximum investment in any one sector was cut to 40%. How would IRR be affected?

3 Consider the following two projects:

	$t=0$	$t=1$	$t=2$	$t=3$	$t=4$	$t=5$	$t=6$	$t=7$
A	-100	5	15	25	55	25	15	5
B	-100	55	25	10	5	10	35	45

(a) Which project would be selected on the payback criterion?
(b) Calculate the NPV for each project at 10% discount and indicate which project would be selected by NPV.
(c) Comment on the results of (a) and (b).

4 Using a discount rate of 10%:
(a) Is the project below acceptable under the finite horizon method (FHM) with a five-year horizon?
(b) Is the project acceptable under FHM with a seven-year horizon?
(c) Do you think that FHM is suitable in this case?

$t=0$	$t=1$	$t=2$	$t=3$	$t=4$	$t=5$	$t=6$	$t=7$	$t=8$
-3000	1650	750	300	150	300	1050	1350	1250

5 Which of the following projects would be selected on the basis of (a) return on capital and (b) accounting rate of return? Assume zero residual values. Do other criteria support the decisions?

		Project	
Year		A	B
$t=0$		-20000	-25000
$t=1$		2000	10000
$t=2$		4000	6000
$t=3$		10000	2000
$t=4$		5000	10000
$t=5$		3000	3000
$t=6$		5000	6000

6 Find the NPV of the following project at 10%:

$$-500 \quad 200 \quad 250 \quad 300 \quad 350$$

Now find the impact on the net present value of risk premiums of (a) 5 percentage points and (b) 10 percentage points.

7 Initial estimates have been made for an investment as follows:

Initial outlay	£100000
Sales price	£30
Sales volumes:	
Year 1	4000 units
Year 2	6000 units
Year 3	3000 units
Unit cost	£20
Discount rate	10%
Life	3 years

The £100 000 buys equipment to make a product at the unit cost and sales price above and selling in the volumes shown.

(a) Calculate the maximum tolerable unfavourable change (as a percentage of the original estimate) in (i) sales price, (ii) unit cost, (iii) sales volume, (iv) initial outlay, (v) project lifetime. Comment on the results. Could the sales volumes be analysed separately?

(b) Now suppose that sales prices are expected to rise by 10% per annum compound, but unit costs are expected to rise at an annual rate of 20% (both starting at $t = 0$). What initial cash subsidy would now be needed for the project to remain viable?

5 EQUITY CAPITAL AND ITS VALUATION

LEARNING OUTCOMES

By the end of this chapter the reader will:

● understand the different forms of equity capital
● be aware of the different ways in which a company can obtain equity capital
● know how to calculate the value of a rights issue
● appreciate the problems of small businesses seeking equity finance

5.1 TYPES OF COMPANY

If a group of individuals wish to work together with the object of carrying on a trade or business to make a profit or earn a living, the two principal forms of association open to them are either a partnership or a company limited by shares.

One of the attractive features about being a company limited by shares is that the owners' liability for the debts and actions of the company is limited in amount to a predetermined share – the nominal value of the shares they own.

The Companies Act 1985 divides companies into 'public companies' and 'private companies'. The vast majority of companies are limited by shares. However, there are two other special types of company: one which is limited by guarantee and one which is not. The latter is referred to as an 'unlimited company'.

Public companies

A public company can be formed by two persons; it is limited by shares and has a share capital. This means that the owners of the company, the shareholders, have only a limited liability for the debts of the company. The owners, in agreeing to purchase a share, are only committing themselves to place funds in the business up to the par value (the nominal value) of that share. If the company should fail and there are not sufficient funds available to pay the creditors, the tax collector, the employees or those who have made loans available to the company, then these people will just have to take what little is available from the sale of the assets of the company. The owners of the company will not have to pay more money into the business to satisfy debts; the owners' private assets cannot be touched.

The name of the company must end with the words 'public limited company', the authorized abbreviation being PLC. A public company cannot restrict the right to transfer its shares.

Private companies

In numerical terms, the majority of companies in the UK are private companies; however, in terms of size, they are usually the smaller companies. There is no minimum amount of share capital for a private company. A private company is restricted in the right to transfer its shares. Therefore any sale of shares by one shareholder to another must be tightly controlled.

If a private company wishes to issue new shares to raise finance, either existing shareholders have to subscribe or the new shares have to be carefully placed. If an existing shareholder wishes to dispose of shares held, he/she has to find another buyer and the price must be negotiated.

It is the ambition of many private companies to go public one day and float their company on the market, but the timing of this step is very difficult. The company needs a good profit record, which means that one or two bad years, perhaps because of an economic depression, can put back the timing of the issue.

Issuing houses and merchant banks are sometimes willing to place the shares of a private company with a few private individuals or institutions, but shares in private companies are not marketable, cannot easily be transferred and are therefore not very attractive to investors. It might be difficult to find buyers of shares in private companies at prices acceptable to the vendors.

5.2 TYPES OF EQUITY SHARE

Ordinary shares

An equity interest in a company can be said to represent a share of the company's assets and a share of any profits earned on those assets after other claims have been met. The equity shareholders are the owners of the business – they purchase shares (commonly called *ordinary shares*), the money is used by the company to buy assets, the assets are used to earn profits, and the assets and profits belong to the ordinary shareholders. Equity shares entail no agreement on the company's part to return to the shareholders the amount of their investment. The directors are under obligation to maintain the assets intact, i.e. not to allow them to drop in value. Whether the original investment in the business keeps its value depends on how well the company is managed and the use to which the funds are put. An equity interest therefore represents a stake in the assets of the business which the shareholder cannot ask the company to repay plus an income stake, i.e. a share in the company's profits.

If an equity shareholder wishes to regain the money he/she has invested, he/she must either find a buyer for the shares or force the company into liquidation. It is possible that the company itself may wish to purchase the shares.

This is possible in certain situations. The ease with which the shareholder will find a buyer depends on the price that he or she is asking for the shares and on the marketability of the particular company's shares. The shares of companies quoted on a stock exchange are more marketable than those that are not, and existing owners, other things being equal, should be able to find buyers. The alternative method of realizing an equity stake – bringing about the liquidation of the company – is of course a very different matter. It means that all the assets of the company are sold, liabilities and prior claims are met and the funds that are left are paid out to the equity shareholders. These are draconian measures indeed, and would be resorted to only in the most serious circumstances.

However, there are some ordinary equity shares in existence which carry no voting rights. Investors buy these risk-bearing shares on the understanding that they have no voice in the management of the company.

This particular point leads to a general one. Equity shares do not, in fact, constitute a homogeneous class of shares. There are several different types of equity shares carrying varying rights to participate in assets and profits; a certain class may, for example, rank in advance of another for the payment of dividends.

Preferred and deferred ordinary shares

Ordinary shares are sometimes subdivided into preferred ordinary and deferred ordinary. The former rank for payment of an agreed rate of dividend before the latter receive anything, but after the preferred shareholders have received their dividend, the deferred holders participate in the allocation of profits. The rate of dividend that the preferred holders receive before the deferred holders are allowed an allocation depends on the particular terms of the capital issues of the company. In some cases, the agreement may also admit the preferred holders to a share in the profits after they have received their priority percentage.

Founders' shares

As equity shares go, founders' shares are a rarity. Normally issued to the original promoters of the business, they draw from the profits, as a rule, only after all other categories of equity shares have received fixed rates of dividend. If the business prospers, there may be profits left over for the owners of the founders' shares. If the business is extremely successful, these shares may be very valuable, since they usually entitle the holders to all or at least a considerable proportion of any surplus profits, the holders' reward for contributing towards the perhaps unforeseeable success of the business.

Non-voting shares

Such non-voting shares that do still exist were usually issued by companies that at one time were family-owned. As the business grew the company needed to increase its equity base, but the family wished to maintain control and one way to do this was to issue non-voting equity shares. With the recognition in recent years of the wider public responsibilities of companies, the idea of ownership without representation has become increasingly unpopular and pressure to discontinue this form of financing has grown. In particular, the large institutional investors do not like this type of share.

Purchase by a company of its own shares

The Companies Act 1981 gave companies the power to purchase their own shares subject to certain restrictions. This benefits private companies where the situation has occurred in which certain shareholders become 'locked in', i.e. are unable to find a purchaser for their shares. It also provides a public company with an alternative way of rewarding shareholders, the company being able to purchase shares rather than pay dividends. The purchase should force up the price of the remaining shares in shareholders' possession. It reduces the number of shares and increases the earning per share.

There have been large buybacks by some companies. In 1994 Boots bought back 9% of their own shares, costing £500 million. At the time they had a large amount of cash available as a result of the sale of a subsidiary.

Shares issued under share option schemes

Many companies offer share option schemes to their executives and certain classes of employees. These options allow those involved to purchase shares of the company at a predetermined price. The options are normally exercisable a number of years after the offer is made. There are tax advantages in not exercising the options within 3 years of issue.

The price at which the offer may be exercised is usually approximately the market price at the time the offer is made. Say Company X makes an offer on 1 January 1994 enabling each of its employees to purchase 100 shares (at the price on that day, of say £1.50) on 1 January 1997. If in 1997 the share price of Company X has risen to say £3.00, an employee would be keen to exercise the option and could purchase the shares from the company at £1.50 and sell them immediately in the market at £3.00. If, however, the price of the shares had fallen, and on 1 January 1997 was only £1.00, the employee would not exercise the option.

Employee share 'schemes' exist for either encouraging or facilitating the holding of shares in a company by, or for the benefit of, employees or former employees of a company or its subsidiaries. The schemes can also apply to spouses, widows, widowers or children of such employees or former employees. There are various advantages of such schemes. Normally a company cannot provide financial assistance to individuals to enable them to buy the shares of a company. However, this is possible in certain circumstances.

5.3 METHODS OF RAISING EQUITY CAPITAL

There are numerous methods by which equity shares can be brought to the stock market in order to raise funds for the company. We will differentiate between methods that can be used by companies that already have equity shares listed, and companies bringing equity shares to the market for the first time.

The London Stock Exchange lists in its Yellow Book the following methods for companies already listed:

1 an offer for sale;
2 an offer for subscription;
3 a placing;
4 an intermediaries offer;
5 a rights issue;
6 an open offer;
7 an acquisition or merger issue (or vendor consideration issue);
8 a vendor consideration placing;
9 a capitalization issue (or bonus or scrip issue) in lieu of dividend or otherwise;
10 an issue for cash;
11 an exercise of options or warrants to subscribe for securities; and
12 such other method as may be approved by the Exchange either generally or in any particular case.

For companies with equity shares not already listed the methods are either an introduction or one of the methods listed below. It should be appreciated that for a company's first issue in the market, sometimes the money raised from the sale of shares is not to be used in the company, but is to be received by the founding shareholders of the company, who are selling the shares they own.

The methods that can be used by new entrants are dependent on the value (at the offer price) of the portion of the equity shares being offered or placed in the United Kingdom. The methods are as follows:

Value of equity shares at offer price	Methods available
Not more than £25 million	offer for sale
	offer for subscription
	placing (which may be combined with an offer for sale, offer for subscription or intermediaries offer)
	intermediaries offer
More than £25 million but not more than £50 million	offer for sale
	offer for subscription
	placing (which must be combined with an offer for sale, offer for subscription or intermediaries offer)
	intermediaries offer
More than £50 million	offer for sale
	offer for subscription

We will now give brief details of the different methods.

Offer for sale and offer for subscription

The company offers shares to an issuing house, which then offers the shares to the general public by advertising a prospectus in which the issue price is shown. The company may take this action because it wishes to change its status to that of a public company – the commonest reason for making an offer for sale – and will therefore be attempting to alter the character of its ownership by making the shares more widely held. In such a case it is not always an issue of new shares but a sale of existing ones to a different group of investors. With an offer for sale on subscription the shares are sold to the issuing house by the existing share-holders at an agreed price; the issuing house then offers them for sale at a slightly higher price to the public; some of the securities may be placed with clients of the sponsor (the issuing house) and any securities house that assists with the offer.

It is possible for existing shareholders, directors, employees and past employees of the issuing company to be placed on a special privileged list. The names on the list receive a preferential allocation of the shares, so long as the allocation does not amount to more than 10% in aggregate of the value of the offer.

Public issue

A public issue is a form of offer for sale. Again the public is being offered shares at an agreed price, only this time the offer is being made directly by the company. The issue is still administered by an issuing house, but this time the public is buying the shares directly from the company, and not from an issuing house. The shares might again either be those belonging to existing shareholders or be new shares, i.e. the vendors of the shares may be either the shareholders or the company.

The issuing house as an agent might advise the company on the issue price, but its influence on this price is obviously not so great as when it owns the shares itself and sells them, as in an offer for sale. This method is normally used only for large issues by well-known companies. The costs can be high: for issues of £10 million, the costs can be in the region of 8% of the money raised. For smaller issues the costs can absorb 14% of the money raised.

Placing

Shares, debentures and other securities are 'placed' when, instead of being offered for sale to the general public, they are sold privately to the clients of the issuing house or broker handling the issue.

Fixed-interest securities tend to be placed mainly with institutions such as insurance companies and pension funds. These institutions, together with investment trusts and unit trusts, are also taking a growing proportion of the offers for sale of ordinary shares. The expenses of an offer for sale are usually higher than for a placing. The Council of the Stock Exchange decides whether permission can be given for a placing or whether the issue has to be made by way of an offer for sale. When the consideration for shares being sold is large, placing permission is unlikely to be given, but this is always subject to the Stock Exchange's discretion.

Stock Exchange introduction

A Stock Exchange introduction may happen when either the shares of the company are already quoted on another stock exchange, or the company already has a wide spread of shareholders and wishes to obtain a quotation. In neither case will new money be raised for the company. The Stock Exchange only permits an introduction in those cases where it is satisfied that there will be, over time, a free market in the shares. In a case where the shares are not already quoted on another market, the stock market will require advertising as for a placing, though of course no new shares are being sold. On certain occasions it will also require shareholders to make shares available as the basis of a free market.

Intermediaries offer

'Intermediary' includes member firms of the Stock Exchange and authorized security houses. An intermediary may apply to the sponsor of an offer for shares in medium-sized offers. They would do this on behalf of their clients who are not on the sponsor's list.

One result of such 'offers' is a wider distribution of ownership of the new shares. The intermediary must allocate the shares to its clients at the issue price.

Open offer

An open offer is similar to a rights issue except in one aspect. It is an offer to existing shareholders to subscribe to the new issue in proportion to their existing issue. But there is not a negotiable document (a right) which can be sold should the existing shareholder not wish to take up the offer.

Tender

Shares are offered to the public and potential investors are invited to name the price that they are willing to pay. The keen buyer will bid high; the less enthusiastic buyer will offer a lower price. Although the company does not suggest or even know the price at which the shares will ultimately sell to the bidder, it does name a reserve price – the minimum price below which they will not be sold. The investor therefore knows the lowest selling price and can, if he or she wishes, make an offer above this level.

The price at which the shares are eventually issued is the highest price which will dispose of all the shares. For example, if a company offers 10 000 shares to the public, and 10 000 investors offer £1 or more for the shares, then all the shares will be sold if the price is set at £1. It is possible that, in total, 20 000 investors offered £0.75 or above for the shares, but the 10 000 who offered between £0.75 and £1 will not receive an allocation. The shareholder does not necessarily have to pay the price he or she offered for the shares: 1000 of the investors may have offered as much as £2 for the shares, but they will only have to pay a price of £1 per share because this was the price which cleared the issue.

The pricing of shares of companies that have not previously had a quotation is very difficult, and the advantage of the tender method is that it leaves the fixing of the price to the public. This price is not determined by an issuing house. The company receives the full benefit of the issue, and if the public forces a high settlement price the company receives the entire amount.

Stags

If the issuing house in charge of an offer or placing underestimates the price that the public is prepared to pay for the shares, the company loses potential capital. If the shares in the example quoted in the section on tenders had been offered to the public at a price of, say, £0.75, they would have been oversubscribed. As soon as dealing began, the excess demand for the shares would force their price up to £1 or more, and the margin between that and the asking price would represent lost opportunities for the company. The company would receive only £0.75 per share – the issuing price. The gains when the price rises above this level accrue to the shareholders who were fortunate enough to receive an allotment.

The breed of speculator known as a 'stag' gambles on situations like this. They subscribe for new issues whose price seems to promise an excessive demand. If they are allocated a number of these shares and if the price does rise as anticipated, they sell their allocation at a profit. If an offer is heavily oversubscribed and the price soars, the stag does very well out of it; if they miscalculate the issue and the demand is unexceptional, they are left with shares whose market value approximates to the price they paid for them.

Offers for sale by tender should reduce the margin between issue price and eventual market price and so reduce the opportunities for stags to make quick profits.

Underwriters

The correct pricing of a new issue of shares is extremely difficult. If the price of an offer for sale is set too high, the demand for the shares will be less than the supply and so not all the shares will be taken up by the public. To avoid the possibility that the company will not dispose of all the shares it is issuing, and so receive less funds than it expected, it is usual to have an issue of shares underwritten.

The lead underwriters are normally the issuing houses, who will usually subcontract the risks to sub-underwriters such as insurance companies and pension funds. They receive a fee based on the value of the issue. In return for the fee they agree to purchase all or a proportion of the issue not taken up by the market. The price that they pay the company for any shares that they purchase is often at a discount on the price quoted in the offer for sale. They receive their underwriting fee whether or not they need to take up any shares.

Vendor placings

Two new methods of raising finance first appeared during the mid-1980s: vendor placings and vendor rights. One reason for their introduction was to overcome a problem that could arise in connection with mergers and takeovers. When one company is taking over another a situation may arise where new shares have to be issued to raise cash. The normal procedure to follow in such a situation is for the acquiring company to call an extraordinary general meeting and to seek the approval of the shareholders to suspend their pre-emptive rights. This can be inconvenient and there is the risk that shareholders will say no. An alternative that emerged was vendor placing and vendor rights.

There were other reasons why these new forms of issue were introduced. One was that a queuing system existed when it came to the issue of new shares. The objective was to avoid too many issues being offered at any one time and so swamping the market. The queuing problem could be inconvenient to companies who wished to raise cash quickly.

Vendor placings can put the small investor – the small shareholder – at a disadvantage. The small shareholder experiences a dilution of his or her holdings. The decision to waive pre-emptive rights taken at the extraordinary general meeting will hardly be influenced by the number of votes of the smaller shareholder. When the vendors eventually place their shares it will most probably be with the large institutional investors. The institutional shareholders therefore need not suffer any dilution in their percentage shareholding. It is the small shareholders who experience this dilution of shareholding power. Vendor placings and vendor rights are discussed further in section 5.6 and in Chapter 22.

5.4 SCRIP DIVIDENDS, SCRIP ISSUES AND CAPITALIZATION ISSUES

One way of issuing new equity shares to existing shareholders is by the distribution of a scrip dividend. As an alternative to paying out cash dividends during a year, a company may choose to pay a scrip dividend. This is essentially a transfer to the shareholder of a number of additional equity shares without the shareholder having to subscribe additional cash.

Advantages to the company include:

1 retaining cash within the business – no cash is distributed to shareholders;
2 a small increase in the permanent share capital base.

Disadvantages to the company include the fact that the administrative costs of scrip dividends can be relatively high.

Advantages to the shareholder include the fact that they receive a dividend which they can convert into cash whenever they wish (although of course they give up the cash they may have received as a dividend). The shareholder does not, of course, have an automatic flow of cash to benefit their bank statement at regular intervals. To realize cash from the scrip dividends entails selling the shares, and flutuations in price could mean that raising urgently needed cash involves selling at a disadvantageous time, though it could also mean the opposite. The company pursuing a policy of issuing scrip dividends would appeal to a different type of investor from a company paying cash dividends.

The key issue arising with this type of dividend payment is the effect of the new shares on the existing share price. If the new shares, the scrip dividend, are issued at the same percentage rate as would be given with a straightforward cash dividend, say 5% so that five new shares are given for every 100 shares held, this does not guarantee a 5% return to the shareholder. The size of the issue ought to be determined by a realistic assessment of the extent by which the shareholder's wealth will be increased as a result: if, for example, the company anticipated that the issue would precipitate a fall in share price, it should offer more than a 5% increase in the number of shares. Scrip dividends are taxed as if they were cash distributions, therefore, from the shareholders' point of view, they are taxed at income tax rates.

Similar to a scrip dividend is a scrip issue of fully paid equity shares, sometimes called a 'capitalization issue' or a 'bonus issue'. A company may decide to capitalize its reserves, using the amount involved to increase the number of its equity shares which are issued to existing shareholders. It is similar to a rights issue where shareholders do not have to pay to take up the additional shares.

The company is not using its current year's profit to support the issue, but is using its capital reserves.

5.5 STOCK SPLITS

A stock split (sometimes called a 'share split'), like a scrip dividend, increases the number of shares in a company without raising any new funds. The procedure is simple: the company reduces the par (nominal) value of each share, and announces that its investors no longer hold, say, one share with a par value of £1; instead, they own two shares with a par value of £0.50 each.

One of the reasons sometimes given for a stock split is to create shares of lower denominations with increased marketability. If the marketability of the company's shares improves, the value of the investor's holding should increase. Suppose, for example, that a shareholder has 100 shares selling at £50 per share; the result of a split (say one additional share for each one held) is that his or her holding is increased quantitatively to 200 shares. Its total value should remain unchanged, with each share now worth £25 instead of £50, but the effects of increased marketability might mean that the price of the 'split' share only falls to £26, in which case, of course, the shareholders' wealth is increased.

Many announcements of stock splits are either accompanied or followed soon after by the announcement of proposed dividend increases. It is well known that once a company increases its dividends, it is extremely reluctant to reduce it. This means that at the suggestion of a stock split either accompanied with a dividend announcement or in anticipation of such an announcement, the share price will usually rise.

5.6 RIGHTS ISSUES

A rights offer is an offer of a company's shares to its existing shareholders. It gives the existing shareholders the first opportunity to purchase a new issue of shares. The terms of the offer are that each existing shareholder has the right to be allotted a certain number of shares upon payment of the asking price. The number of shares they are offered is determined by the percentage of their existing share ownership in relation to the total number of company shares; they are offered a similar percentage of the new shares to be issued. This means that if the shareholder takes up the offer they will maintain their existing percentage ownership of the company. This offer does not have to be accepted personally by the existing shareholders. They may sell the right separately from the share, or sell the share with the rights offer attached.

At times of a depressed stock market, equity capital does not have great appeal either to investors or to issuers. However, in such times, raising equity capital by means of a rights issue does have advantages over the alternative ways of appealing to shareholders for more funds. If the terms of the rights offer are correct and if shareholders have the funds available to take up the offer, the fact that the stock market price is low does not mean that the company is selling a stake in the business to outsiders at a bargain price. The existing shareholders are being given the opportunity to continue to maintain the same percentage holding in the business after the issue as they had before the issue.

Rights issues pose a number of controversial questions. What, for example, is the value of the offer to the shareholder? How many shares should the company issue, and at what price?

The success of a rights issue (where 'success' means selling all the new shares) depends upon the size of the issue, the price asked for the shares and the investors' expectations of the earnings that will result from the use of the funds. The number of shares issued and the price asked for the shares are functions of the amount of funds to be raised. The earnings that will result depend upon the amount of funds raised as well as the expected rate of return. Thus the first problem is the common factor – the amount of funds to be raised.

Funds to be raised

As with all capital expansion programmes, the amount of funds to be raised depends upon the earnings that can be obtained from new investments compared with the cost of the funds. The company must ensure that it can earn on the funds that it obtains a rate at least equal to the cost of this source of capital; it must ensure that the existing shareholders are at least as well off after the issue as they were before. This means that the earnings from the new funds must be sufficient, when capitalized, to increase the market value of the company by at least the amount of the new funds.

The amount of funds that should be raised by a new rights issue is therefore dependent on the earnings of the company on these new funds, and the rate at which the market capitalizes earnings for such a company. It is a matter of the company convincing the market of the earnings that will result from the new funds (see Example 5.1).

Earnings per share

Rights issues present a complication when it comes to calculating earnings per share. Shareholders like to be able to observe how the earnings per share (EPS) of a company have increased over time. Comparative statistics give the EPS for one year and this can be compared with the EPS for the next period. If a rights issue takes place and shares are offered at a price less than the full market price, the shareholders may appear to have received something of a bonus. However, the share in one year is not the same as the share in the year after the rights issue. In order to obtain comparable figures over time, the past EPS figures should be multiplied by a factor which is the ratio of the theoretical ex-rights price of share to the actual cum-rights price on the last day of quotation cum-rights.

This means that if the EPS were 25p in 1996 and in 1997 there was a rights issue, where the theoretical ex-rights price was £1 and the actual cum-rights price on the last day the shares were traded with rights was £1.25, then the adjusted EPS for 1996 would be 20p, i.e. (25p × 1/1.25). This change is necessary because after the rights issue, because of the bonus element, each new share is not claiming quite as much of the earnings as each old share.

Example 5.1

Assume that a company, Stanley Park PLC, contemplating a new issue of capital has the following financial situation. Its balance sheet can be summarized as

Ordinary shares 3000 at £1			
nominal value	£3000	Assets	£9000
Retained earnings	£2000		
Debentures (10%)	£4000		
	£9000		£9000

The net asset value per share is £1.67 (= £5000/3000). The company is earning approximately 17% on its existing total assets, before interest and taxes, made up as follows:

Total earnings	£1508
Interest	£400
	£1108
Tax (35%)	£388
	£720
Earnings per share (£720/3000) = £0.24	

The possible capital issues and their resulting returns are as follows:

New funds (£)	Expected net returns (£)	Average rate of return on new investments
2000	300	15%
3000	360	12%
4500	405	9%

The market's rate of capitalization for a company of this type is 12%.

If the market behaved rationally, valuing the company on 'the capitalized earnings of the firm at the market's normal rate of capitalization for a firm of this type', the total value of the equity before the issue would be

$$720/0.12 = £6000$$

After raising £3000 the value would be

$$£1080/0.12 = £9000$$

Raising this amount of capital satisfies the constraint that the earnings from the new issue must be sufficient, when capitalized, to increase the market value by the amount of the new funds. This would not have been the case if £4500 had been raised:

$$\text{new value} = £1125/0.12 = £9375$$

The new funds raised were £4500 and the increase in market value was only £3375.

If, however, the rate of return on the additional funds had been greater than the market's rate of capitalization, the market value of the firm's shares would have moved upwards. This would have happened if only £2000 had been sought by the rights issue.

Price of rights issue

Having determined the amount that can be raised from a rights issue, it is necessary to determine the number of shares to be issued and to decide on their price. The firm used as an example above could have raised the chosen £3000 through many combinations of number of shares times share price. It is not usual to issue the new shares at the existing market price. In the UK, rights issues are usually priced below the existing market price of the firms' existing shares.

It can be shown that if the market correctly estimates the earnings the company will obtain from investing the new funds, and if the ex-rights share price is based on a correct estimate of future earnings, the price at which the new rights shares are issued need not cause anxiety to the existing shareholders. They will be at least as wealthy after the issue as before, whatever the price of the rights issue. This satisfies the requirement that new issues should leave existing shareholders at least as well off as they were before the rights issue, and this remains true even if the shareholders sell their rights instead of subscribing personally.

To illustrate this point it is necessary to show how the ex-rights price will be arrived at in the market place.

Theoretically the ex-rights price will be equal to a weighted average of the pre-rights price and the rights price, with any adjustment above or below this value depending on the profitability of the project for which the rights are issued compared with the profitability of the rest of the company's investments.

To begin with, it will be assumed that the new funds will earn the same rate of return as the old funds. Then the ex-rights price is

$$P_P \frac{N_O}{N} + P_N \frac{N_N}{N}$$

where P_P is the pre-issue price, P_N is the new issue price, N_O is the number of old shares, N_N is the number of new shares and N is the total number of shares.

Returning to the earlier example of Stanley Park (P_P equals £2, being the total value of equity divided by the number of shares), if in order to raise £3000 an issue of 2000 new shares were issued at £1.50 per share, the ex-rights price would be

$$£2 \times \frac{3000}{5000} + £1.50 \times \frac{2000}{5000} = £1.80 \text{ per share}$$

If the existing shareholders are offered a rights issue of two new shares at a price of £1.50 for every three existing shares, the effect for the shareholders exercising the option would be the equivalent of sacrificing their existing investment plus an additional payment of cash (in total £6000 + £3000) in return for a total of 5000 shares valued at £1.80 per share, i.e. £9000. They should be satisfied with this position; the £9000 now in the company is earning 12%, whereas previously £6000 was earning this rate.

If they exercised only half the option and sold the remaining rights, it would be equivalent to surrendering the original investment of £6000 plus the payment for the new shares of £1500, and in return they would own 4000 shares valued at £1.80 per share (£7200) plus the value of the rights on 1000 new shares which could be sold at £0.30 per right (£300). Therefore they would be no worse off after having given up £7500 and received £7500.

The value of the rights on one new share is simply the difference between the ex-rights market price and the price at which these shares can be purchased under the option – in this example it is £1.80 − £1.50.

The value of a right on one old share can be expressed as

$$\frac{P_e - P_N}{n}$$

where P_e is the expected market price of the share after the rights issue, P_N is the price of the share offered under the rights issue and n is the number of rights on old shares required to purchase one new share. This simply means that, as the share is offered at a reduced price to existing shareholders, the value of that right is the difference between what they are being asked to pay for it and the price at which they can sell the share when the time in which the rights can be exercised has ended.

To determine the value of a right it is necessary to adjust the difference between the possible buying and selling prices of the new shares to existing shareholders in order to allow for the fact that the ownership of one existing share may not entitle the holder to one complete new share. If the offer is, say, one new share for every four existing shares, the value of one right, attached to each existing share, is only a quarter of the price difference.

In the Stanley Park example it can be shown that even with a different asking price, say £1 per share, the existing shareholders will still be no worse off, provided that the market appreciates the earnings the company expects to earn on the new funds. Three thousand shares would need to be issued to raise the £3000. A one-for-one offer is being made. The ex-rights price will be

$$£2 \times \frac{3000}{6000} + £1 \times \frac{3000}{6000} = £1.50 \text{ per share}$$

Taking up the entire option is equivalent to surrendering the £6000 existing investment plus £3000 cash, again £9000, in return for 6000 shares valued at £1.50 (£9000). If only half the option is taken up by existing shareholders, they will give up the existing £6000 plus the new subscription of £1500. In return they will hold 4500 shares worth in total £6750 and receive from the sale of the options £750 (= 1500 × £0.50).

It can be seen, therefore, that in theory neither the number of shares that is issued nor the price at which they are issued is important in affecting the position of existing shareholders. All that matters is that the correct amount of money is raised and that the market is made aware of the earning power of the new investment.

In practice it is necessary that the asking price under the rights offer should appear acceptable; the discount below existing market price should not be so small that it fails to attract shareholders, nor so large that it looks ridiculous and can only raise the necessary amount of capital by the issue of a large number of new shares. If, of course, the shares are offered at a zero price they then resemble a scrip issue where new funds are not being sought but retained earnings are being capitalized. The purpose of a rights issue is to raise new funds. A scrip issue usually has the objective of reducing the price of the company's shares on the market which it achieves by increasing the number of shares without increasing the value of the company.

Options to exercise rights only remain open for a period of time. After that time dealings in the shares become ex-rights.

Rate of return earned on new funds

In the above example only one situation was considered in arriving at the ex-rights price, namely that the yield on new capital is expected to be the same as the yield on old capital. If the two yields are not expected to be the same, the ex-rights price formula needs to be amended to

$$\frac{P_P N_O + P_N N_N (Y_N / Y_O)}{N}$$

where Y_N is the yield on new capital and Y_O is the yield on old capital. If in the example of Stanley Park PLC the company had only raised £2000 worth of new funds by issuing, say, 2000 shares at £1 and invested them to earn extra returns of £300, the new capitalized value of the company would have been £1020/0.12 = £8500, and the price per share would have been £8500/5000 = £1.70. The value of the company would have risen by £2500 as a result of only £2000 of new funds. The ex-rights price would be calculated on the basis of the above formula:

$$\left(£2 \times \frac{3000}{5000} \right) + \left(£1 \times \frac{2000}{5000} \times \frac{15\%}{12\%} \right) = £1.70$$

In this example, where 2000 shares are issued at a price of £1 per share, those shareholders taking up half the offer give up claims to £6000 plus the new subscription of £1000 in cash. In return they receive 4000 shares worth £1.70 per share, and from the sale of rights they receive £700: total value, £7500. The shareholders taking up all the offer would give up £8000 and receive in return shares worth £8500 (5000 × £1.70). Clearly it makes no difference whether the existing shareholders take up all the rights or not; whatever proportion they take up, they will receive the full benefit (if they sell the remaining rights) of the £500 gain in value.

If the £2000 had been raised by the issue of 4000 new shares offered to existing shareholders at a price of £0.50 per share, the existing shareholders would still receive the £500 gain in market value. The ex-rights price would be

$$\left(£2 \times \frac{3000}{7000} \right) + \left(£0.50 \times \frac{4000}{7000} \times \frac{15\%}{12\%} \right) = £1.214$$

The shareholders would again be giving up £8000 and in return hold 7000 shares worth £1.214 each, a total of £8500. If they sold the rights, the rights on each new share would be worth £1.214 − £0.50 = £0.714, and the value of the rights on 4000 shares would be approximately £2858. The 3000 shares are now worth in total £3642. Thus the value of the shares plus the rights shows a £500 gain on the original position, i.e. £3642 + £2858 − £6000.

The crucial factor in this analysis is the expectation of the market about the earnings that will result from the investment of the new funds. In the example it was shown that the existing shareholders could be indifferent to the price of the rights issue. However, the ex-rights share prices of £1.70 and £1.214 were both dependent on the market's expecting the new funds to earn 15%. If the market anticipated earnings of anything less than 15%, thereby casting doubt on the company's expectations, the existing shareholders could lose with a rights issue (if they do not exercise their rights). The size of the opportunities lost by existing shareholders would depend upon the percentage of the rights issue they took up.

Market reaction to a rights issue

From observing actual price behaviour it can be seen that the price of the existing shares of a company often falls slightly when the announcement of a rights issue is made. The price is further adjusted downwards when dealings in the rights start, and again falls when dealings become ex-rights. There are of course exceptions to this, particularly in the case of high-performance companies.

The fact that the share price falls should not be a surprise, as it has already been shown that the price would be expected to fall if the rights issue is offered at a price below the initial market price; the size of the fall depends on the size of the discount. The existing shareholders do not necessarily lose because of the fall in price; what is important is that the ex-rights price should settle quickly at its true value.

If the market anticipates the earnings correctly, then, through the use of the relevant market capitalization rate, the value of the company and thus the value of each share can be assessed. The assumption that the rate of earnings on the new investment would be at least the same as that on the existing investment does not mean that the EPS needs to be maintained. The important variable is the new earnings yield – the relationship between the new earnings per share and the new price. It is this that the company will wish at least to maintain. Consequently, as shown below, if the shares are correctly priced ex-rights, this relationship is in fact maintained.

In the Stanley Park example earnings before the rights issue were £720, the EPS was £0.24 and the price-to-earnings ratio was 8.33:1. On the issue of the new shares, earnings rose to £1020 giving EPS of £0.204; the new ex-rights price was, however, £1.70, which gives a maintained price-to-earnings ratio of 8.33:1 and a maintained earnings yield of 12%.

So far in this chapter we have made rights issues seem a very mechanical and arithmetic affair. But it has to be appreciated that there is a behavioural side to the subject of finance. There can be either enthusiasm in connection with new issues of shares through rights or, as is sometimes the case, criticism by shareholders of rights offerings. Opinions vary because the stock market is not mechanical; it does not always have full information on the possible returns from a new investment, and can therefore react with waves of pessimism and optimism.

A rights offer may lead the shareholders of a fast-growing company to believe that the company is confident and that it will continue to expand; it draws attention to the company's good performance in the past. Psychological factors such as these boost the demand for a company's shares, and so cause prices to rise to a level not justified by the real situation. The psychological factors could of course work the other way. One reason for the frequent fall in share price some time after a rights issue arises out of the shareholders' concern with the latest reported figures and disregard of time lags. Few new investments start to realize returns before some time has elapsed, with the exception of a rights issue in which the funds raised are used to finance an acquisition.

Dividends

Earnings are not the only factor that influences share price, however. Dividends also have an important effect and the dividend statement accompanying the rights issue can influence the ex-rights price. If the dividend per share can be maintained at the rate in effect before the rights issue, with the expected fall in ex-rights price the dividend yield will in fact have risen.

Returning to the Stanley Park example, if the dividends before the rights issue were £300, i.e. £0.10 per share, the dividend yield would be 5% on the £2 share price. After the rights issue it was anticipated that the price would settle at £1.70; if dividends are maintained at £0.10 per share, the dividend yield is now 5.9%. The company would have to distribute £200 of its extra £300 earnings to maintain the same dividend per share, paying a total dividend of £500. To maintain the same dividend yield of 5% on the new price means paying a dividend per share of only £0.085, i.e. a total dividend of £425. To maintain the dividend yield may be all that is needed to satisfy shareholders, and ensure that the market adjusts to a reasonable ex-rights price. This policy also helps the company's cash flow position, which may be crucial in the early years of a new project's life.

A company may state that it will seek to maintain its earnings yield with the new investment, but there is no certainty that it will be able to do this in the first year of a new project's life. However, it may be vital to maintain at least its dividend yield. The dividend is something that the company can control with comparative ease, while the earnings will depend on how long it takes for the project to be brought to its full level of profitability.

Illustration

To illustrate the principles of a rights issue a question taken from the examinations of the Association of Chartered Certified Accountants will now be considered. (Taxation can be ignored in this question.)

Example 5.2

Harris PLC is about to raise finance by increasing its 12 million ordinary shares with a one-for-three rights issue.

The money raised by the rights issue will be used as follows.

1. To fund a new contract to which Harris is already committed and which requires an initial outlay of £1 million. The contract has a profitability index (ratio of present value (PV) of future net cash inflows to PV of initial capital outlay) of 1.4, and full details of the contract have been public knowledge for several months.
2. To reduce borrowings by buying back, at current market value, and cancelling the £10 million debenture issue. The debentures are currently priced in the market to yield 8% per annum, the current yield on such corporate debt.

Total finance required in 1 and 2 will be rounded up to the next whole £100 000 for the purpose of the rights issue. The excess funds raised will be used to reduce short-term borrowings and overdrafts.

The company intends to announce full details of the rights issue on 1 July when the market price per share prior to the announcement is expected to be £5. The company is confident that the whole issue will be purchased, but the managing director is concerned that the discount at which the issue is made may raise the cost of equity capital and hence the weighted-average cost of capital.

(a) Calculate
   (i) the issue price per share;
   (ii) the theoretical ex-rights price per share;
   (iii) the value of the right attached to each Harris share before being traded ex-rights.

(b) Briefly explain whether the concern of the managing director is justified.

Suggested solution

Part (a)
The total funds to be raised are to be used to fund a new contract and to buy back the debentures. The market price of the debentures is not known, but can be estimated. It is assumed that the market is rational and is valuing a debenture at the PV of the cash flow that will be received over the debenture's life. Therefore the total funds to be raised are as follows:

	PV factor 8%		(£million)
To fund contract			1.0
Market value of debentures: interest payments, £1.6m p.a. for nine years	6.247	9.995	
Redemption, £10m in nine years	0.500	5.000	14.995
Total			15.995

Rounded to £16m.

(i) A one-for-three rights issue will increase the number of shares by 4 million and £16 million is needed. Hence the issue price per share must be £4.

As details of the contract are already public knowledge any impact on share price will already have taken place. Similarly, as the repurchasing of the debenture is at market value based on current rates of interest, this is unlikely to affect the share price.

(ii) The total value of equity after rights issue is as follows:

Existing shares	12 million at £5	= £60 million
New shares	4 million at £4	= £16 million
	16 million	= £76 million

The theoretical ex-rights price per share is £76/16 = £4.75.

(iii) Each three shares currently held give the right to purchase, for £4.00, a share which will be worth £4.75. The value of such rights attached to three existing shares is 75p (i.e. £4.75 − £4.00). Hence the value of the right attached to one share is 25p.

Part (b)

The fact that the shares are being offered under the rights issue at a discount on the current price should not affect the cost of equity provided either that the market is efficient in valuing the securities or the existing shareholders take up the entire rights issue. If the market misinterprets the way in which the funds are to be used and some existing shareholders sell the rights, then there could well be a wealth transfer, with a possible reduction in the wealth of existing shareholders.

Pre-emption rights

There is a Stock Exchange requirement that companies wishing to make a further issue of equity shares for cash have to offer them first to existing shareholders. The justification for providing this 'right' is that existing shareholders may wish to maintain a certain percentage holding in the company. By offering them this right they have the chance to do so. If the new issue of shares were offered to all potential investors, existing shareholders could find their percentage holding declining.

The Stock Exchange Yellow Book states:

> Issues for cash of securities having an equity element must, in the absence of exceptional circumstances, be offered in the first place to the existing equity shareholders in proportion to their holdings unless the shareholders have approved other specific proposals. Such approval may take the form of either general disapplication of the statutory pre-emption requirements not more than fifteen months prior to the issue, or prior approval for a specific issue. Holders of other securities having an equity element must be permitted to participate if the rights attached thereto so require.

The financial institutions in the UK, who already own in the region of 70% of all shares, attach considerable importance to these pre-emptive rights. They argue that it means that their voting power is not diluted and that the alternative of selling shares to other shareholders often depresses share prices.

There has been criticism of these rights. It is claimed that it is a restrictive practice, and that the stock markets should be opened up to more competition in the demand for shares by offering new shares to all investors. It is claimed that this would reduce the cost of raising money for the company. Companies themselves point out that if they were not tied by the pre-emptive rights clause they could raise money more quickly and cheaply through placements than through rights issues.

These pre-emptive rights only apply to issues for cash; they do not apply to equity shares issued in exchange for assets. Therefore a share-for-share exchange at the time of a takeover does not contravene the pre-emptive rights. But what if the shareholders of the victim firm want cash rather than shares? It is here where 'vendor placings' have proved to be useful. Vendor placings technically do not offend the rights of pre-emption. The company issuing the new shares is not selling them for cash. The shareholder of the victim company is given shares in the acquiring company in exchange for shares in the victim company. The acquirer has arranged for an institution to be willing to buy these new shares immediately for cash from the shareholder of the victim company. The institution could then sell the shares or perhaps place them with clients. It is even possible for the original shareholders of the acquiring company to buy these new shares from the institution.

With the hectic takeover activity of the 1980s, a number of companies persuaded their investors to waive their pre-emptive rights. But some major UK financial institutions showed that they did not like what was going on by voting against some of the waiver proposals. They did not like a practice that was developing for companies to have the rights of existing UK shareholders waived and then for the new shares to be sold to institutional investors in other countries.

A form of compromise was reached. Guidelines were introduced which stated that any non-rights issues would be limited in any one year to 5% of the company's issued capital. The maximum amount of discount on the pre-issue market price was agreed upon; there would be no deep discounts. Agreement to waive rights for a 12-month period would be obtained from shareholders, and then, provided that the issue was within the guidelines, specific approval would not be required for new issues.

5.7 PREFERENCE SHARES

Preference shares are usually seen as a form of equity capital. They usually entitle their holder to a fixed rate of dividend from the company each year. This dividend ranks for payment before other equity returns, and so the ordinary shareholders receive no dividend until the preference shareholders have been paid their fixed percentage. Preference shares carry part-ownership of the company and allow due participation in the profits of the business. In fact, their dividend is an appropriation of profits and so if a bad year means no profits, it means no dividend for the preference shareholders.

This point constitutes the essential distinction between preference shares and debentures. Debenture holders are not part-owners of the company; their interest claims have to be met whether the company has made a profit or not. Interest payments are not an appropriation of profits. It is for this reason that the tax treatment of each of the two forms of fixed percentage capital is different. Debenture interest, as a charge, is a tax-deductible expense, and like any other form of expenditure it reduces the company's tax bill. Preference dividends, as an appropriation of profits, are not tax-deductible. Tax is payable on the profits figure before the preference dividends are deducted. Consequently, a company earning profits and committed to paying out, say, 8% on capital raised, would usually prefer to be paying it on debentures (for which the interest charge is net of tax) than on preference shares for which the company would have to stand the gross cost.

On cost-of-capital grounds alone a company would not normally choose to issue preference shares unless the dividend rate is less than or equal to the cost of interest (after tax allowance) on a debenture. At present and in the foreseeable future this is unlikely to be the case with the relative risks of the two securities. If a debenture has a coupon rate of, say, 10%, corporation tax at 33% would mean that the cost to the company would be only 6.7%. To offer preference shares with a dividend rate of the order of only 6.7% would be practically out of the question, particularly as debentures are the safer form of investment with prior claims to both interest and capital.

Factors other than cost require consideration, however. The issue of debentures increases leverage, whereas the issue of preference shares increases the equity base: the two forms of capital are not strictly interchangeable. A company might find it impossible to raise more debt capital but still be able to raise preference capital.

Redeemable preference shares

Usually preference shares are irredeemable: they provide permanent capital which does not have to be repaid. If the preference shareholder wishes to dispose of his or her holding they must sell the share in the stock market.

Companies whose articles authorize them to do so can, however, issue redeemable preference shares that either carry a prearranged redemption date or can be redeemed at the company's option. The redeemable preference share would have a price behaviour similar to that of a debenture; the only difference between the two securities, from the investor's viewpoint, is that the debenture would offer the more secure income stream.

Participating redeemable preference shares

Participating redeemable preference shares allow the shareholder to participate in a further share of the profits after they have received a fixed rate of dividend. The fixed rate is usually lower than on an ordinary preference share, because of the added attraction of participation in the general level of profits.

For example, a preference share may carry a dividend rate of 8% and allow the holder to share in additional profits, with the additional profits being divided between equity and preference holders in some specified proportions. Some issues may allow the equity owners to receive a certain dividend before the preference shareholders participate.

Convertible redeemable preference shares

Convertible redeemable preference shares have the added attraction of a right to be converted into ordinary shares at some date. They are in certain aspects similar to convertible debentures.

Cumulative redeemable preference shares

If a cumulative preference share receives no dividends in one year because the company has failed to make a profit, it will receive it in another when the position has improved. The dividends accumulate until the company can afford to pay, and the shareholder then receives the backlog and the current dividend for the year in which payment is made. This does not necessarily apply to all preference shares: it is strictly true only of those that are specified as being cumulative.

The preference shareholder suffers temporary losses by having to wait one or more years for the dividend, although their position is better than that of the equity shareholder who receives nothing back for the dividends lost in years when the company cannot afford to pay.

In their respective claims to dividend, the holders of cumulative preference shares take priority over equity holders, so that only after the cumulative liability for preference dividends has eventually been met can ordinary shareholders again receive any dividend. With non-cumulative preference shares, of course, the dividend rights terminate at the end of each financial year.

Auction market preferred stock (AMPS)

This is one of the complex capital instruments that emerged in the late 1980s. AMPS is a preference share with a floating rate of dividend. From the point of view of the issuing company it is a form of equity. From the point of view of the investor it is similar to debt, except that if the company does not earn sufficient profits no return is received.

Most AMPS are denominated in US dollars, and are traded in the US financial market. They are often issued, however, by non-US companies.

The idea of the floating rate of dividend is attractive to investors (if interest rates rise) and to the issuing company (if interest rates fall). If certain conditions are met, AMPS are attractive from a tax point of view to US-resident investors.

As with many other new financial instruments there are difficulties in deciding whether AMPS should be classified as debt or equity from a financial gearing point of view. The dividends (as opposed to interest) and the non-guarantee of an annual payment suggest it is equity. But the fact that the level of dividend payment floats in line with the level of interest gives it certain debt characteristics.

Because the annual payment to investors depends on whether or not profits are earned, the dividend rate paid has to be higher than the interest rates in the money market. The cost to the company of an AMPS, because of the higher annual payments and the lack of a tax shield, is higher than the cost of short-term debt.

The preference shares are auctioned to investors. Each potential investor states the level of dividend rate they require before they will purchase the AMPS. The auction agent receives these bids from the investors' brokers, and then sets the dividend rate that will be paid. The agent does this on the basis of the lowest possible rate which will clear the entire issue. The AMPS can be redeemed.

5.8 VENTURE CAPITAL

The capital market is good at providing new equity funds for large companies and providing a market for their existing shares. When companies are very small there is a good chance that a few shareholders can provide all the risk capital that is required. However, there is a gap between these two situations which has not really been satisfied. The larger private company or the smaller public company may wish to raise new capital for an investment in which there is a risk. Fixed-interest capital, even if available, is not, therefore, appropriate. The capital required is called 'venture capital'; the providers of this capital are being asked to share in the risks. Merchant (investment) banks were once willing to provide such funds but it is doubtful whether they were ever able to provide funds on a sufficient scale to satisfy the total need.

There has been a gap in the UK for a long time in the provision of funds for venture capital needs. One reason is that an increasing proportion of the available funds flows into the hands of institutions who are not likely to use them for venture capital needs. It is not thought appropriate for pension funds and the like to take these sorts of risks with their contributors' money.

There are practical reasons why newer small firms find it harder to obtain funds to finance their growth than well-established larger firms. A firm is borrowing funds or obtaining new equity in anticipation of being able to realize a prospective stream of future earnings. The capital markets will normally have more confidence in a firm with a known record than in a new entrant. Even though the new firm and the established firm have the same technology and wish to do exactly the same thing with the money raised, the market will take into account that it has experience of one firm but not of the other. Experience is of importance, and unless the existing firm is known to be inept it will have an advantage. Reputation, which is to say prior experience, is of special importance in establishing the terms of finance for transactions that involve large discrete commitments of funds.

The reason for this is that the capital market has incomplete information about companies. The market cannot always distinguish, from the information provided, between a good company and one that is not quite so good. The market is therefore thrown back on its experience of the companies involved. The less well-known applicant will be at a disadvantage: the risks to the provider of funds are high and therefore the costs to the applicant if the funds are obtained will also be high.

The Bank of England uses the expression 'venture-capital investment' to mean a form of investment in which 'investors support entrepreneurial talent with finance and business skills to exploit market opportunities, and thus obtain long-term capital gains'.

The important points about venture-capital investment are as follows:

1 it is high-risk investment – it is not investing in listed companies;
2 it is not passive portfolio investment but involves a close working relationship between the venture capital company and the company receiving the funds;
3 it is not a short-term investment in which the shares will be sold in a matter of months, nor is it a very long-term investment. The venture capital company will be hoping to realize the equity shares it has acquired at a profit in five or so years after it first purchased the shares. It is hoping that either the company will go public or the shares will be bought out by another company or by the other shareholders.

Small companies usually need three different rounds of finance. The term 'venture capital' can apply to satisfying the needs at any of these three stages of development.

1 Seed capital or start-up capital: the finance that a new or young company needs during what can be a lengthy period of research and development. It can also apply to a start-up situation in which the product or idea has been developed and it is thought that it will only be a short period before the firm's cash flow is positive.

   For a small business starting up there can be great difficulties. In order to be able to raise a loan from a bank, it will first be necessary for the entrepreneur to show that he or she has some equity funds. The bank will wish to see that they are sharing the financial risks, not taking them all.

   The traditional sources of equity finance for the small business were the savings of the founder or the savings of their family. With the relative decline in the importance of the private investor and the channelling of personal savings into financial institutions, it is now unlikely that many entrepreneurs with worthwhile projects will have access to sufficient capital, even on a limited scale. Because of this equity gap for small firms, undoubtedly a number of businesses fail to get off the ground.

2 A second round of finance is needed for young companies who have successfully started up and now need additional capital to allow them to begin to grow.

3 The third situation, referred to as the 'development capital situation', is when an established company with a good trading record needs an injection of capital for further expansion.

When a company is referred to as a 'start-up company' it can be a new company or a very young company. In all three situations it is the same type of capital that is needed by the company, namely risk capital. It is just the risks to the venture capital company that vary between the three situations.

Undoubtedly some venture capital is available in the UK for the second and third situations mentioned above, namely finance for the exploitation of products and ideas that have already been researched and developed. As already mentioned, it is difficult, however, to obtain finance in the seed capital situation.

The British Venture Capital Association which represents more than a hundred of the largest venture capital companies has recognized the problem and tries to encourage more of its members to provide such funds. The European Commission also recognized that this is a problem, not just in Britain but across the EU. The Commission backs a number of seed capital funds. This support takes the form of reimbursable interest-free advances of up to 50% of the operating costs of these funds over their first three to five years plus a contribution of up to 25% of their capital needs.

It should be appreciated that not only are the risks high from running a seed capital fund because of the high failure rate, but the operating costs are also high because the investigation and administration costs tend to be at a more or less fixed level whatever the amount borrowed.

A survey of new companies found that only 3% had managed to find venture capital funds as their primary source of finance (even though 45% of them had tried to obtain it). About 55% used personal savings to start up, and 17% obtained funds from the major clearing banks.

Venture capitalists are usually looking for an average return of 35% per annum on their investments. An important question is over what period they are looking for this return. Usually they talk about such average returns on their funds over a three-to-five-year period. Unfortunately in high technology, with a long development stage, it can take more like seven to eight years to achieve this desired level of return. Clearly there is still a gap between those seeking funds and the type of funds that investors will make available.

Another problem from the point of view of the venture capitalist is that small businesses can take up a great deal of their management time. The company will need monitoring and much advice during the early stages of its life.

Venture capitalists are often involved in assisting with the financing of high-risk projects. These companies might not produce profits in the early years of the venture. The financial backers expect a high rate of return to compensate for the risk. They are not always prepared to wait for dividends based on profits, and so sometimes negotiate an annual 'dividend' based on the level of sales.

The venture capital funds

The way in which independent and institutional venture capital companies raise the money that they invest is either through going public and raising the money in the capital markets, by attracting wealthy investors who are taking advantage of tax concessions or by attracting funds from pension funds, investment funds and insurance companies. There are also state-owned agencies who operate such funds, e.g. the Welsh Development Agency and English Estates.

There are a number of financial institutions and banks in the UK who operate venture capital funds and who are willing to invest venture and development capital in the 'right' companies. They are prepared to purchase equity shares in such companies. They are not all, however, prepared to invest in start-up companies. Some are looking for investments in special situations, such as biotechnology, but many will invest in any industry. There are a few examples of what is known as 'corporate venturing', in which large companies provide funds to small businesses.

What a venture capitalist looks at when considering a company for a possible investment is the following:

1 the management team;
2 the product;
3 the markets for that product;
4 a well-developed business plan, covering all aspects including finance;
5 the commitment of the management team – how much of their own money they have invested and how much time they are putting into the venture;
6 the exit routes.

We shall now consider point 6 because of its financial implications.

Exit route

A key question that any venture capitalist has to consider is how to exit, at a profit, from the investment in the company. How is the investor going to be able to dispose of the shares? The possibilities are as follows:

1 the company has its shares floated on a stock exchange;
2 'a trade sale', i.e. the company is sold to a corporate buyer;
3 a management buy-out;
4 refinancing by a new team of backers (investors or new venture capitalists) probably on more favourable terms to the management and entrepreneurs so that the original venture capitalist is replaced;
5 a management buy-in;
6 liquidation.

A trade sale, the purchase of the whole company by another company, is the most common. One problem with a trade sale or any approach that involves finding a replacement investor is agreeing on an appropriate price for the sale. An exit/entry price that pleases both sides and also the continuing equity owners/ managers is not easy. The original venture capitalist wants as much profit as possible; the other parties are thinking of the returns and risks in the future.

Although much talked about, the public flotation has declined in popularity. This has been partly due to the volatile state of the stock market and to the publicity given to the financial difficulties that some newly floated companies have faced shortly after being floated.

Corporate venturing

Corporate venturing occurs when a large company, with cash surplus to its needs for the immediate future, purchases a minority equity stake in a small business. The large company would usually only do this in a business with whom it has contacts, because it is a customer, engaged in related technology or selling in similar markets. On occasion if the large company has the management resources available it will also provide management assistance.

Business angels

This is an expression that originated in the USA. It refers to wealthy individuals who are prepared to help smaller companies by purchasing an equity stake in the company. As is well known, many small companies are over-dependent on loan finance, and find it difficult to attract equity. A 'business angel' is a man or woman who comes to their help.

To venture capital companies, such as 3Is, investing amounts below a certain size is uneconomic. Hence the need for the providers of small amounts of equity capital. Some doubt that 'business angels' really exist in the UK.

In the USA they have made a contribution to the success of many companies, particularly those based on new technology. They often provide technical or managerial support to the companies, not just finance.

Equity capital and its valuation

The Business Expansion Scheme in the UK was designed to encourage wealthy individuals to invest in smaller companies. It gave investors under such a scheme tax advantages. The only trouble was that under the terms of the scheme the advantages ceased the moment the investor offered more than financial support. It prevented investors from contributing knowhow. It did not therefore encourage the business angel.

One problem is how to bring together companies who need support and the business angels. Often this is best done at a local level through regional offices of banks or accounting firms.

5.9 FURTHER READING

Foley, B.J. (1991) *Capital Markets*, Macmillan.

Peasnell, K.V. and Ward, C.W.R. (1985) *British Financial Markets and Institutions*, Prentice-Hall.

Russell, G.R. (1990) *Initial Public Offers: Report of the Review Committee*. The Stock Exchange, London.

Rutterford, J. (1993) *Introduction to Stock Exchange Investment*, 2nd edn, Macmillan, London.

Scott-Quinn, B. (1990) A Strategy for the International Stock Exchange, *National Westminster Quarterly Review*, May, pp. 43–58.

Thomas, W.A. (1989) *The Securities Market*, Philip Allen, Oxford.

5.10 PROBLEMS

[See also problems in Chapter 7.]

1 The issue to the public of an application for shares or debentures in a company must normally be accompanied by a prospectus. What are the main features of a prospectus?

2 Describe the advantages and disadvantages to a medium-sized company of obtaining a quotation.

3 For what reasons, other than the need to raise outside finance, might a private company take the necessary steps to secure a Stock Exchange quotation?

4 In what circumstances might a company make a 'stock split'? What would be the effect of such a decision on the company, the share price and the shareholders' wealth?

5 Clearly distinguish an offer for sale by tender from other methods of raising equity capital and describe the process by which the price is set and the shares allocated in an offer for sale by tender. Outline the circumstances when the use of an issue by tender would be an appropriate way of raising equity.

6 What are the main advantages and disadvantages to a company of raising finance by issuing the following:
   (a) ordinary shares;
   (b) redeemable convertible preference shares;
   (c) deferred ordinary shares;
   (d) convertible debentures.

7 Outline the features of a rights issue of equity capital, and suggest why this method of issuing fresh equity may be preferred by shareholders.

8 (a) Explain the following terms in relation to equity investment:
      (i) dividend yield;
      (ii) price-to-earnings ratio.
   (b) The shares of Company A, which owns and develops commercial property,

show a dividend yield of 1.5% and a price-to-earnings ratio of 40, while those of Company B, a machine-tool manufacturer, yield 6% with a price-to-earnings ratio of 13. Suggest circumstances which might account for those divergent stock market ratings.

9 Cashless PLC is quoted on the Alternative Investment Market. Its share price is £5 and the estimated market capitalization rate applied to its expected earnings is 15%. Cashless announced a rights offer of equity on a one-for-four basis at £4 per share.

(a) Assume that the proceeds of the rights issue will be invested by the company to earn a 15% perpetual return. Identify the theoretical ex-rights price of the shares, and the value of a right attaching to one 'old' share in these circumstances.

(b) Assume instead that the rights offer announcement indicated an intention to invest the proceeds in a new product line offering an expected return of 20% in perpetuity, but having the same risk as that of the present firm. The 'market' is widely regarded as semi-strong efficient, and the company projections are generally regarded as reasonable.

Identify the ex-rights value of each share in these circumstances. What is the value of a right attaching to an 'old' share? What will happen to the share price immediately following the rights announcement? Why?

10 A medium-sized UK company recently made a one-for-four rights issue which was underwritten at 140p to finance one of its growth divisions. The share price prior to the announcement was 173p which was just above the bottom of the shares' 1992–93 trading range. The share price after the announcement was 171p.

The rights issue was the final part of a financial reorganization which included a private placement in the UK capital markets for a slightly larger amount of equity capital than the rights issue and the switching of short-term debt into medium- and long-term borrowings at fixed rates of interest.

A company spokesperson indicated that the immediate affect of the reorganization will be to reduce gearing from 70% to about 20%. Over the next two years gearing will rise to 40% before falling back again.

Required:
(a) Calculate the theoretical share price expected following the rights issue announcement. Provide economically justifiable reasons for any difference you find between your price and the price reported in the above quote. (5 marks)
(b) Several small investors, who are new to the stock market, have expressed concern that they will lose money if they do not subscribe for the new shares. They have asked you for advice on whether or not they should borrow money to take up their rights. Provide full details of the advice you would give them. (5 marks)
(c) The great majority of rights issues are underwritten, which many academics find puzzling because the fees are thought to be high in relation to the risk to which the company is exposed, particularly if the issue is deeply discounted. These academics view the underwriting agreement as an option which is amenable to valuation using option pricing theory. Explain the underwriting agreement as an option and what information is required for its valuation. (6 marks)
(d) Discuss briefly the advantages and disadvantages of a rights issue versus a private placement of shares. (5 marks)
(e) Suggest reasons for the switch from short-term debt to fixed-interest-rate debt, given that the UK yield-to-maturity curve was upward sloping at the time. (4 marks)

6 EQUITY VALUATION

LEARNING OUTCOMES

In this chapter we are concerned with the valuation of the equity of a company. We will look at the problem from three points of view:

1 The issuing company, selling a new issue of its shares in the market place.
2 An investor purchasing a small number of shares in the stock market. This is sometimes referred to as the 'secondary market', one investor selling a share to another investor.
3 An acquiring company interested in purchasing all of the shares of a target company through a takeover or merger.

In one way the valuation process is the same from whichever of the three points of view the problem is approached. But there are differences, so we will look at each case separately.

By the time the reader has read this chapter, he or she will:

● know how to value a listed equity share, based on fundamental information
● know how to value a company
● know how to price an equity share being listed on the stock market for the first time

6.1 WHAT DO WE KNOW ABOUT HOW SHARES ARE VALUED IN THE STOCK MARKET?

Investors buy shares of a company because they expect the price to rise in the future; they sell shares either because they need the cash or because they expect the price to fall in future. On occasions they also buy because they have excess liquidity. Investors receive information on the state of an economy, developments within an industry, and on the future prospects and present financial position of a company. Such information helps investors to decide whether the price of a company's share will rise or fall in the future.

There is much competition in the financial markets. In the major stock markets of the world there are many financial analysts scrutinizing all the information available. These are particularly 'informed' investors. According to the efficient market hypothesis the price of a company's share on any day incorporates all information currently available.

The actual share price reflects the considered opinion of many informed and less informed investors. As in all markets, the price on a day is the one at which the demand to buy the share at that price equals the supply of shares from investors willing to sell at that price. When the price starts to rise it means that there are investors who, having assessed the available information, have raised their expectations about the future prospects of the company. Those who are selling the shares have expectations about the future which are not as high as the buyers'.

Is the actual price of a company's share on any day equal to its 'true' value? We do not really know. We have theories on the subject. We know that in theory the true value of a share is equal to the present value of dividends to be received in the future. But to obtain such a value we need to estimate future dividends, and to agree on the discount rate to obtain the present values.

The true value is sometimes referred to as the 'intrinsic value' (or 'real value', or 'fundamental value'). Unfortunately we do not know this value, we cannot observe such a value, all we can do is make an estimate. Different people will have different expectations about the future. Therefore there will be varying opinions on what is the true value of a share. There is even disagreement on the model that should be used to measure true value.

We can observe an *actual price* for the shares of a company on any day. This price depends upon supply and demand pressures for that share. Who are the investors seeking to buy the shares? Are they rational investors with access to information which is useful for forecasting purposes, or are they irrational investors, following currently fashionable opinions or their own hunches? Those who believe that the major stock markets of the world are efficient believe that the actual equity prices in the markets reflect rational assessments of the fundamental values of a share. Those who are not convinced that such markets are so efficient as is often claimed believe that on occasions actual prices diverge from rational assessments of true values. They believe that many investors are irrational and this gives an opportunity for some investors to make gains. Over time, market prices will fluctuate around their true value, but this means that in the short run opportunities do arise that allow one (particularly the informed investor) to make gains.

In this and the next chapter we will examine this controversy. We will need to consider two issues:

1 Is it possible to determine the true value of a share?
2 Can we explain the movement in share prices over time? It might not matter that we do not know at any point of time what the true value of a share should be, as long as we understand what causes the actual price to move over time.

The rational approach

We begin by considering how equity shares should be valued. In theory the value of a share should be the present value of the dividends to be paid by a company to shareholders in the future. A shareholder is, when buying a share, obtaining a claim to a stream of future cash flows: the only payments made by a company to a shareholder are cash dividends and scrip (stock) dividends. If after a few years the shareholder decides to sell the share, it is the purchaser of the share who will be buying the dividends to be paid by the company in the years following the transaction.

The above is the 'rational' theory of share price determination. Company dividends over time move in line with company earnings. Of course, nobody knows exactly what the future earnings or dividend payments of any company will be. However, the actual price of a share on any day in an efficient stock market should be equal or close to its (intrinsic) value. Why? Because in an efficient market there are many (sufficient) rational investors, who are as informed about the prospects of a company as it is possible to be. These informed investors, with the information they have available, have a collective (consensus) view on what the future earnings and dividends of a company will be, and it is they through their buying and selling of shares that keep the actual share price close to its intrinsic price.

144

The influence on the daily price of the rational investor can be represented as in Figure 6.1. While the price on any one day may not be exactly the same as the intrinsic value, daily prices would be expected either to fluctuate about this true value. Nobody knows the precise true value, but the informed know the range within which it lies. Baumol [1] states that

> earnings do ultimately and solely determine the value to be derived by share-holding and that if shareholders do learn at all well from their experience, their purchasing patterns will, in the long run, force stock prices to conform rather closely to these prospective earnings opportunities of the firms whose shares they buy. We have strong reasons to suspect that in a rough and ready way, security prices do follow closely the developments in company prospects.

This suggests that in the long run the actual share price will move towards its true value as based on expected earnings. The actual share price may be there now, but if it is not there will be movement of the actual price to meet the true value. The movement of price over time as illustrated in Figure 6.1 is rational.

There are some investors who are better informed than others. Financial analysts undertake research in order to be better informed. Some investors are more rational than others. According to theories of finance the rational, better informed, investors keep stock markets in line. It is not possible for anyone to say precisely what should be the true value of a share. But the rational investor knows the price range within which the true value lies and such a person's investment decisions keep the actual price within the correct price range. When the actual price reaches the upper limit of the acceptable range they sell; when it reaches the lower limit they buy.

The above intuitively appealing approach seemed to be justified when the weight of learned opinion believed that the major stock markets were more or less 'efficient'. Fama has argued that it is the sophisticated traders that ensured that actual share prices were close to intrinsic value prices [2]. In the 1980s and 1990s, however, an increasing number of studies have suggested that the stock markets are not as efficient as had previously been thought. A number of studies have shown that the actions of irrational investors could significantly affect share prices and that therefore the price of a company's shares are not always close to its 'intrinsic value'.

In the 1980s there was an increase in interest in the behavioural theory of finance.

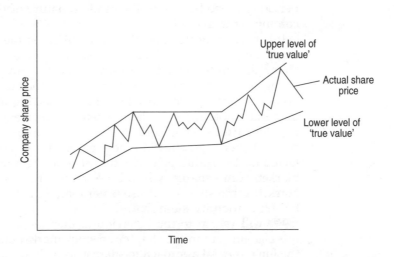

Figure 6.1
Movement of share price within bands of true value

Behavioural theory of share-price determination

The behavioural theorists recognize that actual share prices do on occasions stray away from their theoretical values. There are a number of reasons for this. One is that some investors buy and sell shares on the basis of imperfect information. Such investors are called 'noise traders' or 'trend chasers'. An investor receives a vast amount of information. One investor will consider a certain event or piece of information more important than will another investor. The influence of noise traders can be significant and will not always be effectively counter-balanced by the action of rational investors. The trading activity of the rational investors will not always be large enough to eliminate the effects of the noise traders.

Indeed, the rational investors will sometimes encourage the movement of a company's share price away from its true value. Such behaviour is linked to the 'fads and bubbles' concept. Another explanation for the observed fact that share prices sometimes appear to be higher or lower than would be expected from a rational assessment of the relevant information, or that they do not always move in line with expectations, is because some investors do not behave rationally. The trading activity of the rational investors will not always be large enough to eliminate the effect of noise.

According to the behavioural theorists psychological factors influence price levels and the movement in share prices. Such factors have been referred to as 'herd behaviour', 'fads' and 'fashion'. The behaviourist approach is a recognition that psychological factors, and not just economic facts, might influence prices. Another way of putting it is that 'blockheads' play a major role in the stock market. The level of prices at any time and their movement over time is not just the result of a rational analysis of fundamental information.

A number of studies have shown that the dramatic stock market crash of 1987 (Black Monday) cannot be explained by the release of fundamental economic news. It has also been found that over time it is difficult to link major movements in share prices with the release of economic or other information.

In fact both approaches to share price determination, the fundamental and the behaviourist, provide a useful insight. The intrinsic value approach may not explain the share price on a particular day, but it indicates the direction in which the share price will move over time. The price on any particular day is determined by demand and supply on that day and the demand on a day can in turn depend on rational and less rational investors. Price movement over a short period can also be due to the random nature of the timing of new information coming to the market.

It is because of this uncertainty about when the actual price will approach the true value that many financial analysts have become slightly less enthusiastic about the undervalued shares approach to investment. Many of them have changed the emphasis of their research either towards forecasting the turning points in share price movement or to selecting a balanced portfolio of investments and holding on to them. There has been a growth in the number of index-matching funds being sold to investors. The turning-point idea is that all share prices will change direction more or less at the same time, and so the important factor to determine is when the turn will come. In a bear market (a falling market) some shares will fall less than others, and in a bull market (a rising market) some shares will rise faster than others; therefore it is also important to be able to identity these shares.

We will return to the behavioural theories of share price movement later in this chapter and in the chapter on stock market efficiency. First, we will examine the fundamental approach to share price valuation.

There is no single generally accepted method (theory) for determining the correct true valuation of a company share. It is possible to approach the problem in different ways. A share entitles the owner to a stream of future dividends. Therefore one approach is to take the value of the share as corresponding to the present value of this stream of dividend payments. Obviously there is considerable uncertainty surrounding the size of the future dividends; indeed, it is partly as a result of changing expectations about future dividends that share prices fluctuate.

Of course, the owner of a share at any one point of time will usually consider their returns as accruing not just from dividend payments but from the additional gains resulting from any capital appreciation on the share. Normally, the owner does not intend to hold the share in perpetuity; they wish to sell it and obtain capital gains. But when the share is sold, the buyer is also simply purchasing a stream of future dividend payments and so, once again, the price is determined by future dividend expectations.

This theory can be demonstrated [3]. Suppose that an investor buys a share expecting to hold it for two years: the value of the share to them is the present value of the two dividend payments plus the discounted value of the price they expect to receive on selling the share. If P_0 is the price of the share today, P_2 is the price of the share at the end of the second year, D_1 is the dividend per share to be received at the end of the first year, and i is the discount rate, which is the market capitalization rate (the required rate of return on shares in the risk class being considered), then

$$P_0 = \frac{D_1}{1+i} + \frac{D_2}{(1+i)^2} + \frac{P_2}{(1+i)^2}$$

The investor who buys the share at the end of the second year pays P_2 for it, and expects to hold it for two further years. Therefore, looked at from time zero,

$$\frac{P_2}{(1+i)^2} = \frac{D_3}{(1+i)^3} + \frac{D_4}{(1+i)^4} + \frac{P_4}{(1+i)^4}$$

The price at the end of the fourth year and all future prices are determined in a similar manner. Therefore the equation for the price of the share at the present time can be rewritten as

$$P_0 = \frac{D_1}{1+i} + \frac{D_2}{(1+i)^2} + \frac{D_3}{(1+i)^3} + \frac{D_4}{(1+i)^4} + \ldots = \sum_{t=1}^{\infty} \frac{D_t}{(1+i)^t}$$

Growth in dividends

The dividends of most companies are expected to increase over time. Evaluation of the share price must allow for this, and indeed it is possible to incorporate these growth expectations explicitly in the valuation model. In the model just described the dividends have to be forecast for each year separately. If g is the expected percentage annual rate of growth the formula becomes

$$P_0 = \frac{D_0(1+g)}{1+i} + \frac{D_0(1+g)^2}{(1+i)^2} + \frac{D_0(1+g)^3}{(1+i)^3} + \ldots = \sum_{t=1}^{\infty} \frac{D_0(1+g)^t}{(1+i)^t}$$

This can be rewritten as

$$P_0 = \frac{D_1}{i-g}$$

The above equation can only be used if the growth rate g is lower than the discount rate i. As the formula is written, price is determined at time zero, that is, before the dividend for year one has been declared.

The following illustrates a practical application of the equation. Suppose that a company has a growth rate in dividends of 4% per annum, and that the market's capitalization rate for a company in this risk category is 8%. If the dividend at the end of the first year is expected to be £0.50 per share, the expected share price today would be

$$P_0 = \frac{£0.5}{0.08 - 0.04} = £12.50$$

The dividend yield based on the expected dividend of this company is 4% (0.5/12.50).

The share price now is £12.50 and can be expected to increase by 4% over the next year. The price in one year's time should be

$$P_1 = \frac{D_0(1+g)^2}{(1+i)^2} + \frac{D_0(1+g)^3}{(1+i)^3} + \ldots$$

$$P_1 = \frac{0.5408}{(1.08)^2} + \frac{0.5624}{(1.08)^3} + \ldots$$

which is £13.

The discount rate applicable to a company is a function of the interest rates in effect at the time and the degree of risk associated with that company. In the context of the capital-asset pricing model (CAPM), the risk premium would be related to systematic risk (see Chapter 11).

In fact, some companies, although earning profits, elect not to pay dividends. This is a matter of deliberate financial policy, and not a measure forced upon them by financial difficulties. The above theory of share valuation can still be applied to these companies, since one day presumably they will start paying dividends. This is the only basis on which shareholders can obtain any returns from the company; in the final analysis dividends must be paid or assets realized, otherwise there is no logic in anybody holding the shares. The reason that the price of the shares rises is that with the retention policies of the company, the rapid growth alters investors' expectations about the future size of dividends. At some time in the future, large dividends can be paid. Therefore once again it can be said that dividends determine the company's share price.

It is, of course, a difficult matter to forecast the stream of future dividends payments. Some companies go through periods when their earnings grow at an above-normal rate, and their dividends then, if allowed to, also tend to grow at an above-normal rate. It cannot be assumed, however, that a period of above-average growth will continue into the future. To estimate a level for the share price of a company that is presently enjoying above-average performance it is usual to assume that the above-average growth will continue for a number of years and that the dividend will then revert to a near-normal rate of growth.

Example 6.1

The way in which the share price can be calculated for a company with an above-average growth rate in dividends is as follows. Let us assume that the appropriate market rate of discount is 8%, and that the company is expected to enjoy an above-average performance for eight years, with dividends growing at say 10% per annum. After that time, because of competition and the company losing its present technological or marketing lead, the growth in dividends will revert to the average for all companies – say 4%. The present dividend is £0.1 per share. Three sets of calculations need to be completed before the appropriate share price can be determined.

1 The present value (PV) of dividends over the next eight years is as follows:

Year	Dividend	Discount factor	PV
1	0.110	0.926	0.102
2	0.121	0.857	0.104
3	0.133	0.794	0.106
4	0.146	0.735	0.107
5	0.161	0.681	0.110
6	0.177	0.630	0.112
7	0.195	0.583	0.114
8	0.214	0.540	0.116
			0.871

2 Value of share at end of year 8:

$$P_8 = \frac{D_9}{0.08 - 0.04} = \frac{0.2226}{0.04} = 5.56$$

3 Value today of price at end of year 8:

$$\frac{5.56}{(1.08)^8} = 3.006$$

4 Value of share today = £(0.871 + 3.006) = £3.877.

The growth formula can be used to estimate the market's capitalization rate, i.e. the expected return for companies within a risk class. The formula can be rewritten as

$$i = \frac{D_1}{P_0} + g$$

which indicates that the market capitalization rate equals the expected dividend yield D_1/P_0 plus the expected rate of growth of dividends. This version of the formula is in fact one approach to estimating the cost of capital.

We will use the shares of Guinness PLC to illustrate how this dividend model can be used. During 1996 the price of the company's equity shares ranged from a high of 493p to a low of 430p. The gross dividend for the year ending 31 December 1995 was 18.63p. The share price at the beginning of December 1996 was 444p, which gave a gross dividend yield of 4.2%.

It is difficult to know the expectations of investors with respect to the annual growth rate of dividends. If we observe the gross dividends paid by Guinness in the years prior to 1995 we see that the growth had been steady and at a rate of approximately 6% per annum (it was 14.40p in 1991).

This growth rate would suggest that the dividend D_1 (for the year ending 31 December 1996) would be 19.75p. The market capitalization rate, i.e. the cost of equity capital to the company after corporation tax, would therefore be:

$$i = \frac{19.75}{444.0} + 0.06 = 0.105 = 10.5\%$$

This would be the annual rate of return that shareholders would have expected to earn in 1996 from holding shares in the same risk class as that of Guinness PLC. They would be receiving this return in the form of capital gain plus dividends.

Eurotunnel PLC, in their offer for sale of equity shares in November 1987, made use of this present-value-of-dividend theory. They produced financial projections for the period from when they forecast dividends would first be paid in 1994 to when their concession ends in 2041. They pointed out that the present value of projected dividends over this period, discounted at an annual rate of 12%, would be £24 inclusive of tax credits and £17 excluding tax credits. This, it implied in its offer documents, would be (or should be) the value of the equity shares in mid-1994. It might well have been if the projections had proven to be correct and if the market had believed the projections, if the market had adopted a 12% discount rate, and if the dividend valuation model was used to value shares.

Unfortunately for Eurotunnel the projections proved to be wildly optimistic. The Tunnel was not even open to the public by mid-1994, the project cost over double the estimates, and the financing of the project had to be renegotiated with many acrimonious discussions taking place.

It may be thought that the above equation for valuing shares is naive, based as it is only on the PV of expected future dividends. Theoretically, however, it is correct. It is only through distributions that the shareholders obtain a return from the company. Unfortunately it is not possible to test the theory as we do not know what future dividends will be. Investors have expectations about future dividends, but we do not know what they expect and different investors may well have different expectations. There are many approaches to valuing shares; the approach based on dividend expectations is only one possibility.

Estimating *g*

One way to estimate *g* is by use of the following formula:

$$g = \text{retention ratio} \times \% \text{ return on retained earnings in the past}$$

The retention ratio (sometimes called 'plough-back ratio') = profits retained in business divided by profits available for distribution to shareholders. It is the inverse of the payout ratio i.e. (1 − payout ratio).

A fast-growing new company typically retains a larger proportion of the profits it earns than would a more established company. The rate at which the dividends paid by a company will grow depends not only on the policy with regard to retention but also on the profitability of the projects in which the funds are invested.

A financial analyst can observe a company's past policy with regard to retentions, but would find it difficult to ascertain the rate of return being earned by the company on new investments. An assumption usually made is that the new investments will earn the same rate of return as the present return on equity.

Example 6.2

The management of Fame Electronics, a rapidly growing and profitable private company, is considering applying for a stock market listing. This will provide existing shareholders with an opportunity to sell their shares while allowing the firm to raise the additional funds which will be necessary to finance its planned capital-expenditure programme. The earnings of the firm over the next financial year are expected to be about £8 million, dividends will be limited to £2 million, and £6 million will be reinvested. As It is intended to spend £10 million on new investments next year it is planned to raise £4 million from a new issue of shares. Over the next three years dividends will be limited to 25% of earnings as opportunities to earn above-normal rates of return from new investments are anticipated. No further new issues are planned and it is expected that all investment after next year will be financed from retentions. While the expected rate of return on similar risk shares is about 10%, the management of Fame Electronics anticipate an average rate of return on new investments planned for the next three years of 20%. As competition intensifies it is expected that the return on new projects will fall to 10%. In year four and thereafter it is expected that the firm will continue to grow at above the average rate but new investments are not expected to yield more than 10% per annum and the company plans to revert to 50% payout ratio.

Required:

Ignore taxation.

1 Estimate what the market value of the company should be at the end of year three.
2 What do you consider to be an appropriate market value for the firm today?
3 What proportion of the market value today is due to growth opportunities?
4 Calculate the price/earnings ratio and explain its usefulness and main drawbacks as a valuation model.

Answer

1 We are given sufficient information to be able to estimate the market value of the company using the dividend growth model. We can estimate g for year four and onwards and we are given the market's expected rate of return (10%). We need to calculate the dividend for year four.

	Year			
	1	2	3	4
Earnings	8	10	11.5	13.225
Dividends	2	2.5	2.875	6.6125
Retained earnings	6	7.5	8.625	
New equity	4			
Funds invested	10	7.5	8.625	
Return on new investment (20%)	2	1.5	1.725	

g = retention rate $\times$ expected returns (in future)

$\quad = 0.50 \times 0.10$

$\quad = 0.05$

$$v = \frac{D_4}{i - g} = \frac{6.6125}{0.10 - 0.05} = \text{£}132.25 \text{ million}$$

2 The value today is the discounted sum of the dividends for the next three years and the value at the beginning of year 4 (end year 3)

$$v = \frac{2}{(1.10)} + \frac{2.5}{(1.10)^2} + \frac{2.875}{(1.10)^3} + \frac{132.25}{(1.10)^3}$$

$$= \text{£}105.41 \text{ million}$$

3 Without growth opportunities the company is worth the present value of its current dividends continuing in perpetuity.

$$v = \frac{2}{0.10} = 200 \text{ million}$$

This is 20% of the value with growth. 80% of the price today is due to growth opportunity.

4 The price/earnings ratio is approximately 13 to 1 (i.e. $\frac{105.41}{8}$).

Graham *et al.* [4] wrote in 1962 that the 'predominant role of dividends has found full reflection in a generally accepted theory of investment value which states that a common stock is worth the sum of all the dividends to be paid on it in the future, each discounted to its present worth'.

Not all would agree with the view that dividends have a predominant role in influencing share price. A great deal of theoretical and empirical work over the last 50 years has been concerned with the precise effect of a company's dividend policy on its share price. The research that has been undertaken has found that no single factor explains the level of share price across all companies for all periods of time. In some time periods dividends seem to dominate the market's thinking; in other periods the market seems to be absorbed with earning figures. In some companies the shareholders are more interested in dividends than retained earnings; in other companies the position is reversed. Dividend policy will be discussed in Chapter 14. There is a considerable controversy on the subject. An important proposition, put forward by Modigliani and Miller [5], is that if certain assumptions are made, the dividends decision is irrelevant in determining the share price. This will be considered in Chapter 14.

6.3 EARNINGS PER SHARE AND VALUATION

Probably the most popular approach to valuing a share is by use of the price-to-earnings ratio. This is the earnings multiplier approach, where today's earnings per share are multiplied by a factor which takes into account growth expectations. Investors will be willing to pay a price which is a higher multiple of today's earnings per share for a fast-growing company than for a slow-growth company. Consequently a high price-to-earnings ratio indicates that the market thinks that the company has good growth prospects.

When valuing the shares of a particular company the investor has to begin by making an assessment of what he or she considers to be the appropriate price-to-earnings ratio. The EPS is then multiplied by the appropriate price-to-earnings ratio to arrive at a value. It is, however, not always easy to decide on an appropriate ratio. If the mid price-to-earnings ratio for an industry is taken as the benchmark, we have to be careful to allow for any individual company differences due to such factors as diversification.

The ratio can be used to decide whether a share is undervalued or overvalued. For example, if the appropriate price-to-earnings ratio for a company is assessed as 15:1 and the actual ratio for the company at the current price is 12:1, then the share is being undervalued. The share would have to rise in price by 25% before what is considered the appropriate price-to-earnings (PE) level would be reached.

The example below illustrates the impact of growth expectation on PE ratios.

Example 6.3

Two companies currently have similar dividends per share, £0.50, and similar earnings per share, £1.00. It is thought by the market that one company, ABC, will experience an 8% per annum perpetual growth in dividends and earnings, whereas the other company, XYZ, will only grow at 3% per annum. The risk-adjusted required rate of return for companies similar in nature to ABC and XYZ is 12%.

(i) What are the values of a share in ABC and a share in XYZ?

(ii) What is the price-to-earnings ratio of the two companies?

Answer

(i) $ABC = \dfrac{D_1}{i-g} = \dfrac{0.50 \times 1.08}{0.12 - 0.08} = £13.50$

$XYZ = \dfrac{0.50 \times 1.03}{0.12 - 0.03} = £5.66$

(ii) PE ratio of $ABC = \dfrac{13.50}{1} = 13.5$

PE ratio of $XYZ = \dfrac{5.66}{1} = 5.7$

It can be seen that the company with the higher PE ratio is the expected higher-growth company.

One question that arises is whether the earnings which are used in the calculation should be the last actual earnings figures recorded or some 'normalized' earnings.

The apparent simplicity of the price/earnings ratio approach should not lead to false confidence in its accuracy. It is undoubtedly an easy approach and so not expensive in terms of time and effort, but this says nothing about its accuracy. The method is computationally easier than the PV of dividends approach, but it involves just as many assumptions. Its simplicity merely hides the complexity of the problem.

The dividend valuation model can be reconciled with the price-to-earnings approach. If

$$P_0 = \frac{D_1}{i-g}$$

and K is the payout ratio and E_1 is the expected earnings per share for the current year, then

$$P_0 = \frac{KE_1}{i-g}$$

and so

$$\frac{P_0}{E_1} = \frac{K}{i-g}$$

P_0/E_1 is the price-to earnings ratio based on the expected earnings per share for the current year. The formula emphasizes that expected growth is a key factor in determining the ratio: the higher is g, the greater is the price-to-earnings ratio. To illustrate the use of the equation, let $D_1 = £1$, $K = 0.4$, $i = 15\%$ and $g = 10\%$. Then

$$P_0 = \frac{1}{0.15 - 0.10} = 20$$

$$\frac{P_0}{E_1} = \frac{0.40}{0.15 - 0.10} = 8$$

and

$$E_1 = 2.5$$

If the expected growth rate of the company is 13% then

$$\frac{P_0}{E_1} = \frac{0.40}{0.15 - 0.13} = 20$$

and the price of the share is

$$P_0 = \frac{1}{0.15 - 0.13} = 50$$

Unfortunately the formula cannot be used if $g > i$.

Using the above it is possible to work out what earnings growth assumptions are built into the current price of any share. A similar exercise can be carried out to estimate the dividend growth assumption built into the share price. However, in both methods it is assumed that the price is basically determined by a single variable, either dividends or earnings growth. But other variables do influence the ratio.

6.4 SHARE PRICE AND CASH FLOW

One approach to valuing a company's equity share is to determine what is considered to be an appropriate relationship between share price and operating cash flow. This ratio is sometimes used as an alternative to the price/earnings ratio. A commentary in the *Financial Times* on the price being offered by a Dutch company for TNT, the express mail and logistics company, made the point that the price offered was 11 times the operating cash flow and 19 times operating profits.

UK companies are required to produce annual 'group cash-flow statements'. The operating cash flow figure represents the cash actually generated from normal business activities. It is a cash figure not distorted by depreciation figures and provisions. It is cash generated before deduction of interest payments and of taxation and investment expenditure. It ignores the share of profits of associates.

It is possible to criticize valuations based on accounting earnings figures because earnings are based on many conventions and assumptions. Also it is possible for the management of a company to smooth earnings figures over time and to create a good impression for at least a short period of time. These problems were considered in Chapter 2. To base valuations of shares of companies on earnings can therefore be worrying.

A study in the USA by Kaplan and Roll [6] has indicated that cash flows had more of an impact on a company's share valuation than did reported earnings. They found that a change in accounting reporting practice which affected reported earnings of companies but did not affect their cash flow did not have a lasting effect on share prices. The accounting change initially affected prices, but the change did not fool the market for long and the temporary alteration in value of the shares soon disappeared.

Lee and Lawson [7] have been strong advocates in the UK of cash-flow accounting. They believe that it is much more relevant to the valuation of a company's equity shares than profits based on historical cost figures. Cash-flow figures are supposed to be free from the creative accounting problems that can affect earnings figures.

6.5 THE CAPITAL-ASSET PRICING MODEL AND SHARE VALUES

The dividend model described above is based on a discount rate, which we refer to as the 'market capitalization rate' on shares in the risk class being considered. It is here that we can make use of the CAPM which should assist us in obtaining the correct discount rate. The CAPM gives insights not only into problems of calculating the cost of capital, but also into problems of valuing securities.

The dividend model so far described has not explicitly considered risk. Risk is the possibility that the actual returns, say the actual dividends, will deviate from the expected dividends. In the real world there is uncertainty, and this has to be allowed for in any analysis. With some companies there is a greater risk, a greater possibility that actual outcomes will differ from expectations, than there is with other companies. The CAPM shows one way in which risk can be accommodated in financial analysis. Its particular contribution is that it shows that in market equilibrium a share will be expected to provide a return which is commensurate with its unavoidable risk.

The model explains that risk can be broken down into two components, namely systematic risk and unsystematic risk. The former type of risk represents that which arises because of underlying movements in the economy, in the overall level of share prices. This risk cannot be diversified away by an investor holding the securities of more and more companies. This is the unavoidable risk and is measured by what is known as the 'beta factor'. It is the risk that has to be taken into account when valuing shares.

Unsystematic risk, however, arises from movements in a particular company's returns not associated with general market movements. This arises because of individual company characteristics, and an investor can avoid this type of risk by diversifying his or her shareholdings over a large number of companies.

The impact of this model on investment theory – and so on share price evaluation – has been considerable. The model will be fully discussed in Chapter 11.

If we assume that unsystematic risk is diversified away by the investor, the model states that the expected return on an asset j is

$$\overline{R}_j = R_f + \beta_j(\overline{R}_m - R_f)$$

where R_f is the risk-free rate of return, β_j is the sensitivity of the asset's return to that of a market portfolio, $\overline{R}_m$ is the expected return from holding the market portfolio, and $\overline{R}_j$ is the expected return on asset j.

The way in which this model can be used in share evaluation is that it enables us to determine the relevant discount rate to use in discounting expected returns to arrive at the PV. In Section 6.2 we dealt with the model that relates the market value of a share to the discounted sum of future dividends. The dividends were discounted at a rate i which we described as the market capitalization rate of shares of the class being considered. In fact i equals $\overline{R}_j$. The CAPM enables us to calculate this capitalization rate.

The market price of a share should never fall below the net asset value per share. If this was to happen it would be in the shareholders' interests if the company was liquidated, the assets sold and the proceeds divided amongst the shareholders.

The above statement is based on the liquidation value of the assets less debts. The liquidation value is the price that could be obtained if assets are sold. This is not necessarily the same as the 'book' value of assets. The balance sheet for a company values assets on a mix of bases: some may be valued at original cost less depreciation, others at revalued amounts but at a variety of dates. In Chapter 2 Tobin's Q measure was introduced. This is a ratio of the market price of a company to its net replacement asset value. When this ratio is close to unity or the net asset value is greater than the sum of share and bond valuation the company could be an attractive takeover target.

The point has already been made that values appearing in a company's balance sheet are not, in many industries, a good indicator of the value of the company. Lev [8] has shown that in the USA the acquisition price of companies taken over was on average 4.39 times the book value.

The accounting values are 'relatively informative' in stable industries such as banking, public utilities, oil, paper and department store companies. With banks, for example, the mean ratios of acquisition price to book values of acquired companies was just over 2.00; with department stores it was 2.50. In contrast, in industries that are more dependent on the 'intellectual skills' of employees than on physical assets, the ratio can be very high. Of course, with an acquisition often the acquiring company is forced to pay a high price but the ratios do indicate the limited usefulness of the price to book value per share ratio. The differences arise, of course, because company balance sheets do not usually reflect the value of brands or of the people employed. In some industries it is people and their ideas that influence the value of a company rather than the physical assets being employed.

6.7 PRICING NEW ISSUES

The price at which a new issue of shares is offered to investors through a stock market is based mainly on the price and yields on comparable issues already being traded. It is usually settled in negotiations between the company, the issuing house and the broker. The price in an offer for sale to the public must appear attractive to the underwriters and also, of course, to the public. In a placing, the price must seem attractive to the clients of the brokers and issuing house who are subscribing for the shares. Usually the issuing house would like to see the development of a small premium on the issue price which occurs when the market price settles a little above the issue price. This would give them and their clients a small profit in return for taking up the issue.

In order to make a new issue attractive to investors, the yields offered are usually a little above that of similar traded securities. Investors must be attracted to purchase the new shares in preference to existing securities. If, in a placing, the shares cannot be sold at the desired price, the vendors (the selling shareholders) must accept a lower price or the issue must be abandoned. Either way, it will be embarrassing, since part of the costs will already have been incurred.

Before an issue is made to the public, it is usual to insure against the risk of inadequate subscription by having the issue underwritten.

Although the underwriting or placing of the shares assures the company or the share owners of a certain level proceeds from the issue, this is no guarantee that the issue will be a success. To set the price so high that the issue is left with the underwriters is not necessarily of benefit to the company or the share owners. The latter may obtain the benefit of a high price for their shares in the short run, but the price of the shares is likely to remain weak for a considerable time after the issue. This will, of course, affect the value of any shares still held by the original shareholders and may adversely affect the company's ability to raise money even after the underwriters have succeeded in disposing of their own holdings.

In determining the asking price the company's broker will consider first the market rating of similar companies already quoted, taking into account their relative financial strength, profit record and the future prospects as far as it is possible to judge them. A company may have a magnificent profit record, but if the profit figures or reports recently issued by similar companies indicate a general downturn in profits, this will be an important consideration.

Perhaps the most important factor in determining the flotation price for a company's shares is the forecast of its level of maintainable profits. Such profits are a function of the level of profits on existing assets and the profits expected on any new investment to be financed with the proceeds or part of the proceeds of the new issue. If the shares being sold to the market are those belonging to the existing shareholders of the company, then the company will not receive any increase in its funds; if the shares are new, then the receipts from the sale of these will add to the funds of the company. The profit forecast therefore depends on the use to which the proceeds of the share flotation are to be assigned, with any proceeds intended for new investment adding to the level of maintainable profits.

A simple example will illustrate the issues to be considered when deciding upon a price. Assume a company coming to the market for the first time wishes to raise £500 000. It will be able to maintain profits of £50 000 per annum. (The scale of the amount to be raised does not matter.)

Assume that the forecast net profits of a company are £50 000, after financing a new investment. The company can comfortably rely on maintaining profits at this level and providing a normal rate of profit growth. The policy makers agree that a certain amount of money, in this case say £500 000, is needed, part of which would be used to finance the investment. A crucial decision will involve two variables: the number of shares to be issued, and their price. In theory the desired sum could be raised by many combinations of numbers of shares and share price. In practice, however, there are tacit limits to the range of prices considered appropriate for the shares. There is a feeling, which has only limited logical basis, that below a certain price a new share is too cheap, and above a certain price a new share is too dear. This is of necessity extremely arbitrary.

This ideal price range only applies to a new company coming on to the market. A company that is already traded in the market will issue its shares at or near its existing market price, and so, knowing both the share price and the amount of capital that it wishes to raise, it merely needs to divide the one into the other to determine the number of shares it should issue.

We continue with the example of a company coming to the market for the first time. As a result of the investment, total net profits are expected to be £50 000. If 1 000 000 shares are issued, this will give an EPS of £0.05. If companies in the same risk class have shares with a price-to-earnings ratio of 10:1, the asking price for the new issue could be set at about £0.50 per share. An issue at this price might be feasible, but let us assume that it only just qualifies for the 'ideal' price range. An issue of 500 000 shares would give net EPS of £0.10; with the required price-to-earnings ratio of 10:1, the asking price would be £1.

In both the above circumstances the company would obtain the required amount of funds, £500 000. If, however, a suitable price-to-earnings ratio was only 8:1, the share price in the first case would be only £0.40 and the issue of 1 000 000 shares would realize only £400 000. By issuing more shares the company could still not obtain the £500 000. If 1 250 000 were issued, the net EPS would be £0.04, the share price would be £0.32 and only about £400 000 would be raised. The total amount of funds that can be raised is simply the expected total earnings multiplied by the price-to-earnings ratio. The only way in which the company could hope to raise £500 000 of equity finance, with expected earnings of £50 000 and a price-to-earnings ratio of 8:1, is by disguising its future earnings expectations or by attempting to justify a higher price-to-earnings ratio. The effect on existing shareholders of the price at which new shares are issued is discussed in the sections on rights issues and capital gearing.

The denomination of the shares needs to be considered further. Dividend rates were once expressed in terms of a percentage of the nominal value of a share, and it was considered bad public relations, and certainly embarrassing in trade union negotiations, to declare a dividend of, say, 100% of nominal value. If in the above example 500 000 shares are issued, EPS will be £0.10. If a gross dividend of approximately £0.06 could be paid for a share selling at the price of £1, this gives a gross dividend yield of 6%, which has to be compared with the current level of dividend yields. If the par (nominal) value of the share were set at, say, £0.75, this would give a dividend of 8% of par. If par were set at £0.10, the dividend rate would be 60%, which might give cause for alarm. In fact, the practice has grown of declaring dividends as simply a sum of money per share.

In summary, management has to ascertain

1 the maintainable level of profits;
2 the desired price-to-earnings ratio;
3 the desired dividend cover;
4 the desired dividend yield.

Given all the relevant information on these matters and knowledge of share prices of similar types of company, an asking price for the new shares can be determined. One of the difficulties, here as elsewhere in finance, is the selection of comparable companies that can be used as a guide.

We shall now illustrate an approach to answering questions on the pricing of new issues. The question that follows is taken from a Financial Management paper of the Chartered Association of Certified Accountants.

Example 6.4

At a meeting of the directors of the Alpha Co Ltd, a privately owned company, in May 19X5 the recurrent question is raised as to how the company is going to finance its future growth and at the same time enable the founders of the company to withdraw a substantial part of their investment. A public quotation was discussed in 19X4 but because of the depressed nature of the stock market at that time consideration was deferred. Although the matter is not of immediate urgency the chairman of the company, one of the founders, produces the following information which he has recently obtained from a firm of financial analysts in respect of two publicly quoted companies, Beta and Gamma, which are similar to Alpha Ltd in respect of size, asset composition, financial structure and product mix:

			Beta	Gamma
19X4	Earnings per share		£1.50	£2.50
19X0–4	Average earnings per share		£1.00	£2.00
19X4	Average market price per share		£9.00	£20.00
19X4	Dividends per share		£0.75	£1.25
19X0–4	Average dividends per share		£0.60	£1.20
19X4	Average book value per share		£9.00	£18.00

On the basis of this information the chairman asks what you think Alpha Ltd was worth in 19X4. The only information you have available at the meeting in respect of Alpha Ltd is the final accounts for 19X4 which disclose the following:

Alpha Ltd

Share capital (no variation for 8 years)	100 000 ordinary £1 shares
Post-tax earnings	£400 000
Gross dividends	£100 000
Book value	£3 500 000

From memory you think that the post-tax earnings and gross dividends for 19X4 were at least one-third higher than the average of the previous five years.

Making *full* use of the information above: answer the managing director's question.

Suggested solution

There are three sets of ratios that can be used to give guidance on the appropriate price to ask for the Alpha shares. One is EPS, the second is dividends per share and the third is the asset value per share. We begin with earnings. The EPS of Alpha in 19X4 was £4.00 (i.e. £400 000/100 000). The post-tax earnings in 19X4 were one-third higher than the average of the previous five years. Therefore the average net EPS over the previous five years was £3.00.

The price-to-earnings ratio in 19X4 was 6:1 (i.e. £9:£1.50) for Beta and 8:1 (i.e. £20:£2.50) for Gamma. If one takes the mid-point of these two price-to-earnings ratios, i.e. 7:1, then such a multiple applied to the EPS of £4.00 for Alpha in 19X4 would give a market price of £28. The EPS of Alpha has increased over the last few years, as has been the case for the other two companies.

The gross dividend per share of Alpha in 19X4, was £1 (i.e. £100 000/100 000) and the average for the previous five years was £0.75 (i.e. £75 000/100 000). The dividend yield of Beta in 19X4 was 8.3% (i.e. (£0.75/£9.00) × 100) and the dividend yield of Gamma was 6.3% (i.e. (£1.25/£20.00) × 100). Taking a figure in the middle of these two as one acceptable to the market gives a suggested price for Alpha shares of approximately £13.70, i.e.

$$\frac{\text{£1}}{\text{share price}} \times 100 = 7.3\%$$

This is a much lower value than that obtained based on the price-to-earnings ratio. One reason is that Alpha has appeared to pursue a low-payout policy. In 19X4 they only distributed a quarter of their post-tax earnings to shareholders, whereas both Gamma and Beta distributed half of their available earnings to shareholders. If Alpha announced when going public that they planned to increase their payout ratio it may reduce the fears on dividends of certain investors. Of course, not all investors are interested in high dividends; those investors who have high marginal tax rates may prefer the company to retain the profits and, as a result, for the share price to appreciate. Such shareholders, upon selling their shares, would only be taxed on the increase in their wealth at the capital gains tax rate. Many institutional shareholders like dividends as they have tax advantages, and so it would be as well for Alpha to make some announcement about future dividends if it wished to appeal to the institutional shareholder.

The final set of comparative figures relates to the book values per share. These are £35 for Alpha, £9 for Beta and £18 for Gamma. The ratio of the share price to the book value is 1.00 for Beta and 1.10 for Gamma. The same multiple for Alpha would give a price of approximately £35. This measure is, however, the least important and the least reliable of the three being considered.

On balance it seems that a price in the region of £28 per share would seem the most appropriate, i.e. with the information given in the question. Price-to-earnings ratios move about over time and the issue has to be priced to have appeal at the time of issue. In the stock market conditions of 19X5 and 19X6 a different price-to-earnings multiple might be appropriate.

Underpricing of new issues (the winners' curse)

There is a theory and much empirical evidence that indicates that initial public offerings are underpriced. The theory is referred to as the 'winners' curse'.

The theory is based on the well-accepted assumption that there are two groups of investors, the informed and the uninformed. The former group have information about the companies who are making their first public offering that is not available to the latter group. This informed group only subscribe to an 'initial public offering' when they expect the market price after the issue to exceed the offer price.

In contrast, the uninformed investor is initially tempted to subscribe to all initial public offers. This means that if the actual offer price is above its intrinsic value only the uninformed investors will subscribe. They will finish up holding all the shares. This is referred to as the 'winners' curse'. Over time the uninformed investors when they subscribe to new issues will learn what is happening to them and adjust their investment policies. If companies continue to overprice the new issues, the uninformed investor will have learned to stay out of the new issues market. The new issues therefore become undersubscribed. Over time new issuers and those that advise them learn that to overprice does not benefit them.

In contrast, if the new issue is underpriced, both groups of investors subscribe. Therefore the issue is fully subscribed or oversubscribed. This is one explanation of why most initial public offerings are underpriced.

The model makes a number of assumptions. If an issue is underpriced it is the company or rather the existing shareholders of the company who lose. An important question is whether or not the winners' curse model which is applicable to the new-issues market in general should worry an individual company? Why should an individual company underprice its initial public offering and therefore lose funds it could have raised, just for the benefit of the new-issues market in general? One answer to this question is that it is investment bankers that advise companies on the price of new issues and it is in the bankers' interests to consider the new-issues market in general. Each investment banker will be involved with many new issues. It will be in the bankers' interest therefore to advise on an initial offer price for a particular company which is below the intrinsic value of that share. This underpricing is in the interest of an active new-issues market in general, even though not in the interests of individual companies.

There is much evidence that initial public offerings are underpriced. The above theory offers an explanation as to why this underpricing occurs. Not all writers on the subject of finance accept the theory.

6.8 VALUATION OF A COMPANY

The above analysis has been concerned with valuing a single share. When an investor is buying a single share he or she is buying a stream of future dividends. As a minority shareholder the investor has no influence over the dividend decision. When an investor or another company buys all or, in fact a large enough block of shares to be able to exercise control over the company, again it is a stream of future cash flows that is being purchased. However, this time the investor is in a position to influence the level of these future cash flows. The theory of valuation is the same, namely the present value of future cash flows, but in the latter case the investor may be willing to pay more for each share purchased because with the purchase comes control.

The valuation of a company can be described as 'sophisticated guesswork': it is inevitably an inexact exercise. It is based largely on estimates. There are a number of recognized techniques for arriving at a valuation, all of which can lead to different answers. The final price agreed for the purchase is, of course, the result of negotiation and bargaining; all the techniques can do is provide a framework for discussion. The techniques supply the upper and lower valuations within which the price will eventually be fixed.

An essential preliminary to any purchase or merger negotiation is the valuation of the company to be acquired. This valuation can be based on cash flow, earnings or assets, or on some combination of the three. It is obviously desirable to value the intended purchase by a number of different methods to obtain a range of possible values which will be important in the negotiations. There are a number of standard approaches to the valuation problem, some of which will be explained here.

The value which a company may initially attach to another company is not always the final price at which the purchase is made. If the directors of the company to be purchased resist the initial offer, they can usually obtain better terms for shareholders.

It must not be thought that valuation problems only arise at the time that a business is to be purchased. It may be that a private company needs to be valued for tax purposes. It should also be appreciated that, although valuation disagreements do arise in connection with mergers and takeovers, particularly the well-publicized contested mergers and takeovers, not all acquisitions involve major valuation problems. It is possible to purchase a private company or a small public company simply as a result of amicable negotiations.

Present value of future receipts/operating cash flows

Theoretically the valuation procedure is straightforward. The purchasing company is buying a stream of future returns. The purchaser is buying the difference between its own cash flow before the acquisition and the combined companies' cash flow after the acquisition. The difference needs to be estimated, discounted and summed up to give its PV. The PV of the receipts from the purchase which can be expressed mathematically as

$$PVR = \frac{C}{i}\left[1 - \frac{1}{(1+i)^n}\right]$$

where PVR is the PV of returns, C is the increase in the annual cash flow of the purchasing company as a result of the acquisition, i is the discount factor and n is the number of years.

As an example, assume that the result of purchasing a company will be to increase the annual cash flow by £1000, the appropriate discount rate is 10% and the number of years over which the returns will be taken into account is 50. The value of the acquisition is therefore

$$\frac{1000}{0.10}\left[1 - \frac{1}{(1.10)^{50}}\right] = £9915$$

The purchasing company should be willing to pay up to £9915 for this acquisition, but, given the forecasts, no higher price can be justified.

The approach can be made more realistic by allowing for an annual growth in the cash flow. As a second example, assume that the initial increase in cash flow is £1000 and that this is expected to increase by 4% per annum; the value then is £17 333. The formula that should be used in this situation where the cash flow is growing at a compound rate of g% per annum is

$$\frac{\text{initial increase in cash flow } (1+g)}{i - g}$$

With super growth for four years and then a constant growth at 4%, the equation is:

$$= \frac{1000}{(1.10)} + \frac{1200}{(1.10)^2} + \frac{1500}{(1.10)^3} + \frac{1900}{(1.10)^4} + \frac{2600}{(1.10)^5} + \frac{2600(1.04)}{(1.10)^6} + \dots$$
$$+ \frac{2600(1.04)^{45}}{(1.10)^{50}} = £21\,250$$

The difficulties in the practical application of the approach are as follows:

1 forecasting future annual cash flows;
2 the number of years' cash flows on which the calculation will be based;
3 the appropriate discount rate.

It is not necessary to provide a detailed forecast for many years into the future; either the terminal value can be estimated for some future date, or the cash flows beyond a certain date can be assumed to grow at a constant rate. However, five-year forecasts should not be beyond any company. The budgeting and planning processes of companies are often expressed, at least in part, over five-year periods.

The CAPM has already been discussed at various points in the book and will not now be covered again. The point that is being made is that when valuing a company the effect of the acquisition on the risks of the acquirer needs to be taken into account. The effect can be quantified. A reduction in risk means that the cost of capital is reduced. Investors and bankers may be willing to provide funds at a lower cost after the acquisition than before. The way in which this can be allowed for in calculating the value of the company to be purchased is, with the PV approach, to discount the future cash flow at a lower cost of capital than that being used by the acquiring company before the attempted acquisition. With the price-to-earnings approach the way in which it would be allowed for would be to use a higher multiple to allow for the fact that the market will reassess the company after the acquisition.

Values based on existing share price

It has been found in practice that not all firms actually use the discounted cash flow (DCF) approach when it comes to valuing a company for takeover or merger purposes. This could be because the acquisition decision is a particularly complicated form of investment decision or because the PV techniques them-selves have inherent weaknesses.

If a company to be taken over has an existing market value, i.e. it is a quoted company, then the acquirer will have to pay a price somewhere in the region of this market figure. If only a few changes in the future policy of the acquired company are to be expected, then shareholders and investors would have little reason to expect a much higher valuation than that based on the existing price. If, however, substantial changes are expected to occur in the cash flow or in the financial policies of the acquired company, or if synergy will affect the cash flow, then a considerable premium may well have to be paid above the existing market price.

There are a number of reasons why the market may wish to increase its valua-tion of the company to be acquired above the level existing before the suitor appeared on the scene. These reasons include economies of scale, monopoly strength, changes in investment policies, better management, sale of surplus assets, lower taxes and better information. Equally important is the fact that the merger may reduce the systematic risk of the cash flows of the two companies. There may also be changes in financial policies such as borrowing or dividend policies.

The valuation exercise from the acquiring company's point of view is to estimate the maximum purchase price that they would be willing to pay in order to obtain the company. This is the price that they would pay which would leave their shareholders no worse off after the acquisition than they were before.

If we assume efficient capital markets, then the payment of a premium above the market price in order to purchase a company can be justified only if the acquirer is going to change the growth expectations of the acquired company or alter the risk profile of the combined operations.

Multiple of annual revenue

One question that can be asked is, how do you value a loss-making company? If the company is never expected to make profits then its value is simply the realizable value of its assets less its liabilities. Some adjustment may need to be made in respect of taxation.

If the company is expected to make profits in the future one way to value it would be based on the present value of the future profits or dividends. One loss-making company, Colt Telecommunications, in 1997 was floated on the London Stock Exchange and on NASDAQ (by means of ADRs); see Section 7.4. The company was at that time three years old and had not yet made profits. The company shares were sold at a price which was a multiple of eight times the current annual revenues.

The financial press commented on the method of valuing the company shares and expressed the view that this was a high valuation, but that the company was expected to grow. The money raised by the sale of new shares was to be used to fund planned expansion.

Valuation by capitalizing earnings

One of the simplest methods of assessing the value of a company is to use some predetermined notion of the rate of return that an investor would expect on this particular type of investment, and then, having decided on the earnings of the company, to calculate the capital sum that would result in such a rate of return. The steps used in this approach are as follows.

1. Select a past period for investigation.
2. Estimate the maintainable profits of the company to be acquired, after making any necessary adjustments for such factors as existing levels of directors' remuneration, depreciation or bad debts. It is important to allow for any increased profit potential which may develop with improved management or the possible synergy from the combined operations.
3. Establish the acceptable normal rate of return on capital invested in a similar type of company, allowing for the industry effect, the size of company and the level of capital gearing.
4. Capitalize maintainable profits at a rate established as the acceptable rate of return. If, for example, £10 000 is the maintainable earnings after corporation tax and the normal rate of return in such companies is 8%, then a purchase price of £125 000 would be justified because £10 000/0.08 = £125 000.

The problem with this type of approach is that the estimate of earnings is usually based on historical earnings. Whether this is a straight average of the past five years' earnings or some weighted average attaching greater importance to earnings in more recent years, it is still based on past performance.

Although the estimates are based on established figures, which is important in negotiation, the extent to which the past can assist in determining maintainable future profits is still a debated point.

Price-to-earnings ratio
The capitalized earnings approach is sometimes expressed in a slightly different way. To capitalize earnings at 8% is in fact to multiply the earnings by 12.5. The popular stock market ratio of price to earnings does exactly this – multiplies earnings by some factor. Capitalizing earnings at 8% is exactly the same as adopting a price-to-earnings ratio for the purchase of a company of 12.5.

The price-to-earnings ratio is normally thought of as the multiple of the earnings that an investor would pay for a small number of shares in a company. If the total shares of a company are being purchased, the market price-to-earnings ratio may have to be adjusted. A new management now has control of the assets, and so the earnings and growth potential could well change. Nevertheless, it is not uncommon to hear managers talking in terms of being willing to purchase a company for ten to twelve times its earnings. This is identical with looking for an initial earnings yield of somewhere between 8.33% and 10%.

Asset value

As an alternative to the earnings approach, it could be argued that the purchaser is acquiring a set of assets. It is not the future earnings that the purchasing company is buying, but a collection of assets which have to be managed to achieve the earnings.

If the purchased company is to continue with its existing type of business, the earnings basis would seem more relevant for valuation than the assets basis. If, however, the whole of the purchased company is to be sold, or parts of the purchased company are to be sold, then the realizable value of the assets is important. Earlier it was stated that the existing price of the company's shares should provide a minimum level for valuation purposes. However, it is possible that the price of a share of the company is lower than the net asset value per share. In this case the asset value per share could set the lowest valuation level.

A company is in a bad way if the share price is below the net asset value per share. If the net assets per share, based on balance sheet values, are close to the values that could be realized on the liquidation of the assets, the directors, in the best interests of the shareholders, should liquidate the company and sell off the assets. One of the constraints imposed on management is to ensure that their share price is above the asset value per share. This is the q ratio referred to in the chapter on mergers and acquisitions and in Chapter 2.

Realizable values

The value of the assets as they appear in a balance sheet is not necessarily their liquidation value or realizable value; this would have to be determined by a separate assessment of each asset. The saleable value of property, for example, may be higher with vacant possession than when the property is occupied; once free for some other use, its value might well have increased above that assigned to it on the balance sheet.

Assets are not necessarily shown in balance sheets at their current market values. In fact they very rarely are. They are shown at a mixture of values, with some at the original cost of purchase and others revalued but possibly at different dates. In the UK the reality is that we have a system of selective revaluation, with the assets to be revalued and the dates when this will take place being at the discretion of the directors of the company. Information about significant differences between the values shown in the balance sheet and current market values should be shown in the notes to the financial accounts.

A company should be consistent. This means it should treat all assets within a certain class in a similar way. All assets within a class should be either at historical cost or be revalued at a similar date. Assets which should be revalued at regular intervals include the following classification:

- property (excluding fixed assets specific to the business);
- quoted investments;
- inventory of a commodity nature.

When assets are revalued they should be valued by a qualified valuer.

Unfortunately with the vast majority of companies it is not possible to rely on the asset values shown in the balance sheet to obtain a current value of the business. The net assets and the capital-employed figures of a company are often used in financial ratios, but because of the mixture of valuation methods employed the resulting figures can be suspect.

This, then, is an alternative method of valuing a company: the determination of the value to the purchaser of all the assets. If a price has to be paid for the company above the value of the sum of assets, then an amount has been paid for goodwill. This is where the selling company receives a reward for any above-average performance, for the above-average ability of its managers or for its advantageous market position. Only if a company is to be purchased and its assets liquidated would this asset valuation be the sole criterion for determining valuation. Normally a potential purchaser would consider both the earnings possibilities and the underlying asset values.

Berliner method

The Berliner method is a technique for valuing a company which takes into account both the earnings and the assets of the company to be purchased. The steps involved are as follows.

1 Select a past period for investigation.
2 Estimate the maintainable profits.
3 Determine the acceptable rate of return to an investor on a similar investment.
4 Capitalize the maintainable profits at the rate established in 3. It will be noticed that the procedure so far is exactly similar to that used under a capitalization of earnings.
5 Value the net tangible assets on a going-concern basis.
6 Take the average of the value established at 4 and the value at 5 – the mean of the earnings valuation and the asset valuation.

Clearly, this approach attempts to combine both bases of valuation; not surprisingly, all the difficulties that apply to the two methods separately apply in conjunction here. The averaging of the two methods is not inspired by any particular theory; it is simply a compromise which may provide a practical solution if the bargaining parties cannot agree on the basis of valuation.

Super-profit approach

The final method to be described is similar to the last, but is more widely known and used. The idea behind it is that there is a normal rate of return that can be earned on assets of a certain type, but over a certain number of years it may be possible to earn profits in excess of this normal level. The purchaser will buy in addition to the normalized value of the assets a number of years' super-profits.

The procedure is as follows.

1 Value the net assets of the business on a going-concern basis.
2 Establish an acceptable rate of return on assets of this type.
3 Find the annual profits that would be assumed to result from the use of the assets so as to earn the rate established in 2.
4, Estimate the profits that can be expected to be earned by the business over the next few years.
5 Deduct the acceptable profit figure in 3 from the estimated profits in 4. If the estimate is higher the difference can be regarded as super-profit.
6 Multiply the super-profits by a factor to be agreed – say 3 or 5 – to represent the number of years' super-profits being purchased.
7 The value of the business is 1 plus 6, i.e. the value of the net assets plus, say, five years' purchase of super-profits.

As an example, assume that the net assets of the business are valued at £8000 and the normal rate of return on such an investment is 10%. From step 3 the procedure would be as follows.

3   A 10% return on £8000 results in profits of £800.
4   The profits are estimated as being £1100 for the next few years.
5   The difference between the estimate and the acceptable level is £300.
6   It is agreed to purchase five years' super-profits.
7   The value of the company is £9500 comprising net assets valued at £8000 plus £1500 super-profits (5 × £300).

The value of the super-profits, ultimately the difference between the purchase price and the value of the assets acquired, would be entered in the accounts as goodwill.

The number of years' super-profits to be purchased would, of course, depend on negotiation and the number of years that the purchaser thought the company could maintain the advantageous position. This acknowledges the fact that the above-average level of performance cannot be continued indefinitely – an important point which the earlier simple capitalization of earnings techniques did not explicitly take into account. This is another simple mechanical process that can be employed once the difficult task of estimating profits and deciding on a capitalization rate has been settled. Clearly, the technique would not be greatly complicated if super-profits were also discounted.

Tax consequences

In addition to the asset values and earnings power, which supply the basis for the standard valuation techniques, there are certain other factors to be considered which can increase or reduce the value arrived at by the use of a formula. One such factor is the taxation position of the company to be purchased. It can be worthwhile purchasing a company that has been operating at a loss. The accumulated losses can be offset against the future profits to reduce tax commitments. As a simple example, assume that a company has accumulated tax losses of £50 000. Under certain circumstances it would be worth paying up to £16 500 for this company, if the effective corporation tax rate is 33%. This £50 000 can be offset against future taxable profits and the effect will be to reduce the liability of the purchaser for tax by approximately £16 500. The purchased company may also have capital allowances that can be carried forward and used.

However, the losses and capital allowances carried over can only be used by the purchaser against future profits earned from the transferred business. They cannot be used to reduce tax payable on the profits earned in the main business in which the purchasing company is engaged: the business in which it is engaged before and after the acquisition. Where the purchased business is absorbed into the existing business of the successor company, it may be necessary to apportion the total profits, to ascertain the profits against which the losses can be offset. The transfer is not automatic, however; there are certain conditions that have to be satisfied in order that the unused trading losses and capital allowances can be transferred.

Debt position of company to be purchased

The debt position can work in two ways: either adding to the earnings valuation of the purchase or reducing its value.

The liabilities of the company will have to be taken over, and, as these will have to be met either immediately or at the time specified for redemption in the future, allowance must be made for this repayment. The liability is the present value of the future interest payments plus the present value of the future capital repayment.

The existing debt position of the company to be acquired may add to its purchase value if it is at present undergeared. The acquisition of new assets, paid for by the issue of new shares, will alter the capital gearing of the purchasing company. If the newly acquired assets have not already been used to raise loans, the purchasing company can use them as security for a loan. This will enable the purchasing company to obtain cheaper funds than would have been possible without the purchase. The extent of the opportunity for gearing made available by the new acquisition will depend on the method of payment, the existing borrowing of the purchased company and the financial position of the acquired company.

Example 6.5

The board of directors of Oxclose PLC is considering rnaking an offer to purchase Satac Ltd, a private limited company in the same industry. If Satac is purchased it is proposed to continue operating the company as a going concern in the same line of business.

Summarized details from the most recent financial accounts of Oxclose and Satac are shown below:

	Oxclose PLC Balance sheet as at 31 March (£ million)		Satac Ltd Balance sheet as at 31 March (£000)	
Freehold property		33		460
Plant and equipment (net)		58		1310
Stock	29		330	
Debtors	24		290	
Cash	3		20	
Less: Current liabilities	(31)	25	(518)	122
		116		1892
Financed by				
Ordinary shares[a]		35		160
Reserves		43		964
Shareholders' equity		78		1124
Medium-term bank loans		38		768
		116		1892

[a]Oxclose PLC, 50p ordinary shares; Satac Ltd, 25p ordinary shares.

	Oxclose PLC (£ million)		Satac Ltd (£000)	
	Profit after		Profit after	
Year[b]	tax	Dividend	tax	Dividend
$t-5$	14.30	9.01	143	85
$t-4$	15.56	9.80	162	93.5
$t-3$	16.93	10.67	151	93.5
$t-2$	18.42	11.60	175	102.8
$t-1$	20.04	12.62	183	113.1

[b]$t-5$ is five years ago, $t-1$ is the most recent year, etc.

Satac's shares are owned by a small number of private individuals. The company is dominated by its rnanaging director. The managing director would be replaced if the company were purchased by Oxclose.

The freehold property of Satac has not been revalued for several years and is believed to have a market value of £800 000.

The balance-sheet value of plant and equipment is thought to be a fair reflection of its replacement cost, but its value if sold is not likely to exceed £800 000. Approximately £55 000 of stock is obsolete and could only be sold as scrap for £5000.

The ordinary shares of Oxclose are currently trading at 430p ex-dividend. It is estimated that because of difference in size, risk and other factors the required return on equity by shareholders of Satac is approximately 15% higher than the required return on equity of Oxclose's shareholders (i.e. 115% of Oxclose's required return). Both companies are subject to corporate taxation at a rate of 40%.

(a) Prepare estimates of the value of Satac using three different methods of valuation, and advise the board of Oxclose PLC as to the price, or possible range of prices, that it should be prepared to offer to purchase Satac's shares.

(12 marks)

166

(b) Briefly discuss the theoretical and practical problems of the valuation methods that you have chosen. (6 marks)

(c) Discuss the advantages and disadvantages of the various terms that might be offered to the shareholders of a potential 'victim' company in a takeover situation. (7 marks)

(25 marks)

ACCA

Suggested solution

There are a number of approaches to the problem of valuing a company that does not have a share price determined in the market place. These include the following:

1 PV of expected future cash flows;
2 dividend valuation model;
3 relevant price to earnings ratio;
4 earnings growth basis/super-profits;
5 value of net assets.

Theoretically the first of these is superior. Unfortunately in this question (and in many such examination questions) we do not have sufficient information to be able to adopt this approach.

First, we shall estimate using the dividend valuation model. To do this we need to estimate the appropriate cost of equity K_e per Satac. We know the share price of Oxclose and so we can establish K_e for that company:

$$K_e = \frac{D_1}{P} + g$$

We need to estimate the expected next dividend. The current is 18.03p per share (£12.62 million divided by 70 million shares). The growth in dividends is approximately 8.8% per annum, which gives a D_1 of 19.62p. Therefore for Oxclose

$$K_e = \frac{19.62}{430} + 0.088 = 0.1336$$

We are told that the K_e for Satac should be 15% higher than that for Oxclose. This gives a K_e of 15.36%. Therefore for Satac the total value of equity is

$$P = \frac{D_1}{K_e - g}$$

$$= \frac{124\,410}{0.1536 - 0.10} = £2\,321\,000$$

This estimate is based on a growth rate in dividends of 10% per annum. This growth was achieved except in the year $t - 3$, which we shall assume was an extraordinary year.

We now use the price-to-earnings ratio approach. We need to multiply the current earnings of Satac by an appropriate price-to-earnings factor. The only information we are given on price-to-earnings ratios is that for Oxclose. This gives a multiple of

$$\frac{430p}{28.63p} = 15.02$$

This is higher than we would expect for Satac because Satac is smaller, it is not a quoted company and the past earnings growth of Satac has been less. Let us say that a price-to-earnings ratio of 12.1 is appropriate. Then the price of a Satac share would be given by

$$\frac{P}{28.59p} = 12.00$$

$$P = 343p$$

This gives a total price of £2 195 200.

Net assets basis

	Taking replacement cost (£000)
Plant and equipment	1310
Property	800
Stock	280
Debtors	290
Cash	20
Less: Current liabilities	(518)
Bank loan	(768)
	1414

This assets basis makes no allowance for possible goodwill. As can be seen from the examples above the valuation of a business is far from being an accurate exercise. It depends on many estimates, growth in dividends, appropriate price-to-earnings ratios, future cash flows, etc. In the end the price agreed depends on negotiations. The techniques give a base figure from which to negotiate. In this case a price of between £2 200 000 and £2 500 000 would appear reasonable. The assets basis is more appropriate if the acquired company is to be asset-stripped.

6.9 REFERENCES

1   Baumol, W.J. (1963) *The Stock Market and Economic Efficiency*, Fordham University Press, New York.
2   Fama, E.F. (1970) Efficient capital markets: a review of theory and empirical work, *Journal of Finance*, **25**, May: 383–420.
3   Gordon, M. (1959) Dividends, earnings, and financial policy, *Review of Economics and Statistics*, May.
4   Graham, B., Dodd, D.L. and Cottie, S. (1962) *Security Analysis*, 3rd edn, McGraw-Hill, New York.
5   Modigliani, F. and Miller, M.H. (1958) The cost of capital, corporation finance and the theory of investment, *American Economic Review*, June: 261-97.
    Modigliani, F. and Miller, M.H. (1958) The cost of capital, corporation finance and the theory of investment – reply, *American Economic Review*, September: 655–69.
    Modigliani, F. and Miller, M.H. (1963) Corporate income taxes and the cost of capital: a correction, *American Economic Review*, **53**(3): 433–43.
    Modigliani, F. and Miller, M.H. (1966) Some estimates of the cost of capital to the electric utility industry, *American Economic Review*, **56**: 333–91.
6   Kaplan, R.S. and Roll, R. (1972) Investors' evaluation of accounting information: some empirical evidence, *Journal of Business*, April.
7   Lawson, G.H. (1978) The rationale of cash flow accounting, in *Trends in Managerial and Financial Accounting* (ed. C. Van Dem), Martinus Nijhoff, The Hague.
    Lee, T. (1984) *Cash Flow Accounting*, Chapman and Hall, London.
8   Lev, B. (1989) On the usefulness of earnings and earnings research: lessons and directions from two decades of empirical research, *Journal of Accounting Research*.

6.10 FURTHER READING

Copeland, T.E., Koller, T. and Murrin, J. (1990) *Measuring and Managing the Value of Companies*, Wiley.

6.11 PROBLEMS

1   A company's last dividend was £0.50 per share. Dividends are expected to increase by 10% per annum. The expected rate of return on shares in the same risk class is 20%. What is the market value (market price) of an equity share in this company?

2   A company has recently paid a dividend per share of £0.20. The price of the share in the stock market is £4.00. The par value of the share is £1.00, and it had been initially sold to shareholders for £2.00. The company's policy is to increase dividends by 8% per annum.
    What is the cost of equity capital to the company?

3   A company has issued 1 000 000 equity shares each with a nominal value of 25 pence. The dividend of the company over recent years has been

$$t - 5 = 5.0 \text{ pence}$$
$$t - 4 = 5.5 \text{ pence}$$
$$t - 3 = 6.3 \text{ pence}$$
$$t - 2 = 6.3 \text{ pence}$$
$$t - 1 = 7.2 \text{ pence}$$
$$t = 8.0 \text{ pence}$$

The current market price of the share is £1.00 ex-dividend.

Calculate the cost of equity capital for the company.

4 'A share can be perceived as the present value of a future stream of dividends. However, this does not imply that dividend policy affects the value of the share.'

Discuss.

5 Manu PLC, a quoted company, is considering making an offer for the shares of the privately owned Europa PLC. Relevant financial information on the two companies is as follows:

	£000	
	Manu	*Europa*
Land and buildings	7 600	1200
Plant and machinery	8 400	2420
Current assets	7 420	2100
Current liabilities	4 920	1600
Financed by:		
Ordinary shares*	2 000	540
Share premium	6 500	1600
Revenue reserves	5 300	1980
Long-term debt	4 700	—
*Manu 50 pence shares, Europa 25 pence shares		
Turnover	11 000	2400
Profit after taxation	1 400	500
Dividend	600	200
Retained earnings	800	300
Expected growth in dividends	8%	10%
Market price	350 pence	

Additional information:

Some £200 000 of Europa's inventory is in poor condition and could be sold only for an estimated £20 000. £55 000 of debtors have been outstanding for more than six months and it is expected that only 20% will be recovered. Land and buildings have an estimated market value of £2.0 million. Plant and machinery could be sold for £1.2 million although their replacement cost is £2.8 million.

Required:

(a) Use **three** valuation techniques to estimate a value or range of values for the shares of Europa. Europa's cost of equity is estimated to be 20% higher than Manu's cost of equity.

(b) Comment on the different valuations produced by the three methods.

(c) Assess the extent to which the three methods of valuation you have used provide reliable estimates of economic value.

6 A private company which has an existing share capital of 500 000 shares of £0.50 par value is contemplating seeking a public quotation. It estimates that it needs to raise about £500 000. The earnings have been growing at about 10% per annum and for the last year were £100 000. The price-to-earnings ratios of

companies in the same industry vary between 8:1 and 12:1. The company estimates that it could pay a dividend out of last year's earnings of £60 000.

How many shares would you advise the company to issue and at what price? What information additional to that given in the question would you like to have available?

7 STOCK MARKETS

This is a descriptive chapter. The reader should by the time they have studied the chapter be

- knowledgeable about the international aspects of the world's stock markets
- have detailed knowledge of the workings of the London Stock Exchange
- have some knowledge of stock exchanges in other European countries and in emerging countries

7.1 INTRODUCTION

Companies, governments and international organizations issue securities These securities are sold to investors and the money raised is received by the issuer. This is referred to as a *primary market*.

The first-time buyer of the security may wish to sell the security at some time. This first-time buyer sells to another investor. This is known as a sale in the *secondary market*. The cash that is exchanged does not go to the original issuer of the security.

It is an advantage (but not a necessary condition) to have an organization, to help bring into contact the potential buyer and the potential seller of the securities. Such an organization's role is to assist with the exchange of securities. It is commonly called a *stock exchange*. A stock exchange can be a physical place, it can be a system of telephone links, or, as is becoming more common, it can be a network of computers.

A *stock market* is a place where securities can be bought and sold. It can be in a building, a grand special-purpose building to impress investors. The market can be in the open air. There might not be a physical trading area, just a place to meet.

The securities traded in a stock exchange can be conveniently divided into two categories: equity-type securities and debt-type securities. This distinction has, however, become blurred with new types of securities issued that can under certain circumstances be debt and under other circumstances equity. These new types of security are complex capital instruments, sometimes called 'quasi equity' or 'mezzanine' finance.

There are now more stock markets in developing countries and in the newly industrialized countries than in the older developed countries. The term 'emerging stock markets' is an expression used to refer to the markets in the developing countries, although a few of these markets have existed for a long time (the market in Bombay was established in the nineteenth century).

The major stimulus to the creation of such emerging markets came in the 1980s. With political opinions moving away from a belief in planning as a means of achieving economic growth to a belief in the advantages of the market place, so stock markets were a natural development. The World Bank encourages the creation of such markets. Developing countries could see the success of the stock markets in such countries as Hong Kong, Singapore, Malaysia and South Korea and hoped to be able to repeat the success.

7.2 THE GLOBAL EQUITY MARKET

The global market in equity shares was slower to develop than the global market in bonds. It is also less obvious in that one does not hear or read about Euro-equities or an Asian equity market as often as a Eurobond market or an Asian dollar market. It is also different in that the equity shares concerned in cross-border trading are listed on national markets and are subject to the rules and regulations of that national market; they are not free from national market regulation as are Eurobonds. Nevertheless there is a huge and growing market trading equity securities across national frontiers.

The demand for such shares has come from investors seeking diversification in their portfolios. The supply has come from companies seeking to raise money in different national equity markets.

When we refer to the global (international) equity market, we mean both the listing of equity shares of companies in stock markets other than their own national market (cross-listing) and the movement of portfolio investors funds out of their home country to foreign stock exchanges. The one is the supply of equity shares on a global basis, the other the demand for equity shares on a global basis.

The global equity market is such that on the London Stock Exchange the turnover of foreign equity shares as a percentage of the daily total turnover is on average over 50.0%. London is the national market with the highest level of international activity. The second highest market in terms of international activity is the New York Stock Exchange with the turnover of foreign equities representing 8.0% of total activity.

The USA is attractive to foreign companies seeking a listing. It is important as a global centre because of its wealth. One-third of all the equity shares in the world are held by US investors. The US investors, particularly the financial institutions, can either invest in the shares of foreign companies quoted on the stock exchanges in the USA or they can buy shares of non-US companies listed in markets in other countries.

The USA now wishes its stock exchanges to attract more foreign companies than it has in the past. The regulating body in the USA, namely the Securities and Exchange Commission (SEC), announced in 1993 and 1994 measures to make it easier for foreign companies to be listed in the USA.

With the US actively seeking to have more foreign companies listed on their national stock markets, and with the countries of the European Union accepting the policy of mutual recognition of companies listed in each other's stock exchanges the growth of the international side of national markets seems assured.

The 1990s saw a big growth in new issues on the global (international) equity markets. The new funds raised by cross-border issues increased from £10 billion in 1990 to £60 billion in 1996. One of the main reasons for this growth was the sale of shares in state-owned companies (privatization issues). The amount of money to be raised from the sale of shares in such companies as Deutsch Telekom, ENI and Railtrack was more than the amount that could be supplied in the home national stock exchange of each company.

Integrated markets versus segmented markets

One important question concerning global equity markets is the extent to which they are integrated. Is each national market different, applying different valuation rules, with different levels of taxes and different regulations? Or are the differences so small as not to matter?

If the latter, it would not matter where companies issued shares, the price would be the same (adjusted for foreign exchange rates), the cost of capital would be the same, disclosure requirements would be the same, as would regulations on such matters as insider dealing.

It is generally agreed that the world stock markets are not completely integrated. Taxation differences, different levels of disclosure and different regulations mean that it is not always true that one share has the same price all over the world. Limited arbitrage opportunities exist.

The law of one price

This states that identical assets, whether they are commodities or financial instruments such as shares and bonds should have the same price in all markets. If this is not the situation, profit-seeking individuals can exploit the situation by buying in one market and selling in another market. Such traders would be engaging in what is known as 'arbitrage'.

Many companies have their shares quoted in the stock markets of more than one country. The shares are cross-listed. In theory the shares should be quoted at the same price in each stock market (adjusted for foreign exchange rates); if they are not an arbitrage opportunity exists.

Frost and Pownall [1] found significant price differences in the shares of Smith Kline Beecham between the shares traded in London and those traded in New York. They explained the differences in terms of tax on cash dividends, and differences between the markets in liquidity and investor sentiment towards the company: a mixture of fundamental and behavioural reasons explaining share prices.

7.3 EMERGING STOCK MARKETS

Emerging markets can be classified into a number of different stages of development. There are those at the first stage, which include the former socialist countries located in Central and Eastern Europe. They can be characterized as having few quoted companies, small capitalization, low liquidity and rudimentary financial institutions. Stock markets at a second stage include markets in Brazil, India and Pakistan. They have a variety of quoted companies, attract foreign investors, and have a higher level of liquidity.

The third, and possibly even a fourth, stage consists of markets in Argentina, Indonesia, Malaysia and Thailand. In these the trading volume is higher, capitalization has increased and risk management and hedging instruments exist.

None of these definitions is perfect. There is even disagreement as to whether the markets in Hong Kong, Mexico, Korea and Singapore should be treated as emerging or developed.

Most emerging markets just cater for local national companies, but this is clearly not the case with Hong Kong and Singapore. The emerging markets at early stages have to rely on local finance buying the listed securities, but as they develop they attract foreign funds.

The main advantage of setting up a stock exchange is to help bring together those who have money to invest with those who need finance. The problems of emerging markets are:

1 There is little trading in the shares of some listed companies. The majority of the shares may be controlled by an insider group (possibly members of a family). The market price of a share might not result therefore from a balancing of supply and demand based on economic consideration.
2 The markets might not be well regulated. In many such markets trading on the basis of inside information is not uncommon.
3 Price movements may be extremely volatile, possibly as the result of foreign funds moving in and out. With only low levels of local liquidity, the movement of foreign funds can affect prices dramatically.
4 There are high transaction costs.

7.4 THE US STOCK MARKETS

In the USA shares and bonds are quoted and traded on the organized exchanges or the over-the-counter markets. The New York Stock Exchange (NYSE) is the largest of the organized exchanges, handling in the region of 80% of the activity on the organized exchanges in the USA. The second largest is the American Stock Exchange (AMEX). There are a number of regional exchanges.

The over-the-counter (OTC) market in the USA is large. About 40% by volume of dealing of all share trading in the USA takes place in the OTC market. There are approximately 30 000 issues of equity securities traded in the OTC market, including the shares of almost all the companies listed on the NYSE. The OTC provides price competition for NYSE-listed shares. The shares of a company will be traded on the OTC only if a broker–dealer is willing to make a market in the shares. The majority of the 30 000 securities are seldom traded and their prices are not regularly listed.

There is a computerized communications system for dealing in the securities quoted on the OTC: this is the National Association of Securities Dealers Automated Quotations (NASDAQ) system. This system provides up-to-date dealer quotes for about 5000 companies' equity shares. NASDAQ has listing requirements that need to be met by companies before the securities will be quoted. Only the shares of the better-capitalized companies will be dealt in.

American Depository Receipts (ADR)

When foreign companies wish to have their shares traded in the USA they usually make use of what are called 'American Depository Receipts' or 'American Depository Shares' (ADS). These are negotiable certificates representing ownership rights in non-US companies. One ADR may represent a fraction of one share in the foreign company, one share, or a number of the company shares.

Within the USA they are treated for ownership and transfer purposes in the same way as the share certificates of a US company. The ADRs are issued by a US bank which acts as depository for the foreign shares; the bank either holds the equivalent amount of the foreign shares or they are held in trust in a foreign bank. Under certain circumstances the shares can be in bearer form rather than registered. The ADR is a receipt that the bank issues to the US investor. The bank takes on the responsibility for passing on dividends declared as well as matters relative to rights issues and proxies. When the ADRs are traded it is the certificates that change hands, not the shares. Technically, therefore, the shares are not being traded in the USA.

US investors like ADRs because they are easily tradable, as they are quoted in dollars, with dividends on the shares held against the certificates being paid in dollars. The transaction costs on trading ADRs is less than if the underlying shares needed to be transferred, and there are not the delays that would occur in the USA if a foreign security needed to be transferred. The US investor has the choice of either buying an ADR of a company in the USA or buying the shares of the company in its home stock exchange.

ADRs are not new, they were first issued in New York in 1927, but they did not begin to become popular until the 1970s. In 1990, there were 820 foreign companies that had issued them, and by the end of 1995 there were over 1800.

A non-US company can go through a number of stages with its ADR certificates being traded in the USA before needing to obtain a full listing. First the ADRs can be traded unsponsored. All that is required is to find an investment bank in the USA willing to make a market in the company's equity, A fast-growing UK company might believe it has to appeal to US investors. At this stage only the minimal amount of information has to be filed by the company with the SEC. The costs are not high. The ADRs are being traded in the over-the-counter market.

The second stage which a company might take is to move to obtaining sponsorship with a view to a future listing on an exchange in the USA. This stage requires the company to meet increased costs and to begin to satisfy the SEC listing requirements.

The final step is to obtain a fully sponsored listing of the ADRs on one of the US stock markets. This usually involves either a placement or a public offer of new shares in the company to US investors.

To a UK company issuing such ADR certificates the advantages include:

1. the opportunity to raise dollar capital in the USA;
2. the corporate image of the company in the USA should improve, with its name becoming better known;
3. it is possible to improve the marketability of the company's shares without satisfying the listing requirements of the SEC.

There are certain disadvantages of an ADR. The investor has to appreciate that the price (in dollars) is made up of two elements: the price in the home currency of the company and the foreign exchange rate against the US dollar. There is foreign-exchange risk.

A further problem to an investor can be lack of information about the company. With the 'unsponsored' ADR the only information might be that provided to investors in the home country. This can be a lot less than that usually available to US investors.

7.5 EUROPEAN STOCK EXCHANGES

Details of the different national markets in European countries are shown in Table 7.1. It can be seen that the London Stock Exchange is by far the largest. More information about this market is given in the next section of the chapter. Table 7.1 provides details of the number of listed companies and market capitalization for the major exchanges in Europe and for the USA and Japan. As well as the large exchanges in London, Germany and Paris there are the relatively new stock exchanges of the Central and Eastern European countries.

The reason why traditionally stock exchanges in countries such as Germany have been of less importance than that of the UK is because of a different corporate culture. In Germany the banks in the past have provided much of the longer-term finance needed by the companies. The banks have also owned large blocks of the equity shares. There has been more of a stable long-term

Table 7.1 *Listed shares on leading European and world stock exchanges (main and parallel markets), April 1997*

Exchange	No. of companies with listed shares		Market capitalization of domestic equity shares
	Domestic	*Foreign*	*(Ecu 1000 million)*
Amsterdam	188	156	354
Athens	213	0	28
Brussels	140	128	112
Copenhagen	237	12	66
Germany	675	1499	626
Italy	246	4	235
London	2543	530	1567
Luxembourg	55	221	30
Madrid	366	4	223
Oslo	166	13	51
Paris	680	186	527
Stockholm	223	12	209
Switzerland	213	218	398
Tokyo	1766	67	2550
USA: New York	2602	305	5907
USA: NASDAQ	5140	416	1215

relationship between the providers of finance and the company than there has been in the UK. There has in Germany not been an 'equity culture'. The financial institutions and individuals have not traditionally traded the equity shares they own on a short-term basis. If the owners of equity shares in Germany are not happy with the performance of a company they attempt to change it from within, whereas in the UK and USA shareholders 'vote with their feet', which usually means they walk away from the trouble by selling, possibly to a takeover bidder.

There is a certain amount of cross-listing by European countries: in particular continental European companies being quoted in London. The European Union wishes to encourage greater links in the capital markets within member countries. There are two new international markets that have been opened in Europe. Brief details are given below.

EASDAQ (European Association of Securities Dealers Automated Quotation)

This market opened in October 1996. It operates from Brussels and is modelled on NASDAQ in North America. It is designed to cater for the shares of small firms across Europe. Small and fast-growing firms have suffered for a long time from difficulties in obtaining equity funds to finance growth.

The market is being funded by a consortium of European and US financial institutions. It is hoped that some companies listed on EASDAQ will seek a joint listing in NASDAQ and vice versa.

As the name implies it is a quote-driven system. It is planned that each company listed will have at least two market makers. The flotation costs for a new listing will be in the region of £250 000; the company to be listed will require minimum assets of £2.9 million and capital and reserves of £1.6 million. The company will not need to have been trading for a minimum period, nor will it be required to have had a number of years of continuing profits.

The market planned to start small. A year after it opened it only had 16 companies listed. EASDAQ is in competition with the established stock exchanges around Europe, although it emphasizes it is only competing for the smaller companies.

EURO-NM

In addition to the major stock markets in the various European financial centres, there are, in some of the centres, what have been called 'mini-markets'. These developed during the 1990s, and by 1997 there were four such markets, one in each of France, Germany, the Netherlands and Belgium. These are in addition to EASDAQ. Each of these mini-markets see itself as catering for international businesses, not just domestic. Competition between stock markets is fierce, and it is far from certain that all will survive.

The four mini-markets are to be linked electronically so that trade can take place across markets. As with the EASDAQ link to NASDAQ, trade in the securities of a company listed in one mini-market can be traded in one of the other mini-markets.

Mutual recognition

The European Union has as one of its goals the free movement of capital within member states. This requires the integration of the different national stock exchanges. There are a number of steps they have taken to achieve this goal. One very significant step is the introduction of the principle of mutual recognition. Each national stock exchange has complex national rules regarding the disclosure of information. But as a result of official Directives (and also partly of market pressures) the disclosure documents and annual reports prepared for the stock exchange of a company's home country will now satisfy the requirements of the stock exchanges of all member countries.

This means, for example, the acceptance by the London Stock Exchange of the prospectus and the annual report and accounts prepared by say a German company or an Italian company, according to the laws of those countries, as satisfying the requirements for a listing in London. Whether UK investors understand the complexities of accounting in Germany or Italy is another matter. It is up to the investors to make themselves aware of national differences; it is not up to companies to go through the expensive exercise of preparing statements according to UK standards. Similar harmonization processes are taking place in the banking and insurance sectors.

Global Depository Receipts

The features and purposes of a GDR are similar to those of an ADR. The GDRs are usually listed in Europe, but some are listed in Hong Kong and Singapore.

The first was issued by a Korean company in the London market in 1990. By the end of 1995 there were 27 GDRs listed in London. Seven of these were issued by Indian companies and seven by Korean.

Custodians

These are organizations, usually banks, that will take responsibility for the safe-keeping of clients' shares and bonds. This is particularly important if the securities are bearer securities rather than registered. It has also become more important as financial markets have become global. If, for example, a British investor buys shares listed in the stock market in Italy, he or she might not want the securities sent to the UK: better the securities are deposited with a 'custodian' in Italy.

Custodians have developed their businesses into offering clients a range of services. They were always involved in the settlement business, as clients bought and sold the shares deposited with them. Now they offer to keep the accounting records relating to the investment, cash management and other security services.

This chapter is concerned with the market for equity shares. But it has to be appreciated that the London Stock Exchange deals in securities other than equity. Table 7.2 gives details of the securities dealt with on the Exchange.

As already mentioned, trading of stocks and shares can take place anywhere. It does not have to be on the floor of an exchange building. One financial institution can trade with another via a telephone. Licensed dealers can create a market for shares. In fact, the capital market is any place where negotiable long-term securities of companies and the public sector are traded. Having said this, it is nevertheless the case that the most important part of the capital market in the UK is the official Stock Exchange in London.

The Stock Exchange in London is an independent association of members whose origins go back to the seventeenth century. It is the ambition of most companies in the UK to have their shares listed on the Stock Exchange. The Exchange is the oldest in the world and is one of the largest.

The Official List

There are, in fact, different markets for shares provided by the Stock Exchange in London. This section deals with the main market, with what is known as the 'Official List'. The other markets are dealt with in the following sections.

A company may decide to seek a quotation to satisfy its shareholders who would prefer to hold shares for which a market price has been established and which can easily be sold should the need arise. Major shareholders may wish to sell their shares in the company at some time in order to diversify their portfolios so as to avoid holding the bulk of their wealth in the shares of a single company.

Conditions for listing

A company to be listed must normally have published or filed audited accounts which cover at least three years prior to the listing. These accounts must have been prepared in accordance with the applicant's national law and, in all material respects, with either United Kingdom Accounting Standards, or United States Accounting Standards or International Accounting Standards.

It is possible for a company to have accounts for a period less than three years, but only if the Exchange is satisfied that such acceptance is desirable in the interests of the applicant or of investors and investors have the necessary information available to arrive at an informed judgement concerning the applicant and the securities for which listing is sought.

There are numerous other conditions that must be satisfied, concerning such matters as a need for continuity in management over the period covered by the accounts and the need for the directors of the company to have 'collectively appropriate expertise and experience for the management' of the business.

Market capitalization

Except where securities of the same class are already listed, the expected aggregate market value of all securities to be listed by a company must be at least:

1 £700 000 for shares; and
2 £200 000 for debt securities.

The Exchange may admit securities of lower value if it is satisfied that there will be an adequate market for the securities concerned. The exact requirements will of course change over time.

Table 7.2 Money raised by UK and Irish companies

	Total companies listed		New companies		Other issues		Eurobonds		USM		AIM	
	No.	Money raised (£1.000m)	No.	Money raised (£1.000m)	No.	Money raised (£1000m)	No.	Money raised (£1000m)	No.	Money raised (£1000m)	No.	Money raised (£1000m)
1988	4072	20	129	4	3872	10	71	6	575	2.0		
1989	3956	27	110	8	3749	10	97	9	661	0.8		
1990	3205	28	120	7	2953	7	132	14	453	0.5		
1991	3319	35	101	7	2985	14	233	13	319	0.4		
1992	2876	24	82	3	2488	8	306	13	277	0.2		
1993	2655	48	180	6	1941	18	534	25	212	0.3		
1994	3168	58	256	1	1978	14	934	32	202	0.4		
1995	2803	38	190	3	1710	10	903	35	99	0.2	160	0.1
1996	3029	55	230	11	1773	9	1026	36	55	0.2	389	0.8

Marketability

To be listed, securities must be freely transferable. To be listed, at last 25% of the class of security to be listed must be in the hands of the public when trading in the company's shares begins. The shares must be in the hands of the public in one or more of the member states in the European Union. Shares owned by the public in non-member states may be taken into consideration if these shares are listed in the country concerned.

The prospectus

When the public is asked to subscribe for the shares of or debentures in a company, the invitation involves the issue of a document setting out the advantages to accrue from an investment in the company. This document is termed a 'prospectus' and it is in most cases illegal to issue to the public any form of application for shares or debentures in a company unless it is accompanied by a prospectus complying with the Companies Acts. An issue to existing shareholders or debenture holders need not be accompanied by such a prospectus, nor need an issue which is uniform with shares or debentures previously issued and quoted on a stock exchange.

Rules of the Stock Exchange

The company must undertake to observe the rules of the Stock Exchange. The listing rules (appearing in what is known as the 'Yellow Book') are being continually revised. A new edition of the Book was published in December 1993. The Exchange requires certain information to be provided each year and at times of a new issue additional to that required by law. This information is required in order to give investors the greatest possible knowledge about the company's directors or promoters, the business in which it is engaged, its profit record and the prospects for profits and dividends.

In recent years the number of companies listed on the main London Stock Exchange has been falling. One of the reasons, of course, is that a number of companies disappear through takeovers and mergers. However, this does not hide the fact that there has been evidence of a decline in the appeal of a stock market listing. For smaller companies the costs of obtaining a quotation are relatively high and therefore the potential rewards for successful owners of small and medium-sized businesses from the sale of shares were not providing sufficient compensation for the disadvantages of a listing. The listing rules are demanding and the rules tend to be rigorously applied.

Costs of obtaining and maintaining a quotation on a market arise in two ways: the initial costs and the annual costs. Initially, in order to meet the requirements of the market certain costs need to be incurred. Higher reporting standards need to be met which increases annual costs.

However, there are economies of scale in the issuing of shares. There is a large fixed overhead element in the cost: advertising, administration, the printing of the prospectus, commission fees and legal expenses. Because of the fixed element the costs of raising small amounts of finance can absorb a high proportion of the amounts raised. Having obtained a quotation, annual fees need to be paid to the market and the higher costs of meeting reporting requirements continue. In addition, management time has to be spent on satisfying shareholders' needs, in particular the request for information. Once shares have been sold to the public, in particular to institutions, their interests are only ignored at the directors' peril.

The Alternative Investment Market (AIM)

This market commenced activity in June 1995. It is designed to satisfy the capital needs of the smaller or medium-sized fast-growing company. It replaced the USM, the third market and Rule 4.2. It has minimum listing requirements with respect to the financial and trading record of companies. The cost for companies listed on this market is a lot less than that for a listing on the main London market.

In 1996, the average capitalization of AIM companies was around £11 million. There were four companies capitalized at over £50 million, and at the other extreme twelve companies with a capitalization of under £1.5 million. There is no minimum capitalization requirement, nor a requirement that at least a certain percentage of shares are sold to or placed in public hands. In fact, approximately half the listed companies have sold to the public over 50% of their shares; less than one-fifth have sold less than 20%.

Every company coming to AIM must have a nominated adviser. The company must keep this adviser whilst being listed on this market. The adviser is responsible for confirming that the company complies with all the rules of the AIM. There are over 50 firms of approved advisers, and these include firms of accountants and banks.

Twelve months after the market opened, the number of companies whose shares were traded had increased from 10 to 166. However, the majority of these companies were not entirely new to the Stock Exchange, having previously had their shares traded on Rule 4.2. This, as explained below, was a facility the London Stock Exchange offered to allow an occasional dealing facility in a company's shares. This facility was closed when AIM opened, and so many of the companies involved transferred their dealing arrangements to the AIM. These Rule 4.2 companies were not coming to the AIM to raise money, but were moving in order to continue to have a facility for their shares to be exchanged.

There have, however, been many companies coming to the AIM to raise new money, and the number of market makers in AIM shares has increased. A year after opening, there were over 60% of the AIM companies with at least two market makers quoting prices for their shares. It should be appreciated that it is advantageous for a company to have more than one market maker for its shares. With competition between market makers it is more likely that the market price of a share is close to its true value. The investors in the market consist of private investors (there are tax advantages) and institutions. The market is reasonably liquid, with the institutional investors bringing in increasing funds.

The advantages to a company of having its shares traded in the AIM include the following:

1 Founders of companies can realize cash by selling their shares.
2 Medium-sized companies can obtain equity finance for expansion. Being quoted can also result in banks taking a more favourable attitude towards loan funds as the public standing of the company is increased.
3 A medium-sized company can take over another company by offering shares which have a market in which they can be traded.
4 The company can reward and encourage its employees through share-option schemes.

The disadvantages include the following:

1 An increased amount of financial disclosure is required.
2 As a result, there is an increased possibility of being the target of a takeover bid and with a more dispersed share ownership there is less control over the outcome of the bid.

3 There could be pressure from new share owners for the rate of dividend payments to be increased.
4 There is the danger of less effective management resulting from the divorce of ownership and control.

The Unlisted Securities Market (USM)

This market, which was regulated by the London Stock Exchange, opened in 1980; it enjoyed some success. In 1990, at the height of its success, it had 442 companies listed, with a total market value in excess of £8000 million. The market was closed in 1996. The number of companies coming to the market to obtain a listing declined from over 90 per annum in the early 1980s to only 10 in 1991 and 6 in 1992.

What had gone wrong for the USM? One of the main reasons for its decline was changes that were introduced to the listing requirements to obtain admission to the 'Official List'. These changes made it easier for companies to be quoted on the main London Stock Exchange, and so they made the USM relatively less attractive. The changes were made in order to implement a European Union Listing Directive.

Some companies quoted on the USM when it closed moved to a full listing on the official exchange, and some moved to the AIM.

The third market

A third market had been established by the Stock Exchange in 1987. It was designed to offer an opportunity for listing to companies that might find the entry requirements to the USM too onerous and to provide a market place for young growing companies. In the early 1990s this market was discontinued. This was because proposals were introduced to reduce the trading record requirement for companies seeking admission to the Official List from five to three years, and to the USM from three to two years. With these proposals accepted, new companies could go straight to the USM and miss out the third market.

Rule 4.2

The London Stock Exchange, for many years, allowed trading by members in securities of companies not listed in either the Official List or any of the other lists. Trading was based on what was called 'Rule 4.2', and was allowed in securities of companies in which it was thought there would only be a few transactions.

In 1995, the shares of approximately 300 companies were traded under this rule. The companies included football teams and small breweries, which had regional but not national appeal. Often it was regional stock brokers who would match buying and selling orders.

This rule was introduced in 1950, and ended in 1996. In the region of 80 of the Rule 4.2 companies moved to the AIM. To be listed in the AIM increased the costs of the companies, and increased the disclosure requirements. The majority of the companies chose to have their shares traded 'off the market'.

'Off-the-market' trading in securities

This is sometimes known as the 'over-the-counter market' (OTC). This expression originated years ago when dealers sold securities across a counter. Now it refers to securities being bought and sold but not in an official market. The stock brokers and dealers who make a market in such securities are linked to each other by computers.

It is possible for the shares of any public company to be traded. If a seller can find a buyer, a deal can be arranged. The purpose of an organized market is to make it easier for a seller to find a buyer.

In fact, as explained above, the OTC market in the USA is very large, whereas the OTC market in the UK is not large. One authorized dealer, a recognized market maker, J.P. Jenkins, introduced a dealing service known as 'OFEX'. This is not a recognized market, it is off-the-exchange. It offers facilities for matched bargains. Information on the companies whose shares can be dealt with through OFEX is available on computer screens. The companies concerned have of course to pay for this service. A large number of companies whose securities were previously traded under Rule 4.2 have now moved to OFEX.

Trading system

The various stock exchanges of the world are in competition with one another. They wish to attract companies to list on their exchange, and investors to trade in the shares being listed.

To remain competitive stock markets need to continually change. In 1986, London introduced major changes, referred to as the 'Big Bang'. Prior to these changes most trading took place on the central market floor of the Stock Exchange. It was face-to-face dealing. Jobbers operating on the floor of the Exchange made markets in the shares of companies. If a broker wished to buy or sell shares on behalf of a client he or she walked around the floor of the exchange to enquire the prices being quoted by different jobbers.

The major Big Bang changes were as follows:

1 The separation of member firms into brokers and jobbers ended. All firms could act as brokers, representing clients. They all also became market makers.
2 Ownership of member firms by overseas companies was allowed.
3 A computerized system, the Stock Exchange Automated Quotation (SEAQ), was introduced. Prices were displayed on screens in market makers' offices. Bargains could be completed away from the floor of the Exchange. Face-to-face negotiation became a thing of the past. A broker wishing to buy shares in a particular company could look at a computer screen and see all the prices being quoted by the market makers in that company's shares. This is known as the 'quote-driven' system of trading.

In 1997, further changes were necessary in London's trading system (Big Bang 2). The quote-driven system was considered inferior to the alternative, the order-driven system. It was considered too slow. London moved from the one trading system to the other.

Dealer market – quote-driven

In this market there are dealers (market makers) who will quote a price at which they will buy and sell the shares of a company. They can acquire shares in their own names and sell these. If an investor wishes to buy shares, he or she buys off the dealer at the price at which the dealer quotes. If an investor wishes to sell, he or she sells to a dealer at the price offered by the dealer. NASDAQ is an example of a quote-driven system.

For the equity shares of larger companies there are usually a number of dealers who make a market in the company shares. For frequently traded shares the difference between the buying and selling price quoted by dealers can be small. For infrequently traded shares with only a few market makers the difference can be large.

Auction market – order-driven

Tokyo, Paris and NYSE are examples of such markets. In this type of market prospective buyers of shares place an order quoting a price at which they are willing to buy. Orders are placed on an electronic notice board, which indicates how many shares the individual wishes to buy and at what price. This is matched by computer against orders received from investors who are wishing to sell. If the bidding price of the buyer matches the asking price of a holder of shares who is willing to sell, a deal is completed. Investors sell the shares they own at the bid price established by the buy order of another investor.

Initially the changes in London to this alternative system only apply to shares in the leading companies, but the intention is that eventually all shares will move to the order-driven system.

7.7 REFERENCES

1   Frost, C.A. and Pownell, G. (1996) Interdependencies in the global markets for capital and information: the case of Smithkline Beecham PLC, *Accounting Horizons*, **10**(1): 38–57.

7.8 FURTHER READING

Steil, B. (ed.) (1996) *The European Equity Markets*, Royal Institute of International Affairs, London.

7.9 PROBLEMS

1   The issue to the public of an application for shares or debentures in a company must normally be accompanied by a prospectus. What are the main features of a prospectus?
2   Describe the advantages and disadvantages to a medium-sized company of obtaining a quotation.
3   For what reasons, other than the need to raise outside finance, might a private company take the necessary steps to secure a Stock Exchange quotation?
4   In what circumstances might a company make a 'stock split'? What would be the effect of such a decision on the company, the share price and the share-holders' wealth?
5   Clearly distinguish an offer for sale by tender from other methods of raising equity capital and describe the process by which the price is set and the shares allocated in an offer for sale by tender. Outline the circumstances when the use of an issue by tender would be an appropriate way of raising equity.
6   What are the main advantages and disadvantages to a company of raising finance by issuing the following:
    (a) ordinary shares;
    (b) redeemable convertible preference shares;
    (c) deferred ordinary shares;
    (d) convertible debentures.

7 (a) Coppice PLC plans to obtain a listing on the UK Stock Exchange. The company wishes to raise approximately £3 million, and the Stock Exchange authorities have informally indicated that either an offer for sale or a placing would be permitted. Coppice's finance director has obtained information about the costs associated with new issues. This information is detailed below:

Issuing house commission (not including underwriting)	0.5%
Underwriting commission*	1.5%
Accounting and legal fees:	
Offer for sale	£40 000
Placing	£15 000
Capital duty payable to the government on the proceeds of the issue	1%
Advertising:	
Multiple-page advertisement in a national newspaper	£50 000
Small advertisement in a national or regional newspaper	£3 000
Share-registration costs: £1000 plus £1 per shareholder	
Stock Exchange initial fee:	
Offer for sale	£4 000
Placing	£2 000
Other costs:	
Offer for sale	£25 000
Placing	£10 000

The company pays tax at a rate of 35%

*In an offer for sale, underwriting commission will effectively be deducted from the issue price in determining the price that the company receives.

(i) Discuss how an offer for sale differs from a placing. (6 marks)

(ii) Estimate the total after-tax issue costs if Coppice PLC uses an offer for sale. (3 marks)

(iii) If Coppice PLC decided to seek a listing on the Unlisted Securities Market what difference would this make to the method of issue and to the costs involved? (3 marks)

(b) Coppice eventually decides to enter the stock market by using an offer for sale. Its merchant bank considers that the issue should comprise 2 million shares at a price of 145p per share. The 2 million shares will form half the company's issued ordinary share capital. As an alternative, the merchant bank suggests an offer for sale by tender. The merchant bank is willing to underwrite a tender issue of 2 million shares with a minimum price of 140p per share. Coppice agrees to the issue by tender and receives the following tenders:

Price tendered (pence)	Number of applicants at the price	Number of shares bid for at the price
175	2	22 000
170	84	74 000
165	127	192 000
160	410	724 000
155	1123	928 000
150	2254	1 324 200
145	3520	4 956 000
140	6410	12 230 000

The company decides to allocate the same percentage of the number of shares that were requested to all successful tenders.

(i) Estimate the amount of funds that the company will raise from the tender, net of issue costs, and the average size of shareholding that will result.

(4 marks)

(ii) Suggest reasons why tenders are not the most frequently used method of raising equity finance.

(4 marks)

8 Parbat Ltd has an issued capital of 2 million ordinary shares of 50p each and no fixed-interest securities. It has paid a dividend of 70p per share for several years, and the stock market generally expects that level to continue. The market price is £4.20 per share cum dividend. The firm is now considering the acceptance of a major new investment which would require an outlay of £500 000 and generate net cash receipts of £120 000 per annum for an indefinite period. The additional receipts would be used to increase dividends. Parbat is appraising three alternative sources of finance for the new project.

(a) Retained earnings. The usual annual dividend could be reduced. Parbat currently holds £1.4 million for payment of the dividend which is due in the near future.

(b) A rights issue of ordinary shares. One new share would be offered for every ten shares held at present at a price of £2.50 per share; the new shares would rank for dividend one year after issue, when cash receipts from the new project would first be available.

(c) An issue of ordinary shares to the general public. The new shares would rank for dividend one year after issue.

Assume that, if the project were accepted, the firm's expectations of future results would be discovered and believed by the stock market, and that the market would perceive the risk of the firm to be unaltered.

(a) Estimate the price ex dividend of Parbat's ordinary shares following acceptance of the new project if finance is obtained from (i) retained earnings or (ii) a rights issue.

(b) Calculate the price at which the new shares should be issued under option (c) assuming the objective of maximizing the gain of existing shareholders.

(c) Calculate the gain made by present shareholders under each of the three finance options.

(d) Discuss the advantages and disadvantages of each of the three sources of finance.

Ignore taxation and issue costs of new shares for (a), (b) and (c) but *not* (d).

8 STOCK MARKET EFFICIENCY

LEARNING OUTCOMES

After studying the contents of this chapter the reader will:

- have an understanding of the process of share price determination in the stock market
- understand how in an efficient market it is not possible to consistently obtain above-average performance on investments
- appreciate the fact that no stock market is completely efficient
- understand the behavioural factors that influence the movement in share prices

8.1 INTRODUCTION

In this chapter we consider whether or not stock markets are efficient. This is a very important issue and there is a vast literature on the topic. If a market is efficient investors are taking part in a 'fair game', companies who seek funds obtain them at the correct (fair) price, and the stock market helps promote economic growth by channelling funds to where they can be best used.

Unfortunately we do not really know whether stock markets are efficient. Theories which might help us understand how stock markets work, namely the efficient market hypothesis (EMH), and the capital-assets pricing model, are useful but are highly simplified representations of how stock markets really work.

It is necessary to understand these theories, as they represent a logical approach to how share prices are determined. We will now describe the EMH, and consider both the fundamental and behavioural approach to the price.

8.2 THE EFFICIENT MARKET HYPOTHESIS

We need to be clear what we mean by efficiency. First it should be realized that it is not the same as that well-loved economic concept of the perfect market. For a stock market to be a perfect market the following conditions would need to be satisfied [1]:

1 It would need to be frictionless, i.e. without distortions arising from transaction costs and taxes. There should be no constraining regulations limiting freedom of entry and exit for investors and companies seeking funds.
2 All buyers and sellers should be rational expected-utility maximizers.
3 There should be many buyers and sellers.

4 The market should be informationally efficient, i.e. information should be costless and received simultaneously by all individuals.

No market, whether a stock exchange or any other market, satisfies all the conditions required for it to be classed as perfect. Fortunately a market can be efficient without meeting the conditions necessary to be perfect. We can relax some of the assumptions and still have what is called an 'efficient market'. The assumptions of costless information, a frictionless market place, and many buyers and sellers are not necessary conditions for the existence of an efficient capital market. What therefore is an efficient capital market?

Here we have a problem. There is a wide, generally accepted, dictionary definition of the word 'efficient', but ' "efficient" in connection with the market hypothesis' (EMH) has a narrower meaning which is easier to satisfy. In fact, this hypothesis is one of the most important concepts in the modern literature of finance.

First, we shall consider the wider meaning of the word 'efficiency'. The word in common daily usage, can be defined as 'functioning effectively and with the least waste of effort'. What does 'effectively' mean? Turning to a dictionary again, we find the definition, 'capable of producing a result'. With this definition in mind, we can think of at least five results that we would expect from an 'efficient' stock exchange.

1 Funds coming to the exchange are allocated to where they can be most effectively used. This is first-period [2] or allocational efficiency. Over time there is pressure on firms to employ their resources effectively.
2 Those who provide funds to the market are involved in a fair game. This involves all the familiar tests of stock market efficiency. At any point in time, a share price reflects all information concerning events that have occurred and all events that the market expects to take place in the future. This is pricing efficiency.
3 We would not expect the operation of an efficient market, in itself, to lead to predictable changes in wealth distribution in the second period. This is Mossin's second-period efficiency. With a 'fair game' the distribution of wealth amongst investors in the second period should be similar to that in the first period. In one period some investors will have gained, and some will have lost. In the next period a different group of investors will have gained and a different group lost. No one class of investors is able to maintain a position where they show persistent above-average returns. This is an implication of pricing efficiency.
4 The efficient market should satisfy the social and political goals set for it by the society in which it operates. It may be thought that this is not relevant to the stock exchanges of the developed Western countries, but clearly it is. A stock exchange is seen as a part of the private enterprise system, an important part of a property-owning democracy.
5 The market itself carries out its operations at as low a cost as possible. This is operational efficiency.

It is appreciated that there is a considerable amount of overlap between these five points. For example, 3 might come within 4 in that the government does not want inequalities in wealth distribution to be increased; 3 and 2 are also somewhat interrelated in that if the 'game' is fair, there should be no need to worry about the effect of the stock exchange on wealth distribution. An important issue is how much deviation from a fair game can a market stand before second-period efficiency becomes important?

Allocational efficiency

Three types of efficiency have been identified above: allocational, pricing and operational. Allocational efficiency means that the market channels funds to those firms and organizations with the most promising real investment opportunities. Allocational efficiency requires both pricing efficiency and operational efficiency. The absence of either can lead to the misallocation of resources.

Operational efficiency

Operational efficiency means that buyers and sellers of securities can purchase transaction services at prices that are as low as possible given the costs associated with having these services provided. It requires the bid/ask spread on securities to be as low as possible. It requires a speedy completion of trading transactions. It requires comparatively easy access to the market and easy exit from it, for investors, market makers and companies. The market needs to be administered efficiently.

Pricing efficiency

This is sometimes known as 'fair game' efficiency or 'informational efficiency'. When the efficiency of a stock exchange is discussed in the literature of finance, it is often just concerned with this form of efficiency. Virtually all testing of the EMH has been based on testing for pricing efficiency. Unfortunately the data are not readily available for testing for allocational or operational efficiency. One can in fact even question whether the data are available for testing pricing efficiency.

The efficient market hypothesis states that an efficient stock market is one in which prices of traded securities fully reflect all available information concerning those securities. Thus, by implication, security prices adjust instantaneously and in an unbiased manner to any piece of new information released to the market. Sometimes this is referred to as 'information arbitrage efficiency'; it means abnormal profits cannot be achieved systematically by trading on the basis of available information. A variation on this definition says that prices reflect information up to the point where the marginal costs of obtaining the information exceed the marginal benefits.

How can we test if actual prices do reflect available information? One way would be to see if actual prices are close to what should be the true value based on such information. Unfortunately we do not have an agreed method of determining what is the 'true value' (the intrinsic value) of any share. The value depends on what happens in the future and we do not have an accurate method of estimating the future. Furthermore, we do not have an agreed model to express the relationship between how a company will perform in the future and its share price now.

We can say (a) what the price of a company's share should be relative to its price in the past. For example, when an unexpected dividend increase is announced, the share price will adjust to allow for the change in expectations. We can say (b) what the price of one company's shares should be relative to that of another company's share. This means, in its simplest form, that as information which suggests higher profits for one company becomes available, the price of that company's shares is expected to rise up to a point where the expected earnings yield is comparable with that on other shares in a similar risk class. If information which suggests increased risks for a company becomes available, unless there are also expected higher returns, the share price will fall. This will give a higher expected earnings yield on the share, which should be comparable with that of other shares in the same risk class.

With these above examples we can say that the price of one company's share has adjusted to new information in a correct manner relative to the price of another company's share. We cannot be sure that either the company whose price has changed nor the companies being used for comparative purposes have share prices reflecting their true value.

Fair game model

If the stock market is pricing efficient it is a 'fair game'. In such a situation no player (investor) can expect to continually beat the market. A player might earn above-average returns (excess returns) from his or her investment strategy in one period, but should not expect to do so again in the next period. Returns, of course, equal share price gains plus dividends.

The fair game model states that the excess return (actual return over expected return based on a given set of information) should be zero. The model underlying this fair game is the martingale model. Sometimes it is suggested that the movement of a 'share price' over time can be characterized by movement along a random path. The 'random walk' hypothesis states that in an efficient market successive price changes are independent of one another. This is associated with the 'weak form' test of efficient markets. In fact, since the 1980s the random walk model has been replaced by the martingale model for testing for weak-form efficiency. The latter is a less strict model.

The significance that can be attached to the tests of the efficient market hypothesis and the fair game model depend on the validity of the models that have been used to estimate the true value and the expected returns. Beaver has pointed to other problems with the fair game models [3]. The term 'information set' is not well defined, the meaning of the term 'information' is unclear, and the phrase 'assumed to be fully reflected in prices' is ambiguous. Some markets are clearly more informationally efficient than others, information being disseminated more quickly and more widely.

It is important to appreciate that the EMH only states that it is impossible to invest and consistently achieve above-average returns. This statement is concerned with price movements over time. The EMH does *not* say that the actual price of a share is equal or close to its true (intrinsic) value. Despite the problems with the meaning and the testing of the hypothesis there is a vast literature on the subject of stock market efficiency. The literature has improved our understanding of how stock markets work and of how share prices move over time. One can conclude that unless an investor has access to restricted information it is safer for them to assume that they cannot beat the market than for them to think they can obtain above-average returns.

The tests on the pricing efficiency of markets are usually divided into three categories. What are known as the 'weak-form tests' attempt to ascertain whether knowledge and analysis of past data can be used with advantage to forecast future prices. If it can, it means that the fair game model and the efficient market have to be rejected. It means that the expected excess returns will not be zero for those investors who know how to analyse past data. The semi-strong-form tests examine whether knowledge of all publicly available information can be used to earn excess returns. The strong-form tests consider whether any knowledge, publicly available or not, can be used by those who have it to obtain above-average gains.

Weak-form tests (return predictability)

The weak form of the EMH states that current security prices fully reflect information regarding historical events. Investors, knowing the historical sequence of prices, or of other measures such as dividend yields or interest yields, can neither abnormally enhance their investment return nor improve their ability to select shares. This implies that share price data and other financial data relating to today and the past contain no information that can be used to earn profits in excess of those produced by a naive buy-and-hold strategy. It implies that there are no mechanical rules based on historical patterns which can be used to earn profits in excess of the average market return.

The early statistical studies indicated that the movement of stock prices over time approximated to a random walk. They indicated that, given the price of a share at the end of one period, it was not possible to predict the price at the end of the next period. The hypothesis relates to short time periods, say weeks or months: the very long run is excepted from the predictions of the hypothesis. The study of past movements in price or other fundamental data does not help predict future prices.

Although the prediction of absolute levels is ruled out by the hypothesis, the prediction of relative levels is not. For example, a list of past GEC share prices would not indicate what tomorrow's share price will be, but it might be possible to predict the position of GEC's share-price movement relative to all other company share-price movements.

Of course, over the long term there has been upward movement in share prices, and it is expected that this will continue in the future. This is because the gross national product of most countries increases over time. However, this upward trend can at times be very slow-moving and there can be periods of two or more years when there is a trend the other way. The gradual upward trend may not be fast enough for some investors to be able to use it profitably within their investment horizons. Therefore this predictability of the long-term trend is not very useful to such investors.

Evidence on non-randomness

The early empirical studies produced results which supported the view that the major stock markets of the world were 'weak-form' efficient. The early studies used tests such as serial correlation, run tests and filter tests. However, recent researchers using powerful statistical techniques report that price changes are not always random. They find evidence that successive price changes are on occasions correlated, and that therefore on occasions price levels can be forecast.

An example of a recent study is that of Jegadeesh [4] who tested whether future monthly returns on individual company shares could be predicted from knowledge of past monthly returns and concluded that the returns are to some extent predictable. The results reject the random walk hypothesis.

Another study, by Mills, using data on movements in the UK FTSE index, found that it was possible to predict returns with time horizons varying from three months to over a year [5].

The student of the subject should be careful. Many basic books on the subject state that the major stock markets of the world are weak-form efficient. Fama, writing in 1970, cast doubt on this view [6]. The latest statistical studies on the subject indicate that it is on occasion possible to predict future share prices based on knowledge of the past movement in share prices or other financial data.

There is disagreement on the interpretation of the findings, on the existence or otherwise of random walks. The fact that some evidence has been found that shows it is possible to forecast share prices on the basis of past financial data does not prove that the market is efficient, nor that it is inefficient.

The finding that it is on occasions possible to predict returns can be used to justify both rational stock market behaviour and irrational behaviour. Some evidence of predictability does exist, but the gains to be made according to the published findings are small. It could be, however, that a few 'rocket scientists' employed by financial analysts have found models that are successful at predicting future share prices, but understandably their results are not published.

Time periods

The shortest intervals over which most of the tests of the random walk have been undertaken are daily price changes. The closing price on one day is compared with the closing price on the next day. It has been suggested that this time interval is too long in which to identify the serial correlation in price movements; rather, the price at the end of one hour should be related to the price at the end of the previous hour.

Indeed, research has now been undertaken in which the price is being recorded on a 15-minute basis, and the series of prices obtained is tested to see if the movement is random. Those supporting this idea of non-randomness of price movements over very short periods of time argue that upward and downward trends can be identified within a day. They argue that the price on the hour is not unrelated to the price half an hour earlier.

If it is found that price movements over these very short time intervals are not random, then it would give the opportunity for those investors who are able to follow the movement of prices closely over a day to make above-normal gains. It would give an advantage to those who are close to the market and can respond quickly. Technically the share price at any time is publicly available information, but access to this information is not equally available to all. Only those who know the price hour by hour could benefit. It could be, however, that although predictions can be made over short periods of time, the changes are not large enough to compensate for the transaction costs of trading.

Other independent variables

The recent weak-form literature can be divided into that which attempts to forecast the future level of a share price from past movements in share price, and the more recent research which looks at the ability to forecast share-price movement based on other financial variables such as dividend yield and interest yield [7].

In the late 1980s some studies reported success in predicting share-price movement based on the past movement in certain financial variables. Returns over both short- and long-term horizons were shown to be predictable from dividend yield, from price earnings ratios, from the level of interest rates and from expected inflation rates. As with predictions based on past share prices, forecasts based on these other variables were less successful for short time periods than for longer periods. It has been found that trends in the past level of earnings yields could be used to forecast the future movement in share prices; the forecasts become increasingly reliable the further ahead the period for which one was predicting.

Semi-strong-form tests (event studies)

The semi-strong-form test of the EMH is concerned with whether current prices of shares reflect public knowledge about the underlying company, and whether the speed of price adjustment to events and the public announcement of information is fast enough to eliminate the possibility of abnormal gains. Thus the question of whether it is worth some effort to acquire and analyse this public knowledge with the hope of gaining superior investment results, if answered in the negative, would support the EMH. Generally, the evidence suggests that the share-price adjustment is quick and in the appropriate direction, thus confirming the EMH. The evidence is concerned with how prices react to relevant 'events'.

The first and most important study adopting the semi-strong approach was that of Fama *et al.* [8]. They analysed the adjustment of share prices in the USA in response to the publication of new fundamental information. The information they used was that implied by stock splits. Firth [9] carried out similar tests on stock splits in the UK. He found that share prices adjusted to this new information quickly and that it was not possible to profit from the information once it had been released to the public. Marsh [10] found that in the UK share prices also reacted very quickly to the announcement of a rights issue, and the price behaviour following the announcement was entirely consistent with the semi-strong form of the EMH.

The conclusion is that the market seems to adjust efficiently to this publicly available information. As with the weak tests the market is shown not always to react to these sets of information in quite the way that might be expected. Information of the semi-strong type is little better than weak information when it comes to prediction. Thus again the EMH cannot be rejected: no group of investors can use this class of information to give them above-average gains.

Usefulness of accounting numbers

Good-quality accounting information is necessary to ensure that capital markets remain efficient. Many of the semi-strong tests of the EMH have attempted to determine the link between accounting information and the movement of share prices. How useful are accounting numbers?

On most occasions the announcement of the annual profit figures and the publication of the annual report and accounts will not have a big impact on the share price of a company. As reported in Chapter 2, the results will already have been anticipated by the informed investors [11]. The release of the accounting information is, however, very important as it confirms or verifies the expectation of investors. The better the quality of the accounting information, in terms of reliability and scope, the more useful it is to users.

The amount of information disclosed in the annual report and accounts of companies has increased over time. The notes to the accounts in particular have become more complex. Different users of accounts might well interpret the information in different ways. Nevertheless, event studies have shown that on balance share prices respond rationally to new accounting information.

There is pressure at an international level for greater harmonization between countries in their accounting practices. There are International Accounting Standards and their number is increasing. The reason why such harmonization and more comprehensive reports are required is to protect international investors and lenders. Investors in one country need to be able to understand the financial accounts produced by a company from another contry if cross country portfolio investment is to increase.

The impact on share prices of non-accounting information can sometimes be surprising. For example, the unexpected death of a Chief Executive (CEO) who is a professional manager has been found to be associated with a decrease in the share price of the company. However, the death of a CEO who is also a founder of the company has often been found to lead to an increase in a company's share price. This suggests that the market believes many founders hang onto their business far too long.

Information relating to mergers

In a UK study by Franks *et al.* [12] the EMH was tested using information released at the time of mergers. They analysed the mergers in the brewery and distillery industry in the UK and found that, on average, the market began to anticipate a merger at least three months prior to the announcement date. There was movement in the share price over this three-month period which could not be explained by past behaviour or publicly available knowledge, and the researchers suggest that some information about the proposed merger must have been released to some people. Over this three-month period abnormal share-price returns to the shareholders of the acquired firm averaged 26%. Similar results have been found in studies of mergers in the USA. The fact that abnormal gains prior to the public announcement of a takeover or merger could be obtained might suggest that the market was not efficient. But there are certain other facts that need to be taken into account before coming to this conclusion. The sample used in the study contained only mergers which were concluded and it is possible, indeed most likely, that a number of other mergers reached the stage of being discussed by the parties involved, but the fact that they never got to the stage of completion and announcement meant that they were not included in the sample.

Strong form test

Judging the efficiency of the stock market by observing how share prices adjust to all available information, whether publicly available or not, is known as a 'strong-form test'. It has been found that certain investors do have access either to privileged information or to significant information before other people, and it is not doubted that they can use this to obtain above-average profits. Certain people within companies have access to such information. But there is no evidence that any other class of investor consistently has information which gives them a preferential position in market trading. In the sense that a few people do have information earlier than other investors and so can make an above-average gain, the market may be thought to be inefficient. This is not so, however, for it applies only to a very small group. The vast majority of investors are not in such a favourable position.

A number of researchers have provided evidence that 'insiders' do have what is called 'informational advantage' [13]. This means they are able to use this price-sensitive information to earn 'abnormal' returns from their investments. The law attempts to protect the less informed investors in their dealings with those with inside information. A director of a company knows the up-to-date position of his company, and it would clearly be unfair to allow him to use this information when entering into a buy or sell transaction with an investor who had no such up-to-date information. It would be a form of deception. The position of insiders is examined in Section 8.4.

Of course, one way of making money on the market is to obtain information before other investors, or to react more quickly to the information than other investors. One further prescription for successful trading is to act in the same way as the expert. Usually, however, the uninformed investor finds out too late the way that the informed investor has acted. But it has been shown that it is possible to make a small gain by acting in the same way as the informed investor, but by doing so only one or two days later. It is like standing on the expert's coat-tail – a small amount of gain is left over for other investors after the experts have taken advantage of their knowledge. This trading technique simply states that some money can be made not only by obtaining the information oneself, but by behaving quickly in the same manner as the informed investors.

One type of investor who may be thought to have superior inside information is the newspaper financial journalist, the tipster. The tipster has at least advance knowledge of information to be given in the newspaper for which they write. They know the shares that will be recommended for purchase. They are in a similar position to the investment analyst, whose recommendations can influence the level of a company's share price.

Firth investigated the behaviour of a wide number of tipsters, in particular looking at what happened to the share price of their portfolio recommendations [14]. It is known that the prices of the shares which investors are advised to buy are frequently marked up by market makers the day after the advice is given in the newspapers. This means that either there has been very rapid trading activity or that the market maker has decided to anticipate purchasers' intentions. The result is that by the time most investors have the opportunity to purchase the recommended share, they are buying a correctly priced security and there is little prospect of a further rapid increase in price. The tipster knows that the share price is going to move up after publication of the advice and so the tipster could, if they were so inclined, buy some shares before the article appears and sell them a day or two after it has appeared and so make a gain. City editors tend to ban their tipsters from indulging in such activities. Firth, investigating a number of situations and not one particular case, found no evidence that financial journalists derived profits themselves from trading in the shares that they recommended.

Informed investors

Informed investors are of course different from inside dealers. An efficient market needs informed investors, and one interesting explanation of the random walk phenomenon in share prices distinguishes between two classes of investors, the informed and the uninformed. The informed investors, who have relevant information, anticipate how the trading of the uninformed will be affected by the delays in obtaining the information. They can therefore act on the expected price changes that will eventually result when the uninformed investors obtain the information. The two classes of investors operating in the market could generate the random effect in price movements (as discussed in section 6.1).

Cootner [15] offers a similar explanation. The experts have their own idea of the direction that prices will follow as a result of information not generally available. They will only enter the market if they think that the actual price varies considerably from what they consider to be the correct price. If they think that a price has risen too high they will start to unload the shares at this high price, which will have the effect of pulling the price down. If they think that a price is too low they will start buying the shares at this cheap price, which will have the effect of pushing the price up. There are therefore upper and lower barriers through which it is difficult for the price to move; instead, it moves in a random walk fashion between the barriers. In the short run the price moves in this way because of the uncertainty of the uninformed investors and their resulting random transactions. Over the medium and long run the experts allow the barriers to change. However, perhaps surprisingly, the findings suggest that, except in the very long run, all price movements are random.

The reason that there are upper and lower barriers is that, while it is difficult for the informed investor to name a specific price for a share as the correct value, they do know a price range within which the share is reasonably priced. They will alter the range, the upper and lower barriers, as they receive relevant information. By obtaining this before the non-expert investor, they can make gains on their trading.

Example 8.1

(a) You are required, using the following information, to predict the share prices of Alpha PLC and Beta Engine PLC on day 4, 6 and 12 if the market is:

  (i) semi-strong efficient;
  (ii) strong-form efficient

  Day 1: Alpha PLC has 4 million shares with a market price of £4 per share. Beta Engine PLC has 2 million shares with a market price of £2 per share.

  Day 4: The management of Alpha, meeting in private, decided to make a cash takeover bid for Beta Engine PLC at a price of £4 per share. Both companies have the same earnings per share (EPS) of 40 pence but Alpha has a P/E ratio of 10 while Beta Engine has a P/E ratio of only 5. The management of Alpha also expect to obtain synergistic benefits from the takeover amounting in present value terms to £6 million.

  Day 6: Alpha publicly announces the unconditional offer to purchase all the shares of Beta Engine; details of the expected savings are not announced and therefore are not public knowledge.

  Day 12: Alpha announces details of the savings which will be derived from the takeover.

(b) What would your share-price predictions have been if the purchase consideration, decided upon on day 4 and publicly announced on day 6, had been financed by one newly issued share of Alpha for each Beta Engine share?

Answer

(a) Cash Offer

Alpha

Day 4
Semi-strong: We are told what happened at a private meeting. This is not publicly available information and so the market does not react.

Strong: Price adjusted to reflect 'privately' available information which includes knowledge about the price and the synergistic gains. If it is assumed the bid will be successful then the price immediately moves to its new 'true' value.

  The market value of A before the bid was £16 million and of B £4 million. The combined company is worth £20 million less the cash payment of £8 million. The new company is therefore worth £12 million plus the synergistic gain of £6 million. There are 4 million shares which gives a value per share of £4.50.

Day 6
Semi-strong: The market knows the 'cost' of the bid but not the gains. It believes the value of the combined company to be only £12 million. With 4 million shares the price becomes £3 per share.

Strong: Price remains correctly valued, because all information is reflected in price.

Day 12
Semi-strong: Price moves to its true value of £4.50.

Beta

Day 4
Semi-strong: No change, information of bid not publicly available.

Strong: It is known bid price will be £4, so price moves to this level.

Day 6
Semi-strong: Bid price becomes publicly known, so price adjusts.

Summary

	Semi-strong		Strong market	
	Alpha	Beta	Alpha	Beta
Day 1	£4	£2	£4	£2
Day 4	£4	£2	£4.5	£4
Day 6	£3	£4	£4.5	£4
Day 12	£4.5	£4	£4.5	£4

(b) Share-for-share exchange

Alpha

Day 4
Semi-strong: No change, information not publicly available.

Strong: Price adjusts to reflect privately available information. Value of new company is £26 million (£16 + £4 + £6). Number of shares 6 million. Therefore value per share £4.33.

Day 6
Semi-strong: Public information is only about the bid, not the synergistic gains. Therefore total value £20 million, which gives a value per share of £3.33.

Strong: Price remains at 'true' value.

Day 12
Semi-strong: Price moves to its true value.

Beta

Day 4
Semi-strong: No change.
Strong: Price moves to its true value.

Day 6
Semi-strong: Public know of bid, but not of gains. It is known shareholders of Beta will receive one share in Alpha in exchange for one share in Beta. Market believes on day 6 value of Alpha share will be £3.33.

Day 12
Semi-strong: Price moves to true value.

Summary

	Semi-strong		Strong	
	Alpha	Beta	Alpha	Beta
Day 1	£4	£2	£4	£2
Day 4	£4	£2	£4.33	£4.33
Day 6	£3.33	£3.33	£4.33	£4.33
Day 12	£4.33	£4.33	£4.33	£4.33

8.4 INSIDER DEALING

Insider dealing involves an individual buying or selling shares on the basis of price-sensitive information not yet publicly available. The inside dealer is aiming to exploit the information before it is transmitted to the market. A crucial question is how did the 'insider' obtain the knowledge.

Insider dealing is a very controversial issue. One extreme view is that it is similar to robbery: the insider is taking money away from the person with whom he or she deals who is not aware of certain important facts. Another criticism is that the insider is disturbing the working of a free market: he or she is destroying investors' confidence in the market.

At the other extreme some would argue it is not a crime. Any buyer (and/or seller) of shares in the market should beware. If one trades in any market one takes risks. Why would anybody want to buy a share unless they thought it would lead to gains? It could be argued that the Stock Exchange is all about one person making a gain at someone else's expense. Some economists actually see the practice as beneficial and believe that it should not be prohibited. Insiders can actually be seen as moving the market price in the right direction.

Insider dealing is a way of redistributing wealth. It moves it towards those with inside knowledge and away from those without it.

Why insider dealing is an important issue from the point of view of stock market efficiency is because the strong-form test of the market efficiency is concerned with price movements in response to any information. That is information, whether publicly available or not. It has been found that within limits share prices in the market reflect all publicly available information. They do not, however, reflect information not available to the public. People with access to non-public information (insiders) can therefore make above-average returns. If 'inside dealing' is known to be taking place in the stock market, it will frighten investors without inside knowledge and keep them out of the stock market. The view is taken, therefore, in most stock markets that an individual may not deal in securities of a company if he or she has price-sensitive inside information which is held by virtue of being a connected person or having obtained inside information from such a person. Similarly, an insider must not counsel or procure others to act on inside information and must not communicate such information to anyone else.

In 1990 the Secretary of State argued that he believed the number of insider dealing cases in the UK was 'probably on the decline'. However, many believe that the occurrences of insider dealing have not dropped as markedly as would have been expected since it became illegal in 1980. The international aspects of markets and modern telecommunications have made the crime easier to commit and harder to detect; consequently there can be little confidence that insider dealing is on the decline.

Insider trading in the UK has only been a criminal offence since 1980; prior to that the practice was scarcely frowned upon. The offence now warrants a maximum ten-year jail sentence and a large fine.

The Criminal Justice Act 1993 changed the definition of 'insiders'. The offence was extended to cover anyone who obtains inside information as a result of his or her employment/position. Prior to this change there had to be a more direct 'connection' between an insider and the company whose shares were dealt in. This change greatly increases the scope for investigations.

The 1993 Act increased the scope of the legislation in certain other respects: namely the securities covered; the markets regulated; and the geographical area of the offence. Dealing now includes any off-market deal made through a professional intermediary as well as those on a recognized stock exchange. 'Securities' was given a wider meaning and include debt securities, depositary receipts, options and futures. The offences now cover markets in 19 European countries and extend to any investments made through intermediaries, and disclosure or encouragement made to persons in the UK from anywhere in the world.

Inside information is defined as specific price-sensitive information relating to particular securities which have not been made public. The Act provides that it will be judged price-sensitive when, if made public, it would be likely to have 'a significant effect' on the price of any securities.

An important question is what constitutes price-sensitive information. The regular dialogue between analysts, fund managers and companies is a vital link in the market. Analysts gain specialist knowledge about particular sectors and can advise investors as to the best investments to make. It is claimed the insider dealing rules threaten the very source from which analysts get much of their information, the company.

One group of individuals who will always be (or should always be) knowledgeable about a company are the directors. The Companies Act 1985 required directors to notify the company of any interests that they have in the company's shares. Dealings in the shares and holdings of shares are recorded and are available for inspection at any time. It is unlikely that directors will deal on specific price-sensitive information, but they will always have an overall informational advantage. They will always have better information as to the company's day-to-day activities. The market is aware of the possible significance of such director dealings and much interest is now taken as to just why the director is dealing. The dealings of directors have now become a vital indicator to the market on how a company is really performing. The directors are often dealing on information that is not widely available.

Detection of insider dealing

It is difficult to obtain evidence on illegal insider dealing. The culprits often use foreign-based companies, in say Panama or Guernsey, that are nominee vehicles. This allows the people behind the deal to trade through such companies without being identified.

The culprit could be an employee of a bank or an investment analyst in the UK. The person would buy or sell through a nominee name in an offshore financial centre. This has been made a little more difficult by firms now recording all phone calls through the office. Nevertheless an employee of a merchant bank who knows of a takeover bid that is to take place can pass on the information secretly to someone who would deal through a nominee company. A phone call could be made from a phone box in London to one in, say, Gibraltar.

In the UK it is very difficult to make an insider trading case stick. In the years between 1980 (when such dealing was made illegal) and 1994 the Stock Exchange referred in the region of 200 cases to the DTI. This had led at that time to only 22 convictions, with only one person jailed. That one person was a company chairman who did not try to cover his tracks. In the UK usually the system only catches small transgressions. The USA is more effective in catching insider dealers. They can subpoena witnesses, and settle cases out of court.

8.5 DOUBTS ABOUT STOCK MARKET EFFICIENCY

In 1978 Jensen told us that 'the efficient market hypothesis is the best established fact in all of the social sciences' [16]. In 1988 he went further, telling us that 'no proposition, in any of the sciences is better documented' than the efficient market hypothesis. It is true that there is much research evidence indicating that stock market prices (in the USA in particular) appropriately incorporate all currently available public information. Nevertheless there are sweeping statements; particularly as Jensen does admit in the 1988 study that the evidence is 'not literally 100 percent in support' of the hypothesis [17]. What can we say about the evidence on the efficiency of stock markets?

It is important to appreciate the following.

1 The semi-strong test of the EMH, also referred to as 'information arbitrage efficiency', does not imply rational prices. It does not imply that the share price of a company reflects its fundamental value.

2 At the best the weak-form and semi-strong-form tests indicate that it is not possible to identify persistent opportunities through stock market trading to achieve excess profits. The tests indicate that the EMH cannot be rejected on the basis of the data being used – this does not mean that the tests prove that the market is efficient. The empirical tests in fact can neither confirm nor disconfirm that stock markets are 'efficient'. The tests do not establish that a stock market is efficient. All they show is that it cannot be proved that it is inefficient.

3 There are important differences between the stock markets in Europe and the US stock markets. In the UK the financial institutions own a much higher percentage of the shares of UK companies than is the case with financial institutions in the USA. As Peacock and Bannock point out, this means that in the UK there are not always a large number of buyers or sellers of a company's shares, which, as every first-year economics student knows, is a necessary condition for perfect competition [18]. We should be careful before assuming that findings based on the situation in the USA apply to the UK.

Black caused a stir when, in his presidential address to the American Finance Association, he stated 'I think almost all markets [he was referring to US stock markets] are efficient almost all of the time.' 'Almost all', he explains means at least 90% of the time [19]. In fact, if 10% of the time markets are not efficient this gives a lot of opportunity for 'bargain purchases' of undervalued shares. Black pointed out that a certain amount of trading in shares was motivated by 'noise'. He wished to contrast 'noise' with 'information'. From the market's point of view all trading is good as it makes markets liquid, whether or not the trading is based on facts.

Black's views of what at any point of time the relationship between a true (intrinsic) value and the actual share price should be in an efficient market leaves a lot of room for those engaged in investing in equities to exploit price gaps. Black refers to the market being efficient if it results in the actual price of a company's shares being within a factor of two of its true value. This factor of course represents his view of a reasonable price and Black admits it is arbitrary but he states 'intuitively, though, it seems reasonable to me, in the light of sources of uncertainty about value'. The above comments suggest that either the markets are not so efficient at interpreting the information given in company financial statements or that the statements do not give sufficient information for the intrinsic value to be determined.

Valuation problems

As Stiglitz points out, the existence of asymmetric information means that 'managers can take actions which affect the returns to those who provide capital' [20]. In the 1980s the 'management of earnings disclosure' became an art and unfortunately became not uncommon both in the US and the UK. The manipulation of reported earnings means that one group of market participants have information and an understanding not available to other participants. On the question of understanding, doubts arose particularly in the late 1980s as to whether financial analysts, who had the necessary information, were able to understand its true importance.

Bhattachara, reviewing the literature on the valuation of equities in the stock market, concludes 'the accumulation of evidence presents, in my view, a murky picture vis-à-vis the prevalence of rational [information-efficient] valuation in the stock market' [21]. Roll and other researchers have found that significant movements in individual share price and stock market indices cannot on many occasions be related to public news, and vice versa [22]. The announcement of fundamental news does not on occasions move prices. It is not just news that leads to movements in share prices; the action of uninformed investors also moves prices.

It is claimed by supporters of the efficient markets that the anomalies that have been identified are not of major importance. The ones that have been found only affect a minor part of stock market activity. There does not seem to be anything systematic about them which would give grounds for concern that the stock market is not on the whole a fair game.

It is accepted that discrepancies do exist between actual share prices at any one time and what are thought to be 'true' (intrinsic) values. The research of Bernard and Thomas suggests that the market only allows small discrepancies to arise, which they estimate to be on average up to a 2% difference for larger firms and up to a 6% difference for smaller firms [23].

The studies mentioned above have all been published in the USA and are primarily based on the situation in that country. There has been a vast amount of empirical research in the USA testing the efficient market hypothesis. Whittington, in his overview of financial accounting theory, asserts that 'the empirical approach has become almost a cult among ambitious young academics, especially in the USA' and refers to 'the age of the computer' which facilitates this type of research [24].

There is a certain amount of evidence relating to the efficiency of the London Stock Exchange, but much less evidence on the efficiency of the other stock exchanges in Europe. In fact, the concept of the efficient market hypothesis is of more interest and of more significance in some countries than in others. This is because in some countries stock exchanges are of more importance in the financial system than in others.

Although most of the evidence produced over the last twenty years indicates that the major stock markets of the world are efficient in a weak-form and semi-strong-form sense, doubts are now being raised. It is becoming fashionable to criticize the idea that stock markets are efficient. The problem is that the theory has perhaps been oversold in the past.

One form of criticism relates to the mathematical analysis that has been used in the past to test the hypothesis. New mathematical analysis of stock market prices shows there is often unexpected predictability. This is being explained by the fact that those who trade in the market do not all think the same way [25]. They reason differently about the information they receive, they have different time horizons and different attitudes towards risk. It has been suggested that the more advanced computer models now being developed allow opportunities to outperform the market at least for a while. Such opportunities result from the way in which information is interpreted and used by the participants in the market. The information is efficiently and fairly distributed; it is how it is used that creates opportunities.

The efficient market hypothesis does not say anything about how market participants incorporate news into investment decisions.

8.6 MARKET ANOMALIES

Statistical studies have shown that there is a tendency for mean share-price returns to vary as follows:

1 At different times during the trading day. (It has been found in the USA, dividing a day into 15-minute periods, that the first 45 minutes of trading on Mondays produces negative returns, whilst on other weekdays it is positive. It has also been found that prices rise on all weekdays during the last 15 minutes of trading.)
2 Across the days of the trading week, with below-average return on a Monday.
3 Across the months of the year, with high returns in January in the USA and in April in the UK.

Knowledge of these timing and seasonal patterns means that it would appear to be possible to exploit these inefficiencies to make above average returns. Just an understanding of these patterns in *ex post* share-price returns and the adoption of an arbitrage strategy could lead to 'beating the system'.

Unless we can explain what causes irregularities, we cannot be confident that they will continue to occur. It could just be that they have occurred for chance reasons, with some people being lucky and benefiting from them. It could be that they are unlikely to occur in the future. Unless we have a satisfactory explanation – a theory that explains why they are happening – we have little reason to expect them to recur.

We shall now consider possible explanations for these anomalies.

Hours of the day

As was mentioned above, trading at different times of the day can give above- or below-average returns. Two examples were mentioned; a third is that prices rise between 12.30 p.m. and 1.30 p.m., followed by a fall after lunch between 2.30 p.m. and 3.15 p.m.

A number of research studies have come up with similar conclusions, but with slight variations. For example, the so-called weekend effect has been found by one researcher to begin to take effect on Friday afternoon. Few explanations have been offered for these intra-day effects. Most researchers on the subject have first shown the existence of such patterns and then indicated that further research is required before an explanation can be offered.

Day-of-the-week effect

One explanation for this effect is to be found in the fact that the actions of investors are not consistent throughout the trading week. At weekends investors evaluate their own portfolio and initiate their own 'sell' decisions; they sell first thing on a Monday. 'Buy' decisions, in contrast, are usually initiated by brokers, and such actions are constant throughout the week.

The study by Abraham and Ikenberry [26] found that between 1982 and 1991 share prices on the New York Stock Exchange fell on Mondays by an average of 0.11%. They typically rose during the rest of the week. In fact, 7 of the worst 15 trading days were on a Monday.

It was found that there was disproportionately heavy selling of small amounts of shares on Mondays. Typically the sales were by individual investors, the weekend being the time when individuals consider their investment portfolio.

Months-of-the-year effect

One of the more popular explanations for the patterns that give above-average returns in April in the UK is the tax-loss selling hypothesis. The basis of this is that investors who have accrued losses on certain investments during a year have an incentive to engage in fiscal-year-end selling strategies. They sell the shares on which they show losses in order to create a tax shield against capital gains tax liabilities that arise on shares they hold that have made gains [27].

The result of so many investors in the UK selling shares in March (end of tax-year) is to depress share-price levels. Once into the new financial year the tax reason for selling disappears and the share levels rebound to their price levels before the end of the tax year. This means that buying shares at the beginning of either January (USA) or April (UK) and selling at the end of the respective month produces higher levels of return than can be obtained by adopting a similar strategy in the other months of the year.

Annual effects

Studies covering long time periods illustrate a so-called corrective behaviour of share-price returns. This is that the prices of individual shares or portfolios of shares that perform badly in one year are likely to do well in the next. The reverse also happens for shares that perform well in one year, but the process is asymmetric. It is the losing shares in one period that show the greater positive returns during the next.

Size anomalies

Research has shown that in the long run the returns from investing in smaller companies give a slightly higher return than the average market performance across companies of all sizes. If the market is efficient this should not happen, i.e. unless the market risks from investing in smaller companies is above the average market risk. An investor knowing of this irregularity could devise trading rules to produce consistent above-average returns.

Research in the USA found that smaller companies outperformed other companies over time on average by 4% per annum on a compound basis. Research was later conducted on data from many other countries and similar results were obtained. Dimson and March [28] published results for the UK based on the performance of as many as 1200 companies with market capitalizations of £100 million or less. They found that, on average, the small firms outperformed the larger firms by 6% per annum.

Fama and French have shown that it is possible to predict the prices of the shares of small firms [29].

How can this size effect be explained? Among the explanations that have been offered are the following.

Growth prospects

It is a fact that it is easier for small companies to grow more quickly than large, simply because of the lower starting base. Dividends and earnings of smaller companies do grow faster than those of the average-size company. But this does not really explain the above-average share-price performance we are concerned with. If everyone knows that small companies show faster growth, then investors pay more for their shares, based on current earning levels, than they would for companies with slower growth. This is why faster-growth companies of any size have higher price-to-earnings ratios than lower-growth companies.

Risk

Do smaller companies have higher non-diversifiable risks (betas) than large companies? If this is the case then investors would want an above-average return to compensate for the risk. It has in fact been shown that smaller companies do have above-average betas, but it has also been shown that this difference in betas is not sufficient to give a complete explanation of the size effect [30].

Trading costs

It is more expensive to trade in the shares of small companies than in those of large companies. The reason is that, because of infrequent trading in such securities, the commissions asked by dealers and the spread between the bid and offer price are higher than is the case for the more frequently traded larger companies. To compensate for their higher costs, investors require a higher gross profit on any buy/sell transaction in the shares of small companies. The empirical research that highlights the size effect is based on above-average gross returns. The impact of high trading costs will bring down the net returns on the buying and selling of shares. This could mean that the net return from trading in small-company shares is not very different from the average net return for all companies. If, however, the small-company shares are not traded frequently, but are held for, say, a number of years, then the additional trading cost averaged over the years the shares are held will be low, and above-average net returns can be obtained.

Seasonality

It has been observed in the USA that much of the size effect occurs in the month of January [31]. This means that the price of company shares falls in the last days of December and rises in the early days of January. This seasonal effect has been observed for all companies, not just small ones. As menfioned above, this so-called fiscal-year-end effect occurs in the UK between the end of March and the beginning of April. Possible explanations for this irregularity include actions taken by investors to reduce their capital gains tax bills. At the end of the tax year they realize their losses to be used to offset against gains. This has been referred to as the 'bed and breakfast' technique.

Seasonal irregularity could therefore be part of the explanation of the size irregularity, with institutional and private investors adjusting their portfolios for tax reasons.

The evidence does not come up with support for any one explanation of the size effect. The shares of small companies have been shown to be able to outperform the market. This has been the case for many years in a number of countries. We have a number of possible explanations for this effect, each contributing something to our understanding of the irregularity.

Lack of information

The market has less information about small companies than about large companies. Analysts spend less time studying the financial position of small companies. It is less likely therefore that the market price of smaller companies represents the fundamental value of the share of such a company, than for a large company. This means that there is an opportunity for the aware investor to make above-average returns through investing in smaller companies. For the market to be efficient in the valuation of a company it is necessary to have a number of analysts studying the performance of a company. This is a problem in smaller capital markets, where there may not be enough analysis. It is a problem in the larger markets, because it is not possible for analysts to be knowledgeable about all quoted companies.

8.7 BEHAVIOURAL INFLUENCES ON SHARE PRICE

It has been observed that, in stock markets, share-price movements are more volatile than would be expected if all trading was based on fundamental information. Roll has shown that most idiosyncratic moves in the price of a particular company's shares cannot be explained by public news [32]. There are significant price moves on days when there is no public news that would be expected to influence the share price. Cutler *et al.* [33] found that the days where there is the largest market movement in price are not the days with the most important fundamental news.

The reason for such movements is that prices are influenced by behavioural factors as well as by fundamental factors. Investors can be influenced by moods, sentiment and irrational behaviour. For example, cognitive psychology has shown that individuals systematically over-weight current information and under-weight background information. This has been called the good news/bad news anomaly. It will be discussed later in this section.

Three other behavioural characteristics that affect share prices are bubbles and fads, the herd instinct and excess volatility.

Fads and bubbles

When the movements in share price over time are studied, what are referred to as 'bubbles' can be observed, these being 'explosive' movements in share prices, or deviations from movement based on fundamental information. A number of explanations for such bubbles have been proposed.

One such explanation is noise trading by naive investors. This is called a 'fad'. As mentioned in section 8.2, a number of years ago Cootner referred to informed and uninformed investors. These two classes of investors have been given many names. The uninformed are sometimes called 'noise' traders or 'liquidity' traders. The informed are sometimes called 'arbitrageurs' or 'rational speculators'. It is this latter group who do the work of bringing the company's share price towards its fundamental value. Some shifts in the demand for a share are completely rational, but some are not. The uninformed investor can be irrational – they can introduce a systematic bias into the market. The change in demand can be based on sentiment or the unjustified expectation of uninformed investors. On what is called a 'fad'.

The uninformed investor may be responding to the advice of a stockbroker or a financial guru. The investor might be just following what is seen to be a trend, to be imitating strategies that they believe will leave to above-average returns. One of the strongest tendencies of the less informed investor is to chase the trend. That is, to buy shares following their rise, and to sell shares following a fall. The change in demand is not based on fundamental news, but on noise. Technical analysis can also lead to changes in demand not based on fundamental information.

The informed investors, the arbitrageurs, take advantage of actions of the noise trader. This might not mean to always sell when the uninformed are buying. It might be in the arbitrageur's interest sometimes to jump on the bandwagon for a while. This is called 'feedback trading'. If the uninformed are buying the arbitrageur buys for a while, but has to be careful to sell near the top and take profits. The arbitrageur is for a time therefore helping to feed the 'bubble'; it is only when selling that he or she is helping to bring the price down to its fundamental value.

George Soros, a famous successful investor (investing in the foreign exchange market as well as the stock market), does not always try to counter the irrational waves of buying and selling a security [34]. He is sometimes prepared to ride the wave, but to get out before the uninformed. This tactic has been described as 'pumping up the tulips'.

Booms and crashes in stock market prices are easy to explain if informed investors do on occasions engage in feedback trading – if they do 'pump up the tulips'. They are certainly easier to explain in this way, than by assuming that informed investors always trade to bring an actual market price of a share back to its fundamental value. The informed investor only engages in limited arbitrage. On occasion he or she is willing to go along with the trend, the trend being based on fads, sentiment and noise.

The overreaction hypothesis

Experimental and survey evidence indicates that there is a tendency for individuals to over-weight recent information and under-weight basic data. People overreact. From a stock market point of view this means investors overreact to unexpected earnings figures, and as a result stock prices can and do depart at least in the short run from their underlying fundamental values. The hypothesis states that prices respond to good news or bad news by overshooting their true value. This is as a result of excessive investor optimism or pessimism; after the initial reaction prices move to their true value. This means prices are at some points in time predictable: having fallen too far they will rise, or having risen too far they will fall. Dissanaiki tested this hypothesis with data relating to the largest UK companies, and found support for the overreaction hypothesis [35].

De Bondt and Thaler and other researchers have found evidence that in the USA investors overreact to short-term earnings movements [36]. Investors focus on the immediate past and do not look beyond the immediate future. There is a close correspondence between share-price returns and changes in the short-term earnings outlook. Investors, on average, have an excessively short-term orientation.

These findings are not, of course, what one would expect from an efficient market. But there is now increasing evidence that share prices do take swings away from fundamental values. The evidence is that these 'erroneous' movements away from fundamental values are eventually corrected: there is a mean reversion in share prices.

Poterba and Summers also show that there are transitory components in share prices: that is, there can be a move in the short run away from fundamental values. They found this with UK data as well as US data [37]. These transitory components, these mispricings, are large in relation to what one would expect with stock market efficiency. This overreaction of the market to good and bad short-term earnings figures leads to volatility in investors' returns. The volatility in the market returns for investors is greater than what one would expect if market prices reflected fundamental values.

Herd behaviour

Individuals sometimes suppress their own beliefs and base their decisions on the collective actions in the market. If an individual analyst feels share prices will fall in the future, but all other analysts are buying expecting a bull market to continue, it might be the easiest solution for the individual to also buy.

If the individual analyst does not follow the buy decisions of the market, and is correct in that the market falls, he or she will stand out and be seen as a star. But if the individual analyst goes against the market, and the rest of the market is correct the individual will appear to be a fool and in danger of losing their job. In terms of risk against return it might be safer to follow the herd.

There are often analysts who specialize in obtaining knowledge about shares in a particular sector of the economy. They are seen as lead analysts in that sector. Other analysts tend to follow the earnings forecasts of the specialist.

Excess volatility

The amount and size of share-price fluctuations is often greater than can be justified by changes in fundamentals. What is it that drives the changes in the short run? One explanation is the fact that individuals overreact to news. When the news is good the market prices rise more than can be justified. They subsequently fall to their correct, 'true' level. The opposite happens with bad news.

One interesting event that illustrates a number of aspects of how the market reacts to news occurred in December 1996. The story illustrates that the price of a share partly depends on economy-wide factors, indeed now on global factors. When, in December 1996, Alan Greenspan, chairman of the US Federal Reserve Board delivered a speech in the USA that stock markets were a bubble waiting to burst, the FTSE 100 index (in London) fell during the day following the speech by 170 points. On 'Black Monday' in 1987 it fell by 250 points. In 1992 when the UK withdrew from the ERM it fell by 103 points. The fall following the Greenspan speech clearly indicates the market reacting to new information.

The Greenspan story can be used to illustrate three points relevant to share-price determination. The prices on the London exchange fell quickly in response to information about Greenspan's views. The speech had taken place whilst the London market was closed overnight; as soon as it opened prices began to fall. Prices hit their low just after midday and then rose 80 points by the end of the day's trading. Anecdotal, but an interesting illustration of the market overreaction to bad news.

A second interesting aspect of the event was the use by Greenspan of the word 'bubble'. Why do bubbles occur? Can they happen if the stock markets are efficient?

Greenspan was not concerned in his speech with market efficiency, but he did indicate that he believed the high prices were the result of an 'enthusiasm for buying shares' which amounted to 'irrational exuberance amongst investors'. We have discussed rational and irrational buying behaviour earlier in this section.

Attempts were made, following the speech by Greenspan, to calm down nervous investors. Mr Ruben who was at the time Chief of the Treasury in the USA, said 'over time markets do follow fundamentals'. Those who believe that the markets are influenced by behavioural factors would agree. Over time prices reflect fundamentals but there are, in the short run, movements away from fundamental values.

Considering how important is the level of the share price of a company to many of its decisions and to the future of the management, it is surprising that the process of share-price determination is so subjective. The cost of capital, the potential for growth through external acquisition and the very survival of the company as a separate entity depend on the price of the company's shares. Yet what lies behind one of the key factors by which management is judged, and consequently a factor that determines their survival – namely the share price – is often only vaguely understood.

The 'efficient' market implies that, given the available information, there is an intrinsic value for a share, and that the actual share price will equal that value. This means that a market analyst cannot expect to purchase shares that are underpriced unless he or she has inside information or responds more quickly to new information than other investors. This does not mean that he or she does not or should not try.

Analysts who try to determine the intrinsic worth of a share undertake what is referred to as 'fundamental analysis'. There is another group of analysts who do not concern themselves with the factors that influence the worth of a particular share. They analyse charts and look for patterns in the movement over time of a company's share price. These 'chartists' undertake what is referred to as a 'technical analysis'.

If investors expect a certain thing to happen, the action expressing their expectations can make sure the event does come about: it is a self-fulfilling prophecy. For example, if investors for some reason expect share prices to fall, they will start to sell, a bear market will be created, and prices will duly fall. It is on the basis of these psychological factors influencing share prices that a chartist can be successful. The chartist studies the movement of share prices over time, either the aggregate price level or the prices of a particular company. He or she looks for either recurring patterns of price movements or recurring interrelationships between stock price movements and other market data.

One situation that a chartist would identify, caused by the behaviour of investors, is referred to as a 'resistance zone' or 'supply area'. Suppose, for example, that a share is sold in considerable volume at a price of £1.25, and many investors acquire it at this price. The volume of business in the share then falls, and the price consequently declines. The shareholders will tend to hold onto the share until the price recovers. As the price slowly moves through £0.80 and £0.90 to £1.10 these former buyers will still be reluctant to sell at a loss; it is when the price approaches £1.25 that it would be expected that many of the former buyers would begin to sell. The price of £1.20 or £1.25 has become a 'supply area'.

Another such situation arises where an investor, thinking of buying a particular share at a price of say £0.40, suddenly finds the price has jumped to £0.60. They hear stories explaining the rise and generally boosting the shares of that particular company. The investor is annoyed that they did not buy the share when it first occurred to them. If the price of that company's shares ever gets back to near £0.40, they will buy. The price of £0.40 has become a support area. Investors may not actually think this way but if they act as if they do, the results will be the same.

One technique of the chartists that has been shown statistically to be useful for prediction purposes is the study of advances and declines. Records are kept on most stock exchanges of the number of shares which advance and decline on a particular trading day. Dividing these numbers by the number of shares traded on the exchange on the particular day gives the proportion of shares advancing and declining, and therefore shows the proportion remaining unchanged. It has been demonstrated that given knowledge of these movements in the shares on the market for one day, it is possible to predict the number of advances and declines for the next day.

This analysis of what is called the 'breadth of the market' 'can be used to determine the major turning points in the market as a whole'. The theory is based on the notion of stock market cycles. It is based on the idea that bull markets are long drawn-out affairs, during which time the individual shares gradually reach their peak, with the number of shares reaching their peaks accelerating as the market averages rise towards the turning point. When a share has reached its peak, obviously its next price movement is a decline, so that the number of shares showing a decline in their price accelerates as the market index approaches its turning point.

Chartists survive, along with other types of analysts. Whatever technique they use must be correct a sufficient number of times because chartists remain in business. The techniques that the chartists use, such as 'the head and shoulders' and 'downside breaks', might be given colourful names and be hard to justify in theory, but at least they must have kept investors as satisfied as the apparently more sophisticated approaches.

8.9 THE EFFICIENT MARKET HYPOTHESIS AND THE INVESTMENT STRATEGIES

The efficient market does not mean that investment research should not be undertaken. In fact, paradoxically for the efficient market hypothesis to hold, it is necessary for many people to analyse and attempt to interpret the information that is made available. It is the action of competing investors that makes the market efficient. Each decision maker, each investor, is searching for good companies that will make attractive investments. When they identify such companies, they force up the price of the share to one which, in the end, just leads to average returns. It is important that investors continue to seek good companies. For them not to do so, for them not to try to benefit from knowledge they obtain, would lead to inefficient markets – to share prices that do not reflect all the available information.

In an efficient market, the returns obtained depend upon a number of factors, one being the level of risk of the investments in a portfolio. If an investor is prepared to take heavy risks they can achieve above-average performance for a time. Another factor is luck. A third factor is the level of transaction and management expenses paid for the portfolio management. A large amount of switching of investments increases expenses, and so the gross gains on the share dealings need to be higher to show an average profit net of expenses.

There are two other possible ways in which above-average returns can be earned. One is for the investor to obtain inside information or to have a better understanding than others of publicly available information or of the way the market behaves. This would give the investor the opportunity to earn exceptional returns, but as regulations on trading by insiders are tightened up, this reduces the opportunity for this type of gain. The second way in which such gains can be made is to discover a new form of analysis or to obtain a new insight into the stock market. The person or firm that discovers such methods would use the approach to make gains for themselves, but would probably not wish to make the technique known to others. This is a good reason for investment research. To try to discover such techniques has a cost, of course, and until the new technique gives above-average results the net returns can be quite low.

8.10 REFERENCES

1 Copeland, T.E. and Weston, J.F. (1983) *Financial Theory and Corporate Policy*, 2nd edn, Addison-Wesley, Reading, Mass.
2 Mossin, J. (1977) *The Economic Efficiency of Financial Markets*, Prentice-Hall, Englewood Cliffs, NJ.
3 Beaver, W. (1981) *Financial Reporting: An Accounting Revolution*, Prentice-Hall, Englewood Cliffs, NJ.

4 Jegadeesh, N. (1990) Evidence on predictable behaviour of security returns, *Journal of Finance*, **45**, July 881–98.

5 Mills, T.C. (1991) Assessing the predictability of UK stock market returns, *Applied Financial Economics*, **1**(4), 241–5.

6 Fama, E.F (1970) Efficient capital markets: a review of theory and empirical work, *Journal of Finance*, **25**, May 383–420.

7 Fama, E.F. (1991) Efficient capital markets: II, *Journal of Finance*, **46**(5), 1575–1617.

8 Fama, E.F., Fisher, L., Jensen, M.C. and Roll, R. (1969) The adjustment of stock prices to new information, *International Economic Review*, February.

9 Firth, M.A. (1977) An empirical investigation of the impact of the announcement of capitalization issues on share prices, *Journal of Business Finance and Accounting*, Spring.

10 Marsh, P. (1977) Ph.D. Dissertation, London Graduate School of Business Studies.

11 Ball, R. and Brown, P. (1968) An empirical evaluation of accounting income numbers, *Journal of Accounting Research*, 159–78, Autumn.

12 Franks, J.R., Broyles, J.E. and Hecht, M.J. (1978) An industry study of the profitability of mergers in the United Kingdom, *Journal of Finance*.

13 Finnerty, J.E. (1976) Insiders and market efficiency, *Journal of Finance*, September.
    Jaffe, J.J. (1974) Special information and insider trading, *Journal of Business*, July.
    Lorie, J. and Niederhoffer, V. (1978) Predictive and statistical properties of insider trading, *Journal of Law and Economics*, April.

14 Firth, M.A. (1972) The performance of share recommendations made by investment analysts and the effects on market efficiency, *Journal of Business Finance*, **4**.

15 Cootner, P. (1962) Stock prices: random vs. systematic changes, *Industrial Management Review*, 231–52, Spring.

16 Jensen, M.C. (1978) Some anomalies evidence regarding market efficiency, *Journal of Financial Economics*, **6**, June/Sept., 95–102.

17 Jensen, M.C. (1988) Takeovers: their causes and consequences, *Journal of Economic Perspectives*, **2**(1).

18 Peacock, A. and Bannock, G. (1991) *Corporate Takeovers and the Public Interest*, Aberdeen University Press, Aberdeen.

19 Black, F. (1986) Noise, *Journal of Finance*, **41**, 529–34.

20 Stiglitz, J.E. (1988) Why financial structure matters, *Journal of Economic Perspectives*, **2**(4), 121–6.

21 Bhattachara, S. (1988) Corporate finance and the legacy of Miller and Modigliani, *Journal of Economic Perspectives*, **2**(4), 135–47.

22 Roll, R. (1988) R-squared, *Journal of Finance*, **43**, July, 541–66.

23 Bernard, V.L. and Thomas, J. (1990) Evidence that stock prices do not fully reflect the implications of current earnings, *Journal of Accounting and Economics*, **13**, 305–40.

24 Whittington, G. (1986) Financial accounting theory: an overview, *British Accounting Review*, **18**(2), Autumn, 4–41.

25 *The Economist* (1993) (Supplement) Frontiers of Finance, 9–15, Oct.

26 Abraham, A. and Ikenberry, D. (1994) The individual investor and the weekend effect, *Journal of Financial and Quantitative Analysis*, June.

27 Gultekin, M. and Gultekin, N. (1983) Stock market seasonality: international evidence, *Journal of Financial Economics*, December.
    Haugen, R.A. and Lakonishok, K. (1988) *The Incredible January Effect*, Dow Jones, Irwin, Ill.

28 Dimson, E. and March, P. (1986) Event study methodologies and the size effect, *Journal of Financial Economics*, **17**(1), 113–42.

29 Fama, E.F. and French, K.R. (1988) Permanent and temporary components of stock prices, *Journal of Political Economy*, **96**, 246–73.

30 Roll, R. (1981) A possible explanation for the small firm effect, *Journal of Finance*, September.

Reinganum, M. (1982) A direct test of Roll's conjecture on the firm size effect, *Journal of Finance*, March.

Chan, K.C., Chen, N. and Hsieh, D. (1985) An exploratory investigation of the firm size effect, *Journal of Financial Economics*, September.

31 Keim, D. (1983) Size related anomalies and stock return reasonability: further empirical evidence, *Journal of Financial Economics*, June.

Keim, D. and Stambaugh, R. (1984) A further investigation of the week-end effect in stock returns, *Journal of Finance*, July.

32 Roll, Richard R. (1988) R-squared. *Journal of Finance*, **43**, July, 541–66.

33 Cutler, David M., Porterba, James M. and Summers, Lawrence H. (1989) What moves stock prices? *Journal of Portfolio Management*, **15**, Spring, 4–12.

Cootner, P. – see [15].

De Long, J. Bradford, Shleifer, Andrei, Summers, Lawrence H. and Waldemann, Robert J. (1989) The size and incidence of the losses from noise trading, *Journal of Finance*, **44**, July, 681–96.

34 Soros, George (1987) *The Alchemy of Finance*, New York: Simon & Schuster.

35 Dissanaike, G. (1997) Do stock markets overreact, *Journal of Business Finance and Accounting*, **24**(1): 27–49.

36 De Bondt, W.F. and Thaler, R.H. (1987) Further evidence on investment over-reaction and stock market seasonality, *Journal of Finance*, July.

37 Poterba, J.M. and Summers, L.H. (1988) Mean reversion in stock prices: evidence and implications, *Journal of Financial Economics*, **22**, 27–59.

8.11 FURTHER READING

Thaler, R. (ed.) (1993) *Advances in Behavioural Finance*, Russell Sage Foundation, New York.

Summers, L.H. (1986) Does the stock market rationally reflect fundamental values?, *Journal of Finance*, **41**(3): 591–601.

8.12 PROBLEMS

1 Explain why new equity issues are more common when share prices are high than when the share price index is low. To what extent can the reasons given be considered inconsistent with the efficient markets hypothesis?

2 Describe the efficient market hypothesis and distinguish between its three forms. Discuss the relevance of the hypothesis for the internal financial management of publicly quoted companies.

3 It has not been possible to disprove the efficient market hypothesis in the advanced capital markets of the USA and the UK. Describe the types of empirical research undertaken to test the validity of the hypothesis. Pay attention to the manner in which efficiency is interpreted in the tests you describe.

4 (a) Explain what you understand by the term 'efficient markets model' and compare efficiency in this context with the economist's idealized perfect market model.

   (b) Outline and appraise the types of empirical research undertaken to test the validity of the efficient markets hypothesis.

5 'The results of this paper have indicated that on average managers of unit trusts in the UK have not been able to forecast share prices accurately enough to outperform a simple buy-and-hold policy.' (Firth)

Firth's work seems to confirm Jensen's earlier research on US mutual funds. Discuss the validity of their findings and the implications of their conclusions for unit trust managers and investors if they are correct.

6 (a) Explain the differences between the three forms of the efficient market hypothesis. How does the existence of an efficient capital market assist corporate financial management and planning?

(b) Company A has two million shares in issue and Company B has five million.

On day 1, the market value per share is £1 for A and £2 for B.

On day 2, the management of B decide, at a private meeting, to make a cash takeover bid for A at a price of £1.50 per share. The takeover will produce large operating savings with a present value of £1.6 millions.

On day 4, B publicly announces an unconditional offer to purchase all shares of A at a price of £1.50 per share with settlement on day 15. Details of the large savings are not announced and are not public knowledge.

On day 10, B announces details of the savings which will be derived from the takeover.

Ignoring tax and the time value of money between day 1 and 15, and assuming that the details given are the only factors having an impact on the share prices of A and B, determine the day-2, day-4 and day-10 share prices of A and B if the market is

 (i) semi-strong-form efficient and
(ii) strong-form efficient. (15 marks)

ACCA, Financial Management

7 'Among the investment lessons that the efficient market hypothesis teaches us are the following:

• Random selection of securities is as good as any other. Therefore, practise your dart throwing skill.
• A buy-and-hold policy is as good as any other. Therefore, it is not necessary to follow and keep up with the fundamentals of the companies in which you own securities.'

(a) Explain what you understand by the term 'efficient market hypothesis' and describe the categories of test relating to the model and their significance for the validity of the model.

(b) Examine the validity of the above statements for (i) the investment manager of a large pension fund and (ii) a small private investor.

8 'Recent evidence suggests either that the market is inefficient or that the capital-asset pricing model is inadequate.' Discuss.

9 Discuss the relative merits of an index fund and an actively managed portfolio of quoted investments and comment on the basis on which the manager of an investment portfolio might seek to justify the employment of an investment analyst.

10 Discuss the scope for management action to minimize the cost of capital in an efficient market. In relation to this objective comment specifically on the significance of pre-emptive rights for existing shareholders to subscribe to new issues of equity, the discount to market price at which such new issues are made and the timing of such issues in relation to market 'highs'.

11 The ABC Pharmaceutical Company announces that it is to produce a new drug. It was not known before the announcement that the company had been

successful in its research programme into the effects of this drug. The price of an equity share in ABC before the announcement was £2.30.

Consider the following scenarios:

1. Following the announcement the price of an equity share in ABC jumps to £3, and then over the next week falls back to £2.70.
2. Following the announcement the price of an equity share jumps to £2.70 and stays there.
3. Following the announcement the price slowly climbs to £2.70.

Question
Which scenario indicates an efficient market? Which do not? Why?

12 'The evidence on the capital-asset pricing model is mixed. The theory fits the data fairly well but there are some anomalies.' Comment on the above statement.

13 Discuss the recent attempts to curb insider dealing in the context of a general view that history has demonstrated that it cannot be policed.

14 The 70-year-old chairman, chief executive and founder of a computer company dies. The price of that company's shares falls from £3 to £2. Is this fall in price evidence of an inefficient stock market? Why?

15 The following statement contains several errors. Explain what these errors are.

> According to the efficient market hypothesis all share prices are correct at all times. This is achieved by prices moving randomly when new information is publicly announced. New information from published accounts is the only determinant of the random movements in share price.
>
> Fundamental and technical analysts of the stock market serve no function in making the market efficient and cannot predict future share prices. Corporate financial managers are also unable to predict future share prices.

16 Discuss the implications of the efficient markets hypothesis for managerial decisions in each of the following areas:

(a) the choice of accounting policies;
(b) dividend policy;
(c) the timing of new share issues.

(10 marks)
ICAEW, July 1993

9 DEBT FINANCE

By the end of this chapter the reader should be able to:

- calculate interest yields, and yields to redemption
- calculate the value of a bond
- know about the different types of bonds
- be able to read and understand details published on bond yields and price
- understand the difference between yield curves and the term structure of interest rates

9.1 INTRODUCTION

It is often difficult in the accounting and finance area to draw demarcation lines. One problem arises in drawing a line between long-term, medium-term and short-term funds. The distinction is bound to be to some extent arbitrary. This chapter covering long-term debt finance will consider debentures, loan stock, bonds, loans from banks and other financial institutions, and convertibles and warrants.

Finance provided by mortgages, leasing, commercial bills and certificates of deposit will be considered in the chapter on medium- and short-term finance. It is accepted that this classification is not always perfect; for example, some mortgages may be for a longer time period than some long-term bank loans.

The distinguishing features of debt finance are as follows.

1. From an investor's point of view it is less risky than equity finance. Interest is paid out before dividends, and in the event that the company goes into liquidation the providers of debt finance are paid back before the shareholders receive anything.
2. From the point of view of the borrowing company it is less expensive than equity finance. Because the risks are less, the investor is satisfied with a lower expected rate of return. Further, because interest is an expense, which has to be met whether or not profits are earned, it is tax-deductible.

9.2 DEBENTURES AND BONDS

A debenture is a document issued by a company containing an acknowledge-ment of indebtedness which need not give, although it usually does, a charge on

Debentures and bonds

the assets of the company. The Companies Acts define 'debenture' as including debenture stock and bonds. It is quite common for the expressions 'debenture' and 'bond' to be used interchangeably. Company debentures can also be referred to as 'loan stock'.

Debentures can be secured or unsecured. It is usual to use the expression 'debenture' when referring to the more secure form of issue, and 'loan stock' for less secure issues. When secured, this is by means of a trust deed, the objects of which are to provide security for the money advanced by the debenture holders, to set out the terms of the contract between the company and the debenture holders, and to make provision for such things as the holding of meetings of debenture holders. The advantages of a trust deed are that a prior charge cannot be obtained on the property without the consent of the debenture holders, the events on which the principal is to be repaid are specified, and power is given for the trustees to appoint a receiver and in certain events to carry on the business and enforce contracts. An alternative to receivership is for restructuring or rescheduling to occur, with the terms or the dates for repayment being altered to help the borrower.

Covenants

Almost all bonds and debentures and an increasing percentage of bank-loan agreements contain restrictive 'negative' covenants. These covenants restrict the borrower's right to take certain actions until the debt has been repaid in full. The items covered could include the following:

- the incurring of any further debt unless this is already agreed to in the borrowing agreement;
- the disposal of any assets;
- the payment of cash dividends, redemption of shares, the issue of options, etc., unless already agreed to in the agreement;
- the maintenance of certain levels of working capital;
- the maintenance of a 'loan collateral value', which is the relationship between expected future cash flows and the total level of debt;
- the maintenance of a certain 'debt service ratio', i.e. annual cash flow to annual interest and repayment charges.

These covenants are designed to protect the lenders. They do not protect the lender in the event of default, but they do influence some of the factors that could lead to defaults.

The articles of association usually restrict the power of directors to borrow. The typical wording of a paragraph in the articles is as follows:

> The Director shall restrict the borrowings ... so as to ensure that the aggregate amount of all monies borrowed by the company and/or any of its subsidiaries shall not, at any time, without the previous sanction of an ordinary resolution of the company, exceed the share capital and consolidated reserves.

The goodwill and other intangibles might well have to be deducted from the reserves in working out the base for the borrowing level, the justification being that these are not assets of the company that could easily be realized. Whether or not these assets are excluded depends, of course, on the wishes of those who draw up the articles.

Repayment

A company that issues debentures or loan stock will have to repay the principal at some known date in the future, or in certain circumstances at some earlier date if it so chooses. To provide the funds for repayment the company can either place so much of its profits aside each year (into a sinking fund) which at the time for redemption will be sufficient with interest to repay the amount borrowed, or it can rely on having enough funds on hand at the time of redemption either from the profits of that year or from the proceeds of a new issue of capital. Often a company allows itself a number of years in which to repay; for example, the redemption date may be given as 2010–13, which means the company can repay part of the borrowing in each of the three years. This obviously gives the company a greater choice in planning the necessary repayment.

There is no statutory formality, as in the case of shares, in respect of the issue of debentures at a discount. Provision may be made for the redemption of the debentures at par or at a premium at the end of a specified period; or the company may take power to redeem, at its option, even before the expiration of that period, on certain stated terms. The Act even allows for the debentures to run indefinitely.

During the life of a debenture, in order to secure an early discharge, a company can offer the holders an immediate consideration higher than or equal to the amount originally paid on the debenture. The consideration can either be in the form of cash or fully paid-up shares equal to the value of the consideration.

There is a class of debenture that can be issued that is called 'irredeemable'. This term is, however, confusing for the company does have an option to redeem. As with ordinary debentures there is nothing to stop the company from purchasing the irredeemable debentures from the holders either with their agreement, or by simply purchasing the debentures as they become available on the market. The holder of an irredeemable debenture does not, however, have a date specified by which redemption must take place – he or she cannot demand repayment.

Reference was made above to the fact that debentures and bonds do not have to be redeemed at par, or even at the 'final' redemption date. As an alternative to varying the interest rate, it is possible to vary the amount paid on redemption and the timing of the redemption. One example of this is a £69 million Eurosterling 4.5% subordinated bond redeemable in 2001, which was issued by Storehouse in 1987. Holders were given the option to redeem the bonds on 2 April 1992 at 129.17% (of the £100 nominal value), rather than to wait until 2001 and redeem at 100%. Whether they would wish to do so depended of course on what they thought would happen to interest rates between 1992 and 2001 and on their own liquidity situation.

One-hundred-year bonds

At the end of 1996, IBM issued a $850 million 'century bond'. It was at the time the largest 100-year bond ever issued. Other such securities had been issued by well-known organizations such as Walt Disney, Coca Cola and Yale University.

Why would investors want to buy a security which would not be repaid by the company until 100 years had elapsed? One reason is that they offer high-interest yields. The IBM issue was an 'A'-rated bond, yielding 7.22%. At that time a 30-year US Treasury bond was offering a yield of 6.42%.

To the issuing company such a security is attractive because in some respects it is similar to equity, because of its long duration, but the interest paid on the bond is tax-deductible. It is similar to equity in that the company does not have to worry about finding funds to repay the capital (at least for a very long time). There is always a danger that if the government see such securities as similar in nature to equity they will remove the tax-deductibility allowance on the interest payments.

The market for these very long-term bonds is mainly in the USA. In that country the insurance companies are willing to buy such securities in order to match the life of the long-term assets they hold with the life of their long-term liabilities.

In Europe such long-term bonds are not attractive to investors. In the

Eurobond market investors do not usually buy bonds with maturities of more than 12 years.

9.3 MEDIUM-TERM NOTES

The basic 'plain vanilla' MTN is an unsecured promissory note. A company promises to pay holders of the notes a certain sum at a certain maturity date, or maturity band, a maturity band being a period, say between nine months and a year, within which repayment will take place.

Companies can sell these MTNs in the financial markets. MTNs can be issued at fixed rates of interest, floating rates or zero coupon rates. They can be priced at a premium or a discount. The major currency of issue is the US$. There is a large market in such notes, particularly the floating-rate version (FRNs) in the Euromarkets. The subject is discussed more fully in Chapter 21 on international finance.

The MTNs can be listed on stock exchanges. The particular advantages to the companies issuing such securities are that they are a convenient and not expensive way of meeting working capital needs. If a company is in an industry that takes a long time to develop new products, for example the motor car industry, then MTNs can help satisfy working capital needs between the time when the investment in a new model begins and when the car is launched in the market.

Floating-rate notes (FRNs)

As the name implies these are promissory notes with a floating interest rate. The coupon rate is linked to a floating reference rate, for example LIBOR. In the 1990s these notes have become increasingly popular in the Euromarkets.

Ordinary FRNs share many of the features of MTNs. They are attractive to investors if interest rates are expected to rise, but less attractive to the issuers as they commit the issuer to possible higher funding costs. In fact, FRN issuers have mainly been banks and other financial institutions. They have issued such notes in order to attempt to match their floating-rate assets (deposits) with floating-rate liabilities.

In the 1990s variations on the simple FRN began to appear, termed 'structured FRNs'. These include reverse FRNs (in which coupon rates rise as a reference interest rate falls), collared FRNs and step-up recovery FRNs.

9.4 BANK BORROWING

As well as raising debt finance by the sale of securities in the capital market or by the placement of securities by financial institutions with their clients, it is also possible for a company to borrow directly from a bank or other financial institution. No tradable security is issued. The bank makes the loan and normally carries it on its own books for the life of the loan. The borrower repays the bank. The word 'normally' is introduced because on occasions the bank might try to sell the debt to other investors.

Traditionally commercial banks (high-street banks) have been major suppliers of debt finance to companies. At one time the banks were mainly concerned with short-term loans and overdraft facilities, but in the 1970s they moved into the medium- and longer-term loan business. They have, however, in the 1980s and 1990s faced increasing competition in the corporate debt business from the market place. Larger companies with good credit ratings are able to issue securities in the market place. They prefer to do so because of lower borrowing rates. In the USA the banks' share of corporate debt declined from 19.6% in 1979 to 14.5% in 1994.

It is the smaller and medium-sized companies who are dependent on banks for their debt finance. The markets are not so aware as the banks of the financial creditworthiness of these companies. The banks therefore have an advantage in this so-called middle market.

'Committed facilities'

Large companies with a good credit rating do like to maintain a good working relationship with commercial banks. Commercial banks have, of course, a near monopoly on the payments and settlement system. Banks can provide financial advice in certain areas, and banks can be used to provide a reserve of cash at short notice. Many companies are willing to pay a commitment fee, in order to have a line of credit available should they need it.

Costs

The interest rate on term loans can be fixed or it can be floating. The floating rate is usually in the range of 2–6% above base rate. The exact percentage above base that is charged depends on the creditworthiness of the borrower. On occasions, in addition to the interest charge, an initial arrangement fee or negotiation fee has to be paid. This is usually in the region of 1% of the loan.

Security

Usually the bank will want the loan secured, either on the guarantees of the directors or by a charge over the assets of the business. Under the terms of the government's Loan Guarantee Scheme, it may be possible for a business to obtain a loan without security. The bank may also require the company to sign covenants that restrict the company's rights to issue other debt, to sell assets or perhaps to pay dividends.

Non-recourse debt

This is borrowing by a company, in which the lender cannot, in the event of non-repayment, claim against the assets of the borrower. The repayment of such debt is often dependent on the cash flow generated from a specific project. The borrowing is secured against specific future cash flows. This type of financing is often used in large energy-based projects, such as gas, oil and electricity.

As mentioned above, long-term loans can be obtained from financial institutions other than the main high-street banks. Insurance companies occasionally make loans to businesses for periods up to 20 years. There are also specialist financial institutions who make loans to companies. One of the most well known in the UK is Investors in Industry (3i). There is also the European Investment Bank, which is one of the European Union institutions.

Small business

For the vast majority of small businesses, borrowing from a bank is the most important source of external finance. The banks provide not just the traditional overdraft finance but also a variety of medium- and long-term loans.

Banks are, however, not always helpful to small businesses, particularly those who have only been in existence for a short period. The lack of security for loans combined with the lack of a good track record has meant that a high proportion of loan applications from small businesses are rejected.

In an attempt to alleviate some of the problems of raising finance by new small businesses, successive governments have introduced various schemes aimed at increasing the availability of debt and equity capital. In 1981 the government launched the Loan Guarantee Scheme to boost the amount of debt finance available. Its aim was to help those firm founders who had exhausted other methods of raising funds but nevertheless seemed to have a viable proposition. When it was first introduced the government guaranteed payment of 80% of any approved loan to the institution lending the money, usually a clearing bank. In return the borrower would pay the government a premium of 3% as well as the interest charge to the lender. In this way it was hoped that any claims on the government due to business failure would be covered by the premiums collected and so, in effect, the scheme would finance itself.

Since then the scheme has been changed many times. The government guarantee level has fallen, and the rate of premium has changed. The scheme has been criticized. It is an attempt to fulfil the objectives of 'additionality' and 'viability': additional in that it was to help firms which could not have obtained funding by the more conventional means such as bank loans, viable in the sense that it was to help the potentially prosperous companies. However, identifying which firms are eligible under these preconditions is difficult and subjective. Thus young businesses are still affected by the usual selection policies of financial institutions and their avoidance of high risk. If the borrower has low risks it has been claimed that the bank will grant the loan itself. It is only for the riskier projects, by the bank's definition, that they insist on government guarantees before a loan can be granted. Despite the criticism the scheme has been a success.

There are other specialist financial institutions who help small firms obtain finance. These include the 3i (Investors in Industry) who invest in companies that they believe have a long-term growth potential. In assessing a company they are particularly concerned with the qualities of the management of the venture. If they were willing to support the company an equity involvement is normally sought. They are not looking for control, but just a minority stake. The equity investment is usually accompanied by a medium-term loan. Interest on the loan is charged at commercial rates with the repayments of the principal spread over an agreed period.

The day-to-day running of the business is left to the managers of the company but appropriate guidance is usually offered. Sometimes a non-executive director is appointed to the board.

9.5 BEARER VERSUS REGISTERED SECURITIES

In the UK not only does the existence of a debenture need to be registered, but also a register of who owns the debenture, bond or loan stock needs to be maintained. This is a record of who has a claim against the company. The claims are referred to as registered securities.

In many countries a company has a choice whether to issue what is known as a 'bearer security' or a 'registered security'. As explained above, in the case of a registered security the name of the purchaser is recorded in a register at the company. This means that for tax purposes it is known who is the holder and who will be receiving the dividend or interest payments. In contrast, bearer securities are unregistered. This makes it possible for investors to collect the interest or dividends and for the tax authorities not to know who is receiving this sum of money. A bearer bond has interest coupons attached to it and these are sent to the company or handed to a bank when the holder wishes to obtain interest due. The production of the coupon means that the holder receives interest.

Not surprisingly perhaps, investors are willing to accept lower interest rates on bearer bonds than on registered bonds of comparable risk. The secrecy is of value. However, there is one important danger with bearer securities: if they are lost or stolen it is difficult to prove ownership. Therefore they need to be stored in a safe place. Loss of a registered security is not so crucial: ownership can be proved and a replacement certificate received.

In many countries it is possible for equity shares to be in either a registered form or a bearer form. Again, it is not unusual for bearer equity securities to trade at a higher price than the registered securities.

9.6 BOND MARKETS

The bond markets can be divided into three categories. The first two involve issuing bonds in the national bond markets of a country, the third involves issuing bonds in a truly global market, the Euromarket, a market which is not subject to the rules of any country.

Domestic bonds

These are bonds issued by a domestic borrower in their own national market, denominated in the local currency, that can be purchased by anyone in possession of that currency. The amount of money raised in London by UK companies through bond issues is very variable. Some years the funds raised are considerable, other years they are very little.

Foreign bonds

These are bonds issued in a national market, by a foreign company or government, in the currency of the country in which the market is based. The issues are subject to the regulations and supervision of the national market.

There is nothing new about such issues; for over 200 years foreign governments and companies have been borrowing pounds sterling in London by such means. Such bonds were one of the early forms of international finance. These bonds are now given colourful names. Bonds issued in pounds sterling in London by foreigners are called 'Bulldog bonds'. Bonds issued in New York in dollar denominations by foreigners are called 'Yankee bonds'.

Eurobonds

These are bonds issued by governments and companies, outside their own country, in currencies other than their own. They can be bought by anyone or any organization having the currency available. The bonds are not traded on any one specific bond market.

Eurobonds will be discussed further in Chapter 21 on international finance. One point that should be noted is that if a UK company issues a bond in the UK domestic market, they have to pay interest to the holder of the bond net of taxation. If, however, a UK company issues say a DM bond in the Euromarkets, it can pay interest to the holders of such bonds without tax being deducted. Interest paid on all Eurobonds is on a gross basis. This makes them more attractive to investors than domestic bonds.

Interest rates

One problem that in the past inhibited companies when issuing bonds was the volatile nature of interest rates. It is dangerous for a company to commit itself to pay a particular interest rate which is the current rate at the time of issue when in a short period of time the level in the market place might fall. The company is then committed to service a relatively expensive debt issue.

One solution to the problem of volatile interest rates was to issue index-linked loan stock. The indexing could apply either to the amount that is paid on redemption or to the amount of the annual interest payment. The government issued a number of index-linked securities, but this solution did not prove popular with the corporate borrower. The issue of loan stock (bonds) with options attached to convert into equity, or with warrants attached enabling the holder to purchase equity, turned out to be much more popular.

Companies produced a number of imaginative securities with which to appeal to the investor interested in purchasing debentures and loan stock. These will be referred to in the next few pages. One way around the fixed-interest problem from the point of view of the borrower has been the interest-rate swap. This is a way in which the corporate treasurer can adjust a company's borrowing port-folio to obtain the required balance of fixed-rate versus floating-rate borrowing (see Chapter 17).

Bond dealers

From the point of view of investors, bonds might not seem to be such an exciting security as equity. With equity prices depending on forecasts of profits, and with prices changing when new information reaches the market, equity prices are volatile. Bond prices do move, but move slowly. Bond dealers can, however, make large sums of money. If one is dealing in very large sums of money, a small movement in the price of a bond can mean profits which are considerable. Bond dealers have become quite glamorous figures in the financial community. (A successful popular book by Lewis (1990) dealing with the life of a bond dealer was entitled *Liar's Poker*.)

Unfortunately for some, all investment involves risk, and some dealers make losses. Glaxo announced in July 1994 that it had closed its Bermuda-based treasury operation. It did this after the bond dealers in its treasury department made losses of £100 million on the company's bond portfolio.

The company's treasury department managed the firm's cash portfolio which consisted at times of £2 billion. These funds were invested in a number of finan-cial instruments. The company emphasized that its losses were the result of falling bond prices and not the result of speculation by its treasury department. Nevertheless the company decided to hand over responsibility for the invest-ment of its cash balances to external fund managers.

Bond ratings

Traded bonds are given ratings by Moodys and by Standard & Poor's. The ratings are an assessment of the creditworthiness of the issuing company.

The highest-rated companies by Moodys, are Aaa (Triple A's), then in descending order the ratings are:

   Aa, A, Baa, Ba, B, Caa, Ca, C, D

The highest-rated bonds on Standard & Poor's are AAA, then in descending order:

   AA, A, BBB, BB, B, CCC, CC, C, D

Bonds that are given the highest credit rating benefit in that they can borrow at the lowest cost. Companies try hard to avoid having their credit rating reduced. The companies supply the agencies with the information on which the ratings are based. The information supplied is publicly available, so the ratings supplied by the agencies do not provide new information. The ratings are, however, expressing the opinions of experts, so they are considered important and do affect the rate of interest the company has to offer.

Risk is based on the likelihood that a company will default in the repayment of the loan or fail to pay the interest. The security of the asset backing supporting the loan is also taken into account.

The Aaa and AAA ratings imply the ability to pay both the interest and the principal is very strong. Ca and CC imply a high degree of risk, with such bonds suitable for risky speculation. Such bonds have some quality, but major uncertainties and dangers in adverse conditions dominate their creditworthiness. C bonds are already not paying interest, and D bonds have already defaulted on their repayment of principal.

High-yield bonds

In the late 1990s a high-yield bond market developed in Europe, particularly in bonds denominated in sterling, Deutchmarks and French francs. Such bonds are speculative debt securities issued by companies who have comparatively low credit ratings, for example BBB for Standard and Poor's.

The bonds offer yields several percentage points higher than those available on bonds issued by 'blue chip' companies. These high-yield bonds are a form of mezzanine finance, compensating for the higher risk with higher returns. As in the USA, they are now beginning to be used in Europe to help finance mergers and acquisitions.

Project finance

On a few occasions large projects have been financed through the bond market. Two examples are a £165 million issue by Greenwich Lewisham Rail Link PLC and a £400 million issue by First Hydro Finance PLC, both in 1996.

The funds for such large infrastructure projects would traditionally have been obtained through bank financing. Bank finance has been thought to provide a greater degree of flexibility. Banks also provide a better system of monitoring and control of the funds.

Bondholders have traditionally been passive in terms of monitoring how funds they invest are being used. They buy a bond and only become involved in the case of default. If finance is obtained through the bond market, the investors will require a project agent to be appointed to monitor progress in the project.

Market for secondary debt

This is a market for the bonds that are of extremely high risk, with a strong probability that the issuing company (or government) will not be able to redeem them at their redemption value. It is a market for securities of companies in financial distress. The holder of a bond may feel that rather than wait until redemption date of the bond and then find that the company cannot reply, it is better to sell the security quickly and receive something rather than nothing.

For example, Eurotunnel have experienced financial difficulties for a number of years. They have needed to restructure their capital structure on more than one occasion. The holders of some Eurotunnel debt decided to sell their bonds and obtain what price they could. At one point in 1997 the price of the debt was 36 pence for each pound. This means that for a bond with a redeemable value of £100, it was being sold in the secondary market for £36. In the case of Eurotunnel bonds it was a US investment banker, Bankers Trust, that organized most of the secondary market. It was estimated that in 1996 in the region of £1 billion of the £8 billion total of Eurotunnel debt was being traded in this market.

The secondary market in corporate bonds developed during the 1990s when some of the leveraged buy-outs of the 1980s collapsed or were in trouble.

9.7 MEZZANINE FINANCE AND JUNK BONDS

'Mezzanine finance' is the name attached to a form of finance that combines features of both debt and equity. It is a form of finance that is popular in the following situations:

1 management buy-outs (MBOs);
2 leveraged acquisitions;
3 financing capital-intensive projects;
4 the recapitalization of companies; and
5 when public companies go private.

Mezzanine finance tends to be used when a company has used all the bank borrowing that it can obtain and it does not have access to further equity. It is a form of borrowing that often enables a company to move beyond what is normally considered to be acceptable levels of gearing. It is therefore of higher risk than more traditional forms of borrowing. The features of mezzanine finance are:

- it is often unsecured debt, ranking below senior debt;
- typically the interest rate charged is a floating rate, costing between 2% and 4.5% above LIBOR;
- frequently the return on this high-risk investment includes an 'equity kicker'. This offers equity participation in the company that is borrowing the funds, either through warrants or share options. If the venture being financed turns out to be successful the lender can obtain an equity stake in the company.

One situation in which it is possible to issue such securities is if the company is seen to have a safe and positive future cash flow. This could be the position with an MBO, in which an established business is moving into new hands. With an above-normal level of gearing, a high positive cash flow is normally required in order to pay the high levels of interest payments. Most forms of mezzanine finance result from private placements of debt with investors and direct borrowings from an institution with no secondary market in the debt.

There are investors who may be prepared to lend to companies in an abnormal situation if there is the possibility of very high returns. Such high-risk investors are prepared to buy 'junk bonds'. Junk bonds are a form of mezzanine finance. If events turn out well they pay very high rates of interest. They are bonds which like other bonds can be traded in the market place.

Although a junk-bond market has not developed in the UK, there is considerable interest in other forms of mezzanine finance. It has been estimated that in the region of 40% of MBOs use mezzanine finance, and in the average MBO deal £20 million of funds is provided from this source. The use of mezzanine finance in company restructuring situations will be discussed further in Chapter 23.

As with many new forms of finance, very descriptive names are introduced. With mezzanine finance these include the following.

Strip financing This is a financial arrangement for a company consisting of providing a variety of different types of mezzanine finance, each with different costs and risk characteristics.

Stepped interest This is borrowing with lower levels of interest being charged in the early years of the loan than in the later years. The repayment by instalments of the sum borrowed may also be delayed so that it does not start until the second half of the loan period.

Junior mezzanine This, as the name implies, ranks for repayment below senior mezzanine, which itself ranks for repayment below senior debt. With junior mezzanine there may be little or no interest payments. The return hopefully comes in the form of a possible future equity stake in the company.

The use of mezzanine finance in other countries in Europe has lagged behind its use in the UK. One reason for this is that until the mid-1990s MBOs had not been common on the Continent. Another problem has been that in some countries the legal framework has not helped mezzanine finance: for example, it is not always possible for a lender to take security over an asset.

Figure 9.1 shows the different forms of mezzanine finance. The two extremes of finance are also shown, with equity as high-risk, high-return and senior debt, low-risk, low-return.

Mezzanine debt usually has a maturity of seven to ten years. Often those who provide this form of finance take a second charge over the assets of the borrower. The reason for this is that if the company gets into difficulty and the asset can be sold for an amount that is more than the claim of the lender with the first claim, then there will be some left over to meet the second charge. The lender with the first charge and the one with the second charge often agree on a set of financial covenants.

Most of the individual forms of finance are discussed in detail elsewhere in the book.

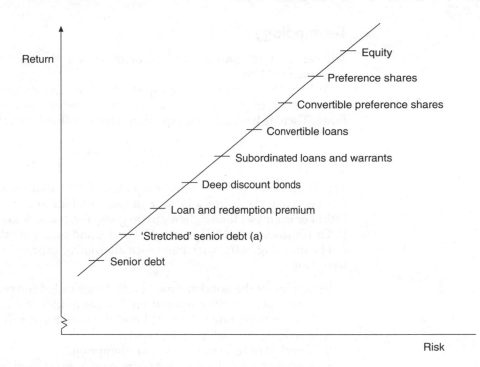

Figure 9.1
Forms of mezzanine finance

Junk bonds

Junk bonds are considered to be high-risk, but they do offer the possibility of high yields. They are usually issued by companies with a low credit rating. In the USA, where such bonds were created, Standard & Poor's gives a credit rating to bonds issued by companies. Bonds issued by top-class companies are given an AAA rating; junk bonds usually have a B rating which is the next to lowest rating, i.e. CC. In return for this level of risk the interest offered on junk bonds can be 5% or more above that on AAA bonds.

Such bonds proved very popular in the USA in the l980s, with issues increasing ninefold between 1980 and 1986. They were particularly popular as a means of raising finance to fund leveraged buy-outs and they financed a large number of corporate raiders. The bonds were popular with some investors and an active secondary market developed in the USA.

The junk-bond market is technically referred to as the 'high-yield bond market'. It has grown in the USA from a small unimportant market in the early 1970s to a 'dynamic continually increasing force in corporate finance'. In 1991 the size of the market was over $209 billion. Its significance can be judged from the fact that in that year this high-yield debt market accounted for 25% of the total corporate debt market.

Junk bonds are now issued in the European capital markets. A company from Switzerland sold DM 158 million in the markets. An above-average rate of interest was being paid on the DM, but the company had the advantage that it had obtained finance that did not have to be repaid for seven years. This form of debt finance is suitable for companies who will have to wait a number of years before the investment being funded reaps profits. Such companies are cable TV and telephone companies, which require large initial investments.

9.8 THE VALUE OF FIXED-INTEREST SECURITIES

Terminology

The valuation of annuities and perpetuities, and the yield to maturity, have been introduced in Chapter 3.

Perhaps the most confusing aspect of valuing bonds for the reader new to the subject is the terminology. A number of expressions are used to mean the same thing. There is basically one equation used to value bonds:

$$V_t = \frac{I_1}{(1+r)} + \frac{I_2}{(1+r)^2} + \frac{I_3}{(1+r)^3} + \frac{R_n}{(1+r)^n}$$

This is the familiar present-value equation. Five variables are involved. A student can be given values for any four of the variables and be asked to calculate the fifth. For example, the student can be given I, r, n and R and be asked to calculate V. Or the student can be given n, V, I and R and asked to calculate r.

The meaning of the variables (with alternative expressions that can be encountered) are

V_t = value of the bond at time t (sometimes called the price at time t);
I = annual amount of interest paid to the holder of a bond (which is equal to the coupon rate (C) on the bond times nominal value of the bond (P));
R = redemption value of the bond;
n = period of time from now to redemption;
r = market capitalization rate/discount rate/annual required rate of return on similar bonds/redemption yield;
C = coupon rate (the rate of interest paid by the company to holders of the bond);
P = par (nominal) value of a bond (sometimes called 'face value').

The following points need to be appreciated by a student new to the subject:

1 It is possible to value a bond at any date after issue. The value (the price) will vary over time.

2 *I* is the annual interest paid on the bond. It is fixed (or the formula that will be used to ascertain the amount to be paid is fixed) at the time the bond is first issued.

   The coupon rate is not the same as *r* which is the market capitalization rate at the time the bond is being valued. *r* will vary over time, depending on such factors as government policy. With a fixed-interest-rate bond neither *I* nor *C* will vary over time.

3 All bonds will have a par (nominal/face) value. In the simplest case a bond will be sold (issued) by the company at its par value. In the simplest case this par value (issue price) will equal the redemption value. It is, however, possible to issue bonds at a discount (issue price less than par value). It is also possible to redeem a bond at a premium (redemption value higher than par value).

4 The coupon rate (*C*) is the rate of interest being offered on the face value of the bond. For example, debenture stock might be issued at a price of say £90 or £110, but be issued in units of £100 nominal value. The interest rate being offered on the £100 unit is referred to as the 'coupon rate'.

   The issue price is the price at which the bonds are initially sold by the company to the investors. Debenture stock can be issued at a premium or a discount, so that the £100 units referred to above can be issued at say £90 or £105 a unit.

5 The market price is the price at which the bond is being traded in the market on a particular day; it is the price which one investor pays another investor. This is a function of the coupon rate which is announced at the time of issue together with the risk class of the particular company issuing the debenture and the current market rate of interest.

Irredeemable bonds (interest in perpetuity)

The vast majority of bonds are referred to as 'dated', which means that a date is given when they will be redeemed. There are, however, some bonds trading in the market that are 'undated'. A well-known example of this is the UK government 3.5% War Loan. This was a bond issued during the Second World War to raise finance to help with the war effort. It was undated and 50 years after the war it has still not been redeemed. It is still, however, traded. The British government continue to pay 3.5% interest per annum to the current holders of the bond. When interest rates in the economy fall (the market capitalization rate) the price of this 3.5% War Loan rises, as do the price of dated securities. No doubt the original purchasers of this bond gave up waiting for the British government to repay and sold to other investors.

One form of undated bond issued by the British government is called a *'consol'*. This is a bond that provides interest in perpetuity. It is never redeemed.

Let us assume that in 1990 a company issued a number of £100 par 8% irredeemable debentures. Investors buying such a security would be acquiring a right to receive an annuity of £8 forever. The amount that they would be willing to pay for such a debenture in 1994 would approximate to

$$P = \frac{100 \times 8.0}{r}$$

where *r* is the rate of interest being offered in 1994 on securities in the same risk class as this particular company's debentures. If in 1994 *r* equals 11.0% then the price of the debenture in the market at that time would be approximately equal to $100 \times 8.0/11.0 = £72.72$.

If in 1995 interest rates were to rise to a level where *r* = 14.0%, then the price of the debenture would fall to approximately

$$P = \frac{100 \times 8.0}{14.0} = £57.14$$

or, to put it another way, the price would fall to a level where the interest yield equalled 14% (i.e. 14% = 8% × 100/57.14).

The interest yield is simply the annual interest received expressed as a percentage of the current market price of the security.

With our security above at the time it was issued in 1990 the interest yield was

$$\frac{8 \times 100}{100} = 8\%$$

In 1994 it was

$$\frac{8}{72.72} \times 100 = 11\%$$

In 1995 it was

$$\frac{8}{57.14} \times 100 = 14\%$$

With an irredeemable bond the interest yield equals the market capitalization rate; that is, the rate currently being offered in the market. This is not the case with a redeemable bond.

Redeemable bonds

For a redeemable security there is a factor other than the interest payment that has to be taken into account. This is the capital repayment. As the date of redemption comes near, an investor will be willing to pay a price for the security higher than that which would give an interest yield equivalent to the existing market rates. This is because the time when the investor is to receive the repayment of the investment is approaching.

As an example let us suppose a government bond with a coupon rate of 5% is redeemable in one year's time. What would be the price of that bond today if the market rate of interest on bonds in a similar risk class is 10%? The holder of the bond will receive in 12 months' time interest plus the redemption value of the bond (£100).

At the beginning of this section we showed an equation; if we substitute the above values in the equation we obtain:

$$V = \frac{5}{(1.10)} + \frac{100}{(1.10)} = 95.46$$

The bond would be selling for £95.46. This only gives an interest yield of

$$\frac{5}{95.46} \times 100 = 5.24\%$$

We might ask why anybody would pay £95.46 for a security giving an interest yield of only just over 5%, when they could obtain a higher yield on other investments. In the example we have assumed the yield on other securities is 10%. The answer is that they are not buying the bond for the £5 interest, but for the £100 that they will receive when the bond is redeemed in 12 months' time. The *Financial Times* quotes two yields for fixed-interest securities: the interest yield and the redemption yield.

The redemption yield (yield to maturity) is the total return (taking into account capital repayment as well as interest payments) that will be obtained from holding on to the security until its redemption. The redemption yield is sometimes above the interest yield and sometimes below it. The relationship depends on the coupon rate on the bond and the current interest yields in the market.

If the coupon rate on a particular bond is above the current interest yields in the market the redemption yield will be lower than the interest yield. If the coupon rate is lower than the current interest yields the redemption yield will be higher than the interest yield. (The reader can check the accuracy of this statement by observing yields quoted in the *Financial Times* for different bonds.)

Let us say that we are now at 1 January 1993 and we are considering purchasing a £100 debenture in Company S which is repayable at par on 31 December 1994. The coupon rate is 12%, payable annually on 31 December. The market price of the debenture is currently £90. We wish to know the redemption yield.

The formula for redemption yield is

$$V_t = \frac{I}{1+r} + \frac{I}{(1+r)^2} + \ldots + \frac{I}{(1+r)^n} + \frac{R}{(1+r)^n}$$

where V_t is the market price of security today, R is the redeemable value, I is the annual interest payment, r is the redemption yield and n is the number of years to redemption. Substituting the values in our example into the above equation gives

$$90 = \frac{12}{1+r} + \frac{112}{(1+r)^2}$$

Solving this equation gives r equal to approximately 18%. The redemption yield on the debenture stock is therefore in the region of 18%.

Semi-annual interest

In fact, the interest on company debentures and government stocks is usually paid in six-monthly instalments. The redemption yield in such cases is found by solving the following equation:

$$P_t = \frac{I/2}{1+r/2} + \frac{I/2}{(1+r/2)^2} + \frac{I/2}{(1+r/2)^3} + \ldots + \frac{I/2+R}{(1+r/2)^n}$$

Illustrating with the same example as above, except that this time the interest is payable semi-annually, gives

$$90 = \frac{6}{1+r/2} + \frac{6}{(1+r/2)^2} + \frac{6}{(1+r/2)^3} + \frac{106}{(1+r/2)^4}$$

We can solve this equation using a present value (PV) of annuity table (Table 3 at the end of the book) and a table to give the PV of a single sum (Table 2 at the end of the book). The PV of £6 to be received at the end of each of four periods, with a 9% interest rate, is £19.44, and the PV of £100 to be received at the end of the fourth period with an interest rate of 9% is £70.84. Summing these two gives £90.28, which is close to the current market price of £90. Therefore $r/2$ is 9%, which means that the redemption yield r is close to 18%.

There is in fact always a difference between redemption yields calculated with interest paid on an annual basis and with interest paid on a semi-annual basis. It is always preferable to receive interest payments earlier rather than later. But, in this example, with the debenture being near to its date of redemption, the effect of the difference is very small.

Financial Times statistics

The prices and yields listed in Table 9.1 relate to government gilt-edged securities, bonds issued by companies and a local authority. In the table by the side of the name of the issue is given the coupon interest rate. The year when the bond will be redeemed is also shown.

The interest yield column is the interest paid each year expressed as a percentage of the closing price of the bond. The redemption yield, as explained in the text, shows the average annual return (as a percentage of the closing price) if the security is held to maturity.

Bond price fluctuations

As can be seen from Figure 9.2, bond prices can fluctuate considerably over time.

The price of a bond is dependent on the current level of interest rates in the market. When interest rates in the market rise, bond prices fall. The longer the time to maturity of the bond the greater will be the fall in price. This is because the longer the life the more annual interest payments to be received at less than current market rates and the further into the future before the redemption value is received.

Long-term bonds fluctuate more in price than short-term bonds. The nearer the time to redemption the more the price is dominated by the redemption sum, the higher its present value. Because the price of bonds does fluctuate they are a security that can be purchased for capital gain as well as the interest payments.

9.9 YIELD CURVES AND THE TERM STRUCTURE OF INTEREST RATES

The question of whether a company, when seeking funds, should at a particular time raise debt or equity is discussed in Chapter 13, where the cost of finance

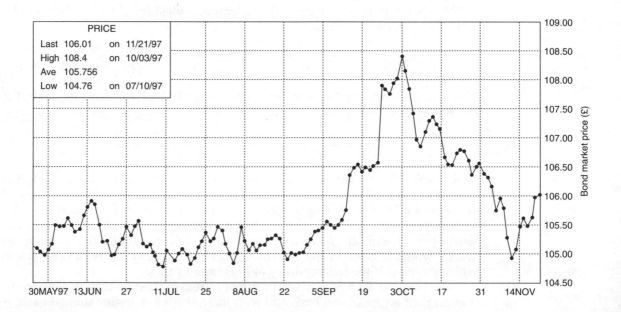

Figure 9.2
Price of Tesco 8¾% Bond (May 1977–Nov 1997)

Debt finance

Table 9.1 *Bond prices and yields, October 1997*

			Yield		Price
			Int.	*Red.*	
Nationwide Anglia	$3\frac{7}{8}$%	2021		3.93	$161\frac{1}{8}$
Birmingham Council	$11\frac{1}{2}$	2012	8.16	7.02	141
Metropolitan Water	3%		3.57	5.80	84
UK gilts					
Treasury	$7\frac{1}{4}$%	1998	7.24	7.01	$100\frac{1}{8}$
Treasury	7%	2001	6.92	6.78	$101\frac{1}{8}$
Treasury	$7\frac{1}{2}$%	2006	7.00	6.45	$107\frac{1}{8}$
Treasury	8%	2015	6.86	6.43	$116\frac{21}{32}$

and the appropriate levels of capital gearing are considered. If a company has decided to borrow, then a further question needs to be settled, namely the maturity of the borrowing. Should the company raise short-term, medium-term or long-term debt? To answer this question we need to know the following:

1 the existing maturity structure of the company's borrowing;
2 how much finance is needed;
3 the use to which the funds are to be put, in particular the likely returns, the risk and the expected time period over which the funds will be needed;
4 the existing level of interest rates on loans of different time periods;
5 the expected future direction of interest rates;
6 the liquidity in the bond market.

In this section we shall concentrate on points 4 and 5, the interest rate aspects of the decision. With regard to point 1, a company will not want all its debts maturing at or near the same date. If all the loans of a company can be phased so that their repayments are spread over a number of years it will make cash-flow management somewhat easier.

The difference between the interest rate on long-term loans and the interest rate on short-term loans can vary over time. The relationship between interest rates and yields and time is expressed in the term structure of interest rates and the yield curve.

Yield curve

This is not the same as the term structure of interest rates. A yield curve shows the relationship between the yield to maturity (YTM) and the period of time before the bond matures.

At any point in time it is possible to observe the yield being earned on bonds of different maturities. In August 1995, the yields to maturity on new UK Treasury Stock issues was

YTM	Time to maturity (years)
6%	4
7%	11
8%	20

This can be plotted, and the line produced is known as the 'yield curve'. In the above example it is upward sloping; this is normally the shape of the curve. The yield curve can, however, on occasions be level (B) or downward sloping (C) (see Figure 9.3).

One reason why it is normally upward sloping is because of liquidity preference. It is reasonable to assume that, the further into the future the lender has to

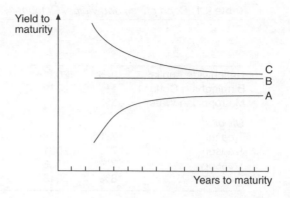

Figure 9.3
Yield curve

wait before the loan is repaid, the greater will be the risks of default and so therefore the greater the return the lender would normally expect to compensate for risk. On most occasions the further into the future is the maturity date on the loan, the greater is the interest that has to be offered by the borrower in order to persuade the lender to part with money. This is known as the 'liquidity preference hypothesis'. An investor has a preference for money now.

The relationship between the differing periods to maturity of loans and their respective redemption yields is called the 'yield curve'. For an accurate comparison of the variation by maturity it is necessary to compare the yields with different dates of repayment but in broadly the same risk class. It should be appreciated that redemption yields only measure the return on a bond if it is held to maturity and the annual interest payments can be reinvested at the rate of the yield.

Spot interest rates and the term structure of interest rates

The spot interest rate is the interest rate offered on a bond in a particular year. It is the spot rate yield. If a bond is sold at par the spot rate yield will equal the coupon rate. But this of course is not always the situation. With a zero coupon bond there is no coupon rate, but a holder of the bond earns a rate of return. The spot rate (i_1) in year 1 might be 8%, but let us suppose interest rates are expected to rise in future, so the expected annual spot interest rate in year two (i_2) might equal 10%. A one-year bond issued now need only offer an 8% yield, but a one-year bond issued in a year's time has to offer 10%. As will be illustrated, the spot interest rate is not necessarily the same thing as yield to maturity. For a bond with a one-year life the two are the same, but this is not necessarily the case for a bond with a life of more than one year.

The expected future spot rate for a year is similar to the forward rate for that year. There might be a small difference due to an investor's liquidity preference.

Example 9.1

Suppose in 1995 the spot rate on a one-year bond in a certain risk class is 10%. Investors expect interest rates to rise during 1996, and it is thought that if a one-year bond in the same risk class were to be issued at the beginning of 1996 it would need to offer a spot rate of 14%.

If a two-year bond was issued at the beginning of 1995 what yield to maturity should be offered to investors to keep them satisfied?

If an investor was to purchase a one-year bond at the beginning of 1995, sell at the year-end and then invest the proceeds in another year bond during 1996, the return would be:

Debt finance

$1 \times 1.10 \times 1.14 = 1.254$

This would be a spot-rate yield in 1995 of 10% with an expected spot rate one year from now of 14%. A bond with a life of two years issued in 1995 needs to offer the same total return as the two one-year bonds, i.e. 25.4%.

This is achieved by offering 12% interest per annum on the two-year bond, i.e.

$1 \times 1.12 \times 1.12 = 1.254$

The average annual return from holding the two 'one-year bonds' is 12%, i.e.

$$100 = \frac{10}{(1.12)} + \frac{14}{(1.12)^2} + \frac{100}{(1.12)^2}$$

The yield to maturity on the two-year bond is also 12%:

$$100 = \frac{12}{(1.12)} + \frac{12}{(1.12)} + \frac{100}{(1.12)^2}$$

The spot-rate interest for the current year (1995) is 10%.

The spot-rate interest on the bond for the year 1996 is 14%.

In this example the YTM on the one-year bond and the YTM on the two-year bond can be used to illustrate the yield curve.

This is not the same as the term structure of interest rates.

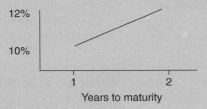

The term structure of interest rates described the future movement of spot interest rates. In our example the term structure is:

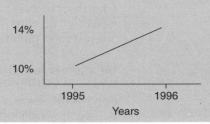

A practical problem arises with the term structure of interest rates in that we do not know what spot interest rates will be in future years. It is because of this problem that the 'yield curve' is used more frequently than the 'term structure'.

We can, however, make estimates of future spot interest rates. We can observe the YTM on bonds with different lives. On the basis of these yields we can calculate the spot interest rates that it is being assumed will arise in future.

Example 9.2

You observe that bonds with one year to maturity have a YTM of 13%, bonds with two years to maturity have a YTM of 14%, and bonds with three years to maturity have a YTM of 15%. What is the market expecting the annual spot interest rates to be in each of the next three years?

To answer the question it must be remembered that the YTM is the annual yield on the bond over its life.

Expected spot interest rate in year 1 = 13%.

Clearly an investor will only invest in the one-year bond if they have to pay a price which results in the same rate of return as can be earned on any other deposit of money for one year. On a one-year bond, the spot interest rate equals the YTM.

Expected spot interest rate in year 2

Two-year bonds give a YTM of 14%. Therefore the total yield over two years of:

$1(1.14)(1.14) = 1.2996$

This final outcome should be the same as that received by an investor who holds a year-one bond and at the end of the year invests the proceeds in another one-year bond (at the expected spot rate of interest in the second year).

Therefore $1(1.13)(1 + i) = 1.2996$
$i = 0.15$

The spot interest rate in the second year is expected to be 15%.

Expected spot interest rate in year 3

$1(1.15)(1.15)(1.15) = 1.5209$
$1(1.13)(1.15)(1 + i) = 1.5209$
$i = 0.17$

The spot interest rate in the third year is expected to be 17%.

The term structure of interest rates and the yield curve are:

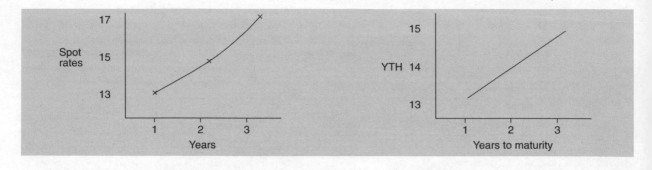

Term structure theories

The three major theories (all of which have some support) that explain the shape of the yield curve are the following.

Liquidity preference

Investors prefer to hold short-term securities because they are more liquid, whereas borrowers prefer long-term securities because they do not have to repay so quickly. Borrowers are willing therefore (and need) to pay higher interest rates on long-term loans.

Inflation expectations

When annual rates of inflation are expected to decline, the yield curve will be downward sloping. When inflation rates are expected to increase the yield curve will be upward sloping.

Market segmentation

This theory states that the market for short-term funds is different from that for long-term funds. The curve would be upward sloping if at a point in time in the short-term market there was a large supply of funds relative to demand, but at the same time there was a shortage of funds in the long-term market.

9.10 BONDS: A VARIETY OF FEATURES

Floating interest rates

Bonds in the UK are normally issued in fixed units of £100 nominal value and, as explained, can be sold at a premium or discount. They can in fact be redeemed at a value which is different from the £100. The interest rate offered is normally set in relation to the current market rates being offered on debentures in the same risk class. It is now becoming not unusual to issue debentures with a floating rate of interest which is tied to a market rate, for example the six months interbank rate. The level of interest paid on the loan can vary over the life of the debenture in line with movements in the rates in the market (US bonds are usually denominated in units of $1000.)

The use of floating rates has become necessary because of the large fluctuations in interest rates over comparatively short periods of time. It is in the interests of investors who may not wish to buy a security with a rate of interest which is fixed for a long period of time and which may therefore become out of line with other rates being offered in the market. It can also be in the issuing company's interest, as it would be reluctant to pay a fixed interest rate over a longer period of time if that rate was above current market rates.

To make the debentures attractive to investors a number of other features are often linked to the security.

Debt finance

Deep discounted bonds

Deep discounted bonds are those where the coupon rate being offered is well below the market rate at the time of issue. There might even be no annual interest being offered, in which case they are referred to as 'zero coupon bonds'. Such bonds, to be attractive, have to be offered to investors at a price which is at a discount compared with the value at which they will be redeemed.

The attraction of these bonds to the investor is that, although low or zero interest yield is being offered, the redemption yield can be high. For example, suppose that in 1990 a company made a debenture stock issue, offering zero interest, redeemable in ten years' time; in 1990 the stock was being offered at £50 to be redeemable at £100. The redemption yield can be calculated using the formula

$$P_t = \frac{I}{1+r} + \frac{I}{(1+r)^2} + \dots + \frac{R}{(1+r)^n}$$

With the annual interest being equal to zero this becomes

$$50 = \frac{100}{(1+r)^{10}}$$

Solving the equation gives $r = 7\%$. This means that the annual interest yield is zero, but at the time of issue the annual redemption yield is 7%. Whether this is attractive to an investor depends on whether or not he or she needs an annual cash flow, and how at the time of issue a 7% annual return compares with current market rates of return on investments with similar risk characteristics.

The attraction of this form of issue to a company is that, if it has current cash-flow problems, it is a way of immediately raising funds that does not result in any short-term cash outflow. It is also attractive to a business that is wishing to raise funds for a long-term project but does not expect to generate cash inflows for a number of years.

Discounted bonds are those issued at a discount which is defined as the difference between the issue price of the security and the amount payable on redemption, excluding any interest. A deep discounted bond is one in which this discount is more than 15% of the amount payable on redemption.

Convertible deep discounted bonds

A variation on the deep discounted bond is a bond issued at a low coupon rate which is convertible into equity shares from a date in the future. Such convertible bonds have been issued by such well-known companies as Burtons, Asda and Lonrho.

The attraction of such securities depends on the terms of the conversion. If the shares to be received are worth much more than the price paid for the bond, the investor is receiving for a number of years the below-market rates of interest in exchange for a gain at the time of the conversion, similar to a deep discount. Alternatively, the terms of the bond may be such that they pay interest rates just below market rates during the life of the bond, with the prospect of a small capital gain when the bond is exchanged for equity shares. A variation offered with some convertible bonds is that, if the holder opts not to convert, it is possible to receive instead an increase in interest rates paid on the bond backdated to the time of issue.

Asset-backed securities that are sold in the market place first appeared in the USA; they were introduced in the UK in 1985. Since then they have become increasingly popular, and the types of asset used for the securitization has widened. The early issues were backed by residential mortgages. Now there are issues backed by car loans, credit-card receivables, company loans and the leasing of railway rolling stock.

Securitization involves putting together a claim on an asset or assets of a company, for this claim to be represented by a security and for this security to be sold in the market place. Prior to this type of arrangement a company would pledge a particular asset or assets to a bank and the bank would advance money on the security of these assets. The disadvantage of this was that the company was having to deal directly with one bank and the bank itself was not in a position to pass on this debt to another party. By putting the assets into a claim and selling the claim in the market place, the seller of the assets should be able to obtain a more competitive price. One reason for this is that the claim is offered to a number of buyers and the initial buyer knows that they should be able to sell the claim to another investor should the need arise. The claim on the company is represented by a security. It is this security that is sold in the market place.

Some securities are sold with a right of recourse, some are sold without such a right. 'Recourse' means that if the asset does not generate sufficient cash flow to pay the interest and to allow the loan to be redeemed, then the purchaser of the security has the right to ask the company that sold the security to make good the cash deficiency. Non-recourse means the purchaser of the security cannot claim off the issuer of the security. The assets sold should generate a sufficient stream of income, for example mortgage repayments or lease payments; but things could go wrong.

If the asset is sold without a right of recourse, then the asset will be removed from the seller's balance sheet; it will be replaced with cash. An obvious benefit to a financial institution selling such a security is to remove an asset with possibly a long maturity from its balance sheet and to receive cash. This clearly improves its liquidity – it can lend again. It also improves its gearing. A market has developed for the exchange of these securities.

If a company, say a financial institution, is able to sell some of its debtors to another company, then clearly the transaction is a sale of an asset; the debtors figure in the balance sheet will be reduced and the cash figure increased. The trouble arises in respect of a sale with a right of recourse. If the purchaser of the debts can come back to the seller if the situation arises where the debts sold cannot be collected, then the seller of the debts has a contingent liability and has to be concerned about possible bad debts.

An interesting 'innovative' example of a securitization issue occurred in the UK at the end of 1996. Stagecoach PLC acquired a leasing company (Porterbrook) which leased out rolling stock to the newly privatized railway operating companies. In the traditional way the leasing company would have received a steady stream of cash over time as the leasing payments were received.

Stagecoach instead transferred these future receipts into a security, which it sold as bonds in the markets for £545 million. The bond is secured by the lease payments. The funds raised were mainly used to pay off a loan that was used to fund the purchase of the leasing company.

Investors will not have recourse to Stagecoach if the projected leasing income does not materialize. The securities were sold without recourse. Holders of the bonds need not worry, however – the government in its eagerness to make the privatization issue a success guaranteed about 80% of the lease payments from the railway companies. The bonds are low-risk.

9.12 REDEMPTION OF BONDS

It is usual to date debentures and bonds, that is, to give the particular year or years in which the security will be redeemed. The cash to repay the debenture or bond holders can be obtained by (a) making a new issue, (b) from funds available as a result of the trading activities in the year of redemption, or (c) funds placed into a sinking fund.

Many debenture issues have a provision in the deed which requires the issuing company to create a sinking fund as a means of discharging the debt. This means that the company creates a separate fund (usually administered by a trustee) into which it makes equal periodic payments over the life of the debenture. The amounts deposited in the fund earn interest, and this amount plus the fund itself could be used either to repay all the debentures at a particular redemption date or to repay a proportion of the debentures in one year, a proportion in the next year, and so on.

In the latter situation the debenture would have been dated for a period, e.g. 1995–8. In such instances individual debenture holders do not know if their debentures will be selected for retirement in a particular year or whether they will even have to wait until the final redemption date. The number of debentures that are to be retired in a particular year depends upon the rate at which the company pays into the sinking fund. With some such issues the company wishes to retire a certain percentage, say 75%, of the securities before the final maturity date. In other cases the annual contribution to the sinking fund may be a fixed percentage of the company's earnings in each year, or sufficient to retire a fixed percentage of the securities outstanding in each year.

9.13 CALL PROVISION

A company does have some choice over the date at which it will redeem its debentures. With the perpetual debenture the company can choose to redeem the debt whenever it so wishes, and the debenture holder is forced to settle. With a redeemable debenture, even after having named a date for redemption in the deed, the company can try to induce a holder to settle at an earlier date by making them an offer.

This is not the same as the option open to US companies. A US company can 'call' in its debenture stock: it can force holders to redeem at any time it so chooses up to and obviously including redemption date. A UK company can merely make an offer to its debenture holder; if the investor does not want to accept the offer, he or she can continue to hold the debenture and only be forced to exchange at the date set for redemption.

This call provision is a tool of financial management that is not usually open to UK companies. It is worth considering the value of this right. It has received considerable attention in US literature, and although UK companies do not have exactly the same opportunities with all debentures, they do with perpetual debentures, and if they can make the offer sufficiently attractive they have some choice with redeemable debentures. Another limited option available to UK companies is the actual date of redemption. As mentioned above often an issue does not give a single date for redemption: rather, a period of time is mentioned during which they will redeem.

This call privilege is also important to borrowers and lenders in mortgage arrangements, lease agreements and many long-term loans. The conditions and terms under which the issuer of the debenture may repay all or part of their obligations before the date of maturity are usually included in the loan agreement. At one extreme the call privilege is not allowed; at the other extreme there is complete freedom to call whenever the borrower wishes. There are several intermediate positions. One may be not to allow redemption until a certain number of years have passed, or to allow the call only a certain number of years before maturity. On occasions the borrower may have to pay a premium if they exercise their call privilege.

The reasons why the borrower may wish to call in the debt early include the following:

1 to take advantage of falls in interest rates by refunding;
2 the borrower's repayment ability may be better than anticipated;
3 business changes may necessitate a change in capital structure;
4 tax changes may encourage refunding;
5 the terms of the debenture may place restrictions on the firm which make refunding desirable or necessary.

The major reason advanced for early repayment is because the opportunity arises to borrow at lower interest rates.

9.14 INTEREST-RATE SWAPS

Interest-rate swaps have increased dramatically in popularity over recent years. There are two principal reasons why a company may wish to engage in such swaps. One is to alter the balance of its portfolio of loans. If a company feels that too many of its loans are at fixed interest rates, and it finds another company that feels that too many of its loans are at variable interest rates, the two companies may be happy to conduct an interest-rate swap.

The second reason is that the situation often occurs where an interest-rate swap results in both companies making savings on their borrowing costs. At first it can seem hard to accept that both companies can gain and nobody loses. It is true, however, and it occurs because of market imperfections. An example below will demonstrate the point.

The subject is discussed more fully in Chapter 17 on treasury management where further examples are to be found.

In its simplest form one party, say Company C, which has borrowed funds at a fixed interest rate, gets together with another party, say Company D, which has borrowed at a floating rate, and the two agree to service each other's loan. In effect, Company C finishes up paying a floating rate of interest and Company D a fixed rate.

In its simplest form the transaction is conducted in just one currency. Both companies, referred to as 'counterparties', will show their own loans in their balance sheets. Some companies disclose their actual interest-rate commitments (resulting from swap agreements) in notes in their annual accounts.

The arrangement becomes slightly more complicated when a bank becomes involved. A bank may act as a broker bringing the two companies together or as one of the principals. One motive behind a swap arrangement is that one company that has borrowed at a fixed rate wishes to service a floating-rate loan. With the other company the position is reversed. We will illustrate this very basic interest-rate swap in example 9.3.

Example 9.3

A company XYZ has borrowed on a line of credit from a UK bank at a floating rate of interest, say the London interbank offered rate (LIBOR) plus a premium. The rate at the time of the swap is 5.5% + 2.5%. Another company, Gresham, has borrowed in the Euromarket at a fixed rate of 8.19%. The directors of XYZ want to transfer from a floating-rate commitment to a fixed-rate loan. This wish could be based on expectations that interest rates will rise dramatically in the future or because it wants a better balance of debts in its porfolio.

The directors at Gresham wish to transter its debts from fixed interest to a floating rate. For the purpose of a swap, an intermediary bank will bring the parties together. The bank will of course charge for its services. XYZ will finish up servicing the fixed-rate debt of Gresham, and Gresham will service the floating-rate debt of XYZ.

The intermediary bank could arrange for XYZ to pay 8.22%, and keep 0.03% for itself, passing on the 8.19% to Gresham to pay the Eurobankers. The counter-arrangement is that with the current interest rates Gresham pay 8.02% to the bank, who pass on 8.00% to XYZ. Of course, with the latter transaction the rate paid by Gresham could change from one period to another as the market interest rates change. XYZ has reduced its risks, as it knows that the maximum amount it will have to pay is 8.22%. In diagrammatic form the transaction appears as in Figure 9.4.

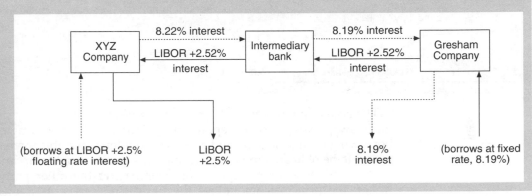

Figure 9.4

We will now use the same example to demonstrate the second reason for an interest-rate swap, namely to save on borrowing costs.

Example 9.4

Let us assume that the XYZ company is larger and has a better reputation than the Gresham company – it can borrow more cheaply (whether fixed- or floating-rate debt). If XYZ wished to borrow in the Euromarket it would have to pay 7.19%. If Gresham wished to borrow at a floating rate from a UK bank it would pay LIBOR + 4.5%.

As can be seen in Table 9.2, XYZ has a comparative advantage of 1% in fixed-rate borrowing and of 2% in floating-rate borrowing. The difference of 1% is the possible gain from a swap transaction.

The rule in a swap is (a) for each company to borrow under the terms with which the company has the greater comparative advantage or the least comparative disadvantage. This means XYZ borrows floating and Gresham borrows fixed; (b) the companies service each other's debts.

Table 9.2 Potential gain

	XYZ	Gresham	XYZ's comparative advantage
Fixed	7.19%	8.19%	1.0%
Floating	LIBOR + 2.5%	LIBOR + 4.5%	2.0%
	Possible net gain		1.0%

We illustrate the gains each company (and the intermediary bank) makes from the swap in Table 9.3. The companies agree to divide the gain more or less equally: i.e.

XYZ borrows at floating rate (LIBOR + 2.5%)
Gresham borrows at fixed rate (8.19%)

One solution, which divides the gain as agreed is for Gresham to pay LIBOR + 4.02% to the intermediary bank.

Table 9.3 Gains from swap

XYZ			
On floating	Pays to UK bank	LIBOR + 2.5%	
	Net receipt from intermediary bank	LIBOR + 4.0%	+ 1.50%
On fixed	Pays to intermediary bank	8.22%	
	Opportunity cost in market	7.19%	
		Loss	− 1.03%
		Net gain	+ 0.47%
Gresham			
On floating	Pays intermediary bank	LIBOR + 4.02%	
	Opportunity cost in market	LIBOR + 4.5%	
		Gain	+0.48%
On fixed	Pays in Euromarket	8.19%	
	Receives from intermediary bank	8.19%	0
		Net gain	+0.48%
Intermediary bank	0.03%	From XYZ	
	0.02%	From Gresham	
		Gain	+ 0.05%

It can be seen that XYZ make a gain on the floating-rate side of the deal, but lose on the fixed-rate side. They are paying Gresham 8.22% fixed rate, whereas if they had gone directly to the market they could have borrowed for 7.19%. On balance, however, they gain.

There net borrowing cost is 6.72% which is 8.22% less than the gain of 1.5%. The net cost to Gresham is LIBOR + 4.02%.

Of course, there are many ways in which the 1% total gain from the transaction can be divided. Who gains most is a matter for negotiation between the two counterparties. Also for any agreed split of the gains there are many different combinations of interest-rate transfer payments that give the desired net outcome.

The accounting treatment of an interest-rate swap is relatively straightforward. Each swap party should report on its balance sheet its original underlying borrowing from its lenders and any accrued interest payable thereon, since it continues to be obligated to pay these amounts. In the usual swap arrangement, the parties do *not* assume responsibility for paying the other party's borrowing: rather, the principal amount of the borrowing serves as a memorandum or notional amount upon which the interest-rate swap payments are based. Thus, one party's balance sheet does not include the other party's principal amount, and vice versa. In the profit and loss account, the net settlement amount under the swap agreement (resulting in a net interest receivable or payable from/to the other swap party) should be accrued each period and reported as a net adjustment to the interest expense for the underlying borrowing. Assuming that the transaction is material, the existence of the swap and its terms (including its impact on the interest cost of the underlying borrowing and the period of the agreement) should be disclosed in the footnotes to the financial statements (usually in the note dealing with debt).

9.15 DEBT–EQUITY SWAPS

One type of financial restructuring arrangement that has proved to be very popular at certain times is the debt–equity swap. With this the holders of a company's debentures and loan stock are invited to exchange that security for equity in the company.

From the company's point of view there are number of advantages.

1 There is a reduction in the level of gearing, with equity replacing debt.
2 When market interest rates are significantly higher than the coupon rate on outstanding debt, it is possible to have an even more favourable effect on the gearing ratios. This is illustrated below.

A 5% bond maturing in 20 years is clearly not worth its par value when current interest rates are, say, at 10%. An approximate indication of the market

Debt finance

price would be £50 for a £100 bond. This means that the company can offer the holders of such a bond equity shares worth just over £50 and it should prove to be attractive. This adjustment has the effect of reducing the level of gearing if the gearing is based on the market values of debt and equity: £50 of debt is replaced with just over £50 worth of equity.

If the debt-to-equity ratio is based on book values, the effect of the re-capitalization is exaggerated. The book value of the debt (£100) is higher than the market value. On book-value calculations, therefore, £100 worth of debt is eliminated from the balance sheet, i.e. the par value of the debt, and replaced with £50 worth of equity.

Another form of financial restructing is a debt-for-debt swap. This again would occur when current interest rates are very much higher than interest rates at the time that the debt was issued.

9.16 REPAYMENT OF LOANS

There are a number of different types of loan, all of which require different methods of repayment. These will be illustrated with examples. Let us assume that a company borrows £100 000 from a bank on 1 January 1994 and the nominal interest rate payable per annum is fixed at 10%. Tax will be ignored.

Term loan

This is the simplest type of loan. The £100 000 is borrowed for a fixed term, in this case four years. The interest is payable on 31 December each year and the capital sum is repayable as a single payment on 31 December 1997. The cash out-flow, what is called the 'annual debt service' of the company, is therefore

End of:	1994	1995	1996	1997
	−£10 000	−£10 000	−£10 000	−£110 000

The borrowing company has to consider how it will repay £100 000 at the end of 1997. As mentioned above, it has at least three options: it could place money aside each year as with a sinking fund; it could hope to be able to repay the amount out of the net cash inflows in the year 1997; it could 'refund' the £100 000 by borrowing again in 1997 and using this cash inflow to repay the 1994 loan.

Mortgage-style loan with equal payment each period

With this method, the annual debt service (the interest and capital repayments combined) is the same each year. This type of loan is similar to those used for purchasing a home by means of a mortgage loan.

Using the same example as above, with the repayment over four years and the first repayment being made at the end of the first year, the annual cash outflow would be as follows:

End of:	1994	1995	1996	1997
	−£31 547	−£31 547	−£31 547	−£31 547

The way in which this annual service charge was arrived at was to calculate the annuity that would be received in each of four years, if a payment of £100 000 was now made with interest at 10% per annum.

The PV of an annuity table (Table 3 at the end of this book) gives the discount factor for four periods, with 10% interest per annum, as 3.1699. Dividing the capital sum of £100 000 by this gives £31 547.

In this problem we were given the PV, the number of years and the interest rate; we then calculated the annual flow. The more usual way in which Table 3 is used is to know the annual flow, the number of years and the interest rate, and then to calculate the present value.

The debt service charge in each year is a mixture of capital repayment and interest. Table 9.4 shows the details of the repayments.

Table 9.4

	Total repayment	Interest	Capital	Capital balance at start of year
1994	£31 547	£10 000	£21 547	£100 000
1995	£31 547	£7845	£23 702	£78 453
1996	£31 547	£5475	£26 072	£54 750
1997	£31 547	£2867	£28 680	£28 680

Payments more frequent than annually

The examples in this section are all based on interest paid on an annual basis. There are of course many loans where interest needs to be paid at more frequent intervals, say six-monthly. The same techniques and the same tables can be used with monthly, quarterly and half-yearly payments as well as with annual payments.

Let us assume in the above mortgage-style loan example that the interest rate is now quoted as 5% semi-annually, with interest and capital repayments over four years at six-monthly intervals. The repayments would now be:

30.6.94	31.12.94	...	30.6.97	31.12.97
−£15 472	−£15 472	...	−£15 472	−£15 472

This service charge has been calculated using Table 3. This time we observe the factor for eight periods at 5% interest per period, which is 6.4632. The £100 000 loan is divided by this factor to give eight payments of £15 472.

Annual equivalent interest rates

It will be noted that this service charge is not one-half of that for the four-year loan with annual repayments. This is because the capital repayments are being made earlier than in the annual repayment case and the effective interest charge is different. It should be appreciated that a 5% interest half-yearly is equivalent to an annual rate of 10.215%, i.e. $(1.05)^2$.

The way that the equivalent annual interest charge can be estimated in the case where interest rates are quoted at intervals shorter than one year is to substitute the quoted rate of interest r and the frequency n of payments in the following equation:

$$\text{equivalent annual interest rate} = (1 + r)^n$$

Therefore a loan with interest quoted at 2% per month compounded is equivalent to an annual rate of 26.82%, i.e. $(1.02)^{12} = 1.2682$. The compounding means that interest is being charged on the interest that has not been paid as well as on the capital. Table 1 at the end of the book gives the amount of 1 at compound interest rates.

The other way in which interest rates might be quoted in loans where equal repayments are required is to quote the annual interest rate but to require payments at intervals more frequently than once a year. Let us say in our above example that the £100 000 is borrowed at an annual interest rate of 10%, but repayments are required quarterly.

Using the equation above we can calculate the quarterly interest rate that is equivalent to an annual rate of 10%:

$$1.10 = (1 + r)^4$$

Table 1 indicates that over four periods, a factor of 1.10 arises somewhere between the 2% and 3% interest rates. In fact, the quarterly compound interest rate is approximately 2.4%. The company is required to repay the £100 000 with 16 equal quarterly payments at an interest rate of 10% per annum. Each payment will be approximately £7600. This can be estimated using Table 3. The relevant factor for an interest rate of 2% is 13.5777 and for an interest rate of 3% is 12.5611. The factor for an interest rate of 2.4% is in the region of 13.16.

Certain loans require the first repayments to be made at the date the contract is signed, i.e. at the beginning of the term of the loan. All subsequent payments are also at the beginning of the payment interval. This is sometimes referred to as an 'annuity due'. The annuity where no payment is needed at the beginning of the term of the loan is an 'ordinary annuity'.

Returning to the example above where the £100 000 was repayable in eight semi-annual instalments with an interest rate of 5% half-yearly, we shall now assume that the first payout is due at 1 January 1994, and then every quarter.

We are now faced with an annuity of eight payments, the first being immediate. PV of annuity tables (such as Table 3) are based on ordinary annuities and do not allow for a payment at the beginning of the term. In fact, what we are faced with is an immediate payout of cash, with the remaining seven payments in the form of an ordinary annuity.

We look up the PV factor for the seven payments, which with interest at 5% is 5.7864; the factor for the first immediate payment is 1.0000. These two factors are added together and divided into the £100 000 to give

$$\frac{£100000}{6.7864} = £14\,735$$

The eight repayments under this type of loan arrangement would each be of £14 735.

Grace periods

Some loans do not require capital repayments during their early years of the term. Loans with grace periods (also called 'rest periods' or 'holiday periods') can sometimes be negotiated when a new business or a small business is borrowing from a bank. Such a grace period could be particularly important when the funds raised are to be used to finance a major project which will take time to develop before it starts to generate cash inflow. Grace periods are also often found in loans by commercial banks to governments. Again, the idea is to allow time for a project to be completed and start to generate returns before needing to worry about capital repayments.

There are at least three variations on loans with grace periods. In one, interest is charged and payable during the grace period but capital repayments do not have to be made during this period. In another, interest is charged but is not payable until the grace period finishes. The interest is accumulated during the grace period and added to the capital repayment, and the total is repaid over the remaining period of the loan. With this latter approach the borrower is in fact borrowing both the capital sum and the interest charge arising during the grace period. The third possibility is for no interest to be charged during the grace period.

We shall illustrate the first and second approaches. Suppose, as in our earlier example, the borrower obtains £100 000. The life of the loan is four years and interest is 10% per annum. The grace period is two years.

Interest charged during grace period
It is being assumed that after the grace period the debt service charge is to be the same in each of the remaining two years of the period of the loan. The cash outflows would be:

31.12.94	31.12.95	31.12.96	31.12.97
−£10 000	−£10 000	−£57 620	−£57 620

The first two years' outflows are simply the interest on the capital sum. The outflows in the last two years are arrived at by obtaining the PV factor for an annuity for two years with interest at 10%. The factor of 1.7355 is divided into the £100 000.

Interest charged but not payable during the grace period
In this situation the interest is accumulated during the grace period and added to the capital sum for eventual repayment. The unpaid interest over the two years accumulates to £21 000 as at January 1996, i.e. $[(1.10)^2 - 1.00] \times £100 000$. The total debt at 1 January 1996 is therefore £121 000. The cash outflows for 1996 and 1997 are again calculated using the PV of an annuity table. The outflows in this case would be:

31.12.94	31.12.95	3.12.96	31.12.97
0	0	−£69 721	−£69 721

Clearly grace periods are a valuable concession to the borrower. In the two examples used as illustrations, they are providing a repayment schedule which should benefit the borrower. It should be appreciated, however, that they are not lowering the interest rate being charged. In both cases illustrated the full nominal rate of 10% per annum is effectively being paid. Grace periods only reduce the effective rate of interest below the nominal rate if no interest is charged during the grace period.

Loans with equal capital repayments each year

This type of loan is somewhat unusual, but can arise particularly in instances where the interest rate charged varies over the life of the loan. The mathematics are relatively simple, with the interest payments each year being based on the balance of the capital remaining to be paid at the beginning of that year.

In the example being used in this section, the annual cash outflow would be:

	31.12.94	31.12.95	31.12.96	31.12.97
Capital repayment	−£25 000	−£25 000	−£25 000	−£25 000
Interest payable	−£10 000	−£7 500	−£5 000	−£2 500
	−£35 000	−£32 500	−£30 000	−£27 500

As can be seen with this method the early years have higher debt service charges than the later years. This could be a disadvantage to the borrower.

Debt finance

To compare the relative advantages of the different types of loan it is necessary to know the expected returns and the timing of the returns from the project to be financed. One approach would be to select the loan with the cash outflows that most closely matched the timing of the cash inflows of the project.

Another approach would be simply to compare the PV of the returns from the project with the PV of the loan costs using conventional discounting methods. The alternative debt service charge schedules could be deducted from the cash inflow figures, and the resulting net figures discounted at the equity cost of the company. This would show the net PV obtained on the shareholders' funds.

In this section we have shown seven different repayment schedules for the same £100 000 loan over a four-year repayment period. A borrower, of course, is most unlikely to be given a choice between the seven alternatives. The borrower, particularly if a small company, could well be offered a loan and given no choice as to how it will be repaid. The situation can arise, however, when a company with some bargaining power does have the opportunity to make a choice between two or three alternative types of loan.

9.17 CONVERTIBLE LOAN STOCK

The characteristics of convertible loan stock issues are that, while they are sold initially as loan stock receiving an appropriate rate of interest, the holder is given the option of converting this loan stock within a given time period into equity shares at a specified price. The advantage to the company of this form of capital is that initially the loan stock assists the capital gearing, and, of course, the interest, with the advantage of the tax shield, reduces the cost of the capital in the years when it remains loan capital. The advantage to the shareholder is that he or she can wait to see how the share price of the company moves before deciding whether to invest in the equity. If the company is successful and the share price rises, the investor will be keen to exercise the option; if not, he or she is free to retain the loan investment. The holder is usually given the opportunity to convert on at least two dates in each year – dates on which the option is exercisable.

Value of convertible security to an investor

The value of a convertible security depends upon what happens to the share price of the issuing company over the life of the security. If the share price rises above the conversion price and the investor expects it to remain above this level, he or she will exercise their option to convert when they are able to. If it does not rise above this level, or they expect any increase above the level to be only temporary, the investor will not wish to exercise the option.

The value of the convertible security depends on expectations regarding the future share price. The *ex ante* yield on the convertible is probabilistic; it depends upon a number of factors. If assumptions are made, for example if it is assumed that the share price grows at a certain rate per annum, then the value of the conversion privilege can be calculated as at any date in the future.

For an investor considering converting the debenture at some time in the future, the yield they can expect to receive can only be determined by forecasting the expected share price. The value of the shares to be received at the time of conversion can be expressed as in the following formula (it is emphasized that this is the total value to be received):

$$C_t = P_0 (1 + g)^n R \qquad (9.1)$$

where C_t is the conversion value of the debenture at time t, P_0 is the share price today, g is the estimated annual percentage rate of growth of share price, R is the number of shares to be received on conversion of one debenture and n is the number of years to conversion.

In addition to receiving the shares at a date in the future if and when the conversion is exercised, the holder also receives in the intervening period the interest on the debenture. This means that the total receipts due to the holder can be expressed as

$$V = I_1 + I_2 + I_3 + \ldots + I_n + P_0(1 + g)^n R \tag{9.2}$$

where I_n is the interest paid on the debenture in year n and V is the total receipts due to the holder. The current price at which the convertible debenture is being sold is known, and so the expected yield to be received from holding such a security can be determined using the following formula:

$$M = \sum_{t=1}^{n} \frac{I}{(1+r)^t} + \frac{P_0(1+g)^n R}{(1+r)^n} \tag{9.3}$$

where M is the price paid for convertible debenture and r is the internal rate of return (yield).

This approach utilizes Brigham's valuation model [1] and can be used to estimate the yield that an investor can expect, given assumptions about the date that he or she will convert and the change in share price over time. The same formula can of course be used to determine the growth in share price that must take place to give a required rate of return to the holder of the convertible debenture. This point is of special interest, because whatever else it may be worth the security has a straight debt value – the price which investors would be willing to pay just to receive the stream of future interest payments plus the redemption of the loan at the end of the period. A useful comparison can therefore be made between the value of the security as loan stock and its value as equity.

Two premiums will be referred to in the analysis:

$$\text{conversion premium} = \frac{\text{market value of convertible loan stock}}{\text{number of shares at conversion date}} - \text{current share price} \tag{9.4}$$

$$\text{rights premium} = \frac{\text{market value of convertible} - \text{value as loan stock}}{\text{number of shares at conversion date}} \tag{9.5}$$

These equations show the premiums per share. To ascertain the premium per unit of convertible loan stock, it is necessary to multiply the premium per share by the number of ordinary shares that can be obtained by converting one unit of loan stock.

To illustrate the use of the above formula, let us assume that a company (Barston PLC) issued a 10% convertible debenture (£100 par) on 1 January 1989. It could be converted into 80 equity shares of Barston at any time between 1 January 1994 and 31 November 1998. The convertible security was being sold for £95 on 1 January 1990. The price of the equity shares on 1 January 1990 was £0.90 and was expected to rise by 10% per annum. The gross yield on the security for an investor purchasing at the 1 January 1990 price can be estimated by using equation (9.3). We shall assume that the convertible debenture is held until the first conversion date, namely 1 January 1994. Then

$$95 = \frac{10}{1+r} + \frac{10}{(1+r)^2} + \frac{10}{(1+r)^3} + \frac{10}{(1+r)^4} + \frac{0.90(1.10)^4}{(1+r)^4} \times 80$$

Solving the equation gives r equal to approximately 11%. The expected yield for the investor buying the convertible at 1 January 1990 at £95 was therefore 11%.

The conversion premium on each Barston convertible debenture as at 1 January 1990 was equal to £0.2875 per share, given by £95/80 − £0.90.

To calculate the rights premium at 1 January 1990, we need to know the value of the convertible as simple loan stock. This depends upon the current interest yields in the market place on loan stock in a similar risk category to that of Barston. We shall assume that such an interest yield is 12%, which means that the value of the simple loan is £83.33. (At this price an interest payment of £10 gives a yield of 12%.)

The rights premium per share is therefore £0.1458, i.e.

$$\frac{£95 - £83.33}{80}$$

The rights premium represents the excess value of the convertible security over an equivalent loan stock with the same rate of interest. The situation is illustrated in Figure 9.5 which depicts the situation in which the increase over time in the price of the company's shares is satisfactory and is expected to continue; consequently, a rights premium exists, since the rights option has a value. The line CM'' represents the conversion value of the convertible security at the various points in time. The market value is higher than the conversion value because investors expect the share price in the future to rise above its present level and so expect the rights to be worth even more.

With the Barston example, the value of conversion to the holders of the security at 1 January 1990 was £72 (80 shares of £0.90 per share). The market value of the convertible is £95. This difference, represented in Figure 9.5 as the gap between the $M'M''$ line and the CM'' line, reflects the required increase in ordinary share value to make conversion worthwhile. As the diagram shows, the two lines move closer together until they meet. At this point, conversion should start to take place.

The rights premium is the difference between the LR line and the $M'M''$ line, i.e. the difference between the convertible security valued as a convertible and as a straight loan stock. In the early years of the security's life, the floor of the conversion value can be determined by its value as a loan stock, but as the share price rises its minimum value will eventually be determined by its worth as a convertible security. While it is still valued as loan stock the conversion premium will exceed the rights premium. However, if the share price rises as expected, as the time for conversion approaches the conversion premium will be lower than the rights premium.

As the conversion value of the security increases, its market value (which begins by being higher) also rises but at a slower rate, and the two values eventually become identical. There are at least two reasons for this. First, with the arrival of the conversion period the holder will be able to exercise the option

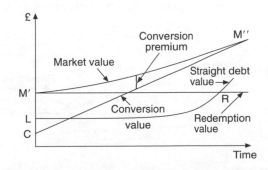

Figure 9.5

Convertible loan stock

245

and receive the conversion value; the market price should be kept from rising too far above this value otherwise the potential holder will be in danger of a loss. This prevents wide spreads arising between the market value and the conversion value. Convertible debentures can be purchased on the stock market on any trading day. On the date that they are first issued by a company, they sell for a premium (the rights premium) above the price which would be paid for a simple debenture that merely secured a stream of interest payments. This is because the investors, at that time of issue, expect benefits to accrue to them through the share-conversion option, and for the same reason the interest yield will be lower on a convertible than on a straight debenture. If, however, the company's share price does not perform well over time, the price of the convertible debenture could well fall to a level giving the same yield as a straight debenture with no options.

Value as a debenture

If the price of the equity shares that are being offered in exchange for the convertible debt should fall or should not rise as much as is necessary to make conversion worthwhile, the value of the convertible security is that of a straight debt issue. The rights premium would be zero, with the value of the convertible equalling the value of loan stock.

The conversion premium in this case represents the recovery required in the ordinary share before conversion becomes an attractive proposition. This situation is illustrated in Figure 9.6 where the market value of the convertible loan stock falls to the value of a straight debenture. This would happen if the share price of the company slumped and the investors considered the value of the right to convert as zero. The rights premium would consequently be zero. There would still be a conversion premium, however, because when the company decided at the time of issue on the number of ordinary shares to be exchanged for the loan stock, the expectations regarding future share price were higher than could later be justified.

The redemption value is simply the amount of debt that will be redeemed at some time in the future. The convertible loan stock can be issued at par value, or at some value below this; in Figure 9.6 it is shown as being issued at par. The market value of the stock falls as expectations change regarding the value of the rights until it becomes valued simply as loan stock. The reason that the value of the convertible as a debenture is shown to rise over time is that convertible securities usually carry a lower interest rate than a pure debt issue. Consequently, as the yield on the convertible is below that on a normal loan, its value as loan stock is initially below par, but as the maturity date approaches, with maturity at par, the two lines move towards each other.

The price of the ordinary shares on the market may rise above the equivalent ordinary share price under the option, but the holder still might not convert. He or she may wish to hold the convertible loan stock, receiving a yield on the loans perhaps greater than the dividend yield on the equity, and convert only on the

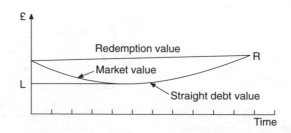

Figure 9.6

Debt finance

final date at which the option can be exercised. As the ordinary share price increases above the equivalent share value, the market value for the convertible will still be equal to the conversion value. The two values will be equal because investors would only be prepared to purchase the convertible in the market at a price equal to the conversion value.

This brings out the second important factor causing the market value and the conversion value to converge, namely the relationship between the yield on the convertible loan stock and the yield on the share for which it can be exchanged. The interest on a convertible is fixed at a certain rate; however, the dividends paid on a share normally rise. This means that the dividend yield on the equivalent share price rises to meet the yield on the fixed-interest loan stock, so that as the time for conversion approaches, the gap between the market value and the conversion value closes, as shown in Figure 9.5.

The exact value L_t of convertible loan stock as a normal debenture can be determined from the following equation:

$$L_t = \sum_{k=1}^{T-t} \frac{I}{(1+i)^k} + \frac{M}{(1+i)^{T-t}}$$

where T is the year of redemption, t is the present year, $T - t$ is the number of years to maturity of the debenture, i is the market interest yield on an equivalent-risk debt issue, I is the interest paid each year and M is the redemption value at maturity.

Advantages of convertibles to the company

If the rate of conversion is correctly determined, this method of finance may offer the company two advantages over other forms of finance. First, as earnings grow the debt is self-liquidating. The ordinary share price will reflect the increasing earnings. When the share price reaches the price at which conversion is worthwhile, debentures will be exchanged for ordinary shares. Therefore the company does not have to find new finance to pay off a debenture when the time for redemption is approaching. By converting, the bondholders are saving the company from having to fund the debt.

It could, of course, be argued that the existing shareholders are being made to suffer by having the debt reduced in this way. It may be in the existing shareholders' interest not to have new equity created but to have a new loan floated to provide the finance to pay off the old loan. This would certainly be the case if the conversion of the debentures, by increasing the number of the shares, lowered their price. A fall in earnings per share, as explained earlier, could well have this effect. However, the empirical studies on this point do not find that the share prices fall after conversion.

The second attractive feature of convertible debentures that offer advantages to the company is that the conversion does not harm the company's capital structure; if anything it helps it. The company has to pay the interest bill on the convertible, but does not have to repay the capital. It is in effect a convenient method of avoiding the need to raise a second round of funds for repayment purposes.

The conversion of debt into equity does not increase the total capital employed of the company. Should the company wish to expand it can now make another issue of debt capital as its gearing will have fallen as a result of the conversion. The use of convertibles became for a time part of a cycle: debt – conversion into equity – new debt – conversion into equity, and so on. To continue such a financial exercise, however, the company needed to produce the earnings performance that enabled the share price to continue to rise.

The type of convertible stock issued by companies has changed over time. Convertibles were once regarded as a special type of borrowing, designed to meet a short-term situation, but they then became looked upon as deferred equity. Early conversion dates gave way to possible conversion over long periods of time. The tax relief available on interest, but not on dividends, undoubtedly contributed to this lengthening in the time in which the conversion option was being offered. A typical convertible stock offers conversion at a price about 10–15% above the market price of the ordinary shares at the time of issue.

Exchangeable bonds/notes

These are a type of convertible bond, where the security to be received upon exchange of the bond is not a share in the issuing company, but some other security.

For example, in 1997, Daimler Benz planned to issue exchangeable notes, in which the notes could be converted into shares in a French software company (Cap Gemini) that it owned. This was the way Daimler Benz intended to dispose of a large equity stake it had in the French company. The issue did not go ahead, however, because of action taken by the other major shareholder in the French company.

The Deutsche Bank, in 1997, sold a convertible bond that was convertible into the shares of an insurance company. The bank owned the insurance company and wished to dispose of all its shares, some being sold in the market, some being exchanged on conversion.

9.18 WARRANTS

A further type of capital issue is loan stock which cannot in itself be converted into equity but which gives the holder the right to subscribe at fixed future dates for ordinary shares at a predetermined price. Many issues have been offered with these terms The subscription rights, called 'warrants', entitle the bondholder to obtain a certain number of the company's ordinary shares at an agreed price. This is different from a convertible issue of loan stock, where the loan stock is given up if the conversion right is exercised. With a warrant the bondholder keeps the original loan stock, and has the choice of using the warrant to obtain ordinary shares in addition.

The advantage to the company of this form of issue is that the loan stock is maintained until the date of redemption. The warrants also enable the company to raise new equity capital: there is no need to substitute one form of capital for another, as there is with a convertible loan. The company retains both forms of capital up to the date of the redemption. The new equity can be used as a base to raise further loan capital in the future. In contrast, convertible loan stock may only help the short-term situation for a company; the loan raises the level of gearing, but when the loan is converted the gearing falls again.

Valuation of warrants

The theoretical value of a warrant is $(M - O)N$, where M is the market price of the ordinary share today, O is the exercise price of the warrant and N is the number of shares that each warrant allows the owner to buy [2].

For example, suppose that a warrant entitles a holder to buy one share at a price of £1. He or she may exercise this warrant at any time over the next three years. The present price of the shares is £2. The value of the warrant appears to be simply £1 = (£2 − £1) × 1. The price of the warrant should not fall below £1, for that is the value of the warrant if it is exercised on the market today.

The price of the warrant can rise above £1 if the prospects for the company are good. If the price of the warrant on the market is £1.50, it means that it is being sold at a premium of £0.50. Is it a good or bad buy at this price? It depends on the present value gained or lost by incurring this expenditure. The holder may not wish to exercise the option to convert into shares with these prices.

If the warrant is to be exercised this has to be completed before an expiry date. If we assume that the holder waits to the end of the period before exercising the option – and a study in the USA [3] showed that almost all warrants remained unexercised until shortly before expiry date – then the PV of exercising the option on expiry date can be calculated. In the above example, £1 has to be paid by the holder of the warrant in three years time. With a cost of money of 10%, the PV of this outlay is £0.75 = £1/(1.10)^3.

The market price of the warrant is £1.50; the PV of the payment on exercising the option at the expiry date is £0.75. The PV of the share is only £2. Someone who purchases the warrant today has a present cost of £2.25 (= £1.50 + £0.75) if they wish to obtain the share at the expiry date.

This is not a good investment with a PV cost of £2.25 to obtain a share with a present value of £2.00.

If the price of the warrant was only £1.20, it would be a good buy, however. Buying an option at £1.20, and paying £1 to the company at the end of year 3, which has a present cost of £0.75, means that for an outlay of £1.95 the investor has access to a share worth £2. The holder of the warrant has to decide whether to exercise the option now or to delay until nearer the expiry date. The choice is between a PV cost of £1.95 and receiving the share in three years' time, or paying £2 and receiving dividends over the three years. They would be indifferent to whether to exercise the option now or later, when the following equation holds:

$$M_0 − P_W = V_D + V_W$$

where M_0 is the price of a share today for which warrant can be exchanged, P_W is the price of the warrant, V_D is the PV of after-tax dividends over the remaining years of the warrant's life and V_W is the PV of the cost of exercising the warrant at the end of its life.

With the above example, this equation gives

$$£2 − £1.20 = x + £0.75$$
$$£0.05 = x$$

Therefore the breakeven PV of the dividends over three years is £0.05, which, with money costing 10%, is a dividend of approximately £0.02 per year. If the company is paying a higher dividend than this per share, it would be in the warrant holder's interest to exercise their option now. If the company is paying a lower dividend rate they should hold the warrant and realize nearer the expiry date.

In the first example, where the warrant had a price of £1.50, there was obviously no question of whether it was worth exercising the option now in order to receive the dividend. It was in the interests of the existing warrant holders if they wanted dividends to sell the warrants and buy shares, for it was only costing them £0.50 to obtain a share this way, whereas with the exercise of the option it would have cost them £1 to obtain a share.

At the beginning of this section it was stated that one approach to valuing a warrant is to take the difference between the market price of the share and the exercise price of the warrant. However, it has been pointed out that this approach is too simplistic. The value of a warrant can rise above this difference. It is partly because of this simple approach to valuing warrants that they are seen as a financial instrument that can lead to very high-percentage capital gains.

To be in line with other valuation techniques in finance, the current price of a warrant should equal the PV of the difference between the future price of the share and the exercise price of the warrant. This relationship can be expressed as

$$P_W = \frac{M_0(1+g)^n - O}{(1+k)^n}$$

where g is the expected growth rate in share price, k is the cost of capital appropriate to the warrant's risk class and n is the number of time periods expiring before the warrant is exercised.

It can be shown that the potential gains from buying a warrant are greater than the potential gains from buying the share to which the warrant relates. Similarly it is possible to make a greater loss. Assume that the price of the warrant at time t_1 equals the current price of the share less the price that would have to be paid when the warrant is exercised plus the premium on the warrant. Assume that the following situation develops:

	t_1	t_2	Change
Share price	£20	£40	+100%
Warrant price	£10	£28	+180%

The exercise price is £12, so that at time t_1 there was a premium of £2 on a warrant, i.e. £22 would have to be paid to obtain a share valued at £20. Time t_2 is the last date for exercise of the warrant, and so at that date the difference between the warrant price and the share price is exactly equal to the subscription price, the cost of exercising the warrant. As can be seen, a greater gain can be made from holding the warrant over the period than from holding the share. With any increase in the price of the share this will be the case.

If, however, the share had fallen in price, a greater loss would have been incurred from holding the warrant rather than holding the share:

	t_1	t_2	Change
Share price	£20	£15	−25%
Warrant price	£10	£3	−66%

This is the gearing effect of warrants.

Certain criticisms can be applied to this approach. It can be argued that if there is an efficient capital market, why in the first situation would the seller of the warrant be prepared to give up such large expected gains? If the buyer and seller have similar knowledge of the affairs of the company, why would the present holder of the warrant sell it for £10 when they have expectations that the warrant will rise in price? We have in the example introduced a premium into the valuation of the warrant, £2. Clearly, with an efficient capital market this premium would not be enough. The situation used in the example could only hold if the buyer and seller had different expectations about the company concerned, i.e. they have different expectations with regard to the growth rate of the company's share price. Given an efficient market, it is unlikely that the holder of the warrant would show a gain of 180% and the holder of the share a gain of 100%.

Equity derivatives

One type of equity derivative is a 'covered warrant'. This is an option on a company's shares sold by a third party (sometimes with the company's permission). The seller of the warrant does have available the necessary quantity of the underlying shares in case the buyer of the option decides to exercise the option. This is why it is referred to as a 'covered warrant'.

It can be contrasted with a 'synthetic warrant', with which the seller of the warrant does not hold the full complement of the underlying shares. The seller of the warrant might have to purchase the shares if the buyer exercises the option, or the seller might at the time of writing the option hedge using existing options or shares.

As mentioned, with this type of derivative, it is not the company whose shares are the subject of the option that is involved in writing the warrant, it is a third party. At the end of the 1980s such options were available on the shares of a wide range of European companies. The attraction of an option is that if the share price rises with a bull market the buyer of the option can make considerable gains, whilst if the share price falls, the loss is limited to the cost of the option premium.

One particular innovation in the market is referred to as the 'basket warrant'. This is an option on a basket of shares, usually in a specific sector of an individual stock market. For example, Salomon Brothers, a merchant bank, issues warrants in London on US food, oil and pharmaceutical baskets.

It should be appreciated that such 'equity derivatives' in no way raise finance for the companies involved, although the speculation in the warrants could affect the price of their shares.

Illustration

A worked example will illustrate the valuation techniques that have been described above with respect to both convertible debentures and warrants. The question used is taken from a Financial Management paper of the Chartered Association of Certified Accountants.

Example 9.5

Conver PLC and Warran PLC each have in issue two million ordinary shares each of £1 nominal value. The only other securities each company has current in issue are as follows.

Conver PLC: 25 000 units of convertible debentures each with a nominal value of £100 and a coupon interest rate of 12% payable yearly. Each £100 unit may be converted into 20 ordinary shares at any time until the date of expiry and any debentures remaining unconverted will be redeemed that day at 105.

Warran PLC: 500 000 warrants each of which provides the holder with an option to subscribe for one ordinary share at a price of £5.00 per share. The warrants can be exercised at any time until the date of expiry.

The ordinary shares of both companies, the convertible debentures and the warrants are all actively traded in the stock market.

(a) Determine the value of each £100 unit of convertible debentures and of each warrant on the date of expiry if the share price for each company immediately prior to the latest time for conversion or exercise were to be (i) £4.40, (ii) £5.20, (iii) £6 and (iv) £6.80. Ignoring any possible taxation consequences, advise holders of the convertibles and warrants whether they should exercise their conversion and option rights in each of the four cases (i)–(iv). (5 marks)

(b) Indicate the likely current market price, or likely range of current market prices, of each £100 unit of convertible debentures if they have a further 5 years before expiry and the current share price is (i) £4.40, (ii) £5.20, (iii) £6 and (iv) £6.80. The appropriate pre-tax rate of interest on a five-year debt security is 8% per annum. (5 marks)

(c) Explain the reasons for any differences between the valuation for the convertible debentures derived in (a) and (b). Outline the major factors which determine the market price of warrants and convertibles. (6 marks)

(d) Show the basic earnings per share for each company:

   (i) in a year when all convertibles and warrants remained outstanding for the whole period;
   (ii) for the first full year following conversion of all convertibles and exercise of all warrants.

Profits for each company can be taken as £1.2 million per year before considering interest payments, taxation and earnings from the investment of any newly raised funds. The corporation tax rate is 50%. Any additional funds will be reinvested within the firm to earn 10% before tax.

(4 marks)
(20 marks)

Suggested solution

Part (a)

The value of the convertible debenture on the date of expiry, namely the final conversion date, depends on whether it is converted into equity or retained as a debenture. If converted its worth is 20 equity shares. If retained as a debenture it is worth £105. The worth of the convertible at the different possible share prices is therefore

	With share price			
	£4.40	£5.20	£6.00	£6.80
As equity	£88	£104	£120	£136
As debt	£105	£105	£105	£105

With the share price at either £4.40 or £5.20 it is not worth converting. With the share price at either £6 or £6.80 it is worth converting.

The warrant entitles the holder to purchase an ordinary share at a price of £5 per share. If the actual share price in the market on the date of expiry is £4.40, the holder of the warrant would not wish to exercise his option. If he wants further equity shares in the company it will be cheaper for him to purchase the share in the market than to exercise his option. In the other three situations given in the question he will wish to exercise the option. The value of the warrant in the three situations is £0.20, £1.00 and £1.80, respectively.

Part (b)

In the question the convertible security still has five years left before expiring. Its value as debt is £119.42, obtained by solving the following equation:

$$V = \frac{12}{1.08} + \frac{12}{(1.08)^2} + \frac{12}{(1.08)^3} + \frac{12}{(1.08)^4} + \frac{12}{(1.08)^5} + \frac{105}{(1.08)^5}$$

(i) If the current share price is £4.40, the value of the security if converted is £88 (i.e. 20 × £4.40). The question asks for the likely current market price, which in the circumstances given would be somewhere in the region of £119.42, its value as a debt issue. There might be a modest premium on this price, but as the equity share price is so far below that at which conversion is just worth while, it would at best be a low premium.

(ii) With the share price at £5.20, the value of the equity obtained upon conversion becomes £104, still below the debenture value. The likely current market price depends upon expectations about the future share price. The market value will be above the straight debt value where the share price is increasing at a 'satisfactory' level. In the situation referred to in this part of the question a larger premium above the £119.42 price might be expected than with the former £4.40 share price.

(iii) In this case the conversion into equity would result in a holding of shares worth £120. Therefore this is the likely minimum market price of the convertible.

(iv) In this case conversion would give £136 worth of equity. Therefore £136 is the likely minimum price of the convertible.

Part (c)

The answer to this part of the question is well covered in the above text.

Part (d)

	Basic earnings per share	
	Before conversion/ exercise	After conversion/ exercise
Convertible	(£000)	(£000)
Earnings	1200	1200
Interest payments	300	–
	900	1200
Tax at 50%	450	600
	450	600
	(000)	(000)
Number of shares	2000	2500
Earnings per share	22.5p	24p
Warrant	(£000)	(£000)
Basic earnings	1200	1200
Return on additional funds £2 500 000 at 10%		250
	1200	1450
Tax at 50%	600	725
	600	725
Number of shares (thousand)	2000	2500
Earnings per share	30p	29p

9.19 REFERENCES

1   Brigham, E.F. (1966) An analysis of convertible debentures: theory and some empirical evidence, *Journal of Finance*, March: 35–54.
2   Samuelson, P.A. (1965) Rational theory of warrant pricing, *Industrial Management Review*, Spring.

Whittaker, J. (1967) The evaluation of warrants, *The Investment Analyst*, October.

3   Kassouf, S.T. (1966) *A Theory and an Econometric Model for Common Stock Purchase Warrants*, Analytical Publishers, New York.

9.20 FURTHER READING

Altman, E.I. (1990) Setting the record straight on junk bonds: a review of the research on default rates and returns, *Journal of Applied Corporate Finance*, Summer: 82–95.

Cordes, J. and Sheffin, S. (1983) Estimating the tax advantages of corporate debt, *Journal of Finance*, March.

Henderson, J. and Scott, J.P. (1988) *Securitization*, Woodhead-Faulkner, Cambridge.

Lewis, M. (1980) *Liar's Poker*, Penguin, London.

McDonald, R.L. (1984) How big is the tax advantage of debt? *Journal of Finance*, July.

Myers, S.C. (1984) The capital structure puzzle, *Journal of Finance*, July.

Rutterford, J. (1985) An international perspective on the capital structure puzzle, *Midland Corporate Finance Journal*, Autumn.

9.21 PROBLEMS

1   An irredeemable £100 bond was issued in 1990, offering a 10% coupon rate. In 1994 the market rate of interest on securities in a similar risk class is 8%. What will be the value of the bond in 1994?

2   A zero coupon bond was issued on 1 January 1990. It is redeemable on 1 January 2000 for £1000. The bond was sold for £463.20 in 1990.

Required:
   (a) What was the market rate of interest on such securities in 1990?
   (b) It is now 1 January 1996, and the market rate of interest on such securities is 12%. What will be the value of the bond?

3   A 12% debenture has three years of its life remaining. The market rate of interest on such securities is now 15%. What will be the value of the bond in the market?

4   A company issued an 8% debenture ten years ago. It is due to be redeemed at par in four years' time. The debenture has a current market price of £100 cum interest. What is the cost of debt capital to the company (ignore tax)?

5   In the above question (4) assume the interest is to be paid semi-annually. What is the annual cost of debt capital to the company?

6   A company has a £100 million bank loan repayable in five years' time. The interest rate payable on the loan is 12% per annum. The company pays corporation tax at 30%. What is the after-tax cost of the bank loan to the company?

7   A company has issued a 15% bond redeemable at par in four years' time. The bond currently sells in the market for £120 ex interest. The corporation tax rate is 30%. What is the after-tax cost of this bond to the company?

8   Suppose that British Telecom sold an issue of bonds with a 10-year maturity, at £100 par value, a 12% coupon rate and annual interest payments.

   (a) What would the market price of bonds be if the going rate of interest on bonds such as these fell to 8% two years after they were issued?

(b) What would the market price of bonds be if the going rate had risen to 14% two years after the initial offering?

9 The Nevel Co Ltd, which is still effectively controlled by the Nevel family although they now own only a minority of shares, is to undertake a substantial new project which requires external finance of about £4 million, a 40% increase in gross assets. The project is to develop and market a new product and is fairly risky. About 70% of the funds required will be spent on land and buildings. The resale value of the land and buildings is expected to remain about, or above, the initial purchase price. Expenditure during the development period of four to seven years will be financed from Nevel's other revenues with a consequent strain on the firm's overall liquidity. If, after the development stage, the project proves unsuccessful, then the project will be terminated and its assets sold. If, as is hoped, the development is successful, the project's assets will be utilized in production and Nevel's profits will rise considerably. However, if the project proves to be extremely successful, then additional finance may be required to expand production facilities further. At present Nevel is all-equity financed. The financial manager is uncertain whether he should seek funds from a financial institution in the form of an equity interest, a loan (long- or short-term) or convertible debentures.

Describe the major factors to be considered by Nevel in deciding on the method of financing the proposed expansion project. Briefly discuss the suitability of equity, loans and convertible debentures for the purposes of financing the project from the viewpoint of (a) Nevel and (b) the provider of finance. Clearly state and justify the type of finance recommended for Nevel.

10 (i) A bond with 4 years of its life remaining is paying a coupon rate of 10%. It is redeemable at par £100 at the end of the fourth year. Plot the value of the bond against interest rates if the market rate of interest is (a) 8%, (b) 11%, (c) 14% and (d) 17%.

(ii) Another bond has 10 years of its life remaining; it is also paying a coupon rate of 10%. It will be redeemable at par £100 at the end of the tenth year. Plot the value of this bond if the market rates of interest are (a) 8%, (b) 11%, (c) 14% and (d) 17%.

(iii) Which bond is more volatile and why?

11 Zero coupon bonds in a government bond market are selling at the following prices. They will be redeemed for £100. Assume that the expectations theory is valid.

Bond	Years to maturity	Price (£)
A	1	94.34
B	2	87.34
C	3	79.38
D	4	73.50

(a) Calculate the one-year, two-year, three-year and four-year yields to maturity.
(b) Calculate the spot rates for one, two and three years hence.
(c) What are the prices of Bond C and Bond D expected to be two years from now?
(d) What annual rate of return can you expect if you buy Bond D now and sell it after three years?

12 Your firm has several different issues of long-term debt as well as a portfolio of short- and medium-term loans at a variety of interest rates, including some variable rates. One issue of debt, the £3 million 9.5% debenture 1993–8 could be redeemed now or at any time up to 1998. The financial director is concerned about the choice of timing for the redemption of this debenture.

(a) Briefly discuss the main advantages and disadvantages of including **fixed-interest** debt finance in the firm's financial structure.

(b) Outline, and describe the impact of, the main factors to be considered when deciding on the timing of debenture redemption. Consider both the case where the redemption must be financed from the issue of further funds and the case where no further funds need be issued.

(c) Discuss the extent to which it is rational for a firm to obtain, at any one time, debt finance from a variety of sources with various durations and at different interest rates rather than utilizing only the source which offers the lowest effective interest charge.

13 Your client is considering the investment of a substantial sum in one of three interest yielding securities. Some details relating to each unit of the three securities are as follows.

	Security		
	A	B	C
	£	£	£
Annual interest:			(Note 2)
years 1–3	30	0	5
Redemption value:			
year 3	(Note 1)	100	100
Expected annual yield over three years	13%	12%	

Note 1: Security A has a life of ten years and will be redeemed for £100. If your client chooses this security then it would be sold immediately after the year-3 interest payment is received at a price sufficient to provide a yield to the purchaser of 14% per annum over its remaining 7 years of life.

Note 2: The interest and redemption values given for security C are quoted in today's money values whereas the actual payments will be directly linked to the level of the retail prices index. This index stands at 100 and expected future levels are as follows:

	Level	Movement in year
End of year 1	110	+10.0%
2	118	+ 7.3%
3	123	+ 4.2%

Each unit of Security C is currently priced at £99.00.

It is thought that interest rates for short-term investment will be as follows: for a two-year investment made at end of year 1, gross annual yield 10%; for a one-year investment made at end of year 2, gross annual yield 9%. Both these yields refer to investments which pay all accumulated interest and repay principal only at time 3.

(a) Calculate the current market prices of securities A and B. Determine the equivalent annual yield on security C expressed in money, rather than real, terms. Advise your client in which of the three securities he should invest if the objective is to maximize wealth at time 3. Ignore taxation.

(b) Indicate the main factors to which you would draw your client's attention if the decision were being carried out as a practical exercise.

ACCA, Financial Management

14 A company is considering issuing a convertible debenture on the terms shown below.

10% £100 convertible debentures 2010, issued and redeemable at par. The debentures are convertible into 60 ordinary shares at any date between

1 January 2002 and 31 December 2004. The debentures are callable for conversion by the company subject to the company's ordinary share price exceeding 200 pence between 1 January 2002 and 31 December 2004, and puttable for redemption by the debenture holders if the share price falls below 100 pence between the same dates.

It is now January 1997, and the market price of the ordinary shares of the company are 96 pence.

(a) Discuss the advantages and disadvantages of convertible debentures.
(b) Explain how the put and call options would work in this case. Why would the company introduce such terms?

ACCA, Dec. 1996

10 RISK AND RETURN

LEARNING OUTCOMES

By the end of this chapter the reader should:

- understand the nature of risk and return in a capital market framework
- be able to calculate expected return and variance of individual securities and portfolios
- be able to explain how better risk–return trade-offs can be obtained by combining assets together
- understand the significance of covariance and correlation in risk reduction
- understand and be able to explain the nature of risk as portfolios become larger

10.1 INTRODUCTION

The reason that risk exists is that project decision-making is based on expectations about the future. The decision maker makes forecasts of cash flows likely to arise from a particular course of action. These forecasts are based on what the decision maker expects to happen given their present state of knowledge. However, in an uncertain world the actual cash flows are almost certain to differ from prior expectations. It is this uncertainty about an investment's actual income that gives rise to risk in business and investment activity generally.

Everyone would agree that where an investor takes on extra risk then this should be acknowledged and rewarded with extra return; however, before this can be done, risk needs to be defined and measured and agreement reached on what extra return should be given per unit of risk.

We begin by posing the question: who is it that ultimately bears the risk of projects undertaken by companies? The answer to this is surely, the investors in companies. In the case of a company financed entirely by equity, risk will ultimately be borne by the providers of this equity, the ordinary shareholders in the company. This can be simply illustrated by Figure 10.1 where investment funds flow from ordinary shareholders to the company; these funds are then invested in real projects by the managers of the company; these projects in turn earn cash returns which will enable the payment of dividends to shareholders and to the extent that funds are retained will lead to an increase in the underlying value of the shares.

This idea can perhaps be more readily appreciated in the context of a company undertaking a single project. In this case the company is merely a convenient device for collecting funds from a number of shareholders to invest in the project. The investors' fortunes are directly related to how well the project performs. For example, we could consider investors who have invested in Eurotunnel, the company formed to build and operate the Channel Tunnel. The

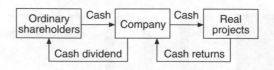

Figure 10.1
Flow of investment funds

company's share-price performance is directly linked to the cost of maintaining the tunnel and net revenues anticipated from traffic using the tunnel.

If we are to try and relate project risk to the risk investors perceive when investing in the equity of companies, we need to establish how such investors measure both the return and risk from an investment in equity shares. We do this in the next section.

10.2 MEASUREMENT OF INVESTOR RETURN AND RISK

Research in both the UK and the USA shows that investors in financial securities demand higher returns from risky investments in equities than from comparatively risk-free government securities [1]. This is not surprising and is what we would expect from risk-averse investors. In both countries the average extra return demanded for investing in equities has been between 8% and 9%. This average risk premium over the risk-free rate of interest might be an appropriate premium to demand for an investment having the same average risk as the equity market generally. Historically, then, investors on average have earned a substantial premium for investing in equities rather than government securities. However, this additional return has been accompanied by a higher volatility in earnings, as the average earnings calculation hides the fact that in some years there have been very high positive returns while in others there have also been high negative returns earned by holders of equity investments. Figure 10.2 shows the UK *ex-post* (historic) risk premium over 1919–92. This illustrates the point just made that the long-run historic average incorporates both high positive and negative returns. Although it was suggested above that the historic risk premium might be used as a guide to current investor requirements, there are at least two problems associated with this. The first is to assume that returns realized are the same as those expected, and the second is to assume that long-run averages give an indication of what is currently required by investors in the market. Both these factors could bias required returns when historic risk

Figure 10.2
The ex-post equity risk premium 1919–92. Equity returns minus long-dated gilt returns
Source: Jenkinson, T. (1993) The cost of equity finance: conventional wisdom reconsidered, *Stock Exchange Quarterly with Quality of Markets Review*, Autumn.

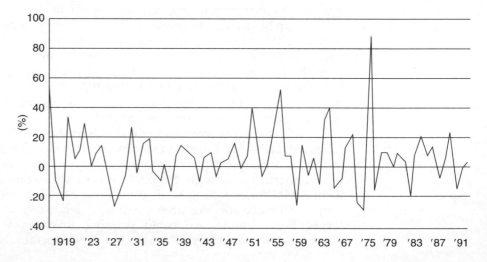

Risk and return

premiums are used to calculate current requirements. We will return to this difficulty in Chapter 12 when we discuss in detail the use of asset pricing models in practical capital budgeting situations.

Measurement of single-period return

It is usual to measure the periodic return from an investor's point of view by taking into consideration both dividends received from the share and any change in value over the period concerned. Thus return in period t_1 can be written as

$$R_1 = \frac{D_1 + V_1 - V_0}{V_0}$$

where R_1 is the return in period t_1, D_1 is the dividend(s) received in the period, V_1 is the value of the share at end of period and V_0 is the value of the share at start of period. This could also be written as

$$R_1 = \frac{D_1}{V_0} + \frac{V_1 - V_0}{V_0}$$

return = dividend yield + capital gain in percentage terms

This return could be an expected (*ex ante*) return based on a subjective probability distribution drawn up by a financial analyst, or it could be measured historically (*ex post*) to assess the performance of the security concerned.

For example, suppose that a dividend of 10p per share was paid during period t_1 on a share whose value was 100p at the start of the period and 150p at the end:

$$R_1 = \frac{10 + 150 - 100}{100} = 0.60\,(60\%)$$

or we could say

$$R_1 = \frac{10}{100} + \frac{150 - 100}{100}$$
$$= 0.10 + 0.50$$
$$= 0.60\,(60\%)$$

i.e. the total return is made up of 10% dividend yield and 50% capital gain.

Because the capital gain/loss element will often be a significant factor in determining the total return on an equity share there is scope for both high positive and high negative returns, given the volatility of stock markets. Thus the crash of 1987 led to average capital losses of 30%, and in some cases losses were very much greater than this figure

Therefore return is expressed in terms of total return bringing in both dividends and capital gains and losses. In the numerical examples above we have calculated return on the basis that dividend income and both beginning- and end-of-period prices are known. This is how historic returns from the ownership of shares are calculated. Calculating estimated returns is a lot more difficult because we shall need to estimate both the dividend expected to be paid during the forthcoming period and also the end-of-period price. In practice, there are a number of different outcomes possible depending upon factors affecting both the individual security and markets generally. Thus the analyst will need to forecast both the range of dividend payments and range of share prices possible during the ensuing period and assign to each value a probability of its occurring.

The risk related to holding an equity share is usually expressed as a measure of the dispersion of expected returns. In the context of expected returns described above, it would be in the form of the variance of expected returns or the square root of the variance, i.e. the standard deviation.

Calculation of expected returns and standard deviation

As described above, if we are trying to estimate the expected returns from holding a security we are likely to consider the possible returns in alternate market conditions and try and assign a probability to each. For example, suppose that we own a share with a current market value of 100p and estimate future possible values and dividends as shown in Table 10.1. We can see that the total return will be 24% if the optimistic version of the market prevails, 12% if normal conditions prevail and 0% if the pessimistic outcome prevails. Before we can make real use of this information we need to estimate the likelihood of each of the different conditions occurring. We do this by using subjective probabilities, i.e. probabilities that are assigned to each possibility by the analyst. They are subjective because they depend upon the decision maker's opinion rather than being based on a large number of observed similar outcomes which might be the case with objective probabilities. We shall see that in practice historic returns are often used to measure variability of share price returns. Measures of variability and other data relating to risk and return are readily available in various forms on a commercial basis (e.g. Datastream and the London Business School Risk Measurement Service referred to in Chapter 12).

Let us suppose that the decision maker assigns probabilities as shown in Table 10.2 to the possible returns. This is a simplified version of the probable outcomes and does not allow, for example, for outcomes other than the three stated and lying between the values given. The probabilities sum to unity and, for illustrative purposes, represent the only outcomes considered possible.

The expected return $\overline{R}$ is calculated by multiplying each outcome R_i by the probability P_i that it occurs and summing:

$$\text{expected return} = \overline{R} = \sum_{i=1}^{n} P_i R_i$$

In this case

$$\overline{R} = 0.25 \times 0.24 + 0.50 \times 0.12 + 0.25 \times 0$$
$$= 0.12 \ (12\%)$$

Table 10.1

Possible market conditions	Conditional end-of-period selling price (p)	Conditional end-of-period dividends receivable (p)	Total end-of-period returns (p)
Optimistic	115	9	124
Normal	107	5	112
Pessimistic	97	3	100

Table 10.2

Market conditions	Probability	Return on investment (%)
Optimistic	0.25	24
Normal	0.50	12
Pessimistic	0.25	0

The expected return (mean) can be regarded as the average outcome or return; in addition we need a measure of how much the individual outcomes differ from the average, i.e. a measure of dispersion. This is usually measured by the variance, or the square root of the variance, i.e. the standard deviation:

$$\text{variance} = \sigma^2 = \sum_{i=1}^{n} P_i(R_i - \overline{R})^2$$

In this case

$$\sigma^2 = 0.25(24 - 12)^2 + 0.50(12 - 12)^2 + 0.25(0 - 12)^2$$
$$= 36 + 0 + 36$$
$$= 72$$

$$\text{standard deviation } \sigma = (\sigma^2)^{1/2}$$

In this case

$$\sigma = \sqrt{72} = 8.49$$

The numerical example used has symmetrical returns, i.e. they are evenly distributed around the most likely outcome. This is termed a 'normal distribution' and is illustrated in Figure 10.3. Normal distributions can be described in terms of their expected return and variance (or standard deviation) alone.

If we assume that investors appraise securities on the basis of expected return and standard deviation of returns, and if we further assume that these investors are risk-averse, then they will prefer high expected returns and low standard deviations. This point is emphasized in Figure 10.4 where two investments are shown which both have the same expected return of 10% but where investment B has a greater dispersion of possible returns. This makes investment B riskier than investment A and this greater dispersion or spread is reflected in the standard deviation of B which is 30% compared with that of A which is 15%. Given that the expected return of both the securities is the same, most investors would opt for A over B.

It should be clear from the foregoing discussion that, other things being equal, investors will prefer an investment giving the highest expected return for a given level of risk or one that has the lowest risk for a given level of expected return. However, these only relate to specific instances where pairs of investments either have the same expected return or the same standard deviation. Where investments have increasing levels of return accompanied by increasing levels of standard deviation then the choice between investments will be a subjective decision based on the investor's attitude to risk.

10.3 RETURN AND RISK OF COMBINING INVESTMENTS

In considering risk/return characteristics of individual investments choice was based on expected return and standard deviation. When combining investments

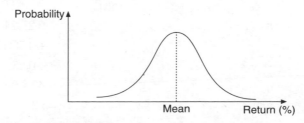

Figure 10.3
A normal distribution

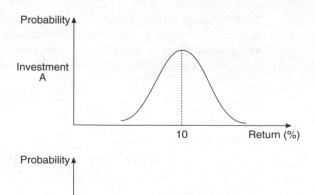

Figure 10.4
The investments have the same expected return but B is riskier

we shall once again be considering the expected return of the combination (or portfolio as it is usually called) and its standard deviation. Table 10.3 gives information about three investments: A, B and C. A might be considered more attractive than C as it has the same expected return as C but a lower standard deviation. However, if we compare the projected returns in alternative possible conditions we can see that A and B have their highest and lowest returns in the same conditions, while C gives high returns when A and B are giving low returns, and low returns when A and B are giving high returns. The important point being made here is that when combining investments together it is not sufficient to look at the standard deviations of the individual investments. We also need to look at how the returns of pairs of securities vary with one another. The expected return on a portfolio of two securities is the value-weighted average of their expected returns. In the general case, if a proportion X was invested in security A and the balance of wealth $1 - X$ in security B, the expected portfolio return would be

$$\overline{R}_p = X\overline{R}_A + (1-X)\overline{R}_B$$

If 0.5 (50%) of wealth was invested in A and $1 - 0.5$ (50%) in B, then

$$\overline{R}_p = 0.5 \times 12 + 0.5 \times 14$$
$$= 13\%$$

However, when we calculate portfolio variance we need to consider not only the individual variances of the investments but also the way in which their returns vary as measured by the covariance. The covariance term for investments A and B is given by

$$\mathrm{cov}(R_A, R_B) = \sum P_R (R_A - \overline{R}_A)(R_B - \overline{R}_B)$$
$$= 0.25(24 - 12)(28 - 14)$$
$$+ 0.50(12 - 12)(12 - 14)$$
$$+ 0.25(0 - 12)(4 - 14)$$
$$= 42 + 0 + 30$$
$$= 72$$

Table 10.3

Market condition	Probability	Return on investments (%) A	B	C
Optimistic	0.25	24	28	4
Normal	0.50	12	12	8
Pessimistic	0.25	0	4	28
Expected return $\bar{R}$		12	14	12
Variance V		72	76	88
Standard deviation σ		8.49	8.72	9.38

The covariance can also be written as

$$\text{cov}(R_A, R_B) = \rho_{AB}\sigma_A\sigma_B$$

It follows that

$$\rho_{AB} = \frac{\text{cov}(R_A, R_B)}{\sigma_A\sigma_B}$$

The term ρ_{AB} is called the 'correlation coefficient' and measures the extent to which the returns of pairs of securities vary with one another. It can take on values between +1 and −1; a correlation coefficient of +1 indicates that the investments move up and down together in perfect positive correlation, while a value of −1 would indicate counter-movement of equal and opposite proportions, i.e. perfect negative correlation.

In this case the correlation coefficient would be

$$\rho_{AB} = \frac{\text{cov}(R_A, R_B)}{\sigma_A\sigma_B}$$
$$= \frac{72}{8.49 \times 8.72}$$
$$= 0.97$$

Investments A and B therefore have high positive correlation and the scope for risk reduction is limited. Remembering that we have X invested in A and $1 - X$ invested in B, the variance of this two-security portfolio is given by

$$V_P = X^2 V_A + (1-X)^2 V_B + 2X(1-X)\text{cov}(R_A, R_B)$$

or, using the standard deviation symbols

$$\sigma_P^2 = X^2\sigma_A^2 + (1-X)^2\sigma_B^2 + 2X(1-X)\text{cov}(R_A, R_B)$$

and substituting $\text{cov}(R_A, R_B) = \rho_{AB}\sigma_A\sigma_B$, we obtain

$$\sigma_P^2 = X^2\sigma_A^2 + (1-X)^2\sigma_B^2 + 2X(1-X)\rho_{AB}\sigma_A\sigma_B$$

The first two terms in the equation are the individual variances weighted by the square of the proportion invested in each. The third term is more interesting as it considers the way in which the returns of each pair of securities vary with one another. The term is always twice the product of the proportions invested in each as it considers the covariance of A with B and of B with A. These are always the same, of course.

If we now calculate the variance of our portfolio of A and B we obtain

$$\sigma_P^2 = (0.5)^2 \times (8.49)^2 + (0.5)^2 \times (8.72)^2 + (2 \times 0.5 \times 0.5 \times 72)$$
$$= 73\%$$
$$\sigma_P = \sqrt{73} = 8.54\%$$

The standard deviation of the portfolio, 8.54, is very close to the weighted average of the standard deviations of A and B; this is because the returns are closely related, as evidenced by the correlation coefficient of 0.97. Let us now examine what happens when we hold B and C in equal amounts. First of all the expected return is as before:

$$\overline{R}_P = X\overline{R}_B + (1 - X)\overline{R}_C$$
$$= 0.5 \times 14 + 0.5 \times 12$$
$$= 13\%$$

However, we shall find that the covariance and hence the correlation coefficient are both much lower:

$$\text{cov}(R_B, R_C) = 0.25(28 - 14)(4 - 12)$$
$$+ 0.50(12 - 14)(8 - 12)$$
$$+ 0.25(4 - 14)(28 - 12)$$
$$= -28 + 4 - 40$$
$$= -64\%$$

(covariances can be negative as well as positive). We can also calculate the correlation coefficient between B and C:

$$\rho_{BC} = \frac{-64}{8.27 \times 9.38}$$
$$= -0.82$$

B and C have a high negative correlation and the resulting variance of the portfolio reflects this:

$$\sigma_P^2 = (0.5)^2 \times (8.72)^2 + (0.5)^2$$
$$\times (9.38)^2 + (2 \times 0.5 \times 0.5 \times -64)$$
$$= 9\%$$
$$\sigma_P = 3\%$$

When we combine investments B and C together in equal amounts the standard deviation of the portfolio is only 3%; thus while the expected returns of portfolios of A and B and B and C are the same (13%) the risk of a portfolio of B and C is only about one-third of the risk of a portfolio of A and B. This is due to the high negative correlation between the returns of B and C, whereas the returns of A and B have high positive correlation.

In our example we considered only two security portfolios, but the principles remain the same when larger portfolios are considered. As portfolios increase in size so the opportunity for risk reduction also increases. The formulae for N investment portfolios are as follows:

$$\overline{R}_P = \sum_{i=1}^{N} X_i \overline{R}_i$$

$$\sigma_P^2 = \sum_{i=1}^{N} X_i^2 \sigma_i^2 + \sum_{i=1, j \neq i}^{N} \sum_{j=1}^{N} X_i X_j \text{cov}(R_i, R_j)$$

where X_i is the proportion of wealth invested in investment i.

The first term in the variance formula is the sum of the individual investment variances multiplied by the square of the amount invested in each. The second term is the covariance term. Each covariance term is multiplied by twice the product invested in each investment. Although a 2 does not appear in the equation the double summation brings in the covariance between securities 1 and 2 and 2 and 1 which, of course, are the same. For example, with a three-security portfolio the double-summation term would be

$$\sum_{\substack{i=1 \\ j\neq i}}^{3} \sum_{j=1}^{3} X_i X_j \, \mathrm{cov}(R_i, R_j)$$

$$= X_1 X_2 \, \mathrm{cov}(R_1 R_2) + X_1 X_3 \, \mathrm{cov}(R_1, R_3) + X_2 X_3 \, \mathrm{cov}(R_2, R_3)$$
$$+ X_2 X_1 \, \mathrm{cov}(R_2, R_1) + X_3 X_1 \, \mathrm{cov}(R_3, R_1) + X_3 X_2 \, \mathrm{cov}(R_3, R_2)$$

As $\mathrm{cov}(R_1, R_2)$ is the same as $\mathrm{cov}(R_2, R_1)$ and so on,

$$\sum_{\substack{i=1 \\ j\neq i}}^{3} \sum_{j=1}^{3} X_i X_j \, \mathrm{cov}(R_i, R_j)$$

$$= 2X_1 X_2 \, \mathrm{cov}(R_1 R_2) + 2X_1 X_3 \, \mathrm{cov}(R_1, R_3) + 2X_2 X_3 \, \mathrm{cov}(R_2, R_3)$$

Implications of very large portfolios

Let us consider a case where equal amounts are invested in a large portfolio. Then

$$\sigma_P^2 = \sum_{i=1}^{N} \left(\frac{1}{N}\right)^2 \sigma_i^2 + \sum_{i=1}^{N} \sum_{\substack{j=1 \\ j\neq i}}^{N} \frac{1}{N}\frac{1}{N} \, \mathrm{cov}(R_i, R_j)$$

First of all suppose that investments are independent and therefore all the covariance terms are zero. In this case the value of the second term in the above equation is zero and

$$\sigma_P^2 = \sum_{i=1}^{N} \left(\frac{1}{N}\right)^2 \sigma_i^2 = \frac{1}{N}\bar{\sigma}_j^2,$$

where $\bar{\sigma}_i^2$ is the average variance of the investments. As N becomes larger the variance of the portfolio becomes smaller and with a very large portfolio approaches zero.

Therefore with a very large portfolio of independent investments we could have zero variance. However, we find that in most markets investments have some positive correlation and the covariance term is positive. If we now reconsider the variance calculation including the second term we begin with

$$\sigma_P^2 = \sum_{i=1}^{N} \left(\frac{1}{N}\right)^2 \sigma_i^2 + \sum_{i=1}^{N} \sum_{\substack{j=1 \\ j\neq i}}^{N} \frac{1}{N}\frac{1}{N} \, \mathrm{cov}(R_i, R_j)$$

$$= \frac{1}{N}\bar{\sigma}_i^2 + \frac{N-1}{N} \sum_{i=1}^{N} \sum_{\substack{j=1 \\ j\neq i}}^{N} \frac{\mathrm{cov}(R_i, R_j)}{N(N-1)}$$

We have previously seen that the first term is the average variance; the final term is also an average. There are N values of i and $N - 1$ values of j; remember that there is one less value of j since it cannot equal i. The final term is therefore the sum of the covariances divided by the number of covariances; it is the average covariance. Rewriting, we have

$$\sigma_P^2 = \frac{1}{N}\bar{\sigma}_j^2 + \frac{N-1}{N} \overline{\mathrm{cov}}(R_i, R_j)$$

We have previously stated that as N becomes very large the first term tends towards zero while the second term will approach the average covariance. We can see that in a large portfolio the individual risk of investments can be diversified away, but the risk contributed by the covariance terms will remain.

As we have seen, the covariance term reflects the way in which investment returns move together. Most securities will tend to move in the same direction to a greater or lesser degree because of common macroeconomic factors affecting all securities; however, the individual risk of securities can be diversified away by holding a sufficiently large portfolio.

Figure 10.5 illustrates the risk reduction from holding a portfolio of UK securities. The vertical axis measures the risk of the portfolio as a percentage of the risk of an individual security, while the horizontal axis shows the number of securities in the portfolio. We can see that risk can be substantially reduced by holding a comparatively small portfolio of between 10 and 15 securities. However, the diagram shows that the marginal benefit decreases as more securities are added and that there seems to be a limit to the benefits of diversification. This is because, although unique risk relating to individual securities can be diversified away, the risk relating to the common association between securities, which is often called 'market or systematic risk', remains.

10.4 SUMMARY AND CONCLUSIONS

Investors require extra return for taking on higher levels of perceived risk. In the case of equity investors risk will be related to the business activities being undertaken by the company. Research supports this view as average returns on risky (equity) investments have exceeded returns on risk-free (government) securities by between 8% and 9%.

Investors measure their expected return on the basis of both expected dividend and capital gain/loss. Dividends tend to be more predictable than changes in share prices, and therefore the risk of equity investment is related to the volatility of share prices. This volatility is expressed as a measure of variance or standard deviation of returns. It can be calculated on the basis of a distribution of *ex-ante* expected returns or, as is more usual, from historic returns.

Investors will therefore select investments on the basis of expected return and

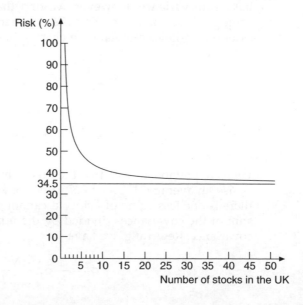

Figure 10.5
Portfolio risk
reduction

Risk and return

standard deviation of returns. Where one investment dominates by either having a higher return for a given risk (standard deviation) than any other or a lower risk for a given level of return choice will be easy. However, where securities have increasing levels of risk as return increases the choice is not so obvious.

When securities are held in combination, while expected return is simply the weighted average of the expected returns of the two or more securities involved, the standard deviation depends crucially on the covariance or correlation between each pair of securities. By holding securities together it is possible to reduce risk, and this reduction is greater the lower the correlation between securities. When very large portfolios are held it is found that risk unique to individual securities can be eliminated and that the only risk that remains is the covariance risk relating to securities' common association with each other. The ideas that have been introduced in this chapter are very important for an understanding of the capital-asset pricing model which we examine in the next chapter.

10.5 REFERENCES

1 Dimson, E. and Brealey, R.A. (1978) The risk premium on UK equities, *Investment Analyst*, **52**: 14–18, December.
Allen, D., Day, R., Hirst, I. and Kwiatkowski, J. (1986) Equity, gilts, treasury bills and inflation, *Investment Analyst*, **83**: 11–18, October.
Ibbotson, R.G. and Sinquefield, R.A. (1992) *Stocks, Bonds, Bills and Inflation*, Ibbotson Associates, Chicago. (Updated annually.)

10.6 FURTHER READING

Brealey, R. (1983) *An Introduction to Risk and Return*, 2nd edn, Blackwell, Oxford.
Elton, E.J. and Gruber, M.J. (1991) *Modern Portfolio Theory and Investment Analysis*, 4th edn, Wiley, New York (an introduction to risk and return is given in the early chapters).

10.7 PROBLEMS

1 A share had a price of 250p at the start of the year, paid a dividend of 12p during the year and had a price of 235p at the end of the year. What is the percentage return on the share for the year?

2 Probus shares currently sell for 520p per share. You intend to buy the shares today and hold for two years. During those two years, you expect to receive dividends at the year-ends that total 55p per share. Finally, you expect to sell the Probus shares for 548p per share. What is your expected holding-period return on Probus shares?

3 The probability that the economy will experience moderate growth next year is 0.4. The probability of a recession is 0.3, and the probability of a rapid expansion is also 0.3. If the economy falls into a recession, you can expect to receive a return on your portfolio of 2%. With moderate growth your return will be 5%. If there is a rapid expansion, your portfolio will return 10%.
(a) What is your expected return?
(b) What is the standard deviation of that return?

4 Suppose the expected returns and variances of shares A and B are

$$\bar{R}_A = 0.2, \bar{R}_B = 0.3, \sigma_A^2 = 0.1, \text{ and } \sigma_B^2 = 0.2, \text{ respectively.}$$

(a) Calculate the expected return and variance of a portfolio that is composed of 60% A and 40% B when the correlation coefficient between the stocks is -0.5.

(b) Calculate the expected return and variance of a portfolio that is composed of 60% A and 40% B when the correlation coefficient between the shares is -0.6.

(c) How does the correlation coefficient affect the variance of the portfolio?

5 Shown below are the possible rates of return that you might obtain over the next year from investing in shares V and Z.

State of economy	Probability of state occurring	Share V return if state occurs	Share Z return if state occurs
Recession	0.3	-10%	10%
Normal	0.4	20%	10%
Boom	0.3	50%	10%

(a) Determine the expected return, variance and standard deviation for share V.

(b) Determine the expected return, variance and standard deviation for share Z.

(c) Determine the covariance and correlation between the returns of share V and share Z.

(d) Determine the expected return and standard deviation of an equally weighted portfolio of share V and share Z.

6 If a portfolio has a positive weight for each asset, can the expected return on the portfolio be greater than the return on the asset in the portfolio that has the highest return? Can the expected return on the portfolio be less than the return on the asset in the portfolio with the lowest return? Explain.

7 You are faced with a choice of shares from among the three detailed below:

Market condition	Probability	Return Share A	Share B	Share C
Optimistic	0.25	16	4	20
Normal	0.50	12	6	14
Pessimistic	0.25	8	8	8

(a) Calculate the expected return and standard deviation for each share.

(b) Calculate the correlation coefficient and covariance between each pair of investments.

(c) Calculate the expected return and standard deviation of the two- and three-share portfolios formed by combining together equal proportions of the shares (i.e. two-security portfolios, half and half; three-security portfolio, one-third, one-third and one-third).

8 Is the variance of a well-diversified portfolio determined by the variance of the individual securities? Explain and discuss.

9 Standard deviation as a measure of risk pays as much attention to upside risk as to downside risk. As investors are more concerned with downside risk and the likelihood of losing their money it follows that standard deviation is not a satisfactory measure of risk. Explain and discuss.

10 The following information relates to the actual price at the end of each month and dividends paid during month of two securities over the past seven months.

Month	Security D Price (p)	Security D Dividend (p)	Security E Price (p)	Security E Dividend (p)
1	123		57	
2	119	1	62	
3	121		70	1
4	123		72	
5	125		81	
6	126	3	86	
7	126		92	

(a) Calculate the rate of return for both securities for each month.

(b) Calculate the average rate of return for both securities and the standard deviation of returns.

(c) Calculate the correlation coefficient between the two securities.

(d) Calculate the average return and standard deviation of an equally weighted portfolio of D and E.

11 You have £10 000 to invest in either or both of two securities Wye and Zee with expected returns and standard deviations as follows:

	$\bar{R}$	σ
Wye	10%	20%
Zee	12%	25%

The correlation ρ between the returns of the two securities is 0.5.

(a) Calculate the expected return and standard deviation of the following portfolios:

Wye	Zee
100%	–
–	100%
50%	50%
25%	75%
75%	25%

(b) Use the values calculated in (a) to plot the set of portfolios and identify the efficient set.

11 RISK AND THE CAPITAL-ASSET PRICING MODEL

LEARNING OUTCOMES

By the end of this chapter the reader should:

- be able to distinguish between non-market and market risk
- explain the nature of beta and how it measures risk
- know how to compute beta from basic data
- be able to discuss beta in a portfolio context

11.1 INTRODUCTION

In Chapter 10 we saw that the risk–return characteristics of financial securities could be expressed in terms of a security's expected return and the variance or standard deviation thereof. Investors would prefer those securities offering higher return and lower standard deviation when faced with a choice between single investments. It was also observed that when securities were held together, while the expected return of the resulting combination was merely the value-weighted average of the expected returns of each individual security, the risk of the combination as measured by the standard deviation could be less than a simple weighted average if the expected returns on the securities were less than perfectly correlated. In this chapter we continue to develop these ideas with a view to determining how rational risk-averse investors would manage their affairs given these opportunities to reduce the risk of their overall investment holding.

11.2 THE CAPITAL-ASSET PRICING MODEL

In Chapter 10 we discussed how the total risk of a security could be divided between market and non-market risk. Figure 11.1 stresses this point that as increasing numbers of securities are added to a portfolio the non-market or unsystematic risk decreases while the level of systematic or market risk remains unchanged. The unsystematic risk relates to risk unique to the security (the term 'specific risk' is also sometimes used). This risk will relate to unexpected pieces of good and bad news relating specifically to the company or the industry in which it is engaged. If a portfolio is held, unexpected pieces of bad news pertaining to some companies are cancelled out by unexpected pieces of good news relating to others. However, no matter how many securities are held in the portfolio, market risk remains. This risk reflects market-wide economic factors affecting all securities to some extent. Some securities will be more sensitive to market factors than others and will therefore have a high market or systematic risk, while others will not be so dependent upon mainstream economic activity and will have a lower systematic risk. Examples of market factors would include news on changes in rates of interest, inflation and other macroeconomic factors including expectation of a change in government!

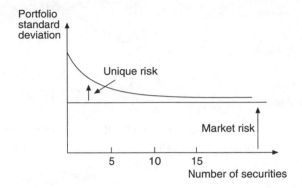

Figure 11.1
Unique risk
eliminated but market
risk remains

Rational investors will seek to improve their risk–return trade-off by holding a diversified portfolio of securities; as securities are added to the portfolio so unique risk will be reduced and will be eliminated completely when the market portfolio of all risky securities is held. However, although unique risk can be diversified away, market risk remains. In this situation individual risky assets will be priced by reference to their relationship to the market generally, i.e. on the basis of their market risk alone, since any unsystematic risk will have been diversified away by incorporating them in the market portfolio. In this context a security's standard deviation, which reflects both unsystematic and systematic risk, is no longer the appropriate measure of risk. It is the covariance of the individual securities with the market which is now the appropriate measure of risk. This measure of risk is called 'beta' and is usually represented by the symbol β.

The CAPM was originally developed independently by Sharpe, Mossin and Lintner [1] and is often referred to as the Sharpe–Mossin–Lintner form of the CAPM. The CAPM equation or security market line (SML) is usually written as

$$\overline{R}_i = R_f + \beta_i(\overline{R}_m - R_f)$$

where $\overline{R}_i$ is the expected return on the ith risky asset, R_f is the rate of return on a risk-free asset, $\overline{R}_m$ is the expected return on the market portfolio and

$$\beta_i = \frac{\text{cov}(R_i, R_m)}{\sigma_m^2} = \frac{\rho_{im}\sigma_i\sigma_m}{\sigma_m^2} = \frac{\rho_{im}\sigma_i}{\sigma_m}$$

The SML is plotted in Figure 11.2. It should be noted that the measure of risk used is beta; by definition the beta of the market portfolio is equal to unity. In equilibrium all securities will be priced so that they plot along the SML. Remember that expected return in the CAPM context depends upon the market-risk beta, and that it is quite possible for securities with different levels of total risk to have the same measure of market risk and hence the same required return.

The SML equation can be rewritten using the expanded definition of beta given above:

$$\overline{R}_i = R_f + \beta_i(\overline{R}_m - R_f)$$
$$= R_f + (\overline{R}_m - R_f)\frac{\text{cov}(R_i, R_m)}{\sigma_m^2}$$

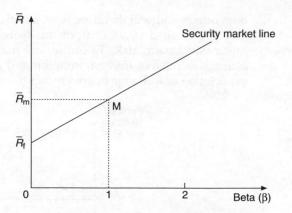

Figure 11.2
Security market line

Remember that $\text{cov}(R_i, R_m) = \rho_{im}\sigma_i\sigma_m$ where ρ_{im} is the correlation between the return on security i and the market. The equation then becomes

$$\bar{R}_i = R_f + (\bar{R}_m - R_f)\frac{\rho_{im}\sigma_i\sigma_m}{\sigma_m^2}$$

$$= R_f + (\bar{R}_m - R_f)\frac{\rho_{im}\sigma_i}{\sigma_m}$$

This can also be written as

$$\bar{R}_i = R_f + \frac{\bar{R}_m - R_f}{\sigma_m}\rho_{im}\sigma_i$$

In the SML the risk premium depends not only on the standard deviation of the security but also on its relationship with the market as reflected in the value of the correlation coefficient. This explains why it is possible for securities with high total risk measured by their standard deviation to have low market risk when measured by beta. We shall illustrate these points with a numerical example.

Suppose that we are given the following information about security i, the market and the risk-free rate of return: $\bar{R}_m = 20\%$, $R_f = 12\%$, $\sigma_m = 25\%$, $\sigma_i = 30\%$ and $\rho_{im} = +0.75$. First of all we calculate the beta of security i:

$$\beta_i = \frac{\rho_{im}\sigma_i}{\sigma_m}$$

$$= \frac{0.75 \times 0.30}{0.25}$$

$$= 0.90$$

We can then calculate the expected return of security i:

$$\bar{R}_i = R_f + \beta_i(\bar{R}_m - R_f)$$

$$= 0.12 + 0.90(0.20 - 0.12)$$

$$= 0.192(19.2\%)$$

Note that $\beta_i < 1$ and therefore its market risk is below average; because of this the expected return of i at 19.2% is lower than the expected market return. Although the total risk of i at 30% is greater than the market standard deviation, because correlation with the market is less than unity this compensates for the higher total risk.

The total risk of any security or portfolio can thus be broken down into two components as follows:

total risk = market risk + unique risk

For security i this would be expressed by the following equation:

$$\sigma_i^2 = \beta_i^2 \sigma_m^2 + \sigma_{DI}^2$$

The unique risk can be calculated by substituting the values for total risk, beta and market risk from above:

$$(0.30)^2 = (0.9)^2(0.25)^2 + \sigma_{DI}^2$$

$$\sigma_{DI} = 0.198(19.8\%)$$

It is this unique diversifiable risk that can be eliminated by holding security i in a sufficiently large portfolio, leaving only market risk which depends on i's relationship with the market.

11.3 IMPLICATIONS OF THE CAPITAL-ASSET PRICING MODEL

In order to calculate the variance of a portfolio it was necessary not only to know the standard deviation of each security in the portfolio but also the covariance or correlation of each pair of securities. However, when we use the CAPM the measure of risk used is beta which, if calculated directly for each individual security, greatly reduces the number of computations necessary. Also, the beta of a portfolio of securities is merely the value-weighted average of the betas of the individual securities in the portfolio:

$$\beta_p = \Sigma W_i \beta_i$$

In terms of risk of individual securities those with high betas, i.e. greater than unity, will be regarded as high-risk high-return securities. The expectation would be that the securities would show above-average gains in a rising market and greater-than-average falls in a declining market; such securities are sometimes referred to as 'aggressive securities'. However, securities with betas less than unity are referred to as 'defensive securities' as they can be expected to show smaller-than-average losses in a falling market but will generally experience lower-than-average gains in a rising market. Investors will thus be able to assess the risk of their portfolios and make any adjustments necessary to bring it to a desired level of risk.

When we began our discussion on risk and return in Chapter 10 the point was made that in assessing the risk of projects managers should be seeking to identify how investors assess the risk of investing in companies specializing in particular lines of business activity. It was initially suggested that risk might be measured in terms of standard deviation of expected returns. However, when we extended our analysis to the CAPM it was found that the measure of risk as far as shareholders was concerned changed from standard deviation to beta. The reason for this is that shareholders are regarded as rational and risk-averse and will therefore hold portfolios of securities so that unsystematic risk can be diversified away. The result of this will be that investors face only systematic risk; the required return on individual shares will therefore be based on systematic risk rather than total risk as measured by standard deviation. If we assume an all-equity company producing a single product, then the required return on projects will reflect the required return by investors in the equity of the company. It would therefore be appropriate for managers to use beta as a measure of the project risk in such a situation. Therefore, given the beta of the equity of such a company, all that would be required would be a measure of the risk-free rate of return and the expected market return to enable the manager to calculate a project rate of return. The application of the CAPM to capital budgeting is dealt with in the next chapter. We shall also discuss how betas are measured in practice and examine some of the problems associated with the use of the theoretical CAPM in a practical situation.

11.4 SUMMARY AND CONCLUSIONS

The CAPM divides risk between systematic/market risk and diversifiable/ unique risk. The latter can be diversified away in a portfolio but market risk, measured by beta, cannot. In equilibrium conditions return will be priced by reference to market risk alone which relates to an asset's sensitivity to the market generally. This relationship is summarized in the SML equation

$$\overline{R}_i = R_f + \beta_i(\overline{R}_m - R_f)$$

11.5 REFERENCES

1   Sharpe, W.F. (1964) Capital asset prices: a theory of market equilibrium under conditions of risk, *Journal of Finance*, **19**: 425–42, September.
    Mossin, J. (1966) Equilibrium in a capital asset market, *Econometrica*, **34**: 768–83, October.
    Lintner, J. (1965) The valuation of risk assets and the selection of risky investments in stock portfolios and capital budgets, *Review of Economics and Statistics*, **47**: 13–37, February.

11.6 FURTHER READING

The serious student is referred to the original articles listed above. There are many textbooks explaining both the original theories and some simplifications of them. Good coverage is contained in the following.

Elton, E.J. and Gruber, M.J. (1991) *Modern Portfolio Theory and Investment Analysis*, 4th edn, Wiley, New York.
Modigliani, F. and Pogue, C.A. (1974) An introduction to risk and return, *Financial Analysts Journal*, **30**: 68–80, March–April 1974; 69–88, May–June.
Wagner, W.H. and Lau, S.C. (1971) The effect of diversification on risk, *Financial Analysts Journal*, **27**, November–December.

11.7 PROBLEMS

1   Define 'systematic' and 'unsystematic' risk.
2   Which of the following statements is true and which is false?
    (a) The expected return on a share with a beta of 2 is twice that of the market portfolio.
    (b) A share plotting above the SML is overvalued.
    (c) A share held as a sole investment and having a beta of 2 is twice as risky as holding the market portfolio.
    (d) The total risk of a share determines its contribution to the risk of a well-diversified portfolio.
3   Comment on the following advice:
    (a) An investor holding a portfolio need only consider the systematic risk of securities.

(b) Only unsystematic risk is relevant to the investor holding just one security.

(c) A cautious investor should always consider total risk.

(d) No one should hold an asset that gives an expected return below the risk-free rate of return.

(e) Never buy an asset if its expected return is less than that on the market as a whole.

4 Two particular assets, A and B, are known to lie on the SML. A, which has a beta of 0.5, carries a risk premium of 4%. B has an expected return of 20% along with a beta of 1.75. In the light of this information, determine whether the securities below are overpriced or underpriced:

Security	Expected return	Beta
1	20	2.00
2	14	0.75
3	15	1.25
4	5	−0.25
5	31	3.25

5 As an investor in an equilibrium market containing many different assets, you currently have 50% of your wealth in a risk-free asset and 50% in the four assets below:

Asset	Expected return	β asset	Invested in asset
A	7.6%	0.2	10%
B	12.4%	0.8	10%
C	15.6%	1.2	10%
D	18.8%	1.6	20%

(a) Calculate the current β and expected return of your portfolio.

(b) Assume that you want an expected return of 12% and intend to obtain it by selling some of the risk-free asset and using the proceeds to buy the market portfolio. Calculate the set of weights in the revised portfolio.

(c) If you hold only the risk-free asset and the market portfolio, what set of weghts would give you an expected return of 12%?

(d) Explain the significance, if any, of the beta concept to investors in quoted securities.

12 COST OF CAPITAL

By the end of this chapter the reader should:

- be able to compute returns using the capital-asset pricing model (CAPM)
- explain the problems of using the CAPM to compute costs of finance
- be able to ungear equity betas
- be able to compute a weighted-average cost of capital (WACC)
- understand the problems of using a single WACC as company cost of capital
- appreciate the factors affecting the value of betas

12.1 INTRODUCTION

In the previous chapter we discussed how the capital-asset pricing model could be used to estimate asset returns. We could use the model to estimate the return on an ordinary share or a project by using respectively an equity share beta or a project beta. In a company carrying out business activities having a common risk and financed entirely by equity the share and project betas should be identical. If the all-equity company carried out many different activities then the equity beta should reflect this and be a value-weighted average of the betas of each activity. Of course, most companies are financed by a mix of equity and debt and in these circumstances the cost of equity capital will increase with the level of debt as financial risk increases. In these circumstances project rates of return will need to be computed using adjusted (ungeared) equity betas or a composite cost of capital obtained by combining together the cost of equity and debt into a weighted-average cost of capital.

The capital-asset pricing model (CAPM) approach which is developed in this chapter can be summarized as follows:

1   The return managers should require on projects should be related to that required by investors in the company.
2   Investors are assumed to hold diversified portfolios to reduce the risk of their total investment.
3   Rational investors will diversify away all non-market or specific risk.
4   The market will therefore price risk on the basis of systematic or market risk only.

5   The measure of risk used will be beta (b) which measures the covariance of returns with the market as a whole.

In this context the expected return on any asset i can be written as

$$\bar{R}_i = R_f + \beta_i(\bar{R}_m - R_f)$$

where $\bar{R}_i$ is the expected return on asset i, R_f is the risk-free rate of interest, β_i is the beta of asset i and R_m is the expected return on the market portfolio of risky assets.

12.2 PROJECT RISK AND RETURN

In the previous section it was stressed that the return on projects which managers should aim at should be related to a return required by investors in the company. If we first of all consider the case of a company financed entirely by equity or ordinary shares, then both the risk and return currently demanded will reflect the perceived risk of the current activities being undertaken by the company. If we further assume that the company is undertaking a single business activity then the beta of the equity share held by the investor should be identical with the beta of the project currently being undertaken by the company. In this context the company can merely be seen as a device for collecting investment funds from different investors and investing the total of such funds in a particular business activity.

Given the basic CAPM equation, then both the return required by an investor in the equity of the company and the return required from the business activity undertaken by the company can be represented by the now familiar basic CAPM equation:

$$\bar{R}_i = R_f + \beta_i(\bar{R}_m - R_f)$$

It is clear that for a financial manager in a company to make use of the theory to calculate a project cost of capital it is necessary to estimate R_f, β_i and $\bar{R}_m$. The CAPM equation is forward-looking, i.e. it is seeking to measure the expected return on an asset over the next period of time. This is the return that the manager will require, but whereas the CAPM model deals only with a single period, in most cases the manager will be looking at projects which span a number of years. It is clear then that some assumptions are necessary when adapting the single-period CAPM to multi-period use.

In the context of the CAPM it is usual to represent the risk-free rate R_f by the rate of return currently required on three-month treasury bills. These are short-term government securities and are regarded as the nearest thing to a risk-free investment that is possible in an inherently uncertain world. In the context of the model this is fine; however, it has just been pointed out that in most instances projects will extend over several years rather than just a single short period. In these circumstances the risk-free return could be related to a government security having the same maturity as the life of the project. For example, with a five-year project the risk-free rate could be related to the yield to maturity on a five-year government security. Many companies use real rates of return in project appraisal. In these circumstances the real risk-free rate of return can be approximated by using the redemption yield on an appropriate index-linked government security.

In theory the beta of the project could be calculated by drawing up a subjective probability distribution for both the project and the market and then calculating the variance and standard deviation of market returns and project returns and the covariance of the market and project returns. This clearly requires forecasting the expected market return and distribution thereof for a number of years where a multi-period project is concerned. It is more usual to base the beta measurement on historic betas calculated using regression analysis. That is, the responsiveness of returns on any particular ordinary share could be obtained by plotting the return on the individual security against the market return.

The final part of the formula, $R_m - R_f$, is termed the 'market risk premium' and in theory is the expected excess return on the market portfolio over the risk-free rate of return. However, once again there are forecasting problems in determining this risk premium term, and in applying the theory historical measures are frequently used. The historic average for the UK has been estimated by Dimson and Brealey over a 60-year period at 9% and by Allan *et al.* for 1919–84 at 9.15% [1]. These estimates are comparable with the 8.4% risk premium on US shares estimated on a long-term basis by Ibbotson and Sinquefield [2]. It must be stressed that the figure of around 9% is a long-term historic average rather than the expected risk premium used in the theoretical model. It is necessary in using this figure as a risk premium to assume that long-run historic averages reflect *ex-ante* expectations and that these average risk premiums reflect current and future expected risk premiums.

Over the past decade many texts on corporate finance and other books written for practitioners have suggested that a market risk premium of between 8% and 9% based on historic data could be used in determining cost of capital in a CAPM framework. The effect of this can be illustrated for a project of expected life of ten years and average market risk (beta of one) using 1994 yields on government securities. The redemption yield on conventional gilts maturing in 10 years in August 1994 was 8.4% while index-linked gilts of the same maturity yielded 3.7%. Assuming a market risk premium of 9% and a beta of one implies costs of capital as follows:

market or money rate of return:
$8.4 + 1 \times 9 = 17.4\%$
real rate of return (allowing for inflation):
$3.7 + 1 \times 9 = 12.7\%$

These figures suggest that average projects in late 1994 should have been appraised using a real discount rate of 12.7% or if cash flows had been adjusted for inflation a money rate of return of 17.4%. Although these rates may not be very different from rates being used by UK companies they have been criticized as exaggerating the returns actually expected by investors in the summer of 1994. This is not a trivial point as the use of an excessively high discount rate could lead to the rejection of potentially profitable projects, particularly longer-term projects where high discount rates penalize them relative to short-run projects. The reason that long-run average historic risk premia are used is that obtaining estimates of expected future risk premia is very difficult. How do you do it? One way is to ask investors and in fact this approach was taken by the UK Monopolies and Mergers Commission (MMC) in their report on the rate of return that should be applied to the privatized British Gas pipe lines. The MMC surveyed eight fund managers and asked them what real (pre-tax) rate of return they expected on equity investments. The target rates ranged between 6 and 8% except for one fund whose target was 5 or 6%. Assuming a real risk-free return of 3.5% this would imply an equity risk premium from 2 to 4%. This is much lower than the 9% often assumed and would have a huge effect on project hurdle rates implying an increase in UK investment rates if adopted. However, it could be argued that a sample of only eight is too small to adopt completely new criteria for assessing risk.

The use of the 9% historic risk premium is justified on the basis that although expected returns should be used expected returns cannot be observed while historic returns can be observed. Additionally, by taking long-run returns covering over 80 years it is assumed that investors are unlikely to be systematically mistaken in their expectations. This approach also assumes that risk premium is relatively consistent over time. Table 12.1 shows the real ex-post returns on equities and gilts (UK government securities) from 1919 to 1992. In addition, figures are shown for the periods 1946–92 and 1963–92. The figures in the table reflect a number of interesting points.

First, the figure of 9% risk premium is based on arithmetic average returns: annual returns are added and divided by the number of years' returns. This will always produce higher returns than geometric averages; given the volatile nature of equity markets this is an important point. For example, suppose we consider a two-year period; in the first period prices increase by 100% while in the second they decrease by 50%. The arithmetic average is 100 + (−50)/2 = +25%; however, the geometric return is zero as prices will be back where they started. Another significant reason why the *ex-post* estimates of equity risk premium are so large is that there have been significant periods during which gilt returns have, on average, been very low or negative in real terms. This suggests that investors suffer due to unexpected inflation which they systematically underestimate. However, it could be argued that the introduction of index-linked gilts makes this less likely to occur in the future as investors will be using the real returns available on these securities as a yardstick for their required returns on conventional gilts.

Table 12.1 *Real ex-post returns on equities and gilts 1919–92*

	1919–92 %	1946–92 %	1963–92 %
Geometric averages			
Equity returns	7.3	6.3	5.9
Gilt returns	1.5	−0.4	1.3
Ex-post risk premium	5.8	6.7	4.6
Arithmetic averages			
Equity returns	9.7	8.9	9.1
Gilt returns	2.4	0.3	2.0
Ex-post risk premium	7.3	8.6	7.1

Source: Jenkinson, T. (1993) The cost of equity finance: conventional wisdom reconsidered, *Stock Exchange Quarterly with Quality of Markets Review*, Autumn.

The effect of a systematic error in estimating gilt returns will have meant an overestimation of the risk premium measured using historic returns. There could even have been a greater exaggeration if equity returns were underestimated. We can also see that the average risk premia are not consistent over time with the 1963–92 period producing significantly lower figures than the longer-run averages.

Taken together, these points suggest that there is quite a strong case for suggesting that the use of long-run historical data may not be the most appropriate way of estimating future returns expected by investors. As the use of models incorporating risk premia based on historic data is fairly popular this suggests that the cost of equity may be being overstated in many cases.

In the above example the project beta was assumed to be one; in the next section we examine how project betas can be identified using available information.

12.3 MEASURING EQUITY BETAS

In this section we discuss how betas can be obtained for use in project evaluation. Let us assume that our company is financed entirely by equity and that we are considering an expansion which has the same average level of risk as the company as a whole. In these circumstances it would be appropriate to use the beta of the equity share capital as a measure of the project risk.

The equity beta could be measured by comparing its price movement with market movements over a period of time. The returns of two hypothetical securities are plotted against the market return in Figures 12.1 and 12.2. A scatter diagram is produced and a line of best fit is drawn through the points. The slope of the line represents the beta of the security. In Figure 12.1 a low-beta security is represented while in Figure 12.2 a high-beta security is shown. In fact in most cases calculations of beta are already available. The London Business School (LBS) publishes a quarterly *Risk Measurement Service* containing calculations of betas and other statistical information for most UK companies of any significance. The betas are calculated using a standard least-squares regression program. The monthly returns for each security over the previous five years (i.e. 60 observations) are regressed against the monthly market returns as represented by the FT actuaries all-share index. Other databases also include beta measurements and other useful information; see for instance Datastream. In many instances company managers will therefore have direct access to the beta of their equity shares.

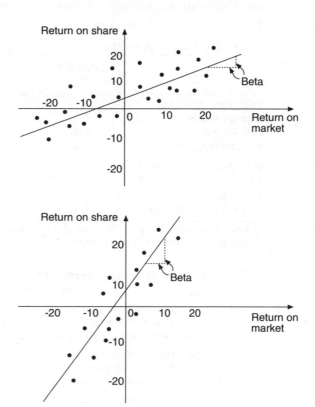

Figure 12.1
Low beta share

Figure 12.2
High beta share

As well as data relating to individual companies information is also available relating to industries. Table 12.2 shows industry betas available through the LBS risk measurement service. Industry betas could be preferred where there is some doubt over the accuracy of individual company betas as measurement errors tend to cancel out when betas of portfolios are used. The availability of industry betas also allows analysts advising companies without a stock market quotation to use CAPM by selecting a beta appropriate to the project under discussion.

Another reason for using industry betas is that the financial manager will wish to relate the measure of risk to the particular type of project being appraised; unless the project is identical with the average risk level of the company, the beta

Cost of capital

of the company would not be appropriate. Many companies carry out a wide range of different activities; these companies are often split into operating divisions. The beta of the equity of such a company would reflect these different activities, and in an all-equity company the beta of the equity could be written as

$$\beta_e = \Sigma W_a \beta_a$$

where β_e is the beta of equity, W_a is the proportion of value in activity A and β_a is the beta of activity A.

Table 12.2 *London Business School, Risk Measurement Service, industry betas*

Gold mining	0.77
Oil	0.79
Building and construction	1.29
Diversified engineering	1.13
Engineering contractors	1.10
Vehicle components and assembly	1.25
Breweries	0.97
Spirits, wines and ciders	1.03
Food retailers	0.75
Food manufacturers	0.82
Electricity utilities	0.89
Gas distribution	0.94
Tobacco	0.90
Healthcare	0.83
Hotels and caterers	1.24
Textiles	1.17
Banks	1.40
Property	1.06
Leisure	1.18

The use of ordinary share or equity betas in this section has usually been prefaced by the assumption that the company is all equity. The reason for this is that when a company is financed partly by debt and partly by equity then the beta of the equity as well as reflecting the business risk of the particular activities undertaken will also reflect the financial risk of the equity shareholders resulting from the existence of debt in the capital structure. This problem is examined in the next section.

12.4 UNGEARING EQUITY BETAS

The point has just been made that the beta of the equity of a geared company will be higher than that of an equivalent ungeared company because of the financial risk involved. In fact, this idea can be illustrated in the context of portfolio betas.

Suppose first of all that an all-equity company invests half its funds in a risky project with a beta of 1.2 and the other half in the risk-free asset. We would expect the beta of equity to be calculated as follows:

$$\beta_e = 0.5 \times 1.2 + 0.5 \times 0$$

$$= 0.6$$

In this case the shareholders' funds are invested half in a risky asset and half in a risk-free asset, and the beta of the equity will be the value-weighted average of the two.

Now suppose that a hitherto all-equity company borrows at the risk-free rate so that the amount borrowed is equal to shareholders' funds and invests the amount borrowed plus shareholders' funds in risky projects. The borrowing can be regarded as a negative investment and the beta of the equity could be written as follows:

$$\beta_e = 2 \times 1.2 + (-1 \times 0)$$

$$= 2.4$$

Figure 12.3 illustrates the point just made using the security market line (SML). The actual risky project has a beta of 1.2; if half the equity shareholders' funds are invested in this and half are lent at the risk-free rate, then the equity beta will be 0.6, reflecting a weighted average of the betas of the securities invested in. If, however, the company borrows and invests the original shareholders' funds plus an equal amount borrowed into the risky project, then the shareholders' funds will be riskier and will have a beta of 2.4. The borrowing moves the equity beta further up the SML to the right. Therefore, if we have the equity beta of a company with borrowing in its capital structure and wish to obtain the beta of the risky assets being invested in, we would need to write β_e as follows:

$$\beta_e = \beta_a \frac{E+D}{E} - \beta_d \frac{D}{E}$$

where E and D are the market values of equity and debt respectively. Rearranging to express the beta of the asset, we have

$$\beta_a = \beta_e \frac{E}{E+D} + \beta_d \frac{D}{E+D}$$

For example, if we are told that the equity beta of a company carrying out a single business activity is 1.8 and that the total values of equity and debt are £8 million and £4 million respectively, we could calculate an asset beta as follows:

$$\beta_a = 1.8 \times \frac{8}{8+4} + 0 \times \frac{4}{8+4}$$

$$= 1.8 \times \frac{8}{12} + 0 \times \frac{4}{12}$$

$$= 1.2$$

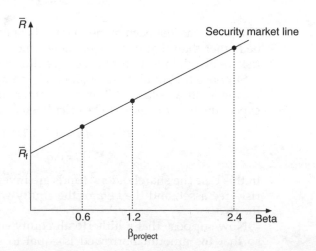

Figure 12.3
Equity beta and debt

Cost of capital

This chapter has examined in some detail the CAPM approach to cost of capital computation. The existence of debt in the capital structure required equity betas to be ungeared to arrive at asset betas and in practice this might require assumptions concerning future rates of taxation and risk of various types of debt. Companies often obtain their funds from many different sources including ordinary shares, convertibles, secured and unsecured loans, borrowings in different currencies, and so on.

All these sources of finance will have different costs depending on the risk to investors; from a company perspective it is the overall or average cost which is of significance as this indicates the return the company must earn from its business activities to cover its total financing costs. It would be incorrect to use the cost of a single source of finance, for example the most recent tranche of borrowing, in project appraisal as individual rates are affected by the overall financing package the company has in place.

In this approach the cost of each source of capital is calculated separately and then weighted by the proportion of total capital coming from that source. Although it is possible to use book values or market values in the weighted-average calculations it is incorrect and potentially misleading to use book values. Although book values of debt may approximate to market values, particularly for example in the case of floating-rate bonds, equity market values may be quite different from book values. It should also be borne in mind that the costs of finance will be market-determined and therefore to be consistent market values should be used throughout the calculations.

The weighted-average cost of capital calculation requires three steps as follows:

1 Compute cost of each individual source of finance using appropriate models. The cost of equity could be obtained using an equity beta and the CAPM model; alternatively the dividend growth model could be used. Bond valuation models can be used to compute the redemption yield on fixed-interest issues.
2 Compute total market value of each source of finance used by the company; for equity this will be number of shares in issue multiplied by market price, for bonds nominal values in issue adjusted for current market values.
3 Combine 1 and 2 together by weighting individual costs by proportion of value.

We shall now show how the weighted-average cost of capital can be calculated from available data (see Table 12.3).

Table 12.3

	Penn PLC	
	Financial statements information	Market-based information
Number of ordinary shares issued	2 million	
Total dividends paid	£0.44 million	
8% Non-redeemable debt	£5 million	
Market value per share		£3
Market value of debt		£80
Equity beta		1.5
Risk-free interest rate		7%

Overall cost of capital: weighted-average cost approach

Future dividends are expected to grow at an annual rate of 8%. The current market risk premium is estimated to be 6%. Corporation tax is 30%.

1   The cost of equity can be calculated using both CAPM and the dividend growth model as follows:

$$\text{Current dividend per share} = \frac{0.44}{2} = 0.22 \ (22\text{p})$$

Using the Gordon growth model where $P_o = \dfrac{D_1}{r-g}$ and $r = \dfrac{D_1}{P_o} + g$

$$\text{Cost of equity} = \frac{22 \times 1.08}{300} + 0.08$$

$$= 0.16 \ (16\%)$$

CAPM in this case gives the same result:

Cost of equity = 7 + 1.5 (6)

$$= 16\%$$

As the debt is perpetual:

$$\text{Cost of debt} = \frac{8}{80}$$

$$= 0.1, \ (10\%) \text{ before tax, relief}$$

2   Market values are as follows:

	£ (million)
Equity	
2 × £3	6
Debt	
5 × $\dfrac{80}{100}$	4
	10

3   Weighted-average cost of capital (WACC)

$$\text{WACC} = \frac{6 \times 16 + 4 \times 10(1 - 0.3)}{10}$$

$$= 12.4\%$$

Note that cost of debt is reduced from 10% to 7% when relief is given for corporation tax of 30%.

12.6 SINGLE-COMPANY COST OF CAPITAL AND THE CAPITAL-ASSET PRICING MODEL

CAPM assesses risk by expressing the relationship between individual project returns and the market for risky assets as a whole. This approach is forward-looking and related to the risk of the project and its forthcoming returns. It does not necessarily relate required return on projects to be undertaken to the return currently being earned by investors in the company as indicated by the weighted-average cost of capital. The latter approach would only be correct where the new project to be undertaken has the same level of risk as the average risk of projects currently being undertaken by the company and is financed by the same mix of securities. Even if the new project is an expansion of an activity already being undertaken, the overall single-company cost of capital may not be appropriate because it may reflect the average return currently required from a variety of different activities.

Figure 12.4 compares the use of a single-company cost of capital with the CAPM approach. Use of a single-company cost of capital would require projects to earn a rate of return of R_i or more to be adopted. That is, all projects would face the same hurdle rate irrespective of their level of risk. However, if the CAPM approach is used, then for adoption the project rate of return would have to plot either on or above the SML; in this case the rate of return would be tied to risk as measured by beta. Figure 12.4 contains two shaded areas, A and B. Area A contains low-risk projects having an expected rate of return lower than the single-company cost of capital. If the latter was used as the hurdle rate, then these projects would be rejected. However, projects in that area lie above the SML; and therefore have a return equal to or greater than that required for their level of risk. In contrast, area B will contain projects lying above the single-company cost-of-capital line but below the SML. These projects would be accepted using a single-company cost-of-capital criterion but rejected using the CAPM approach. If single-company cost of capital is used there could be a tendency to accept high-risk projects which, although giving a return greater than an average cost of capital, do not give a high enough return to compensate for their level of risk, while low-risk low-return projects would be rejected.

Although companies not using the CAPM approach might use varying hurdle rates, these are often intuitive and not based on any sound basis. The CAPM provides a rational framework for evaluating individual project risk.

Factors affecting beta

There are two factors which are likely to affect the systematic risk of a project more than any others.

1 The relationship between expected project revenues and mainstream economic activity. If the sales of a project are likely to be buoyant when the economy as a whole is buoyant but to fall sharply when main-line economic activity falls, a high beta activity is indicated. However, if demand for the product or service is likely to be unaffected by the level of economic activity, then a low-beta project would be indicated. Of course, if an activity can be identified giving higher returns when the economy as a whole is doing badly, then this would be regarded as a very valuable constituent of a portfolio; the activity would have a low beta and a low required rate of return.

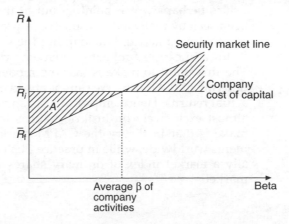

Figure 12.4
CAPM compared with
single cost of capital

2   The second factor which can affect the value of beta relates to the proportion of fixed costs in the project cost structure. The higher the proportion of fixed costs the higher the project beta that can be expected. We discussed in Section 12.3 how fixed finance costs in the form of debt lead to a higher-equity beta. Fixed costs in the project cost structure have the same affect on the beta of the project.

If we combine these two factors we can see that a project with revenues strongly associated with mainstream market activities and a high proportion of fixed costs would be particularly risky and an appropriately higher rate of return should be demanded for such a project. A capital goods manufacturer with a high level of fixed costs would be an example of such business activity. However, a business activity having low correlation with the market and low fixed cost would be expected to have an appropriately low beta and lower rate of return. An example here might be a gold mining company employing casual labour which can easily be hired and fired. Gold is a good example because historically it has been purchased by investors uneasy about market conditions in times of economic and political instability. Typically, gold mining shares have high total risk as measured by standard deviation but low market risk as measured by beta.

A consideration of these two factors gives some indications as to why betas might change over time. For example, activities whose cash flows have a high correlation with mainstream economic activity might include the sale of certain luxury items. If these luxury items over time become regarded as mere necessities, then the beta of the activities might be expected to change. Similarly, if the cost structure of a business changes from one having a high proportion of fixed costs to a low proportion or vice versa, then once again the beta of the particular activity can be expected to change.

12.7 REALISM OF THE CAPITAL-ASSET PRICING MODEL

For some years the CAPM has been regarded as a useful tool for both analysts of financial securities and financial managers in business organizations. However, it is not without its critics and will doubtless be replaced when another model is developed which improves on its theoretical appropriateness and practical usefulness. It is this combination of theory and its practical application which so far have maintained the interest in CAPM. Another model, the arbitrage pricing model, might take over the mantle of CAPM in the future, but there may be a little time to go before this happens.

It is perhaps worth pointing out at this stage that, although the CAPM has been seen by many as a reasonable approximation of reality, there are a number of problems that exist in adapting the theoretical model for practical use. This factor also causes problems when empirical tests of the model are undertaken. The first point to make is that the model is *ex-ante*, i.e. it is based on expectations about the future. We cannot observe expectations but we do have access to actual returns. Hence empirical tests and data for practical use tend to be based almost exclusively on historic returns (*ex-post* information). Another point to make is that in theory the CAPM market portfolio includes all risky investments worldwide, while in practice this is replaced by a surrogate which is usually a market index of ordinary shares relating to a particular national stock market.

12.8 SUMMARY AND CONCLUSIONS

It was emphasized that risk and return are related to the type of business activity undertaken and will determine the rate of return demanded by investors which should also be used by company managers in project appraisal. Risk should be related to non-diversifiable risk (market risk in a CAPM framework) as unique risk can be diversified away by holding a portfolio of securities.

The use of CAPM involves adaptation of a single-period *ex-ante* model to appraise multi-period future projects. In these circumstances it is necessary to use a surrogate risk-free return, perhaps relating to a yield to maturity on government securities. In addition, betas tend to be measured using past returns and it is necessary to assume some sort of stability if they are to be used as a risk measure for future activities. The market risk premium term $\bar{R}_m - R_f$ is often based on historical averages, and again it is necessary to assume that the actual premiums realized reflect expectations and that long-run average premiums give an indication of current and future premiums.

Commercial beta books, e.g. the LBS publication, are a useful source of information but need to be used with care. Because of potential measurement errors and difficulty of classification, industry betas might be more satisfactory than individual company equity betas. A company's equity beta will reflect all business activities undertaken and also any borrowing in the financial structure. Equity betas of geared companies (i.e. those with borrowing) can be ungeared to give betas which relate solely to the risk of underlying business activities; a project rate of return could be calculated based on the ungeared beta.

An alternative way of calculating a company's cost of capital is to compute a weighted-average cost of capital (WACC). With this method the cost of each type of finance is calculated using an appropriate valuation model. The individual costs are then weighted by the proportion of each source of finance based on market values. Allowance can be made for tax relief where appropriate and a composite cost of capital obtained. This cost represents current activities, risks, capital structure and tax rates. To the extent that any of these factors is different in the new project under review the use of the current WACC will not be entirely appropriate.

12.9 REFERENCES

1 Dimson, E. and Brealey, R.A. (1978) The risk premium on UK equities, *Investment Analyst*, **52**: 14–18, December.
   Allen, D., Day, R., Hirst, I. and Kwiatkowski, J. (1986) Equity, gilts, treasury bills and inflation, *Investment Analyst*, **83**: 11–18, October.
2 Ibbotson, R.G. and Sinquefield, R.A. *Stocks, Bonds, Bills and Inflation: 1996 Yearbook*, Ibbotson Associates, Chicago.

12.10 FURTHER READING

Black, F., Jensen, M.C. and Scholes, M. (1972) The capital asset pricing model: some empirical tests. In *Studies in the Theory of Capital Markets*, ed. M.C. Jensen, Praeger, New York.
Fama, E.F. and MacBeth, J. (1973) Risk return and equilibrium: empirical tests, *Journal of Political Economy*, **71**: 607–36, May–June.

Roll, R. (1977) A critique of the asset pricing theory's tests; Part I: On past and potential testability of the theory, *Journal of Financial Economics*, **4**(2): 129–76, March.

Ross, S.A. (1976) Arbitrage theory of capital asset pricing, *Journal of Economic Theory*, **13**: 341–60, December.

12.11 PROBLEMS

1 Midland Industries has three operating divisions:

Division	Percentage of firm value
Food	50
Chemicals	30
Machine tools	20

The Finance Director wishes to estimate divisional costs of capital and has identified three companies carrying out similar activities:

	Equity beta	Debt/ equity
Amalgamated Foods	0.9	0.40
Sludge Chemicals	1.2	0.25
Chunky Tools	1.4	0.50

(a) Estimate asset betas for each of Midland's divisions on the assumption that debt can be regarded as risk free.
(b) If Midland's debt to equity ratio is 0.25 what is its equity beta?
(c) If the risk-free rate of return is 10% and the expected return on the market is 18%, what is the cost of capital for each of Midland's divisions?
(d) How reliable do you consider the costs of capital calculated in (c)?

2 Until about a year ago Victoria PLC operated only in the light engineering industry but, owing to expansion, now operates three separate divisions – light engineering, food retailing and luxury goods. Victoria has previously utilized the weighted-average cost of capital to appraise the expected cash flows of all investment projects and the use of this discount rate had been considered successful. However, this year the use of the weighted-average cost of capital as the discount rate had produced results whereby all proposals from the fairly risky luxury goods division and a few proposals from the medium-risk light engineering division appear acceptable. Most projects from light engineering and all proposals submitted by the low-risk food retailing division have been rejected. The management of Victoria are wondering whether their project selection procedures are correct and are considering the suggestion that 'investment projects be appraised using a discount rate equal to the after-tax cost of debt finance because this year all projects are being financed either by newly raised debt or by zero-cost retained earnings. The cost of debt is therefore a sufficiently conservative indication of the cost of capital.'

(a) Comment on the suggestion to use the cost of debt as the discount rate for appraisal purposes and on the assertion concerning the cost of retained earnings. Discuss the validity of Victoria's use of a weighted-average cost of capital discount rate:
 (i) in the past when only one division was operating;
 (ii) now that three separate divisions are in operation.
(b) Explain how the discount rate for use in the financial aspects of project

appraisal should be determined for use in Victoria's three unequally risky divisions. Explain how this approach may be applied in practice and specify what constitutes risk for discount rate determination purposes.

(*ACCA, Financial Management, June 1983*)

3 The average equity β value for a group of similar companies in the motor industry is 1.32; their average debt to equity ratio is 0.20. The debt-to-equity ratio of Arden Motors is 0.30 while the risk-free rate of return is currently 12%. The market risk premium can be assumed to be 9%.
   (a) What is the required return on the assets of Arden Motors?
   (b) What is the required return on the equity of Arden Motors?

4 A firm is considering the following projects, and the expected returns calculated by way of IRRs are as follows:

Project	Beta	Expected return
A	0.5	12%
B	0.8	13%
C	1.2	18%
D	1.6	19%

   (a) Which projects have a higher expected return than the firm's current 15% single cost of capital?
   (b) Which projects should be accepted?
   (c) Which projects could be accepted or rejected incorrectly on the basis of the cost of capital as hurdle rate?

   You may assume that the risk-free rate is 8% and the market risk premium is 7%.

5 The total market value of the equity of Lucav PLC is £6 million and the total value of its debt is £4 million. The beta value of the equity is estimated to be 1.5 and the expected market risk premium is 10%. The risk-free rate of interest is 8%.
   (a) What is the required return on the Lucav equity?
   (b) What is the beta of the company's existing portfolio of assets?
   (c) Estimate the company's cost of capital.
   (d) Estimate the discount rate for an expansion of the company's present business.
   (e) Suppose that the company replaces £3 million debt with equity. Does the beta of the equity change?
   (f) What would the company cost of capital be now?
   (g) If the company wishes to diversify into another industry with a beta value of 1.2, what would be the required rate of return?

6 An all-equity company is expected to generate £48.5 million in dividends per annum in perpetuity and has a beta coefficient of 1.85. Another company, also all-equity, is expected to generate £37.8 million in perpetuity and has a beta coefficient of 0.68. The risk-free rate of return is 7.5% and the expected return on the market is 13.8%.
   (a) If the two firms were to merge, and if no scale economies or managerial synergies were expected from the merger, what would be the value of the combined firm?
   (b) If the merger of the two firms were to result in managerial synergies that are expected to increase the annual dividends of the combined firm by £3.85 million but to leave its systematic risk unaltered, what would be the value of the combined firm?

(c) Compare the results obtained in (a) and (b) with the sum of the values of the two companies as separate entities. Explain any differences which arise and comment on the benefits of mergers to investors in the context of the CAPM.

13 CAPITAL STRUCTURE

LEARNING OUTCOMES

By the end of this chapter the reader should:

- be able to explain and discuss the alternative views and theories on the benefit and risk of debt in a corporate capital structure
- be able to discuss and evaluate the impact of corporate taxes on the debt decision
- understand the effect of increasing levels of debt on the risk of the company and its cost of finance
- be able to explain the effect of potential bankruptcy on the company's level of debt
- understand and be able to explain pecking order theory and agency costs associated with increasing levels of debt

13.1 INTRODUCTION

In the previous chapter we examined the cost of capital of a company and how an average cost of capital could be computed using the estimated costs of equity and debt. In this chapter we discuss alternative ways of financing the company and whether any of these alternatives lead to a reduction in the average cost of capital and by implication an increase in the overall value of the company.

An important factor in reducing cost of capital was identified as the tax deductibility of debt interest. The combination of lower-cost debt and interest relief appear to favour debt over equity as a source of finance. However, we also need to consider the effect on risk and hence return demanded by equity shareholders as the level of debt increases in the capital structure.

The terms 'gearing' and 'leverage' are both used to refer to the level of debt in a company's capital structure. Both terms are used in the UK while 'leverage' is the favoured term in the USA. High gearing or leverage indicates a high proportion of debt in a company's capital structure. Low gearing or leverage the opposite.

13.2 CAPITAL STRUCTURE IMPLICATIONS

Higher levels of leverage have been advocated for a number of reasons, some more valid than others. Tax deductibility of debt interest can create extra shareholder value as long as company profits exist to offset the interest paid. Increasing earnings per share through borrowing is more debatable: borrowing adds financial risk to the company and its shareholders who will normally expect compensation in the form of higher returns for the additional risk assumed. There may be agency benefits in taking on higher levels of debt in that corporate managers will have to create value to pay debt interest and make repayments; it could be said that in these circumstances there is less financial slack in the system and managers have an incentive to perform and survive.

Although historically UK and US companies have had lower levels of debt than their counterparts in Japan and continental Europe there has been more realization of the potential benefits borrowing brings to the corporate structure and many companies in both the UK and the US have been adopting higher levels of debt.

Example 13.1

We shall now illustrate a number of the issues raised so far with the help of the example shown in Table 13.1. The example considers three possible levels of gearing and examines the effect of these on profits and earnings per share. Capital structure A involves no debt, while B and C use increasing amounts of debt.

Table 13.1

Alternative balance sheet projections

	A	B	C
Ordinary shares of £1 each	100 000	80 000	50 000
12% debt	–	20 000	50 000
	£100 000	£100 000	£100 000
debt-to-total assets	–	0.20	0.50
debt-to-equity	–	0.25	1.00

Effect on income and earnings per share of different levels of gearing and earnings

	A			B			C		
	(i)	(ii)	(iii)	(i)	(ii)	(iii)	(i)	(ii)	(iii)
1 Earnings	8000	12 000	16 000	8000	12 000	16 000	8000	12 000	16 000
2 Interest at 12%	–	–	–	2400	2 400	2 400	6000	6 000	6 000
3	8000	12 000	16 000	5600	9 600	13 600	2000	6 000	10 000
4 Taxation 33%	2640	3 960	5 280	1848	3 168	4 488	660	1 980	3 300
5	5360	8 040	10 720	3752	6 432	9 112	1340	4 020	6 700
EPS	5.4p	8.0p	10.7p	4.7p	8.0p	11.4p	2.7p	8.0p	13.4p
Interest cover	–	–	–	3.3	5	6.7	1.3	2	2.7

The table illustrates the effect on earnings per share (EPS) under each capital structure assuming three possible levels of profits. These are shown for each of the three structures under the three columns. A charge for taxation has also been included in the illustration. If we assume that the range of earnings shown represents lowest outcome, expected outcome and highest outcome respectively we can examine the effect on returns to ordinary shareholders as represented by EPS.

We can see that with structure A the EPS ranges from 5.4p to 10.7p. With increasing levels of debt in the capital structure, as in B and C, EPS at the lowest level of profitability declines while EPS at higher levels of profitability increases. One argument advanced for high levels of gearing is that it leads to an increase in EPS for ordinary shareholders. The example shows that this is the case only when the rate of return earned on assets is higher than the level of interest paid on debt. The second column for all three structures shows the same EPS at 8.0p; this is where total profits are £12 000, a return of 12% on assets employed and the return required on debt. Where the company earns less than this, higher levels of gearing will lead to a decrease in EPS; where the company earns more higher gearing will indeed increase EPS. It may be thought that if the company is optimistic about future profitability, then higher levels of gearing should be taken on. However, the example illustrates another factor related to gearing in that increasing levels of gearing also increase the risk as far as ordinary shareholders are concerned. This is illustrated by the way in which the range of EPS values increases with the level of gearing. It would seem that rational investors should require an increase in return on equity as the risk increases. Increasing levels of risk are also reflected in the declining interest cover ratios shown for different levels of gearing. External analysts, whether representing potential shareholders

Capital structure

Another interesting point which we can also gain from the illustration is the effect of different levels of gearing on the total return paid to providers of capital, both debt and equity. Let us consider the second column for A, B and C. In A the total payment to providers of capital will be the £8040 paid to ordinary shareholders shown in row 5. In capital structures B and C rows 2 and 5 will show the amounts earned by providers of debt and equity respectively. In structure B this is £8832, and in C it is £10 020. The reason that the total earnings to providers of capital increases in this case is entirely due to the tax shield provided on interest payments.

A number of factors have been determined relating to the effect of debt in the capital structure; among these are the lower return required on debt because of lower perceived risk, that debt interest is deductible against corporation tax, that debt in the capital structure increases the risk of equity shareholders and that debt increases EPS provided that the return on assets is greater than the coupon rate on debt.

We shall proceed to review and analyse the alternative views on the effect of debt in the capital structure, beginning with the traditional view that it is possible to identify an optimum level of debt for each company. In the analysis which follows the value of equity and debt will be related to market value. While ratio analysis tends to use accounting numbers, financial theory is concerned with the value of companies as indicated by markets which gives a direct measure of investor wealth.

13.3 TRADITIONAL VIEW OF CAPITAL STRUCTURE

The traditional view of company capital structure suggests that the average cost of capital does depend on the level of gearing. The implication is that there is an individual company optimum level of gearing at which cost of capital will be minimized and the value of the firm maximized. When a company has both equity and debt in its capital structure, then the cost of capital can be expressed as a weighted-average cost of capital where the cost of each type of capital in the company is weighted by its proportional value in the total value of the company. This is normally expressed as follows:

$$\text{weighted-average cost of capital} = K_0$$

$$K_0 = K_e \frac{V_e}{V_e + V_d} + K_d \frac{V_d}{V_e + V_d}$$

where K_e is the cost of equity capital, K_d is the cost of debt capital, V_e is the market value of equity and V_d is the market value of debt.

The above formula does not consider taxation, and if this is to be taken into account then the after-tax cost of debt should be used in the calculation. This would be $K_d(1 - t)$ where t is the rate of corporation tax. The formula becomes:

$$K_0 = K_e \frac{V_e}{V_e + V_d} + K_d(1-t) \frac{V_d}{V_e + V_d}$$

We will use these formulae in the analysis which follows.

The traditional view of capital structure was that as the level of gearing increased over moderate debt ranges the average cost of capital fell because of the lower cost of debt capital compared with equity capital. It was assumed that moderate amounts of debt did not add significantly to the risks attached to holding equity, so that initially the company would not have to offer higher returns to its equity shareholders. This would cause the weighted-average cost of capital to decline, thus increasing the value of the company. As the proportion of debt in the capital structure rises, two things happen: first, the equity shareholders realize that their investment is becoming riskier and therefore demand a higher rate of return from the company; second, lenders advancing money to an already geared company will also recognize increasing risk on their investment as the level of gearing rises and expect a higher rate of return on succeeding tranches of debt advanced. The result of this on the cost of capital is that the increasing cost of both debt and equity will tend to cancel out the advantage gained by substituting lower-cost debt for equity. Thus, although traditionalists claim that overall cost of capital is initially reduced by introducing debt into the capital structure, it is recognized that as the level of debt increases the total cost of capital no longer decreases and eventually starts to rise again at higher levels of debt. This view is summarized in Figure 13.1 which shows a U-shaped cost-of-capital curve; the optimal level of gearing is where the average cost of capital is at its lowest point, at the trough of the U. Figure 13.2 illustrates the effect of the traditional approach on the value of the firm at different levels of gearing. If the traditional approach is accepted, then there is a level of gearing for each firm at which the cost per unit of capital is at its lowest point. Managers would therefore have to identify this optimum level of gearing and ensure that their company maintained its capital structure at this level.

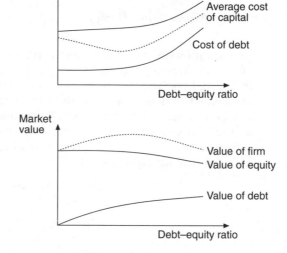

Figure 13.1
Traditional view of debt and cost of capital

Figure 13.2
Traditional view of debt and value of firm

13.4 CAPITAL STRUCTURE IN PERFECT CAPITAL MARKETS

Modigliani and Miller [1] were the first to carry out a rigorous analysis of the effect of gearing on cost of capital and firm value. MM criticized the traditional view which was the accepted wisdom of the time and questioned whether it was possible for firms to reduce the cost of capital in the way that was described in the previous section.

MM argued that, under a restrictive set of assumptions, gearing would have no effect on either cost of capital or firm value. The assumptions on which they base their arguments are important and they are as follows.

1. Perfect capital markets exist where individuals and companies can borrow unlimited amounts at the same rate of interest.

2   There are no taxes or transaction costs.
3   Personal borrowing is a perfect substitute for corporate borrowing.
4   Firms exist with the same business or systematic risk but different levels of gearing.
5   All projects and cash flows relating thereto are perpetuities, and any debt borrowed is also perpetual.

Under such assumptions MM demonstrated that it was the income generated by the firm from its business activities which determined value, rather than the way in which this income was split between providers of capital. If two firms with the same level of business risk but different levels of gearing sold for different values, then shareholders would move from the overvalued to the undervalued firm and adjust their level of borrowing through the market to maintain financial risk at the same level. In this way shareholders would increase their income while maintaining their net investment and risk at the same level. This process of arbitrage would drive the price of the two firms to a common equilibrium total value. The example below illustrates the MM arbitrage process. In the illustration both companies generate the same level of income and have the same business risk, but Thompson, the geared company, is valued in total at £1 million more than Lilley.

Example 13.2 Illustration of MM arbitrage in perfect capital markets

Lilley and Thompson are companies in the same class of business risk. Both companies have annual earnings before interest of £1 million but different capital structures. The companies are currently valued on the market as follows:

	Lilley	Thompson
Equity	5 000 000	4 000 000
8%debt	–	2 000 000
	£5 000 000	£6 000 000

Let us suppose that Chappell owns 5% of Thompson's equity. His income will be

Total Thompson earnings	1 000 000
Less: debt interest at 8%	160 000
	£840 000

$$\times \frac{5}{100} = £42\,000$$

MM would say that Lilley and Thompson should both have the same total market value because they have identical levels of earnings and risk.

Chappell could sell his equity in Thompson for £200 000 (5% of £4 million), borrow £100 000 at 8% from the market to maintain his total risk (business and financial) at the same level and invest the whole £300 000 in Lilley's equity. He will then own 6% of Lilley (6% × £5 million = £300 000).

Chappell's income would then be

Total Lilley income		£1 000 000
$\times \dfrac{6}{100}$		60 000
Less: interest on personal loan 8% × £100 000		8 000
		£52 000

Chappell could increase his income by £10 000 while maintaining total risk at the same level. MM said that this arbitrage would result in the total values of Lilley and Thompson moving to the same equilibrium value.

MM would say that under their assumptions it would be possible for an equity holder in Thompson to sell his holding, borrow on the market to maintain his total risk at the same level, i.e. business and financial risk, and invest the total in Lilley. The shareholder will then be able to increase his total income after paying interest on the personal loan while maintaining his overall risk at the same level. The result of this arbitrage process would be that the equity value of the overvalued company, in this case Thompson, would decrease while the equity value of the undervalued company, Lilley, would increase until a point was reached where the total value of both companies was the same. For ease of illustration it has been assumed that the companies are of the same size. This is not necessary. All that is required is that there exist companies in the same risk class. For example, if Lilley's cash flows had been twice those of Thompson the expectation would be that Lilley's value should be twice that of Thompson.

Let us assume that in this example Thompson's debt and Lilley's equity are trading at equilibrium prices and the selling arbitrage results in Thompson's equity declining in value to £3 million. The resulting values and cost of capital will be as follows:

	Lilley	Thompson
Equity	5 000 000	3 000 000
8%debt	–	2 000 000
	£5 000 000	£5 000 000
Cost of equity	1 M/5 M	(1 M − 0.16 M)/3 M
	= 0.2 (20%)	= 0.28 (28%)
Cost of debt		0.16/2 M
		= 0.08 (8%)

As Lilley is financed solely by equity its weighted-average cost of capital (WACC) will be the cost of equity, i.e. 20%. In Thompson's case

$$\text{WACC} = 0.28 \times \frac{3}{5} + 0.08 \times \frac{2}{5} = 0.2 \ (20\%)$$

Thus MM say that the weighted-average cost of capital is the same irrespective of the level of gearing and is equal to the equity rate of return in an ungeared firm. Also, the value of a firm in a particular risk class is equal to the annual cash flow income discounted at the rate of return required from an ungeared firm. In the case of Lilley and Thompson

$$\text{total market value} = \frac{1\,000\,000}{0.2} = \text{£5 000 000}$$

MM express their conclusions on gearing, cost of capital and the value of the firm in the form of three propositions as follows.

Proposition 1

The market value of any firm is independent of its capital structure. Further, the market value of any firm is given by capitalizing its expected total earnings at the capitalization rate appropriate to an all-equity company of that risk class. This result is ensured by the operation of the arbitrage process previously described.

Proposition 2

The expected rate of return on equity increases linearly with the gearing ratio. This can be illustrated using the weighted-average cost-of-capital formula previously examined. If K_u is the return required on the equity of an ungeared firm, then we know that this is equal to the weighted-average cost of capital of all geared firms in the same risk class. We can write

$$K_0 = K_u = K_e \frac{V_e}{V_e + V_d} + K_d \frac{V_d}{V_e + V_d}$$

Multiplying throughout by $V_e + V_d$ we obtain

$$K_u V_e + K_u V_d = V_e K_e + V_d K_d$$

Dividing by V_e gives

$$K_u + \frac{K_u V_d}{V_e} = K_e + \frac{V_d K_d}{V_e}$$

$$K_e = K_u + \frac{V_d}{V_e}(K_u - K_d)$$

This expression shows that the expected return on the equity of a geared company is equal to the expected return on a pure equity stream plus a risk premium dependent on the level of debt in the capital structure. The effect on the cost of equity of introducing debt into the capital structure is that the cost of equity rises linearly to offset the lower-cost debt directly, giving a constant weighted-average cost of capital irrespective of the level of gearing.

Proposition 3

The cut-off rate to be used in investment appraisal is the rate of return appropriate to an all-equity firm. This is the case because in an MM world the weighted-average cost of capital is constant and equal to the cost of equity in an all-equity firm. This follows from Proposition 2 where the cost of equity increases linearly to offset exactly the advantage of lower-cost debt financing. The three propositions are therefore entirely consistent and tie in with the arbitrage idea previously discussed. Figure 13.3 illustrates the effect of gearing on cost of capital while Figure 13.4 shows the effect on the value of the firms. The figures stress that in the MM framework both overall cost of capital and firm value are constant irrespective of the level of gearing.

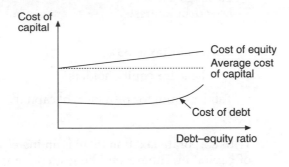

Figure 13.3
MM (no taxation) and
cost of capital

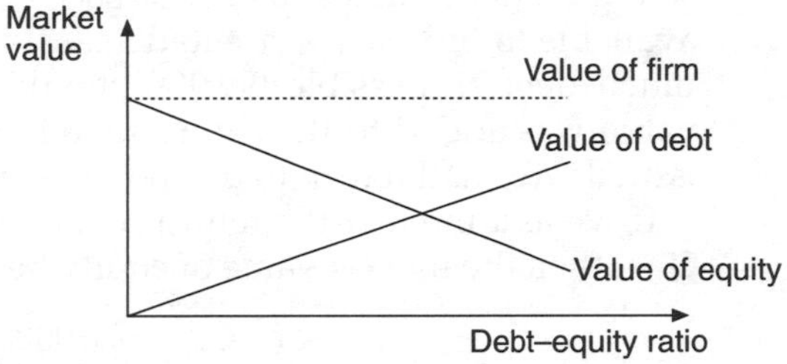

Figure 13.4
MM (no taxation) and
value of firm

The important point being made is that it is the business activities undertaken by the firm which determine value rather than the way in which the fruits of these activities are packaged between the providers of capital. Managers will make more money for their shareholders by concentrating on identifying profitable projects rather than trying to increase wealth through dividend and financing decisions. Of course, it must be admitted that MM theory was derived by making simplified assumptions which could be criticized as follows.

1 It could be questioned whether personal borrowing is a substitute for corporate borrowing, given the corporate sector's limited liability and its ability to borrow at keener rates of interest than the personal sector.
2 Is it possible to identify companies in the same risk class? Is there such a thing as two identical companies?
3 In the real world taxes and transaction costs exist and these need to be considered.

Despite the criticisms which can be levelled at the unrealistic assumptions made by MM there is almost universal acceptance of their conclusions, given the assumptions made. If different levels of capital structure are to affect both cost of capital and the value of the firm, then we must identify the imperfections in the world assumed by MM. We begin this in the next section where we examine the impact of corporate taxes on the capital structure decision.

Corporation taxation

The original MM model discussed in Section 13.3 did not consider the influence of taxation. When this was pointed out they simply corrected their earlier analysis to allow for corporate taxation [2]. What are the effects of corporate taxation on debt in the capital structure? If we return to the example of the ungeared Lilley and the geared Thompson we can examine the effects of introducing corporation tax of 33% into our analysis.

	Lilley	Thompson
Earnings	1 000 000	1 000 000
Less: debt interest	–	160 000
	1 000 000	840 000
Corporate Tax at 33%	330 000	277 200
Available for equity holders	£670 000	£562 800
Total amount for providers of capital	£670 000	£722 800

$$(160\,000 + 562\,800)$$

With corporate taxation there is an increase of £52 800 in cash flows to providers of capital in Thompson, the geared company. This increase arises from the tax shield on debt interest paid (160 000 × 33% = £52 800) and increases the amount available to ordinary shareholders. MM suggested that, with corporation tax, as much debt as possible (99.9%) should be included in the capital structure as value was added to the equity shareholders' interest with each £1 of extra debt issued. We shall return to this point later.

If we assume that the return required by equity investors in Lilley remains at 20%, then the market value of equity becomes

$$V_u = \frac{670\,000}{0.2} = £3.35 \text{ million}$$

where V_u is the value of the ungeared company. If the value of debt in Thompson and the required return on debt are also unchanged, then designating V_g as the value of a geared company:

value of Thompson = V_g = value of ungeared company + PV of tax shield on debt interest

$$= 3\,350\,000 + \frac{52\,800}{0.08}$$
$$= 3\,350\,000 + 660\,000$$
$$= £4.01 \text{ million}$$

This assumes that debt is perpetual and that the tax shield has the same risk as debt.

value of Thompson = value of equity + value of debt

and

value of debt = £2 million

Therefore

value of equity = £4 010 000 − £2 000 000

$$= £2.01 \text{ million}$$

The present value (PV) of the tax shield above is given by

$$PV = \frac{0.08 \times 2\,000\,000 \times 0.33}{0.08}$$

The 0.08 terms in the numerator and the denominator cancel out, leaving,

$$PV = 2\,000\,000 \times 0.33$$
$$= £660\,000$$

Thus generally,

$$V_g = V_u + V_d t_c$$

where t_c is the rate of corporation tax.

How do these findings affect the three MM propositions outlined in the previous section?

MM Proposition 1 with corporate taxes

The market value of a firm is no longer independent of its capital structure. Value is increased as debt is added to the capital structure because of the PV of the tax shield on interest payments. The market value of a firm is now given by summing its value if all equity and the value of tax shield on interest payments.

MM Proposition 2 with corporate taxes

Although the expected return on equity increases as debt is added to the capital structure the rate of increase is lower because of the existence of corporate taxes:

$$K_e = K_u + (1 - t_c)(K_u - K_d)\frac{V_d}{V_e}$$

The average cost of capital K_g in a geared company also declines with debt financing as follows:

$$K_g = K_u(1 - t_c L)$$

where

$$L = \frac{V_d}{V_e + V_d}$$

Alternatively, the weighted-average cost of capital of a geared firm can be written as

$$K_g = K_e \frac{V_d}{V_e + V_d} + K_d(1 - t_c)\frac{V_d}{V_e + V_d}$$

Using the data for Lilley and Thompson we can calculate the cost of equity and the average cost of capital of Thompson as follows:

$$K_u = 0.2 \text{ (given)}$$
$$K_d = 0.08 \text{ (given)}$$
$$K_e = 0.2 + (1 - 0.33)(0.2 - 0.08)\frac{2.0}{2.01}$$
$$= 0.28 \text{ or } 28\%$$
$$K_g = 0.2\left(1 - 0.33 \times \frac{2.00}{4.01}\right)$$
$$= 0.167 \text{ or } 16.7\%$$

or

$$K_g = 0.28 \times \frac{2.01}{4.01} + 0.08(1 - 0.33)\frac{2.00}{4.01}$$
$$= 0.1403 + 0.0267$$
$$= 0.167 \text{ or } 16.7\%$$

MM Proposition 3 with corporate taxes

The implications of Proposition 3 without taxes was that the weighted-average cost of capital was constant irrespective of gearing and that the appropriate cost of capital was that rate appropriate to an all-equity firm. We have just seen in the discussion above that tax deductibility of debt interest leads to a progressive reduction in overall cost of capital. What rate of return should be used in project appraisal?

The use of either formula for K_g given above would result in the mingling of benefits and risks relating to both the project and the means of financing. In addition it would reflect the average risk of existing projects and their financing mix.

MM developed their ideas well before the capital-asset pricing model (CAPM) was available for use. The original tendency was to use the weighted-average cost of capital to calculate K_g to obtain a project discount rate, and assume that the project and its financing were identical in terms of risk and gearing to the existing firm. However, it is suggested that the more appropriate approach is to split the project and financing; the project should still be evaluated as though all-equity using an appropriate cost of capital, with separate and explicit adjustment being made for any financing involved.

The result of introducing tax deductibility of debt interest seems to suggest that as much debt as possible should be included in the capital structure. However, debt ratios in the UK rarely exceed 50% and vary considerably between companies. In their analysis MM assumed that it was certain that firms would be able to obtain benefit for the tax shields in each and every succeeding financial period and that no additional disadvantages accrued with higher levels of gearing. In the past it has not been unusual for UK companies, particularly manufacturing companies, to pay little or no UK tax because of the availability of high allowances for capital expenditure or the existence of double tax relief on overseas income. Tax shields only have value if the company is in a tax-paying position; thus the higher are the levels of gearing the higher is the probability that in at least some periods in the future the company will not be able to benefit from the interest tax shields. Another factor which needs to be considered is that from an investor's point of view debt interest and equity income might be taxed differently, thus leading to investor preferences when personal as well as corporate taxes are considered. A further point we need to consider is that as more debt is added to the capital structure the possibility of potential bankruptcy or financial distress increases.

13.6 CAPITAL STRUCTURE AND FINANCIAL DISTRESS

In their 1963 paper MM [2] agreed that when there is corporation tax relief on interest payments then the cost of capital is not independent of the debt-to-equity ratio. The existence of this tax relief provides advantages which favour borrowing. However, as the proportion of debt in the capital structure increases, then not only do the risks of equity owners increase but also those of succeeding providers of debt. With increasing proportions of debt the likelihood of incurring costs of financial distress increase, as does the cost of the ultimate financial distress, bankruptcy. Potential financial distress has a cost, and as companies take on higher and higher levels of debt this cost will have a negative effect on firm value, offsetting the value of the tax shield from extra interest payments made. In these circumstances the value of a geared firm can be written as

value of a geared firm = value if firm is all equity financed + PV of tax shield on borrowing − PV of costs of financial distress

The chances of financial distress increase as gearing increases because with debt capital a fixed-interest payment has to be made annually whatever the profit or cash-flow position of the company, whereas it is possible to postpone a dividend payment.

The costs of financial distress can be divided into direct and indirect costs. The direct costs include fees for lawyers and accountants, other professional fees and the managerial time used in administration. The indirect costs are less tangible and arise because of uncertainties in the minds of suppliers and customers. They include lost sales, lost profits and lost goodwill. The presence of these possible distress costs is likely to increase the cost of capital because the shareholders will want a greater return for what they see as additional risk. This means that whether bankruptcy costs are a threat or not, the shareholders perceive them as a threat as the level of gearing increases, and it is likely to lead to an increase in the cost of capital.

As can be seen from the equation above, the threat of financial-distress costs reduces the benefits of tax relief on debt achieved by higher levels of gearing. Proponents of the importance of distress and bankruptcy costs argue that there is an optimal level of gearing at which the bankruptcy costs, the cost of capital and the tax relief are balanced. Therefore the cost of capital is not independent of the capital structure.

In the previous section we were concerned with the effect of taxation on the optimal capital structure; in this section we have been concerned with the effect of financial distress. The joint effect of taxation and financial distress is illustrated in Figure 13.5. This illustration shows the trade-off between the increase in value arising as a result of the tax-shield effect on debt interest paid and the increase in costs of financial distress as the proportion of debt in the capital structure increases. An optimal level of capital gearing is shown at point B. In practice an optimal level of capital gearing for a firm does appear to exist. One reason why optimal levels of capital gearing do exist is because of institutional restrictions; these are discussed below.

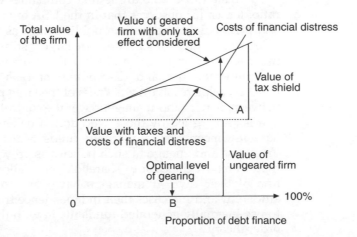

Figure 13.5
Value of firm with taxes and financial distress

Students of company finance for over twenty years have had to answer questions on the intricate theories of capital structure. Students, whether at university or studying for professional examinations, have been expected to understand the ideas of Modigliani and Miller.

There has, however, been disagreement among researchers as to whether firms actually behave as if there is an optimal level of gearing. It is accepted that the MM model does not predict the actual level of gearing of the typical firm, but this is not really surprising. Individual firms have to make allowances for their own potential level of bankruptcy costs (both the legal and administrative costs and the effect on their ability to do business) and of the tax shield effects of debt. Nevertheless there are those who argue that firms behave as if there is a target debt/equity ratio.

One explanation for a target gearing level is provided by the trade-off theory. Financial managers can think of the firm's debt/equity decision as a trade-off – the tax advantages of debt balanced against the risks of distress. There is some controversy as to how valuable are tax shields and what are the costs of financial distress but these disagreements are only variations on a theme. This trade-off theory of capital structure recognizes that target debt ratios may vary from firm to firm. Companies with safe, tangible assets and plenty of taxable income to shield ought to have high target gearing ratios. Companies with variable profits and risky, intangible assets ought to rely primarily on equity financing.

If there were no costs of adjusting capital structure, then each firm should always be at its target debt ratio. However, there are costs, and therefore delays in adjusting to the optimum. Firms cannot immediately offset the random events that move them away from their capital structure targets, so we should see random differences in actual debt ratios even among firms having the same target debt ratios. Because of this adjustment process it is not easy for researchers to identify target ratios.

There is some evidence that companies appear to make their choice of financing instruments as if they have target levels of debt in mind. If this is the case, then in principle companies needing new finance should issue equity if they are above their target debt level and debt if they are below. With no flotation costs, such adjustments could be made instantaneously and continuously. In practice, however, the existence of significant flotation costs gives rise to infrequent 'lumpy' issues, with the consequence that debt ratios fluctuate over time around their target level.

There are those who argue that companies do not have a target debt/equity ratio. Jensen [3] observes that in the USA organizations have been using public and private debt, rather than public equity, as their major source of capital. The primary providers of such debt are large institutions who designate the agents to manage on their behalf and bind those agents with covenants and contracts governing the use and distribution of cash and profits. This trend, Jensen believes, helps resolve a weakness of the large public corporation, i.e. the conflict between owners and managers over the control and use of corporate resources.

It is also argued by those who do not believe in a target ratio that managers have few incentives to distribute funds. Managers seem to prefer to retain any 'free' cash and engage in such policies as growth through diversification, rather than to return the cash to shareholders to allow them to undertake diversification of their own. If managers have cash to retain this increases their own autonomy and increases their independence from the capital markets. This wish to use internally generated funds fits in with the ideas expressed in the pecking order theory.

Pecking order theory

The pecking order theory was first proposed by Donaldson in 1961 [4]. The pecking order theory argues against a target debt/equity ratio. The theory suggests that firms rely for finance as much as they can on internally generated funds. If not enough internally generated funds are available then they will move to additional debt finance. It is only when these two sources cannot provide enough funds to satisfy needs that the company will seek to obtain new equity finance. This theory of course contrasts sharply with the theories which indicate that there is an optimal capital structure for a firm.

One explanation of this 'pecking order' for the supply of finance is issue costs. Internally generated funds have the lowest issue cost and new equity the highest. Firms obtain as much as they can of the easiest and least expensive finance, mainly retained earnings, before moving to the next least expensive debt.

Myers [5] has suggested that firms follow a 'modified pecking order' in their approach to financing. Although Donaldson [6] originally argued that reliance on internal finance enables professional managers to avoid subjecting themselves to the discipline of the capital market, Myers has suggested asymmetric information as an explanation for heavy reliance on retentions. There may be a situation where managers, because of their access to more information about the firm, know that the value of the shares is greater than the current market value based on semi-strong market information. In the case of a new project, for example, managers' forecasts may be higher and more realistic than that of the market. If new shares were issued in this situation there is the possibility that they would be issued at too low a price, thus transferring wealth from existing shareholders to new shareholders. In these circumstances there might be a natural preference for internally generated funds over new issues. The use of internal funds also ensures that there is a regular source of funds which might be in line with a particular company's expansion or renewal programme. If additional funds are required over and above internally generated funds, then borrowing would be the next alternative under this pecking order approach. If management is averse to making equity issues when in possession of favourable inside information, market participants might assume that management will be more likely to favour new issues when they are in possession of unfavourable inside information which leads to the suggestion that new issues might be regarded as a signal of bad news! Managers may therefore wish to rely primarily on internally generated funds supplemented by borrowing, with issues of new equity as a last resort.

Myers and Majluf [7] demonstrate that with asymmetric information, equity issues are interpreted by the market as bad news, since managers are only motivated to make equity issues when shares are undervalued. Asquith and Mullins [8] empirically observed that announcements of new equity issues are greeted by sharp declines in stock prices. Thus, equity issues are comparatively rare among large established companies.

Agency costs

A further explanation that has been offered for the pecking order is agency costs. These are costs, either direct or indirect, of ensuring that company management act in the best interests of the providers of finance. These costs cover the costs of reporting and being accountable to shareholders, and the costs of the providers of debt monitoring and restricting (bonding) the managers through covenants.

There is, however, disagreement as to whether the agency costs associated with debt are greater or less than those associated with equity.

Jensen and Meckling [9] drew attention to a number of ways in which agency problems may restrict the level of debt taken on by companies. Agency costs are additional expenses, either direct or indirect, which are incurred in ensuring that agents, in this case company management, act in the best interests of principals, in this case the suppliers of debt. The reason for the existence of these costs is that it would be possible for company management to undertake policies detrimental to providers of debt if constraints of some sort were not placed upon them. For example, it would be possible for the position of debtholders to be adversely affected *vis-à-vis* equity holders by entering into a riskier investment programme. Table 13.2 helps illustrate this point. It shows two possible projects; both have an expected value of £40 000 but project 2's higher risk is indicated by the wider distribution of potential returns. If the required investment in each project is £30 000, to be financed by borrowing, we can see that both the projects have positive net present values (NPVs). However, in the case of project 1, lenders are sure of repayment whichever outcome occurs; with project 2 there is only a 0.5 chance of there being sufficient funds to repay the lenders. We can see that equity holders might prefer project 2 because, if the higher outcome occurs, they will receive £40 000 after paying off debtholders while in project 1 they would receive only £10 000. If the lower outcome occurs in project 2 they would be protected by limited liability from having to contribute to the shortfall due to debtholders while with project 1 the smaller outcome would go totally to the debtholders. It would be particularly difficult if debtholders provided funds in the expectation that project 1 was to be adopted but the firm then undertook project 2 instead. This change would result in a transfer of wealth from debtholders to shareholders. This type of risk shifting, and there are others, explains why debtholders require certain kinds of covenants in debt contracts to protect their position. Agency costs are the cost of writing and enforcing such agreements. An example might be the requirement that dividend payments are limited so that companies cannot pay out excessive dividends, thus diminishing the capital base and increasing the risk of debtholders. Restrictions on the issue of further debt might also be imposed.

Table 13.2

Probability	Project 1	Project 2
0.5	30 000	10 000
0.5	50 000	70 000

Baskin [10] undertook an empirical study in which he regressed the level of gearing against profits. He found that as profits increased the level of gearing declined. The debt-to-equity ratio was inversely related to profits. This is not the finding one would expect if firms had a target debt/equity ratio. If there was a target, as retained profits increased (i.e. equity) one would expect the level of borrowing to increase. Baskin concluded that the empirical evidence is entirely consistent with the prediction of the pecking order hypothesis.

13.8 SUMMARY AND CONCLUSIONS

In this chapter we have examined the effect of gearing on company profitability, cost of capital and value. We began by illustrating the effects of gearing on profit and earnings-per-share calculations, noting that as gearing increased so did volatility of earnings per share. We then moved on to discuss the alternative views on the effect of debt on company value and cost of capital.

The original traditional view seems to be based upon the idea that higher earnings per share could be generated by the use of debt, but this approach seems to ignore risk as the increasing levels of debt add to the variability of earnings.

MM's papers [1, 2] provided an analytical framework for examining the effect of debt on the value of the firm. Their paper on debt and taxes probably overstates the value of the tax shield to most companies. In suggesting that the value of the firm increased by $V_d t$ it was assumed that the benefit of debt was perpetual and that there were no constraints on being able to use the debt tax shield in each and every succeeding future period. In addition, it was assumed that the rate of corporate taxation would remain unchanged. In fact, it is almost certain that the rate of taxation used should be lower than the current rate of corporate taxation, but the estimation of an effective rate of tax to use in the calculation is very difficult.

The tax shield will only have value if there are taxable profits to offset interest payments against. An established firm may feel reasonably confident that it will be able to cover reasonable levels of debt interest; however, smaller firms and firms with a high variability of earnings may find that in some years their taxable profit may not be sufficient to cover debt interest. Clearly, another factor here will be the number of other opportunities available to companies to shield income.

We saw that a further factor limiting the amount of debt taken into the capital structure would be the potential costs of financial distress. The higher these potential costs, the lower the level of debt a firm would be encouraged to take on. The level of these costs could be affected by the type of asset involved, being lower for tangible saleable assets than for intangible unsaleable assets.

The foregoing suggests that large companies using tangible saleable assets and having a low earnings volatility might be expected to have a higher level of debt than a smaller company with intangible assets and a high earnings volatility. These are broad categories, and the main purpose of the examples is to highlight the factors which one would expect to affect debt policy.

A final suggestion was that there might be some pecking order which indicated preferred ways in which directors might seek to finance the companies they manage. Retentions are the favoured form of finance followed by debt and as a last resort new equity issues. Retentions are a convenient form of finance as they allow for planned expansion at a pace with which directors feel comfortable. Use of retentions minimizes issue costs and also allows scope for an emergency issue should one be needed. The pecking order approach avoids potential issues of undervalued shares caused by asymmetric information between directors and shareholders.

13.9 REFERENCES

1 Modigliani, F. and Miller, M.H. (1958) The cost of capital, corporation finance and the theory of investment, *American Economic Review*, **48**: 261–96.
2 Modigliani, F. and Miller, M.H. (1963) Taxes and the cost of capital: a correction, *American Economic Review*, **53**: 433–43.
3 Jensen, M.C. (1989) Eclipse of the public corporation, *Harvard Business Review*, **5**: 61–74.
4 Donaldson, G. (1961) *Corporate Debt Capacity*, Harvard University Press, Cambridge, Mass.
5 Myers, S.C. (1984) The capital structure puzzle, *Journal of Finance*, **39**: 575–92.
6 Donaldson, G. (1971) *Strategy for Financial Mobility*, Irwin, Homewood, Ill.
7 Myers, S. and Majluf, N. (1984) Corporate financing and investment

decisions when firms have information investors do not have, *Journal of Financial Economics*, June, 187–221.

8 Asquith, P. and Mullins, D.W. (1983) The impact of initiating dividend payments on shareholder wealth, *Journal of Business*, **56**: 77–96.

9 Jensen, M.C. and Meckling, W. (1976) Theory of the firm: managerial behaviour, agency costs and ownership structure, *Journal of Financial Economics*, 305–60.

10 Baskin, J.B. (1989) An empirical investigation of the pecking order hypothesis, *Financial Management*, **18**: 26–35.

13.10 FURTHER READING

A suitable starting point is the two MM papers:

Modigliani, F. and Miller, M.H. (1958) The cost of capital, corporation finance and the theory of investment, *American Economic Review*, **48**: 261–96; and (1963) Taxes and the cost of capital: a correction, *American Economic Review*, **53**: 433–43.

Personal as well as corporate taxes are considered in:

Miller, M.H. (1977) Debt and taxes, *Journal of Finance*, **32**: 261–76.

A number of readable papers on contemporary financial issues are contained in Stern and Chew.

Stern, J.M. and Chew, D.H., Jr. (1986) *The Revolution in Corporate Finance*, Basil Blackwell, Oxford.

including:

Myers, S.C. (1984) The capital structure puzzle, *Journal of Finance*, **39**: 575–92.

13.11 PROBLEMS

1 ABC PLC and XYZ PLC are two firms which operate in the same industry and are both considered to be in the same risk class. Both companies have gross operating profit of £100 000 per annum. ABC PLC relies on equity sources in its finance while XYZ PLC uses both loan and equity sources. Their capital structure is as follows

ABC PLC: equity	<u>£700 000</u> (market value)
XYZ PLC: equity	£400 000 (market value)
8% debenture	<u>£400 000</u> (nominal value – currently traded at par)
	<u>£800 000</u>

At the present time you hold 4% of XYZ's share capital. Assume that both companies pay out all their profit after interest in dividends.

(a) Determine the weighted-average cost of capital of both companies; then comment whether these two companies' ordinary shares are in equilibrium or not.

(b) Show how you may gain from arbitrage whilst keeping your current level of finance risk constant. Assume that you can borrow money at an annual interest rate of 8%.

(Ignore taxation.)

2 ABC PLC and XYZ PLC are two companies with identical levels of business risk. The two companies have different capital structures as ABC has an all-

equity capital structure while XYZ is very highly geared. You are given the following information about earnings, dividends, interest payments and market values of both companies:

	ABC PLC Years 1–∞	XYZ PLC Years 1–∞
Annual dividends	£360 000	£200 000
Annual interest	—	£160 000
Total annual cash earnings	£360 000	£360 000
Total market value of equity	£3 600 000	£1 200 000
Total market value of debt	—	£2 000 000
	£3 600 000	£3 200 000

Assume that the capital market is perfect (no taxation, no transaction costs). Assume also that markets for the ordinary shares of ABC PLC and the debentures of XYZ PLC are in equilibrium.

(a) What do you think is the best decision for shareholders in both the companies to make?

(b) Assume that Mr Money holds shares having a market value of £4000 in both of the above companies. Show Mr Money how he can improve his financial position whilst keeping his current level of financial risk unchanged.

(c) Explain how the above is used to confirm the proposal that a company's cost of equity capital in equilibrium can be estimated by the expression

$$K_e = K_0 + (K_0 - K_d)\frac{D}{E}$$

3 The board of directors of Rickery PLC is discussing whether to alter the company's capital structure. Corporate legislation permits Rickery PLC to repurchase its own shares and it is proposed to issue £5 million of new debentures at par, and to use the funds to repurchase ordinary shares.

A summary of Rickery's current balance sheet is shown below:

	£000
Fixed assets (net)	24 500
Current assets	12 300
Current liabilities	(8 600)
	28 200
Financed by:	
25p Ordinary shares	4 500
Reserves	14 325
	18 825
5% Debentures 1997	9 375
	28 200

The company's current ordinary share price is 167p and the debenture price is £80. Rickery's finance director does not expect the market price of the existing ordinary shares or debentures to change as a result of the proposed issue of new debentures. The company expects to pay a premium of 2.5% over the risk-free rate of interest for its new debentures. Rickery's equity beta is estimated by a leading firm of stockbrokers to be 1.24, and the estimated market return is 15%. Debenture interest is payable annually. Issue costs and transactions costs can be ignored.

(a) Evaluate the probable effect on the cost of capital of Rickery PLC if the company restructures its capital:
  (i) if the company pays tax at a rate of 35%;

(ii) if the company does not expect to pay corporate taxes for the foreseeable future.

All the relevant calculations must be shown. State clearly any assumptions that you make. (12 marks)

(b) Rickery's finance director believes that the market price of the company's existing ordinary shares and debentures will not change. Explain why he might be wrong in his belief and suggest what changes might occur.

(8 marks)

(c) What are the arguments for and against the use of book values and market values in establishing a company's target capital structure? (5 marks)

(Total 25 marks)

ACCA, Dec. 1987

4 (a) A colleague has been taken ill. Your managing director has asked you to take over from the colleague and to provide urgently needed estimates of the discount rate to be used in appraising a large new capital investment. You have been given your colleague's working notes, which you believe to be numerically accurate.

Estimates for the next five years (annual averages)

Stock market total return on equity	16%
Own company dividend yield	7%
Own company share price rise	14%
Standard deviation of total stock market return on equity	10%
Standard deviation of own company total return on equity	20%
Correlation coefficient between total own company return on equity and total stock market return on equity	0.7
Correlation coefficient between total return on the new capital investment and total market return on equity	0.5
Growth rate of own company earnings	12%
Growth rate of own company dividends	11%
Growth rate of own company sales	13%
Treasury bill yield	12%

The company's gearing level (by market values) is 1:2 debt to equity, and after-tax earnings available to ordinary shareholders in the most recent year were £5 400 000 of which £2 140 000 was distributed as ordinary dividends. The company has ten million issued ordinary shares which are currently trading on the Stock Exchange at 321p. Corporate debt can be assumed to be risk-free. The company pays tax at 35% and personal taxation can be ignored.

Estimate the company's weighted average cost of capital using

(a) the dividend valuation model

(b) the capital-asset pricing model.

State clearly any assumptions that you make.

Under what circumstances would these models be expected to produce similar values for the weighted-average cost of capital? (10 marks)

ACCA, Dec. 1986

5 (a) Berlan PLC has annual earnings before interest and tax of £15 million. These earnings are expected to remain constant. The market price of the company's ordinary shares is 86 pence per share cum. div. and of debentures £105.50 per debenture ex. interest. An interim dividend of six pence per share has been declared. Corporate tax is at the rate of 35% and all available earnings are distributed as dividends.

Berlan's long-term, capital structure is shown below:

	£000
Ordinary shares (25 pence par value)	12 500
Reserves	24 300
	36 800
16% debenture 31.12.94 (£100 par value)	23 697
	60 497

Required:
Calculate the cost of capital of Berlan PLC according to the traditional theory of capital structure. Assume that it is now 31 December 1991.

(8 marks)

(b) Canalot PLC is an all-equity company with an equilibrium market value of £32.5 million and a cost of capital of 18% per year.

The company proposes to repurchase £5 million of equity and to replace it with 13% irredeemable loan stock.

Canalot's earnings before interest and tax are expected to be constant for the foreseeable future. Corporate tax is at the rate of 35%. All profits are paid out as dividends.

Required:
Using the assumptions of Modigliani and Miller explain and demonstrate how this change in capital structure will affect:

● the market value
● the cost of equity
● the cost of capital

of Canalot PLC. (7 marks)

(c) Explain any weaknesses of both the traditional and Modigliani and Miller theories and discuss how useful they might be in the determination of the appropriate capital structure for a company. (10 marks)

(25 marks)

ACCA, Dec. 1991

6 The government has just announced that corporation tax is being reduced from 33% per year to 30% per year and the directors of Varis PLC wish to know the likely effect of this change on the company's share price and cost of capital.

The company's current capital structure is

	£m
Ordinary shares (50 pence par value)	30
Share premium	48
Other reserves	62
Shareholders' equity	140
10% debenture (irredeemable)	40
	180

The company's shares are trading at 320 pence ex-div, and the debentures at £125 ex interest.

Prior to the tax change Varis's beta equity was 1.2. The market return is 13% per year. The tax cut itself is expected to increase the net present value of Varis's operating cash flows by £15 million.

Assume that the cost of debt and market price of debt do not change as a result of this tax change. Ignore advance corporation tax.

Varis's debt may be assumed to be risk free.

Required:

(a) Estimate the company's current cost of capital. (5 marks)

(b) Using Modigliani and Miller's theory of capital structure (with tax) estimate:

    (i) the expected share price after the tax change; (3 marks)

    (ii) the company's expected cost of capital after the tax change. (6 marks)

(c) Explain the reasons for the difference between the old and new cost of capital. (3 marks)

(d) Briefly discuss

    (i) the main limitations of this analysis; (5 marks)

    (ii) the importance in investment decisions of accurate estimates of the cost of capital. (3 marks)

(25 marks)

ACCA, Dec. 1993

14 DISTRIBUTION POLICY

LEARNING OUTCOMES

By the end of this chapter the reader should:

- be able to explain the nature and significance of a company's dividend policy
- understand and be able to distinguish between alternative views on the significance of dividends to shareholders
- know the significance of tax and tax systems to the dividend decision
- be able to explain the factors affecting dividend payments in practice
- understand share re-purchase strategies and scrip dividends

14.1 INTRODUCTION

This chapter deals with the distributions made by companies to ordinary shareholders. Although much of the discussion covers cash dividend payments other strategies exist, the current most significant one being share repurchase and this is also dealt with in this chapter.

Unlike preference shares and other forms of capital, ordinary shares carry no specific dividend rights. The payment of ordinary dividends is a matter of company policy and depends upon such factors as the availability of distributable profits, the liquidity of the company and the existence of profitable investment opportunities to the company.

The proportion of profits paid out as dividends can vary considerably from one company to another. At first sight it might appear that the highest dividend possible would be best for shareholders, particularly as valuation models of equity are often based on the present value of future dividends. However, it is the pattern of dividends over time which creates the highest present value which maximizes shareholder wealth; if the payment of a high dividend in the current year means that investment must be forgone in a profitable project, then a low or even zero dividend might be preferable. Other factors which could affect dividend payments are taxation, both personal and corporate, and the way in which dividends may be used as providers of information in uncertain conditions.

The value of dividend payments to shareholders continues to provoke lively discussion and controversy. Initially there was a reasonable degree of acceptance among finance practitioners and academics that high dividends increased shareholder wealth but other persuasive views have been advanced. Miller and Modigliani (MM) [1] suggested that dividend payments were value-neutral and irrelevant to shareholder value while another school of thought advanced the view that dividends reduce shareholder wealth because dividend income was taxed more highly than equivalent capital gains. We will discuss these views in the context of current market conditions and tax legislation.

14.2 DIVIDEND IRRELEVANCY IN PERFECT CAPITAL MARKETS

MM began by examining the effects of differences in dividend policy on the current price of shares in an ideal economy characterized by perfect capital markets, rational behaviour and perfect certainty. Under such a set of restrictive conditions they concluded that dividend policy was irrelevant in that the share price was independent of the particular policy followed.

The rationale behind the MM theorem is that it is the value created by the company which is important rather than how this value is packaged between dividends and retentions with the latter being reflected in share price. Given the perfect world that is assumed, higher dividends will be reflected in a lower share price and a need to replace cash by a new issue of shares. Thus any change in dividend payment will lead to an equal and opposite change in the amount of money raised from new issues. Suppose that a company is currently valued at £1 million and has in issue 1 million shares valued at £1 each. Further suppose that the company's current income exactly covers its investment requirement. Any dividend to be paid by the company will have to be met by a new issue of equity.

Let us examine the implications of the company's paying a dividend of 20p per share:

	Company	Individual share
Current value	1 000 000	1.00
Less: Dividend payment	200 000	20
	800 000	80p
New issue	200 000	
	£1 000 000	

Simultaneously with the payment of the dividend a new issue will be made of 200 000/0.80 = 250 000 shares, i.e. to raise £200 000 the company will have to issue 250 000 shares priced at 80p per share, which is the value of shares after allowing for the dividend payment to 'old' shareholders. The value of the company after dividend payment and new issue remains at £1 million; there are now 1 250 000 shares in issue valued at 80p per share. 'Old' shareholders have received a cash dividend of 20p per share and their shares have declined in value from £1 to 80p; their total wealth is unaltered. 'New' shareholders have purchased shares at a price which reflects the true value of the company.

If the company did not pay a dividend, existing shareholders could 'manufacture' their own dividend by selling some of their shares on the market to new shareholders (Table 14.1). A holder of 100 shares would need to sell 20 shares at £1 each to obtain the cash equivalent of a dividend of 20p per share. The shareholder would be left with 80 shares valued at £1 plus £20 cash. This would be the same position as if a dividend had been paid, except that in that case the residual holding would be 100 shares at 80p. This result relies entirely on the assumptions set out in detail at the beginning of this section. Perfect capital markets are necessary so that costless transactions can be undertaken at correct prices; the prices in turn reflect the perfect certainty enjoyed by all participants in the market with investors indifferent between dividends and capital gains.

Given the assumptions there is now almost complete agreement that MM are

Distribution policy

correct, and in recent years the dividend issue has concentrated on imperfections in their assumptions. In particular, the existence of taxes, both corporate and personal, needs to be considered as does the absence of certainty about the future. Both these factors are discussed in later sections, beginning with the traditional view of dividends which regarded them as more valuable than the equivalent retention partly because they were regarded as less risky and resolved, to some extent, uncertainty about the future.

Table 14.1

	Holder of 100 shares, cash dividend		'Homemade' dividend by selling through market
Value prior to dividend/sale	100		100
Cash dividend at 20p per share	20	Sale of 20 shares at £1	20
Residual value	80		80

14.3 DIVIDEND PAYMENTS MAY INCREASE SHAREHOLDER WEALTH

The irrelevancy conclusions of MM challenged the conventional wisdom of the time. Up to that point there had been almost complete agreement by both finance theorists and corporate managers that investors preferred dividends to capital gains and that companies could increase or at least maintain the market value of their shares by choosing a generous dividend payout policy. The popular view was that dividends represented a more certain form of income than equivalent capital gains and that therefore they would be valued more highly than the equivalent amount of uncertain and riskier capital gains.

This view was summarized by Graham and Dodd [2] in their now classic text on security analysis when they wrote:

> the considered and continuous verdict of the stock market is overwhelmingly in favor of liberal dividends as opposed to niggardly ones. The common stock investor must take this judgment into account in the valuation of stock for purchase. It is now becoming a standard practice to evaluate common stock by applying one multiplier to that proportion of the earnings paid out in dividends and a much smaller multiplier to the undistributed balance.

Support for the 'bird-in-hand' argument came from Myron Gordon [3] who argued that investors will apply a lower rate of discount to the expected stream of future dividends than the more distant capital gains. This view is encapsulated in the Gordon valuation model which places higher values on securities offering higher dividend growth.

The belief in the importance of dividend policy seems to be reinforced by the actions of business-people, investors and government. Company directors, as we shall see later, seem to regard dividend payments as important. Shareholders and their advisers frequently seek to persuade directors to increase dividend payments.

It might appear initially that Gordon's argument demands support and that MM chose to ignore the differential risks of dividends and capital gains. However, the MM analysis stressed that provided that the investment policy could be taken as given, then any change in dividend policy had to be reflected by an equal change in the amount of fresh equity raised by the company. Thus any increase in dividend payment would be reflected by an equal additional issue of equity. If existing shareholders were to gain by an increase in dividend payment, then new shareholders would have to be persuaded to take on additional risk without receiving full recompense for it. There would thus be a transfer of risk from existing to new shareholders. This intuitive approach suggests that risk is not related to whether return is received in the form of dividend or capital gain but depends crucially on the type of activity being undertaken by the company, i.e. the rate of return which shareholders expect depends not on the form in which increases in wealth accrue but on the risk of the investment activities undertaken by companies. This approach was stressed in the earlier chapters on risk in project appraisal.

There is wide acceptance for MM's conclusion of dividend irrelevancy given their assumption of perfect and efficient capital markets. However, there would again be agreement that in the real world their model would be deficient. In fact, the extent of this deficiency would vary according to the country examined. In the UK and the USA markets are widely accepted as efficient if not perfect, but in other countries around the world the degree of efficiency has often been considered to be at a lower level than in the more sophisticated markets of the UK and the USA. The dividend debate can therefore be considered in terms of both market imperfections and inefficiencies or, as has been suggested by at least one author, in terms of whether shareholders are fully rational.

There may be natural clienteles for both high- and low-payout stocks. For example, tax-exempt investors, trust funds, because of the way in which income is defined, and retired investors looking for income to live on, all prefer companies with high-payout policies. It could be argued that if investors require cash then this could be obtained by selling securities in line with the MM argument. However, it is both more convenient and less costly (because of transaction costs) for companies to pay higher dividends to those shareholders requiring them. It has also been argued in the past that a clientele exists for low-payout shares and that younger investors paying higher marginal rates of income tax might prefer to have lower dividends and higher capital gains. The existence of clienteles was acknowledged by MM who suggested that shareholders would be attracted to the policy which best suited them and that there would be sufficient companies with different policies to satisfy all clienteles. In the circumstances no company could increase its value by changing its policy.

The role of dividends in conveying information has been noted by a number of writers [4]. In this context a change in the level of dividend payment is regarded as conveying information on how company directors view future prospects. An increase in dividend would be regarded as conveying optimism about future profitability, while a decline in dividend would signify pessimism about the future.

14.4 DIVIDEND PAYMENTS MAY REDUCE SHAREHOLDER WEALTH

This view was developed mainly in the USA [5] and concerned the different tax treatment of dividends and capital gains. In many countries capital gains have or continue to be taxed at lower rates than dividend income. It has therefore been claimed that in these circumstances shareholders would be better off with lower dividends, thus receiving more of their return in the form of capital gains. In order to evaluate this point of view it is necessary to evaluate more fully the impact of taxation on dividend policy.

14.5 DIVIDEND PAYMENTS AND TAXATION

In the UK companies are taxed under an imputation system of corporation tax. A progressive system of personal income tax is in force with the first £4100 of tax-

Distribution policy

able income being assessed at 20%, the next £22 000 at 23% and the balance at 40%. This is in fact much less progressive than at times in the past when it was possible for very rich people to pay over 90% on marginal income. Capital gains are now taxed at the taxpayer's marginal income tax rate, whereas prior to the Finance Act 1988 they were taxed at a proportional rate which was often lower than the taxpayer's marginal income tax rate. One advantage of capital gains which still continues is that they are taxed only on realization, i.e. sale of the security. Thus, deferring taking a profit defers the payment of capital gains tax and additionally capital losses can be offset against gains; there is also an exemption limit of the first £6500 realized in any year. The major difference in the USA is that there is a classical system of corporate taxation which was in fact the system operative in the UK up until 1973. The development of personal taxation in the USA has followed similar lines to that in the UK, so that the distinction between the taxation of dividends and capital gains is much less pronounced.

The main difference between the two systems of corporation tax can be illustrated using a numerical example:

	Classical system	Imputation system
	£000	£000
Profit before corporation tax	5000	5000
Less: corporation tax at 33%	1650	1650
	3350	3350
Less: dividend	1000	800
	2350	2550

(assuming ACT of $\frac{20}{80}$ under imputation system)

Under the classical system there is no connection between the corporate and personal systems. The payment of the dividend would be regarded as gross income for tax purposes and subject to income tax at the shareholder's marginal tax rates. However, under the imputation system the dividend paid has a tax credit attaching to it of $\frac{20}{80}$ ($\frac{1}{4}$) of the cash payment. If the receiving shareholder does not pay tax in the 40% tax band no further tax will be payable. However, if tax is payable at this higher rate a further 20% becomes payable; for example, a higher-rate taxpayer receiving cash dividends of £800 would be assessed on £1000 dividend income, £800 plus tax credit of £200 ($\frac{1}{4}$ × £800). The tax liability would be:

£1000 at 40%	400
Less: imputed tax credit	200
Additional tax payable	£200

Until July 1997 if shareholders did not pay tax then a refund equivalent to the tax credit could be reclaimed from the Inland Revenue. Thus, tax-exempt pension funds receiving cash dividends of £800 could reclaim the tax credit of £200, giving a total benefit of £1000. However, in the first budget presented by Chancellor Gordon Brown it was announced that pension funds would no longer be able to claim refunds of the tax credits attaching to dividend payments. Although for the moment individual taxpayers can continue to claim refunds this signalled a new attitude and, given the significance of pension-fund investors in the equity market, could lead to a change in attitude towards dividend policy in the United Kingdom.

The UK tax regulations require companies to pay over advance corporation tax (ACT) when making distributions (including dividends). These payments of ACT can be offset against future payments of mainstream corporation tax. The imputation system thus links together the corporate and personal systems.

However, the UK government announced in November 1997 that ACT would be abolished from 6 April 1999. From this date a lower, non-refundable, tax credit of one-ninth of the dividend will attach to dividends paid by companies. No further tax will be paid by basic rate taxpayers but higher rate tax payers will pay 25% of the cash dividend received.

14.6 PRACTICAL ISSUES IN DIVIDEND POLICY

Dividend payments

UK companies have normally declared and paid two dividends in respect of each financial year. An interim dividend is paid during the financial year and is normally the smaller of the two. At the end of the financial year it is usual for a final dividend to be recommended which will be included in the annual accounts as a provision. While a board of directors is empowered to declare and pay interim dividends, shareholders' approval must be obtained at the annual general meeting before payment of the final dividend. With the growing international nature of financial markets some large UK companies are now moving to the US system of quarterly dividend payments, but this is likely to affect only a comparatively small number of companies.

Distributable profits

The Companies Act 1985 requires that dividends only be paid out of accumulated net realized profits. This includes the realized profits for both the current year and previous years. Essentially profits calculated in accordance with generally accepted accounting principles will be regarded as realized profits. Profits available for distribution are calculated after deducting any accumulated realized losses from previous years. In addition, for public companies a distribution may only be made to the extent that accumulated distributable profits exceed net unrealized losses.

Liquidity

The distinction between profits and cash has been stressed in an earlier chapter. Because a company is showing a high level of profitability it does not necessarily mean that the company will have large amounts of cash at its disposal. It is frequently the most profitable rapidly expanding companies which are most pressed for liquid funds. In order to pay a dividend a company clearly requires cash, and therefore the availability of cash resources within the company will be a factor in determining dividend payments. It could be argued from a theoretical point of view that provided that the company is profitable it will be able to borrow in capital markets to enable it to pay whatever rate of dividend it wishes. However, for a variety of reasons the directors may not wish to adopt such a strategy and prefer to meet any dividend payments from the company's current resources.

Current debt obligations

The company may already have debt obligations which require repayment. It may intend to replace current debt with another security issue on maturity or alternatively may be setting aside amounts to a sinking fund to fund repayment on maturity. If the company's policy is to repay the debt by transferring amounts to a sinking fund this will usually require a higher level of earnings to be retained.

When making existing borrowings the company may have had to make covenants with regard to the level of cash dividends paid to ordinary shareholders. A covenant of this kind is designed to protect the lender and may limit the level of payments, define the earnings from which dividend payments can be made, or require certain liquidity ratios to be maintained at certain minimum levels.

Investment opportunities

Growth companies faced with many investment opportunities may prefer to finance their expansion by retaining a large proportion of profits. The alternative would be higher levels of dividend payments followed by rights issues to shareholders. As an expanding company is likely to require a regular flow of new money for projects, it is likely that a low dividend payout policy will be adopted by smaller rapidly expanding companies. There is the additional point that smaller companies are likely to find it costly and difficult to raise funds from outside the company in the form of either debt or equity, while larger well-established companies with a longer track record are likely to find it easier to gain access to capital markets.

Volatility

Shareholders do not like unpleasant surprises. (Of course, like everyone else they just love pleasant surprises!) Company directors are therefore wary about setting a level of dividend payment which they think may in some circumstances be unsustainable. A company with relatively stable earnings will therefore be more likely to adopt a higher payout policy than a company with a volatile pattern of earnings.

Control

The control of a company is determined by the ownership of the ordinary share capital. The way in which a company chooses to finance its activities may have an impact on the control of the company. If shares have to be sold to new shareholders outside the present group of shareholders then this could lead to dilution of control within the company. It is also possible that high levels of debt may also restrict the freedom of activity of the owners of the company with regard to certain policies. These may be additional reasons to encourage particularly smaller companies to adopt a lower payout policy.

Taxation

The potential effect of taxation on dividend payments has been discussed in a previous section. The current UK position has been complicated by the proposed abolition of ACT. Although for the immediate future no extra income tax will be paid by individuals, as the effective rate of capital gains tax is likely to be below the shareholders' marginal tax rate, some shareholders may prefer capital gains to dividends. More recently the removal of the right of pension funds to reclaim tax on dividends paid to them, coupled with the phasing out of foreign-income dividends, has further muddied the waters surrounding dividend payments. Different groups of shareholders may prefer different dividend policies depending on their rates of taxation, and it is the directors of companies who will have to resolve any potential conflicts of interest which arise. To some extent there may be a 'clientele effect' whereby shareholders with low tax rates are attracted to high-payout companies and shareholders with high tax rates are attracted to low-payout companies. However, the effectiveness of a clientele policy will to some extent be determined by portfolio considerations.

14.7 SHARE REPURCHASE AND SCRIP DIVIDENDS

In addition to the payment of cash dividends to shareholders other strategies available include scrip dividends and share repurchase. Both of these were introduced in Chapter 5 on equity capital. A scrip dividend is a small scrip or bonus issue which capitalizes distributable profits in the form of extra shares, leaving it to the shareholder to decide on whether to keep the extra shares or sell on the market for cash. Prior to 1965 scrip dividends were not treated as income and thus there were tax advantages for shareholders in this form of issue. Shareholders accepting extra shares instead of a cash dividend are normally treated as receiving a dividend equal to the cash that could have been taken. Tax is deemed to have been paid at the basic rate. If the value of the shares taken as stock dividend differs from the cash dividend by 15% or more the shareholder is deemed to have received a dividend equal to the value of the shares at the date of issue. Therefore enhanced scrip dividends, provided the enhancement is below 15% of the cash dividend, will not give rise to any additional income tax liabilities. This will be most beneficial and therefore attractive to higher-rate taxpayers.

Another possible strategy arises from the ability of companies to repurchase their own shares following the provisions included in the 1981 Companies Act. This option has long been permissible and widely practised in the USA and it is gaining increasing significance in the UK as company managements recognize its potential in an integrated financial strategy. The discussion which follows concentrates on share repurchase by quoted companies.

A number of reasons have been suggested for share repurchases, including the following:

1 return of surplus cash to shareholders;
2 increase of earnings per share (EPS) and hence share price;
3 buyout of large holdings of unwelcome shareholders;
4 achievement of desired capital structure.

In the first case, share repurchase can be seen as an alternative to a higher dividend payment or leaving the cash on deposit. Share repurchase may involve higher transaction costs than dividend payments but may be more flexible in that there are different methods of repurchase which may not involve all shareholders and which allow choice to be influenced by tax implications which may be significant.

Share price could be improved over time if company management had access to positive information unknown to the market. However, this would effectively be insider trading and could benefit remaining shareholders at the expense of those bought out. The EPS advantage is debatable in that it is an accounting measure and not necessarily related to any increase in the value of the company. It has been suggested that 'the EPS benefits of share re-purchases are minimal for most companies' [6].

Share repurchase of large holdings has taken place in the USA to ward off unwanted takeover threats (so-called greenmail). However, this type of activity is to be discouraged rather than encouraged as it tends to promote speculative activity by arbitrageurs taking positions in companies in the hope of being bought out by management at an enhanced price. A UK example of a large share repurchase was the 1989 purchase by BP of 790 million shares built up by the Kuwait Investment Office, a move forced on BP by the UK government.

In 1994 many of the electricity distribution companies took powers to buy back substantial amounts of shares. These companies generate substantial cash flows from their trading activities but a contributory factor may have been the large cash mountain caused by consumers prepaying electricity bills in March 1994 to avoid value added tax levied on payments from 1 April 1994 onwards. The companies therefore had substantial cash resources surplus to immediate requirements and likely to increase from normal trading activities. With short-term interest rates low and managers confident about the future of their companies, share repurchase could be argued to be the best use for these surplus funds.

The ability to adjust capital structure through share repurchase gives management an additional way of increasing the proportion of debt in the capital structure (gearing). The alternative would be to take on extra borrowing.

Of great importance to listed companies contemplating share repurchases are the regulation and tax consequences of such transactions. Regulations are necessary to ensure that creditors and remaining shareholders are not disadvantaged by share repurchases with which they may not be directly involved. Tax laws have sought to maintain treatment consistent with cash dividend payments. UK quoted companies can repurchase shares in three ways:

1   purchase in the stock market;
2   arrangements with individual shareholders;
3   tender offers to all shareholders.

Prior permission must be obtained for any repurchase from shareholders and holders of any warrants, options or convertibles. Prior clearance is also necessary from the Takeover Panel. Payments for repurchased shares must be made from distributable profits and all repurchased shares must be cancelled.

14.8 EVIDENCE ON DIVIDEND PAYMENTS

Lintner [7] conducted interviews with 28 companies to investigate how they determined dividend policy. The work carried out by him suggested the following.

1   Managers concern themselves with change in the existing dividend payout rate rather than the amount of the newly established payout as such.
2   Most management sought to avoid making changes in dividend rates that might have to be reversed within a year or two.
3   Major changes in earnings were the most important determinants of the companies' dividend decisions.
4   Investment requirements generally had little effect on changing the pattern of dividend behaviour.

Lintner's findings suggest that the US company management interviewed at the time regarded dividends as an important decision, that dividends were paid irrespective of forecast levels of investment and that management were reluctant to increase dividends uuless they were reasonably sure that they would be able to maintain the higher level of payment permanently. Lintner developed a simple explanatory model consistent with the findings outlined above:

$$D_t - D_{t-1} = C(BE_1 - D_{t-1})$$

where D_t and D_{t-1} are the dividends payable in the years signified by the subscripts, C is the rate of adjustment adopted by the company, B is the target payout ratio and E_1 is the earnings per share for that year. The equation states that companies will adjust their dividend payout gradually as earnings change rather than by immediately increasing their dividend by the percentage increase in earnings. The more conservative the company, the more slowly would the adjustment take place and therefore the lower would be the adjustment rate C. Fama and Babiak [8] investigated a number of different models for explaining dividend behaviour. Of the many models used, Lintner's proved to be one of the two best.

The conclusion is that the US corporations examined increased dividends only after they were reasonably sure that they would be able to maintain them permanently at the new level. The research suggests that not only do company directors think that dividends are important but they recognize that market participants also regard them as being important and are therefore anxious not to convey bad information by having to alter the trend of dividends once they have been established.

More recent work undertaken by Farrelly et al. [9] has expanded and updated Lintner's study. A questionnaire mailed to 562 firms listed on the New York Stock Exchange yielded 318 responses. The views obtained were supportive of Lintner's earlier findings and indicated that managers believe that dividend policy is relevant and influences the value of share prices.

14.9 SUMMARY AND CONCLUSIONS

Research and behaviour indicate that market participants consider dividends to be important. Lintner's study suggested that company managers considered decisions on dividends to be important and there seems no reason to change this view. Managers seek to smooth dividend payments from year to year by only adjusting gradually to changes in earnings. Unexpected fluctuations are avoided wherever possible because of the potentially adverse information that might be conveyed, leading to uncertainty and a volatile share price.

MM demonstrated that in perfect capital markets dividend payments were irrelevant to shareholder wealth; however, when imperfections are considered the position is less clear-cut. Taxation, corporate and personal, can make a difference.

A consistent dividend policy does not mean that all companies will have similar payout ratios. Expanding companies with many investment opportunities are likely to pay out a lower proportion of earnings than companies with few or perhaps no investment opportunities. Retentions are a favoured source of finance for new investment, and company directors will try and adopt a dividend policy which satisfies shareholders yet at the same time leaves sufficient retentions for investment purposes.

Investors in small high-growth companies will usually expect a low-dividend policy and be prepared to sacrifice current income for the prospect of higher capital gains in the future. In time, growth will tend to level off, perhaps because of competition, and a higher payout policy might then be adopted. Investors are unlikely to complain if a previous high-growth low-payout company subsequently increases its dividend payout; however, if a previous high-payout company changed policy and decided to cut dividends, perhaps to reduce borrowing or to obviate the need for an equity rights issue, shareholders might not necessarily agree. Any change of this sort would need careful preparation and explanation to major shareholders to avoid potential adverse effects on share price.

14.10 REFERENCES

1   Miller, M.H. and Modigliani, F. (1961) Dividend policy, growth and the valuation of shares, *Journal of Business*, **34**: 411–33, October.

2   Graham, B. and Dodd, D.L. (1951) *Security Analysis: Principles and Techniques*, 3rd edn, McGraw-Hill, New York.
3   Gordon, M.J. (1959) Dividends, earnings and stock prices, *Review of Economics and Statistics*, **41**: 99–105, May.
4   Hakansson, N. (1982) To pay or not to pay dividends, *Journal of Finance*, 415–28, May.
5   Miller, M. and Scholes, M. (1978) Dividends and taxes, *Journal of Financial Economics*, 333–64, December.
6   Dodd, J. (1989) Does share repurchase boost EPS? *Professional Investor*, November.
7   Lintner, J. (1956) Distribution of incomes of corporations among dividends, retained earnings and taxes, *American Economic Review*, 97–113, May.
8   Fama, E.F. and Babiak, H. (1968) Dividend policy: an empirical analysis, *Journal of the American Statistical Association*, 1132–61, December.
9   Farrelly, G.E., Baker, H.K. and Edelman, R.B. (1986) Corporate dividends: views of the policy-makers, *Akron Business and Economic Review*, 62–74, Winter.

14.11 FURTHER READING

An analysis of the effects of corporate and personal taxes on dividends (and financing) is given by King. A number of readable and up-to-date articles, particularly those by Miller and Brealey, are contained in Stern and Chew. The rationale for share repurchases and the legal and taxation framework are discussed in a Bank of England publication.

The original analysis of dividend policy in a perfect capital market is contained in:

Miller, M.H. and Modigliani, F. (1961) Dividend policy, growth and the valuation of shares, *Journal of Business*, **34**: 411–33, October.

The traditional view on the value of dividends is put in:

Bank of England (1988) Share repurchase by quoted companies, *Bank of England Quarterly Bulletin*, August.
Brealey, R.H. (1986) Does dividend policy matter? In *The Revolution in Corporate Finance* (eds J.M. Stern and D.H. Chew Jr), Basil Blackwell, Oxford.
Gordon, M.J. (1959) Dividends, earnings and stock prices, *Review of Economics and Statistics*, **41**: 99–105, May.
King, M. (1977) *Public Policy and the Corporation*, Chapman and Hall, London.
Miller, M.H. (1986) Can management use dividends to influence the value of the firm? In *The Revolution in Corporate Finance* (eds J.M. Stern and D.H. Chew Jr), Basil Blackwell, Oxford.
Stern, J.M. and Chew, D.H., Jr. (eds) (1986) *The Revolution in Corporate Finance*, Basil Blackwell, Oxford.

For an analysis of how companies set dividend payments see:

Lintner, J. (1956) Distribution of incomes of corporations among dividends, retained earnings and taxes, *American Economic Review*, **46**: 97–113, May.

1 Over the past decade Radnor PLC has achieved an average annual growth in dividends of approximately 7% and is about to declare a dividend 8% higher than that paid last year. This level is consistent with expectations contained in recent press comment. However, Radnor is offered an opportunity to invest in a project which promises a discounted cash-flow return considerably above the weighted-average cost of capital but which will produce no significant cash flows for about three years. The only funds available are those which would otherwise be used for the dividend, and undertaking the project would entail not paying a dividend at all this year. The managing director is of the opinion that shareholders deserve some reward and suggests that if the dividend is passed (i.e. not paid this year) the company should make a bonus issue of shares to give shareholders 'a dividend of a capital nature'.

   Advise Radnor on the major theoretical and practical factors to be considered before arriving at a decision concerning undertaking the project or paying a dividend. Comment on the managing director's suggestion for rewarding shareholders.   (20 marks)

   (Chartered Association of Certified Accountants, Dec. 1982)

2 The chairman of the board of Oak Tree Ltd has announced that the company will change its dividend policy from paying a target proportion of 'normalized' earnings per share. Instead, dividends will be paid out as a residual, i.e. any cash flows left over after the firm has undertaken all profitable investments will be paid out to shareholders. In view of the increased variability of dividends to be paid in future years analyse the possible effects of the change in policy on the value of the firm. Your analysis should contain reference to both the certainty and uncertainty cases.

3 'Dividend policy is irrelevant.' Discuss this statement, paying particular attention to the assumptions required to support it.

4 XYZ Ltd have just paid a dividend of £0.20 per share. The market expects this dividend to grow constantly in each future year at the rate of 6% per annum. The cost of capital for XYZ Ltd is currently 8%. As soon as the dividend was paid, however, the board of XYZ Ltd decided to finance a new project by retaining the next three annual dividend payments. The project is seen by the market to be of the same risk quality as the existing projects and it is expected that the dividend declared at the end of the fourth year from now will be £0.25 per share and will grow at the rate of 7% per annum from then on. You hold 1000 shares in XYZ Ltd and your personal circumstances require that you receive at least £200 each year from this investment.

   (a) Assuming that there is a perfect market in XYZ Ltd's shares and that the market uses a dividend valuation model, show how the market value of its shares has been affected by the board's decision.

   (b) Show how you can still achieve your desired consumption pattern in the first three years while improving your expected dividend stream from then on.

5 About nine years ago Haaste PLC, a large and old-established firm, ceased paying dividends because of its poor financial performance and mounting losses. Following considerable reorganization and investment the firm is now an efficient, profitable and soundly managed organization. Consideration is being given to recommencing the payment of dividends, but when initially discussed at board level there was no agreement on the merits of this step. Three main views were expressed:

- a stable dividend policy should be introduced as soon as possible;
- dividends are irrelevant to shareholders;
- dividends should be paid only when the firm has no investment opportunities which promise a return equal to or greater than that required by shareholders; this situation is unlikely to arise for several years.

(a) Outline, and explain the importance of, the main points which should be considered when deciding upon corporate dividend policy. Comment on the three main views expressed by Haaste's board. (15 marks)

(b) It is proposed that there be a change in taxation to a system which penalizes corporate retained earnings and favours distribution of profits, thereby effectively forcing all companies to distribute all earnings. Examine the implications of such a change from the viewpoint of (i) corporate financial management, (ii) shareholders and (iii) the workings of the financial system and financial institutions. (10 marks)

(Total 25 marks)

(Chartered Association of Certified Accountants, Financial Management, June 1984)

6 In the past when governments have enacted incomes policies they have invariably also restricted the level of dividend increases that companies can make. The argument has been that it is only fair that the 'wages of investors' (dividends) should be under the same restraint as wages paid to work-people. Discuss the reasoning behind the dividend restraint policy and comment on its scope for providing equity with an incomes policy.

7 Supporters of dividends as enhancers of shareholder wealth have supported their view by pointing out that shares with high dividend yields tend to have above-average price-to-earnings ratios. Discuss the validity of this evidence.

8 Many quoted companies with small capitalization value either pay no dividends at all or have very low payout policies. Discuss why this might be and whether this policy could be expected to continue.

9 UK companies, like their US counterparts, can now use share repurchase as part of their financial strategy. One motivation suggested for share repurchase is to increase earnings per share. Consider the following information relating to a company:

Profit after tax	£5 million
Number of shares in issue	10 million
Earnings per share	50p
Share price	£6
Price-to-earnings ratio	12

Suppose that the company repurchases 2 million shares at £6 per share. The number of shares in issue will now be 8 million and the earnings per share will increase to 62.5p; if the price-to-earnings ratio remains at 12, the share price will rise to £7.50. Discuss this analysis and the general view expressed that share repurchase can boost earnings per share.

15 FINANCIAL PLANNING

By the time the reader has studied this chapter they should:

- have a basic understanding of the role of strategic planning in a business (this is a big subject and this chapter can do no more than act as an introduction)
- know how to plan for long-term and short-term financial needs
- be able to calculate the working capital requirements of a business
- appreciate the differing needs for finance during the operating cycles and the life cycles of a firm

15.1 STRATEGIC PLANNING

It is now quite common for companies and other organizations to produce mission statements, which they often publish. A mission statement shows a company's objectives.

Long-term strategic planning attempts to ensure that the company meets these objectives. There is a vast and growing literature on the subject of strategic planning, which basically involves studying the strengths and weaknesses of the company and ascertaining the company's position within a particular market and industry. When the opportunities and dangers have been explicitly identified strategies are developed to achieve the objectives.

There are three inputs required in the planning exercise:

- the objectives of the company;
- the characteristics of the industry and markets in which the company is engaged;
- the strengths and weaknesses of the company.

Objectives

The company's objectives can be expressed in financial terms or in 'grander terms'. The mission statements of some companies are expressed in terms of contributing to society's well-being. If a company wishes to publish a mission statement it is for a purpose and these grand objectives are presumably to show the company in a good light – to show that the company is not just there to make profits.

For many companies the main objective is simply to survive, although it would not be written in such terms in a published mission statement. Most businesses give as key objectives the wish to achieve a certain rate of return on investments and to grow at a certain rate. Smaller companies may have objectives such as to achieve a stock market listing. There can of course be all sorts of sub-objectives, such as to achieve a certain market share or to introduce new products or to improve the levels of service offered to customers, or to improve the management of the company.

Industry and market analysis

The planning exercise involves studying the strengths and weaknesses of the company relative to competitor companies engaged in the same industry or industries. The position of suppliers has to be considered. What changes are taking place in supplier businesses? What is the relative bargaining strength of the supplier companies in relation to one's own company?

The requirements of customers in terms of quality requirements, service and price need to be researched. Any changes in customer tastes has to be carefully monitored, as do technological developments and possible new products.

It would not hurt a planning department to study the literature on company failure. There are certain reasons why companies fail, which are discussed later in this book. Failure after failure can be blamed on the same few causes. It is possible for companies to avoid some of these pitfalls if they plan ahead. Obvious problems arise if companies ignore changes in technology in their industry and ignore changes in taste and needs in the markets in which they sell.

Company analysis

When researching what is happening in the industry and markets around the company it is also important to analyse the strengths and weaknesses of one's own company. It is the opportunity for competitive advantage that the planner wishes to identify. Of course, equally important, as mentioned above, is competitive disadvantage. The issues to be considered would include:

- technology;
- distribution channels;
- access to raw materials;
- management structure and succession.

Strategy

Having determined the company's objectives, and analysed its strengths and weaknesses, the next step is to develop strategies to achieve these objectives. Broad strategies could include:

- reducing the range of products or markets in which the company operates;
- expanding into new markets;
- reducing costs so as to achieve a price advantage over competitors;
- a marketing campaign to differentiate the company's products from competitors';
- increasing research and development expenditure to obtain a technological advantage;
- trying to improve market share through acquisition.

Planning

Once a strategy has been agreed it will be written into a plan. This will involve forecasting the company's performance over the medium and long term (Figure 15.1).

Strategies are written into plans and an important element of any plan will be the financial plan. There will be sales plans and production plans, but in this book we are concerned only with the financial plans.

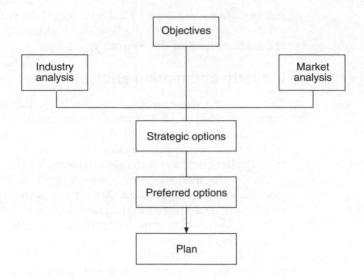

Figure 15.1
The strategic
planning process

15.2 LONG-TERM AND MEDIUM-TERM FINANCIAL PLANNING

Management consists of three types of operations: planning, decision making and control. Planning is concerned with exploring alternative future situations or outcomes and the course of action or sequence of management actions necessary to attain the outcomes. Decision making refers to the selection of one course of action from the candidate set of conceivable courses of action. Such a decision can only be taken rationally if there is an explicitly stated objective on the basis of which the outcomes can be compared. The complexity of decision making in the financial area is such that a planning model will often prove useful in appraising the relative merits of different outcomes.

Broadly speaking, the role of financial management in a firm concerns the prudent administration of the flow of funds through the firm. This includes the determination of what constitutes desirable present and future utilization of funds and determining the most advantageous present and future sources of funding. Fund utilization is conveniently classified into investment in fixed assets (capital budgeting) and in working capital. Fund generation can of course be achieved either by internal means through revenues raised or by external means. The capital structure decision on externally raised finance, i.e. the optimal proportions of equity and debt components, constitutes the principal financing decision of the firm. Allied closely to that decision is the determination of dividend policy – assessing the required dividend for distribution to equity shareholders.

But the financing and investment decisions need to be taken in accordance with the firm's financial objective. Thus a policy statement on financial objectives is of paramount importance.

Financial planning involves the following:

1   determining the company's financial goals;
2   forecasting certain key variables;
3   analysing the choices open to the company in terms of investment opportunities and finance available;
4   comparing the projected outcomes under the different opportunities available;
5   deciding what action needs to be taken;
6   comparing subsequent performance against the plan.

Financial planning can be divided into the following:

1 medium- to long-term planning;
2 short-term planning including cash budgets.

The medium- to longer-term aspects of financial planning which involve answering questions such as the following.

1 When should a new issue of equity shares be made?
2 What should the dividend policy of the company be?
3 What should the level of borrowing for the company be, and should it be short-dated or long-dated?
4 Should the interest paid be fixed or floating?

In earlier chapters we have considered each of these questions. Financial planning brings them all together.

Many decisions have a long lead time. For example, if a car assembly company wants to construct a plant in a new country, the search process, the negotiating process and the construction period can well take up to five years. The company has to have plans as to how it will finance the project over that period.

15.3 FINANCIAL MODELLING

The planning process can be supported by a financial model. The directors of a company can use the model to estimate the effects of the alternative decisions they might make. Alternative policies and assumptions can be fed into the model to see how close are the outcomes to meeting the goals of the company. Different sales and cost estimates can be imputed into the model to see, for example, how they affect the profit figures and balance-sheet figures.

It is not very difficult to produce such pro forma statements for a one-year plan, but it is tedious to extend it into longer periods. Fortunately, there are many computer programs that enable such projections to be made. The computer models allow many different assumptions to be made and the impact of the assumptions on the financial statements to be observed. The computer model also allows us to alter the inputs and so undertake sensitivity analysis.

The aim of planning is to ensure that a given objective is attained with as much certainty as is possible. In almost all financial models the uncertainty with regard to future period sales represents the single most potent problem. Therefore it is customary in even the most simple model to relate variables explicitly to sales wherever possible so that sensitivity analysis can be tested on the model with respect to the uncertain sales variable.

Sensitivity analysis would be prohibitively difficult if the model user had to perform manual adjustments on the values of several variables which are jointly determined. However, a computer program allows us to solve a set of simultaneous equations.

15.4 SHORT-TERM FINANCIAL PLANNING

Short-term financial planning involves considering and answering questions such as the following:

1 What level of cash needs to be on call at various dates during the next planning period?

2 What level of inventory do we need to maintain?
3 How quickly can we pay off the bank overdraft?
4 What period of credit do we grant to our debtors?
5 Should we pay our suppliers quickly and take advantage of the cash discount being offered?
6 What proportion of current assets should be financed by short-term funds?
7 What is working capital and what influences its level?

Short-term financial planning is concerned with what is referred to as 'working capital'. Working capital can be defined as the excess of current assets over current liabilities. It is the same as net current assets. It represents the investment of a company's funds in assets which are expected to be realized within a relatively short period of time. It is not an investment in an asset with a long life but, as the name implies, represents funds which are continually in use and are turned over many times in a year. It is capital used to finance production, to support levels of stock and to provide credit for customers. The three main current assets are stock, debtors and cash. They can be funded by short-term finance, i.e. current liabilities, or by medium- and long-term finance. The working capital cycle is illustrated in Figure 15.2:

$$\text{working capital} = \text{cash} + \text{debtors} + \text{stock} - \text{short-term liabilities}$$

It can also be defined as

$$\text{working capital} = \text{equity} + \text{long- and medium-term debt} - \text{fixed assets}$$

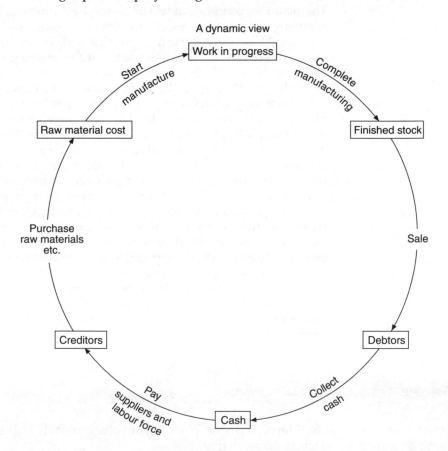

Figure 15.2

As can be seen from the above equations, the more of a business's finance is invested in working capital, the less is available for investing in long-term assets

Financial planning

such as buildings, plant and machinery. At most times it is believed that the profits to be earned from investing in long-term assets are greater than the profits to be earned from investing in working capital. At such times, therefore, a business wishes to minimize its own investment in working capital and to concentrate its resources on investments with a longer life than current assets, with as much as is safe of the current assets being financed by current liabilities.

15.5 FINANCIAL RISK MANAGEMENT

Planning involves more than considering the implications of what is expected to happen in the future, it also involves being prepared for the unexpected. The financial risks a company might face include:

- physical damage, due to explosions, earthquakes, terrorism, etc;
- product liability;
- employers' liability – worker compensation;
- business interruption – explosions, sabotage;
- environmental liability – pollution;
- exchange-rate risks;
- interest-rate risks;
- commodity risks.

A company can hedge against some of these risks using, for example, financial derivatives or insurance. It can also prepare 'damage limitation' plans – steps to be taken as soon as there is knowledge of the losses.

Some of the above risks are usually covered by financial hedging techniques, for example interest-rate risk and foreign-exchange risk; these are discussed elsewhere in the book. Other risks, which also can have serious financial consequences have traditionally been covered by insurance policies, for example physical damage, product and environmental liability and employers' liability.

Companies can suffer from sudden disasters, which can be called 'catastrophes'. For example the sinking in 1989 of the *Exxon Valdez* and the resulting pollution. The estimated financial cost of this disaster was over $11 billion. The oil and chemical industries are particularly vulnerable to catastrophes; other examples in that industry include an explosion and resulting fires on an oil rig (Phillips Petroleum) and an explosion at a chemical factory at Bhopal in India (Union Carbide). Companies in other industries have suffered from acts of terrorism, (Pan Am – the Lockerbie bombing), from product defects (Perrier – chemical in water) and negligence (P & O Ferries – loss of the *Herald of Free Enterprise* at Zeebrugge).

Lloyd's of London are the largest single providers worldwide of catastrophe insurance. In fact, in the period from 1988 to 1990 there were so many major expensive catastrophes that Lloyd's and many of their underwriters encountered financial problems in meeting the claims.

Risk financing needs to become part of the long-term strategic plan of a company. For most companies, insurance against certain types of risk is essential. Some very large companies have, however, decided to insure themselves against catastrophe exposures. BP made such a decision in 1991. BP recognized that the size of its catastrophe exposures was beyond the capacity of the insurance market to cover. They decided to insure exposures below US $10 million in the market, and to retain exposures above this level within the company. Now a large number of large multinational companies own what are called 'captive insurance companies', and carry part of their risk exposure themselves.

Rather than pay insurance premiums to an insurance company outside the group with the premiums being set at a level which gives the outside insurance company a profit, better to pay the premiums to a 'captured' insurance company owned within the group. All profits are then kept within the group of companies. Many of these captive insurance companies have been set up in tax haven countries.

This policy works, as long as the group of companies is big enough in total to be able to absorb any financial loss, without leading to the collapse of the group. If not, it is not really insurance.

Companies are using financial derivatives to hedge against interest-rate, exchange-rate and commodity-price risk. Finance directors are becoming more familiar with these tools of risk management, and the products available are becoming more sophisticated.

Companies have benefited from the increased opportunities to hedge. A few companies have, however, lost money in the derivative market, either through a lack of understanding of the instruments being traded, or through fraud and lack of adequate internal control and monitoring procedures.

Table 15.1 shows a sample of the major derivative losses that have occurred since 1990. It will be seen that companies from a number of countries have suffered losses. It is ironic that derivative contracts are entered into to reduce risk and if they are not understood or controlled they can increase risk. Risk management is complex.

Table 15.1 *Some of the major derivatives losses since 1990*

Organization	Loss (US$m)	Type of instrument
Sumitomo Corporation	2600	Copper futures
Orange County, USA	1700	Interest rate derivatives
Showa Shell Sekiyu	1700	Foreign exchange forwards
Metallgesellschaft	1570	Oil futures
Kashima Oil	1500	US dollar futures
Barings Bank	1400	Futures on Nikkei index
Daiwa Bank	1100	US government bonds
Allied Lyons (now Allied Domecq)	265	Foreign-exchange options
Eastman Kodak	220	Swaps and options
Glaxo (now Glaxo-Wellcome)	182	Interest-rate futures
Procter & Gamble	102	Interest-rate swaps

15.6 WORKING CAPITAL REQUIREMENTS

Table 15.2 lists the factors that influence working capital items. When considering the control of debtors and stocks it is possible to calculate ratios which can be used to monitor movements in these items. For example, the average length of credit being allowed on debtors can be seen from the ratio of debtors to sales. Unfortunately it is not possible to introduce meaningful monitoring ratios for the control of creditors.

Purchases, and consequently the creditors' figure, are made up of a mixture of items: materials for stock; materials for consumption; wages and salaries; payment for services, energy, rent; purchase of capital equipment, etc.

Of course the type of working capital required can vary from one industry to another. These industry differences have to he allowed for in any comparisons across companies. What is an acceptable working capital position in, say, the retailing industry would not be acceptable in a manufacturing industry.

To determine the level of cash that a company requires, it is necessary to prepare a cash budget where the minimum balances needed from month to month will be defined. If expenditures are lumpy or business is seasonal, cash

Financial planning

Table 15.2 *Controllability of working capital*

Element	Influence
Debtors	Volume of sales
	Length of credit given
	Effective credit control and cash collection
Stocks	Lead time
	Variability of demand
	Production cycle
	No. of product lines
	Volume of planned output
	actual output
	sales
Payables	Volume of purchases
	Length of credit allowed
	Length of credit taken
Short-term finance	All the above
	Other payments/receipts
	Availability of credit
	Interest rates

shortages may arise in certain periods. Generally it is thought better to keep only sufficient cash to satisfy short-term needs, and to borrow if longer-term requirements occur. Maintaining a very large cash balance to meet every eventuality likely to arise throughout the planning period is thus discouraged in favour of *ad-hoc* borrowing. The problem, of course, is to balance the cost of this borrowing against any income that might be obtained from investing the cash balances. Since cash needs can hardly ever be predicted with absolute certainty, some firms will no doubt opt for a safety stock of cash with which to meet the unexpected. Like any other insurance premium this particular brand of peace of mind involves an opportunity cost.

The management of inventories is as important for the company's short-term financial situation as the management of cash, and again a balance has to be found: this time between tying up money which is not earning anything and losing sales, and profits, through not being able to meet an order when it comes in. This problem is discussed in Chapter 18.

The other side of the working capital problem concerns obtaining short-term funds. Every source of finance, including taking credit from suppliers, has a cost; the point is to keep this cost to the minimum. The cost involved in using trade credit might include forfeiting the discount normally given for prompt payment, or loss of goodwill through relying on this strategy to the point of abuse. Some other sources of short-term funds are bank credit, overdrafts and loans from other institutions. These can be unsecured or secured, with charges made against inventories, specific assets or general assets.

The short-term financial problem is one of balancing the options. Cash requirements with seasonal patterns involve deciding whether to use short-term funds, take credit, offer varying discounts, employ factors or maintain large balances. Given the forecasting requirements and the alternative costs, it is theoretically possible to make an optimal decision.

15.7 FROM RULE OF THUMB TO PLANNING MODELS

In fact there are a wide variety of approaches to working capital planning and control that management can adopt. These range from simple rule of thumb methods to sophisticated mathematical and computer models.

The simple approach relies on keeping working capital levels within certain limits, determined by ratio analysis. A number of the commonly used ratios were discussed in Chapter 2. This approach is based on the idea that working capital should be funded in one way and long-term assets in another way. To fund long-term assets with current liabilities would be seen as dangerous, and to fund non-permanent working capital with long-term funds would be seen as a waste. This approach is often found in practice: the disadvantage is that the ratios used as guides are to some extent rules of thumb. However, at any time there are a set of generally accepted levels for certain ratios which can be useful as a guide for planning and control purposes.

One fairly accurate way of estimating working capital needs is first to determine the relationships between debtors and sales, creditors and sales, and inventory and sales. The company has a budget or a plan which will show the expected increase in sales over the next period, and by using the relationship determined between sales and the relevant items of current assets and current liabilities, it is possible to estimate the extra working capital needed to finance the expected increase in sales.

It must not be thought that over time this relationship between sales and the funds required as working capital remains static even in the short run. The relationship can vary at different stages of a company's sales cycle and the economic cycle. The funds required for working capital need to be planned in advance of knowledge of actual sales. The level of working capital at any time is based on estimated sales. For example, raw material stocks are partly based on estimates of production levels and work in progress, and finished goods are based on expected sales. Therefore, at times of downturns in economic activity there could well be overstocking.

This is not desirable and the successful company adjusts its stock levels as quickly as possible to the new level of activity. The point being made is that at such times the working-capital to sales relationship could well be out of line with the planned level.

One other word of warning is needed when using this practical approach, and that is concerned with the fact that the company may not be satisfied with its existing position.

This does not represent all of a growing company's needs for additional finance. In addition to increases in working capital to meet higher levels of sales, it may also be necessary to increase fixed capital to satisfy higher levels of sales. The increases required in fixed investment, i.e. in buildings, plant and equipment, are, of course, lumpy – they do not increase in direct proportion with sales. Certain equipment is purchased which will be able to produce x units of goods. It is not necessary to purchase an additional piece of this equipment until sales have increased by x units. At certain times businesses need to increase their production capacity and this requires quite large expenditures on capital equipment. When this new investment has been undertaken the company then has capacity greater than its present needs and it will not have to invest in additional capital equipment until some time has elapsed. The need for funds to satisfy working capital requirements increases in a more direct relationship with sales than does the need for funds for fixed investment.

However, it can be helpful to analyse the relationship between fixed investment and sales in order to see what growth it implies in financial terms. It must be recognized, however, that the cash outflow for fixed investment will not necessarily coincide with the cash inflow from sales.

It can, however, be helpful in financial planning to know that, for example, for every £100 increase in sales, an extra £25 of new funds needs to be provided in order to sustain the rate of growth, i.e. £20 working capital and £5 new fixed investment.

Financial planning

A more sophisticated approach, but not necessarily a more useful one, is to introduce mathematical programming techniques. This enables us to build constraints into the model. We can say, for example, that we need to maximize profits subject to maintaining a minimum level of cash on hand or on short call. We can make the model dynamic and say that in one period cash at short call should be at least £x, and in another period, because of greater market opportunities, it should be £x + £y. The objective function can also be adjusted to include multiple goals. The models can also take into account the probabilities of different outcomes.

A computer-based information retrieval system is well suited to this task as the computer database of liabilities can readily be segregated. It is a straightforward matter to rearrange the list of liabilities according to planned repayment dates. Segregation into different classes will facilitate the optimal funding by allowing consideration of postponement of certain non-statutory creditors.

To conclude, the corporate treasurer has a number of tools to assist in the management of working capital, ranging from simple ratio analysis to simulation models.

15.8 THE OPERATING CYCLE

The operating cycle is the length of time that elapses between the company's outlay on raw materials, wages and other expenditures and the inflow of cash from the sale of the goods. In a manufacturing business this is the average time that raw materials remain in stock less the period of credit taken from suppliers plus the time taken for producing the goods plus the time the goods remain in finished inventory plus the time taken by customers to pay for the goods. On some occasions this cycle is referred to as the 'cash cycle'.

This is an important concept for the management of cash or working capital because the longer the operating cycle the more financial resources the company needs. Management needs to watch that this cycle does not become too long.

The operating cycle can be calculated approximately as shown in Table 15.3. Allowances should be made for any significant changes in the level of stocks taking place over the period. If, for example, the company is deliberately building up its level of stocks, this will lengthen the operating cycle.

Some writers advocate computation of an annual operating cycle and of a cycle for each quarter, since with a seasonal business the cycle would vary over different periods. The numerators in the equations can be found by taking the arithmetic mean of the opening and closing balances for stocks, creditors and debtors. If a quarterly statement is being prepared, the opening and closing balances for the quarter would be used.

It is difficult to calculate the operating cycle from the annual accounts of a company, as in the UK the inventory figure is not often broken down into its different elements and the purchases figure is not given. Take as an example a company with the figures shown in Table 15.4 where the necessary inventory and purchasing figures have been given. The operating cycle for the year is as follows:

$$\text{Turnover of raw materials} = \frac{19\,200}{240} = 80 \text{ days}$$

$$\textit{less credit granted by suppliers} = \frac{12\,000}{240} = \textbf{50 days}$$

$$\overline{30 \text{ days}}$$

$$\text{Period of production} = \frac{13\,500}{363} = 37 \text{ days}$$

$$\text{Turnover of finished goods} = \frac{12\,500}{363} = 34 \text{ days}$$

$$\text{Credit taken by customers} = \frac{28\,000}{400} = 70 \text{ days}$$

$$\overline{171 \text{ days}}$$

A number of steps could be taken to shorten this operating cycle. The amount of debtors could be cut by a quicker collection of accounts, finished goods could be turned over more rapidly, the level of raw material inventory could be reduced, or the production period could be shortened.

The operating cycle is only the *time-span* between production costs and cash returns; it says nothing in itself of the amount of working capital that will be needed over this period. In fact less will be required at the beginning than at the end. Initially, the only expenditure is on materials, but as wages and other expenses are incurred the amount of working capital required increases over the cycle.

It is not necessary to have as available cash at the beginning of the period a sum equal to the estimated cash costs of the production, although over the cycle as a whole it must be possible for the company to have access to such an amount. Short-term working capital is required to support a given level of turnover, i.e. to pay for the goods and services before the cash is received from sales to customers. To determine the amount required it is necessary to know the estimated sales for the period, and the characteristics and scale of the operating cycle.

Table 15.3 *Calculating the operating cycle for a period*

				Days
1. Raw materials period of turnover of raw material stock	=	$\dfrac{\text{average value of raw material stock}}{\text{purchase of raw materials per day}}$	=	
Less: period of credit granted by suppliers	=	$\dfrac{\text{average level of creditors}}{\text{purchase of raw materials per day}}$	=	
2. Period of production	=	$\dfrac{\text{average value of work in progress}}{\text{average cost of goods sold per day}}$	=	
3. Period of turnover of finished goods stock	=	$\dfrac{\text{average value of stock of finished goods}}{\text{average cost of goods sold per day}}$	=	
4. Period of credit taken by customers	=	$\dfrac{\text{average value of debtors}}{\text{average value of sales per day}}$	=	
Total operating cycle			=	

The successful control of working capital or cash depends on detailed budgets which must be as accurate as possible. These are needed for planning balance-sheet and profit-and-loss accounts, and consequently it is common practice for the conventional budgetary system to include estimates of the component parts of working capital. All that is needed for the management of working capital as a whole is that the parts should be put together.

Sources of medium-term working capital include retained profits and funds put aside as depreciation provisions. These are funds which are retained in the business not specifically to be used for short-term expenditures. The funds are reduced by expenditures on capital replacements, and dividend and tax payments. The required levels of medium-term working capital at different points in time can again be ascertained by preparing budgets.

Table 15.4 *Figures from which an operating cycle can be calculated*

	1998	1999	Mean
Raw material inventory	18 000	20 400	19 200
Work-in-progress inventory	12 500	14 500	13 500
Finished goods inventory	10 000	15 000	12 500
Debtors	26 500	29 500	28 000
Creditors	11 000	13 000	12 000
Sales	136 000	156 000	146 000
Purchase of raw material	85 000	90 200	87 600
Costs of goods sold	125 000	140 000	132 500

The total working capital required is compared with the net current assets plus overdraft limit to show the required borrowing, or, alternatively, the funds that can be lent and for what period. If the difference between needs and funds available is not large when expressed as a percentage of the budgeted amounts, then no action need be taken. The difference can be assumed to lie within the normal range of forecasting error. If the surplus is large and continuous, however, it would suggest that working capital is in excess of needs.

A company therefore needs to forecast its short-term and long-term working capital needs. The cash budget is obviously a key part of this planning exercise. To prepare such a budget it is first necessary to estimate the future level of sales, and so determine the amount and timing of the funds flowing into the business. It is next necessary to forecast the future expenditures. Certain costs will vary directly with the level of sales, perhaps with a linear relationship, other costs vary but in a less than linear relationship because of economies, and yet other costs remain fixed, at least over certain ranges of output. The future cash budget can be developed in this way after allowing for capital expenditure and irregular payments such as dividends and taxation. Cash budgets are discussed further in Chapter 17.

To estimate a funds-flow statement for a future period it is necessary to forecast the expected changes in the balance sheet items. The level of future sales and production activity will be known from the sales and production budgets. Decisions then have to be made on how each balance sheet item will vary with the sales activity.

15.9 THE LIFE CYCLE OF A FIRM

It is useful to be able to identify the life cycle of the typical firm, as the financial needs usually vary at the different stages of a firm's life. Figure 15.3, plotting sales against time, shows a typical pattern. It is possible to identify five stages. The first is the experimentation period, the introductory period. The second is the exploitation period, the take-off. The third is the slow-down – the dynamic stage is now over. For a well managed company, the fourth stage is the move into maturity with either a steady (but not spectacular) growth in sales or static sales. It is hoped that the company does not move into the next stage indicated in the figure, namely the decline.

Figure 15.4 shows the cash-flow position for the same firm during the life cycle. In the first stage the company needs start-up capital, which usually means the personal savings of the proprietor and possibly some venture capital. Once the source of equity investment can be identified the company can approach the banks for loans. Some form of guarantee will usually be required on such loans; in many cases it will need to be a personal guarantee, but in some cases these loans may be covered by government guarantees. The new firm will usually be dependent not only on the banks for finance but also on trade credit from suppliers. During this

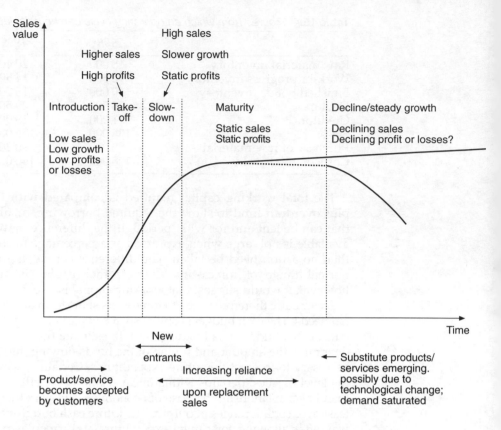

Figure 15.3

start-up phase there are other financing possibilities which include leasing, hire purchase and factoring. There are also a few private- and public-sector financial institutions which can and do provide funds for some newly launched firms.

During this early stage in the life cycle of the firm it is essential to introduce an adequate system of financial planning and control. Cash budgets must be produced and the actual cash flows must be carefully monitored. The large accounting firms have now moved into the market, offering financial advisory services to small businesses in this first stage of growth. They offer to produce business and financial plans, to keep the books and to help control the financial position of the small business.

During the second phase of the company's life, the rapid-growth phase, finance will continue to come from the sources indicated for the first phase and in addition from retained earnings, further trade credit and bank loans, and

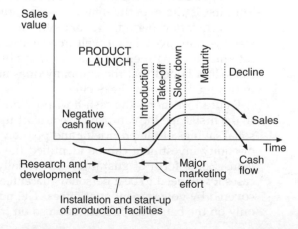

Figure 15.4

specialist financial institutions and government schemes. The larger small businesses will be able to approach merchant banks and the venture capital companies.

As the firm approaches maturity it may be thinking of selling shares to the public or to financial institutions and raising further equity through this means. In addition, it will be in a position to obtain medium- and long-term loans from the banks and the other financial institutions.

15.10 FURTHER READING

A selection of articles and books on corporate strategy and financial planning is given below.

Barwise, P., Marsh, P.R. and Wensely R. (1989) Must finance and strategy clash? *Harvard Business Review*, Sept.-Oct.

Bhaskhar, K., Pope, P. and Morris, R. (1982) *Financial Modelling with Computers*, Economist Intelligence Unit.

Davidson, K. (1985) Strategic investment theories, *Journal of Business Strategy*, Summer.

Gentry, J.R. (1988) The state of the art of short run financial management, *Financial Management*, Summer.

Johnson, G. and Scholes, K. (1993) *Exploring Corporate Strategy*, Prentice-Hill.

Lee, C.F. (1985) *Financial Analysis and Planning: Theory and Applications*. Addison-Wesley.

Myers, S.C. (1987) Finance theory and financial strategy, *Midland Corporate Finance Journal*, Spring, pp. 6–13.

Porter, M.E. (1985) *Competitive Advantage*, Free Press.

Smith, K.V. (1979) *Guide to Working Capital Management*, McGraw-Hill.

Smith, K.V. and Callinger, C.W. (1988) *Readings on Short term Financial Management*, 3rd edn, West Publishing.

Thompson, J. (1993) *Strategic Management: Awareness and Chance*, Chapman and Hall, London.

15.11 PROBLEMS

1

	Supermarket chain	Heavy manufacturing	Hotel	Bank
Fixed assets				
Land and buildings	299	132	562	1 329
Plant and machinery	207	312	212	506
	506	444	774	1 849
Associated companies	–	6	117	–
Current assets				
Stocks	180	59	26	
Debtors	10	68	148	132 806
	190	127	174	132 806
Current liabilities	339	76	195	116 663
Net current assets	(149)	51	(21)	16 143
	357	501	870	17 992
Share capital and retained reserves				
Loan capital				
Short-term borrowing				
	357	501	870	17 992

For each company complete what you think would be an appropriate amount of equity (i.e. share capital and retained reserves), loan capital and short-term borrowings.

2 (a) What is meant by business risk? Outline the major factors that determine a company's business risk and comment upon how controllable these factors are by a company. (8 marks)

(b) Discuss to what extent business risk is of relevance to an investor owning a well-diversified portfolio. (3 marks)

(c) Huckbul Ltd plans to purchase a new machine in the near future which will reduce the company's direct labour costs, but will increase fixed costs by £85 000 per annum. Direct labour costs are expected to fall by 20% per unit of production. The new machine will cost £820 000 and will be financed by a five-year fixed-rate loan at an interest cost of 15% per year, with the principal repayable at the maturity of the loan. The company normally pays half of after-tax earnings as dividends, subject to the constraint that if after-tax earnings fall the dividend per share is kept constant. Huckbul expects its volume of sales to increase by 15% during the current financial year. Summarized extracts from the company's most recent financial accounts are detailed below.

Profit and loss account	£000	£000
Turnover		3381
Operating expenses		
Wages and salaries	1220	
Raw materials	873	
Direct selling expenses	100	
General administration (all fixed)	346	
Other costs (all fixed)	380	
		2919
Profit before interest and tax		462
Interest		84
Profit before tax		378
Corporation tax		151
Profit available to ordinary shareholders		227

Balance sheet	£000	£000
Fixed assets (net)		1480
Current assets	1720	
Less current liabilities	1120	
		600
		2080
Long-term debt		570
Net assets		1510
Capital and reserves		
Ordinary shares (25p)		800
Share premium account		320
Other reserves		390
		1510

The company is subject to taxation at a rate of 40%.

(i) Evaluate the effect of the purchase of the machine on both the degree of operating gearing and the financial gearing of Huckbul Ltd, comparing the position at the start of the current financial year with the expected position at the end of the current financial year. (9 marks)

(ii) What are the implications for the ordinary shareholders of Huckbul as a result of the purchase of the machine:
(1) if turnover increases by the expected 15%?
(2) if turnover falls by 10%? (5 marks)
State clearly any assumptions that you make. (25 marks)

ACCA, June 1987

3 The relevant figures for a company are:

From profit and loss account:	(000s)	(000s)
Sales	8000	
Cost of goods sold	5000	
Materials purchased	3000	

From balance sheet:		
Stock – finished goods	1200	
WIP	600	
Raw materials	1000	2800

Debtors		2000
Creditors		600

(a) Determine the operating cycle of the company and comment on its importance.

(b) Target figures are:

	Days
Raw materials in stock	20
WIP materials in stock	12
Finished goods in stock	45
Credit granted to customers	40
Credit taken from suppliers	60

If the targets are achieved what will be the impact on the level of working capital? What will it cost, or save, per year if interest rates are 7%?

4 The directors of CDX PLC are examining the company's estimated financial position for the next year.

	£000	
	Current year	Next year
Sales	3500	4400
Cost of goods sold	2980	3300
Purchases	1900	2200
Debtors	680	890
Creditors	450	580
Raw material stock	510	630
Work in progress	200	270
Finished goods stock	380	450

Required:
(a) The company's board of directors considers that the estimate is very favourable as operating profit is expected to increase significantly.

Explain whether you agree with the board of directors, and highlight any factors that you would draw to the board's attention, with recommendations for any action to be taken. Relevant calculations should support your analysis.

(b) The directors are also considering an operational plan for the short-term investment of surplus funds. Prepare a brief report for the directors, discussing the major influences on the selection of short-term investments.

16 INTRODUCTION TO DERIVATIVES AND OPTION THEORY

By the end of this chapter the reader should:

- be able to explain the nature of derivatives and distinguish between forwards, futures and options
- know the risks and benefits of buying and writing options
- be able to undertake basic option strategies
- appreciate the factors that affect option values
- be able to value options using a simple binomial model
- understand the application of option theory to corporate financial decisions

16.1 INTRODUCTION

Derivatives are securities whose value depends on the value of other more basic variables; these include the value of linked assets, for example, commodities, ordinary shares, bonds, currencies, etc. Derivatives include forward contracts, futures contracts, swaps and options. Although our main concern in this chapter is with options we begin with a review of derivatives in general.

Some derivatives are traded on exchanges where contracts are standardized and completion of the contract guaranteed by the exchange; futures and options are examples of derivatives which are traded on specialist exchanges. Some derivative transactions are 'over-the-counter' (OTC) transactions where a financial intermediary puts together a transaction which is tailored precisely to the needs of the client; futures and swaps are increasingly OTC transactions.

What are derivatives and how do they work?

The simplest derivative security is a forward contract. This is an agreement to buy or sell an asset at a fixed future date at a price agreed now. For example, an exporter receiving payment at a future date in a foreign currency may choose to sell the currency forward at a price agreed now, thus fixing the amount to be received in terms of the domestic currency. Conversely an importer with a future bill to pay in a foreign currency may choose to buy the currency forward. Both these would be examples of covered positions where gain or loss on the forward would be offset by an equal and opposite loss or gain on the amount to be received or paid. Forward contracts are also available on interest-bearing securities; for example, companies may enter into forward rate agreements where interest rates are agreed now for deposits or loans to be made at a future date.

Futures contracts are similar to forward contracts in that there is an agreement between two parties to buy or sell an asset at a future date at a price fixed now. Futures are more liquid in that they are usually traded on a regulated exchange. The exchange guarantees the integrity of the contract in that if one party was to go bankrupt it would not affect the other party.

Although the ability to trade futures provides flexibility they may be less flexible in other aspects as futures contracts are standardized. This means that the amount, quality of asset and delivery date of futures contracts are pre-specified and a hedger may not be able to obtain perfect cover by using futures. Forward contracts, on the other hand, can be agreed precisely to cover the risk faced by the hedger. It is possible that futures may be more readily available to some companies than forwards and where risk exposures are changing rapidly may enable the company to cover these risks more quickly.

With a futures contract the broker will require an initial deposit in a margin account. As the futures price changes the margin account will be debited or credited with losses or profits on a daily basis; this is called 'marking to market'. The investor can withdraw any balance exceeding the initial margin but will have to make good the deficit should the margin fall below a pre-set limit.

A more recent derivative development has been the use of swaps. A swap is an agreement between two parties to exchange cash flows at stated future times in accordance with the terms of the agreement. Swaps are typically entered into for currencies and interest rates. The simplest type of swap is an ordinary or 'plain vanilla' interest rate swap whereby one party agrees to pay another party cash flows equal to a fixed rate of interest on a notional sum for a number of years in return for receiving interest at a floating rate on the same notional sum for the same period of time. On each interest payment date one party sends the other the difference between the two interest payments. Note that no exchange of principal is involved.

The use of derivatives in managing risk is covered in Chapters 17 and 20 and many worked examples are shown of how they can be used. Unfortunately some companies have suffered losses by going beyond the hedging use of derivatives and trying to boost profits through position taking in commodities, currencies or interest rates. Companies need clear policies on the use of derivatives and internal controls to ensure that these policies are being followed. This is not always easy as many new derivative products are being produced which are difficult for even corporate treasury specialists to understand fully. This can make the monitoring process very difficult. We now turn to the main discussion of this chapter which concerns options and their valuation.

16.2 TYPES OF OPTIONS

An option is a contract giving the holder a right to buy or sell a stated security at a specified price, called the 'striking' or 'exercise' price, on or before a specified date. The value of any option is directly related to the value of its underlying security. Options represent a claim against the underlying security and thus are often called 'contingent claim contracts'. Although complex option-trading strategies are common, all the strategies can be analysed in terms of basic put and call options and the underlying security.

Call options

A call option gives the holder the right to buy a fixed number of shares at a specified price, either before or at a fixed future date. American and European

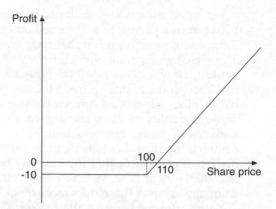

Figure 16.1
Call option holder

options differ in that European options can only be exercised at expiry date whereas American options can be exercised any time up to and including expiry date. A call option with an exercise price below the current market value is referred to as an 'in-the-money option'; however, where the exercise price is above the current market value the option is referred to as an 'out-of-the-money option'.

If a call option is exercised, then the exchange of shares is between two investors. It is thus a secondary market activity and there is no effect whatsoever on the company which has issued the securities. The investor who issues the call is known as the 'writer' of the call, while the other investor 'purchases' the call. Figure 16.1 shows the profit per share arising to the holder of a call option at expiry date. The figure assumes that the call option was purchased originally for £10 with an exercise price of £100.

The holder of the call option will not exercise the option unless the share price is at least £100 at exercise date. At any price below £100 it would be cheaper to buy on the market rather than exercise the option. The holder would just break-even if the market price at expiry was £110. The holder would be able to buy the underlying security for £100 and sell on the market for £110, thus just covering the price paid for the option of £10. For the moment we are ignoring both transaction costs and the time value of money. We can see that as the price rises above £100, so the value of the option increases on a pound-for-pound basis.

Let us now examine the position of the writer of the call option. Figure 16.2 shows the position of the writer of the call option. The writer of the call option receives the purchase price of the option and will be called upon to supply the shares if the price at expiry is £100 or greater. We can see that the position of the writer is a mirror image of that of the purchaser of the call option. Any profit made by the holder of the call will result in an equal and opposite loss by the writer of the call. Option dealing can therefore be referred to as a 'zero-sum game'.

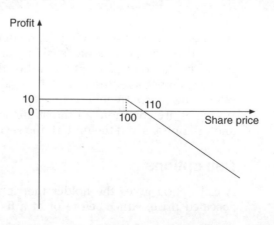

Figure 16.2
Writer of call option

Introduction to derivatives and option theory

If the option is an American option exercisable before expiration date, then if the share price was above £100 then a profit could be made by exercising the option. However, with traded options it is usual for the option to be sold on the market. The sale may be to an individual who wishes to take a position in the option or it could be to an investor who has written an option and wishes to liquidate the position.

Although option transactions are entered into between individuals, because they involve the passage of time it is still possible that decisions taken by companies will affect the value of the underlying shares. For example, both bonus/scrip issues and dividends will affect the share value. A one-for-one bonus issue would normally be expected to result in the share halving in value; cash dividends will normally result in a lower ex-dividend market price. Most options are protected against bonus/scrip issues by an automatic adjustment in the exercise price and the number of shares that can be purchased with one option. It is less usual to make adjustment for cash dividends and no adjustments are made to traded options. The possible impact of dividend payments will have more significance the longer the option has to run to expiry. This would be the case where option valuation models are adapted to value warrants and convertibles.

Put options

A put option gives the holder the right to sell shares at a specified price on or before a specified date. Figures 16.3 and 16.4 show the profit at expiry date for a put with an exercise price of £100 that originally cost £10. Figure 16.4 shows the profit to the writer of a put which would never be greater than the premium received for writing the put. However, Figure 16.3 shows that for prices above £100 the owner of the put would be better off selling shares in the market as the price received would be greater. Therefore for prices above £100 the exercise value is zero. However, for prices below £100 the owner of the put would wish to exercise the option instead of selling on the open market. For prices between £100 and £90 a loss would be made because of the £10 premium paid, but below £90 the owner of the put would make money on a pound-for-pound basis as the price becomes lower. Once again the payoff for the owner and writer of the put are exactly opposite. One makes money as the other loses.

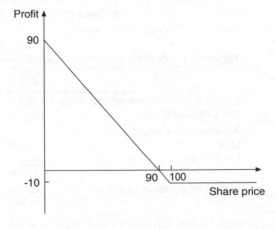

Figure 16.3
Put option holder

Puts, like calls, are rarely exercised before expiration. If the share price declined then the value of the put option would rise, but instead of exercising the option the owner would sell the right on the market.

With both types of option the longer to expiry the greater is the value as there is more time in which significant price changes may take place.

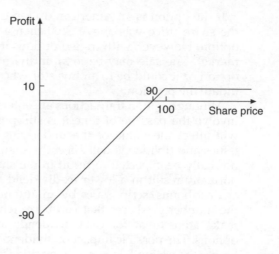

Figure 16.4
Writer of put option

16.3 SIMPLE OPTION STRATEGIES

Table 16.1 contrasts the investment of £1000 in call options with a similar amount invested in the underlying security. It is assumed that call options with an exercise price of 105p can be purchased for 10p on a security currently trading at 100p. If the price was to rise to 150p by exercise date then an investment in options would yield a total profit of £3500 and a return of 350%, while an investment in the underlying security would yield a profit of £500 and a return of 50%. However, suppose that the price at exercise date was only 105p. As the exercise price and market price were the same, the option would go unexercised and the option buyer would lose the premium paid of £1000. A loss of 100%! However, the buyer of the security would experience a gain of £50 or 5%. Any gains made by the holder of the call option would of course be reflected in identical losses made by the writer of the option. Holding options on their own can therefore be seen to be a risky investment. Both high returns and large losses are possible, and therefore an investor in options should expect to receive a high rate of return to compensate for the level of risk involved. However, we shall see that when options are held in combination or with the underlying share, then a low-risk strategy can result.

Table 16.1 *Option trading compared with purchase of shares*

	Options		*Shares*
Purchase of 10 000 call options at 10p	1 000	Purchase of 1000 shares at £1	1000
Exercise price £1.05	—		—
Assume price at exercise date £1.50			
Cost of options	1 000	Cost of shares	1000
Exercise price, 10 000 at £1.05	10 500		
	11 500		
Sale at market value 10 000 at £1.50	15 000	Sale at market value 1000 at £1.50	1500
Profit	£3 500	Profit	£500
	350%		50%
Assume price at exercise date £1.05			
Cost of options	1 000	Cost of shares	1000
As current price equals exercise price price option not exercised	—	Sale at market value 1000 at £1.05	1050
Loss	£1 000	Profit	£50
	100%		5%

Introduction to derivatives and option theory

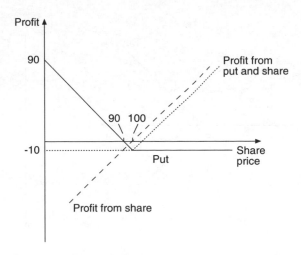

Figure 16.5
Share and put option

As well as being held in combination, options can also be combined with the share on which they represent a claim. Figure 16.5 shows the payoff resulting from owning a put and also owning the share. An exercise price of £100 is assumed together with a current share price of £100 and a put premium of £10. The figure shows three lines: one for the share (or long position), one for the put purchased and one for the combination. The strategy reduces the return at higher share prices but limits potential losses should the share fall in price.

Another example of this type of strategy involves holding the share and writing a call option on the share. This is referred to as 'writing a covered call'. Figure 16.6 shows the payoff arising from this strategy, and again three separate lines, one for the share, one for the call written and one for the combination, are shown. As can be seen, an investor who follows this strategy, rather than just owning the share, increases the return at low share prices while reducing returns at higher share prices. This strategy might be used by a portfolio investor in slack markets to try and increase portfolio return.

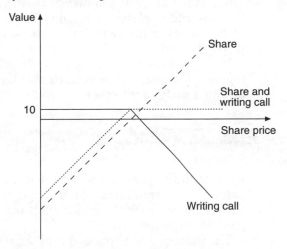

Figure 16.6
Share and writing call
option

16.4 CALL OPTIONS AND FUTURES COMPARED

A mistake is sometimes made by regarding futures and options contracts as identical. This is definitely not the case. With futures both parties are obligated to complete the transaction, either by a reversing trade or an actual delivery.

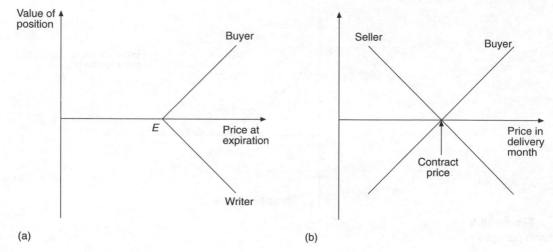

(a)   (b)

Figure 16.7 Call option and futures compares

Figure 16.7 contrasts the situations faced by (a) the buyer and writer for a call option and (b) the buyer and seller of a futures contract. The option shows the position at expiration date, while the futures position is shown at delivery date.

As shown in Fig. 16.7(a), no matter what the price of the underlying stock, at expiration an option buyer cannot lose and an option writer cannot gain. Option buyers pay writers for putting themselves in this position with a premium at the outset of the contract. The exercise price is set more or less arbitrarily and the premium negotiated. In a broader sense, the premium is the equilibrating factor, bringing quantity demanded and quantity supplied together in the options market.

The situation is quite different with a futures contract. As shown in Figure 16.7(b) the buyer may gain or lose, depending on the price in the delivery month, and so may the seller. The higher is the original contract price, the greater is the likelihood that the buyer will lose and the seller will gain. The lower is the original contract price, the greater is the likelihood that the seller will lose and the buyer will gain. The contract price is negotiated in the attempt to find a value that will lead both parties to consider the resulting prospects worth their while.

In the futures market, the contract price is the equilibrating factor, bringing together the quantity demanded and the quantity supplied. No money is paid by either party to the other.

16.5 FACTORS AFFECTING OPTION VALUES

We saw in the previous section that the option price or premium is the factor determining equilibrium in the option market. It is therefore important to determine those factors which affect option value so that appropriate valuation models can be derived.

The value of a call option at expiry date can be stated as follows:

$$V_o = \max(V_s - E, 0)$$

where V_o is the value of the option at expiration, V_s is the value of the underlying share at expiration, E is the exercise price and max means the maximum of $V_s - E$ and zero. Options always have a minimum value of zero as the holder will only enforce the option if it is profitable.

Option values clearly depend on the share price and the exercise price.

Introduction to derivatives and option theory

However, this is only looking at the position at expiration of the option. We are interested in obtaining a value prior to expiration. When we consider the situation one period prior to expiration we do not (cannot) know what the value will be at expiry, but instead will formulate some sort of probabilistic belief about the value one period hence.

Suppose that we hold an option expiring in 90 days' time with an exercise price of £10 and that the current market value is also £10. If this position was to hold at expiration the option value would be zero. However, with time to run to expiry as long as a probability exists that the price will exceed £10 before expiry, the option should have a positive value. If the expected value of the share at expiry was £10 represented by the distribution

$$
\begin{aligned}
0.3 \times £5 &= £1.5 \\
0.4 \times £10 &= £4.0 \\
0.3 \times £15 &= £4.5 \\
\hline
&£10.0 \text{ expected value}
\end{aligned}
$$

then the expected value of the option at expiry date would be

$$0 \times 0.3 + 0 \times 0.4 + (15 - 10) \times 0.3 = £1.50$$

Remember that $V_o = \max(V_s - E, 0)$.

Now consider another share, also with an exercise price, market value and expected valued of £10 at expiration date, but having the distribution

$$
\begin{aligned}
0.3 \times £0 &= £0.00 \\
0.4 \times £10 &= £4.00 \\
0.3 \times £20 &= £6.00 \\
\hline
&£10.00 \text{ expected value}
\end{aligned}
$$

In this case the expected value of the option at expiry date would be

$$0 \times 0.3 + 0 \times 0.4 + (20 - 10) \times 0.3 = £3.00$$

Both shares have the same expected value but the expected option value of the second security is twice that of the first. Why should this be? If we examine the respective probability distributions, we can see that the second security has a wider dispersion around the mean. This higher volatility makes the option more valuable. It should be noted that although there is the possibility of a lower value in the second share than the first, this does not matter as the option value cannot be less than zero; it is the possibility of a higher value which makes the option more valuable.

The holding of a call option can also be regarded as a deferred purchase of the underlying security as the exercise price does not have to be paid until a later date. This means that the option value will be affected by the level of interest rates. The higher are the interest rates the greater will be the value of the option because the present value of the exercise price will be lower. Clearly the longer the time to expiration the higher will be the option value as again the present value of the exercise price will be reduced. In addition, the longer is the time to expiration the greater will be the opportunity for higher share values to result from share volatility. Our discussion to date suggests that option values are determined by the following:

1 the current price of the share;
2 the exercise price of the option;
3 the volatility (variance) of returns on share;
4 the time to expiration;
5 the short-term interest rate.

Figure 16.8 sets out the limits of the value of a call option and also the more

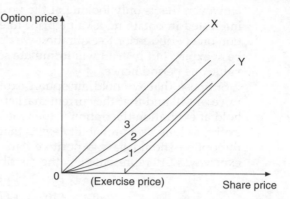

Figure 16.8
Limits of option
valuation

usual pattern of valuation. The highest possible value is shown by line X, indicating a value equal to the underlying share. This value would occur only if there was a very long time to expiration (perhaps a perpetual option) and if exercise was not expected in the near future, i.e. the present value (PV) of the exercise price approaches zero.

The lowest value that the option can have is that represented by line Y: zero up to exercise price and Y for values greater than exercise price. This would be the value at expiry. Most options will lie between these two bands represented by lines 1, 2 and 3, indicating a convex relationship where the value of the option commands the greatest premium over the theoretical value at exercise price and where the premium declines with increases in the value of the share beyond that point.

16.6 BINOMIAL VALUATION FORMULA [2]

We now move on to consider option-pricing formulae. The simplest of these is the binomial option-pricing formula and we shall present a detailed derivation in this section. The basis of this valuation formula and also the more rigorous Black and Scholes formula [1] is that it is possible to construct a risk-free hedged portfolio by buying shares and writing call options on the shares. As the resulting portfolio is risk-free it would be expected that only a risk-free rate of return would be obtained. This then enables us to obtain a value for the call option.

Both models to be discussed are for the European call. As traded options are of the American variety it may seem that there is more academic than practical merit in this approach. However, Merton [3] made a number of observations on the comparison of European and American options. The first point to make is that the American call is a European call with the additional opportunity to exercise before expiry date. It follows that an American call cannot be worth less than a European call having the same expiry date and exercise price. Another conclusion is that it never pays to exercise an American call before expiry date provided that the share does not pay dividends or the exercise price is adjusted for dividend payments. The reason for this is that, although the share price might be trading above the exercise price prior to expiry, there is still the chance that the price will rise further before expiry. Suppose that an investor holds an American call with an exercise price of £10 on a share currently selling for £12. It would seem that the investor should exercise the call immediately rather than holding it and exercising at a later date. However, with a traded option there is the opportunity to sell the call to another investor. The American call will have two sources of value; the value of an immediate call (£2) plus the value of the chance to call from now to expiration date. Therefore provided that an American

Introduction to derivatives and option theory

call will not pay dividends before the expiration date or the exercise price is dividend protected it can be valued as a European call. Having established the relevance of European call option valuation models we shall proceed to examine the binomial option-pricing formula.

It is required to value a call one period before expiration given the following information: present price of share, £10; exercise price of call option, £10; risk-free interest rate, 25%. Assume that the share price will either increase to £15 or decrease to £5 by the exercise date. It should be possible to construct a fully hedged position by buying shares and writing call options. Table 16.2 shows the cash flows at the beginning of the period and the end of period where one share is purchased and two calls written. It can be seen that at the end of the period the net outcome will be the same irrespective of whether the £15 price or the £5 price prevails. The reason for this is that if the share price at the end of the period is £15 then the share purchased will be worth £15 while the holder of the call written will require two shares to be delivered for which £20 will be paid (2 × £10). These shares will have to be purchased in the market at the price of £15 each and a total cost of £30, giving a loss of £10. However, if the price at exercise date is £5 then the value of the one share held will be £5, and the calls will go unexercised and will have a value of zero. Because the strategy results in a certain outcome whichever possible share price results, the return on the strategy should be the certain return, i.e. the risk-free rate of return. We can therefore say

$$(10 - 2C)1.25 = 5$$

$$C = £3$$

We can see from the above equation that we have a net investment of £4, i.e. the cost of one share minus the premium received on writing two calls, and as the outcome of this net investment is certain we would expect to earn the risk-free rate of return. In this case we required one share for every two calls written. The shares-to-option ratio is often called the 'hedge ratio' or 'option delta'. In our example the option delta is 0.5. Options will have to be priced in accordance with this model, otherwise opportunities would occur for dealers to earn riskless profits. Arbitrage activity would ensure that all options are priced in accordance with the formula above.

Table 16.2 *Cash flows in fully hedged position*

| | | *Flows at t_1* | |
| | | *Possible share prices* | |
	Flows at t_0	*£15*	*£5*
Buy one share	−10	15	5
Write two calls	+2C	−10	−
		5	5

A general formula for the value of a call option with one period to expiry can be written as

$$C_0 = H\left(P_0 - \frac{P_L}{1+r}\right)$$

where C_0 is the value of the call option with one period to expiry, r is the risk-free rate of interest, P_0 is the current share price, P_L is the lower value of the share at end of period and $H = (C_u - C_L)/(P_u - P_L)$ is the hedging ratio. C_u is the upper value of the option at the end of the period and C_L is the lower value of the option at the end of the period; P_u is the upper value of the share at the end of the period.

While the foregoing illustrates the principles of option valuation it makes the unrealistic assumption that there are only two possible prices for the share at the end of the period. Fortunately Black and Scholes have devised an option-valuation formula which assumes that a share's returns are normally distributed, and this allows for a more realistic assessment of option values. Detailed consideration of this model is beyond the scope of this particular text but it is based on the principle discussed above that if capital markets are in equilibrium the call option will be priced so that the rate of return on hedged portfolios is equal to the risk-free rate of return.

16.7 APPLICATION OF OPTION PRICING THEORY TO CORPORATE FINANCE

It has become increasingly recognized that a knowledge of options and their value can be useful for managers in companies. This is because managers encounter options in their day-to-day activities concerning both projects and their financing. It may be that in some circumstances the existence of options is not clearly recognized or that they are not valued correctly. These options could include the following.

The option to expand

A small project or even an apparently unprofitable project can be made more valuable if it gives the company the option to expand when economic prospects improve. That option to expand in the future clearly has a value. When valuing a current activity, perhaps to decide whether to continue, any option of this kind should be included in the value of the activity to the business. For example, it may not be immediately profitable to enter a particular field of high-technology activity, but if the company does not proceed it will lose its option to expand in what promises to be a growing market. It would be possible, given the necessary estimates for the five factors determining option value, to use a model to calculate the value of a project's option to expand. This, of course, is a call option. Some care needs to be exercised as the manager will have to incorporate more estimates into his or her calculation because of the lack of a market for projects.

The option to abandon

The option to abandon represents a put option on the project. This option may be very valuable on some projects where it may be possible to abandon a project and sell off assets rather than continue with a project which is yielding negative net present values (NPVs).

Underwriting costs

When a company arranges for a new issue to be underwritten it is essentially buying a put option from the underwriters. The fee paid in the past has often been based on a percentage of the issue proceeds, whereas in fact the actual value of the option will depend upon the five factors previously discussed. If the issue price is a rights issue at a reasonable discount on current market value and there is only a short time from announcement to issue, underwriting fees based on a fixed percentage of issue proceeds might lead to an overpayment by management for the put option facility. There is a clear scope for negotiation based on the use of a model to value the option.

Equity as a call option on the firm's assets

Because of the existence of limited liability ordinary shareholders in a geared company can be regarded as holding a call option on the company's assets. By paying off the debtholders they can gain possession of the assets; if the assets become worth less than the debt, liability shareholders can 'put' the assets back to the debtholders who have effectively written this put. We can represent this relationship in the equation:

$$W = V - (B - P)$$

where W is the value of equity in the form of a long-run call on the company's assets, V is the value of assets, B is the value of debt if risk-free, and P is the value of European put option.

It should be noted that any investments undertaken by a geared firm which lead to an increase in specific or non-market risk will increase the wealth of shareholders at the expense of debtholders, even if the total value of the firm is unaltered. These are just a few examples of options which occur in the corporate financial environment. Others will include warrants which are long-run call options but have the added complication of changing the capital structure when exercised and convertibles which can be regarded as a fixed-interest security with a call option attached. In fact, debt instruments have become increasingly complex. For example, during the 1980s many companies issued so-called puttable convertibles enabling holders to convert into equity at a later date but also carrying the right to have the company buy back the bonds at a premium on issue price. The holders of the bonds therefore have a call option enabling them to convert into equity and also a put option allowing them to sell the bonds back to the company at a higher value. There are implications with this type of issue not only for the way in which it is valued by the investor and the issuing company alike, but also for the way in which it is treated in the accounts of the company.

16.8 SUMMARY AND CONCLUSIONS

We have seen that options give the holder the right to buy or sell assets at a fixed price on or before a specified date. Share options are the most familiar type of options and the put option gives the holder the right to sell shares while the call option gives the holder the right to buy shares at the exercise price. Options do not have to be exercised, and if the share price is below the exercise price in the case of a call option at expiry the holder will not be forced to exercise their option. This contrasts with futures where there is an obligation by both parties to complete the contract. It was noted that American options can be exercised at any time up to and including the expiry date, while European options can only be exercised on the expiry date. The factors affecting option value were identified as the current price of the share, the exercise price of the option, the volatility (variance) of returns on the share, the time to expiration and the short-term interest rate.

It was noted that, while options held on their own are very risky investments, by holding them either in combination or with the underlying security it was possible to reduce risk. This was an important factor in developing valuation models where it was noted that by holding the underlying share and at the same time writing call options it was possible to produce a fully hedged portfolio.

In addition to using option valuation models to value the options on shares it was noted that managers in companies are frequently dealing with options, although they may not necessarily be explicitly recognized as such. Examples given and discussed were the option to expand a project and the option to abandon a project, which are a call option and a put option respectively. It was also noted that the equity of any geared firm could be regarded as a call option on the firm's assets.

16.9 REFERENCES

1   Black, F. and Scholes, M. (1973) The pricing of options and corporate liabilities, *Journal of Political Economy*, **18**: 637–54, May–June.
2   Cox, J.C., Ross, S.A. and Rubinstein, M. (1979) Option pricing: a simplified approach, *Journal of Financial Economics*, **7**: 229–63, September.
3   Merton, R.C. (1973) Theory of rational option pricing, *Bell Journal of Economics and Management Science*, **4**: 141–83, Spring.

16.10 FURTHER READING

Black, R. and Scholes, M. (1973) The pricing of options and corporate liabilities, *Journal of Political Economy*, **18**: 637–54, May–June.
Cox, J.C., Ross, S.A. and Rubinstein, M. (1979) Option pricing: a simplified approach, *Journal of Financial Economics*, **7**: 229–63, September.
Hull, J. (1993) *Options, Futures and Other Derivative Securities*, 2nd edn. Prentice-Hall, Englewood Cliffs, NJ.

16.11 PROBLEMS

1   Six months ago you purchased a call option on 1000 shares in Frisky PLC at 10p per share. The share price six months ago was £1.10 while the exercise price is £1.20. The current price, just before expiry, is £1.35.
    (a) Should the option be exercised?
    (b) What is the profit/loss on the option dealing?
    (c) Compare the result in (b) with the strategy of investing the same amount of cash in shares six months ago.
2   Analyse the relative risk and payoff of the following strategies:
    (a) buy share;
    (b) buy call;
    (c) buy share and buy put option on the share;
    (d) buy share, buy put and write call;
    (e) buy share and write call option on the share;
    (f) sell put.
3   (a) Critically appraise the factors which determine the theoretical value of options highlighting any problems that might be encountered in incorporating them in a formal valuation model.
    (b) Explain how option theory might be useful in evaluating underwriting fees to be paid in connection with a proposed rights issue.
4   A financial dealer recently advised a client holding a well-diversified portfolio of shares to write calls on all the share holdings he owned or as many as were traded on the LIFFE. He explained that the client could not lose money but would benefit from the premiums received. Evaluate this strategy and the dealer's view that the client could not lose. If only a few options were traded on the portfolio shares, what alternative strategy would you suggest?
5   Using the binomial pricing model calculate the hedging ratio and the value of a call option with one year to expiry from the following data: current share price, £5; exercise price, £6; value expected at expiration, either £8 or £4; risk-free rate of return 10%.
6   Explain how call options differ from futures and evaluate their use in hedging risk.

17 CASH AND INTEREST-RATE MANAGEMENT

LEARNING OUTCOMES

By the end of this chapter the reader will:

- understand the significance of cash management
- know how to prepare a cash budget
- appreciate the cash cycle which can affect companies
- understand the problems caused to companies by volatile interest rates
- understand the mechanics of interest-rate futures contracts
- know how to calculate the benefits from interest-rate swaps

17.1 THE TREASURY FUNCTION

The growth in treasury specialization over the last thirty years can be linked to the increasing complexity and volatility of financial markets. Treasury management is responsible for:

1 management of cash while obtaining the optimum return from any surplus funds;
2 management of exchange rate risks in accordance with group policy;
3 providing both long- and short-term funds for the business at minimum cost;
4 maintaining good relationships with banks and other providers of finance including shareholders;
5 advising on aspects of corporate finance including capital structure, mergers and acquisitions.

Cash management
The efficient collection and payment of cash both inside the group and to third parties will concern the treasury department. The involvement of the department with the detail of receivables and payables will be a matter of policy. There may be complete centralization within a group treasury or the treasury may simply advise subsidiaries and divisions on policy (collection/payment periods, discounts, etc.). Any position between these two extremes would be possible. Treasury will normally manage surplus funds in an investment portfolio. Investment policy will consider future need for liquid funds and acceptable levels of risk as determined by company policy.

Currency management
The treasury will manage the foreign currency risk exposure of the company. In a large multinational company (MNC) the first step will usually be to set off

intra-group indebtedness. The use of matching receipts and payments in the same currency will save transaction costs. Treasury might advise on the currency to be used when invoicing overseas sales. Possibilities include home-company currency, customer-country currency or common currency (e.g. US$ as in oil prices). Competition and accepted trade practices are likely to influence the method adopted.

The treasury will manage any net exchange exposures in accordance with company policy. If risks are to be minimized then forward contracts can be used either to buy or sell currency forward. Forward contracts are available in most major currencies but not in less traded or very volatile currencies. An alternative strategy to forward contracts is to use one of the other forms of derivative.

Funding management

Treasury will be responsible for planning and sourcing the company's short-, medium-and long-term cash needs. Treasury will also participate in the decision on capital structure and forecast future interest and foreign currency rates. The last decade has seen the introduction of more complex capital issues requiring careful analysis.

Banking

It is important that a company maintains a good relationship with its bankers. Treasury will carry out negotiations with bankers and act as the initial point of contact with them. Short-term finance can come in the form of bank loans or through the sale of commercial paper in the money market. Companies usually pay a 'commitment fee' to the bank to have short-term facilities available. Companies can also arrange with a bank or group of banks a multiple option facility (MOF) which gives them a choice of interest rates and loans of different duration.

Corporate finance

Treasury will be involved with both acquisition and divestment activities within the group. In addition it will often have responsibility for investor relations. The latter activity has assumed increased importance in markets where share-price performance is regarded as crucial and may affect the company's ability to undertake acquisition activity or, if the price falls drastically, render it vulnerable to a hostile bid.

Treasury organization and control

A central treasury department normally exists within a large company. Although the treasury section may be staffed by a comparatively small number of people these staff are usually well qualified and costly to employ. The decision on whether to operate a separate treasury function and the scope of this function should be taken by comparing the incremental costs of establishing the section with the benefits to be obtained.

The structure of treasury departments can vary quite considerably. Responsibility may be retained by operating units with central treasury merely providing advice, while there may be a fully centralized treasury department with operating units reporting positions to treasury and acting on their instructions.

The tendency is for increasing centralization of corporate treasuries, offering potential for greater gains given that most of the treasury costs are likely to be fixed. Centralization itself can take a number of forms, two of which are the central agent and central banker models.

Where treasury acts as central agent it transacts business on behalf of operating units rather than these units dealing direct. This approach requires the treasury to transact all the operating units' business with banks or other appropriate organizations. Where the central banker model is adopted then effectively the treasury acts as the group's central banker.

The model adopted may determine the status of treasury within the organization. Where an agency role is adopted then treasury might be regarded as a service cost centre. However, as the model becomes like that of a central banker the status may change to that of profit centre with treasury covering its costs of operation by charging operating units for services undertaken and profiting from netting off procedures (which are discussed in Chapter 21).Care must be exercised and clear guidelines laid down as more autonomy is given to the treasury department. If company philosophy is for risks (e.g. foreign currency, interest rate, etc.) to be minimized with business results not affected by movements in financial markets, this must be clearly stated and treasury act accordingly. A potential danger of treasury being a profit centre is that managers may be judged on results and have an element of profit-related pay, thus providing temptation to engage in speculation by, for example, taking on exposure in foreign exchange which goes well beyond any hedging requirements of the business. This strategy could make big profits but on the other hand can lead to spectacular losses should the exchange rate move in the wrong direction. Large and well-publicized losses made by treasury functions in both public- and private-sector organizations highlight the need for knowledgeable and highly trained staff operating within dear guidelines established at the highest level of the organization (see section 15.5).

Measuring treasury performance

This is a controversial issue. Management needs to be able to judge the effectiveness of its treasury function. This of course depends on the objectives set for the function. If it is seen as just another profit centre within the group the company has to be very careful to define the levels of risk in which the treasury can operate. Reward has to be traded off against risk. A treasury can hedge, become involved in arbitrage opportunities, spread its trading (this involves taking limited risks – for example, betting on a rise in interest rates by borrowing now for one year, and then investing the funds for short periods as the interest rates rise) and even become involved in speculation. The treasury can take high levels of risk; for a time it can beat the market and show profits; the danger is that it will then lose to the market and show losses.

Where the treasury is centralized and is seen as acting as a banker to the group it should not be seeking to maximize profits. The treasury should charge companies within the group a rate for the services offered that is similar to the scale of a bank's charges. This gives confidence to the managers of companies in the group that they are not being exploited. The treasury can make a profit, as does a bank by netting transactions, dealing with the outside markets in bulk, and undertaking a certain amount of investment with the short-term funds it has available; but it should not make a profit from high charges to group companies.

Control of treasury function

The responsibility for controlling the treasury function rests with the board of directors. A few cases occur each year in which a company reports that its treasury department has made large losses on its activities. The board usually claims surprise at the size of the losses. In order to avoid such surprises the board should ensure internal controls have been established and the actual performance is constantly monitored.

One area where controls are necessary is in the dealing function (in foreign currencies, the money markets and commodities). Many large treasury losses have resulted from unauthorized dealing. Dealing is difficult to control if it is permitted at subsidiary level. This is one argument for a centralized function.

The names of the personnel authorized to deal, and the limits of their authority, should be established. These individuals should be given dealing mandates. Counterparties must be made aware of who in the company is authorized to deal and of the limit on the amount of dealing permitted with that counterparty. The dealers should need to report regularly to superiors on their activities.

Limits may need to be divided between those for immediate settlement and those for different forward periods. The limits should be based on the level of loss the company is prepared to accept.

A dealer makes a deal. Behind him or her is what is called a 'back office' which is responsible for the settlement of the transactions. This office sends out the confirmation to the counterparties. The work of this office needs to be kept separate from the dealer. If it is not it is relatively easy for a dealer to breach approved limits without other staff being aware of it. The 1995 example of losses by one dealer employed by Barings illustrates the problem of control.

17.2 THE MANAGEMENT OF CASH

There are three basic reasons why a company would wish to hold some of its assets in the form of cash or cash equivalent. These reasons, according to economic theory, are the transaction motive, the precaution motive and the speculative motive.

The firm must be able to conduct its purchases and sales, and the management of this process involves an analysis of flow of cash in and out of the firm. Any firm needs working capital whatever its form of trading or manufacture. It is not just sufficient to acquire plant and machinery; a sum of working capital initially in the form of cash must be put aside to pay the wages, to buy materials and to meet any other expenses. A product is manufactured. The product might need to be placed in inventory before it is eventually sold. If the sale is for credit the company may have to wait some time before the cash is received. The cash cycle, the time that elapses between when the company pays its costs and when it receives the cash from sales, indicates the need for cash for transaction purposes. We shall return to this subject when cash budgets are considered.

It is impossible to forecast accurately cash inflow and cash outflow, and the less certain the predictions the greater is the balance that needs to be maintained as a precaution. The nearness of cash on short call will affect the amount that needs to be held for this purpose. If a large amount of securities or other assets can be converted into cash within a day or two, the amount that needs to be held as a cash balance will be less. Some companies rely heavily on bank overdrafts as a source of finance. These companies can often offer as security assets which are easily convertible into cash at short notice. Some types of inventory are very illiquid and take time to convert into cash. Other inventories, such as raw materials and commodities, can quickly be converted into cash and so can act as ideal security for short-term loans.

17.3 THE COLLECTION AND PAYMENT CYCLES

The corporate treasurer will attempt to control the flow of cash in and out of the business. He or she will wish to delay payments for as long as it is an advantage to do so, and to collect cash as quickly as possible.

Cash and interest-rate management

The collection cycle

The collection cycle consists of the following:

- receipt of the order;
- credit approval – acceptance of customer, and agreement on discount and price;
- dispatch of goods and documentation;
- posting of invoices stating credit terms and method of payment;
- debtor control;
- enforcement procedures;
- collection and banking of cash.

As the collection cycle can take 100 days or more, any steps that can be taken to reduce its length are important. Many aspects of the problem will be dealt with in Chapter 18 on the management of debtors, and at this point we shall concentrate on the movement of the cash.

'Float' is a term used to describe the money tied up in the process of collecting debts. It can arise because of the time interval that elapses between the day a customer, a purchaser, posts the cheque to the supplier and the day when the supplier can use the funds for their own purposes. First there can be the time required for postal delivery, which in the UK is between one and three days in most cases. When the supplier receives the cheque and banks it, he or she will have to wait for the bank to clear the cheque before they can draw on the funds they have deposited. In the UK the total time delay can be expected to vary between four and nine days depending on the postal service, the speed at which the cheque is deposited and delays due to weekends.

Let us say that a customer sends a cheque for £10 000 to his or her supplier. If the cheque can be cleared within four days rather than nine days, this is earning profits for the receiving company. If interest rates are 10%, then the saving of five days is worth approximately £14:

$$£10\,000 \times \frac{5}{365} \times 0.10 = £14$$

With a large sale to a particular customer, it is clearly important to reduce the size of the float as much as is possible. In the USA, where the problem is potentially of greater significance than in the UK because of the possible longer distance between companies' finance offices and so greater postal delays, many firms have reduced the size of the float by means of decentralized collection and regional banking. This avoids unnecessary cross-country transfer of funds. When large single payments are involved firms have been known to use messengers travelling by air to avoid possible postal delays.

One way in which a company can improve its cash position is through the system of collecting and depositing receipts from its divisional offices. Some small companies only deposit funds at the bank once or twice a week. If the company has an overdraft, the effect of rapidly depositing receipts is obvious: the overdraft is reduced, and so is the interest payment that the company has to make. If the company has a positive cash balance the effect of early deposits is just as important. The early deposit can earn interest on deposit account, enable the company to take advantage of cash discounts by payment of accounts on time or enable the company to carry out further investment of its own.

Payments cycle

The payments cycle consists of the following:

- placing the order;
- credit control – deciding on priority invoices to be paid quickly and calculating the benefit of discounts;
- method of payment – cheque, direct debit or standing order;
- payment frequency and timing – policy and past experiences with the creditor.

The time taken to pay is referred to as the 'reverse float'. It should be the result of a policy decision, taking into account the available funds, the discounts on offer and the relationship with the supplier. The time taken to pay can be a function of the efficiency of the administration handling payment. The administration is a cost to the business, but savings should not be made to the extent that unintentional delays in payment harm relationships with suppliers.

17.4 CASH TRANSMISSION TECHNIQUES

The final stage of the collection of debts and the payment of suppliers is the movement of cash. In large companies the treasury management function is usually well aware of the opportunities for earning returns through the fast movement of cash.

There are a number of cash transmission techniques. These include netting, cash pooling and direct debiting.

Netting involves netting the flow of funds between units within the same company, and only settling the net amount. It reduces the costs that the company has to pay. Bank charges for fund transfers and foreign-exchange transactions involve a fixed charge per transaction and a variable charge based on the size of the transaction. Netting will reduce the variable charge.

Cash pooling operates within a group. All the units in the group transfer their net funds to a central account. This enables surplus funds to be invested to their best advantage and means that one part of the group is not paying interest on an overdraft, whilst another part is earning interest on a cash balance.

As is apparent at some supermarkets and large stores the developments in computer applications have been applied to cash management. It is now possible to have electronic fund transfers. At the time of purchasing goods, the purchaser's account at a bank can be instantly debited through the use of computers. At the moment this system is in its early days, but there are moves to increase its use. It is a natural extension of the use of credit cards.

The management of cash in the USA presents many opportunities not available in the UK. The size of the country and the variety of banking institutions and services offered create different opportunities from those in the UK. For example, if a treasurer in the USA wished to delay payment of a debt to a supplier, he or she could draw a cheque on a bank situated far from the creditor, thus increasing the delay in clearing the cheque. To overcome this problem US companies have introduced a number of measures. Many companies charge interest on overdue accounts. Banks offer locked-box facilities. This means that a debtor is given the address of a bank or post office located much nearer to them than is the supplier. The cheque is to be sent to the locked box. The box is opened regularly by a bank official who will quickly credit the supplying company's bank account with cheques received. The locked-box arrangement is offered by the bank on a regional basis and helps overcome delays in the postal service brought about by the distances involved.

17.5 CASH BUDGET

The following decisions have to be made.

Cash and interest-rate management

1 How much cash should be held on hand or at short call?
2 How much should be invested in money-market securities?
3 What portfolio of securities should be held? What should the balance be between securities with different maturity dates?

Determining the amount of cash that a firm needs at a particular time is a difficult matter. As already explained, if a firm has too little cash it can be in liquidity difficulties; if it has too much cash it is missing opportunities to earn profits. The problem is to determine how much cash is too much cash. There are many opportunities for lending funds, even for short periods of time, which can all earn interest and so profits for the company.

The key to successful cash management is planning. Money can be earned not only through the manufacture or distribution of products but also through the management of all the assets that it employs. Through its cash budgets, a company can decide on the funds that it will have available for short-term investment. If the business is seasonal or trade is cyclical, cash budgets will show when the surplus funds are available, and what length of time will elapse before they are required. Some companies borrow to satisfy their seasonal or cyclical needs – to finance the build-up in inventories and debtors. They manufacture during the slack sales period and have to wait for the high sales period to arrive before the cash starts to flow back into the business. Other companies accumulate cash during the selling period, invest it and realize these investments to meet the need for cash during the slack sales period.

A simplified example will be shown. A company decides on a policy of maintaining the outflow of cash constant throughout the year, which means that production is to be even throughout the year. The inflow of cash is seasonal because sales are seasonal. The net cash-flow is illustrated in Figure 17.1.

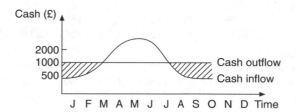

Figure 17.1

The company will not have enough cash flowing in during the period from August to March to meet current needs for outgoings. It can either borrow funds during this period and pay back in April–July, or it can accumulate funds during April–July, putting them into short-term investments and realizing these investments to meet its need for cash in August–March. Cash budgets revealing the demand and supply of cash will show the quantity of funds free for investment and the periods when they are likely to be available.

The same type of decision situation arises when the fluctuations are of longer duration – a cyclical, not a seasonal demand. Of course, the choice of policy depends on investment and borrowing opportunities.

The key statements by which management can be kept informed about the cash position of the company are the cash budget and the cash-flow statement. It is necessary to have these information statements as quickly as possible and as up to date as possible, so that action can be taken on the figures. The cash budget involves estimating what the inflow and outflow of cash will be at fixed intervals over the next planning period. Budgeting over short intervals – weekly or monthly – gives management a better chance to control any surplus of cash or to arrange to meet any expected shortages.

Table 17.1 shows a typical cash budget, analysed by monthly periods. The business is seasonal, with the vast majority of the sales taking place in the third and fourth quarters of the year. The row indicating the collection of cash from debtors shows how the receipts from sales were spread out over time, after allowing for the expected delays in payment by customers. Production was planned to be more or less constant throughout the year. The actual balance sheet at the commencement of the period is shown in Table 17.2, as are the estimated balance sheets at the end of each of the four quarters. The budgeted profit-and-loss accounts are given in Table 17.3. The differences in the values of the balance sheet items from one date to another highlight the difficulty of analysing the accounts of a seasonal business. The impression to be drawn depends so much on the day in the year when the balance sheet is constructed.

Table 17.1 *M company cash budget*

| | First quarter | | | Second quarter | | | Third quarter | | | Fourth quarter | | |
	Jan.	Feb.	Mar.	Apr.	May	June	July	Aug.	Sept.	Oct.	Nov.	Dec.
Cash sources												
Collections from debtors	226	122	22	21	12	13	20	15	15	210	210	815
Dividends received	–	–	100	–	–	–	–	–	100	–	–	–
Sale of plant	–	–	–	–	100	–	–	–	–	–	–	–
Total sources	226	122	122	21	112	13	20	15	115	210	210	815
Cash uses												
Cash expenses (labour and other)	76	92	92	71	84	51	50	55	55	40	40	55
Payment to creditors	–	–	–	–	–	–	80	150	150	150	100	100
Taxes	100	–	–	–	–	–	–	–	–	–	–	–
Equipment	–	–	–	–	–	250	–	–	–	–	–	–
Total uses	176	92	92	71	84	301	130	205	205	190	140	155
Beginning balance	200	150	150	150	150	150	150	150	150	150	150	150
+ Source of cash	226	122	122	21	112	13	20	15	115	210	210	815
– Use of cash	(176)	(92)	(92)	(71)	(84)	(301)	(130)	(205)	(205)	(190)	(140)	(155)
Cash balance before loans or repayments	250	180	180	100	178	(138)	40	(40)	60	170	220	810
Desired cash balance	(150)	(150)	(150)	(150)	(150)	(150)	(150)	(150)	(150)	(150)	(150)	(150)
Cash borrowed	–	–	–	50	–	288	110	190	90	–	–	–
Loans repaid	100	30	30	–	28	–	–	–	–	20	70	610
Cash in excess at 31 December												50

Table 17.2 *M company budgeted balance sheet*

	Opening 1 Jan.	First quarter	Second quarter	Third quarter	Fourth quarter
Fixed assets	800	750	850	800	750
Stock	200	550	650	800	300
Debtors	310	90	300	700	500
Dividends due	50	–	50	–	50
Cash	200	150	150	150	200
	1560	1540	2000	2450	1800
Capital and reserves	1250	1315	1340	1375	1650
Bank loans	160	0	310	700	0
Provision for tax	100	25	50	75	100
Creditors	50	200	300	300	50
	1560	1540	2000	2450	1800

Table 17.3 *M company budgeted profit-and-loss account*

	First quarter	Second quarter	Third quarter	Fourth quarter
Opening stock	200	550	650	800
Purchases	150	100	380	100
Depreciation	50	50	50	50
Expenses	260	206	160	135
	660	906	1240	1085
Sales	150	256	450	1035
Closing stock	550	650	800	300
Dividends received	50	50	50	50
	750	956	1300	1385
Profit before tax	90	50	60	300
Tax	25	25	25	25
Profit after tax	65	25	35	275

In the example the company has an opening cash balance of £200. After balancing the needs of liquidity and profitability, and discussing with the bank the overdraft facilities available, the management decides that a cash balance of £150 should be maintained.

Once the required cash balance is decided on, the forecast of the cash inflow and outflow will enable the company to see how much money it needs to borrow and how much it has to invest. As can be seen, the company commenced the year with a short-term bank loan of £160. The selling season is over, but the cash still has to come into the business from many of the sales; when this flows in during the first quarter, the company is able to repay the loan. In the second quarter little cash is coming into the business, and the constant level of production, together with the acquisition of new capital equipment, means that cash borrowings need to be made.

It is important to be aware of weaknesses in the normal approach to cash budgeting. One-figure forecasting is generally out of date. It is advisable to look at a range of possible outcomes, at the situation that may develop under a number of sets of assumptions. Unexpected events can occur, good or bad, which can affect the firm's cash flow. For most companies, the key area of uncertainty affecting the cash budget is the volume of sales. Cash flow is particularly sensitive to changes in sales volume. Not all cash dispersements are proportional to the volume of sales. If the volume of sales falls, certain items of expenses will still have to be met and cannot be reduced proportionately. There are fixed payments that have to be made. Wages are increasingly becoming a fixed element. A company is not able to reduce its labour force in the short run and so reduce its costs. Other fixed items of expenditure include rents and rates.

In handling uncertainty in cash budgets, one can vary the assumptions about sales volume and produce a range of possible cash-flow figures. There are many computer simulation approaches to this problem. The sales figures are varied by a certain percentage and the effect on cash flows can be measured. However, this may not be sufficient by itself. It may be important to have a probability estimate attached to the different sales figures and so to the different cash forecasts.

17.6 CASH CYCLE

The five balance sheets shown in Table 17.2 demonstrate very clearly how dramatically the financial structure of a company can change during a cash cycle. The cash cycle is shaped by seasonal demand, cyclical demand over time and the stages of a product's development. The cash cycle in the above example was created by seasonal demand.

The phrases of the cash cycle can be described, in very general terms, as follows. Orders are placed with the firm, which by this early stage has already had to meet the considerable cost of capital equipment. (It is not always necessary to pay for this in cash – other methods, such as leasing, are available – but at least part of the equipment will involve outright settlement.) The orders require the purchase of raw materials. This purchase generates creditors. Labour is employed and paid for, and the work-in-progress inventory increases. The goods are completed, having entailed further cash outlays for direct and indirect overheads, and then move into finished inventories. Many of the manufacturing costs will already have been paid. If the goods are produced to order they will be shipped out of the factory, debtors will increase and perhaps 90 days hence the cash from the sale will be received.

The influence of sales on the level of current assets is illustrated in Figure 17.2. Over time sales increase but there are fluctuations around a rising long-term trend. There should be a parallel increase in fixed assets, which should eventually be financed by long-term funds. As sales increase, so will the level of current assets. Some of this increase in the permanent current assets will have to be financed out of long-term capital, equity or loan. There is a constraint on the relationship between current assets and current liabilities, for a ratio of 1:1 would certainly be considered dangerous by creditors and bondholders. Only a proportion of the increase in permanent current assets will be financed by current liabilities through the increase in creditors, accrued tax and wages. The temporary increase in current assets, fluctuating through the cash cycle, should certainly be financed by short-term liabilities. It can be dangerous to finance long-term needs out of short-term finance; it is expensive, and so uneconomical, to finance short-term needs out of long-term finance.

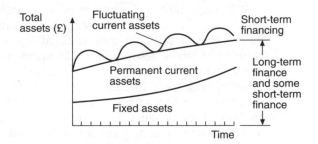

Figure 17.2

Product life cycle

A company's capital budgeting decision normally involves choosing the batch of projects that will produce the highest net present value within the limits of the amount of capital available. Each of the projects will normally need a certain amount of working capital to be set aside for their use; this is in addition to the initial capital cost of the project. Thinking in cash-flow terms is an important aspect of managing the company's finances so as to ensure the availability not only of sufficient long-term capital to finance the selected projects but also of adequate working capital to span each project's life. A new product, whether it is accepted for production or abandoned in the development stage, results in a cash outflow for the company, and some products demand heavy cash commitments, especially during the development stage.

This leads to the concept of threshold development cost, which implies that there is a minimum size of firm that can afford certain types of research and development activity. The relevant size depends of course on the speed of technological advance and the industry being considered. The size of the firm needs to be sufficient to be able to spend large quantities on research: it is difficult for a firm below a certain size to undertake successful research activity.

At various stages of a product's development decisions have to be made on whether the expected future returns justify the commitment of any more cash or capital resources. Even when the product has been developed, there is still a period when the net cash flows will be negative, and this applies even to products of a fairly uncomplicated character requiring little development expenditure. When manufacturing begins, work-in-progress builds up and finished goods are produced. Sales are made, debtors accumulate and eventually the cash flows into the firm.

The cash flows over a product's life cycle are illustrated in Figure 17.3. The investment decision on whether to go ahead with the product will involve forecasting the cash inflows and outflows over the entire life of the project, and discounting at an appropriate rate to obtain their present worth. In the illustration, the flows are shown as their estimated value for each year of the product's life, which is not, of course, the same as their present value at the time that the decision is made to go ahead.

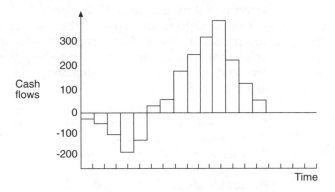

Figure 17.3

17.7 FUNDS-FLOW AND CASH-FLOW STATEMENTS

A funds-flow statement can take one of two forms. One is a historical document showing what has happened in the past, where the funds have come from and where they have been used. The second type of funds statement is as a tool for financial management, for financial planning. One type of statement relates to the past, the other relates to the future. The statements will disclose the extent to which long-term funds have been used or are to be used to finance working capital needs or vice versa. It will show whether the purchase of long-term assets has been or will be financed with short-term funds. It will show the movement of funds within the working capital items and whether working capital in total is being increased or decreased.

A funds-flow statement differs from a cash-flow statement. There are, however, two types of cash-flow statement: one relates to the past, and the other to the future. The one concerned with the future is called a 'cash budget'. A cash budget is essentially a document for assisting management in planning short-term financial needs and opportunities. For longer-term financial planning, management needs to produce a funds-flow statement to cover the needs of the next few years. A funds-flow statement does-not go into detail concerning the movement of cash: it is more interested in where the funds are coming from over the next few years and how they are to be used. It is necessary to estimate the funds that will be retained in the business each year, which are a function of profitability, depreciation policy and, where appropriate, dividend policies. The need for funds will depend upon capital investment plans and working capital needs, which are both a function of the planned rate of growth, and with longer-term investments, which are a function of the replacement cycle of the capital equipment. Funds may also be needed to redeem debentures.

Any gap between the anticipated use of funds and internally generated finance has to be met from external finance. It is in order to obtain an indication of the amount of external finance required and when it will be needed that companies need to undertake funds-flow projections. They can take the necessary steps to ensure that when they will need to raise new equity or issue new loan stock or borrow from their bankers, they are not rushing about at the last minute. Funds-flow projections are concerned with these longer-term capital-type items, whereas cash budgets are more involved with short-term cash management.

Cash budgets and projected funds-flow statements are essential for financial planning. Historic cash-flow and funds-flow statements can also be useful. They may indicate something to management that they may have missed if they had concentrated their analysis on just the balance sheet and profit-and-loss account. Historical cash-flow and funds-flow statements can also be useful ways of presenting information to shareholders. The cash-flow statement of British Telecom is shown in Table 17.4.

This is a good example of the type of cash-flow statement published by companies. It shows clearly the areas of activity which generated cash and the areas that used up cash. In order to help the reader of accounts, companies are required to produce such statements in a standard form. Cash flows are analysed under a number of headings:

- net cash flow from operating activities;
- net cash flow for returns on investments and servicing of finance;
- taxation;
- capital expenditure and financial investment;
- acquisitions and disposals;
- dividends paid;
- financing activities;
- the management of liquid resources.

17.8 INTEREST-RATE RISK MANAGEMENT

Interest rates in the future are uncertain. A company could be heavily dependent on floating-rate debt; if interest rates rise in the future the company has a higher interest cost than it need have done. Alternatively a company could now borrow large amounts of money at fixed-interest rates, only to find that interest in the market begin to fall. Again the company is faced with higher interest costs than are necessary.

There are now a number of arrangements and financial techniques available to the treasury manager, to enable him or her to reduce the impact of movements in interest rates. These techniques can be used to hedge against losses, or to speculate in the hope of making gains.

The techniques include:

- forward forward loans;
- forward rate agreements;
- interest-rate guarantees;

Cash and interest-rate management

Table 17.4 *British Telecom Group cash-flow statement for the year ended 31 March 1997*

	Notes	1997 £m	1996 £m
Net cash inflow from operating activities	8	**6,192**	5,834
Returns on investments and servicing of finance			
Interest received		**196**	202
Interest paid, including finance costs		**(342)**	(332)
Premium paid on repurchase of bonds		**(60)**	–
Dividends paid to minorities		**(14)**	(20)
Net cash outflow for returns on investments and servicing of finance		**(220)**	(150)
Taxation			
UK corporation tax paid		**(1,032)**	(738)
Overseas tax paid		**(13)**	(46)
Tax paid		**(1,045)**	(784)
Capital expenditure and financial investment			
Purchase of tangible fixed assets		**(2,823)**	(2,547)
Sale of tangible fixed assets		**124**	88
Purchase of fixed asset investments		**(172)**	(85)
Disposal of fixed asset investments		**51**	44
Net cash outflow for capital expenditure and financial investment		**(2,820)**	(2,500)
Acquisitions and disposals			
Purchase of subsidiary undertakings, net of £2m (1996 – £1m) cash acquired		**(126)**	(26)
Purchase of associated undertakings		**(148)**	(122)
Sale of subsidiary undertakings		**11**	16
Sale of associated undertakings		**11**	–
Net cash outflow for acquisitions and disposals		**(252)**	(132)
Equity dividends paid		**(1,217)**	(1,138)
Cash inflow before use of liquid resources and financing		**638**	1,130
Management of liquid resources	9	**(504)**	(1,317)
Financing			
Issue of ordinary share capital		**160**	130
Minority shares issued		**51**	59
New loans		**235**	177
Loan repayments		**(670)**	(151)
Net cash inflow (outflow) from financing		**(224)**	215
Increase (decrease) in cash in the period		**(90)**	28
Decrease in net debt in the period	10	**849**	1,319

- caps, collars and floors;
- interest-rate futures;
- interest-rate swaps.

We will now examine each of these techniques.

Forward forward loans

A company may know that it will need to borrow in future. Let us say its cash-flow forecasts indicate that in three months' time it will need to borrow £1 million for a six-month period. The treasurer is worried that interest rates will rise over the next three months. The company is faced with an interest-rate risk. It can avoid this by borrowing the £1 million now at today's interest rates for a nine-month period.

It does not need the funds for the first three months so it can invest for these. If interest rates rise, as expected, it will gain from the higher interest rates through the interest earned for three months. It will not have to pay the higher interest rates on its borrowed funds because it has agreed now the terms of a fixed interest rate loan.

Such a forward forward agreement means the company knows the interest rates it will have to pay in the future. It takes away the uncertainty. It does not mean that it takes away the risk of an opportunity loss. if interest rates fall in future, against the company's expectations, it will finish up paying higher interest charges than it need have done. If it had waited the three months until it needed the money, before it borrowed, it would have borrowed at lower interest rates.

Forward rate agreements (FRA)

These are arrangements whereby a company can lock itself into borrowing at a future date at an interest rate that is agreed now. They differ from forward forward agreements, in that the funds are not obtained now, but when they are needed. It is the rate of interest to be charged in the future that is agreed now. Clearly this takes away the uncertainty.

Similarly FRAs can be arranged for investing money. For example, a company may know now that it will have £10 million available in one year's time. It is worried that interest rates will fall over the next 12 months. The FRA will fix now the rate of interest that it will earn in the future when the company invests the money.

FRAs are usually supplied by banks. It has to be appreciated that the FRA is a different transaction from the actual borrowing (or the lending) of the funds. The borrowing or lending can be with one bank and the FRA with another bank.

The way in which the FRA works is that it is only the difference between the agreed interest that would be paid at the forward rate and the interest actually paid on the borrowing that is transferred between the company and the bank who enter into the FR arrangement. The FRA does not involve the lending of the principal sum or the actual interest paid on this sum.

Let us say a company enters into an FRA agreement with Bank A. That means it will borrow £1 million at say 12% in six months' time. The period of the loan will be twelve months. In six months' time if the market rate of interest is 14%, the company will borrow from Bank B at 14%, and have to pay Bank B £140 000 interest over the year It will receive 'compensation', however, from Bank A of £20 000 (the difference between interest at 14% and the agreed 12%).

If on the other hand the market rate of interest falls to 9%, the company will borrow from Bank B at 9% and pay Bank B £90 000 interest over the year. It will also, however, have to pay 'compensation' to Bank A of £30 000.

As can be seen the FRA agreement between the company and Bank A means that the company eliminates the uncertainty. It knows precisely what the cost of its borrowing will be in six months' time. An FRA does not mean the company necessarily gains financially over what it could have achieved without the agreement.

In fact, the FRA market is mainly an interbank market. Non-bank businesses can often get their banker to quote a 'forward' loan interest rate. This means that not only will a bank tell a customer how much it will cost to borrow today, but also how much it will charge if the customer wishes to borrow in six months' time. In the example, therefore, the company should be able to get Bank B to agree that it will lend in six months' time at a predetermined interest rate. This eliminates uncertainly, making an FRA unnecessary.

Interest-rate guarantees

Interest-rate guarantees (IRGs) are short-term options, usually with a maximum maturity of one year. If a company wants longer-term guarantees it can use caps, collars or floors.

Interest-rate guarantees and interest-rate options (IROs) allow a borrowing company to hedge against upward movements in interest rates. The company can do this without losing (other than the cost of the guarantee or option) if there is a downward movement in interest rate. They are similar in this respect to other forms of options.

Similarly if a company plans to invest funds in the future an IRG or IRO will allow the company to hedge against downward movements in interest rates. If interest rates should rise, the company just invests in the market, earns higher interest and pays the cost of the option.

The IRG involves the payment of a premium to the seller of the guarantee, which has to be paid whether or not the option element of the guarantee is exercised.

A major difference between IRGs and FRAs is that although both protect against downside risk, only the IRG allows the holder the opportunity to gain from a favourable movement in interest rates. If a borrower is worried about interest rates rising by the time the company needs to borrow, both the IRG and FRA will 'lock' the company into the maximum amount of interest that will need to be paid.

If, however, having entered into an FRA or IRG the interest rates fall by the time the company wishes to borrow, only the IRG will allow the company to benefit.

Caps, collars and floors

These are hedging techniques that can be used to cover risk on longer-term borrowing. As the names imply, a 'cap' is an upper-level interest rate and a 'floor' a lower-level interest rate. With a collar a company enters into an arrangement such that it will borrow for a period of time with a floating interest rate, but it knows it will not have to pay more than the 'cap' rate, but on the other hand it will not be able to pay less than the 'floor' rate.

A cap

Let us assume Booker PLC wishes to borrow £10 million for five years. The company's bank will only lend the money at a floating rate, of say LIBOR + $2\frac{1}{2}$%. The company's treasurer is worried that interest rates will rise in future.

One solution for the treasurer is to take the loan on the bank's terms, but also to buy an interest-rate 'cap' agreement. The cap is for a rate of let us say 14%. At the present time LIBOR is 10%, so the company is paying $12\frac{1}{2}$% interest per annum. Let us say interest rates rise in future and in year 3 of the loan LIBOR rises to 12%. In this situation the cap agreement will become operative.

Booker PLC will only have to pay 14%, not the $14\frac{1}{2}$% which is the level of the floating rate. A 'cap' sets an upper limit on the interest to be paid, but allows the company to benefit from falling interest rates. The company has to pay to enter a 'cap' agreement. How much it will pay depends on how close the level of interest agreed as a cap is to the level of interest rates in the market at the date the agreement is signed.

A collar

It is possible for a company to reduce the cost of hedging with a cap agreement, by simultaneously entering into a floor agreement. The bank's risk in an interest-rate cap agreement is that it will lose if interest rates rise in the market but will not gain if interest rates fall. If interest rates fall over time all the bank receives is the premium paid when the agreement is signed.

If the company wishing to borrow enters into an interest-rate floor agreement with a bank at the same time that it enters into an interest-rate cap agreement with the bank, it will reduce the premium paid for entering into the hedge. It will be improving the bank's expected financial outcome.

In the example above let us say Booker PLC enters into a 'floor' agreement with the bank at say a level of 9.5%; it will improve the bank's position and therefore reduce the premium that the company has to pay. We have described above what happens if interest rates rise. Now with this floor agreement, let us say interest rates begin to fall. Assume LIBOR drops to 6%. Without the floor agreement Booker will only be paying the bank $8\frac{1}{2}\%$ on its borrowings. It has, however, entered into a floor agreement. Booker therefore has to pay the 9.5% agreed lower level.

This arrangement whereby a company enters simultaneously into both a cap agreement and a floor agreement is known as a 'collar'.

17.9 INTEREST-RATE FUTURES CONTRACTS

The nature and purpose of futures contracts were outlined in Chapter 16. In this chapter the use of one form of futures contract will be considered. An interest-rate futures contract has, in common with all contracts, a buyer and a seller. The buyer agrees to receive the interest on a particular sum of money on an agreed future date. The seller of the contract agrees to pay the interest on the sum of money on the agreed future date. The rate of interest is specified in the contract.

Futures contracts are legally binding agreements. Unlike options it is not possible for one of the parties to decide not to exercise the futures contract. The buyer and seller will make profits or losses depending on how interest rates move in the money market between the time when the contract is taken out and when it is time for delivery.

The interest-rate futures (IRF) contract is not concerned with the borrowing or lending of the capital sum. As with an FRA the futures deal involves a separate contract, additional to the agreement to borrow or lend a sum of money. An IRF offers the opportunity to hedge against interest-rate risk.

When hedging by means of futures two separate sets of transactions take place, one in the money market (the borrowing or lending of the principal sum) and the other in the futures market. The futures market deal is approximately equal in size to the money market transaction, but is designed to be in the opposite direction. This means that if the company loses in the money market it gains in the futures market. But if it gains in the money market it loses in the futures market.

There are a number of futures markets around the world. The London Financial Futures Exchange (LIFFE) was established in 1982. It is the futures exchange in Europe offering the widest range of futures contracts. The Exchange offers six types of short-term interest-rate contracts, six types of bond futures contracts, and one type of stock market index-linked futures contract.

The contract

Table 17.5 shows an extract from the *Financial Times* in October 1997. The heading shows the name of the contract and the market in which the contract is

Cash and interest-rate management

Table 17.5 *Extract from Financial Times – futures contracts*

THREE MONTH STERLING FUTURES (LIFFE) £500,000 points of 100%

	Open	Sett price	Change	High	Low	Est. vol	Open int.
Dec	92.66	92.64	−0.02	92.66	92.62	19041	134327
Mar	92.62	92.62	−0.01	92.65	92.60	21632	114497
Jun	92.65	92.65	−0.01	92.68	92.62	23267	84197
Sep	92.68	92.70	–	92.74	92.67	9579	63269
Dec	92.79	92.80	−0.01	92.83	92.78	5940	62838

Also traded on APT. All open interest figs. are for previous day.

THREE MONTH EURODOLLAR (IMM) $lm points of 100%

	Open	sett price	Change	High	Low	Est. vol	Open int.
Dec	94.10	94.09	—	94.11	94.08	62.031	573,799
Mar	94.01	94.01	–	94.03	94.00	66.301	439.140
Jun	93.92	93.92	–	93.93	93.90	36.834	345.267

listed. The first futures contract referred to is listed on LIFFE, the second is listed on the International Money Market (IMM). The IMM is located in Chicago and is the most important futures market in the world.

The currencies to which the interest-rate futures refer is shown in the headings. The statistics shown include the opening prices of a contract, the change in the day in the price of the contract, intra-day highs and lows, and the estimated volume of trading in the contract on the previous day.

All short-term futures contracts are based on borrowing or lending for a three-month period. This means that the interest rate for borrowing or lending is fixed for a three-month period starting from an agreed future date. Let us say a company enters into such a contract in October 1997. It will be determining the rate of interest at which it will borrow for a three-month period starting at a future date, either December 1997 or March or June 1998.

In the LIFFE the dates for all futures contracts follow a March/June/September/December cycle. The buyer of such a contract on 1 October 1997 could choose a contract with a December starting date. This is the earliest futures contract it could enter into. They would be fixing the interest rate for the first three months of 1998. The contract with a starting date the furthest into the future would be one for 18 months ahead of the next starting date. This means that in October 1997 the borrower could be locking into an interest rate it will pay for three months from the end of June 1999.

It should be appreciated that LIFFE (as are all future exchanges) is a market place. There is a primary market in which buyers and sellers agree on new contracts. There is also a secondary market in which futures contracts already in existence can be bought and sold before their expiry date. A company that enters into the initial contract to sell a futures at an agreed future date could therefore pass on this commitment to another party, by selling the contract before the expiry date.

It is important to remember that an interest-rate futures contract is in fact buying and selling only the cash flow associated with the interest-rate payments. The actual loan has to be obtained from another source. A fully hedged position involves two separate sets of transactions, (1) borrowing *or* lending in the money markets, (2) buying *and* selling in the futures market.

The company entering into futures contracts is seeking to ensure that they will only have to pay interest on a loan at a rate of say 10%. If interest rates in the money market rise to say 12% by the time the company needs the funds the company obtaining the loan will have to pay the lender the 12%, but will make a profit of 2% on the futures contracts. LIFFE and other futures exchanges guarantee this position, so if the counterparty in the futures contracts goes out of business, the exchange authorities will pay the 2% difference.

The tick

The prices of the contracts are not quoted in terms of interest rates. The convention is that they are priced at 100 minus the annual interest rate to be paid. So a contract shown as being priced at 90 is effectively quoting a forward interest rate of 10% per annum (i.e. 100 − 90). This 10% is the borrowing rate. The normal spread in this market is $\frac{1}{8}$ of 1%, which means the interest paid on an investment for the same period would be 9.875% (i.e. 10% − 0.125%).

In Table 17.5 the three-months Eurodollar is quoted for December on IMM as 94.10. This means a borrowing rate of 5.90%.

The movement allowed in these futures prices is in units of one basis point – of one-hundredth of 1% (i.e. 0.01%) of the base of 100. This means that the smallest movement in a contract with a price of 90 is to 89.99 or 90.01. This smallest movement is known as the 'tick size' (0.01).

The profit or loss with such movements in futures contracts prices needs to be converted into money. The three-month sterling interest futures market is based on a contract size of £500 000 (see Table 17.5). A movement of one basis point therefore means £50. A further complication is that the price is based on annual interest rates, whereas the contracts are only for three months. This gives a value per tick (per basis point) on a three-month contract of £12.50.

Example

If interest rates fall by 0.5%, that is, by 50 ticks (0.5% ÷ 0.01), an investor who has bought 20 such contracts will therefore gain by 20 × 50 × £12.50 = £12 500 (i.e. the number of contracts × number of ticks × value per tick).

A futures contract will rise in value as interest rates fall in value, the price being 100 less the interest rate. Buying a futures contract does not mean that a sum of money, such as £500 000 × 90, ever has to be paid. The only cash that ever has to transfer between the buyer and seller is the amount covering interest payments.

The hedge

For a company wishing to hedge a loan it will initially sell futures if it expects interest rates to rise. If a company wishes to hedge funds deposited against falling interest rates they will initially buy futures contracts.

The price of a contract (say 90) represents the interest to be paid on a sum of money (i.e. 10%). It is being quoted on an index basis. What a company is buying or selling is the interest over a period of time on a sum of money. The purchaser of the contract will receive that sum of money. The seller will deliver that sum of money. The sum of money is due for delivery in the middle of the agreed month. Very few contracts are in fact left to mature. Offsetting transactions are usually entered into and only the balance of money is transferred. This offsetting is illustrated in Example 17.1.

Example 17.1

We will demonstrate how a short-term interest-rate futures contract can be used to hedge against interest-rate risk. The treasurer of Atkinson PLC plans to borrow £1 million in two months' time for a period of three months. It is now 1 March. She believes that interest rates will rise in future and wishes to take out a future contract on LIFFE to minimize the company's risk.

The following prices are being quoted on 1 March.

Cash and interest-rate management

3-month £ sterling futures contract (£500 000)

Mar.	92.00
June	91.00
Sept.	90.00

The current interest rate (in March) is 8%. The market clearly expects interest rates to rise in value. In March the market expects interest rates in June to be 9%. (That is why it is quoting a price of 91.00.) In May interest rates in fact rise to 10%. This will mean the price of June futures contracts being quoted in May will fall to 90.0. Interest rates have risen more quickly than the market expects.

Required

Show how an interest-rate futures contract can be used as a hedge by Atkinson PLC.

Necessary steps to answer questions

The first step is to calculate the target interest cost. The second step is to decide on the number of futures contracts that need to be bought or sold, to complete a hedge. The third step is to decide the appropriate date for the contracts. The fourth step, and perhaps the most difficult, is to decide whether the company needs to be a buyer or seller of a futures contract.

The rule with regard to buying or selling is that if the company wishes to hedge against rising interest rates it will initially sell futures contracts. (This is called a 'short hedge'.) If the company wishes to hedge against falling interest rates it will initially buy futures contracts (called a 'long hedge'). Why this rule?

If interest rates rise over time, the price of futures contracts fall (100 − interest rate) over time. We initially agree to sell at a future date (something at present we do not own). As the date for delivery gets nearer (the expiry date of the contract), the price of the futures contracts will have fallen. We will then be able to buy in the market a contract with the same expiry date at a cheaper price than we agreed to sell it for. We settle for the difference, a profit. This profit compensates for the higher interest rates we are paying on the actual borrowing.

Let us say that Atkinson PLC expects interest rates to rise. It is now 1 March. The company wishes to borrow on 1 May and repay on 1 August.

The treasurer will now sell futures contracts for delivery in June now at a price of 91. In May the treasurer will buy futures contracts at a price of 90. The gain on futures helps offset the higher interest charge paid on the borrowings.

Answer

Step 1

The interest target is 8% × £1 000 000 × $\frac{1}{4}$ = £20 000. This is based on interest rates at 1 March.

Step 2

Two contracts need to be entered into to cover the £1 million.

Step 3

The company as at 1 March could choose contracts dated March, June or September. The March date is no use as the contracts will have expired by the time the company needs to borrow. Any interest-rate movement affecting borrowing in May will affect futures prices only after the March contracts have expired. It would be normal to choose the June contract, as the contract with the next expiry date following the date the loan is required.

Step 4

The treasurer wishes to hedge against rising interest rates and so will initially agree to sell futures contracts. Futures contracts will fall in value, if as expected, interest rates rise. The treasurer will then enter into an offsetting futures transaction by buying futures.

Transactions

Money market On 1 May the company borrows £1 000 000 at 10% for a three-month period. Interest costs £100 000 × $\frac{1}{4}$ = £25 000. Loss against target £5000.

Futures market

- *On 1 March* Sell two sterling contracts at £91 to be delivered in June. £91
- *In May* Buy two contracts at £90 for delivery in June. £90
- *In June* Close contracts. 1 = 100 ticks

Total profit = 2 (Contracts) × 100 × £12.50 = £2500

This gain of £2500 provides some compensation for the target loss of £5000.

Efficiency of hedge

It should be noted that a futures hedge is not always a perfect hedge. It does not always fully compensate for the changes in interest cost resulting from the changes in interest rates in the money market.

The efficiency of the hedge depends on two factors:

1 How close is the movement in the price of future contracts to the movement in actual interest rates? In the Atkinson example, we assumed that the movement in interest rates between March and May was from 8% to 10%. However, we only allowed for movement in the June futures price from 91.0 to 90.0, a much smaller movement. In fact in the market the movement in futures prices is approximately in line with changes in interest rates in the money market.

If we had allowed the interest rates and the futures price to move at the same rate we would have had a perfect hedge, the June futures price moving from 91.0 in March to 89.0 in May:

1 March: Sell two contracts at   £91
May: Buy two contracts at   £89
                 £2 = 200 ticks

June: Close the contracts
    Profit = 2 (contracts) × 200 (ticks) × 12.50 = £5000

It should be appreciated the movement in futures prices is not always exactly in line with the movement in interest rates. It is not usual, therefore, to obtain a perfect hedge.

2 The second factor on which the efficiency of the hedge depends is how close is the amount of money covered in the hedge (number of contracts × size of contract) to the amount of money borrowed or deposited. In our example we had an exact match. The £1 000 000 borrowed equalled two contracts each for £500 000. This is unusual. In futures markets contracts are for standard sizes and so it is not always possible to match the amount to be hedged with an exact number of contracts. It may be necessary to enter into contracts for a greater or lesser amount than the sum at risk.

It might be possible to obtain an exact match in the over-the-counter market.

Over-the-counter

There is nothing new about futures and options contracts. They have long existed in the commodities market with deals made between farmers and food processors. The first futures exchange that offered deals in other derivatives, that is in currencies, interest rates and stock market indices, was established in Chicago in 1973.

What is relatively new is what is called the 'over-the-counter' (OTC) market. This is a market, not based around a specific exchange, in which trades are arranged in any size between a bank and its customer; or between two banks. Such deals are not subject to the regulation of an exchange.

In the OTC market, prices are negotiated between the parties and the terms are 'customized' to suit the needs of the parties. This is in contrast to deals in established exchanges, where prices are quoted, and the terms are standardized.

Example 17.2

The corporate treasurer of Cradley PLC plans to borrow 10 million Italian lire in three months' time for a period of three months. There is a possibility of a change in government in Italy and interest rates have recently been volatile. The treasurer has received a number of suggestions as to how to protect against interest rate risk. These include:

1. an FRA in Italian lire;
2. futures contracts in Italian lire;
3. an interest-rate guarantee in Italy;
4. a collar OTC interest rate option in Italy.

The following prices are available. It is now 1 April.

FRA in three months for periods of up to six months at 86.25

Futures
Italian 3 months futures (Lire 1 000 000 contract)

June	88.00
September	87.75

Interest-rate guarantee
A guarantee at 13.75% is available at a premium of 0.25% of the amount to be borrowed.

Collar
A collar, with a ceiling exercise price of 13.9% and a floor of 12%, is available at a premium of 0.1% of the amount to be borrowed.

The current base rate in Italy is 12%. Cradley can borrow in Italy at base plus $\frac{1}{2}$%.

Required

Evaluate with hindsight the effects of the four alternative hedging strategies that have been suggested to the treasurer, if:

1. interest rates in Italy increase in three months' time to a base rate of 14%;
2. interest rates in Italy decrease in three months' time to a base rate 11%.

Comment on your findings. State any assumptions you make.

Answer

1. *Forward rate agreement in Italian lire*

Effective cost $100 - 86.25 = 13.75\%$
Cost of 3 months loan $= $ L 10 million $\times 13.75\% \times \frac{3}{12} = $ 343 750 lire

This is the cost whatever happens to the level of interest rates in the future.

If interest rates rise to 14%, Cradley will borrow in the market at 14.5% and receive compensation from the bank with whom it has an FRA – for the difference of 0.75%. If interest rates fall to 11%, Cradley will borrow in the market at 11.5% and pay compensation of 2.25% to the bank with whom it has the agreement.

2. *Futures contracts in Italian lire*

(a) Target outcome
$$10\,000\,000 \times 12\tfrac{1}{2}\% \times \tfrac{3}{12} \qquad = \text{L } 312\,500$$

With 14% rates in future:

(b) Expect interest rates to rise, so sell futures now for September delivery.
Need 10 contacts (loan 10 million lire, each contract for 1 million lire).
At beginning of July, at the time of borrowing in the money market, undertake reverse futures agreement. That is, buy futures for September date.

(c) *Transactions*
Money market
Borrow L 10 million on 1 July
Cost

$10\,000\,000 \times 14\tfrac{1}{2}\% \times \tfrac{3}{12}$	$= \text{L } 362500$
Loss against target	$= \text{L } 50\,000$

Futures market
1 April
Sell 10 futures at 87.75 for September
1 July
Buy 10 futures at 85.75 for September

Note: It is assumed the futures contract moves by the same amount (2%) as the move in the interest rates in the money market.

30 September
Close transactions:
- Move of 200 ticks (i.e. 2%)
- Tick size
  $\text{L } 1\,000\,000 \times (100 \text{ of } 1\%) \times \tfrac{3}{12}$
  $= \text{Lire } 25$
- 10 contracts

Outcome: profit on futures of:

$10 \times 200 \times 25$ lire	$= \text{Lire } 50\,000$

(d) *Overall cost*

L 10 million $\times 14.5\% \times \tfrac{3}{12}$	$= \text{L } 362\,500$
Less profit on futures	50 000
	L 312 500

With 11% base rate in future
(b) Sell futures now for September delivery. On 1 July buy futures for September delivery.

(c) Transactions

Money market
Cost of borrowing on 1 July
L 10 million $\times$ $11\frac{1}{2}$% $\times$ $\frac{3}{12}$ = L 287 500
Gain against target   = L 25 000

Futures market
1 April
Sell 10 futures at 87.75 for September
1 July
Buy 10 futures at 88.75 for September
(Assume futures contract price moves by same percentage points as move in interest rates, i.e. 1%)
30 September
Close transaction:

    Move of 100 ticks
    Outcome: loss of:
    10 $\times$ 100 $\times$ 25   = L 25 000

(d) Overall cost
L 10 million $\times$ 11.5% $\times$ $\frac{3}{12}$ = 287 500
Plus loss on futures   25 000
     312 500

3. *Interest-rate guarantee*
Market rates rise to 14%.

The company has the choice of either borrowing in the market at 14.5% and paying the cost of the option, or borrowing under the terms of the guarantee at 13.75% and paying the cost of the option. Clearly the latter is preferable. The option will be exercised. The cost will be:

L 10 million $\times$ 13.75 $\times$ $\frac{3}{12}$ = 343 750
plus
cost of guarantee L 10 million $\times$ 0.25%   = 25 000
     368 750

Market rates fall to 11%
The option will not be exercised. The cost of the finance will be

L 10 million $\times$ 11.5% $\times$ $\frac{3}{12}$ =287 500
plus
cost of guarantee   = 25 000
     312 500

4. *Collar*
Interest rates rise to 14%
The option will be exercised. Choice is between borrowing in the market at 14.5% plus premium, or borrowing at 13.9% plus premium.

Cost
Lire 10 million $\times$ 13.9% $\times$ $\frac{3}{12}$ = 347 500
plus
10 million $\times$ 0.1%   = 10 000
     357 500

Interest rates fall to 11%
Collar will be effective. It guaranteed that the most Cradley would have to pay was 13.9% (plus premium) and the least Cradley would have to pay would be 12% (plus premium). Cradley having entered into a 'collar' contract cannot take advantage of the opportunity to borrow in market at 11.5%.

Cost with 'floor'

Lire 10 million $\times$ 12% $\times$ $\frac{3}{12}$ = 300 000
plus
Premium   = 10 000
     310 000

Summary of costs

	Base rate 14%	Base rate 11%
FRA	343 750	343 750
Futures	312 500	312 500
Interest-rate guarantee	368 750	312 500
Collar	357 500	310 000

With the rates given in the question clearly the FRA is unattractive. The interest-rate guarantee is Inferior to the futures contract, because although they have the same cost with interest rates at 11%, the futures contracts have the lower cost at the higher interest rates. The choice is between the collar and the futures. Futures give a lower cost at higher interest rates (the difference between borrowing at 12.5% and 13.9%, plus premium). The collar gives a lower cost at lower interest rates (the difference between 12% plus premium and 12.5%).

17.10 DURATION

We have seen that firms can hedge interest-rate risk by using interest-rate futures contracts. It is also possible to hedge interest-rate risk by matching the duration of liabilities with the duration of assets. Interest-rate risk is affected by both the maturity date and the coupon rate of debt instruments. A risk measure that takes both these factors into consideration is called 'duration'. Duration measures the weighted-average maturity of an asset's or liability's cash flows. The weights are determined by present-value factors and expressed in years and fractions of years.

The greater the duration the greater the risk; zero coupon bonds will have a duration equal to the time to maturity while the duration of an interest-paying bond will be less than the time to maturity with higher coupon bonds having lower durations. Overall risk can be established by calculating the duration of a group of assets or liabilities. This can be done by calculating an average of the duration of the individual items weighted by the market value of each item.

The concept of duration is particularly useful for financial institutions who receive deposits and invest these in a portfolio of securities. They will seek to immunize themselves from interest-rate risk. Immunization occurs when:

$$\text{duration of assets} \times \text{market value of assets} = \text{duration of liabilities} \times \text{market value of liabilities}$$

The maturity of a bond is clearly a factor to take into account when making an investment decision. It does, however, only indicate when the final cash flow (the redemption) is to be made. It ignores all the interim cash flows resulting from the payment of interest. Duration measures the weighted-average time of the cash flow payments. The weights are the present value of the cash flows themselves.

The formula for duration is

$$\sum_{t=1}^{n} \frac{t \times PVCF_t}{K \times TPVCF}$$

where K is number of periods per annum (i.e. number of interest payments per annum), n is number of periods, until maturity ($K \times$ number of years to maturity), t is period when cash-flow is to be received, $PVCF_t$ is present value of cash flow in period t (discounted at yield to maturity) and TPVCF is total PV of all the cash flows. This looks complicated but is not. The numerator is simply the sum of the time until the receipt (t) of each cash-flow multiplied by the present value of the cash flow for the period (t). The denominator is the sum of the PV of the cash-flows times K, which is equal to the price of the bond.

We will illustrate the concept of duration with an example. Let us assume we are considering a 9% debenture with 5 years to go before maturity. Interest is paid semi-annually. The price of the bond today is £100. The interest yield and the yield to maturity equal 9%. We are asked to calculate the 'duration' of the debenture.

(1) Periods each of six months	(2) Cash flow per debenture (£)	(3) PV factor at interest rate of 4.5%	(4) PV (column 3 × column 2)	(5) (t × PV) = (column 4 × column 1)
1	4.50	0.957	4.31	4.31
2	4.50	0.916	4.12	8.24
3	4.50	0.876	3.94	11.83
4	4.50	0.839	3.78	15.12
5	4.50	0.802	3.61	18.50
6	4.50	0.768	3.46	20.76
7	4.50	0.735	3.31	23.17
8	4.50	0.703	3.16	25.28
9	4.50	0.673	3.03	27.27
10	104.50	0.644	67.30	673.00
Total			100.00	826.88

$$\text{Duration} = \frac{826.8}{2 \times 100} = 4.13 \text{ years}$$

This is the weighed-average time of the cash-flow payments. The big payment is of course the redemption. As can be seen this so-called Macauley duration is less than its maturity (5 years). For a zero coupon bond the duration is equal to its maturity, this being the only cash payment. If other factors are held constant the lower the coupon rate, the greater the duration of the bond, and the closer it is to its time to maturity.

This measure of duration is used by analysts to measure the volatility of a fixed-interest security, the relationship being

$$\frac{-1}{\left(1 + \dfrac{\text{yield}}{K}\right)} \times \text{Macauley duration} \times \text{yield change} \times 100$$

$$= \text{percentage change in price of bond}$$

We will illustrate the use of this formula by continuing with the above example. Let us say there is a change in the market's required yield to maturity from 9% to 10%. Substituting in the equation:

$$\frac{-1}{\left(\dfrac{1 + 0.09}{2}\right)} \times 4.13 \times (+0.010) \times 100$$

The estimate is very accurate for small changes in yields, but is less accurate for large changes.

17.11 INTEREST-RATE SWAPS

The size of the market for interest rate swaps is huge and yet when they are first explained to those new to the subject few believe such arrangements can work. Here is a situation in which everyone gains and nobody loses. Two companies can come to an arrangement such that both companies reduce their costs of borrowing. The fact that such opportunities exist is due to imperfection in the money market. Basically it is because the risk premiums charged to a company in the fixed rate borrowing market are not necessarily the same as the risk premiums charged in the floating rate market. One example has already been given in Chapter 9.

Example 17.3

You are the new finance director of Douglas PLC. The company wishes to borrow £100 million for five years. At a fixed rate of interest this will cost 14% per annum and at a floating rate of LIBOR + 1¼%. A bank has offered to arrange an interest-rate swap for two years with a smaller company Wight PLC which can borrow floating-rate debt at LIBOR + 2%, and fixed-rate borrowing at 15¾%. The bank charges will be ignored.

Because of the existing balance of their debt portfolios Douglas wishes to service a floating-rate loan. Wight wishes to service a fixed-rate loan.

Required

Do you think there is an opportunity for an interest-rate swap contract? Assume any savings would be shared equally between the companies.

Answer

	Douglas	Wight	Difference
Fixed	14%	15.75%	1.75%
Floating	LIBOR + 1.25%	LIBOR + 2%	0.75%
	Potential saving		1.00%

Douglas can borrow more cheaply than Wight both fixed- and floating-rate loans, but its comparative advantage is In fixed-rate borrowing. For both companies to gain from a swap it is necessary for Douglas PLC to borrow at fixed rates and to service the floating-rate debt.

One solution, which will divide the gains equally, is for Wight to pay Douglas 15¼% fixed, and for Douglas to pay Wight LIBOR + 2%. It should be appreciated, however, that there are many alternative solutions which will result in the gains being shared equally.

Solution

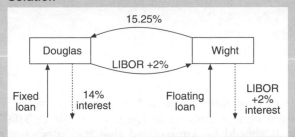

It should be noted that Douglas borrows a fixed-rate loan, even though it services (as is the wish of the company) the floating-rate loan. Douglas's cash outflow now varies over time according to the movement in interest rates.

The fact that these particular inter-company payments result in an equal share of the gain can be proven as follows:

Douglas	Fixed-rate borrowing		
	Pay the lender	14%	
	Receive from Wight	15.25%	
	Gain		1.25%
	Floating		
	Pay Wight	LIBOR + 2%	
	Opportunity cost	LIBOR + 1.25%	
	Opportunity loss		0.75%
	Net gain		0.50%
Wight	Fixed rate		
	Pay Douglas	15.25%	
	Opportunity cost	15.75%	
	Gain		0.50%
	Floating rate		
	Pay lender	LIBOR + 2.0%	
	Receive from Douglas	LIBOR + 2.0% 0	
	Net gain		0.50%

Two things need explaining. First, the opportunity cost represents the cost to the company if it had gone to the market and borrowed that form of finance. For example, If Wight had gone to the market for fixed-rate finance it would have cost 15.75%, whereas Wight is only paying Douglas 15.25%. This is giving it a saving in servicing fixed-rate borrowing of 0.5%.

The second issue is a practical one. A simple approach to working out the rates of interest paid by one company to the other is to hold the rate on the one form of borrowing at the market rate. For example, in this problem the payment from Douglas to Wight to service the floating-rate debt (LIBOR + 2%) is the same as the rate paid by Wight to the market. The gains are then all based on the rates for the other form of borrowing.

Remember, Douglas actually borrows the fixed-rate funds from the market because it can obtain fixed-rate borrowing more cheaply than Wight. The issue to be settled Is the swap arrangement – how much will Wight transfer to Douglas to service this fixed-rate borrowing?

Solution (based on monetary amounts)

The above was based on interest rates. We will now substitute monetary amounts to prove to the doubters that interest-rate swaps work. The question told us that £100 million was to be borrowed (and the interest-rate streams swapped). Let us assume LIBOR is 12%. It should be appreciated that the capital sums borrowed do not need to be swapped as both companies borrow the same amount (in the same currency).

The cash-flows are:

Douglas		£ million
Fixed		
Pay lender	–	14.00
Receive from Wight	+	15.25
Floating		
Pay Wight	–	14.00
Net cost		12.75

New cost of floating-rate capital 12.75%

This results in a saving of £0.50 million on the cost of floating-rate borrowing without a swap (13.25%).

Wight		£ million
Pay lender	–	14.00
Receive from Douglas	+	14.00
Pay Douglas	–	15.25
Net cost	–	15.25

This results in a saving of £0.50 million on the cost of fixed-rate borrowing without a swap. It reduces Wight's cost of fixed-rate borrowed capital from 15.75% to 15.25%.

Let us now assume LIBOR equals 15%.

Douglas		£ million
Pay lender	–	14.00
Receive from Wight	+	15.25
Pay Wight	–	17.00
The cost of capital is now 15.75%	–	15.75

This again gives a saving of £0.50 million on floating-rate debt without a swap (16.25%). It is, however, more expensive than if Douglas had borrowed at fixed rates.

The company is paying 15.75% for floating-rate debt whereas it could have borrowed fixed at 14%. But the company decided before the swap was agreed that it wished to service floating-rate debt. If the market rates of interest rise the cost of floating-rate debt could well be above the cost of fixed-rate debt. The point about the swap arrangement is that for Douglas it has reduced the cost of its floating-rate debt – the issue is not whether fixed costs more or less than floating.

For Wight with LIBOR at 15%		£ million
Pay lender	–	17.00
Receive from Douglas	+	17.00
Pay Douglas	–	15.25
Net cost	–	15.25

This again gives a saving of £0.50 million over the cost of fixed-rate borrowing without a swap.

17.12 THE MARKET FOR DERIVATIVES

The growth in the markets for interest-rate swaps and for currency swaps is dramatic. The markets grew from almost nothing in the early 1980s to $1000 billion markets ten years later. It should be appreciated that the interest-rate swap market is four times the size of the currency swap market.

The growth reflects not only the use of the market by industrial and commercial companies, but also by financial institutions and public-sector entities. All use these instruments for funding and risk-management purposes.

In the interest-rate swap market approximately half of the deals are interbank and half what are termed 'end-users' (that is, one non-financial company with another non-financial company). Of course in the 'end-user' market banks often act as an intermediary, charging an arrangement fee.

Worries about derivatives!

There are in fact many other types of derivative, with names such as:

- corridors;
- range-forwards;
- cylinders;
- barrier options;
- compound options.

New, more 'exotic' versions are being created all the time. They are all variations on the themes described in this and other chapters in the book.

A swap is a financial derivative. Financial regulators are concerned with certain aspects of the derivative markets, in particular the swap, futures and options markets. They appreciate the value of derivatives to the parties involved, but are concerned about the following issues.

1 The adequacy of risk management practices in the firms involved, and the level of disclosure of the firms' involvement.
2 The pricing models used to value derivative products, with the assumptions made including that on liquidity in the market. The option models become less valid the greater the volatility in the price of the underlying asset. Not all option writers cover their position. With volatility some can face substantial losses. Who will meet these losses if the writers cannot?
3 The deepening linkages across markets that result from derivatives.
4 The lack of transparency (of disclosure) in the derivative markets.

5 They are concerned that, although there is competition for business between option and swap markets and between countries, there is also an increasing level of cooperation. For example in 1993 the International Swap Dealers Association reached agreement which clarified the rights and obligations of swap counterparties in the event of default. This issue resulted from a dispute in the USA in which one counterparty defaulted. The legal issue was whether or not a swap should be considered a futures contract. In the end it was decided that a swap contract was not a form of futures contract.

Many economists and politicians are concerned about the impact of derivatives on the international financial system. The flexibility and linkages between markets mean that they can distort underlying price movements, and limit an individual national government's ability to manage its own economy. This is a general problem as financial markets become global. What derivatives can do is add to volatility in foreign-exchange rates, and reduce the effect of government attempts to manage interest rates within a country.

It is also possible for those who play in the derivatives market to lose money. In Chapter 15, a list is shown of the major losses on derivatives.

Proctor & Gamble blamed outside derivative dealers for selling the company risky financial instruments! A failure that attracted a great deal of attention in 1994 was the case of Metallgesellschaft, a German metals, mining and industrial group. The company lost DM 2.3 billion through trading in oil derivatives. The size of the losses was so great that it nearly led to the financial collapse of the company. The company in 1992 began negotiating long-term fixed-price contracts to sell fuel to petrol stations and small businesses. In order to lock into the profit the company hedged by buying oil futures on the New York mercantile exchange.

Oil prices began to fall sharply in the market in 1993, reducing the value of the futures contracts. There is disagreement as to why the company lost. Some argue that there was a mismatch between the short-term hedge and the long-term liability, others argue that the company became concerned about the losses too early. If it had continued to invest in futures, and to pay the margins required by the counterparties the end result would have been satisfactory. One outcome was that the company sacked its treasury managers.

17.13 FURTHER READING

The corporate treasury function has assumed greater prominence with the increased volatility of foreign-exchange rates and interest rates. A selection of books and articles dealing with the issues and techniques is shown below.

Block, S.B. and Gallagher, T.J. (1986) The use or interest rate futures and options by corporate financial management, *Financial Management*, Autumn.

Collier, P.A., Cooke T.E. and Glynn, J.J. (1988) *Financial and Treasury Management*, Heinemann Professional Publishing.

Davis, E.W. and Collier, P.A. (1982) *Treasury Management in the UK*, Association of Corporate Treasurers.

Donaldson, J.A. (1988) *The Corporate Treasury Function*, ICAS.

Galitz L. (1993) *Financial Engineering: Tools and Techniques to Manage Financial Risk*, Pitman/Financial Times, London.

Hartley, W.C.F. and Meltzer, Y. (1987) *Cash Management*, Prentice-Hall.

Hull, J. (1989) *Options, Futures and Other Derivative Securities*, Prentice-Hall, Englewood Cliffs, NJ.

Kallberg, J.G. and Parkinson, K. (1984) *Current Asset Management*, Wiley.

Ross, D. (1987) *International Treasury Management* , Woodhead-Faulkner Ltd, Cambridge.

Smith, K.V. (1988) *Readings on Short-term Financial Management*; West Publishing Company.

Watson, A. and Altringham, R. (1986) *Treasury Management, International Banking Operations*, The Institute of Bankers.

Wall L.D. and Pringle, J.J. (1989) Alternative explanations of interest rate swaps: a theoretical and empirical analysis, *Financial Management*, Summer.

17.14 PROBLEMS

1 Elmdon Heath Ltd. run a chain of golf supply shops. Their business is seasonal in nature. Their forecast sales for 1995 are as follows:

	£000s		£000s
January	20	July	160
February	12	Aug	100
March	12	Sept	48
April	20	Oct	12
May	32	Nov	12
June	100	Dec	48

50% of the company sales are on cash terms, and 50% on credit terms. Of the sales on credit 50% pay during the first month following sale and 50% during the second month.

The company purchases goods 3 months prior to when they are expected to be sold, and pays for them 2 months after purchase. The cost of purchases amounts to 60% of the sales price. Wages and administrative costs amount to £10 000 per month. Deprecation costs are £5000 per month. A tax payment of £20 000 needs to be made in April.

Required

(a) Prepare a cash budget for 1995. The opening cash balance is £20 000. Assume sales in the last few months of 1994 were similar to those forecast for the final months of 1995.

(b) What are the maximum and minimum monthly cash balances for the year? What policy would you advise with respect to these balances?

(c) How should depreciation costs be treated in a cash budget?

(d) The cash budget is a forecast. If sales in the early months of the year show signs of falling below forecasts how might the company act to protect its liquidity position? How would you allow for uncertainty in preparing a cash budget?

2 The finance director of Pondwood Ltd wishes to prepare an estimate of next year's working capital requirements. Sales for the next year are expected to be 85 500 units at a basic unit price of £50. Direct materials, direct wages and direct energy costs are expected to be £15.51 per unit, £17.35 per unit and £4.95 per unit respectively. Administrative salaries are forecast to be £264 000, and distribution and other overheads a total of £92 000. Corporate taxation is at a rate of 35%, payable one year in arrears. The current year's profit before taxation, after deducting interest payments of £118 000 for the company's overdraft, is £311 000. Pondwood offers its customers a 2.5% cash discount for payment within 14 days. On average 40% of customers take this discount, and the remainder take an average of 10 weeks to pay for their goods.

Stocks of raw materials equivalent to four weeks' usage are held, and finished goods equivalent to eight weeks' demand. The production process takes an average of four weeks. Work in progress is valued at the cost of materials for the full period of the production process and the cost of wages and energy for half the period of the production process. Pondwood is allowed eight weeks' credit from its suppliers of raw materials and six weeks' credit for distribution and other fixed costs. Energy bills are payable quarterly in arrears. The company pays wages one week in arrears and salaries one month in arrears (one month may be assumed to be four weeks).

Pondwood's existing overdraft facility has recently been extended to cover the next financial year. The interest rate payable on the company's overdraft has remained at 11% per annum during the past year, and is not expected to change during the foreseeable future. The company has utilized its full overdraft facility during the past year.

(a) Evaluate whether, on the basis of the above information, the company's overdraft facility is likely to be large enough to finance the company's working capital needs for the next year. State clearly any assumptions that you make. A monthly cash budget is not required as part of your evaluation. (15 marks)

(b) What other information would be helpful in the assessment of the company's overdraft requirements? (3 marks)

(c) Discuss what is meant by (i) an overdraft and (ii) an acceptance credit. What are the advantages and disadvantages of these forms of short-term finance? (7 marks)

ACCA

3 (a) Manling PLC has £14 million of fixed rate loans at an interest rate of 12% per year which are due to mature in one year. The company's treasurer believes that interest rates are going to fall, but does not wish to redeem the loans because large penalties exist for early redemption. Manling's bank has offered to arrange an interest-rate swap for one year with a company that has obtained floating-rate finance at London Interbank Offered Rate (LIBOR) plus $1\frac{1}{8}$%. The bank will charge each of the companies an arrangement fee of £20 000 and the proposed terms of the swap are that Manling will pay LIBOR plus $1\frac{1}{2}$% to the other company and receive from the company $11\frac{5}{8}$%.

Manling could issue floating-rate debt at LIBOR plus 2% and the other company could issue fixed-rate debt at $11\frac{3}{4}$%. Assume that any tax relief is immediately available.

Required:
(i) Evaluate whether Manling PLC would benefit from the interest-rate swap
(1) if LIBOR remains at 10% for the whole year;
(2) if LIBOR falls to 9% after six months. (6 marks)

(ii) If LIBOR remains at 10% evaluate whether both companies could benefit from the interest-rate swap if the terms of the swap were altered. Any benefit would be equally shared. (6 marks)

(b) Manling expects to have £1 million surplus funds for three months prior to making a tax payment. Discuss possible short-term investments for these funds. (5 marks)

ACCA, June 1990

4 (a) Discuss the possible advantages and disadvantages of centralizing the finance functions of a group of companies. (11 marks)

(b) If you were the managing director of a group of companies suggest, giving reasons for your suggestions, what financial ratios (or combinations of financial ratios) you might find useful in order to monitor, evaluate and control the activities of the group. (8 marks)

What problems might exist with the use of financial ratios as a financial control system within a group of companies? (6 marks)

ACCA

5 In three months' time your company will need to borrow £5 million for a six-month period. Current interest rates are around 9% p.a. and this annual rate currently applies to all spot and forward rates for up to 18 months.

Your firm is concerned that interest rates may rise from the level of 9% per annum before the loan is obtained.

Advise the treasurer on the financial instruments/securities which may be useful to him in managing this potential interest-rate risk and explain the characteristics of each of them. (15 marks)

6 (a) It is now 31 December 1991 and the corporate treasurer of Omniown PLC is concerned about the volatility of interest rates. His company needs in three months' time to borrow £5 million for a six-month period. Current interest rates are 14% per year for the type of loan Omniown would use, and the treasurer does not wish to pay more than this.

He is considering using either:
  (i) a forward-rate agreement (FRA), or
  (ii) interest-rate futures, or
  (iii) an interest-rate guarantee (short-term cap).

Required:
Explain briefly how each of these three alternatives might be useful to Omniown PLC. (10 marks)

(b) The corporate treasurer of Omniown PLC expects interest rates to increase by 2% during the next three months and has decided to hedge the interest rate risk using interest-rate futures.

March sterling three months time deposit futures are currently priced at 86.25. The standard contract size is £500 000 and the minimum price movement is one tick (the value of one tick is 0.01% per year of the contract size).

Required:
Show the effect of using the futures market to hedge against interest-rate movements:
  (i) If interest rates increase by 2% and the futures market price also moves by 2%;
  (ii) if interest rates increase by 2% and the futures market moves by 1.5%.
  (iii) if interest rates fall by 1% and the futures market moves by 0.75%.
In each case estimate the hedge efficiency.

Taxation, margin requirements, and the time value of money are to be ignored. (10 marks)

(c) If, as an alternative to interest-rate futures, the corporate treasurer had been able to purchase interest-rate guarantees at 14% for a premium of 0.2% of the size of the loan to be guaranteed, calculate whether the total cost of the loan after hedging in each of situations (i) to (iii) in (b) above would have been less with the futures hedge or with the guarantee. The guarantee would be effective for the entire six-month period of the loan.

Taxation, margin requirements and the time value of money are to be ignored. (5 marks)

ACCA, Dec.1997

Cash and interest-rate management

7 Panon PLC has a commitment to borrow £6 million in five months' time for a period of four months. A general election is due in four months' time, and the managers of Panon are concerned that interest rates could significantly increase just after the election.

Panon can currently borrow at LIBOR + 1%. Three month LIBOR is at 7.5%

Current LIFFE £500 000 sterling three-month futures prices are:

September   92.60
December   92.10.

Assume that it is now the end of June and that futures contracts mature at the end of the relevant month.

Required:
(a) Illustrate how Panon PLC could use a futures hedge to protect against its potential interest-rate risk. The type and number of contacts must be included in your illustration.   (5 marks)
(b) Estimate the basis risk for this hedge both now and at the time the contract is likely to be closed out. Comment upon the significance of your estimates for Panon PLC. Illustrate your answer with reference to the impact of a 2% increase in LIBOR.   (5 marks)

                                                                  (10 marks)
                                                          ACCA, June 1997

8 Noswis PLC borrowed two million Deutschmarks in four-year floating-rate Euro-Deutschmark (EDM) funds nine months ago at an interest rate LIBOR plus 1 %, in an attempt to reduce the level of interest paid on its loans. At that time EDM LIBOR was 6%. Unfortunately EDM LIBOR interest-rates have increased since that time to 7.2%. The company wishes to protect itself from further interest-rate volatility, but does not wish to lose the benefit of possible interest-rate reductions that might occur in a few months' time. An adviser has suggested the use of a six-month American-style DM swaption at 8.5% with a premium of DM50 000, commencing in three months' time and with a maturity date the same as the floating-rate EDM loan.

Required:
Briefly explain what is meant by a swaption, and illustrate under what circumstances this proposed swaption would benefit Noswis. The time value of money may be ignored.   (10 marks)
                                                          ACCA, Dec. 1995

18 MANAGEMENT OF DEBTORS AND INVENTORY

LEARNING OUTCOMES

By the end of this chapter the reader should:

- appreciate the importance of credit management
- be able to judge acceptable levels of risk, credit insurance and the terms of sale
- know the main sources of information for credit applicants
- be able to evaluate policies on the collection of debts
- understand the importance of efficient inventory management
- be familiar with and be able to use a range of stock control models
- understand the principles of the just-in-time philosophy

18.1 DEBTORS: THE PROBLEM

The typical company in the UK has a ratio of debtors to total assets in the region of 20–25%. This represents a considerable investment of funds, and so the management of this asset can have a significant effect on the profit performance of a company.

By international standards, the UK does not have a good record for the collection of debts. In the UK manufacturing sector it takes on average about 60 days for a company to collect the funds due from a debtor. In contrast, in the USA the average collection period for manufacturing industry is in the region of 40 days.

In the USA there seems to be a more professional approach towards credit management than in the UK. However, it might not be just a matter of more effective chasing up of creditors. It could be that in the UK there are different standards when it comes to paying debts. In the UK attitudes have developed such that the debtor often feels that it is acceptable to delay settlement beyond an agreed period. On occasion, the agreed credit terms are ignored.

The company that is selling will attach payment terms to the sale. It can, however, be a problem to enforce these terms. UK-listed companies are required to give details in their annual report and accounts of their policy with regard to payment of trade creditors. The difference in attitude to payment is illustrated by the statements made by two companies: Marks and Spencer in their 1995 accounts state 'it is the Company policy to: Agree the terms of payment at the start of business with that supplier. Ensure that suppliers are aware of the terms of payment. Pay in accordance with its contractual and other legal obligations.' In contrast, Halma PLC, a company in the engineering and aerospace industry, state that they have: 'due regard to the payment terms of supplies and generally settles all undisputed accounts within 30 days of the due date for payment.' The words 'generally' and 'within 30 days' would not give much comfort to suppliers.

It has to be remembered that most businesses not only have customers owing them money but they themselves owe money to suppliers, employees and the tax collector. Companies not only have to manage their debtors, they also have to manage their creditors.

A company has to pay its employees by the end of a week or a month and it is in trouble if it is late with its tax payments. It does, however, have some freedom as to when it pays its trade creditors. The subject of purchasing (or procurement) policy and the method of payment of suppliers is one which has become of increasing importance. We are making the point that there can be a connection between the terms offered on sales and the policy towards payment of suppliers. In the case of Marks and Spencers the funds tied up in debtors will be comparatively low because most of their sales are for cash. They can therefore afford to be more generous when it comes to paying suppliers than can Halma, for whom most sales are on credit.

Credit management is a problem of balancing profitability and liquidity. Credit terms are a sales attraction, and so the longer the time a company allows its customers to pay, the greater are the sales and the possible profits. However, the longer the credit terms the greater is the amount of debtors (accounts receivable) and the greater the possible strain on the company's liquidity.

The credit-issuing policy of a company should answer several questions. For instance, to whom should credit be extended? How much credit should be allowed (at an individual level and in total)? How long should the credit be for? What is to be done about defaulting debtors? The objective of the company is assumed to be to choose the credit policy that, taken in conjunction with its other policy decisions, maximizes its expected profits.

By setting the 'terms of sale' the company can to some extent control its level of debtors (accounts receivable). If it only allows 7 days to pay, it rules out customers who want 30 days to pay. By offering only 30 days' credit, it rules out customers who require 60 days to pay. An example of this process is a supermarket, which usually does not offer credit at all and so has few or no debtors. A trading company may even adopt the policy with a particular company or class of companies that it will only supply goods if payment is received in advance.

The relative bargaining strengths of the credit giver and credit receiver are important. If a customer firm with alternative sources of supply takes a large proportion of the output of a manufacturer geared to producing for them, the customer may be able to dictate the terms of credit.

It is always possible that the buyer will ignore the terms of sale and the credit terms offered. It is not unknown for some companies to deduct a cash discount when making a payment, even though the period of time over which the discount was offered has elapsed. The administrative costs to the seller in challenging such a practice can exceed the amount of the discount being contested. Whether such practices can be repeated in future dealings depends on the relative bargaining strengths of the buyer and the seller. Unfortunately a seller who is heavily dependent on one buyer cannot do very much when the buyer continually takes 120 days to pay bills and deducts a cash discount offered for payment within 30 days!

The problem of the late payment is particularly crucial to the smaller businesses. They do not have the bargaining strength to demand payment on time. Periodically, the government of the day comes forward with proposals designed to help the smaller business. In 1997, there were proposals to give small firms a statutory right of interest (SRI) on late payment of bills.

The proposals were that small companies would be able to charge interest, at the rate of 4% over base rate, on overdue accounts. Where no credit period has been specified in the sales agreement, the period before interest could be charged would be 30 days from the day of invoice or delivery of goods, whichever is the later.

The proposals were met with criticisms. Worries expressed were that large firms would push up their payment terms from 30 days from receipt of invoice to a much longer period and that it would be difficult, and perhaps counter-productive in the long term, for small companies to enforce payment of interest.

A company has at least four factors under its control that can influence the number of its debtors and the level of debt:

1 the customers to whom it is prepared to sell;
2 the terms of credit offered on the sale;
3 the cash discount offered to prompt payment;
4 the follow-up procedure on slow payment.

These decision variables will now be considered.

18.2 DECIDING AN ACCEPTABLE LEVEL OF RISK

The choice of which customers to sell to is really a question of the level of risk of non-payment that is considered acceptable. With every sale there is some risk that the customer will not be able to pay, but with most large companies the risk is so small that it is not even considered. With certain small illiquid companies the risk of non-payment might be so high that there is no question of selling to them. At some point between these two extremes the company is faced with a difficult choice of whether to sell or not. A £50 order cannot be viewed as simply a £50 cash inflow. The company must consider the present value (PV) of the future volume of sales from the customer. If they accept this order, goodwill is created and future sales may result. However, there is also the chance that the £50 may not be received and so, with a PV approach, the order may not be worth as much as £50.

A method of estimating the probability that a particular company will turn out to be a bad payer, perhaps even a bad debt, is required. If a credit risk can be attached to the customer, then a rational decision can be made about whether to trade with them. For example, suppose that a group of customers can be associated with a 10% credit risk, i.e. there is a 1 in 10 chance that they will not pay; then a decision can be made about whether to trade with this group.

Added sales by trading with this 10% risk group		£2000
Amounts on average uncollected (by definition 10%)		£200
Additional revenue		£1800
Marginal production and selling costs associated with the orders (60% of sales)	£1200	
Added collection costs	£300	
		£1500
Net annual incremental profit		£300

In this situation it would be worth trading with the 10% risk class of customers. As the level of production changes, a different decision may be made. If sales increase and production rises, then, because the company is working nearer the level of full capacity, the additional production costs may also increase; this could mean that it is no longer worth trading with this group. In the reverse situation, as soon as there is a danger that total sales will fall, the company may be willing to sell to a riskier class of customer in order to keep up its production level and so be able to keep down its cost per unit.

The following question is taken from an examination paper of the Association of Certified Accountants. The solution that follows the question illustrates one way of tackling the problem.

Example 18.1

The summary forecast profit statement and balance sheet of the AB Co. Ltd for the next 12 months is as follows.

Summary profit forecast for next 12 months

	£	£
Sales income (100 000 units)		1 200 000
Less: Variable costs	900 000	
Fixed costs	150 000	1 050 000
Profit		£150 000

Summary balance sheet

	£	£
Investment in fixed assets		1 500 000
Investment in working capital		
Debtors	200 000	
Stock	80 000	
Cash	24 000	
	304 000	
Less: Creditors	60 000	
		244 000
Total investment		£1 744 000

Profit as return on investment = 8.6%

The directors are concerned about the low return on investment, particularly because of the under-utilization of the investment in fixed assets. There is little likelihood of significant alterations to selling prices and costs, and the only apparent way of improving the situation is increased sales. All sales are on credit and the company operates a very strict credit control procedure which has virtually eliminated bad debts. Because of this a number of potential customers have had to be refused and some existing customers have taken their business elsewhere. The suggestion has been made that a relaxation of the credit control policy could increase sales substantially. Specifically, if the company were to introduce a scheme whereby a 2% discount were given on accounts paid within ten days – at present no discount is given –and if the company were willing to accept 'riskier' customers, the sales would increase by 40%. Probably 65% of the customers would avail themselves of the discount and the average collection period of the remainder would be half of what it is at present. Bad debts would be of the order of 2–6% of total sales.

Comment on the above situation making full use of the information given and highlighting any matters that should be brought to the attention of the directors.

Suggested solution

We shall begin by calculating the profit that will result if the new policy is accepted. Sales will increase by 40%.

	£	£
Sales income (140 000 units)		1 680 000
Less: Variable costs	1 260 000	
Fixed costs	150 000	
		1 410 000
		270 000
Less: Cash discount		
(0.02 × 0.65 × £1 680 000)		21 840
Profit		£248 160

This £248 160 is the profit before allowing for bad debts. It is estimated that bad debts will vary between 2% and 6% of sales. If bad debts equal 2% of sales that will amount to £33 600 and result in net profit of approximately £214 560. If bad debts equal 6% of sales, that will amount to £100 800 and reduce profits to approximately £147 360. This is lower than the present profit figure. Some adjustment would be required to the estimated profits to allow for the fact that the percentage of companies taking advantage of cash discounts is an estimate, and the estimate of 65% of customers would probably need to be reduced a little if a percentage of the customers turn out to be bad debts. The amounts involved in this adjustment would be small and so will be ignored. It is assumed that fixed costs will not increase even though there has been a 40% increase in sales.

The position is therefore that with a bad debts figure equal to 2% of sales, the policy is clearly worthwhile, showing a higher absolute profit figure and a higher return on net assets than with the present policy. With bad debts as 6% of sales, the policy is marginal, the return on net assets has marginally increased, but the absolute profit figure has fallen. If bad debts are expected to be below 5%, it can be shown that the new policy is worthwhile from both a return and an absolute profit point of view.

The company would need to consider the probabilities of the different levels of bad debts arising. It would also need to consider carefully whether its assumption with regard to the future level of debtors is justified. One reason why the new policy appears advantageous is that the total level of investment is reduced because of the reduction in the level of debtors. Is it realistic to believe that all customers, other than bad debtors, will pay within one month, and that 65% will wish to take advantage of the cash discount?

The problem of placing a potential customer in a particular risk category is not easy. However, there are a number of sources of information which may be useful.

Trade references

A new customer can be asked to supply one or two references from other companies with whom they have had business. The wording of the references and the standing of the companies who supplied them will give a guide to the creditworthiness of the customer.

Bank references or banker's opinion

A bank may be asked to comment on the financial standing of its customer. This is of limited use, however, because it only reflects on the behaviour of the company with one particular bank, and the manager of a bank may be reluctant to report unfavourably on one of its own customers. The situation could be very difficult for the bank manager, particularly if the bank itself had funds tied up in the company. In fact, banks have a number of standard letters that they send in response to enquiries on their customers' financial standing. The letters are very carefully worded, but the particular letter that is sent in reply reflects the banker's view of the relative creditworthiness of the company. The bank can also say whether a company has pledged its inventory or debtors to secure a loan.

Credit bureau reports or registers

A number of credit bureaux operate in the UK. The selling company can make use of one of these bureaux (one is Dun and Bradstreet) who publish lists showing relevant financial details of many companies, including a credit rating. This is a service that is continually updated and covers many companies. Should the enquiring company require additional information, it can ask for a special credit report on any company. The information given is based upon the record of transactions of creditors of the company, on special enquiries and on published financial information.

Salespeople's opinions

The opinions and impressions formed by sales staff when visiting a customer can be useful additional information.

Published information

The annual accounts can of course be analysed to determine the liquidity position of the customer. The accounts of listed companies also often include a statement on the payment policy of the company. The interpretation of such information is discussed elsewhere in this book. The Registrar of Companies keeps records of charges on the assets of a company and details of the directors, as well as the annual reports; these records can be examined. The records provide a useful insight into the financial position of any company. In fact, when an agency is asked to provide a special credit report it often relies heavily on the information in Companies House.

Company's own sales ledger

An examination of how well the customer has paid in the past might give some guide to how well they will pay in the future. It should show at least their willingness to pay. The financial situation of the customer may have changed, however, and so the ability to pay may have altered. A computer is sometimes used within a company to control debts. The computer can store up-to-date information on a customer's creditworthiness: it can store the latest information on the financial position of the customers, and report when a customer's liquidity position becomes dangerous. By keeping a record of the previous experience with the customer, the time they take to pay and the highest amount of credit previously allowed, information can quickly be provided when any new decisions have to be made on the sales terms for a particular customer. This information could save the company a loss on a possible bad debt.

Traditionally in the UK firms have asked to be supplied with the names of two traders and one banker when deciding on the suitability of a customer for credit. The supplier can perhaps obtain additional information from a credit agency. Discussions with managers of other companies or perhaps divisions within the same company that trade with the same customer can provide useful information. So can visits to the buyer by credit personnel and sales representatives. If a large amount of trade credit is likely to be required over a period of time, then a detailed investigation is obviously necessary. Financial statements of the company may be helpful. The larger the credit investigation the greater is the cost, but if a company placing an order is unknown or has a record of bad debts, then an investigation could well be worthwhile. If the supplying company has many investigations that need to be carried out in a year, it may set up its own investigation unit.

In the UK the banks have traditionally been conservative in providing information on companies. They do not wish to upset the customers and they have a fear of legal action being taken against them as the result of an unfavourable report. Opinions in the UK differ on the usefulness of bank references. There are those who argue that they are of no use whatever, and others who argue that, if you read between the lines, the statements can be useful. In the USA, in contrast, many banks will provide information regarding their customer's approximate cash balance together with an indication of the amount of activity in the account and any known loan commitments that the customer has already entered into. Therefore the seller of goods on credit in the USA has a considerable amount of information when it comes to deciding on the period of credit that it is worth offering to any customer.

Having obtained as much relevant information as possible, the company must decide whether the customer falls within an acceptable risk class. In recent years a good deal of effort has been expended on the problem of devising numerical credit-scoring systems for evaluating creditworthiness at the consumer level. Biographical data as well as credit history are employed. Success with these systems has been mixed. There is no reason in principle why a numerical credit-scoring system should not be developed to assess business loans. It might prove especially valuable to a company with a large number of small debtor companies. It is amusing to speculate what would be relevant 'biographical' data at company level! For the time being, however, the creditworthiness decision has to be largely a matter of judgement.

18.4 TERMS OF SALE

Having decided to sell to a customer, the company has next to decide on the credit terms that will be offered and the level of cash discount. First, we shall look at credit terms, i.e. the length of time the buyer is given in which to pay. Often credit terms and conditions of sale are settled by the usual terms of trade of the particular industry. A company just adopts the normal standards. Traditionally the majority of trade credit granted in the UK is on monthly terms. This means payment on or before the last day of the month following the date of the invoice. For example, if goods were dispatched during March, which on average means the 15th or 16th day of the month, and invoices are sent out at the end of that month, then payment should be expected by the end of April. This unusually fast processing would lead on average to 45 days' credit. If, however, invoices for goods dispatched on 15 March cannot be prepared by the end of that month and are not sent out until some date in April, it could well be that payment is not received until the end of May, which is 75 days' credit. The purchasing company needs time to process the invoice, and usually this takes a few weeks.

The time taken to collect a debt clearly depends to a large extent on the credit terms being offered by the supplier. Here again, from a seller's point of view the UK compares unfavourably with the USA. In the vast majority of cases in the USA, the stipulated terms are net 30 days. This means that the account should be paid 30 days after delivery or invoice. If cash discounts are offered, they are usually restricted to payment within 10 days and the rate offered is usually in the range of 0.5% to 2%. If an account in the USA is overdue, which usually means that it has not been paid 30 days after the receipt of the goods or the invoice, it is very frequent for an interest charge to be levied on the overdue amount.

In the UK, although monthly terms are the most usual, as explained above, the purchasers tend to regard this as meaning the end of the month following delivery. This is not the same as 30 days after delivery, for if goods are delivered on, say, 15 March, the UK interpretation would be that the payment is expected at the end of April, i.e. 30 days after the end of the month following delivery. A few large suppliers have tried to improve their cash position by informing purchasers that they are expecting to be paid on the 20th of the month following delivery, and a few are trying to move to the 10th day of the month following delivery.

With most transactions in the UK the method of payment required is not specified on the invoice. It is generally assumed that the payment will be by cheque, but there is increasing use of direct bank transfer methods. With the bank transfer, the purchaser agrees that the supplier should send the invoice directly to his or her bank and that the bank will settle within a specified number of days. This is a credit transfer system. The buying company receives a copy of the invoice that has been sent to the bank so that it can be verified.

Of course, the ability of the supplier to encourage customers to use this form of payment depends strongly on the supply situation. If the supplier is in a powerful position, they can insist on this method of payment.

Cash discount

Traditionally, cash discounts have been offered by the seller to the buyer to encourage early payment. This is to encourage payment before the end of the period of credit. Cash discounts have a cost to the seller and are of value to the buyer. Whether the buyer decides to pay early and take advantage of the cash discount being offered, or to wait until the end of the credit period before paying, depends to some extent on the size of the discount. We shall use an examination question to illustrate how the value of a cash discount can be determined.

Management of debtors and inventory

Example 18.2

The Claridge PLC wishes to speed up the collection of its debtors. It is considering offering cash discounts for early payment. In 1996/97 its sales were £2 million per annum and its debtors at year-end £500 000.

It is thinking of offering a 4% discount for payment within 10 days, and a 2.5% discount for payment within 30 days. It is estimated that customers representing 30% of sales will take advantage of payment within 10 days, and a further 20% will pay within 30 days. The remaining customers will not change their payment policy. The cost of finance for Claridge is 12%.

The management of the company have asked you to advise them on the financial result of this policy.

Answer

(a) At present the debtor collection period is 91 days

$$\left(\frac{£0.5}{£2.0} \times 365 \right)$$

(b) The proposed scheme would lower this to 54.5 days

> 10 days for 30% of customers
> 30 days for 20% of customers
> 91 days for 50% of customers

This equals (30% × 10) + (20% × 30) + (50% × 91)

(c) This would reduce the debtors figure to £298 630

$$\left(\frac{54.5}{365} \times £2.0 \text{ million} \right)$$

(d) The interest saving would be:

(£500 000 − £298 630) × 12% = £24 164

(e) The cost of the discounts would be:

(4% × 30% × £2m) + (2.5% × 20% × £2m)

= £34 000

(f) The discount policy is not therefore worthwhile.

In the USA and sometimes in other countries, it is usual for the supplier of goods to express its terms of sale in the following form:

5/10, net 30

This means the supplier is offering a 5% cash discount if the account is paid within 10 days. The final date for settlement being 30 days.

Companies that decide not to take advantage of the cash discounts being offered are in fact borrowing funds from their supplier. In the above example if the purchasing company decides to pay in 30 days rather than 10 it is receiving a 20-day loan. There is, however, a cost, namely the extra amount that needs to be paid if payment is made on the 30th day rather than the 10th.

To illustrate the effective rate of interest the purchaser pays if the cash discount is not taken, assume the goods purchased cost £100. If the company pays in 10 days the cost is £95. Waiting up to an extra 20 days increases the payment by:

5/95 = 0.0526 or 5.26%.

The implicit interest being charged is 5.26% for 20 days. There are just over 18 twenty-day periods in a year. So the effective annual rate of interest being paid in taking credit rather than benefiting from the cash discount is over 150%:

$$(1.0526)^{18} - 1 = 1.516175$$

In fact, the use of cash discounts in the UK has declined in recent years. This is largely because of the practice of some purchasers of taking discounts, whether or not they have paid within the specified time. If this happens it is very difficult for the supplier to try to obtain the amount which has incorrectly been taken as a discount. Buyers have taken the full credit period to pay, say in the above example, after the change, the full 90 days, and have then only paid the amount of the debt less the value of the discount. As a result many suppliers have abandoned cash discounts. Quantity discounts have become fashionable; buyers of large quantities are able to obtain large reductions in the unit price of the goods they buy.

Once the sale has been made and the terms offered, the company will wish to ensure that the cash is received as quickly as possible. This sometimes means sending reminders to customers. Chasing bad debts can be an expensive process. The company must ensure that the selling price is adequate to cover all expenses and credit losses. A certain proportion of debts will turn out to be bad, and these losses must be adequately covered by gains elsewhere. In fixing a selling price, allowance should therefore be made for the fact that on average only a proportion, say only 97%, of sales revenue is collected. This means that the company should show a profit on 97% of the sales price. This is assuming that an averaging system is being used by the company with regard to bad debts; in other words a system of cross-subsidization is being employed.

If it is thought bad policy to charge a higher price than is reasonable to customers who pay promptly, i.e. making them pay a proportion of the bad-debt expense, then different prices or at least different discounts may have to be offered to different risk categories of customers. For example, the 10% risk class of customers will have to cover the bad debts of this group between them. If, on average, only 90% of the revenue from this group is collected, then the company must ensure that profits on sales to this group are obtained when 90% of the sales revenue is received. This could be achieved by either charging a higher sales price to risky customers than to less risky customers, or by offering lower discounts and poorer credit terms.

One obvious management tool in the control of receivables is a record of the age of outstanding debts. Each month the debtors figures should be broken down to show the proportion of debts that have received various periods of credit, as for example in Tables 18.1 and 18.2.

Table 18.1 *Analysis of age of debts*

Number of days account has been outstanding	Percentage of total debtors figure (%)	Number of accounts
up to 29	58	1 000
30–59	20	400
60–89	15	200
90 and over	7	40

Table 18.2 *Collection rate – 'outstandings'*

Month	Sales (£000)	Still outstanding (£000)	Proportion (%)
Current	300	295	98.3
−1	280	220	78.6
−2	290	105	36.2
−3	300	50	16.7
−4	270	25	9.3
−5	275	15	5.5
−6	310	15	4.8
		725	

Steps would then be taken to collect the accounts that are considered to have been outstanding for longer than an acceptable length of time. The first attempt to collect payment would be a simple reminder; later, more serious attempts would include threatening legal action and finally court action itself. It is possible to carry out an exercise to show after what period of time attempts should be made to collect the outstanding accounts. The costs at each stage in the follow-up process should be balanced with the expected returns from the action, i.e. the probability of successfully obtaining payment as a result of the action multiplied by the interest that can be earned from obtaining money now rather than as a result of the next in the order of actions in the follow-up process. If we ignore deterrent effects, which may, however, be quite significant although difficult to evaluate, it is worth spending more in seeking to obtain payment than the expected returns from chasing the debt. The question of a default policy will be returned to later.

One way to encourage customers to pay on time, i.e. by the end of the agreed credit period, is to charge interest on overdue accounts. If the credit period is for 60 days, say, then at the end of that time, if the invoice has not been paid, the supplier will charge interest at some agreed rate on the amount of the debt. This condition would have to be agreed by the buyer at the time of sale.

This practice of charging interest on overdue accounts has never been very common in the UK. However, the practice is used extensively elsewhere in the EU and in the USA. In fact, in the UK the Law Commission recommended in 1976 that a scheme of statutory interest on contract debts should be introduced. The recommendation was to the effect that interest would start to be paid from a date agreed between the buyer and seller. The recommendation has not been acted upon.

Although this practice is not common in the UK, in recent years a number of companies have been introducing such terms into sale agreements. The extent to which it is possible to introduce such interest charges depends, of course, on the relative strengths of the buyer and seller.

One decision that a company has to make is concerned with how much trouble it should go to in chasing up debtors. When should reminders be sent out? When, if at all, should a debt-collecting agency be used? At what stage should legal action be taken to recover an outstanding debt?

The decision on more effective chasing of overdue accounts involves balancing the returns from receiving a payment earlier than one would have done otherwise against the costs of the action taken.

18.6 CREDIT INSURANCE

If a company is worried about non-payments it can always take out credit insurance. There are a number of specialist companies that offer such insurance. The service is not cheap, and the actual costs depend upon the type of policy taken out. The credit insurance company does not want to take all the high-risk business and will want the option to be able to refuse insurance or invoices sent to particular customers. There are two types of policy.

Credit insurance on export sales is discussed in Chapter 19. One insurer of export sales is the Export Credit Guarantee Department (ECGD). They are merely concerned with insurance of medium-term and long-term credits. It is private-sector insurers that cover short-term export credit sales and domestic credit sales.

Private-sector credit insurers not only provide guarantees, they also provide advice. They will evaluate potential customers in any country. They will comment on the strengths and weaknesses of the exporter's distribution chain. They will provide both political and commercial risk cover for sales to most countries of the world. They of course charge for all the services they provide.

Whole-turnover policy

In this type of policy the premium is a percentage of the insured company's whole turnover. The insured is given a limit of discretion on the value of an invoice. Any account below this amount will be automatically insured as long as the company taking out the insurance uses approved sources of information to assess the buyer's creditworthiness. This may slightly increase costs to the insured as it may mean obtaining more expensive information. For accounts with a value which is above the limit of discretion the insured company must apply to the insurance company for approval for this particular buyer.

Specific account

In this type of policy the insured company can select those buyers' debts which it wishes to insure. The credit underwriter can of course refuse to take the policy. If the debt is insured the premium charged is a percentage of the sales to the particular buyer. Usually the rate of premium charged is higher than for a whole-turnover policy as it is usually the riskier debts that are insured.

18.7 DEBTORS: CONCLUDING REMARKS

The management of credit is an important part of financial management. Companies, particularly fast-growing ones, can find their liquidity position under considerable strain if the level of their debtors is not kept in hand. A fast-growing company has to produce for a higher level of future sales than past sales; therefore it invests in equipment and building up inventories to meet these future demands. The company has to pay for these purchases and other manufacturing costs, and if it does not collect receipts from the past lower level of sales in a reasonable time it can find itself with a liquidity crisis.

The management of debtors is essentially a practical problem. Consequently a considerable amount of this chapter has been concerned with the normal routine process of credit management, i.e. investigating customers, deciding on the credit terms to be offered and keeping records of outstanding accounts. Only a small part of the chapter has been devoted to theoretical ideas on debt management. The subject has not been one in which many advanced analytical ideas have been developed or even proposed. This is because of the facts of life of debt management. Whatever credit terms a company may like to offer it can be limited by the practice of the industry. Whatever a company may feel about a certain debtor's always taking a long time to pay, if that customer is an important purchaser, the selling company's bargaining position is very weak.

18.8 INTRODUCTION TO INVENTORY MANAGEMENT

Successful management of manufacturing and distribution requires efficient stock control. Inventory can represent up to 20% or 25% of the total assets of manufacturing companies. This proportion can rise to 40% in retail distribution. So efficiency gains in inventory management can bring significant improvements to overall company financial performance.

Inventory can be classified into three main types depending on the stage of the manufacturing process at which it is held. We can distinguish *pre-production inventory, in-process inventory and finished goods inventory*. Pre-production inventory includes raw materials, bought in components and other inputs secured from outside the firm. In-process inventory is *work in progress* and may be held at points within the production process. Finished-goods inventory consists of the firm's products from which sales are drawn. In general, *any* temporarily idle resource could be thought of as an inventory. Stocks have been described as 'money in disguise' and indeed the stock may be of money itself, as in the holding of cash. Some cash management problems can, in principle, fit a classical stock control framework.

A main purpose of inventory is to allow each stage of the production and sales process to operate economically, decoupled from different or varying rates of activity at other stages. Finished-goods inventory, for example, stands between production and sales. Even when demand is at a constant rate it may be uneconomical to produce continually at that rate. For example, if a manufacturer makes 50 different sizes of wheel, economies of scale can be gained by making a year's supply of each in 50 separate one-week production runs. But stocks should not be a cover-up for poorly co-ordinated processes. One of the benefits of the *just-in-time* approach has been to bring new thinking to the levels of stock needed in well-managed production.

Apart from situations where flexible manufacturing systems (FMSs) are used in the production of durable goods in a demand-led environment, erratic or periodic sales will mean that it is unduly expensive to keep production rigidly in step with demand. Inventory gives the ability to satisfy demand promptly without unrealistic variations in rates of production. Similar considerations apply within the production process itself. If a product must be processed on several machines which operate at different rates or at different times or with differing reliability, in-process inventory can be useful.

The production process may need to be decoupled from irregularities of supply. The price of this security is the cost of holding pre-production inventory. Where security of supply is not a problem, as when sourcing is from well-integrated suppliers or other parts of the same organization, a just-in-time (JIT) approach may save considerable sums. Raw materials may also be held for speculative reasons if there are expectations of rising commodity prices.

There are valid and invalid reasons for holding stock. It has rightly been said that 'stocks buy organization' to the extent that inefficient production and distribution can be masked and sustained by excessive stock levels. But it is not possible to operate efficiently at zero stock levels in all cases. The stock control problem is to find the ideal balance between the costs and benefits of inventory. We shall be looking for the best obtainable stock control policies in a variety of situations. A stock control policy is a rule or collection of rules which determine:

1 the size of stock replenishments;
2 the timing of replenishments;
3 the consequences of out-of-stock situations.

In the main, models here are expressed in terms of finished-goods inventory for a single product. Similar principles apply to in-process or pre-production inventory although materials requirement planning (MRP) methods may be particularly relevant in this case.

18.9 THE CLASSICAL MODEL

This elemental stock control model forms the basis of a number of more advanced models and its assumptions are:

1 a single item of stock;
2 all parameters known and constant;
3 instantaneous replenishment of stock;
4 no variable re-order costs.

The parameters of assumption 2 are data for costs and the rate of demand for stock. Figure 18.1 shows the graph of inventory level against time and has a characteristic 'saw-tooth' shape.

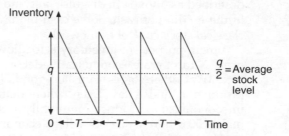

Figure 18.1

The problem is to determine the best value of the replenishment size q. Figure 18.1 starts with inventory at its maximum level which then declines at a uniform rate. When stocks have fallen to zero, it is assumed that they are immediately replenished in full. The length of time required for stocks to go from peak to peak (or from trough to trough) is one *inventory cycle*. But we do not aim to minimize costs per cycle, as this could be achieved by setting $q = 0$ and keeping no inventory at all! Rather, the objective is to minimize costs per annum (or some other suitable length of time).

Costs fall into two categories: holding costs and replenishment costs. Holding costs include storage, insurance, deterioration and interest charges. There will normally be a fixed and a variable component to replenishment costs. Administrative costs of placing an order (if supplies are brought in from outside) or the set-up costs of machinery (if the goods are produced by the firm) are considered fixed in the short term. Variable costs depend on the amount re-ordered. We shall use the following notation:

C_m is the cost of procuring one unit of the item;
iC_m is the cost of holding one item in stock for one year;
C_o is the fixed cost of a replenishment order of *any* size;
A is the annual rate of demand.

Use of the notation iC_m for the holding cost reflects the view that it is often the case that annual holding costs are proportional to the value (cost) of an item stocked. The factor of proportionality, i, is typically around 0.2 or 0.3. In terms of annual holding costs it is as if half the maximum level of inventory was being held throughout the year, so that

$$\text{total holding costs per annum} = \frac{q}{2}iC_m$$

Assumption 4 of the model means that (for the moment) procurement costs will be ignored so annual replenishment costs will be C_o times the number of stock refills needed. If annual demand is for A units of stock and replenishment size is q units, then n replenishments will be needed, where

$$n = \frac{A}{q}$$

n is the number of inventory cycles per annum, so

$$\text{total replenishment costs per annum} = \frac{C_o A}{q}$$

Overall, total costs per annum, C, are:

$$C = \frac{q}{2}iC_m + \frac{C_o A}{q}$$

The only unknown on the right-hand side is q, and we seek the value of q which minimizes C (which is more fully described as *total annual relevant costs*). The situation is plotted in Figure 18.2.

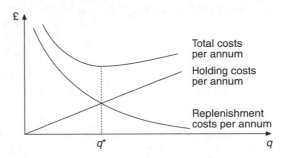

Figure 18.2

Total cost and its components are plotted against replenishment size q. The ideal value of q is that giving the lowest point on the total cost curve (marked as q^*). Although it happens that with this model the minimum of the total cost curve is above the intersection point of the holding and replenishment cost curves, it is *rates of change* that are important. What is being sought is an optimal balance or trade-off between those costs which rise with q (holding costs) and those which fall with q (replenishment costs). The best balance is struck where the rate at which holding costs are going up is equal to the rate at which replenishment costs are coming down. There is a convenient formula for q^*:

$$q^* = \sqrt{\left[\frac{2AC_o}{iC_m}\right]}$$

which is known as the *square root rule* and q^* is the *economic order quantity* (EOQ). Economic lot size (ELS) and economic batch size (EBS) are alternative descriptions of the square root rule and reflect different contexts in which the rule is used. Note that the optimal level of inventory varies inversely with iC_m and directly with C_o. Putting the EOQ into the cost expression gives a formula for the minimum of annual costs. This is:

$$C^* = \sqrt{(2AC_o iC_m)}$$

which varies directly with both C_o and iC_m – in both cases damped by the square root. Consider an example. A company faces a demand for 2000 items per annum. Replenishment costs are £100 per replenishment. It costs £2.50 to hold one item in stock for one year. So in this case:

$$C_o = 100 \qquad A = 2000 \qquad iC_m = 2.5$$

and substituting in the EOQ formula gives:

$$q^* = \sqrt{\left[\frac{2(100)(2000)}{2.5}\right]} = 400$$

The EOQ is 400 units, five replenishments (2000/400) are needed each year and the minimum level of annual costs is £1000. Note that if annual sales double to 4000 units per annum with nothing else changed, the optimal level of inventory increases by a factor of $\sqrt{2}$ to 565.69. The square root rule confutes a common-sense idea that if sales double so should stocks. So if demand did double to 4000, optimal costs would be £1414.21 but if an order quantity of 800 had been used, annual costs would be £1500.

Consider another example. A company's stock is depleted at a constant rate of 10 units per day. Storage costs per unit per calendar month are 40p and the cost per re-order is £150. At what intervals should replenishments be made and what would be the minimum level of annual costs achievable? On an annual basis:

$$A = 3650 \qquad iC_m = 4.8 \qquad \text{and } C_o = 150$$

First find the EOQ. This will be:

$$q^* = \sqrt{\left[\frac{2(150)(3650)}{4.8}\right]} = 477.62$$

Ignoring the problem of fractions, a replenishment size of 477.62 with an annual demand of 3650 means that the number of stock replenishments per annum, n, will be:

$$n = \frac{3650}{477.62} = 7.64$$

This gives a cycle length of 47.76 days. The minimum level of annual costs is £2292.60. The change in costs if these figures were rounded off to $q = 480$ ordered every 48 days is trivial, as may be confirmed. Annual costs C are not sensitive to small variations in q. The damping effect of the square root means that the EOQ rule is robust with respect to minor errors in parameter values.

18.10 VARIABLE RE-ORDER COSTS

Re-order costs normally vary with re-order size because in addition to C_o the firm usually pays an amount C_m per unit. If the firm makes the good itself, then C_m is the unit variable cost of production. If the firm is a distributor or retailer then C_m is the supplier's charge per unit ordered. Costs for a re-order of size q are now:

$$C_o + qC_m$$

A/q re-orders per annum will still be needed and total annual costs are:

$$C = \frac{q}{2}iC_m + (C_o + qC_m)\frac{A}{q}$$
$$= \frac{q}{2}iC_m + \frac{C_o A}{q} + C_m A$$

Since $C_m A$ is a constant term, the EOQ is unchanged and the square root formula still applies. If C_o is unchanged, annual costs rise but it pays to replenish stock in the original quantities (assuming that the firm intends to satisfy total annual demand). This does not mean that the unit cost figure can be ignored, but what it does show is that the usefulness of a model cannot always be measured by the plausibility of its assumptions.

Example 18.3

A builders' merchant holds stocks of taps, demand for which is at the rate of 250 units per quarter. It costs £2 to hold one tap for a year and the merchant's own costs of placing a re-order are £10. The manufacturer charges £3 per tap plus £30 per re-order but has offered an alternative scheme of charges. The price per tap would come down to £2.50 but the charge per tap

re-order would go up to £120. Is this new arrangement desirable? To find out, the EOQ and annual cost figures must be worked out under each arrangement. In the first instance:

$$iC_m = £2 \quad C_o = £40 \quad C_m = £3 \quad \text{and } A = 1000$$

Note that the C_o value includes the manufacturer's charge. The resulting EOQ is:

Management of debtors and inventory

$$q^* = \sqrt{\left[\frac{2(40)(1000)}{2}\right]} = 200$$

and annual costs are:

$$C = \frac{200}{2}2 + \frac{40(1000)}{200} + 3(1000)$$

$$= 3400$$

Under the alternative scheme the EOQ would be:

$$q^* = \sqrt{\left[\frac{2(160)(1000)}{2}\right]} = 400$$

Annual costs here are:

$$C = \frac{400}{2}2 + \frac{160(1000)}{400} + 2.5(1000)$$

$$= 3300$$

So the alternative gives a saving of £100 per annum for the merchant. Although both holding costs and re-order costs have increased, this has been more than compensated by the reduced unit cost C_m.

18.11 CASH MANAGEMENT MODEL

Cash management has similarities to stock control and the classical model can give useful insight and order-of-magnitude results. The following example continues the theme of variable re-order costs, and shows how the model can deal with inflows as well as outflows.

Example 18.4

A company receives inflows of cash at a steady rate of £350 000 per annum. The cash can be invested in securities to earn 12% per annum. Each time an investment is made there is a brokerage charge of £50 plus 1% of the sum invested. How many investments of cash should the company make annually? An alternative scheme of brokerage charges is £100 plus 0.8% of the sum invested. Which scheme would the company prefer?

The cash is not placed in securities immediately because of the fixed part of the brokerage charges. The company needs to know the ideal size of investment and hence, with the given annual inflow, the number of investments each year. Figure 18.3 plots the position with q as investment size.

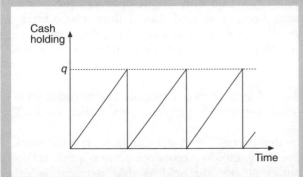

Figure 18.3

The average cash holding is $q/2$ and the cost of holding £1 in cash for one year is the lost interest, £0.12. Note that to invest each pound costs £0.01. So in the original scheme:

$$C_m = 0.01 \quad A = 350\,000 \quad C_o = 50 \quad iC_m = 0.12$$

The square root formula produces:

$$q^* = \sqrt{\left[\frac{2(50)(350\,000)}{0.12}\right]} = 17\,078$$

So the optimum number of investments per annum will be:

$$\frac{350\,000}{17\,078} \approx 20.49$$

or about 41 in two years. The total cost works out at:

$$C = \frac{17\,078}{2}0.12 + \frac{50(350\,000)}{17\,078} + 0.01(350\,000)$$

$$= £5549$$

For the alternative:

$$C_m = 0.008 \quad A = 350\,000 \quad C_o = 100 \quad iC_m = 0.12$$

the square root formula produces:

$$q^* = \sqrt{\left[\frac{2(100)(350\,000)}{0.12}\right]} = 24\,152$$

So the optimum number of investments per annum under this scheme would be:

18.12 LEAD TIME AND BUFFER STOCKS

Now consider relaxing the instantaneous replenishment assumption. *Lead time* is the delay between placing an order and the arrival of the goods in stock. Instant replenishment means zero lead time. Suppose that lead time is a fixed number of weeks, L. A fixed lead time leaves re-order quantity unchanged. Frequency of re-orders, the intervals between them and the costs are also the same. But the order for replenishment must now be placed when the amount of inventory falls to the level of lead-time demand. The level of lead-time demand is the *re-order level* (also known as the re-order point), R. This is shown in Figure 18.4.

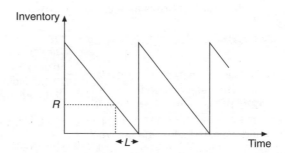

Figure 18.4

Suppose that in the builders' merchant case there is a lead time of three weeks ($L = 3$). If a 50-week working year is assumed, weekly demand is for 20 units so that demand during lead time, the re-order level, would be 60 units. The EOQ remains at 400. All this assumes a fixed lead time. In practice lead time may be variable and a stochastic model would result.

In the classical model all parameters are known and constant – it is a deterministic model. Buffer stocks come in when we relax this assumption. Buffer or safety stocks are additional inventory held against unforeseen events such as a surge in demand or a longer-than-usual lead time. In the deterministic world of the classical model, buffer stocks are not needed, but if they *were* added in, inventory would never fall below the level of buffer stock. Both the average level of stock and the re-order level are shifted up by the amount of buffer stock, B, so:

$$R = LW + B$$

in which L is lead time in weeks and W is weekly demand. The re-order level is then lead-time demand (expected demand in general) plus buffer stock. The model is graphed in Figure 18.5.

EOQ is unchanged. Lead-time demand is $R - B$, the minimum level of stock is B and the maximum level is now $B + q$. Holding costs per annum and total costs rise by £BiC_m. The reason buffer stocks are held is that demand is often uncertain, as may be lead time. Demand in any period is usually a random variable, although the *average* rate may be known. So the saw-tooth diagram now has ragged edges as in Figure 18.6.

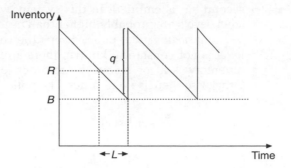

Figure 18.5

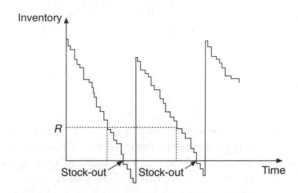

Figure 18.6

If re-order level is now set at *average* lead-time demand and there is no buffer stock, then if demand during lead time happens to be brisk, all orders during this period cannot be filled straight away – a *stock- out* occurs. Figure 18.6 assumes that orders received when out of stock can be filled when supplies arrive. This is *backlogged demand* which will not always apply as some orders may be lost and there will usually be costs associated with stock-outs. These costs relate to lost custom in the future, possible failure to meet contracts, compensation for delay, etc. Any estimate of stock-out costs is questionable – a fact which must be taken into account. But it would be unwise to ignore these costs and so assume they are zero. The larger is buffer stock the smaller is the chance of a stock-out each cycle and expected stock-out costs are reduced, but holding costs rise. The problem is again to find the best balance – the level of buffer stock which minimizes

buffer stock holding cost + expected stock-out costs

in which the buffer stock holding costs and expected stock-out costs are *additional* to the holding and re-order costs and which can be seen as *uncertainty costs* which more advanced models can take into account.

18.13 PERIODIC REVIEW MODELS

The classical model with random demand is an example of a *re-order level* model. The policy is to place a replenishment order when the stock falls to or below the re-order level. The size of the order is given by the square root rule and is the same each time a stock re-order is made. Re-order level policies require continuous monitoring of stock level. This could be implemented as a simple *two-bin system* where two containers or 'bins' full of the item are used. When one bin becomes empty an order for stock is placed. This should arrive before the second bin is emptied. In this system, while monitoring costs are low, average stock levels are probably higher than necessary.

The *periodic review* policy keeps the concept of a re-order level but the stock level is not constantly known; there are periodic *stock-takings*. If at stocktaking inventory is at or below the re-order level, a re-order of fixed size is placed. Otherwise there is no re-order. The policy is illustrated in Figure 18.7.

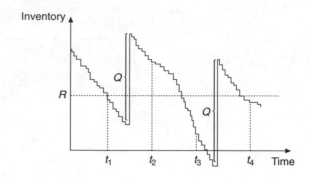

Figure 18.7

At time t_1 there is a stocktaking which reveals inventory level below R so that a replenishment order of size Q is placed. This arrives after a random period of lead time. At the next review, at time t_2, stock is above the re-order level so that no replenishment order is placed at this time. The next review is at t_3 and an order is placed but a lead time stock-out arises. The next review is at t_4. The interval between reviews is fixed in this model and has to be determined, as do both Q and the re-order level R. In comparison with the re-order level policy, information costs are reduced but this is at the expense of holding more stock on average and/or having increased stock-out costs.

The *re-order cycle* policy dispenses with a re-order level and a re-order is placed at each review, but the size of the replenishment is now variable. The amount of stock ordered is the difference between a maximum inventory level, S, and the level of stock at review. The situation is shown in Figure 18.8.

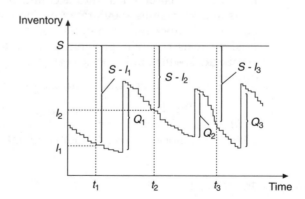

Figure 18.8

The amount ordered is Q_1 at t_1, where

$$Q_1 = S - I_1$$

and Q_2 at t_2, where

$$Q_2 = S - I_2$$

Compared to the periodic review policy there is less chance of a stock-out. If the interval between reviews is similar in the two models (it may tend to be longer in the re-order cycle case) the average level of stocks and hence stockholding costs would tend to be higher, although this depends on the value of S. If the interval between reviews is similar then re-order costs will be higher.

The s, S policy combines features of the periodic review and re-order cycle policies. In this case inventory is again reviewed at regular intervals but an order for replenishment is only placed if the stock level at review is at or below the level s. The amount re-ordered, if there is a re-order, is calculated as in the re-order cycle policy – an amount sufficient to bring the stock on hand at review up to the level S. Therefore the amount re-ordered, Q, is given by:

$$Q = \begin{cases} S - I \text{ if } I < s \\ 0 \quad \text{if } I > s \end{cases}$$

The s, S model is illustrated in Figure 18.9.

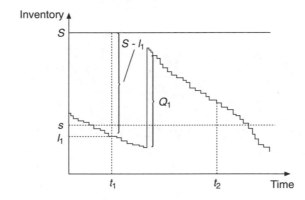

Figure 18.9

It will be seen that no order for stock is placed at time t_2. The classical static model is a special case of the s, S model with $s = 0$ and $S = $ EOQ. While s would normally be positive in the s, S model, if backlogged demand is allowed, a decision is required as to what *negative* level s should take. Again, a balance has to be struck between holding costs which will diminish as s falls and shortage costs which will rise as s falls.

The choice between these and other stock control models depends on the company or system under investigation. Although the s, S approach is often appropriate, the other models, or variants of them, may on occasion better exploit the peculiarities of an individual system.

18.14 THE ABC CLASSIFICATION SYSTEM

Where more than one good is stocked, optimization can proceed individually for each good if they do not compete for a common scarce resource such as storage space. If there is competition for a scarce resource, methods of constrained optimization may be usable if only a few products are involved.

Where many products are stored, a different approach may be needed. Some chemical companies may have over 20 000 items in stock and in such cases detailed analysis of all products may not be warranted. One method that has gained popularity is the *ABC classification* method originally developed by the General Electric Corporation. In this approach items of stock are ranked by turnover as follows:

Category A: those items that account for most of the turnover (in value terms). It is often the case that just 10% of the product range accounts for 70% of total turnover.

Category B: this is the intermediate section of the product range with, say, 30% of the total number of items stocked accounting for around 20% of total turnover.

Category C: a large part of the product range by number, perhaps 60%, may account for only a small proportion of turnover, say 10%. These are the category C items.

The ABC classification scheme is shown in Figure 18.10. The curve is called the *Pareto curve* (the ABC method is also called *Pareto analysis*) and ABC and other variations on this theme are sometimes referred to as *grouping methods.*

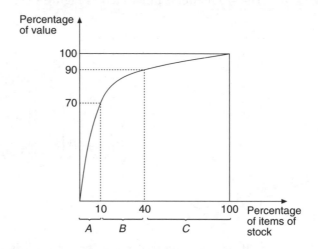

Figure 18.10

The precise shape of the Pareto curve and the break points between categories will vary between firms but the general point that a small percentage of items make up most of the value is generally true. The measure of value itself may be turnover, profits, capital invested or another measure that the company may decide.

The purpose of the classification is to direct management effort to where the best results will be obtained. Category A items should receive most attention with sophisticated forecasting and recording systems and detailed analysis of order quantities and buffer stocks. Category B items would receive less detailed treatment with simpler forecasting methods and rougher estimates of EOQs.

Only simple treatment would be warranted for the category C items. A possibility here is a two-bin system where the re-order level is $q/2$. This produces fairly large, infrequent orders with minimal cost consequences. No forecasting methods need be used, just an estimate of annual demand. For category C there may not even be a formal system of recording stocks, with sample-based estimates sufficing for audit purposes.

Computer-based systems will be used for at least part of the stock range. Category A and possibly category B items would be included, the nuts, bolts and slow-moving items of category C might not, but as computing costs decline, the range of items worth recording in detail continues to expand.

Management of debtors and inventory

Where a finished product consists of components manufactured and brought together in a multi-stage production process, the materials requirement planning (MRP) method can bring substantial reductions in stock holding. If many components are involved in a finished product, management of the stock process should reflect the interdependent nature of the demand for the components rather than controlling stock for the components independently through a re-order level system.

Materials requirement planning, which has its origins in the 1960s, is a computerized planning system which explicitly recognizes demand for components as interdependent and derived from that for the final product(s) of the firm. A master production schedule follows from the quantity and timing of the demand for the final products, and from this the requirements for components and materials are derived in a materials requirement plan which takes into account existing stocks, lead time, etc., and on the basis of which re-orders or re-runs are triggered as necessary to maintain manufacturing flow.

A detailed production schedule is required, along with estimates of lead times for bought-in components. The computer-based MRP package derives orders for sub-assemblies, components and materials from the production schedule, level by level. This operation, a requirement generation run, might be performed at monthly or perhaps weekly intervals. Stocks of components, materials and work in progress can be reduced substantially (30% or more) and for some items can be eliminated altogether if the production plan shows significant periods in which an item is not required. Staff savings are also likely. However, it should be noted that changes in the master production schedule (or additional, separate, demand for spare parts) will still mean that some component inventory will be necessary.

The MRP approach (also termed 'MRP I') was extended to cover the management of all resources used in manufacturing. Manufacturing resource planning (MRP II) is a more comprehensive, systems-oriented, package taking in production, marketing, human resources and finance in companies manufacturing high-volume complex products (such as cars). MRP II, implemented as part of a programme of computer-integrated manufacturing (CIM), usually also has an emphasis on higher product quality. An appropriate MRP software package is selected and adapted to meet the requirements of the user company.

As with any complex exercise there can be difficulties with implementing MRP II which can mean increased costs (for as long as two years) before the main benefits are realized. MRP II requires reliable and appropriate systems and accurate data and may necessitate considerable managerial reorganization.

18.16 JUST-IN TIME MANAGEMENT

The just-in-time (JIT) approach to achieving profit, quality and customer-satisfaction goals originated in Japan in the late 1960s when, because of excess capacity in steel making, shipbuilders were able to get fast delivery of orders and so managed to reduce their inventories tenfold from about 30 days to 3 days. Car makers followed suit and the philosophy evolved with Taiichi Ohno (a vice-president of Toyota) writing extensively on JIT, mediated in English to the West by Richard Schonberger [1].

JIT is a managerial strategy, not just a set of techniques. Cheng and Podolsky [2] describe JIT as: 'a Japanese management philosophy applied in manufacturing which involves having the right items of the right quality and quantity in the right place and at the right time.' It is a customer-led production-to-order approach that has the objective of eliminating idle resources throughout the company. It is the antithesis of 'just-in-case' management which calls for stock to be held in case something goes wrong. The JIT view is that low or non-existent stock levels show up problems and areas of weakness hidden by high inventory levels.

The JIT approach seeks continuous improvement in manufacturing system operation and design. There is a particular concern with waste and the three undesirables: excess (*muri*), waste (*muda*) and unevenness (*mura*). JIT can bring very big savings in costs and waste along with increases in quality and the elimination of non-value-added activities – for example, time spent in inspecting, moving, waiting and storing (in contrast to the value-adding production time). The ultimate aims of JIT can be expressed as:

Materials purchased	JIT	to produce parts
Parts made	JIT	for sub-assemblies
Sub-assemblies ready	JIT	for final assembly
Finished products made	JIT	for sale

JIT has been described as 'stockless production' – inventory being seen as wasted investment that could be released for ploughing back elsewhere.

With JIT, a new method of handling and keeping track of items needs to be introduced – the Kanban system. A Kanban (Japanese for 'visible record') is part of JIT implementation but is not the most important aspect of JIT. Kanbans, introduced by Toyota in 1981, smooth the flow of materials through the production process where a downstream assembly station makes a demand to a point upstream in what is a 'pull' manufacturing system of flow lines of dissimilar machines (rather than the more traditional functional groupings of similar machines) in a cellular manufacturing system. Kanbans follow parts through the system and are returned to trigger more supply when the parts are used up. A Kanban can take a variety of forms – for example, it may be a card or a container. If an operator has no Kanbans they can be working on improvement projects or maintenance. The JIT approach regards such 'idle' time as preferable to higher-than-necessary stocks. Kanbans are well suited to inexpensive, high-turnover components. Low-use items could use a re-order point system or MRP.

JIT does not take for granted assumptions in the more traditional EOQ approaches (which originated around 1915) and goes for the reduction of set-up times (set-up costs being equivalent to the fixed component of re-order costs). The JIT view is that most things are measurable and an EOQ approach will miss opportunities to improve quality, productivity and motivation. Where JIT can be applied, savings can be substantial – Rover, for example, cut their inventories by £40m. JIT sees EOQ as wasteful. Lot sizes can be smaller (with an ultimate goal of one unit). Fresh thinking (with regular involvement of the workforce and a possible one-off cost of modifying machinery) can cut set-up times by a factor of five or more. Stocks of work in progress (WIP) are seen as masking unevenness in production and perpetuating bad practices.

Quality improvements (total quality) are an integral part of JIT and the absence of buffers gives direct feedback to employees on the quality of their work with peer-pressure incentives not to allow disruptive defects. Activities can be carried out more effectively if safety stock is reduced. Specifically:

scheduling is improved;
handling is improved with fewer movements and damage reduced;
recording costs and ordering paperwork are reduced (through suppliers having long-term contracts);
storage space requirements are reduced;
plant layout is more effective;
product quality is improved.

Through these effects, further savings of 30% or more are often possible over and above those arising from the saving from reduced stock levels. Advanced manufacturing technology (AMT) facilitates reduced set-up times and costs, lower capacity loss during set-up and the smaller batch sizes inherent in JIT. The smaller batch sizes themselves mean less WIP and finished-goods inventory.

JIT can take time to implement properly. Indeed, it can push up costs and magnify problems if it is not appropriately introduced. It can be difficult to introduce if plant is near full capacity – but the JIT programme should enhance capacity and can trigger-off a huge range of improvements. EOQs are progressively reduced. JIT can bring challenges to the management accounting, budgeting, operational control, performance measurement and costing processes.

JIT is a philosophy that extends beyond the individual company, calling for a close and well-managed relationship with suppliers. Under JIT, suppliers will be fewer in number (half or less) and will have long-term contracts in return for delivering high-quality components (inspected at source) reliably, quickly, frequently and in smaller batches. With components delivered to the production line there is no need for movement into store or the storage space.

This need for suppliers to deliver quality-assured components to match the production schedules of the purchaser requires improved inter-company information flow and has organizational consequences for suppliers.

Ideally, stocks should not in effect be pushed down to suppliers – every part of the manufacturing chain works just in time, with no one having stocks passed down to them. It is possible that a supplier may relocate plant closer to the purchasing company. In other cases, there may be undesired external effects of JIT such as worsening traffic congestion and pollution through more frequent deliveries. Elements of a JIT approach are now adopted by two out of three UK companies.

18.17 INVENTORY: CONCLUDING REMARKS

Which approach to use? The situations of companies differ widely – for example, in how far management policies in other companies in the manufacturing chain could be influenced to accommodate a JIT strategy. An MRP approach is indicated in organizations making durable products containing many parts. An EOQ methodology is indicated for a stockholder with a 10 000-product range. Each approach can contribute to effective inventory management within the same organization.

For a company making a range of products of varying complexity, those products with independent demand would be controlled adequately with an EOQ-based system such as re-order level or periodic review. Even for raw-materials inventory a re-order level or similar system may still be best if the final product is uncomplicated and has a fairly stable pattern of demand. However, an MRP–JIT approach is indicated for products with complex production processes and a consequent need for a large number of demand-dependent items.

Rapidly improving computer hardware and software and ever-diminishing IT costs have not only allowed the development of MRP and related methods but have also benefited smaller firms using EOQ-based PC packages.

18.18 REFERENCES

1   Schonberger, R.J. (1982) *Japanese Manufacturing Techniques: Nine Hidden Lessons in Simplicity*, The Free Press, New York.

2   Cheng, T.C.E. and Podolsky, S. (1993) *Just-in-time Manufacturing: An Introduction*, Chapman and Hall, London.

18.19 FURTHER READING

Anderson, D.R., Sweeney, D.J. and Williams, T.A. (1994) *An Introduction to Management Science* , (7th edn), West Publishing.

Bass, R.M.V. (1979) *Credit Management*, Business Books.

Clarke, B.W. (ed.) (1989) *Handbook of International Credit Management*, Gower Publishing.

Dear, A. (1988) *Working towards Just-in-time*, Kogan Page, London.

Dear, A. (1990) *Inventory Management Demystified*, Chapman and Hall, London.

Drury, C. (1992) *Management and Cost Accounting*, 3rd edn, Chapman and Hall, London.

Lewis, C.D. (1981) *Scientific Inventory Control*, 2nd edn, Butterworth, London.

Kirkman, P.R.A. (1977) *Modern Credit Management under Inflation*, Allen and Unwin: Chartered Association of Certified Accountants, London.

Littlechild, S.C. and Shutler, M.F. (eds) (1991) *Operations Research in Management*, Prentice-Hall.

Samuels, J.M., Wilkes, F.M. and Brayshaw, R.E. (1995) *Management of Company Finance*, 6th edn, International Thomson Business Press, London.

Schniederjans, M.J. (1993) *Topics in Just in time Management*, Allyn and Bacon.

Wilkes, F.M. and Brayshaw, R. (1986) *Company Finance and its Management*, Van Nostrand Reinhold.

18.20 PROBLEMS

1   Calculate the implicit interest rate being charged to customers that do not take advantage of cash discounts with the following terms of sale: (a) 5/20, net 45; (b) 4/20, net 30; (c) 3/15, net 30.

2   Quansit Pty is reviewing its credit policy. Currently it extends credit terms of 30 days from invoice date and is considering extending this to 60 days. Current sales are 10 000 units a month, priced at £12. Direct costs are 90% of sales price. The marketing director believes that if the credit period is extended sales will increase by 12%. If the current cost of funds to the company is 11%, should the company extend the credit period:

   (a)   (i) if the extended credit is only applied to new sales?
         (ii) if the extended credit is applied to existing sales as well?

   (b) What other issues should be brought into the discussion, and which other departments in the company should have an input?

3   Softtouch Ltd buys products from manufacturers and sells on credit to customers at an average rate of gross profit of 30%. The company is considering relaxing its credit standards and its collection policies and asks for your advice. At present, sales amount to £1 200 000 per year and debtors pay on average 60 days after the date of invoice, except for 1% of sales representing bad debts. The proposed relaxation of credit and collection policies should increase sales by 10%, but debtors are expected to pay 90 days after invoice, and an estimated 2% of sales should prove to be bad debts. The relevant capital cost for this decision is 12% per year. Softtouch pays its creditors 30 days after receiving delivery, and has a policy of holding inventory equal to 50 days of projected sales requirements.

Management of debtors and inventory

(i) Identify the cash flows relating to each month's sales for the existing policy and for the new policy, assuming that the purchasing and stock-holding policies have adapted completely to the new sales level.

(ii) Advise Softtouch Ltd.

4 Comfylot PLC produces garden seats which are sold in both domestic and export markets. Sales during the next year are forecast to be £16 million, 70% to the UK domestic market and 30% to the export market, and are expected to occur steadily throughout the year. Of UK sales 80% are on credit terms, with payment due in 30 days. On average UK domestic customers take 57 days to make payment. An initial deposit of 15% of the sales price is paid by all export customers. All export sales are on 60 days credit with an average collection period for credit sales of 75 days. Bad debts are currently 0.75% of UK credit sales, and 1.25% of export sales (net of the deposit). Comfylot wishes to investigate the effects of each of three possible operational changes:

(a) Domestic credit management could be undertaken by a non-recourse factoring company. The factor would charge a service fee of 1.5% and would provide finance on 80% of the debts factored at a cost of base rate + 2.5%. The finance element must be taken as part of the agreement with the factor. Using a factor would save an initial £85 000 per year in administration costs, but would lead to immediate redundancy payments of £15 000.

(b) As an alternative to using the factor a cash discount of 1.5% for payment in seven days could be offered on UK domestic sales. It is expected that 40% of domestic credit customers would use the cash discount. The discount would cost an additional £25 000 per year to administer, and would reduce bad debts to 0.50% of UK credit sales.

(c) Extra advertising could be undertaken to stimulate export sales. Comfylot has been approached by a European satellite TV company which believes that £300 000 of advertising could increase export sales in the coming year by up to 30%. There is a 0.2 chance of a 20% increase in export sales, a 0.5 chance of a 25% increase and a 0.3 chance of a 30% increase. Direct costs of production are 65% of the sales price. Administration costs would increase by £30 000, £40 000 and £50 000 for the 20%, 25% and 30% increases in export sales, respectively. Increased export sales are likely to result in the average collection period of the credit element of all exports lengthening by five days, and bad debts increasing to 1.5% of all export credit sales.

Bank base rate is currently 13% per year, and Comfylot can borrow overdraft finance at 15% per year. These rates are not expected to change in the near future. Taxation may be ignored.

Required:

(a) Discuss whether any of the suggested changes should be adopted by Comfylot PLC. All relevant calculations must be shown. (19 marks)

(b) Explain what is meant by 'forfeiting' and comment upon whether it could be of value to Comfylot PLC. (6 marks)

(25 marks)

ACCA, June 1992

5 A company has annual demand for 2500 units of the one product that it stocks. The replenishment cost for inventory is fixed at £400 regardless of the size of the replenishment. Annual holding costs are £8 per unit. Find (a) the economic order quantity, (b) the optimum number of replenishments per annum and the length of an inventory cycle, and (c) the lowest level of inventory costs.

6 The annual demand for a company's only item of stock is 1000 units. It costs the company £6 to hold one unit of stock for one year. Each time that a replenishment order is made the company incurs a fixed cost of £75.

(a) Find the economic order quantity.

(b) Find the number of re-orders per annum and optimal costs.

(c) Suppose that the company's supplier introduces a condition of no more than five orders for stock per annum. How much would the company be prepared to pay to escape this condition?

7 A company receives a steady inflow of cash of £250 000 per annum. The cash can be invested at 12.5% per annum. Each time the company makes an investment there is a brokerage charge of £25 plus 1% of the sum invested (both sums payable at the time the investment is made).

(a) What is the best size of investment and how many investments of cash should be made per annum?

(b) If the brokerage charges were £100 plus 0.75% of the sum invested, at what annual rate should investments now be made?

(c) Which scheme of charges would the company prefer?

19 SHORT- AND MEDIUM-TERM SOURCES OF FINANCE

LEARNING OUTCOMES

This is mainly a descriptive chapter. The expressions 'short term' and 'medium term' are not precise. Short term is usually taken to mean finance which is available for up to one year, and medium-term finance is available for one to five years.

By the end of this chapter the reader should:

- be aware of the different sources of short- and medium-term finance
- know how to calculate the true interest cost on borrowed funds and trade credit
- know how to calculate whether it is better to lease an asset than to purchase the asset
- be aware of how to finance the export of goods and services

19.1 BANK OVERDRAFTS

Companies in the UK rely more on short-term financing than do companies in other European countries. A survey in 1994 indicated that 70% of UK business relies heavily on overdrafts, compared with 37% in Germany relying on short-term funds. The trouble with short-term finance is that it can be unreliable. This is a particular problem for the medium or smaller-sized company which can be dependent on this form of finance.

Short-term borrowing of the kind made available principally by the commercial banks in the form of overdrafts is very flexible. When the borrowed funds are no longer required they can quickly and easily be repaid. It is also comparatively cheap because the risks to the lender are less than on long-term loans, and loan interest is a tax-deductible expense. The banks issue overdrafts with the right to call them in at short notice. Such advances are, in fact, legally repayable on demand, although enforcing the letter of the law on this point is often impractical since it would hardly be in the bank's interest to drive its client into a dangerous financial position if that looked likely. Normally the bank assures the borrower that he or she can rely on the overdraft not being recalled for a certain period of time, say one year or six months.

However, the borrower must be careful of what he/she does with the money obtained on these terms. If it is recalled, the company has to be able to repay, which would be awkward if the funds had been used to purchase fixed assets. In such a case the company might have to sell assets it had obtained for long-term use, or at least dispose of inventory in an unpalatable hurry. Any plans that involve an overdraft or other form of short-term loan should therefore refer closely to the company's cash-flow analysis so that it is quite clear how long the funds will be needed and when they can be repaid.

Banks from the early 1990s tried to encourage borrowers to switch from the very popular short-term overdraft facility to term loans. They tried to do this by charging very high interest rates on unauthorized overdrawing on overdraft facilities. Other incentives used included relaxed collateral arrangements on term loans, and interest holidays on term loans.

The banks have been very successful with this policy of reducing the use of overdrafts. One bank reduced the total amount advanced on overdrafts in a year by 43%. The switch was to term loans, with some loans being of a medium to long-term duration.

For many companies bank borrowing is the cheapest form of short-term finance for a company, the only exception being that under certain conditions finance may be available for export purposes at a cheaper rate. Interest on bank borrowing is charged only on the outstanding balance. Alternative sources of finance are usually for a fixed term, and interest has to be paid on the borrowed funds over the full term of the loan. With a bank overdraft any cash that flows into the company can easily be used to reduce the balance of the advance and so reduce the interest that has to be paid.

The lending decision

We will now briefly consider the factors a bank takes into account when deciding whether or not to make a loan available to a company. There are qualitative factors the banker will take into account as well as quantitative. First, there are some general issues to be considered:

1 How much is to be borrowed, and for how long?
2 What is the purpose of the advance?
3 *Source of repayment* This depends on the bank's approach to lending, which may be, on the one hand, based on so called 'liquidation analysis' and on the other hand on 'going-concern analysis'. The former, in its simplest form, values a company on what it would be worth in liquidation whereas the latter is trying to establish the long-term financial strength of the firm.
4 *Creditworthiness* This is the critical point of the whole procedure. The bank's lending officers will, in order to form a picture of clients' credit-worthiness, rely on several sources of information and will attach varying degrees of importance to them.
5 *Borrower's own contribution* Normally the borrower is expected to put some money in the project or the venture. This is an indicator of the borrower's confidence in the future success of the plan.
6 *What security is being offered?* In most cases bank advances are not totally secured. Many loans approved are based purely on the creditworthiness of the borrower. The purpose of asking for some sort of security is of course to provide the bank with an asset which can produce the funds with which to repay the advances should the customer *fail* to do so. A problem is that in the last resort the value of any security can be massively discounted when liquidation arises. An example is in the late 1980's recession in the UK where the values of property dropped between 25% and 50%.

Some bankers like to employ a checklist approach to lending. One form of classification which has been advocated is the four Cs of credit which later became seven Cs. These cover:

- character
- capacity
- capital
- conditions

- customer relationships
- competition
- collateral

These are proposed as the factors to be looked at by a lending officer. However, many bankers have commented that they are not in favour of these kinds of mnemonics. They tend to consider them as 'unwieldy tick-lists which would lead to a superficial approach to their job'. A list which was produced in the 1930s had temperance as a key factor to consider!

A more financial-statement-oriented approach is urged by many. The Committee of London Clearing Bankers suggested that the financial analysis should be conducted following two different approaches: the liquidation approach and the going concern approach. According to the former, the accounting value of the company's assets is expected to exceed by a decent margin the value of the liabilities. This is sometimes known as 'asset-based lending'. The going-concern approach, on the other hand, focuses on the analysis of the company's future viability, which is reflected ultimately in the ability to generate profits and cash. If this is the case, the financial statements (in particular the cash-flow statement) are used as a guide in order to form views about a company s future performance.

Credit rating systems

Increasingly banks are using credit scoring systems in deciding on business loans. It is argued that it reduces the human factor which involves subjectivity. The supporters of the new technology claim that it can help not only with the pure lending decisions but also offers administrative advantages and portfolio control over loan officers. As far as the administrative advantages are concerned it means banks can use and allocate their human resources more efficiently. For example, on-line expert systems can be used as substitutes for senior officers' involvement in the preliminary stages of credit decisions and may be done by less experienced officers. Credit assessment systems may help in getting rid of the paperwork involved in such decisions and in setting credit authorization criteria.

The latest feature of these systems is their interactive ability as well as the fact that they try to capture the qualitative dimension of the lending decision. Much of the time they are designed to engage in a question-and-answer session with the user. The system may ask crucial questions like: is the company in a growth industry? To this question the loan officer can answer with various degrees of certainty; even vagueness and uncertainty are accepted. The most recent developments in the field of artificial intelligence are the so called neural networks. These are systems with built-in logic. Score cards are recalculated as conditions change.

19.2 REVOLVING UNDERWRITING FACILITY

With the revolving underwriting facility (RUF), rather than offer a borrower a loan over a set period of years, a bank will underwrite the borrower's access to funds at a specified rate in the short-term commercial paper market throughout an agreed period. This type of arrangement is only likely to be available to large companies. Although the borrower may be well known to its lead bank (the underwriter) and even to the first purchaser of the notes, the notes can be sold in the secondary market and further purchasers may not be familiar with the corporate name or its rating. It is the name of the underwriting bank that helps sell the security.

During the period of the arrangement the borrower will issue a successive series of short-dated promissory notes up to the total of the facility. These notes will bear interest at a rate agreed at the outset, probably linked to the London interbank offer rate (LIBOR). At each new issue the interest rate is likely to be different, depending on movements in LIBOR. However, the spread, again agreed at the outset, will remain constant. The bank undertakes to sell the notes in the market at a price fixed by the RUF agreement and underwrites the issues by agreeing to purchase the instruments themselves should the market fail to take them up. In many respects this is similar to the acceptance credit tender panels which are gaining popularity among borrowers. What the banks are doing under an RUF is not giving an undertaking to lend funds themselves but merely guaranteeing the borrower's credit rating and in doing so ensuring that the company will be able to sell the notes and so obtain finance.

The bank offering the RUF is paid an underwriting fee and commission on the sale of the notes. In theory both the bank and the borrower benefit from this arrangement: the borrower is provided with direct access to finance, and the bank is supporting a customer without necessarily reducing its own liquidity. It is part of the move to securitization.

19.3 MEDIUM-TERM BANK BORROWING

Since the 1970s most UK and foreign commercial banks have been willing to make medium-term loan finance available to companies. The loans are usually secured by a fixed or floating charge on the company. In addition, borrowers often have to covenant to maintain a prescribed level of interest cover and possibly current-assets cover.

Many of the bank loan schemes that are offered can be taken out not just for medium periods of time but also for long periods. For example, development loans can be for terms of from one to twenty years.

Fixed-term lending by the clearing banks has grown in importance both to borrowers and as a proportion of the banks' total advances. It is now a welcomed source of finance to companies. These term loans can either be repayable in a lump sum at the end of the loan period or repayable in periodic instalments. The borrower can negotiate with the bank to obtain the terms best suited to the expected future cash flow. It is possible to arrange 'rest' periods during which time only the interest on the loan is payable. The capital repayments by instalments do not begin until the rest period ends. This type of rest period followed by repayment by instalments is more common than the method of repayment by a single lump sum at the end of the term.

19.4 BILLS OF EXCHANGE

A post-dated cheque is a simple example of a bill of exchange. When a cheque signed on 1 January is dated 1 April or 1 July, the signatory is asking his bank to pay the prescribed amount in three or six months' time. The signatory, a buying company, can send this cheque to a supplier who will dispatch goods; the supplier is in fact giving three or six months' credit, and can choose either to retain the cheque and present it for payment on the due date, or to sell it to a bank or discount house. With a commercial bill of exchange, however, the supplier prepares the bill. A bill is defined as 'an unconditional order in writing, addressed by one person to another, signed by the person giving it, requiring the person to whom it is addressed to pay on demand, or at a fixed or determinable future time, a sum certain in money to or to the order of a specified person, or to bearer' (Bills of Exchange Act 1882, section 3).

Short- and medium-term sources of finance

Bills of exchange are now used mainly in connection with overseas shipments. The seller of the goods can obtain cash immediately after the goods are dispatched, either because the bill has an early maturity date or because he or she discounts the bill. The buyer of the goods can delay payment of the bill, which is particularly important with overseas orders, because the buyer may have to wait some time before receiving the goods. The bill of exchange therefore helps both buyer and seller with their finance, which is valuable for all transactions but is of added importance if the goods are a long time in transit and neither party has possession of them.

The cost of funds provided by a bill of exchange depends upon the rate at which the bill is discounted. If the seller of the goods presents the bill to a bank, which buys it at a discount rate of 2%, a £100 bill payable in three months' time would have a cost of $2/98 = 2.04\%$. The seller has had to surrender £2 to receive £98. This is equivalent to an annual interest rate of $(1.0204)^4 - 1 = 8.4\%$.

Bills cover periods ranging from 60 to 180 days, but are usually for 90 days. They are usually for over £75 000 in value. The discounts charged on a 90-day bill would be based on the three-month interbank rate, and usually are at a rate somewhere between 1.5% and 4% above this interbank rate. The actual discount rate would depend upon the risks involved, mainly the creditworthiness of the seller and buyer. If credit insurance is arranged, it results in a 'finer' discount rate.

19.5 ACCEPTANCE CREDITS

An acceptance credit has much in common with a bill of exchange. To obtain finance under this type of arrangement a company draws a bill of exchange on a bank. The bank accepts the bill, thereby promising to pay out the amount of the bill to the holder at some specified future date. The bill itself is then worth something as the holder is to receive a sum of money at a future date. This bill can then be sold by the company either at once or when the funds are needed. It is sold in the money market to, say, the discount houses. It is similar to an ordinary bill of exchange between two companies, but now one of the parties is a bank. A bill bearing a reputable bank's name can be sold in the money markets at a lower discount rate than a bill bearing the name of a medium- or small-sized company because of the reduced risk.

Merchant banks were the first to offer this sort of finance. They would sign bills promising to pay a sum of money to the holder of the bill at some future date. These credits (bills) were then sold in the market so that the money could be made available at once to the company who was the other party to the bill. When the date mentioned in the bill arrived, say one year after issue, the company would pay the accepting bank the value of the bill and the bank would pay the current holder of the bill its face value. The leading merchant banks still dominate this field, but other banks, including the clearing banks, now also offer acceptance credits. Sometimes a syndicate of banks issues the credit.

Of course, the company drawing the bill has to be able to satisfy the bank providing the credit that their money is safe both from the point of view of capital repayment and interest payments. It is unlikely, therefore, that a company that has been unable to satisfy its own bankers that it is safe for a loan will be able to satisfy another bank or a syndicate of bankers that it is safe to make available a certain level of credit. The point about acceptance credits that is particularly interesting is that the company can be sure that the credit will be made available for a longer period than the usual bank overdraft. This type of syndicated credit is quite common in Germany.

The company that draws up the bill does not have to sell the bill immediately it is issued; it can retain it and use it as part of its credit facilities. From the company's point of view these acceptance credits are similar in nature to a medium-term overdraft with either a fixed or a variable rate of interest. The bank signing the bill is helping to make available to the company a certain level of credit. The company can then use these funds as it requires them, up to the agreed maximum. The length of period over which the credit is made available depends on negotiations, but can be as long as five years. From the company's point of view it represents an alternative source of finance: money is being obtained from a source other than the company's banker.

Acceptance credit facilities have proved to be very popular. Companies have found that they can often borrow more cheaply in the money market, for periods of from one month to six months, through using acceptance credits than through a traditional bank overdraft. Of course, the company may be locked into a fixed interest rate for the period of the credit rather than the variable interest rate applying to overdrafts.

Bank borrowing versus capital markets borrowing

Large companies have direct access to borrowing in the capital market. They have become less dependent on borrowing direct from a bank. Medium-term notes and floating-rate notes have already been discussed in Chapter 9. The banks have responded to the competition by offering very competitively priced loans to the large businesses. This has been to some extent at the cost of smaller and medium-sized firms. The cost of bank borrowing to this sector has been relatively high. Due to fierce competition between the banks, the large firms have faced very competitive loan supply conditions.

Disintermediation

This clumsy word means cutting out the role of financial intermediaries. The word refers to the process of companies lending to and borrowing from other companies. A company with surplus cash will lend to another company. This cuts out the bank or other financial intermediary. Clearly it means the borrowing rates will be less than if a bank was involved because the costs of the intermediary have been avoided.

Rather than a simple loan, it is often a financial security that is traded. The one company (usually a well-known company) that wishes to obtain finance now will issue a promissory note, in which it promises to pay a certain sum of money at a specified future date. This note is then sold at a discount in the market place. It could be purchased by another (non-financial) company. This is known as 'commercial paper'. The paper might be resold a number of times during its life. It is usually used for short-term borrowing. At the maturity of the note the issuing company pays its face value to whoever is the holder at that moment.

19.6 TRADE CREDIT

One of the most important forms of short-term finance in the economy is the trade credit extended by one company to another on the purchase and sale of goods and equipment.

To receive goods and delay payment of the account is a recognized form of short-term financing: the goods can be used to provide returns or benefits throughout the period that elapses before the bill has to be settled. For the receiving company this is similar to buying goods with a bank overdraft, except that an overdraft carries the obvious interest charge. When the finance is provided by another company, the cost is not so obvious.

If, however, a cash discount is offered to encourage early payment and the receiving company does not take advantage of this, then there is a clear cost. Assume that a 1% cash discount is offered for payment within 30 days. The cost of capital for credit taken for these 30 days is

$$\frac{1\%}{100\% - 1\%} = \frac{1}{99} = 1.01\%$$

Taking such credit for 30 days is the equivalent to an annual interest rate of $(1.01)^{12} - 1 = 12.7\%$.

Trade credit is not necessarily a cheap source of finance. On occasions, trade credit is taken because the buyer is not aware of the real costs involved, if he were he might turn to alternative sources to finance trade. However, other forms of finance are not always available, and for a company that has borrowed as much as possible trade credit may be the only choice left. This is an important source of funds for many small companies.

At one time large companies often played an important role as informal benefactors by allowing small companies periods of credit. This has changed. Certain large companies now have a notorious reputation among small firms for taking a long time to pay as creditors but demanding ruthlessly prompt payment when the position is reversed.

A company which provides credit to another is in fact putting itself in the position of a banker whose advance takes the form not of cash but of goods for which payment will be deferred. This use of trade credit between companies is extremely important from both an industrial and a national point of view.

Advantages of trade credit

When the customer's creditworthiness is well established, trade credit becomes a convenient informal affair, and is indeed a normal part of business in most industries. The offer of trade credit by a seller is part of the terms of sale – a sales promotion device by which he or she hopes to attract business. The amount of credit offered will depend on the risks associated with the customer. In certain cases, the seller may agree to sell only a 'safe' quantity of goods.

Trade credit is, however, double-edged. It is for the seller a device used to attract customers and for the buyer a desirable source of funds, and as such could conceivably cause a company both profit and loss simultaneously. In the role of buyer, a company would want to obtain as much credit as possible without losing too much discount or goodwill; as seller, it would prefer its customers not to take too long over paying their accounts.

Terms of credit

Terms of credit vary considerably from industry to industry. Theoretically, four main factors determine the length of credit allowed.

1 *The economic nature of the product:* products with a high sales turnover are sold on short credit terms. If the seller is relying on a low profit margin and a high sales turnover, he or she cannot afford to offer customers a long time to pay.
2 *The financial circumstances of the seller:* if the seller's liquidity position is weak he or she will find it difficult to allow very much credit and will prefer an early cash settlement. (If credit terms are being used as a sales

promotion device by the seller's competitors, the seller may have to allow credit, and try to improve his or her liquidity by some other method.)

3 *The financial position of the buyer:* if the buyer is in a weak liquidity position he or she may have to take a long period in which to pay. The seller may not wish to deal with customers of this kind, but if he or she is prepared to take the risk so as to obtain the sale, the seller will have to grant credit.

4 *Cash discounts:* when cash discounts are taken into account, the cost of trade credit can be surprisingly high. The higher the cash discount being offered the smaller is the period of trade credit likely to be taken.

In many industries, credit terms are recommended by trade associations. In others, established custom defines the normally accepted conditions. In some industries where a there is a long time lag between the purchase of materials or commodities and the sale of the finished product, the suppliers may be prepared to give long-term credit.

19.7 FACTORING

Factoring involves raising funds on the security of the company's debts, so that cash is received earlier than if the company waited for the debtors to pay. Basically most factors offer three services:

1 sales-ledger accounting, dispatching invoices and making sure the bills are paid;
2 credit management, including guarantees against bad debts;
3 the provision of finance, advancing clients up to 80% of the value of the debts that they are collecting.

The client need not use all these services; it can choose whichever it requires.

Sales-ledger administration

The factor providing sales-ledger administration will take on responsibility for the sales accounting records, credit control and the collection of the debts. It is claimed that, with their experience, the factor will be able to obtain payment from customers more quickly than if the company were to be responsible for the collection.

The cost of this administrative service is a fee based on the total value of debts assigned to the factor. The fee is usually between 1% and 3%. It is based on the amount of work that needs to be carried out.

Credit management/insurance

For a fee the factor can provide up to 100% protection against non-payment on approved sales. Of course, the factor has to decide whether the debt is worth covering. The credit standing of the company's individual customers will be analysed carefully before a guarantee can be obtained.

Provision of finance

Provision of finance is the main reason why companies use the service of factors. For a small fast growing company a factor provides a good means of releasing funds tied up in debtors. It provides a good source of working capital.

Factors will provide finance if required, thus improving a company's liquidity position, but this finance is not cheap, and since bank borrowing is both flexible and less expensive, any company in liquidity difficulties should approach a bank first. However, factoring can be particularly useful when a company has exhausted its overdraft and is not yet in a position to raise new equity.

Factors assess every client and, in fact, turn down many applicants. They do not see themselves as the last financial resort for companies in difficulties; they are not interested in bad companies. The implications for a company when it obtains funds through factoring are not similar in all respects to the implications of normal borrowing. The charges do not have to be registered, and the client's borrowing ratios are not affected.

The factor usually allows 80% of the value of debts to be borrowed when the invoice is dispatched to the customer. The remaining 20%, less charges, will be paid either after a specified period or when the invoice is paid by the customer. The charge is based on the amounts borrowed at a particular time, with the interest rate 2 to 5% above base rate.

Confidential invoice factoring

In the conventional factoring procedure the factor sends a statement to the customer who purchased goods from the factor's client, and the customer repays the factor. With *confidential* invoice factoring, the customer is unaware that a factor has intervened in the transaction. No third party is introduced into the buyer–seller relationship. The client receives an advance on the copy invoices he or she sends to the factor, but is still responsible for collecting the debt. The client is now acting as an agent for the factor: he or she sends the invoice to the purchaser, collects the debt and then forwards the receipts, to the extent of the advance, to the factor.

The maximum amount which can be raised by a company through factoring depends on its annual turnover and its average collection period for debts. If it takes on average 90 days to collect a debt, then on any one day approximately a quarter of the annual turnover will be debtors. A factor will normally advance up to 80% of this debtors figure, or, to put it another way, as much as 20% of the annual turnover of the company could be made available in the form of cash.

The cost of this confidential invoicing depends, of course, on the cost of money at the time and on the standing of both the borrower and the borrower's customers. It is usually based on a percentage per month charged on the money used for as long as the debt remains outstanding. Of course, the factor has to cover the cost of their borrowing and administrative costs, and to earn a suitable profit for the risks they are taking.

19.8 INVOICE DISCOUNTING AND CREDIT INSURANCE

Invoice discounting is purely a financial arrangement which benefits the liquidity position of the user. Again, it is designed to overcome the problem of tying up working capital in book debts.

A company can convert an invoice into cash through specialized finance companies. Either separate invoices or a proportion of a company's book debts can be discounted, although the full face value of the invoice is not usually advanced. The company makes an offer to the finance house by sending it the respective invoices and agreeing to guarantee payment of any debts that are purchased. If the finance house accepts the offer, it makes an immediate first payment of about 75% of the value of the invoices. The company then accepts as collateral security a bill of exchange for this 75%, which means that at a specified future date, say after 90 days, the loan must be repaid. The company is responsible for collecting the debt and for returning the amount advanced, whether the debt is collected or not.

The cost of this service depends upon the risks and administrative costs involved; it includes an interest charge on the amount advanced plus a service charge. The cost is not cheap. For invoice discounting, the cost of funds advanced can be between 3% and 6% above the base rate. A potential borrower offering a book debt as security will find that any lending institution – bank, factor or finance house – will be more willing to make the advance if the debt is insured. The procedure is familiar enough: the client pays a premium to the insurance company in return for the amount of the invoice. The cost of the insurance will depend on the amounts involved and the risks attached to the debt.

19.9 DEFERRED TAX PAYMENTS

Another source of short-term funds similar in character to trade credit is the credit supplied by the tax authorities. This is created by the interval that elapses between the earning of the profits by the company and the payment of the taxes due on them.

As long as the company continues to earn stable or expanding profits, tax payment deferred in this way comprises a virtually permanent source of finance. The tax bill for one period can be paid out of next period's profits. Consequently, although a part of any period's profits will be reserved for tax payment purposes, these funds do not have to be relinquished to the tax authorities immediately and so can be used by the company to earn profits. The company must ensure however, that when the time for payment arises it has liquid resources available.

19.10 MERCHANT (INVESTMENT) BANKS

Merchant banks (which include acceptance houses) have historically been more associated with the provision of risk 'venture' capital than have the high-street (commercial) banks. However, the amount of money that the merchant banks have available to invest compared with the resources of the clearing banks is comparatively small. It is often commented in the UK that there has not been sufficient finance available in the venture-capital market.

The merchant banks are selective when it comes to making investments. Their lending policies vary enormously from one bank to another. Many of the large merchant banks take the view that the provision of finance of less than £250 000 is not worth bothering with. It is reported that, of the total number of loans of the largest merchant banks, only about 25% are to small firms. However, there are smaller merchant banks that are willing to invest smaller amounts of money. There are those who would be willing to invest in the region of £50 000. In order to make large sums of money, say £3 million or more, available to a company, merchant banks sometimes combine together to form a syndicate.

It is hard to define the typical investment that they will undertake. At one time they would only provide loans if they could obtain a minority equity stake, and the package was usually composed of equity funds and loan money. Now, the bank is not usually looking for a permanent stake in the company but rather a profitable investment, and it is likely that it will attempt to dispose of its equity investment in a company five or so years after making the investment. The bank hopes to obtain its return through capital appreciation over this period. If a suitable return within this period is not possible the bank may not be interested in longer-term investment. When the bank thinks that it is time to dispose of the shares, the existing owners of the company will, in most cases, be given the chance to buy them before they are offered to outsiders. This is referred to as the 'exit route'.

Short- and medium-term sources of finance

3i

The Industrial and Commercial Finance Corporation (ICFC) was set up in the UK in 1945 specifically to assist the smaller company seeking loan and equity capital. Undoubtedly ICFC was successful. In 1983 a company Investors in Industry (3i) was formed to take over ICFC and another merchant bank, Finance for Industry (FF1). The 31s was 85% owned by the English and Scottish clearing banks and 15% owned by the Bank of England.

In the summer of 1994, the 3i company was floated on the London Stock Exchange as an investment trust. The company floated 45% of its equity.

Almost a quarter of the value of its portfolio is in companies with sales of less than £5 million. It makes investments in some companies without insisting on a timetable for flotation. It claims that it is able to put such investments in its 'bottom drawer' and to pull them out only when they begin to perform well. It is able to do this because of its wide investments base: it is much bigger than the traditional venture-capital company.

Because it has a network of regional offices it is in a better position to be able to identify and work with companies at a local level. But, as with all venture-capital companies, it has its failures.

19.11 EXPORT FINANCE

This is a complex subject. In this section we will deal briefly with the issues involved. When a company sells goods to a company in another country, it could just dispatch the goods and wait for the payment to be received. This, however, could be an expensive and a risky approach. Expensive because it could take a long time before the payment is received; risky because often less is known about the financial status of a foreign customer than that of a domestic customer.

To overcome the problem of expense it is often possible for a company to obtain a loan to help it fund itself during the period between dispatch of the goods and receipt of payment. To overcome the risk of non-payment it is sometimes possible to obtain a guarantee.

Indeed, one way in which it is possible to increase the probability that a bank will lend money to finance a company during the period between the production and dispatch of goods for export and the receipt of cash from the foreign buyer is through the use of an export credit guarantee.

In fact, in the region of 85% of UK exports are financed by traditional bank overdrafts. Most banks seek security for such loans. They like credit insurance on the debts of the overseas buyer as security. Without such insurance on the amount to be received they are reluctant to lend to support exports.

The government and exporting

The central government of a country has a role to play in encouraging and helping its companies export. In fact, some governments do more to help their companies than do other governments. British companies complain that they are at a competitive disadvantage to their continental competitors in that the British government does not do enough. It is often claimed, for example, that French companies receive greater export credit insurance support, with greater availability at lower cost, from their government, than do British companies from the UK government.

The argument for the government to become involved is that exporting is not only important to the company involved but also to the country. The balance-of-payments position of a country is crucial to the economic well-being of the country. It helps determine what policies a government can afford to pursue. Exporting is not just for private benefit, but also for the public's benefit.

It is for this reason that governments support their companies in export markets. It becomes a competition for business not just between a company in one country and a company in another country, but also between one government and another government.

The ways in which the government can help, include:

- trade counsellors in embassies in a country helping business-people when they visit that country;
- giving advice to companies on how to export, and on the conditions and requirements in a particular country;
- assistance with finance, in particular export guarantee cover.

The government does not provide the finance. But because the government provides a guarantee of payment the banks are willing to lend money.

Insurance

The Export Credit Guarantee Department (ECGD) is a government department that has the role of assisting companies with their exporting. It issues guarantees appropriate to the terms of sale, and with these guarantees the exporting company is able to borrow from a bank

With an ECGD guarantee behind a company's exports, the banks may be willing to advance up to 100% of the value of an individual invoice and to advance up to 90% of the value of an invoice for trading on open account. The amount actually advanced will depend upon the type of goods exported, the length of the credit period being made available to the purchaser, and the country to which the goods are being shipped.

In the late 1980s the UK government divided the export credit insurance business into two. ECGD withdrew from the short-term insurance business, leaving this to the private sector. The short-term insurance division of the ECGD was sold off to the Dutch insurance company NCM. In fact, however, the UK government has found it necessary to continue to support, indirectly, the short-term business. It does this by providing reinsurance support to NCM to underpin its operations. It has been thought necessary to do this because of a lack of capacity in the private reinsurance market.

The UK government in response to criticism that it does not do enough to help British exporters, doubled, in the five years between 1991/92 and 1996/97 the amount of money available for ECGD cover. A portion of this cover was tied aid targeted for use only in certain overseas markets.

Another way in which government helps exporters is through making credit available to purchasers. Governments in developed countries provide financial aid to developing countries. Financial aid is not the same as a grant; the funds are not necessarily free. Aid is defined as finance made available at favourable terms, where 'favourable' means at an effective cost which is 25% or more less than commercial rates.

Such aid is usually tied. This means it can only be used to purchase goods or services from companies from the country providing aid. The UK government will make a loan available to a country at favourable terms. The money borrowed is to be used to purchase UK-made goods. One source of finance therefore for UK companies is through obtaining contracts in developing countries in which the UK government has provided aid finance.

Supplier credits

The ECGD and NCM (a private insurance company) are not themselves a source of finance for companies. They do not offer loans but make it easier for companies to obtain loans from the banks. When exporting, a company has to be able to offer an attractive deal to the overseas buyer. The factors influencing whether or not the exporting company obtains the business include the quality of the product, the price, the delivery date and possibly the credit terms attached to the sale. Does the UK supplier wish to be paid by the buyer immediately on the goods and documents being delivered or one month after delivery, or are they offering a period of credit? If a period of credit is being offered to the foreign buyer, say six months, then the exporter will need sufficient working capital to be able to finance the production of goods and to be able to pay interest or sacrifice earnings on the funds tied up in the sale. This credit may be carried by the exporter through their normal overdraft arrangement with a bank, or possibly the bank will discount the invoice. An alternative approach is for the exporter to obtain from the ECGD or NCM a guarantee that the bank will have any loan it advances repaid even if the overseas buyer does not pay for the goods or contract work at the end of the period of credit. It is the bank that makes the loan to the company and the insurer that provides the guarantee. On shorter-term business the buyer gives a promissory note or accepts a bill of exchange; the insurer is then prepared to give an unconditional guarantee to the exporter's bank that it will pay 90% of the value of the invoice when it becomes six months overdue.

Most of the credit insurance provided is what is described as 'comprehensive short term'. 'Short term' refers to goods sold on credit of up to six months. 'Comprehensive' means that the exporter does not have to inform the insurer of each individual sale. There is an agreed upper credit limit for a 12-month period. It is only when a large amount of credit is being advanced to a new customer that the insurer will need to be informed.

Buyer credits

For larger business deals an alternative way for companies to finance their export sales is by means of buyer credit financing. This is possible on major projects and on capital goods business where the contract value is over £250 000. Under this arrangement the exporter is paid by the buyer in cash immediately upon delivery of the goods or satisfactory completion of the contract. To enable this to happen the exporter, the exporter's bank and the ECGD or private insurer will arrange for a loan to be made to the overseas buyer. Instead of buyers being offered deferred payment terms, they are now offered a loan to enable them to pay the exporter as soon as they are satisfied with the goods or the contract work. Buyer credit guarantees are available to banks making such loans to the foreign purchaser.

Under this buyer credit arrangement, the overseas buyer is normally required to pay the supplier 15–20% of the contract price out of their own resources. The remainder is to be paid to the exporter from funds made available from a loan either to the overseas buyer or to a bank in the buyer's country. The funds have been lent by a UK bank and guaranteed. The loan is normally for less than the value of the goods and services supplied by the UK exporter.

Countertrade

Countertrade is a method of financing trade, but goods rather than money are used to fund the transaction. It is a form of barter. Goods are exchanged for other goods. This was particularly fashionable in the 1980s, when many deals exchanging petroleum for manufactured goods took place. These deals were outside the OPEC export quotas set for the countries concerned. It was a way of avoiding the quotas on sales. Countertrade was also popular in deals with developing countries and East European countries as both groups were short of foreign exchange and so keen to resort to barter. They wished to import and had goods that they wished to export. Negotiation determined how much of one good was exchanged for the other.

The spectacular growth period of this form of trade has now passed. A number of companies engaged in this business as intermediaries lost money and found themselves with goods they could not move. Countertrade is now a normal part of international trade, accounting for some 10–15% of the total. There are many forms of countertrade, one of which is a triangular management, A ships goods to B, who ships goods to C. Then C ships goods back to A in return for the original transaction.

Forfeiting

With forfeiting a bank purchases a number of sales invoices or promissory notes from a company. The selling company obtains immediate cash, and the purchasing bank has a claim to a stream of income to be received in the future. Usually the bank purchasing the debts would only do so if the banks of the companies purchasing the goods guaranteed payment of the invoices. The invoices involved are often concerned with export transactions. The bank which has purchased the invoices can in fact sell them to another party. They become a security to be traded in the market place.

Factoring

An alternative form of financing is through a factor. The factor will buy the overseas debt and in return make an immediate cash payment to the exporter of part of the value of the receivable. They will of course also, if required, take over the record keeping, the credit control and the debt collection. Factoring has the reputation of being expensive.

A typical exporting situation and the choice faced by a company will be explained. A company exports 90% of its £2 million turnover to large multinational companies. The company receives payment on average within 90 days from the time when the goods are dispatched. This means on average its level of debtors is £500 000 ($= \frac{90}{360} \times$ £2 million). The company can fund this either by taking time to pay its suppliers, by short-term borrowing, or by using the services of a factor.

The first of these alternatives is risky. Let us say the company has an overdraft facility of only £100 000. It could ask the bank for a larger overdraft arrangement, but there is the possibility that the bank would be reluctant because of the large proportion of overseas debts. The exporter could turn to other short-term borrowing arrangements or to a factor. The company could expect the factor to grant a facility covering up to 80% of the value of its debtors, with an agreed upper limit. The factor would provide finance and a debt collection service in the buyer's country.

19.12 PROJECT FINANCE

Project finance is a form of medium-term borrowing that has been developed for a particular purpose. The underlying idea behind this type of finance is that the security against which the funds are advanced is a project rather than the standing or potential of the borrower, or an asset of the business. With most loan applications, it is the credit standing of the borrower that is the factor that decides whether the money will be advanced, but with project finance, although the credit standing of the borrower is of some importance, the key consideration is the financial viability of the project.

Short- and medium-term sources of finance

This type of finance grew in importance during the 1970s, particularly in international business. One reason for its growth was the increasing size of many investment projects that required funding. Many of the North Sea oil developments were funded with this type of finance. Many small companies participated in North Sea oil investment and they were of such a size that it would not have been possible for them to raise the finance required against the security of their own balance sheets. However, such companies were able to generate the necessary borrowings against the security of the oil that they were seeking to extract. The banks making the loans were taking certain risks: first whether or not the exploration work would lead to the discovery of oil, and second that the future price levels for oil would justify the expenditure. Because the investments were long-term ventures, there was uncertainty with regard to the cost of the exploration work. With this type of loan the banks do not have the usual recourse to the assets of the borrower if the project fails. They are taking risks above those which they are normally willing to incur. The banks have traditionally been reluctant to enter into long-term lending and even when venturing into medium-term lending have not usually been interested in projects maturing beyond seven years. This traditional time horizon was not long enough for oil and other natural-resource projects.

The largest single source of project finance is said to be the World Bank. However, some of their loans are not strictly project finance, as they are funding of larger-scale operations. Project finance is limited to those cases where it is possible to identify a particular project and to be able to identify an income stream that results from it. The banks need to be able to identify the various risks associated with the particular project. This is different from the usual type of financial risk analysis that the lender normally undertakes, which is assessing the creditworthiness of a company. To compensate for the higher levels of risk in project finance over their traditional means of providing finance, the banks frequently require higher returns on their loans than is normal, and on occasion seek returns in the form of royalties over and above the interest payments. Banking syndicates are formed in order to provide the finance for very large projects.

Often energy developments are funded with this type of finance, for example nuclear power stations and hydroelectric schemes. The development of project finance has enabled small companies to bid for very large contracts and it has also become possible for small countries to engage in the development of their natural resources. An alternative name for this method of financing is 'natural-resource financing'.

It is possible to identify alternative forms of project financing depending on who takes the risks. At one extreme there is the situation where the borrower takes no risks at all. If the project is not a success, it is the lender that loses the money. The lender takes all the commercial and political risks. A second type of loan involves the borrower in taking a certain amount of the risk. The borrower may be at risk until the project comes on stream. Once the commercial operations begin, it is the lender that takes on the risk. This type of financing is often arranged for complex industrial projects which involve new or untried technological methods. It is reasonable in such cases for the constructor, the borrowing company, to cover the risk as to whether or not the project will work. It was this division of risk that was accepted in financing many of the North Sea pipeline projects. The third type of situation arises where the borrower takes the commercial risks while the lender assumes the political risks. This would be particularly important in projects in developing countries where there is always the threat of nationalization. Finally, there is the project where the lender takes no risk at all, but advances the money on the guarantee of some third party that the loan will be repaid if there is default. The guarantee may be provided by governments or by some state agency in the country where the work is taking place.

Hire purchase is a source of medium-term credit sometimes used for the purchase of plant and equipment. Initially a hire-purchase company purchases the required equipment, but it can immediately be used by the hiree, who after a series of regular payments, which includes an interest charge, becomes the owner of the equipment. The hiree has the advantage of the use of the equipment over the period that they are making the payments, and so obtains the benefits from using the equipment without having to incur a large capital outlay.

The legal framework of the hire-purchase agreement is that the hire-purchase company hires out the equipment to the intended purchaser, who is given an option to purchase the equipment for a nominal sum when the hiring rents have been paid. The legal title to the equipment does not rest in the hiree until the completion of the agreement.

In terms of cash flow the hiree has to make an initial payment and a series of instalments, rather than one large cash outlay at the time of first using the equipment. The funds that can be saved by only having to make a small initial payment at the beginning of the period rather than the full purchase price are available for investment elsewhere. However, hire purchase tends to be an expensive form of finance. The eventual purchasing company (the hiree) is entitled to claim taxation relief in respect of any investment allowances. It can also obtain tax relief on the interest element in the payments it makes.

The significance of hire purchase in the financial structure of the economy is that it is a convenient source of medium term credit on fixed terms for the purchase of equipment, where the equipment itself can provide adequate security for the loan and the loan can be paid off by regular instalments.

The security on any loan is important. For the equipment itself to provide the security, the life of the asset must be greater than the period of the agreement, so that if the agreement is broken there is still an asset in existence which has a value. It is desirable that the value of the asset is at all times greater than the amount of the outstanding indebtedness. However, this requirement is not always enforced.

Effective rates of interest

With an overdraft and many types of loan, the interest charge is based on the outstanding balance of the debt at particular points of time. As a company reduces its overdraft at the bank, so its interest charge falls. Providers of instalment credit calculate interest in a way which differs from that on overdrafts and term loans. Interest is charged on the amount of the full loan for the whole period of the agreement, even though the borrower is, in fact, repaying the capital at intervals throughout the period of the agreement. Each payment is a mixture of capital and interest. Interest is being charged as though the amount of the loan was not repaid until the end of the period, even though in fact the amount of the loan is being reduced throughout the period.

An example will illustrate this point. Assume that a company enters a hire purchase agreement to acquire a piece of equipment and the equipment cost is £1 000. The period of the hire-purchase agreement is three years. If the finance company mentions a rate of 12% interest on the agreement, it means that the total interest charge will be £360, i.e. £1 000 × 0.12 × 3. The company will have to repay £1 360 over the three years, i.e. 36 monthly payments of £37.77.

If L is the initial value of the equipment, i is the 'add-on' interest rate, t is the length of the agreement and n is the number of payments each year, then total interest charged = Lit

total value being advanced = $L(1 + it)$

size of each payment = $L(1 + it)\, tn$

In each monthly payment the company is repaying part loan and part interest and yet the interest is still being calculated on the full value of the capital sum advanced.

The 'true' rate of interest (the effective rate) can be determined by calculating the discount rate that equates the present value of the series of payments with the initial loan. The discount tables at the end of this book provide figures for returns and payments for different time periods. They can be used for monthly periods as well as annual. With the hire-purchase example it can be seen that with this method of payment, the 36 monthly approach, they give a true rate of interest well above the 'add on' rate. The true rate for the 36-month case is 23.8%.

We can obtain an approximate answer using an annuity table. The £1000 capital sum divided by the monthly payment of £37.77 gives a factor of 26.48. Table 3 shows 35 periods but not 36. The factor of 26.48 approximates to the factor for 35 periods with a 2% rate of interest. Each payment is for a monthly period. This rate of just under 2% per month gives 23.8% per annum. In this example the effective rate is approximately twice the add-on rate.

19.14 SALE AND LEASE-BACK

It is possible to convert certain assets which a company owns into funds, and yet for the company to still continue to use the assets. For example, if a building is sold to an insurance company or some other financial intermediary and then leased back from the purchaser, the company has secured an immediate cash inflow. The only cash outflow is the rental payments that it now has to make. These rental payments are allowed as a tax deductible expense. However, the company may be subject to capital gains tax, which will arise if the sale price is in excess of the written-down value as agreed by the tax authorities.

This financing possibility is particularly applicable to assets which appreciate in value, such as land, buildings or some other form of property. It is particularly appropriate to companies owning the properties freehold, and to institutions such as insurance companies or pension funds which are interested in holding long-term secure assets. The property is leased back by the seller at a negotiated annual rental, although with long lease-backs there will need to be a provision for the revision of the rental at certain intervals of time. Clearly the sale and lease-back releases funds which can be used for some other investment. A number of takeovers have been financed by this means. Assets were sold and leased back: the cash obtained from the sale was used to finance the purchase of another company. If the acquired company had substantial property so much the better, for this property could then be sold to an insurance company and leased back.

With sale and lease-back, funds are released for use elsewhere in the business, and in the short run the assets used by the company do not change. It must be remembered, however, that the leased asset no longer belongs to the company; the lease may one day come to an end and then alternative assets will have to be obtained. Also, the company is no longer obtaining the possible capital appreciation on the asset. Therefore there are costs to this process in addition to the lease payments that have to be made. The costs have to be compared with the increase in profits that can be obtained by having more working capital available.

As an example of a sale and lease-back arrangement, assume that a trading company owning a commercial property is offered £150 000 for the sale of the premises by an insurance company. The company is then to be allowed to rent the property from the insurance company, with the rental being fixed at a level of £13 000 per annum for the next five years and then being subject to review. This rental is giving the insurance company a 'yield' of 8.7% on its investment, which at the time is considered reasonable. This yield figure, which is often quoted in such transactions, is a crude yield; it is not discounted, and it is based simply on the first year's rent against initial investment.

From the trading company's point of view, it has to decide whether the profits it could make each year from investing the £150 000 cash it would obtain would be greater than the amount of the annual rental it had to pay. The amount of the rental payments after the fifth year are not known with certainty, but then neither are the profits. Taxation has to be taken into account, the rental payment being a tax-deductible expense, and the profits earned being subject to tax. Terms offered can be quite favourable to companies wishing to enter into such agreements. For example, if the owner–occupier of a property sold that property to an institution for £1 million and then leased it back, the initial rent could probably be arranged to be comparatively low. A number of companies have used such arrangements to help their short-term profit performance. Had the occupier wished to raise the £1 million by borrowing, the annual interest charge would be higher. Sale and lease-back can therefore be a profitable way for the occupier and owner of property to raise funds when rents, interest rates and the value of property are right. One problem with the sale and lease-back arrangement, however, is that there are rent reviews to be taken into account. Although in the above example the owner–occupier may initially be able to obtain a rent at only 5% of the sum realized, it is possible that at the first rent review after, say, five years, the rent charge could double.

An alternative way of raising money on a property is through a mortgage. There are disadvantages to mortgages. One is that a mortgage has an adverse effect on the debt-to-equity ratio of a company. The mortgage obligation appears as a debt in the company's balance sheet and so increases the total debt in relation to the shareholders' fund. Under a sale or lease-back arrangement, no debt arises. One asset disappears from the balance sheet and is replaced by cash. Sale and lease-back arrangements convert the fixed assets of a company into liquid assets.

One variation on the conventional sale and lease-back arrangement is for the occupier to retain the freehold title of the property. The institution merely buys a long leasehold and then rents the property back. This does not always appeal to institutions but, if it can be arranged, the occupier does retain the long-term reversion of the property.

19.15 MORTGAGING PROPERTY

An alternative to sale and lease-back is, as mentioned above, mortgaging. It may be possible for a company to arrange to borrow money by means of a mortgage on freehold property. The most likely institutions prepared to lend on such a basis are insurance companies, investment companies and pension funds. Building societies are reluctant to lend to companies; they may be more willing to grant mortgages to the proprietors of small unincorporated businesses. Repayments of principal plus interest may be spread over a long period of time. The rate charged is somewhat in excess of the base interest rate.

The main advantage of a mortgage is that ownership of the property remains with the mortgagor and therefore the benefits that come from the ownership of a rapidly appreciating capital asset are not lost. In addition, as with any other long-term borrowing, the real cost of making repayments of principal will be reduced over time by inflation, and the cost of paying interest will be reduced by tax relief. However, since capital repayment is involved, instalments together with interest will represent a considerably higher annual cost than the initial rentals payable under a sale and lease-back arrangement, especially if the mortgage is for a relatively short period.

This means that less money will be available for investment within the business in the early years under a mortgaging arrangement than with a sale and lease-back. However, over time the advantages may well swing back in favour of mortgaging. Under a sale and lease-back transaction the company becomes a tenant paying a rental. The company receives the sale price of the property but has to finance rental payments which may be expected to increase in line with movements in market rents at each review. With inflation reducing the real costs of repayment, and with rental payments increasing over time and continuing indefinitely, the cash outflow under a sale and lease-back arrangement could be higher in the later years than under a mortgage arrangement.

19.6 LEASING

Leasing is a popular form of medium- or short-term finance. The distinguishing feature of a lease agreement is that one party (the lessee) obtains the use of an asset for a period of time, whereas the legal ownership of that asset remains with the other party (the lessor). The leasing agreement, unlike a hire-purchase arrangement, does not give the lessee the right to final ownership. If a manufacturing company is satisfied to be able to use a particular asset without owning that asset, then leasing is a possibility.

Leasing accounts for between 20% and 25% of all new assets acquired. The reasons for leasing will be considered below, but first we define some terminology.

The lessee is the company making use of the equipment, and in return paying a rental to the lessor. The lessor, typically a finance company, initially purchases the equipment and then leases it out for a period of time. It is up to the two parties to agree on the terms of the agreement. A leasing agreement can be for a period running from only a few months to the entire expected economic life of the asset.

At the end of the period of the lease the ownership of the assets still remains with the lessor. Therefore normally any residual value of the underlying leased asset belongs to the lessor. For legal and tax reasons it is necessary to ensure that leasing arrangements appear as proper arm's-length rental transactions. With long-term leases it is quite common for the lessee to be given an option to enter into a 'secondary lease' when the period of the 'primary' lease has expired. This means that the lessee can continue to use the equipment, even though still not the legal owner. The rental payments required during the period of the secondary lease are usually very low, and are often referred to as 'peppercorn' rents. This effectively means that although the lessee has not been given the option to purchase the asset at the end of the first agreement, he/she is given the opportunity to continue to use the asset at almost negligible cost, which, as far as use of the asset is concerned, is not so different from ownership.

Any attempt to classify leases into categories must, to some extent be arbitrary, but two broad classifications can be identified, namely 'finance leases' and 'operating leases'. A finance lease can usually be identified by the fact that the lessor is assured by the initial agreement of the full recovery of the capital outlay plus a suitable return on the funds invested. Sometimes it is referred to as a 'full payout' lease. The risks and rewards of ownership have effectively passed to the lessee. The risks and rewards from the use of the asset are, of course, also with the lessee. The lessee has signed an agreement covering more or less the full economic life of the asset and has agreed to pay fixed annual amounts. The lessor knows the return that will be obtained.

The second type of lease, known as an 'operating lease', is usually for a shorter period of time than a finance lease: certainly it is for less than the estimated economic life of the asset. During the period of the lease agreement the net cost of the equipment to the lessor is not fully recovered. It is the lessor that retains the usual risks and rewards that come from the ownership of the asset as distinct from the use of the asset. If the life of the asset turns out to be less than expected, perhaps because of obsolescence or damage, it is the lessor that loses. Consequently it is usually the lessor that takes on responsibility for repairs, maintenance and insurance under an operating lease. If the secondhand value of the asset turns out to be less than expected, it is the lessor who loses.

The life of an operating lease agreement is not always known at the outset, for the lease may be cancelled or cover only a short period with the options open for a succession of short periods, each being less than the economic life of the asset. Where rental periods are extended, these will be on a negotiated economic basis. The rental payments, together with the tax and any other benefits received by the lessor over the period of a particular lease, will not necessarily cover the cost of the asset. The lessor may sell the asset at the end of any of the short periods of a lease. When the operating lease agreement is signed the lessor does not know whether they will recover their capital and earn a return. There are future agreements to be negotiated and a sale to be arranged.

Reasons for leasing

There are at least four reasons why leasing has grown in popularity.

1   A company may not actually have the funds available to purchase the asset. It may not have any other alternative sources of funds. The purchase of large pieces of equipment such as Boeing 747 aircraft and large oil tankers can be very expensive. The purchase of a large mainframe computer can be beyond the means of small companies. Leasing is therefore a source of finance, a way of being able to obtain the use of an asset upon payment of the first rental. Even if a company has funds available, it may prefer to use these funds for some other purpose, either where they can be more profitably used or where the acquisition of the other asset cannot be linked to a particular form of finance such as leasing.

2   There can be considerable tax advantages in leasing. If a company has not been showing taxable profits in the years prior to its decision to acquire an asset, it will not be able to obtain the immediate advantages of any investment allowances. The lessor company had profits: it purchased the asset, obtained the tax allowances, and passed the advantages of the lower net cost on to the lessee in lower rental payments. Subsequent examples will illustrate the way in which this works.

3   A company may not wish to own a certain type of asset, for example a computer. These machines can quickly become out of date, and the company may wish always to have available the most up-to-date equipment. There are always some companies who are willing to use secondhand computers. Therefore it is convenient to lease a new computer for, say, four years and then to replace it by leasing another new machine. The lessor takes the machine back at the end of the four years and leases or sells it to another customer. This takes the risks and trouble out of the hands of the lessee.

Short- and medium-term sources of finance

4 It was once the case that leasing did not interfere with other possible borrowing or credit facilities. Traditionally leasing was seen as 'off-the-balance-sheet' financing. A company did not need to record the asset with its other fixed assets in its annual balance sheet. The company has use of the equipment, just as much as if it owned the equipment itself – the equipment is used to earn the profits that appear in the accounts, but because the company does not have a legal title, the equipment was traditionally not shown as one of the assets of the company. This could affect the profit-to-loss asset ratio of a company. A company that leases its equipment could show in its accounts a higher return on its assets than a company that purchases the equipment. If the earnings from using the asset exceed the rental, a profit would be shown and the assets in the balance sheet would not reflect the use of the leased asset.

This 'off-the-balance-sheet' aspect of leasing has now to some extent disappeared in the UK. Finance leases have to be capitalized. The leased asset appears in the balance sheet as do the obligations arising under the leasing deal. The asset appears on one side of the balance sheet, and the liability on the other.

It is emphasized that the capitalization of the leased assets only applies to finance leases and not to operating leases. There are major companies who as a result of this capitalization requirement structured their new leasing deals so that they could be classed as operating leases and so kept off the balance sheet. The decision to capitalize leased assets was controversial. The major issue of principle that had to be decided was whether a lease is in essence the transfer of a right to use property. If it is, then it can be argued that the lessee should recognize in their accounts that they have the use of an asset and also that there is a liability to meet. In legal terms the lessee company does not own the asset, but in substance the company has a legal right to use the asset. The controversy revolves around whether one believes that a balance sheet should only list items which are legally owned.

Anybody wishing to lend money to a company that has leased assets should be in a position to know what payments the company is already committed to. The accounting standard requires the lease obligations to be shown. The lease payments are a regular commitment similar to interest payments on loans. It is a legal obligation to pay a certain sum of money each year. It is normal for a prospective lender to calculate the interest cover of the borrowing company, i.e. the excess of profits over interest payments. If a borrower has lease payments to make, it is important that the prospective lender should know this so that they have the information to enable them to determine the risks involved.

Leasing versus buying

We shall illustrate the financial decision-making technique required at the time when purchasing or leasing is being considered with an example.

Example 19.1

At 1 January 1997 a new machine cost £50 000 to buy. The machine would also require an input of £10 000 working capital throughout its life. It is estimated that if acquired it would earn the following pre-tax operating net cash-flows:

Year	
1	£20 500
2	£22 860
3	£24 210
4	£23 410

The company is considering whether to lease or buy the machine. A lease could be arranged in which the company, the lessee, would pay an annual rental of £15 000 per annum for four years, with each payment being at the beginning of the respective year. If the company were to purchase the machine it would obtain the finance through a term loan at a fixed rate of interest of 11% per annum. The company believes that the appropriate after-tax cost of capital for a machine with the risk characteristics of the one being considered is 12%. Corporation tax is payable at the rate of 35% one year in arrears, and capital allowances are available at 25% on a reducing balance basis. It is not anticipated that the machine will have any value at the end of the lease period, but if it does still have a useful life the lessee would be able to enter into a secondary leasing agreement. Both the lessor and the lessee can ignore the financial consequences of a secondary leasing agreement. If the machine is in a satisfactory condition, it can be used during a secondary lease period, but the rental will only be a small nominal amount. The leasing company has to budget to recover its cash outlay and earn a reasonable profit during the period of the primary lease; any rental receipts beyond that are just a bonus. This is a typical situation in a finance lease.

There are a number of approaches to solving a lease-versus-purchase problem. We shall illustrate the more popular approach. In this leasing is regarded as a source of finance. This requires two decisions to be made. First we shall decide whether, if we do wish to obtain the use of the machine under consideration, we should purchase it or lease it. Which is the less expensive: purchasing or leasing? Having decided on the less expensive method of financing the use of the machine, we can then compare the costs with the returns expected to be earned for the use of the machine. The second question is: do the returns justify the cost?

There are a number of cash-flow streams to consider:

1 the net cash-flow stream resulting from the financing method being adopted;
2 the net cash-flow resulting from operating the asset;
3 the investment of working capital;
4 any residual value.

These cash-flow streams (with the exception of working capital) can have taxation implications.

We shall begin by calculating the cash-flow streams associated with the methods of financing. The PV of the cash-flow associated with leasing is to be compared with the PV of the cash-flow associated with purchasing. This can be expressed as

$$NPV = \left[\sum_{i=0}^{t} \frac{P_i}{(1+m)^i} + \sum_{i=0}^{t+1} \frac{T(P_i)}{(1+q)^i} \right] - \left[\sum_{i=0}^{t} \frac{L_i}{(1+n)^i} + \sum_{i=0}^{t+1} \frac{T(L_i)}{(1+q)^i} \right]$$

where P_i is the cash flow in year i resulting from a decision to purchase the equipment, $T(P)_i$ is the cash flow in year i resulting from investment allowances, L_i is the cash flow in year i resulting from a decision to lease the equipment, $T(L)_i$ is the cash flow in year resulting from a tax saving on lease payments, m is the discount rate appropriate to cash flow with the properties of the purchasing cash-flow stream, n is the discount rate appropriate to cash flow with the risk properties of the leasing cash-flow stream and q is the discount rate appropriate to tax savings. There are two parts to this equation: the after-tax cost of purchase and the after-tax cost of leasing. We shall calculate them separately.

First, we shall determine the appropriate discount rates. The lessee's borrowing cost is 11%, which gives an after-tax cost of 7.15%, i.e. 11%(1 − 0.35) = 7.15%. We shall take this as m. For practical purposes q will be taken as equal to n or m. It will be argued in the next section that leasing is usually a direct replacement for borrowing. Therefore m can be taken as equal to n. As will be explained below, this assumption is only valid if investors regard the lease and the loans as being perfect substitutes for each other from the point of view of capital structure and the riskiness of the cash flows. Table 19.1 shows the net cost of purchase and Table 19.2 the net cost of leasing. As can be seen the NPV of the costs of leasing are slightly greater (by £104) than the NPV of the costs of purchase. If the company wishes to use the machine, on financial grounds it should purchase it.

We now move to the second stage of the decision-making process (Table 19.3). We shall decide whether or not the machine is a good investment. The NPV of the after-tax operating cash flow needs to be calculated. This cash-flow stream will need to be discounted at the rate appropriate to the business operating risks. These will be different from the risk associated with leasing or purchase cash flows.

The risk associated with the annual tax payments has two elements. One is risk associated with changes in the rate of corporation tax, and the other is associated with the operating cash flow on which the tax calculation is based. The tax payment figure is the corporation tax rate multiplied by the taxable profits. Although it can be argued that the tax-rate risks may be low and therefore an interest-rate-based discount rate would be appropriate, it can also be argued that the level of taxable profits is higher risk and therefore the operating cash-flow stream discount rate is more

Table 19.1

Year	1 Investment	2 Capital allowance	3 Tax shield on allowance (35%)	(1)+(3) Net cash flow	× PV factor =	PV of cash flow
0	−50 000			−50 000	1.000	−50 000
1		12 500			0.933	
2		9 375	+4375	+4 375	0.871	+3 811
3		7 031	+3281	+3 281	0.813	+2 667
4		21 094[a]	+2461	+2 461	0.759	+1 868
5			+7383	+7 383	0.708	+5 227
						−36 427

(a) with balancing allowance.

Table 19.2

Year	Lease payment	Tax shield	Net cash flow	× PV factor =	PV of cash flow
0	−15 000		−15 000	1.000	−15 000
1	−15 000	+5250	−9 750	0.933	−9 097
2	−15 000	+5250	−9 750	0.871	−8 492
3	−15 000	+5250	−9 750	0.813	−7 927
4		+5250	+5 250	0.759	+3 985
					−36 531

Table. 19.3

Year	Operating cash flow	Tax payable	Net	PV factor 12%	PV
1	+20 500		+20 500	0.893	+18 307
2	+22 860	−7175	+15 685	0.797	+12 501
3	+24 210	−8001	+16 209	0.712	+11 541
4	+23 410	−8474	+14 936	0.636	+9 499
5		−8194	−8 194	0.567	−4 646
					+47 202

appropriate. We shall use the same discount rate for the operating cash-flow stream and the tax payable on that stream.

The discount rate to use to obtain the PV of this cost-saving stream is not the one that is to be used for discounting the payments associated with leasing or purchasing the machine. The reason that a different rate is used is that whereas the lease payments and the interest payments are known with certainty, the costs that can be saved by operating the new machine are very much estimates. The predictability of the two streams are very different. Whereas the discount rate for the more certain stream can be taken as the cost of borrowing, we will take as the discount rate for anticipated revenues or cost saving the firm's cost of capital. We are told in this example that the after-tax cost is 12%. The PV of the returns clearly exceeds the PV of the costs of finance.

There is one more cash-flow stream to take into account, and that is the working capital. This money was invested at the commencement of the project and it is assumed that it will be returned at the end of the project's life. This involves a cost to the company. The PV of the outflow is £10 000, and the PV of the inflow, discounted at the same rate as the operating cash flow, is

$$10\ 000 \times 0.636 = £6360$$

This is an NPV of −£3640.

We can combine the three PVs that we have obtained to evaluate whether or not the investment in the machine is profitable:

NPV of net operating cash flows	+47 202
NPV of purchasing the machine	−36 427
NPV of working capital investment	−3 640
Overall NPV	+£7 135

The investment is clearly profitable, and should be financed by borrowing.

Leasing versus borrowing

In the above example the discount rate applied to the cash-flow stream resulting from purchase is the same rate that has been applied to the cash-flow stream resulting from leasing. This is assuming that the cost of capital in both cases is the same, which is assuming that leasing is a direct replacement for debt finance. It is assuming that the risks attached to both cash flows are the same. In most cases this assumption is correct.

When a company enters into a finance leasing arrangement, it is required to record on the liabilities side of the balance sheet the obligations under leasing contracts. To the user of the accounts this is clearly seen as a form of borrowing. Companies have target gearing ratios. The precise level of the target ratio might depend on ideas regarding an optimal level, it might depend on institutional constraints in that banks are not prepared to lend more than a certain percentage of the shareholders' funds, or it might depend on restrictions written into a company's articles of association.

Discount rate

The discount rate that should be used in all investment decisions is the opportunity cost. If the firm is not in a capital rationing situation and if it can obtain additional funds should it need them, then we have argued above that leasing is a direct substitute for borrowing and so the opportunity cost of leasing is the cost of borrowing. There can be a complication when, say, £100 worth of leasing is not replacing £100 worth of borrowing. It could be that the debt capacity of the kind of equipment being leased is different from that of the existing assets of the company. The leased equipment could then either increase or decrease the gearing possibilities of the lessee. If £100 of lease liability is a substitute for less than £100 of debt, then a cost of capital other than the borrowing rate will need to be used.

The point being made is that the borrowing rate is only justified if the leasing deal on a particular project does not have financial side-effects, i.e. if it does not disturb the normal gearing and cost of capital of the lessee. If the leasing deal does have financial side-effects then the appropriate discount rate is the borrowing rate adjusted for these side-effects.

One formula which can be used for estimating the appropriate discount rate for such a leasing deal is:

$$r^* = r(1 - T_\text{C}Lj)$$

where r^* is the adjusted after-tax discount rate, r is the opportunity cost of capital for a similar deal with no side effects, T_C is the marginal corporation tax rate and L_j is the particular leasing deal's proportional contribution to the company's borrowing power. L represents the effect of leasing on the borrowing power of the company. If £100 of leasing only replaces £80 of debt capacity, $L = 1/0.80$. It is sometimes suggested that £100 of leasing does not have as much impact on future borrowing possibilities as £100 of borrowing. Alternatively, perhaps because of risk considerations, the £100 of leasing might replace £120 of debt, in which case $L = 1/1.20$. It should be emphasized that this formula is only one technique for making some allowance for the possible financial side-effects of leasing. In most cases, in practice it is assumed that $L = 1$, in which case the appropriate discount rate in a leasing decision is the after-tax cost of borrowing.

If a company believes that lease finance is not a substitute for loan finance, then the appropriate discount rate would either be the company's weighted-average cost of capital or, using the capital-asset pricing model approach, the risk-adjusted cost appropriate to the type of asset being leased.

If a company is in a capital rationing situation and is still able to lease, then clearly leasing is not a substitute for debt. To the company leasing is the only possible way of funding the use of the asset, in which case the discount rate should, as just explained, be either the weighted-average cost of capital or the risk adjusted cost appropriate to the asset. Technically such a company is not in a capital rationing situation, as it is still able to obtain the use of assets through leasing arrangements. In a true capital rationing situation, where financing the use of an asset through a leasing deal means that some other investment cannot be undertaken, the discount rate to use is the return that would have been earned on the investment that is not to be undertaken. This is the clear opportunity cost of obtaining the use of one asset by leasing, rather than the use of some other asset by other financing means.

It has been argued in this section that in the vast majority of cases the discount rate that should be used in leasing decisions is the after-tax cost of borrowing. This is certainly the most straightforward approach, but the assumptions that are being made should be remembered when adopting this approach.

Lessor's decisions

In Example 19.1, the lessor's cash flow ignoring tax is

$$-50\,000 + 15\,000 + \frac{15\,000}{1+i} + \frac{15\,000}{(1+i)^2} + \frac{15\,000}{(1+i)^3}$$

The lessor invests £50 000 at time zero and immediately receives the first lease payment of £15 000. The next three lease payments are received in each of the next years. What is the lessor's cost of capital and tax position?

If the lessee can claim the same capital allowances as the lessor, both may well have the same cost of capital, and if the leasing company does not add on a profit percentage or if the cost of capital to the lessee plus the add on percentage is the same as the cost of capital to the lessor, then the lessee will be indifferent whether to lease or buy. Leasing can be attractive when the lessee is faced with different cash flows from those of the lessor.

A number of factors in practice mean that a difference usually arises. These include:

1 Different costs of capital for lessor and lessee. It is often assumed that because many leasing companies are subsidiaries of banks, and so are able to obtain funds at a lower cost than the lessee, the discount rate they use should be lower than the lessee's. In fact, the lessor does face risks when purchasing an asset and leasing it out. They are risks associated with non-payment and with the probable residual value of the asset. If the lessor is using a risk-adjusted cost of capital to calculate the required lease payments the difference between the discount rate of the lessor and lessee may not be very great.

2 Differences in tax rates between the lessor and lessee. If the lessor pays at a higher marginal tax rate than the lessee, then both lessors and lessees can benefit from a leasing deal. It is the Inland Revenue that loses in that it collects less tax than it would have done if the desired user of the asset had made a purchase.

3 Utilization of capital allowances was once one of the most popular reasons for leasing as opposed to purchasing. If the lessee had insufficient taxable profits to be able to take advantage of the full depreciation possibility in the year of purchase or shortly afterwards, it was usually beneficial to lease the asset rather than purchase it. Leasing companies usually had the taxable capacity and could pass on the benefits of the early tax allowances

in lower lease payments. This has become less important with lower levels of initial allowances.

4 Residual values at end of the primary leasing contract. If a company buys an asset, at any point in time the value of that asset belongs to the company. The value of the asset depends on obsolescence, maintenance and the market conditions at the time. The owner of an asset is unsure of the future value of the asset. In a leasing deal the asset belongs to the lessor during the period of the lease period. However, who obtains any residual value of the asset at the end of the leasing agreement is a matter of agreement between the lessor and lessee. It is not possible to generalize on this matter, but, on occasions, the lessee can negotiate for a generous residual value to be paid over by the lessor at the end of the leasing period. Agreements with regard to residual value can help to determine whether leasing is preferable to purchase.

19.17 BRITISH GOVERNMENT SOURCES

Central government and local government attempt to encourage industry to invest. Central government wishes to encourage the 'right' kind of investment, for example investment in new technology, and also wishes to encourage companies to set up factories in depressed areas of the country. It can encourage companies by making finance available, by reducing taxation or by direct controls.

Local government wishes to create wealth and employment in the area for which it is responsible; again, it can offer financial incentives. It should be appreciated that some government schemes for making funds available to industry have a comparatively short life. Different governments have different views on the necessity of helping industry and on the best way of achieving this, and in addition the need for government finance varies with the health of the economy.

The government, through taxation, has an influence on the extent to which a company can finance itself. Investment grants and allowances, permissible depreciation deductions are matters of government policy that influence the level of retained profits.

The government can vary the level of corporate taxation and it can also vary the investment allowances to affect the profits left over after taxation. A government's policy on investment incentives and depreciation allowances affects the flow of funds between the two sectors.

When operating through the tax system, with say investment allowances, assistance is being provided on a national scale. Often governments wish to be more selective and support will depend upon the location of a project, upon the sector of industry or type of business activity.

19.18 EUROPEAN SOURCES

The European Investment Bank

The European Investment Bank (EIB) was created in 1958 with the object of making loans available to public and private borrowers. The EIB does not seek to attract deposits from the public. Its finance is derived from two sources: first, that subscribed by member states of the EU, and second, that borrowed on the international capital markets. Member states each agree to subscribe a certain amount of money; Germany, France and the UK subscribe the largest amounts of capital and each agrees to put in an equal amount. In addition to the subscribed funds the EIB has borrowed extensively in international capital markets.

The bank is non-profit-making and seeks only to cover its expenses and to set aside sufficient reserves to deal with any possible loss from defaults on loans. It finances projects for developing the less developed regions of the EU, for modernizing or converting existing undertakings, for developing fresh activities within the EU and for supporting projects of common interest to several member states.

It is a source of long- to medium-term loans with money being advanced for periods of between seven and twelve years. The interest rates charged on loans are reasonable since the EIB is non-profit-making.

One problem with the EIB's loans is that they have to be repaid in the currency in which they are borrowed. Therefore a borrower has to take into account not only the interest charge but the possible exchange loss from movements in the value of currencies.

At one time the EIB was criticized for only providing large sums of money to very large creditworthy customers. A change in policy took place, however, when the EIB announced that it would make a large sum of money available to finance small- and medium-scale industrial ventures. The sum would be specially earmarked for smaller and medium-sized firms. The EIB operates this scheme through agency arrangements. Barclays and the 3i act as UK agents. A customer who wants a smaller EIB-funded loan applies to one of these agency banks.

19.19 FURTHER READING

To keep up to date with changes that are taking place in the methods of financing companies it is necessary to read current journals. These include the *Bank of England Quarterly*, the quarterly publications of the leading banks and *Business Weekly*, the publication of the Department of Trade and Industry. A selection of interesting books and articles is given below.

Look what credit scoring can do now, *ABA Banking Journal*, May 1994.
Bank of England (1990) Venture capital in the United Kingdom, *Bank of England Quarterly Bulletin*, Feb. 78–83.
Collet, N. and Schell, C. (1992) *Corporate Credit Analysts*, Euromoney Books.
Donaldson, T.H. (1983) *The Medium-Term Loan Market*, Macmillan.
Economist Newspaper (1989) How banks lend, *Economist*, 4 Feb.
National Westminster Bank (1992) Banks and small to medium sized business financing in the UK, *National Westminister Bank Quarterly Review*, Feb.

For discussion on the leasing issue, see:

James, A.N.G. and Peterson, P.P. (1984) The leasing puzzle, *Journal of Finance*, 39.
Hochman, S. and Rabinovitch, R. (1984) Financial leasing under inflation, *Financial Management*, Spring.
McConnell, J.J. and Schalheim, J.S. (1983) Valuation of asset leasing contracts, *Journal of Financial Economics*, Aug.

19.20 PROBLEMS

1 Beaver PLC is considering entering into an agreement with a factoring company. The main details of the proposed factoring agreement are:

(a) The agreement will be for a minimum period of 2 years, thereafter cancellable at three months' notice.

(b) Basic factoring services will be provided for a charge of $1\frac{1}{2}$% of Beaver's annual turnover, the charge payable annually in arrears. Entering into the factoring agreement will enable Beaver to save £60 000 per year in office and other expenses – the savings being effected in a lump sum each year-end.

(c) The factor is willing to advance Beaver up to 80% of the invoice value of factored debts immediately a sale is invoiced. A commission of $2\frac{1}{2}$% will be deducted from the gross amount of any funds advanced (i.e. up to 80% of invoice value). The factor will also charge interest at 15% per annum, applied on a simple monthly basis, on the gross funds advanced, i.e. before deduction of the $2\frac{1}{2}$% commission. Both interest charge and commission will be deducted from the funds advanced to Beaver.

(d) The factor is confident that the average collection period will be reduced from the current figure of 90 days to 70 days, or perhaps to only 60 days, although a transition period of up to 6 months will be required before the reduction is fully effected. On receipt of cash from Beaver's invoiced debtors the factor will immediately pay to Beaver all sums outstanding concerning that invoice.

Beaver's annual credit sales amount to £7.2 million which are spread evenly throughout the year.

Required:

(a) Calculate the effective annual factoring cost, as a percentage of the funds improvement caused by factoring, for a full year after any transition period under each of the following separate conditions:

  (i) Beaver will not take advantage of the factor's willingness to advance funds but the factor will reduce the average collection period to 70 days. (3 marks)

  (ii) Beaver will take full advantage of the factor's willingness to advance funds and the average collection period:

    (a) remains at 90 days, and (4 marks)

    (b) is reduced to 60 days. (4 marks)

(b) Beaver can borrow at 16% per annum and could, by spending £30 000 per annum payable at the end of each year, reduce the average collection period to 80 days without factoring whereas the factor would reduce the collection period to 70 days. Advise Beaver whether it should enter into the factoring agreement and, if so, whether funds should be obtained from the factor rather than by borrowing. (9 marks)

(You may assume a 360-day year split into 12 equal months. Taxation may be ignored.) *(ACCA, Financial Management)*

2 Corcoran Ltd is a small manufacturing company which is experiencing a short-term liquidity crisis during 1994. The company accountant has estimated that by the end of October 1994 a further £200 000 of extra funds will be required. Since the company already has a large overdraft, its banker will not advance any more funds. Three solutions to the problem have been put forward:

(a) Option 1. A short-term loan of £200 000 could be raised for 6 months from 1 September 1994 at an annual interest rate of 18%. This would be obtained through a finance company, but there would be no costs involved in raising the funds.

(b) Option 2. The company could forgo cash discounts of 2% which are obtained from suppliers of raw materials for payment within 30 days. The maximum credit which could safely be taken is 90 days. Monthly purchases of raw materials amount to £102 041 before discounts. Corcoran Ltd would forgo the discount for 6 months before reviewing the position again.

(c) Option 3. The company could factor its trade debtors. A factor has been found who would be prepared, for a period of 6 months from 1 September, to advance Corcoran Ltd 75% of the value of its invoices less the deduction of factoring charges, immediately on receipt of the invoices. (You may assume that all invoices are sent out at the end of the month of sale.) The factoring charges would consist of:

  (i) an interest charge of 15% p.a. on the amount of money advanced, calculated on a day to day basis, and deducted in advance;

  (ii) a fee for taking on the task of collecting debts, amounting to 2% of the total invoices and deducted in advance. Monthly sales are expected to be £300 000. The factor would pay the balance owing on the invoices on receipt of the money from the debtors. On average, debtors pay at the end of the month following the month of sale. As a result of using the factor, Corcoran Ltd estimates that there would be savings in administration costs of £4 000 per month.

Any surplus funds in excess of the £200 000 required would be used to reduce the bank overdraft, which costs 1% per month.

Required:

(a) Show which of the three options is cheapest. (15 marks)

(b) If the factoring arrangement is the option preferred, what would be the cash-flow position for receipts for the period September 1994–April 1995? (5 marks)

(c) Briefly explain the other considerations which should be taken into account when choosing between the three options. (5 marks)

Ignore taxation. (25 marks)

3 Newlean Ltd has experienced difficulty with the collection of debts from export customers. At present the company makes no special arrangements for export sales.

As a result the company is considering either:

(a) employing the services of a non-recourse export factoring company;

(b) insuring its exports against non-payment through a government agency.

The two alternatives also provide new possible ways of financing export sales. An export factor will, if required, provide immediate finance of 80% of export credit sales at an interest rate of 2% above bank base rate. The service fee for the debt collection is $2\frac{1}{2}$% of credit sales. If the factor is used administrative savings of £12 500 per year should be possible. The government agency short-term comprehensive insurance policy costs 35 pence per £100 insured and covers 90% of the risk of non-payment for exports. For a further payment of 25 pence per £100 insured the agency will provide its guarantee which enables bank finance for the insured exports to be raised at $\frac{5}{8}$% above bank base rate. The finance is only available in conjunction with the government agency comprehensive insurance policy. Newlean normally has to pay $2\frac{1}{2}$% above base rate for its overdraft finance.

Newlean's annual exports total £650 000. All export orders are subject to a 15% initial deposit.

Export sales are on open account terms of 45 days credit, but on average payment has been 30 days late. Approximately $\frac{1}{2}$%, by value, of credit sales result in bad debts which have to be written off.

Clearing bank base rate is 10%.

Required:

(a) Determine which combination of export administration and financing Newlean Ltd should use. (15 marks)

(b) Outline the main debt collection techniques with respect to sales in the home market that are available to financial managers. (5 marks)

(c) Discuss how a manufacturing company might devise an effective debt collection system. (5 marks)

(25 marks)

4 (a) Describe and discuss the arguments advanced in favour of equipment leasing. Do all these arguments stand up to rigorous scrutiny?

(b) Selly Oak University needs a new computer. It can either buy it for £520 000 or lease it from Compulease. The lease terms require Selly Oak to make five annual payments (first instalment payable immediately) of £140 000. Selly Oak has charitable status and pays no tax. Compulease pays corporation tax at 50% with a 12-month lag and can claim 100% capital allowances for tax purposes. The computer will have no residual value at the end of year 4. The bank has quoted an interest rate of 20% for loan facilities.

   (i) Should Selly Oak University lease or buy the equipment?

   (ii) How much money is the lessor making from the lease?

5 The West Midland Company is considering a proposal to acquire a new machine. Because of the shortage in cash available to purchase the machine, the lease financing alternative will have to be considered as well. The finance department has been able to provide the following estimates:

Expected useful life	5 years
Purchase price	£230 000
Lease payments (per annum)	£72 000
Annual operating costs (if purchased)	£26 000 (fixed for the five years)
Annual operating costs (if leased)	£6 000
Scrap value	NIL

In addition you are given the following information:

   (i) The cash flows take place at the end of each year, except the initial capital expenditure and the lease payments being required at the beginning of the year.

   (ii) The machine, if purchased, would qualify for a 100% first-year capital allowance.

   (iii) The corporation tax rate is 50%.

   (iv) There is a 12-month lag in the payment of taxes and in the receipt of tax allowances.

   (v) The company's cost of capital is 20%, and its current net of tax long-term borrowing rate is 8%.

You are required to advise the company whether it should purchase or lease the machine.

Show calculations in arriving at your recommendation, identifying any important assumptions.

20 FOREIGN EXCHANGE MANAGEMENT

LEARNING OUTCOMES

After studying this chapter you should be able to:

- read and understand foreign exchange quotations
- appreciate the fundamental factors that influence the rate of exchange of a currency
- understand the relationship between spot rates of exchange, interest rates, inflation rates and forward rates
- advice on basic hedging techniques that companies can employ to reduce foreign exchange risk
- understand simple options and futures transactions

20.1 FOREIGN EXCHANGE MARKETS

The size and level of activity in the foreign exchange markets (FOREX) grew dramatically during the 1980s. Until the early 1970s many countries had currencies whose rates of exchange were fixed by their governments or linked to movements in a major currency, so there was little volatility in exchange rates. The 1980s saw (a) floating exchange rates with the rate of exchange determined by the market, (b) increasing levels of international business, and (c) the ending of restrictions in many countries on the outflow and inflow of direct and portfolio investment. In 1995 the daily volume of FOREX dealings worldwide was well in excess of $1000 billion. Of this the daily trading values in London were in the region of $460 billion, in New York, $244 billion and in Tokyo $161 billion. In 1986 the daily volumes had only been in London $90 billion, in New York $60 billion and in Tokyo $50 billion.

It has been estimated that somewhere between 10% and 20% of FOREX transactions involve as one of their parties a company, an institution or an individual. Most of the transactions are, however, interbank, with one bank laying off their foreign exchange exposure with another bank. Let us say Barclays Bank may find at the end of the day that as a result of normal exchange activity it is holding more US dollars than is its wish. It will therefore attempt to sell these dollars (at the best price) to other banks who may feel they are short of dollars in their currency portfolio.

In the volatile FOREX markets in 1997, there was much talk of speculators. Let us say the government of Italy has been defending the value of the lira, it has been buying its own currency to increase the demand for it, in an attempt to maintain the present rates of exchange. Mr S (a speculator?) believes that on the basis of fundamentals the lira is overvalued. He believes that at some point the lira will fall dramatically against the pound sterling.

The three-month forward rate of exchange quoted today (say 1 January) is 2700 lire equal £1. Mr S is a fund manager, attempting to make profits for the people or institutions whose funds he controls. He will agree to sell lire forward. He will enter into a transaction to deliver 2700 lire in three months' time (1 April) in exchange for £1. He at the present time does not have lira – he is 'selling short'.

If Mr S is correct, and that in the end economic fundamentals factors and not politicians determine exchange rates, then at some time the lira will fall in value. Mr S hopes that within three months this fall will occur. Let us say such a devaluation in the lira does occur.

On 1 April the spot rate of exchange is 3000 lire equal £1. On that day Mr S will be able to sell pounds sterling, receiving 3000 lire for every £1 (if he does not have pounds he can borrow them). He will then be able to complete his forward deal. He will deliver 2700 lire to the counterparty and receive £1. He will have made 300 lire profit on each £1.

This is speculation. Mr S could have lost money if the exchange rate did not move in the direction he expected.

But what about people such as pension-fund managers or treasury managers of companies? Are they speculators? They also can see when a currency is over-valued. They look at the same economic indicators as Mr S. All agree on what are the fundamental factors that affect exchange rates. They also have a responsi-bility to manage funds under their control. If in the above situation they have lira, are they supposed to hold on to them, and suffer a loss when the lira falls in value. If a company has sold goods to Italy and is due to receive lira in three-months' time, is the treasury manager supposed to do nothing and wait until she receives the lira and then exchange at the spot rate at the time when 3000 lire equal £1. If the treasury manager is doing her job properly she will also enter a forward deal on 1 January.

Finally, what about an Italian company that has sold goods to the UK. The company will receive pounds on say 1 January. Is the treasury manager of that Italian company supposed to exchange each pound for 2700 lire on that day, or to hold on to the pounds for three months and then sell them in exchange for 3000 lire.

It is convenient for politicians to be able to blame 'speculators' when their currency falls in value. The reality is different. So-called speculators are often used as an excuse by politicians, in an attempt to divert attention from mistakes that they have made in managing their country's economy.

It should be appreciated that the amount of funds in the hands of speculators is very small compared with the huge amounts of company and bank money that is traded in the FOREX markets every day. If it was just speculators who tried to anticipate what was happening and acted accordingly they could not move by very much the rates of exchange of the major currencies.

If a UK-based pension fund that is looking after pensioners' assets happens to have £1 million liquid, and it sees the UK government struggling to protect the value of the pound, are they supposed to keep the pounds and be patriotic, or are they supposed to protect the value of the pensioner's assets? In the example at the beginning of this section let us say it is a pension's fund rather than Mr S that has the £1 million. Fund managers who are accused of speculation can clearly say, 'We are just doing our job.'

20.2 QUOTATIONS

The price of a foreign currency is usually expressed in terms of local currency. In Table 20.1 the exchange rate is shown between pounds sterling and the US dollar, the French franc and the Deutschmark as quoted on 1 October 1997. The closing spot rate between the pound and the US dollar is shown as £1–$1.6154. (This is known as an indirect quote.) The change in the rate of exchange during the previous day's trading is also shown. As can be seen, the pound fell in value against the dollar by 0.11 cent on that day.

A bid/offer spread is also given in the extract (namely 150-158). This means that the bid price is £1 equals $1.6150, and the offer price $1.6158. (The last three digits in the mid price are adjusted.) The lower price is the one at which the foreign exchange dealer is willing to sell dollars in exchange for pounds. The higher dollar price is the one which the dealer wishes to receive when selling pounds (the customer will have to give $1.6158 dollars to receive £1).

Table 20.1 *Exchange rates against the pound (1 October 1997)*

	Closing mid point	Change on day	Bid/Offer spread	One month	Three months	One year
US dollar	1.6154	−0.0011	150–158	1.6133	1.6092	1.5921
French franc	9.5829	+0.0338	781–877	9.5499	9.4929	9.2174
German mark	2.8531	+0.0099	518–543	2.8438	2.8247	2.7378

The size of the spread between the two quoted prices will depend on the exchange dealer and the type of market in which they are operating. The one-month, three-month and one-year forward rates are also given.

In the above example we have expressed the pound in terms of a number of dollars. This would be referred to in London as an 'indirect quote', one unit of the home currency being equal to a variable number of units of the away currency. The reciprocal rate to the above, means expressing the exchange rate in reverse terms. Taking the mid-point of £1 = $1.6154 we could express the dollar in terms of a number of pounds sterling. The reciprocal is $1.6154 = 1/x$. Solving this equation gives $x = 0.6190$. In other words $1 = £0.6190. This would be known in London as a 'direct quote'.

The UK usually expresses FOREX rates in the indirect form. This is sometimes known as 'European terms'. The USA traditionally quotes foreign exchange rates using the direct form. This is sometimes known as 'American terms'. In fact, both the expressions 'European' and 'American' can be misleading.

Technical definitions are:

- direct quote is the number of units of home currency to deal in one unit of away currency;
- indirect quote is the number of units of away currency to deal in one unit of home currency.

These terms can, however, confuse the student. A quote of £1 = $1.50 is 'indirect' when quoted in London, the pound being the home currency. It would be 'direct' if quoted this way around in New York, the dollar being the home currency. Would it be direct or indirect if quoted this way in Tokyo, where neither currency involved is 'home'?

Unfortunately, despite the growth of global financial markets, there has been only a little standardization between countries in the way they quote currencies. In some countries (including the UK) is it usual to see quotations written in the indirect form. In others it is more usual to see the use of the direct form. The US uses direct quotes in some situations and indirect in others. With the growth in worldwide data systems such as 'Reuters', the US banks have increasingly moved to quoting in the 'indirect' form.

The definitional problem can cause difficulties for new students of the subject. The difficulties are not always resolved by the textbooks on the subject.

Spot and forward

The spot rate is the exchange price for transactions to be settled quickly. This normally means that (in the example we are using) the dollar and the pound are to be exchanged within two business days, although in practice deals to be settled within a week are often still called 'spot transactions'.

The alternative to the spot price is the forward price. The forward price applies to a deal which is agreed upon now, but where the actual exchange of the currency is not to take place until an agreed time period has elapsed. The exchange at the date in the future will be at the price agreed upon now. The exchange rates shown below, quote the one-month forward price as $1.554 = £1 (these are October 1996 rates). There is very little difference between this rate and the spot rate. There is, however, a small difference with the dollar becoming stronger. This means that the dollar was trading at a forward premium on the pound. This means that if an agreement was made now to exchange pounds for dollars in one month's time, less dollars would be paid per pound than if the pounds were to be exchanged at the spot price.

The rate of exchange of the US dollar against the pound at the mid-point was:

spot rate	1.5544
one month forward	1.5540
three-month forward	1.5538
one-year forward	1.5562

The dollar premium between the spot and one-month forward rate is 0.04 cent. However, there is a dollar discount between the spot and the one-year forward of 0.18 cent. This difference between spot and forward rates is sometimes known as the 'swap rate'. We either add the swap rate to, or deduct it from, the spot rate to arrive at the appropriate forward rate.

It is important not to confuse the use of the word 'swap' in this context with its use in expressions such as 'interest-rate swaps' and 'currency swaps'. Its use here is limited to the simple monetary difference between spot and forward rates of exchange.

With a forward exchange deal it is possible to make an opportunity gain or loss. Suppose that a UK businessman has purchased goods from the USA which he will have to pay for in dollars in three months' time. The value of the goods is $10 000. He has three choices: he could buy the dollars now at the spot rate, which would cost £6433 = 10 000/1.5544; he could enter into a deal now for dollars to be delivered in three months' time, buying at the appropriate forward exchange rate, which would cost him £6436 (= 10 000/1.5538) in three months or he could wait three months and buy dollars at whatever the spot rate is at that time. If he follows the first option he could earn interest on the dollars for three months at the interest rate on the dollar. It could be that the value of the dollar falls in future and in three months he could buy at spot at a cost of say £6300. If this was the case and he had already bought at spot at the time of the purchase or bought in the forward market he would have made an opportunity loss. At the time of the purchase he is not to know this. By entering into a FOREX agreement at the time of purchase he is avoiding risk. But risk could result in a loss or a gain.

Cross rates

Exchange rates between currencies are quoted in many markets around the world. These exchange rates have to be in line with each other to prevent dealers making easy gains. One opportunity to exploit possible differences arises in relation to what are known as 'cross rates'. This can be illustrated with three currencies and let us say three different markets.

In London	£1 = $1.5
In New York	$1 = DM 2
In Frankfurt	1 DM = £0.30

In this situation the market is not in equilibrium. The opportunity exists for what is known as 'cross-rate' (triangular) arbitrage.

A dealer in Frankfurt with pounds would sell £0.30 and buy 1 DM. They could take the 1 DM to New York and buy $0.50. They could then take the $0.50 to London and buy £0.33. They would have made a gain of £0.03 on the cross-market dealings.

The problem is that the pound is overvalued against the DM. The equilibrium rate of exchange is 1 DM = £0.33. This disequilibrium situation should not arise; if it did it would only be for a brief moment of time. The arbitrage dealers in selling pounds and buying DMs would depress the price of the pound and increase the price of the DM.

20.3 FACTORS INFLUENCING EXCHANGE RATES

As with any commodity the price of a country's currency depends on demand and supply. The foreign exchange market is rational. In the short run governments, through using reserves and borrowed funds, may be able to boost the demand for their currency. In the short run behavioural factors can affect exchange rates. In the long run, however, the price depends on fundamental factors.

These fundamentals include the balance of payments position of a country, the capital inflows and outflows, interest rates and inflation rates. Also of importance is the confidence the foreign exchange dealers have in the economic policies being pursued by the government of a country.

We will briefly consider each of the economic factors.

The balance-of-payments position

A country may have a balance-of-payments deficit with its imports exceeding its exports. It has to pay for its imports in foreign currencies and its exports do not earn sufficient foreign exchange to pay for the imports. Therefore it has a shortage of foreign currency. The demand for foreign currency increases. In the absence of other factors, this will tend to put upward pressures on the price of foreign currency against the domestic currency. The country's own currency will fall in value.

Purchasing power parity

This is a complicated theory. However, it basically means that if the rate of inflation in country A is greater than the rate of inflation in country B, the rate of exchange of the currency of country A will fall against the currency of country B.

In its simplest version it is based on the idea that in terms of an international price a product should cost the same wherever it is produced. Let us suppose, for example, that a washing machine was initially priced the same whether it was produced in Germany or the UK (the same price at the then rate of exchange). Both countries export washing machines. Let us assume that in the next year inflation was higher in the UK than in Germany, and so the monetary cost of product became higher in the UK than in Germany and the monetary price became higher. Then, if the exchange rates remain constant, consumers in a third country will buy the less expensive product from Germany rather than the more expensive UK product. This means that sales of the UK product will fall. The demand from foreigners for Deutschmarks to buy the German product will rise and the demand for sterling by foreigners to buy the UK product will fall. This will mean that, in consequence, the price of the Deutschmark will over time rise against the pound.

The above example refers to the effect of inflation on one product. Of course, we would not expect the price of one product to affect the exchange rate. However, the general level of inflation would be expected to have an effect over time on the relationship between exchange rates.

According to the theory the expected difference in the inflation rate approximates to the expected change in the exchange rates.

Market expectations

It can be argued that the price of one currency relative to another depends upon what is expected to happen in the future. For example, an election to be held in the near future in country X introduces a note of uncertainty, which could affect the exchange rate. A government could be elected which would change policies with respect to such things as inflation, foreign trade and public-sector deficits. Those buying and selling the currency of country X will have their own expectations of the future economic position of the country. This will affect the supply and demand for the currency and the relationship between the spot rate and the forward rate.

Some market traders will be willing to accept more risk than others. Some have different expectations to others. It is the interaction of the different traders' expectations that will determine the rates of exchange. Because of the differing expectations, and the consequent problems of forecasting, the best forecast of the future spot rate is the current forward exchange rate. In other words, so many factors can influence the spot rate that will apply in, say, three months' time, with many of the factors counterbalancing each other, that if one wants a forecast of the spot rate that will exist in three months' time one may as well use today's three-month forward rate. This reflects the expectations in the market.

Interest rate

The interest rates within a country are determined in the money market. The price of money, like anything else, is determined by supply and demand, although in many countries governments do try to manage the interest rate. The demand for money depends on such factors as levels of investment, inflation and public-sector borrowing. The supply depends on such factors as the government's policy on money supply, the efficiency of the financial institutions, and the customs and habits within a country.

Interrelationship between factors influencing exchange rates

There is a relationship between exchange rates, interest rates and inflation rates. These interconnecting relationships are illustrated in Figure 20.1. It should be appreciated that the equations shown in the figure are those that apply when the UK is the home (base) country and we are expressing the rate of exchange as the number of dollars to be received per pound (e.g. £1 = \$1.50). If we were to express the rate of exchange the other way around, i.e. how many pounds we needed to exchange to obtain one dollar, we would need to alter the equations in which the exchange rate appears. For example, the forward premium/discount formula would be $\frac{(S_o - F_o)}{F_o}$ and the expected change in spot rates $\frac{(S_o - S_T)}{S_T}$.

We shall now examine each of the individual relationships and show the significance of the points just made.

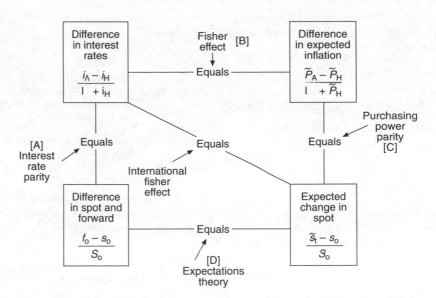

Figure 20.1
The four way model in
the FOREX market (in
equilibrium)

Where H = home country
A = away country
and home country
currency quoted in
indirect form

Relationship between exchange rates and interest rates (A)

There is a strong relationship between the FOREX market and the money market. The relationship between the interest rates in two countries affects (a) the rate of exchange of the currencies involved and (b) the relationship between the spot rate of exchange and the forward rate of exchange.

The currency with the higher interest rate will sell at a discount in the forward market against the currency with the lower interest rate or, to put it the other way, the currency with the lower interest rate will sell at a premium in the forward market against the currency with the higher interest rate.

The reason that these relationships hold is that operators in the money market are free to invest or borrow in the currency that offers them the most favourable interest rates. This will affect the forward exchange rates, as will be illustrated in the following example in which it is assumed that only interest-rate differentials affect forward exchange rates.

Example 20.1

Suppose that on 1 January the spot rate is £1 = $1.50. The interest rates on money deposited is 13% per annum for pounds sterling and 10% for US dollars. What would we expect the three-month forward rate to be that is being quoted on 1 January, if what is known as the interest-rate parity theory applies? The forward rate equals the spot rate plus or minus the swap rate. The swap rate reflects the interest-rate differential.

The swap rate can be determined using the following formula:

spot rate × % difference in interest rates × effective time fraction of one year = swap rate

Thus,

$$\$1.5 \times \frac{0.10 - 0.13}{1.13} \times \frac{3}{12} = -\$0.009\,956$$

The way in which the difference in interest rates is calculated should be noted. It can be approximated by taking the simple difference of 3%, but the above method gives a more precise measure. The US interest rate is 2.65% below that for the UK (i.e. (0.13 − 0.10)/1.13).

In this case the forward pound would be selling at a discount against the dollar, with the fall in the value of the pound over the three-month period balancing the interest-rate differential. To determine the forward rate we deduct the swap rate from the spot rate:

Spot rate £1	$1.500 000
Swap rate	−$0.009 956
Three-month forward rate	$1.490 044

which we shall round off to $1.49.

To prove that this approach works, we shall show that, with the exchange rates adjusted in line with

---

interest-rate differentials, it is not possible for gains to be made:

1 January

| Step 1. | Sell | $1500 |
| Step 2. | Receive and deposit | £1000 |

1 April

Step 3.	Interest received	£32.5
Step 4.	Sell	£1032.5
Step 5.	Receive	
	(at $1.49 = £1)	$1538

The investor would have been just as well off if he/she had invested their dollars for three months in the USA at the lower interest rate of 10%. The difference between the spot rate and the forward rate being quoted on 1 January reflects the differences in interest rates.

This is known as the 'interest-rate parity theory': it states that in equilibrium the difference in interest rates between two countries is equal to the difference between the forward and spot rates of exchange. It can be expressed mathematically (when the indirect quote is being used in the home country) as

$$\frac{i_A - i_H}{1 + i_H} = \frac{F_0 - S_0}{S_0}$$

where i_H is the current interest rate on the currency of the home country and i_A is the current interest rate on the currency of the away country: F_0 is the current forward rate of exchange between the two currencies.

One detail over which we have to be careful is what time T we are considering. The equations we shall introduce will work for any time period ahead: three months, six months or 12 months. However, we must be careful to use the interest rates (adjusted if necessary) for the same time period as the period for the forward rates.

Substituting the values in the above example into the interest-rate equation, and taking the USA as the away country and the UK as the home country gives

$$\frac{0.10 - 0.13}{1.13} \times \frac{3}{12} = \frac{1.490044 - 1.50000}{1.5000} = -0.00664$$

It should be noted that the difference between the annual interest rates has in this case been adjusted to give the difference over a three-month period. The forward rate being used was for three months.

The above appears to be straightforward. There are, however, at least three possible pitfalls for the student when attempting to answer questions on interest-rate parity or on the related issue of covered interest-rate arbitrage.

(a) There are two ways of writing the interest-rate differential formula. Either is acceptable. They both always give the same answer. The alternatives are given by:

$$\frac{i_A - i_H}{1 + i_H} = \left[\frac{1 + i_A}{1 + i_H}\right] - 1$$

In the problem above, the interest rates are being compared with a three-month forward exchange rate. It must be remembered that the figures to be used in the equations may need to be adjusted to allow for the time period. For example,

$$\left[\frac{1.10}{1.13}\right] - 1 \times \frac{3}{12} = 0.00664$$

(b) Second possible problem: there are two ways of writing the formula for the difference between spot rates and forward rates. There is a problem in that they give different results. The formula can be written as $\frac{(F - S)}{S}$ as above, or as $\frac{(S - F)}{F}$.

The first of these should be used when the home currency (in our example pound sterling) is being quoted in 'indirect' form. In our example the UK is the home country and it is the number of units of the dollar (1.50 or 1.49) that is being used to deal in one unit of the home currency (one pound sterling).

The alternative version of the formula should be used when the home currency is being quoted in a 'direct' form.

Let us remain in London with the pound as the home currency. The direct quotes on the dollar would be

$$\text{Spot} \quad \$1 = £0.6667$$
$$\text{three-month forward} \quad \$1 = £0.6711$$

The appropriate equations for a three-month period when the direct quote is being used in the home country are:

$$\frac{3}{12} \times \frac{i_A - i_H}{1 + i_H} = \frac{S - F}{F}$$

$$-0.006\,64 = \frac{0.6667 - 0.6711}{0.6711}$$

There is a small difference in the alternative answer due to rounding-off errors.

Conclusion on the second possible pitfall. Identify a home or away rate of interest. Then select the appropriate formula for the difference in spot forward rate quotes.

(c) The third pitfall: what do we do when there is no obvious home or away currency, when the quote is in the currency of a third country? The simple answer is to be careful.

There are two possible rules to follow:

One rule that can be applied is always to express the movement in the exchange rate such that the premium/discount equals $\frac{(F-S)}{S}$ and then to remember that the interest rate used as the first number in the numerator of the interest differential formula is the one for the currency expressed as the variable unit. The second interest rate used in the numerator (and as the denominator) is the currency that is quoted as a whole number.

Let us say that in a third country, say Germany, £1 is being quoted in the spot market as 10 FF. The annual interest rate on the pound is 20%, and on the French franc is 10%. We are asked what would be the one-year forward rate if the market was in equilibrium.

Adopting the above guide, the pound has the indirect quote (£1 = 10 FF), we use $\frac{(F-S)}{S}$. The variable unit is the French franc and therefore the first interest rate used in the numerator is that for the franc. Therefore:

$$\frac{F - 10}{10} = \frac{0.10 - 0.20}{1.20}$$

$$\frac{F - 10}{10} = -0.083\,33$$

$$F = 9.1667$$

The one-year forward rate of exchange in equilibrium is therefore £1 = 9.1667 FF.

Interest-rate arbitrage

If the money market and the foreign exchange markets are not in equilibrium, then arbitrage is possible. Let us suppose in the above example, the one-year forward rate of exchange was £1 = 9.50 FF. Then a player in the foreign exchange market could take the following steps.

1 January	Step 1	Borrow 10 000 FF
	Step 2	Convert to pounds at the spot rate
	Step 3	Invest the £1000

31 December   Step 4   Cash in the pound sterling investment and receive £1000 + £200

                 Step 5   Convert the £1200 into FF at the agreed rate for the forward deal of 9.50. Receive 11 400 FF

                 Step 6   Repay the FF loan plus interest (10 000 + 1000) FF
Profit = 400 FF

Tests of the interest rate parity theory show that this relationship is usually found to hold in exchange rate markets. When it does not this can usually be explained by government restrictions, transaction costs and tax policies which often mean that it is not easy for investors to exchange currencies and transmit interest and profits to take advantage of opportunities created by interest and exchange rate differences. In the Eurocurrency markets, which are free from government interference, the interest-rate parity concept is almost always found to hold.

Relationship between interest rates and inflation rates (B)

Why do nominal interest rates vary between one country and another? One school of economic thought attributes such variations to different expectations with regard to the rates of inflation within countries. If investors could move their funds freely from one country to another, they would move towards countries where they could expect to obtain the highest real rate of interest (nominal rate of interest less the inflation rate). With competition to attract funds, that would mean that the real rates of interest would move so that they were equal in all countries. An investor would not leave money in a country that was paying lower real returns than could be obtained elsewhere.

Let us say that France and the UK are offering interest rates of 15% and 10% respectively, and the inflation rate is the same in both countries. Investors will move their money to France where they can earn more on their money. However, if the inflation rate in France is expected to be 10% and that in the UK is only 4%, the investors can earn a greater real return in the UK. France would need to raise its nominal interest rates to 16% in order to prevent investors taking their funds out of the country.

The difference in interest rates between two countries is equal in equilibrium to the expected difference in inflation rates between these countries. The equation representing the Fisher effect is

$$\frac{i_A - i_H}{1 + i_H} = \frac{\Delta P_A - \Delta P_H}{1 + \Delta P_H}$$

The effect of this is that, with the free movement of capital, the interest rates in a country should be equal to the international real rate of interest adjusted for the difference in the expected rate of inflation in that country compared with the inflation rate worldwide.

Given information on interest rates we are in a position to forecast differences between expected inflation rates, which leads to our being able to forecast differences between forward and spot rates. If we were given information on expected inflation rates we could forecast both differences in interest rates and expected changes in spot rates.

In Example 20.1 we have been given the interest rates, and so we can forecast differences in expected inflation rates. Let us assume that the expected annual rate of inflation in the UK is 8%; then we can calculate that in equilibrium the expected rate of inflation in the USA must be in the region of 5.1%. It should be noted that both the interest rates and the expected inflation rates are annual rates.

Substituting these values in the relevant equations, and taking the UK as the home country,

$$\frac{0.10 - 0.13}{1.13} = \frac{\Delta P_A - 0.08}{1.08}$$

$$0.051 = \Delta P_A$$

Relationship between exchange rates and inflation rates (C)

This relationship is expressed in the purchasing power parity theory which has already been referred to.

The hypothesis is that the expected difference in inflation rates between two countries equals, in equilibrium, the expected movement in spot rates. It can be expressed in an equation as

$$\frac{\Delta P_A - \Delta P_H}{1 + \Delta P_H} = \frac{S_T - S_0}{S_0}$$

We shall now substitute the values used in our example into the equation to obtain an estimate of S_T the expected spot rate of exchange at time T. It should be noted that the inflation rate figures we are using are annual rates. Therefore we shall obtain an estimate of the expected spot rate in 12 months' time. We shall then adjust this expected spot rate in order to reconcile the estimate with the three-month figures that we have used elsewhere in the example. It should be remembered that in our example the UK is being used as the home country. Then:

$$\frac{0.051 - 0.080}{1.08} = \frac{\overline{S}_T - 1.5}{1.5}$$

$$-0.02685 = \frac{\overline{S}_T - 1.5}{1.5}$$

$$1.46 = \overline{S}_T$$

We therefore expect that, in equilibrium, the spot rate of exchange in 12 months' time will be £1 = \$1.46. The three-month spot rate should therefore be in the region of £1 = \$1.49, i.e. a quarter of the movement over the year.

Sometimes a simplified version of the equation is used to measure the difference between inflation rates. This is simply the difference between the two expected inflation rates. An example will be given to illustrate the alternative simplified approach.

Let us say the expected annual inflation rate in the UK was 8% per annum and in France it was 3%. If the spot rate of exchange today was £1 = 8 FF according to the theory of purchasing power parity the spot rate of exchange in one year's time would be (using the full formula) approximately £1 = 7.63 FF.

$$\frac{0.03 - 0.08}{1.08} = \frac{\overline{S}_T - 8}{8}$$

$$-0.046\,29 = \frac{\overline{S}_T - 8}{8}$$

$$-0.370\,32 = \overline{S}_T - 8$$

$$7.63 = \overline{S}_T$$

Using the simplified approach the 5% difference between the two annual inflation rates equals the expected change in spot rates. Therefore

$$0.05 = \frac{\overline{S}_T - 8}{8}$$

$$7.60 = \overline{S}_T$$

The mathematics is that for low rates of inflation this simplified relationship gives a reasonable estimate, but for higher rates of inflation it does not.

In fact, the purchasing power parity theory provides reasonable estimates of the movement in exchange rates only over longer periods of time, but does not over shorter periods. There is certainly not a close enough relationship to provide useful short-term forecasts of future exchange rates.

Relationship between the forward rate of exchange and the expected change in spot rates (D)

We know from the theoretical relationships that we have developed that the difference at any time between the forward and spot rates is equal to the expected change in spot rates. If the three other relationships hold, these two variables must be equal. Indeed it is *a priori* what we would expect. If we knew with certainty what the pound–dollar spot rate would be in, say, six months, that would be the forward rate today. If we know we can buy $1.70 for £1 in six months, we would only be willing to enter into a six-month forward deal today at that price. We would certainly not want to enter into a deal if we were offered less than $1.70, and the dealer would not want to offer us more. Of course, this is ignoring risk: the forward deal hedges against risk, from the buyer's point of view; waiting for the future spot price does not.

The expectations theory indicates that the percentage difference today between the forward rate and the spot rate is the change expected in the spot rate. The forward rate of exchange for, say, six months is what collective opinions in the market expect the spot rate to be in six months. In fact in six months' time the actual spot rate can turn out to be different from this expectation.

20.4 MANAGING TRANSACTION RISK

Transaction exposure occurs when there is a time delay between the sale of goods or services and the receipt of the payments, and it will occur in all foreign trading. The question is: who carries the risk? If an importer agrees to pay in the currency of the supplier then it is the importer who is taking the risk. Alternatively, if a supplier agrees to be paid in the buyer's own currency, then the exporter is taking the risk. Which currency is used for invoicing depends on the bargaining strength of the two parties to the transaction. Usually, in order to sell a product, the exporter quotes a price in the currency of the purchaser. For example, a UK company ships goods to a French purchaser on 1 January and the terms of the sale, which is invoiced in French francs, mean that the French buyer will not transmit the funds until 1 April. The UK company is exposed to an exchange risk during the three-month period. If the franc becomes weaker against the pound, the UK company will lose. If the franc becomes stronger against the pound the UK company will gain. Means of hedging against this type of exposure will be discussed.

Transaction exposure can occur within multinational companies with inter-company trading, and with the payment of dividends from subsidiaries to the parent company. In the latter case hedging can again be used. The date of dividend payments will be known in advance, as will the approximate amounts. Arrangements can be made in advance of the date, so that the parent company will not make a monetary loss as a result of any movements in the exchange rates.

A businessman exposed to transaction risk can either run the risk of exchange rate movements or he can take steps to protect his future cash flows from exchange rate fluctuations. If he has sold goods abroad and is prepared to gamble he could, in addition to the profit on the sale of the goods, find that he had made a currency gain. This would happen if the rate of exchange had moved in his favour between the time that he delivered the goods and the time when he is paid. However, it could be that the rate of exchange moves the other way, giving him a currency loss and perhaps meaning that the payment he receives when converted into his own currency does not cover his costs. It is to avoid this possibility that many business-people seek to avoid the risks of currency movements by adopting one of a number of possible hedging techniques.

Covering in the forward foreign exchange market

Covering in the forward market is the procedure for balancing either sales and the receipt of foreign currency or purchases and the payment of foreign currency, so that there is no net open position with regard to the movement of exchange rates.

Suppose that on 1 January 19X0 a UK exporter sells goods to a US customer, invoiced at $150 000, payment to be made in dollars on 1 April 19X0. The spot rate of exchange on 1 January 19X0 is, say, $1.50 = £1. The exporter, in deciding to sell the goods, has in mind a sales price of £100 000, and will base any decisions on the profitability of the deal on this amount. The rate of exchange will most probably vary between 1 January and 1 April, with the size and direction of the move being uncertain. If the pound strengthens against the dollar, the UK exporter makes a currency loss on the deal. If on 1 April £1 = $1.60, the purchaser receives dollars worth only £93 750. However, if the dollar strengthens against the pound and the spot rate on 1 April is £1 = $1.40, the purchaser will make a profit, as the $150 000 will be worth £107 143. They have made a profit on the foreign exchange transaction of £7143.

Rather than run the risk of a possible loss on the currency side of the deal, the exporter may decide to cover the deal. Let us assume that at the time of making the sale on 1 January, they enter into a forward currency deal. They promise to sell $150 000 against pounds to be delivered on 1 April. On 1 January the three-month forward rate is £1 = $1.45. The dollar is expected to become stronger against the pound. This forward contract will mean that they receive £103 448. On April the exporter receives a cheque for $150 000 from the purchaser. The exporter delivers $150 000 against the forward contract, and receives in exchange £103 448.

From the beginning of the transaction the exporter knew that they would receive £103 448. It could be that they make an opportunity gain on the deal, as during the three months that they were waiting for payment the dollar became weaker against the pound. They may have made an opportunity loss. They sold the dollar in the forward market at a price of $1.45. They were uncertain what the spot price would be on 1 April; if it had turned out that the £1 equalled only £1.40, as a result of hedging they would have made an opportunity loss. If they had waited and sold the $150 000 in the spot market, they would have received £107 143. Hedging by selling in the forward market has resulted in an opportunity loss of £3695.

However, the exporter was uncertain about the movement of the two currencies, and covering the sale in the market was a form of insurance. They could not know what the future spot rates would be. If the company had not hedged and the pound had strengthened against the dollar, with say a spot rate on 1 April of £1 = $1.55, it would only have received £96 774. A hedge through a forward deal would have resulted in an opportunity gain of £6674 (i.e. £103 448 − £96 774).

Opportunity gains and losses can only be calculated when the eventual spot price is known; it is just looking at the transaction with hindsight. By dealing in the forward market, the exporter is avoiding the risk of losing as a result of movements in the exchange rate. They are also, of course, giving up the chance of gaining as a result of a favourable movement. They are taking a neutral position.

It is the exchange dealer who is taking the risk. They enter a transaction on 1 January agreeing to accept in three months' time a certain number of US dollars, not knowing what the exchange rate will be in April when they have to hand over an agreed number of pounds to a business-person. It is the commercial banks that help make the foreign exchange markets work. They are willing to deal in foreign exchange; sometimes they are willing to speculate. Often, however, it is individual dealers who are the speculators.

Covering in the money markets

An exporter is to receive dollars. They do not know what the dollars will be worth in three months' time. They could borrow dollars on 1 January and convert these to pounds at the spot rate on that day. They will have incurred a dollar debt, but that does not matter because they can repay this borrowing when they receive the dollars from the debtor. They will have hedged by converting the dollars to pounds at the 1 January rate; they need not worry about future exchange-rate movements.

To illustrate the technique, we shall continue with the example in the previous subsection. The spot and forward rates are as above, the borrowing rate on US dollars is 8% and the rate paid on investments in pounds is 12%. The following steps will need to be taken:

1 January	Step 1.	Borrow $147 056 for three months
	Step 2.	Convert these dollars at the spot rate of £1 = $1.50 to give £98 037
	Step 3.	Invest the £98 037 in the UK for three months
1 April	Step 4.	Receive $150 000 from US customer
	Step 5.	Repay the dollar loan of $147 056 plus three months' interest of $2944
	Step 6.	Realize the investment in the UK and receive £98 037 plus interest of £2941, a total of £100 978

Again, the exporter has taken out a form of insurance. Having borrowed in dollars they do not need to bother what happens to the exchange rate between dollars and pounds as their net exposure in the foreign currency during the three-month period is zero. They are owed dollars by their customer and owe in turn a similar amount of dollars to a US bank. They can match their cash flows. Depending on the movement in exchange rates, however, they might make an opportunity gain or loss.

Covering in the options market

There are markets in options for many assets, commodities, shares and foreign currencies. In Chapter 16 both the theoretical aspects of options and details of trading in the options market for shares were described in considerable detail. The theory described applies to options in currencies as well as in shares. The trading techniques are similar. A company engaged in international trade, which is exposed to possible losses, can take out an option as an alternative to hedging in the forward or money market.

In the example above, the UK exporter would have the opportunity to buy an option to be able to sell dollars in three months' time. The writer of the option agrees that they will be willing to purchase dollars in three months' time at a price agreed now. The exporter buys the option to be able to sell the dollars at an agreed rate. This will limit their loss if the dollar were to fall. They will have to pay a commission to the writer of the option.

If, in fact, the dollar becomes stronger rather than weaker against the pound, the exporter need not exercise the option. The cost to the exporter for peace of mind during the three months' spent waiting for payment is the option writer's commission.

Hedging examples

Two problems will now be considered to show how the alternative hedging techniques work.

Example 20.2

Albion Ltd is expanding its operations in France and has ordered the construction of a new factory near Lille. The final payment of 5 000 000 French francs is due in three months' time. Albion currently only possesses sufficient liquid funds to finance normal working capital requirements, although £0.5 million, the proceeds from a sale and lease-back deal, should be received in approximately three months' time.

Current foreign exchange market rates applicable to Albion Ltd and money market rates are detailed below:

Foreign exchange market	French francs/£1
Spot	11.121–11.150
Two months forward	11.035–11.065
Three months forward	10.948–10.976

Money market	Borrowing	Lending
UK clearing bank	16%	11%
French banque de depôts	11%	8%
Eurofranc	11%	9%
Eurosterling	15.5%	12%
UK treasury bill	–	12%
1 year French bond	–	9.5%

Prepare a report discussing the advantages and disadvantages of the alternatives that are available to Albion Ltd for making payment. Recommend which alternative Albion Ltd should choose.

Suggested solution

There are at least four possibilities open to Albion Ltd.

1 The company could do nothing now. It could wait until the three months had elapsed and then buy French francs at the spot rate at that time. This policy involves taking a considerable risk, as the company does not know If the French franc will become stronger over time against the pound, which could involve them in needing to pay more than if they were to hedge. However, if the French franc were to become weaker against the pound, it would be in Albion's interests to delay payment as long as possible (referred to as a 'lag in payment').

2 The company could take cover in the forward foreign exchange market. This means agreeing now to buy francs in three months' time at a rate of FF 10.948 = £1. This could cost £456 704. At the current spot rate the debt is £449 600, The forward exchange cover therefore has a cost of £7104 above the current spot rate.

3 If the company expects the French franc to appreciate in value, then Albion might decide to accelerate payment of the FF 5 million. This is referred to as a 'lead payment'. Albion would need to borrow £449 600 now. It would convert these pounds into French francs and pay off the debt, but it would not be able to repay the borrowing until three months had elapsed. With the cost of borrowing in the Eurosterling market at 15.5%, the cost of this policy would be the interest payment of £17 422. This would appear to be an expensive policy.

4 A further possibility is for Albion Ltd to obtain money-market cover. It could borrow pounds now in the UK and immediately convert these into French francs. The money-market approach is to invest these French francs in the Eurofranc market rather than to pay the French company. The company needs FF 5 million in three months' time. If it exchanges £ for FF now, it eliminates uncertainty about exchange rate movements. It can invest these FF to earn interest. it can earn 2.25% over three months in the Eurofranc market. This means it only needs FF 4.890 million now. To obtain FF 4.890 million now the company needs £439 700 (converted at spot). It borrows this amount now and pays interest. The steps in the money-market hedge are:

Step 1. Now Borrow £439 700 at 3.875% interest
     2. Now Convert to FF 4.890 million
     3. Now Invest in Eurofranc market
     4.   In 3 months: cash in Eurofranc invest-
             ment (4.890 million +0.110 million)
     5.   Pay for factory
     6.   Repay £ loan plus interest = £456 738

(Note the above steps are shown in the time sequence but this is not the sequence in which the calculations are made. As shown above the first calculation involves determining how much needs to be invested in FF now to be able to pay the debt on the due date.)

The company does not know what is going to happen to the exchange rate over the next three months. It is only after the elapse of the three months that the opportunity costs of the different policies could be worked out, and so the real least expensive alternative determined. At the time of making the decision, the company can either take a risk with possibility 1 or take some cover with either 2 or 4. Possibilities 2 and 4 cost more or less the same because the money market and the FOREX market are in equilibrium.

Example 20.3

Fidden is a medium-sized UK company with export and import trade with the USA. The following trans-actions are due within the next six months. Transactions are in the currency specified.

Purchase of finished goods for resale, cash payment due in six months: $447 000.

Sale of finished goods, cash receipt due in six months: $154 000.

Exchange rates (London market)

	$/£
Spot	1.7106 – 1.7140
Three months forward	0.82 – 0.77 cents premium
Six months forward	1.39 – 1.34 cents premium

Interest rates per annum

	Borrowing	Lending
Sterling	12.5%	9.5%
Dollars	9%	6%

Foreign currency option prices (New York market)
Prices are cents per £, contract size £12 500

Exercise price($)	Calls March	June	Sept.	Puts March	June	Sept.
1.60	–	15.20	–	–	–	2.75
1.70	5.65	7.75	–	–	3.45	6.40
1.80	1.70	3.60	7.90	–	9.32	15.35

Assume that it is now December with six months to expiry of the June contract and that the option price is not payable until the end of the option period, or when the option is exercised.

Required

(i) Calculate the net sterling receipts/payments that Fidden might expect for its six-month transactions if the company hedges foreign exchange risk on
  (1) the forward foreign exchange market;
  (2) the money market.

(ii) If the actual spot rate in six months' time was with hindsight exactly the present six months forward rate, calculate whether Fidden would have been better to hedge through foreign currency options rather than the forward market or money market.

ACCA, Dec. 1989

Answer

The net position of Fidden is that a cash payment of $293 000 must be made in six months' time.
(i) (1) Forward market
        Buy $293 000 at $1.6967   = £172 688
    (2) Money market
        Step 1. Borrow £166 296 at
                12.5% p.a. (now)
             2. Convert to dollars at
                $1.7106   = $284 466
             3. Invest dollars at 6% p.a
             4. Cash-in dollar investment
                (in June)   = $293 000
             5. Pay US supplier
             6. Repay UK loan + interest = £176 690

Conclusion
The forward market is less expensive than the money market.

(ii) Options
Need to buy $ and sell £. Therefore a put option on £ sterling for exercise in June. Prices available $1.70 and $1.80.

Step 1 At $1.70 we need 14 contracts i.e.

$293 000 at $1.70 = £172 353

$$\frac{£172\ 353}{£12\ 500} = 14 \text{ (to nearest higher number)}$$

Step 2 Cost of option

$(14 \times £12\ 500 \times 3.45 \text{ cents}) = \$6037.5$

$= £3530$

Step 3 The 14 contracts will give us 4500 more dollars than we need (297 500 − 293 000). These will be worth £2646 at the spot rate in six months' time.

Step 4 Total cost

(£175 000 + £3530 − £2646) = £175 884

Conclusion

Options at $1.70 are more expensive than the forward market.

Option at $1.80 = £1

Step 1 Number of contacts

$$\frac{\$293\,000}{\$1.80} = £162\,778$$

$$\frac{£162\,778}{£12\,500} = 13.02$$

This is so close to 13 that it should be possible to take out 13 contracts and deal with the balance in the forward market.

Cost of 13 = (£12 500 × 13) = £162 500

Step 2 Cost of option

(13 × £12 500 × 9.32 cents) = $15 145

= £8 854

Step 3 The contacts will give approximately the number of dollars we need

(13 × £12 500 × $1.80) = $292 500

The extra $500 will cost approximately £294.

Step 4 the total cost equals

£162 500 + £8 854 + £294 = £171 648

Conclusion

This is the least expensive. With hindsight the company should have hedged with a $1.80 option.

Note: In both option situations we have ignored the small amount of interest arising if the option price had to be paid at the time the option contract is signed.

20.5 CURRENCY FUTURES CONTRACTS

The first point to make is that this form of foreign exchange hedging is not often used. The London International Financial Futures Exchange (LIFFE) closed down its futures currency market in 1990 because of a lack of business. In London the forward currency market dominates. However, there are futures markets in other countries that offer the opportunity to trade in currencies, for example the markets in Philadelphia and Chicago. It is also possible to arrange an over-the-counter currency futures contract in London and many other cities.

A second point to make is that technically there is much in common between a currency futures hedge and an interest-rate futures hedge.

When hedging in the futures market two separate activities will be taking place. One will be a transaction at a future date in the cash market at the spot rate at the time of the transaction. The other activity will be two transactions taking an equal and opposite position in the futures market. 'Equal' means the transactions are of an approximately similar size. 'Opposite' means that if the exchange rate moves so that the person hedging makes a loss on spot rates in the cash market, then the person hedging makes a net gain on the transactions in the futures market. Of course, if the person hedging gains on the movements in spot rates in the cash market they lose in the futures market.

The hedge does not usually result in a perfect match of gains and losses. The price for currency in the cash market and the price in the futures markets tend to move in roughly parallel fashion, but not always at precisely the same rate. There can also be a mismatch resulting from the fact that in the traded futures market contracts are for a standard amount of currency and this amount might not equal the exact amount to be hedged.

To repeat, with a forward hedge, basically two sets of transactions are taking place. One transaction is the exchange of currency at the spot rate. Let us say a UK manufacturing company makes a sale and will receive US$ in three months' time. These dollars will be exchanged into pounds at the spot rate in three months' time. The second transaction, or rather transactions, are in the futures market with a purchase and a sale of futures contracts, one at one date, one at another, the intention being that any loss on the spot deal is balanced by a net gain on the two futures contracts. We will illustrate a currency futures hedge with an example in which a company is to receive a foreign currency.

The steps we need to take to arrive at the exact details of the futures contracts are:

1. Ascertain the target outcome.
2. Decide for the first futures contract which currency we will be buying and which we will be selling.
3. Determine the appropriate date for closing the two contracts.
4. Ascertain the number of contracts we need to buy and sell.

Example 20.4

Fry PLC sells goods to the USA on 1 January. It invoices the US purchaser for $150 000 with payment to be received on 1 May. The management of Fry is worried that the dollar will fall in value against the pound over the next few months. They decide to hedge in the futures market.

On 1 January the relevant foreign exchange cash and futures rates were:

FOREX (cash market)

Spot	$1.59–$1.60
3-month forward	$1.60–$1.61
6-month forward	$1.61–$1.62

Sterling futures

Mar.	1.585
June	1.602
Sept.	1.612

It should be appreciated that the price of futures contracts moves in line with prices in the cash market, but that they are not usually exactly the same. For example, the six-month forward rate of exchange will only approximate to the rate of exchange quoted for a futures contract expiring at the same date.

On 1 May the actual spot rate turns out to be $1.615–1.625 and the price of June futures contracts $1.620. On 30 June the actual spot rate is $1.620–$1.630.

The first thing to calculate is the target outcome.

This is based on the spot exchange rate on the day of the sale. As at 1 January the company could expect to receive from the sale $150 000/1.60 = £93 750. Subsequent outcomes will be measured against this target.

On 1 May the company will be buying pounds and selling dollars in the spot market. We wish to hedge against loss against the target outcome. We have to decide upon the details of two futures contracts. One futures contract will be taken out now, the other at (or near) the date of the spot transaction. Both deals will be closed at a date beyond the spot deal.

There are two possible alternatives. One is to agree now to (a) enter a forward contract to buy sterling and sell dollars at some future date (say 30 June) and (b) to carry out the opposite futures deal for the same sterling amount on 1 May also for settlement at 30 June. If the dollar becomes weaker over time against the pound we will receive a better price quoted in January for selling dollars in June than will be quoted to us in May when we wish to enter the second of the forward contracts to buy dollars on 30 June. We will make a gain when we close the forward deal on 30 June which will balance the loss we make in the spot market on 1 May.

The reader should be able to work out that the alternative possibility agreeing now (1 January) to buy dollars in June and on 1 May agreeing to sell dollars in June has exactly the opposite effect to that required. It leads to a loss on the futures deals which will add to the loss on the spot deal.

The rule is that if in the cash market you will be selling a currency at a future date, then the initial futures contracts is also to sell that currency. If on the spot market one is to buy a currency, then the first futures contract is to buy that currency.

In this example our first futures deal is therefore to buy sterling and sell dollars with a June futures contract. Why June? It is usual to fix the date to close out our two opposite futures deals as the first available date after the invoiced amount is received (or has been paid).

To ascertain the number of contracts we need to buy we convert the dollars to be received into sterling, and we usually use the futures price to do this.

$$\frac{\$150\,000}{1.602} = £93\,632$$

Each futures contract is for £25 000; therefore we need to buy four contracts.

Transactions

In futures market

1 January: Enter four sterling futures June contracts, to purchase pounds at a price of $1.602 to £1.

1 May: Enter four sterling futures June contracts to sell pounds and buy dollars at a price of $1.620 to £1.

30 June: Close out the two futures contracts.

In spot market

1 May: Sell $150 000 at $1.625 (equals £92 593).

20.6 FOREIGN EXCHANGE RISK

There are three types of FOREX exposure, each of which results in risks for a company. Transaction risk has already been referred to. The other types of exposure and risk are as follows.

Accounting (translation) exposure

Accounting exposure arises not as a result of conversion of currencies but as a result of financial data denominated in one currency needing to be expressed in terms of another currency. Such translation of currencies occurs at the end of each accounting year when the accounts of all subsidiaries have to be expressed in the currency of the parent company in order to present the consolidated accounts of the group. The important question that arises is at what rate of exchange the accounts should be translated. For balance sheet purposes the rate at the end of the accounting year is the most popular. For purposes of calculating profit some average for the year is most common.

Economic exposure

The economic value of an asset, or collection of assets, is based on the present value (PV) of the future cash flows that such assets will generate. This approach was discussed in Chapter 3. A company is an asset; therefore in theory its value as a going concern is the PV of its future cash flows. However, for a multinational the question arises of the appropriate currency in which to measure the cash flows. The owner of an overseas subsidiary will wish at some time to be able to convert the cash flows generated in the host-country currency into another currency. Therefore the value of the future cash flows is not just influenced by business risks, but also by exchange-rate risks. The value of any business at any time depends upon the future cash flows and the expected future exchange rates. We will return to translation (accounting) risk and economic risk in Chapter 21. Companies vary in the way they deal with translation and economic risk.

A company faces transaction exposure in a number of situations. These include:

1 normal trade with countries with different currencies;
2 repaying foreign-currency loans;
3 sale of fixed assets of subsidiaries in foreign countries;
4 repatriation of profits, and payment of royalties and management charges by foreign subsidiary to parent company.

Most companies have a policy towards hedging against such risks. Most large companies tell their shareholders about this policy in their Annual Report and Accounts. As explained above, there are a variety of hedging techniques a company can employ, ranging from forward contracts to currency swaps.

Most companies hedge against transaction risk. They wish to make their profits from manufacturing and trading, not foreign exchange dealing. There are, however, a few companies that speculate in the foreign exchange markets. Undoubtedly some make gains in some years. However, when they make losses and the losses are disclosed they are very heavily criticized.

In 1987 Volkswagen made FOREX losses of DM 473 million. In 1991 Allied-Lyons disclosed FOREX losses of £150 million. Allied-Lyons lost as a result of aggressive profit seeking and an inadequate system of internal controls. It was estimated that their exposure against the US dollar was at one time in the region of £1.5 billion. Allied-Lyons had sold call options against the dollar.

As mentioned earlier, financial derivatives can be useful for hedging purposes. But they can also be dangerous. It is not just lack of skills that can lead to losses, it is also judgement. Bankers also make mistakes.

In 1994 the Governor of the Bank of Malaysia resigned. This was because the bank had lost £1.3 billion on foreign exchange deals in 1993, and this followed even larger losses in the previous year.

20.7 FURTHER READING

There are excellent textbooks on the subject of international finance and the finance of multinational business that have sections dealing with foreign exchange markets. These books include:

Bank of England Quarterly Bulletin (1995), **35**(4), November.

Buckley, A. (1992) *Multinational Finance*, 2nd edn, Prentice-Hall.

Chalmin, P. and Gombeaud, J.L. (1988) *The Global Market*, Prentice-Hall.

Clark, E., Levasseur, M. and Rousseau, P. (1993) *International Finance*, 1, International Thomson Business Press, London.

Demirag, I. and Goddard, S. (1994) *Financial Management for International Business*, McGraw-Hill.

Eiteman, D., Stonehill, A.I. and Moffett, M.H. (1998) *Multinational Business Finance*, 8th edn, Addison-Wesley.

Hamilton, A. (1986) *The Financial Revolution*, Penguin, London.

Holland, J.B. (1986) *International Financial Management*, Blackwell, Oxford.

Rodriguez, R.M. and Carter, E.E. (1984) *International Financial Management*, 3rd edn, Prentice-Hall.

Shapiro, A.C. (1992) *Multinational Financial Management*, 4th edn, Allyn and Bacon, Boston.

Tucker, A.L., Madura, J. and Chiang, T.C. (1991) *International Financial Markets*, West.

20.8 PROBLEMS

1 Who are the players in the foreign exchange markets? What objective is each trying to achieve? What tactics do they adopt to achieve their objectives?

2 Explain what is meant by the terms 'foreign exchange translation exposure', 'transactions exposure' and 'economic exposure'. What is the significance of these different types of exposure to the financial manager?

3 'As foreign exchange markets are efficient, it is not possible for a company to accurately predict future spot rates.'
Discuss.

4 Your managing director has received forecasts of US$ exchange rates in two years' time from three leading banks.

$/£ forecasts 30 June 1999
Pallbank   1.25
Superbank   1.55
Emubank   1.68

The current spot mid-rate (June 1997) is $1.5240/£

A non-executive director of your company has suggested that in order to forecast future exchange rates, the interest rate differential between countries should be used. She states that 'as short-term interest rates are currently 6% in the UK, and 8.5% in the USA, the exchange rate in two years time will be $1.597/£'.

Required
You have been asked by your managing director to prepare a brief report discussing the likely validity of the non-executive director's estimate.   (6 marks)
ACCA, Jan. 1997

5 You have been asked to give advice to a medium-sized glass manufacturer in Italy that is tendering for an order in Kuwait. The tender conditions state that payment will be made in Kuwait dinars in 18 months from now. The company is unsure as to what price to tender. The marginal cost of producing the glass at that time is estimated to be 581 million lire and a 25% mark-up is normal for the company.

	Exchange rates *Lira/Dinar*
Spot	5467 – 5503

No forward rate exists for 18 months' time.

	Italy	*Kuwait*
Annual inflation rates	9%	3%
Annual interest rates available to the glass manufacturer:		
Borrowing	14%	9%
Lending	9%	3.5%

Required:
Discuss how the glass manufacturer might protect itself against foreign exchange rate changes, and recommend what tender price should be used.

(10 marks)
ACCA, Dec. 1996

6 You have been provided with the following information, which suggests that price levels in Japan are expected to rise by 0.5% over the next twelve months, and in the USA by 4.5% over the same period. The one year Euro-Yen nominal rate of interest is 2.5% and the Euro-dollar twelve-month rate is quoted at 7.5%). The spot rate for the yen is 99.075/$, and the yen is quoted at 96.00/$ twelve months forward.

Required
(a) Are the foreign exchange and money market in equilibrium? Explain.

(b) (i) If the markets are in disequilibrium show how investors can make a riskless profit. (You may assume any amount to trade with.)
   (ii) Explain the impact that arbitrageurs' actions will have on both interest rates and exchange rates.
(c) Based on the information given in the case, calculate the equilibrium twelve-month forward rate, assuming interest rates are as given.

7

Currency	Spot	1 month		3 months	
£/$	1.5015–25	3	6	13	17
$/DKr	9.3600–25	90	130	320	360
$/Yen	231.87–97	63	59	185	180

(a) Explain the terms 'spot' and '3 months'.
(b) Determine the outright forward rates for all three currencies.
(c) Assume your firm is dealing in the foreign exchange markets with a dealer who has given the above quotations. At what rate would you deal?
   (i) You buy yen for $ spot.
   (ii) You buy DKr for $ 1 month forward.
   (iii) You sell $ for £ 3 months forward.
   (iv) You buy yen for $ 1 month forward, option over the first month.
   (v) You sell $ for DKr 3 months forward, option over the whole period.
(d) (i) Calculate the spot £/yen exchange rate.
   (ii) Calculate the £/DKr 1 month forward rate.
(e) UK interest rates are 12% per annum. Using the data given above, determine the annual rate of interest to be expected on a three-month US deposit. Explain.
   If the actual rate was 3% per annum higher than you have calculated what would be your best course of action?

8 A UK company has £8 000 000 excess cash available for a period of six months. It is uncertain whether to invest the capital in the UK or to invest it in the USA in order to take advantage of higher interest rates. The rates are:

£/$ spot	1.7800–1.8000
£/$ 6 months forward rate	10–20 Dis
Sterling interest rate	$8–8\frac{1}{4}\%$ p.a.
US$ interest rate	$9\frac{1}{4}–9\frac{1}{2}\%$ p.a.

Advise the company on whether it should invest its excess cash in the USA or within the UK.

9 Assume that on your first week at work in one of the UK major banks, you were assigned to the foreign exchange department. A couple of weeks later the head of the research department was suggesting that he is convinced that the German mark is presently overvalued relative to the US dollar. Your boss wants you to take action on the basis of the following expectations and facts.

Exchange market

Spot rate	DM 1.7483/$
Three month – forward rate	DM 1.7593/$
Expected spot rate in three months' time	DM 1.8095/$

Money market
German rates (p.a.)

Three months	5.8%
Six months	5.6%
Twelve months	5.3%

US rates (p.a.)

Three months	3.0
Six months	$3\frac{5}{16}$
Twelve months	$3\frac{5}{8}$

Required

(a) Are the exchange and money markets in equilibrium? Why?   (4 marks)

(b) (i) Is there any way to take advantage of the situation? If so, how? (Without speculating, you can assume any amount to trade with.)
    (8 marks)

    (ii) What exchange and interest rate trends would appear in the market if a large number of investors took similar action?   (5 marks)

(c) How can the bank profit from its forecast of the future spot rate?
    (4 marks)

10 Runswick Ltd is an importer of clock mechanisms from Switzerland. The company has contracted to purchase 3000 mechanisms at a unit price of 18 Swiss francs. Three months' credit is allowed before payment is due. Runswick currently has no surplus cash, but can borrow short-term at 2% above bank base rate or invest short-term at 2% below bank base rate in either the UK or Switzerland.

Current exchange rates

	Swiss franc/£
Spot	2.97–2.99
1 month forward	$2\frac{1}{2}$–$1\frac{1}{2}$ premium
3 months forward	$4\frac{1}{2}$–$3\frac{1}{2}$ premium

(The premium relates to the Swiss franc.)

Current bank base rates

Switzerland	6% per year
United Kingdom	10% per year

(i) Explain and illustrate three policies that Runswick Ltd might adopt with respect to the foreign exchange exposure of this transaction. Recommend which policy the company should adopt. Calculations should be included wherever relevant. Assume that interest rates will not change during the next three months.   (9 marks)

(ii) If the Swiss supplier were to offer 2.5% discount on the purchase price for payment within one month evaluate whether you would alter your recommendation in (i).   (5 marks)

(c) If annual inflation levels are currently at 2% in Switzerland and 6% in the UK, and the levels move during the next year to 3% in Switzerland and 9% in the UK, what effect are these changes in inflation likely to have on the relative value of the Swiss franc and the pound?   (3 marks)

ACCA

11 (a) Explain briefly what is meant by foreign currency options and give examples of the advantages and disadvantages of exchange-traded foreign-currency options to the financial manager.   (5 marks)

(b) Exchange-traded foreign-currency option prices in Philadelphia for dollar/sterling contracts are shown below:

Sterling (£12 500) contracts

	Calls		Puts	
Exercise price ($)	September	December	September	December
1.90	5.55	7.95	0.42	1.95
1.95	2.75	3.85	4.15	3.80
2.00	0.25	1.00	9.40	–
2.05	–	0.20	–	–

Option prices are in cents per £. The current spot exchange rate is $1.9405–$1.9425/£.

Required:

Assume that you work for a US company that has exported goods to the UK and is due to receive a payment of £1 625 000 in three months' time. It is now the end of June.

Calculate and explain whether your company should hedge its sterling exposure on the foreign currency option market if the company's treasurer believes the spot rate in three months' time will be:

(i) $1.8950–$1.8970/£

(ii) $2.0240–$2.0260/£

(7.5 marks)

ACCA, June 1992

21 INTERNATIONAL FINANCE

By the end of this chapter the reader should:

- have an understanding of what are referred to as the 'global financial markets'
- appreciate the opportunities available for large companies to obtain finance in the global markets
- be able to appraise foreign capital investment projects
- be able to evaluate political and foreign exchange risk
- know how to hedge against foreign exchange risk
- understand the basis of international taxation

21.1 INTRODUCTION

Multinational companies (MNCs) are increasing in importance. The largest 100 companies in the world (all of whom are multinational) become responsible each year for an increasing proportion of the world's trade (much of it being transfers within a company). They also are becoming responsible for an increasing proportion of the world's direct investment. Even smaller and medium-sized companies are becoming more international in their activities.

A company might produce all its goods in one country, but sell some of its goods in other countries. If the foreign sales are invoiced in the currency of the buyer, it will be exposed to exchange rate risk which is known as 'transaction exposure'. As the company grows it might set up an office in the overseas country, even if just for marketing purposes. It now has assets in that country. What will happen to the value of those assets if the currency of the host country moves against the currency of the home country?

The setting up of an overseas subsidiary, with or without a foreign partner clearly makes the enterprise a multinational business. The country where the investment takes place is referred to as the 'host country'. The country where the company which ultimately has control of the investment is registered is referred to as the 'home country'.

The result of these trends is that the international aspects of financial management is now of major importance. It is, for example, not possible to understand the financial decision of an MNC without understanding something about (a) the way the global financial markets work and (b) the way in which taxation operates internationally.

We will begin by exploring the growth of the global financial markets and consider the way in which large companies can make use of the markets. We will then consider how MNCs make investment decisions, the influence of taxation, and the ways in which MNCs control their subsidiaries in many different countries.

The sources of finance available to small and medium-sized enterprises are usually limited to those available within their own domestic market. Larger companies are in a position to obtain funds in international and foreign financial markets. These funds are sometimes obtained, not to finance overseas investment, but to bring back to the home country.

From a company's point of view financial markets can now be divided into three groups (of which the last two are international):

1 their own domestic 'national' market;
2 national markets in other countries that are open to foreigners;
3 global capital and money markets.

The fact that large internationally known companies can obtain funds from any of these three markets puts them at a competitive advantage over smaller companies. If interest rates and the cost of capital are comparatively high in the domestic market, the larger firm will move to the global markets to keep costs down.

There is nothing new about the idea of markets in some countries being open to foreigners who wish to obtain the currency of that domestic market. The London market has for centuries been open to foreign governments and companies who wish to obtain pounds sterling. Similarly New York has been open to foreign borrowers for many decades, and those UK companies who have been in a position to do so have often taken advantage of this opportunity. What has changed in recent years is that with the 'deregulation' of monetary and legal controls more countries have opened up their markets to foreigners, and have also allowed their own nationals to purchase securities in foreign markets. Japan, a major financial power, only opened up its markets in the 1980s.

1 Motives of firms to obtain funds outside home country:
   (a) growth of transnational companies, operating around the world;
   (b) access to funds – sometimes the domestic capital markets of a firm are not large enough to raise the amounts of funds required;
   (c) funds raised can be cheaper: the funds are raised in large amounts and there is an absence of regulations in some international markets;
   (d) natural hedge to international investment;
   (e) becoming known internationally; borrow in same currency as assets valued;
   (f) taxation advantages.
2 Motives for investors to invest outside home country:
   (a) diversification;
   (b) high potential returns from investing in growth economies of the world;
   (c) possible gains from exchange-rate movements;
   (d) avoid taxation.

The global markets began with foreign bond issues in national markets. A government may have wished to borrow. It may not have wished to raise the money in its own domestic market and so it went to one of the large financial centres such as New York or London. The money raised would of course be dollars in the former and pounds sterling in the latter. This type of activity fits the definition of an international financial market; it is the raising of domestic currency for a non-resident borrower. It is not, however, part of the Euromarkets.

For many years the US capital market was a world market. Issuers from any country in the world could offer securities in New York and obtain the dollars they required. These were called 'foreign bond issues', and they were treated on an equal footing to issues by US residents. Companies from outside the USA did not in fact make great use of this source of finance; it was mainly of service to national governments.

There were a number of reasons why foreign firms did not use New York, of which one was that the Securities and Exchange Commission was comparatively demanding in the information that it required from companies offering securities in the USA.

In the 1960s, with the expansion of national economies and multinational companies, the demand for finance was growing. Many national capital markets were inadequate. Therefore companies, as well as public authorities and governments, needed an international capital market, or at least a market in some form, that could supply them with large amounts of money without too much regulation or political interference. The USA was setting controls on interest rates and countries such as Russia were worried about depositing dollars in the USA. Banks in Europe were happy to receive dollars, and so the Euromarkets began.

The markets received a major boost in the 1970s with the dramatic increases in oil prices. This resulted in a few oil rich countries having large balance-of-payments surpluses that they needed to invest. The Euromarkets offered the opportunity for these funds to be invested in other countries. Many countries, particularly in the Third World, needed finance to support their economic development and to cover their balance-of-payments deficits. As is known, they borrowed heavily in the international marketplace. The international money and capital markets helped recycle funds.

The next major boost to the growth of these markets came in the 1980s with change in communication techniques, deregulation, companies seeing themselves as transnational, developing countries in the market place to borrow and new centres of financial power emerging. The money and capital markets became truly global.

We shall briefly look at these contributing factors.

Change in political support

The political climate in many countries in the 1970s and 1980s moved towards supporting the ideology that decisions should be made in the free marketplace and hence that controls and regulations should be ended. From a finance point of view deregulation means removing restrictions on the import and export of currency. In the past, UK investors, financial institutions and companies were prevented by law from moving funds out of the UK to invest in a foreign country. The UK ended such restrictions in 1979. Prior to that, in 1974, the USA ended its restrictions; Germany ended its restrictions in 1981, and Japan in 1984.

The change in Japan was particularly important as the Japanese people have traditionally been savers of large amounts of money. With deregulation Japanese financial institutions were able to move the savings out of Japan and invest anywhere in the world.

Of course, the other side of deregulation is that a country opens up its economy to the inflow of funds, both direct and portfolio investment. Foreigners are given access to the domestic markets of a country.

A further major change in political ideology occurred when the centrally planned economies of Central and Eastern Europe, and of China, moved to support the ideas of free markets. This meant funds could flow into these countries and out of them without restriction. They became part of the global market place.

Technological change

It became technically possible for various agencies to provide computer networks that allowed trading to be conducted so that buyers and sellers could complete bargains anywhere in the world at any time. The trading could be in shares, bonds, commodities or foreign exchange. When New York is closing, Tokyo is opening; when Tokyo is closing, London opens, and so on. Funds in London at 5.00 p.m. local time, as offices are closing, can be invested at overnight rates, and that money can be moved around the world, through New York and Tokyo, and be back in London plus interest at 8.00 a.m. the next morning as offices are re-opening. Of course, the money does not physically move; it is just that various accounts are being debited and credited.

There was a time when buying and selling of shares was a face-to-face activity. A broker acting for a buyer would find a jobber who was willing to sell, and a price was agreed. The Stock Exchange in London, which grew out of coffee houses in the City in the eighteenth century, had as its code: 'My word is my bond'. Now there are no words. Buying and selling does not involve face-to-face contact. The buyer sits in front of one computer terminal, and the seller in front of another. Computers are not limited by distance; they can be activated around the world. The buyer could be in London, and the seller in Japan. Computer trading therefore made global markets technically possible.

Other factors

Other factors that boosted the growth of global markets were as follows.

1 There was a move to floating exchange rates between currencies.
2 Banks became multinational businesses. Some banks, e.g. Barclays, always had a large multinational operation, but a boost came in the 1980s with the expanding multinational role of the Japanese banks and security houses.
3 There have been financial innovations, including securitization, the growth in the interest rate and currency swap markets, and in the use of futures and options.
4 Privatization issues have meant, because of the size of the issues, that shares had to be sold in more than one market.
5 There has been a big increase in the amount of funds searching for investment opportunities. These arose partly because of the growth in pension funds, mutual funds and units trusts in the USA and the UK. It also became accepted that there were advantages in holding in a portfolio a percentage of foreign securities.
6 Emerging country capital markets increased in number, as did the securities being offered. Portfolio funds were attracted to these markets by the prospect of high rates of return.

The growth of global markets

In the chapter on equity we made reference to the global equity market, and in the chapter on debt we made brief reference to the Eurobond market. We will now consider these two markets in more detail. Global markets consist of (a) the true international financial markets, with no national base, and (b) the foreign aspects of national financial markets.

There is nothing new about international trade and international borrowing. For centuries nations have traded with each other. Bankers in one country have lent to borrowers in another country. The centre of such trade and commerce has changed over time from one part of the world to another. These centres were not originally seen as global markets, but national markets open to international business. The changes that have occurred over the last three decades have, however, introduced a new dimension. What has changed is the speed and manner in which money moves around the world, the organization of the financial system to facilitate this movement and the amount of money involved.

The growth of global markets is not without its problems, which include the following.

1 Interdependence: a slump in a domestic market in one country can have repercussions in many other markets around the world. This could be seen following the collapse in Wall Street on 19 October 1987. On that day the Dow-Jones index fell by a record amount, in both absolute and percentage terms. In one trading session it fell by 23%, a larger fall than that in the Wall Street crash of 1929. The immediate cause of the crash is said to be the publication of the US trade-deficit figures for the month of August. There were other factors such as share prices being at very high levels on Wall Street, despite a weak economy. There was also evidence that many computers in dealers' offices had been programmed to produce sell orders when certain events happened; they therefore all acted together when the poor trade figures were announced. The collapse in New York led to falling prices in stock markets around the world. As so often happens, dealers in the markets overreacted; there was panic.

A similar situation arose in 1997, when problems in the foreign exchange markets and stock exchanges of certain South East Asian countries led to a collapse of share prices in London, New York and other mature stock markets. The stock markets in New York and in Europe, on this occasion, soon recovered. One reason for this was that lessons had been learnt from the collapse ten years earlier. In New York the Stock Exchange had introduced the idea of a 30-minute cooling-off period if the market fell during a day by more than a certain percentage. During this 'rest' period the market players were able to reassess the situation. Also, certain forms of programmed trading had been banned.

2 Another problem resulting from the growth of multinational banking is the danger that it will lead to a situation in which a few very large banks dominate the world banking scene.

3 Money now moves quickly around the world looking for growth opportunities. Large amounts can move from one centre to another, thereby increasing the volatility of security prices, interest and exchange rates in any one centre.

4 Companies who have access to global markets will be able to obtain less expensive funds than those who can only use domestic markets. This gives an advantage to big business, possibly leading to increasing concentration.

5 A further problem is who regulates the global markets. Companies operate in many countries. Each government wishes to retain its right to regulate within its own country. Companies can play off one country against another: it is called 'regulation arbitrage'. One of the reasons why BCCI was able to operate in a dishonest manner for a number of years was that no one regulator was responsible for controlling the total banking operation.

21.3 INTERNATIONAL MONEY MARKETS

In order to demonstrate the role of the international markets we shall consider what are called 'Euromarkets'. These are markets for short-, medium- and long-term debt. They involve borrowers and lenders from all parts of the world. They are called 'Euro' because they were first organized by banks located in Europe, even though they initially dealt mainly in dollars. The dollars deposited often come from oil-rich countries located outside Europe, and the lending was often to the developing countries of Africa and South America.

Even though banks located in Europe still lead in the Euromarket business, there is some competition from international markets centred in other parts of the world. There is, for example, an Asian currency market centred around Singapore. This market started in 1968 and was then known as the 'Asian dollar market'. It grew in importance because of the time zone it occupied between the USA and Europe and because of the economic growth in the region leading to a large supply and demand for dollars.

Most of the funds deposited with banks in the Asian currency market are lent to Asian borrowers, but there are also strong links with the Eurocurrency centres based in Europe. Other centres for the Asian dollar market include Hong Kong.

The international money market

The international financial markets can be divided by the activities they undertake into the international money markets, sometimes called the 'international banking market' or the Eurocurrency market, and the international securities markets. We will consider the securities markets in the next section.

The money market is concerned with the short- to medium-term end of international activity and is by far the largest element of the international financial markets. Suppliers of funds to the market are able to place their money on deposit with a bank for periods of time varying from overnight to a number of years. Borrowers in this market usually only want funds for short periods of time, although loans can be arranged for periods of three years or even more. Because there are so many interbank transactions, it is difficult to be precise about the size of the international banking market. When securities are involved it is possible to count the value of the securities. However, in the case of bank lending, there can be a considerable amount of double counting with the same money changing hands several times. Most of this involves cross-border lending and borrowing by banks.

The largest part of the interbank business in this market is in overnight to three-months money. The Eurocurrency market is one part of the international money market, and the dollar is the currency that is most often used in transactions. A Eurodollar arises when a bank physically outside the USA receives a deposit of dollars. The receiving bank, which of course can be an overseas branch of a US bank, wishes to make use of such a deposit. It lends it to somebody, say a company or a government. The initial deposit of dollars can lead to the creation of much more purchasing power than its actual value. The receiver of the first loan could well deposit all or part of the dollars received in another bank. This other bank would then feel free to lend part of the sum involved again. Each bank through which the money flows may wish to maintain a reserve ratio between the amount of Eurodollars it lends and the amount of Eurodollars deposited with it.

An example of how the chain of borrowing and lending might commence would be a European company selling to the USA, receiving payment in dollars and deciding to deposit these with its European bank. The bank may lend the funds to another bank, which in turn lends them to another company that wishes to invest in the USA and so needs dollars. The money or credit allowed could change hands many times.

Syndicated credits

These are usually included in the 'international banking market' classification rather than the 'international securities market' because there are no securities resulting from the borrowing and lending. There are no securities to be traded in the marketplace.

Syndicated credits are medium-term credits with the borrower being allowed to draw on funds as required up to an agreed upper limit. A loan is different from a credit. A loan can be identified by the actual movement of a specific sum of money from the lender to the borrower at a particular time. The full amount of the loan is known from the outset and interest has to be paid on it for the entire period of the borrowing. With a credit the borrower can borrow funds when required, and might never draw the total amount agreed as the upper limit.

Syndicated Eurocredits are an important source of finance in international markets. Because large amounts may be required by individual borrowers the lenders often work as a group to provide the funds: they work as a syndicate. They provide medium-term finance for periods usually in the region of from three to five years. Usually, the interest rates are variable over time and are tied to some basic market rate such as LIBOR.

Large companies frequently use this market when engaged in takeover activity. They can obtain standby credit, which they will use to fund the purchase if the takeover bid is successful. The market has seen a growth in merger-related credits. Companies also use this market to refinance debts incurred in earlier acquisitions, when they have not been able to obtain other funds to pay off the debts. Highly geared companies frequently use this market, and as a result they can be charged relatively high margins above LIBOR by the lenders.

21.4 INTERNATIONAL (SECURITIES) CAPITAL MARKETS

There are international markets in

- short- and medium-term notes;
- bonds;
- derivative instruments;
- equities.

Short- and medium-term notes

This is a very large market. By far the most popular form of note issue was the Euro medium-term note (EMTN). The medium-term note market far exceeds in size the market for short-term notes (including Euro-commercial paper).

Short-term Euronotes

This covers the short-term end of the securities market. The notes are sometimes called 'European commercial paper' (ECP). A company writes a note promising to pay to the holder of the note a certain sum of money at a certain date or dates in the near future. This note is then sold in the market and subsequently can be traded. The note is not usually underwritten. It may be written in respect of one currency, or it can be a multiple-component facility which enables borrowers to draw funds in a variety of forms and a number of currencies. The market is mainly limited to leading companies, who are referred to as 'prime borrowers'.

Euronotes have been issued with interesting features. One of the Japanese security houses has issued ECP with which the return offered is linked to a Japanese government bond futures contract. Holders of such ECPs would benefit if the value of the futures contract rises.

Euro-medium-term notes

To some extent the medium-term Euronote market is competing with the Eurobond market. It fills a gap between short-term notes and long-term bonds. The medium-term notes are continuously issued notes, which are usually unsecured, with maturities ranging from nine months to ten years. They allow the borrower flexibility with respect to maturity profiles and the size and timing of issues.

Some companies see this form of medium-term borrowing as a way of matching the time period of the sources of finance with the time period of the credit they make available to customers. For example, these medium-term loans are a useful tool of treasury management for a company selling cars and allowing two to three years for the customer to pay, as they allow the cash inflow and outflow to be matched. An alternative approach would be for the company to securitize the accounts receivable.

The market has a lower minimum size requirement than the Eurobond market and in the market there are investors who are prepared to lend to borrowers with a slightly lower credit rating than needed for Eurobonds; for example, they would issue the notes of a company with BBB rating whereas the Eurobond market looks for AAA borrowers.

Bond market

The most common currency of issue for the Eurobond is the US dollar, with the next three most popular being the Swiss franc, the yen and the Deutschmark. There are also issues in pounds sterling and the ECU. The borrowers in the market include large multinational companies, national governments and international institutions such as the World Bank and the EU.

Many Eurobond and floating-rate note (FRN) issues have novel features such as zero coupon rates, convertibility into equity and bonds with warrants attached. Most FRN issues have a call option which gives the issuer the right to redeem the note prior to maturity. Some issues offer a put option which gives the buyer of the note the option to obtain repayment prior to the maturity date.

The technique of making an issue through the Eurobond market is not like that of a public issue in the UK; it is more similar to the technique of placing. The bank or consortium of banks who are managing the issue invite a large number of other banks and institutions each to take up a part of the issue. These banks and institutions who are approached by the issuing bank or banks can then, if they accept the offer, either keep the bonds themselves or sell them to their clients. Underwriters are appointed by the issuing bank or banks in case the issue is not taken up through these private placings. A number of interesting features can be linked to the underwriting. These include a revolving underwriting facility which allows the issue and the underwriting to be spread over time.

The funds raised by the borrower are in a specific currency; if the borrower wishes to use that particular currency they need take no further action. If, however, the borrower wishes to obtain, say, pounds to invest in the UK and the loan obtained is in Deutschmarks, they will have to convert the currency. They have to repay the loan in the currency of issue, which means that they run the risk of an exchange loss (or even an exchange gain) if significant movement in either of the currencies occurs between the time of the borrowing and the time of repayment.

There is a secondary market for the Eurobonds with a number of market makers. This secondary market has in the past been criticized for its lack of liquidity; this means that there is a shortage of funds attracted to the secondary market to buy bonds. As a result, sellers could not always obtain the price that they expected and often found it necessary to spread a large sale of bonds between a number of market makers.

Dealers are located all around the world. It is very much a telephone market. As with all Euromarkets there is no central market place – dealers communicate with each other by telephone, telex and fax. In order to improve the liquidity almost all Eurobond public issues are listed on at least one major stock exchange.

Convertible bonds

These have increased in popularity in the Euromarkets. In 1991 $10 billion was raised through such issues; by 1996 this had risen to $60 billion. The reasons for the growth include, the high level of equity share prices, a well-developed secondary market and the safety level such bonds offer if equity prices collapse. Novel features include 'conversion resets' in which the number of shares offered on conversion will be increased if share prices fall. There is with some issues redemption of the bond at a premium if the equity share price fails to reach a predetermined level.

International equity

This is sometimes referred to as the 'Euroequity market', but this is a misleading title. There is no list of Euroequity issues. When we refer to 'international (global) equity' we are referring to companies cross-listing in a number of national markets and investors from one country buying securities in foreign markets.

Many stock markets in the world are open to security issues by foreigners who wish to raise funds in the currency of that market. These markets are also open to foreigners who wish to invest funds and buy domestic securities. It is this that constitutes the international (global) equity market; not a market free from the rules or regulations of any government (as is the Eurobond market).

In the early days of the Euromarket, attempts were made to place in Europe large blocks of shares of US companies; of course, these were offered in exchange for payment in dollars. These placings did not work because of the arbitrage opportunity of selling these shares back in the US stock markets. The Japanese company shares that were issued in Europe also had a rather unsuccessful history. Many of these shares issued in Europe were eventually sold in the domestic Japanese market. The difficulty is that there is not really a large independent market for such equity shares in Europe. Dealings in such shares in Europe tend to be dominated by what is happening in the large home stock market for the same shares.

The equity shares issued in the international market that flow back to the market in the home country of the issuer is known, not surprisingly, as 'flowback'. Despite the flowback problem there are now each year a number of so-called Euroequity issues.

The 1990s saw a big increase in these international equity (cross-listing) issues. In 1983 the amount raised by such issues was $2 billion; this had risen to $10 billion by 1990 and to $60 billion in 1996.

Reasons for the increase included large privatization issues, too big for a single stock market to handle, the sale by large multinational companies of subsidiaries, the high valuation of equity shares and the large amount of portfolio funds looking for investment opportunities.

Because the shares being sold need to meet the listing requirements of each country in which they are offered to the public, this form of selling shares is expensive. Companies and governments obviously believe that with large issues the costs are justified.

In the region of 20% of the total number of companies quoted on the major stock exchanges of the EU countries are foreign companies, i.e. they are not registered in the country in which they are being quoted. Of these foreign companies, approximately 25% are based in the USA. Some companies are quoted in more than one market; for example, Du Pont, General Motors and Occidental are all quoted in three or more exchanges.

The reasons why a company might make such an issue rather than an issue in just its own domestic markets include:

- larger issues will be possible than if the issue is limited to just one market;
- wider distribution of shareholders;
- queuing procedures which exist in some national markets may be avoided;
- to become better known internationally.

A foreign listing for a share can enable a company to raise finance in another market place. Another reason is that a company seems less foreign when it has a domestic listing, and there will be an opportunity for nationals of the country to buy shares in the company. It will improve the company's image. Once a foreign company is accepted in a country, and it discloses all the information in the form required in that country, then there is an increasing likelihood that it will continue to expand. There is little point in obtaining such a foreign listing unless a company already trades in the country where it wishes to be listed. However, once a large company is established in a country there can be political advantages from a listing. A third advantage arises in that a listing can create a wider market for a company's shares. It may well be that only a small secondary market develops initially, but as the company name becomes better known it can attract a wider group of shareholders. It will broaden the shareholder base. A listing will also allow a company to use its shares in the country's national capital market to make share-for-share acquisitions of other companies in that country or to enter into, say, a joint venture with a local company. Shares can be offered to nationals in exchange for shares in a domestic company, and these new shares will be acceptable as they can be traded in the domestic market. Finally, the listing of a company's shares will simply help to make that company better known amongst the financial community of the country; it is a form of promotional exercise. The prospectus or other documents presented at the time of the listing will help the foreign company to become more understood.

Global market for derivative instruments

There has been a rapid growth in the markets for financial futures, options and swaps. Many of the markets are outside the USA. Many of the instruments are related to interest rates in, and currencies of, European countries.

As well as this level of activity in organized derivative exchanges, there has been a rapid growth in activity in the over-the-counter derivative markets. These developments are discussed elsewhere in the book.

As the Barings case demonstrated, the derivatives market is truly international. Nick Leeson, a trader for a British bank, was operating out of Singapore, seeking to make money out of arbitrage opportunities. He was trading in Nikkei cash and futures securities, seeking to find gaps between the prices of these securities in the Singapore, Osaka and Tokyo markets.

Issues by foreigners in national markets

As explained at the beginning of Section 21.1 many national capital markets are open to foreigners. These are part of the global markets, indeed they were the beginning of the international market. The use of such markets for the cross-listing of equity issues has just been described.

In a foreign debt issue a foreign borrower raises funds on the domestic capital market of another country. The borrower obtains funds in the currency of that market. The market jargon for a foreign issue in the US domestic market is 'Yankee bond'. Issues by foreigners of yen securities in Tokyo are referred to as 'samurai issues', and issues of bonds by foreigners in London for sterling are known as 'bulldog issues'.

The overseas operation can be financed as follows.

1. Funds generated by the subsidiary: retained earnings and depreciation.
2. Funds transferred within the group: equity and loans from the parent company; loans from other subsidiary companies; leads and lags in the payment for intercompany transactions.
3. Funds from outside the group: borrowing from host-country sources or international financial markets; local equity issues.

In practice most investment in foreign subsidiaries is initially financed by a mixture of parent-company equity (either in the form of cash or the transfer of equipment) and foreign borrowing. As the subsidiary grows, additional finance is usually obtained through local borrowing and internally generated funds.

Local borrowing

One approach to investing in a foreign country is to borrow as much as possible in local markets. There are two advantages of this approach. One is that it would reduce the adverse effects if nationalization of the subsidiary's assets were to take place. With nationalization the local loans would not be repaid. A second advantage is that if the interest and repayments can be covered by revenue earned in the local currency, then it will not affect the parent-company cash flows. Any movements in exchange rates would be immaterial. The alternative of borrowing from sources in other countries can lead to exchange losses if the local currency is depreciating against the currency in which the borrowing is made.

The parent company should not automatically borrow as much locally as it can. The cost of borrowing in the host country should be compared with the costs of borrowing outside the country. It could be that it would be cheaper to borrow in international money markets or in the home country. The possible rate of devaluation of the host-country currency would then have to be compared with the interest savings resulting from borrowing in a foreign currency and transferring the money into the host country. The resulting earnings from the investment will probably mostly be in the currency of the host country. If this currency falls in value it will make the repayment of the foreign currency loan more expensive.

The effective cost of foreign borrowing is given by the formula

effective cost = interest rate on borrowing
± appreciation/depreciation in exchange rates between home and host-country

For example, if the cost of borrowing in the UK is 10% and the Kenyan shilling is expected to depreciate against the pound by 10% per annum, the effective cost to a company of raising funds in London, converting these to shillings in order to invest in Kenya and using the cash flow earned in shillings to service the debt, is approximately 20%. If the cost of borrowing in Kenya is less than 20% it would pay to borrow locally. However, if the cost of borrowing in Kenya is above 20% it would pay to borrow in London and convert the funds to the required shillings.

This is demonstrated in the following example. We borrow, say, £1000 in London, have to pay £100 interest at the end of each of two years and repay the debt at the end of the second year. The pounds sterling are converted into shillings and the debt is serviced from Kenya. At the time of converting the loans into shillings and investing in Kenya the rate of exchange is £1 = 12 shillings. With the 10% devaluation of the shilling per annum the rates of exchange at the end of the next two years becomes £1 = 13.2 shillings and £1 = 14.52 shillings. The cash flows are as follows:

Years	London Interest	Loan	Kenya Interest	Loan
0		+£1000		+12 000
1	−£100		−1320	
2	−£100	−£1000	−1452	−14 520

To obtain the effective cost of servicing the loan we need to solve the following equation (representing the cash flow in shillings) and find r:

$$+12\,000 = \frac{1320}{1+r} + \frac{15\,972}{(1+r)^2}$$

Hence r is just under 21%. As mentioned above, adding together the nominal interest rate and the percentage devaluated/appreciation gives an approximate solution.

Local equity

Another way of raising finance locally is through the issues of shares. Such shares could either be sold to local individuals or institutions through a stock market or could be sold to partners in a local joint venture.

In some countries of the world the equity shares in the subsidiary are not sold to local nationals, but given away to people with connections with key local politicians or establishment figures. This in some countries is a necessary step in order to obtain the necessary licences to operate in the country. In one country the typical distribution of equity shares for a subsidiary of an MNC wishing to operate in that country would be 51% with the multinational parent company, 25% with the families of important people, 15% with institutional investors and 9% with the public.

The shares can be issued with or without a quotation on the local stock market.

Local equity listing by subsidiary company
The advantages to a company of obtaining a listing are:

- with ownership shared with local investors investment risk can be reduced – the company is less likely to be discriminated against as a foreign company;
- it can overcome problems of restrictions on moving cash flow into and out of the host country;
- it can mean that less information needs to be disclosed in the host country. The subsidiary will need to meet local listing requirements, but this can mean the parent company needs to disclose less about group activities;
- it can be a source of finance, and if the group should one day wish to exit the host country it will be easier to find buyers if shares are listed.

Disadvantages

- When a subsidiary becomes a public company it cannot be managed in the same way as when it is wholly owned. For example, it would be more difficult to use transfer pricing to the advantage of the group.
- It will be necessary to demonstrate that significant decisions are made locally, not by the group headquarters. The MNC might lose control of the subsidiary.
- The interests of minority shareholders need to be taken into account. There will be local stock exchange rules on this point.
- It could lead to takeover of the subsidiary unless sufficient shares are still owned by the parent.

Movement of funds within a group

When setting up a subsidiary abroad, it needs to be remembered that at some future date it will probably be necessary to repatriate at least some of the funds to the parent. The cash could be needed to pay dividends or fund investments in the home country. The remittance could be in the form of dividends, royalties, interest, management fees, inflated transfer prices or loans. The incidence of tax on each of these ways of fund transference should be examined closely, as should the question of whether there is an absolute or proportional limit for each type of payment. When, finally, the exchange risk and any other legislative regulations about remittances have been taken into account, it will be possible to make decisions on such issues as from where in the group funds should be transferred and indeed who should own the new subsidiary. For example, suppose that the UK does not have a double taxation agreement with country X, but France, Holland or the Bahamas, say, does. A UK company which has a subsidiary in one of these latter countries may find it cheaper for that subsidiary to set up the new subsidiary in country X. Remitting its dividends, interest, etc., via the subsidiary in France, Holland or the Bahamas could be cheaper than remitting its earnings directly to the UK.

Royalties, fees and transfer prices for goods offer ways in which a company can control its flow of funds. They constitute payment for specific goods or services which do not always have an easily determined market value. They are pre-tax charges against profit which may or may not be the subject of withholding tax.

The intra-company transfer of funds is a very important part of multinational financial management. A multinational also aims to produce an optimal relationship between its monetary assets and monetary liabilities. Its assets and liabilities are in many different currencies, some hard, some soft, some within the group, some external. Wherever possible a company tries to have its assets in hard currencies and its liabilities in soft currencies in order to minimize the exchange risk.

The timing of the company transfer of funds is very important, and it can be achieved without the constraint of the legal onus of payment that a normal third-party debtor works under. For example, if devaluation is a possibility in the country where a subsidiary is based, or at least the spot price (in the currency to be paid) seems likely to decline, then the multinational can withhold payment to its subsidiary until such time as it feels it is advantageous to pay, or until the financial needs of the subsidiary cannot be satisfied by any cheaper means.

21.6 CURRENCY SWAPS

One way of obtaining borrowed funds in a foreign currency is by way of a currency swap. This involves the exchange of debt from one currency to another. Swaps comprise contracts to exchange cash flows relating to the debt obligations of the two counterparties to the agreement. Although swaps are contracts between the two parties, they do not alter the direct responsibilities that each party has for the debt obligation that it has personally incurred.

Let us assume that a well-respected UK company wants to borrow French francs, but is not well known in France. If there is a company in France that wishes to borrow pounds sterling but is unknown in the UK, there is the possibility of a swap. If the UK company borrowed in France it would have to pay a relatively high interest rate, reflecting its poor credit rating. Similarly, the French company would have to pay a relatively high interest rate on its borrowing in the UK. From an interest-rate point of view it is better if the French company borrows the francs and the UK company borrows the pounds sterling. The two companies then swap currencies and the payments related to them. The UK company pays the interest and eventually repays the French loan and vice versa.

The simplest method of servicing the loans would be for the UK company to pay the interest on the French franc loan and for the French company to pay the interest on the sterling loan. In fact, each counterparty is paying interest on the other's loans as if it were the borrower. They are both paying lower interest charges than if they themselves had borrowed the currencies they needed.

The French company has borrowed francs and the UK company has borrowed sterling. They swap the currencies, and the simplest basis of doing this is at the spot price at the time of making the deal. When it comes to repayment, the easiest method is for the UK company (that has been earning FF) to make the francs available to repay the loan. The French company has to repay in francs, and the UK company makes the appropriate amount of francs available to the French company. The French company makes the sterling available.

An example of a simple cross-currency swap is shown in Figure 21.1. The UK company wishes to finance a subsidiary in Germany. The German company wishes to have pounds sterling to invest. Both companies are better known in their own country than in the other country.

Under the agreement, the UK company contracts to pay the interest on the Deutschmark borrowing and the German company pays the interest on the sterling borrowing. The UK company passes on the proceeds of the sterling loan to the German company, which agrees to service the debt and repay the debt at the appropriate time. The companies agree in advance the appropriate exchange rates for the transactions.

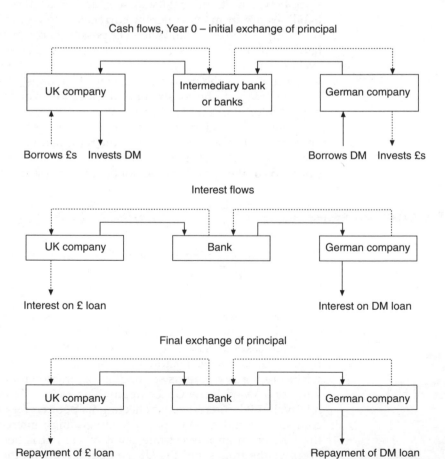

Figure 21.1

A currency swap can be constructed as a series of forward exchange contracts. If it reduces exposure it is a form of hedging. The term of currency swaps can vary. The swap document should clarify the rate of exchange that will be used. Normally one currency is recorded as the fixed principal amount, with an agreed rate of exchange for calculating the amounts in the second currency.

One of the objectives of the currency swap is to take advantage of lower interest rates; another objective is to restructure the currency base of a company's liabilities. If a UK-based multinational found that nearly all its borrowing were in sterling, it would become worried if the pound was becoming stronger against the currencies in which it was generating its earnings. Therefore it might attempt to swap some of its sterling debts into debts in other currencies. It would be attempting to reduce its risks due to exchange-rate exposure.

In restructuring the debts to balance its exchange-rate exposure, the company could also take the opportunity to alter the structure of its interest-rate liabilities. If many of its loans were at fixed interest rates and it was believed that interest rates would fall in the future, at the same time as swapping currencies it could move from fixed-rate obligations to floating-rate commitments. As implied above, we can have three types of currency swaps: a cross-currency fixed to floating; a cross-currency fixed to fixed; a cross-currency floating to floating.

Growth of the swap market

The reasons why a very large swap market has developed over recent years include:

1 Inconsistencies in the global debt market. A company can receive a different credit rating in one country from that it receives in another country. The company may be better known in one place than in the other.

There are differences in the abilities of individual companies to raise money in different financial centres. For example, some US companies might be highly rated in the US markets but are less well known and less well regarded in Europe. An interesting example of this occurred in connection with World Bank activities. The World Bank wished to borrow Deutschmarks and Swiss francs but found itself at a relative disadvantage in European markets. It could borrow easily and relatively cheaply in the large US dollar markets. These circumstances meant that the Bank became a counterparty to European companies which could borrow easily either in Swiss francs or Deutschmarks. The European company would borrow Deutschmarks, say, and make these available to the World Bank. The World Bank would borrow dollars and make them available to the European company.

2 Another important reason for the growth of the swap market occurred because of demand-side pressures. As part of treasury management many companies wanted to obtain a better, less risky, balance between fixed-interest and floating-interest debts, and between debts in one currency and those in another currency.

A variation on the above is a 'back-to-back' loan or what is sometimes called a 'credit swap'. This is a simultaneous spot and forward loan transaction between the company and a bank. Basically, the company lends a sum of money to the bank in the UK which converts it into the required foreign currency at the spot rate. The company's foreign subsidiary then draws on this loan from the bank's foreign office or the office of one of the banks in its consortium.

There are numerous permutations on this type of currency swap and back-to-back deal. Arbi-loans or international interest arbitrage financing is a variation on a currency swap. It is useful for a company operating in a country where interest rates are high and credit is tight. The scheme is for a subsidiary in a low-interest country to borrow the required amount and convert it at the spot rate into sterling, say, and then the UK parent signs the document promising to repay in the foreign currency at the end of the term. The parent then purchases a forward contract which will provide the right foreign currency for repayment at the repayment date. Therefore the lender, in addition to their promissory note, has the forward foreign-currency purchase contract which gives the lender additional security.

One variation on the currency swap theme is a *swaption*. This, as the name implies, integrates features of a swap with those of an option. It is referred to as a 'hybrid derivative product'.

The buyer of a swaption has the right to enter into a swap contract (a currency swap or an interest-rate swap) at any time within a specified period, at a rate of exchange and/or under terms agreed when the swaption deal is agreed. The buyer of the swaption has to pay to the writer of the contract an up-front premium.

These contracts are not available on the established option exchanges, but are available in the over-the-counter market.

21.7 COST OF CAPITAL

The first point to make is that it is difficult to calculate the cost of capital for a domestic project. It is even more difficult to calculate a figure for a foreign project. An estimate can, and should be made, but it is only an estimate.

There are a number of issues that need to be considered, these include:

- *Issue A*
  Should the decision to invest be based on cash flows that are free to be remitted to the parent company or on the project cash flows in the host country?
  Answer
  Parent-company cash flows should be the most important factor. The company will not normally undertake a project which is profitable in host-country terms, but which, because of remittance restrictions, tax or other problems, is unprofitable to the parent.
- *Issue B*
  Should the discount rate used for the parent-country analysis be the parent-company cost of capital?
  Answer
  It should be the parent-company cost of capital adjusted for certain factors.

The parent company will want a return on its equity investment in a project in a foreign country which is at least equal to its opportunity cost of capital. This opportunity cost for a multinational company will be based on the risk-free rate of return available in its home country plus a premium to cover risk. If the foreign project or subsidiary is in a developed country then the premium could well be similar to the premium in the home country. If the foreign subsidiary is in a developing country then the premium would probably be higher.

If the home country and the host country are similar, then the opportunity cost of equity could well be more or less the same in the two countries. This might be the situation if a UK company were investing in the USA. However, the point is being made that if a UK company was investing equity funds in, say, Thailand, then the opportunity cost of equity capital would be different between the two countries, and it is the UK cost (adjusted for risk) that would be used to evaluate the cash flows generated from the investment in Thailand.

- *Issue C*
  A related question is: should the cost of capital be calculated based on the capital gearing of the group or of the subsidiary undertaking the project?

Answer

It should be based on the capital structure of the overall group.

The gearing of a foreign subsidiary may be much higher than is considered normal in the home country. This could be because of subsidized loans provided by the host government in order to encourage foreign investment into the country. The MNC will wish to obtain the cheapest sources of finance available. But in calculating the cost of capital to use in a subsidiary, the subsidized finance should be allowed for, not by taking a distorted gearing ratio, but by allowing credit in the cash-flow calculations for the saving in interest costs. This can be achieved using the adjusted present value (APV) technique.

Another reason why a high gearing level of a subsidiary should not be used as a basis for a cost of capital calculation is because often the high level of borrowings is only obtained because of parent-company guarantees (explicit or implicit). The balance sheet of the subsidiary is therefore misleading. The borrowings have been obtained not on the strength of the subsidiary's asset base but on the strength of the group's assets.

Another reason why a foreign subsidiary may have a high level of gearing is because the equity of the subsidiary is not listed on the local stock exchange. It may not wish to raise local equity funds. The decision may have been reached to borrow as much as possible locally; this of course has foreign exchange advantages.

The MNC should aim to achieve an optimal capital structure on its consolidated operations. As explained above, the capital structure of a subsidiary may deviate from this overall optimum. It is the global capital structure that is important to creditors and investors in determining the financial strength of a company. It is also this global structure that should be used as a base for determining the cost of capital.

The MNC should not worry about its local debt–equity ratios. It should borrow wherever it can as cheaply as possible. However, it has to be aware of its consolidated position. So if it has high levels of gearing in some countries (for example, those offering interest-rate subsidies) it will need to have low levels of gearing in other countries.

- *Issue D*

  What are the factors that need to be taken into account when evaluating a foreign investment that make it different from evaluating a domestic investment?

  Answer

  1 Foreign exchange risk;
  2 political risk, ranging from loss of assets to restrictions on dividend remittances and on other forms of repatriating income;
  3 host-government subsidized loans;
  4 host-country levels of capital gearing;
  5 host-country tax incentives.

All these factors need to be allowed for in the investment appraisal exercise.

- *Issue E*

  Should these complex factors be allowed for by adjusting the discount rate or by adjusting the cash-flows?

  Answer

  There are at least two approaches to this problem:

  1 The simplest approach is to take the overall cost of capital of the group and add on a single premium, the size of which depends on where the project is to be located and the business risks of the project involved. For example, a UK company with a cost of capital in the UK of 20%, before

tax, might add on a 3% premium if it invests in Zambia and a 5% premium if it invests in Bosnia. The cash flows of the project are discounted by this simple risk-adjusted rate.

2 The above approach is theoretically incorrect. An alternative often suggested in the international finance literature is to make some adjustments for risk through the parent company's cost of capital and some adjustments through the cash-flows.

The adjustment to the parent company's cost of capital is to allow for the business risk associated with the project. The business risks involved in some business activities are greater than in others (e.g. a retail store versus a coal mine).

With foreign investment there is a major problem in deciding on the size of the risk premium to be added for business risk. It should be appreciated that it is only the systematic component of total risk that needs to be taken into account (based on the project beta). The risks of investing in foreign countries due to economic factors associated with individual countries can cancel themselves out. If a company invests in a number of countries, when some countries are doing badly others will be doing well. Following a diversification argument the business risks of a well diversified MNC are hopefully less than those of a company dependent on one country. The presence of international diversification could, therefore, other things being equal, reduce the cost of capital.

Having determined a suitable discount rate, all other factors that characterize an overseas project can be allowed for either by adjusting the cash flows or through employing sensitivity analysis. This means adopting the APV technique for evaluating foreign investment projects. The APV first calculates the value of the project as if it was all equity-financed, and then adds or deducts amounts from this value to allow for the actual method of financing the project.

It is particularly important to take the intricacies of the financing package into account for overseas projects. The decision on whether to go ahead with the project will depend on remittable cash flows, and these depend on the method of financing the project.

The factors to be allowed for in the cash flow calculations include:

1 different tax rates in home and host countries;
2 the contribution of the project to the borrowing capacity of the group;
3 the value of concessionary loans in foreign currencies (interest-rate subsidies).

The APV approach is based on calculating the PV as if the project were financed entirely by equity and then adjusting for these factors mentioned above. It can be expressed in an equation as:

$$\text{APV} = (-)\,\text{PV of cost investment outlay} + \text{PV of remittable cash flows}$$
$$+ \text{PV of interest tax shields} + \text{PV of subsidies on project}$$
$$+ \text{PV of effect of project on debt capacity of group}$$

Certain other factors affecting cash flow can be introduced to extend the equation. The different components in the equation may need to be discounted at different rates to reflect their different levels of risk. It is the remittable cash-flow stream that is discounted at the appropriate cost of equity capital.

It should be noted that we have not allowed for foreign exchange risk and political risk in the above APV equation. The reason is that these are probably best taken into account using sensitivity analysis. Questions such as 'What if exchange rates move against the home currency by 2% per annum more than expected?' or 'What if remittances cease after five years?' can best be handled by sensitivity analysis.

In fact, the overall impact on a group of companies of political risk and foreign exchange risk can also be reduced somewhat by diversification.

As mentioned at the beginning of this section, computing the cost of capital for an individual foreign investment is very difficult. There are still many unresolved issues. Usually the project will not have been repeated many times so it is difficult to estimate a risk premium to use in determining the equity cost. It is difficult to estimate a measure for systematic risk. In addition, decisions on hedging against exchange-rate risk and decisions on the management of political risk could affect the cost.

It is difficult to allow for such factors as political risk in a single discount figure. As suggested one approach to this problem is to undertake sensitivity analysis to determine the impact on cash flows of different levels of political interference at different times. An alternative approach is to take out insurance. Yet another approach is to ignore such risk, arguing that the company has a well-diversified international portfolio of investments.

- *Issue F*
  Should the decision whether or not to undertake the project be based solely on the cash flows free to be remitted to other companies in the group and the parent-company cost of capital?
  Answer
  The evaluation is a two-stage process – first, the cash flows in the host country, and then, the cash flows than can be remitted to the home country or other countries in which subsidiaries are based. In practice companies do take into account, in the decision-making process, the returns earned in the host country.

A company is judged in the short run by its reported earnings. In consolidated company accounts the earnings of all companies in a group are added together. A project undertaken by a foreign subsidiary can therefore either add to group profits or reduce group profits. Clearly the group would prefer the former. This is why the profitability or otherwise of the project in the host country is important.

It should be noted that the answer above is in terms of profitability in the host country. Profitability is not the same thing as cash flow. Profitability is important in the host country, and remittable cash flow is important to the parent company.

We will now consider a worked example. One approach to estimating the cost of capital is to use the CAPM model. Let us say a major MNC based in the UK is considering undertaking a large capital investment project in Indonesia. The MNC will invest equity. It will appraise the project using the APV approach.

It is necessary therefore to calculate the project cost of equity. The systematic risk beta of the project is estimated to be 1.625. This is not necessarily the same systematic risk measure as would be used on domestic projects; it reflects any additional business risk of investing in Indonesia. The risk-free rate of return available from investing the parent company's funds is 7%. The market expected rate of return on equity is 15%.

The CAPM model indicates the cost of equity on the Indonesian project is

$$7\% + (15\% - 7\%)\,1.625 = 20\%.$$

This is the discount rate that would be used to discount returns earned on the parent equity investment. In arriving at the cash-flow stream available to equity deductions would have been made for taxation (in home country and in Indonesia) and interest payments on debt. The cash-flow stream would have been converted into pounds sterling at the expected spot rates of exchange or possibly at agreed forward rates.

Using this cost with the APV approach means that the cash-flow stream would be adjusted to reflect the level of gearing. The cash benefits resulting from the tax shield on interest payments would be added to the cash flow from operations.

A UN study [1] published in 1994 highlighted how a small number of multi-national companies dominate the world economy. It was found that transnational corporations (TNCs) account for one-third of global output. This global network of TNCs consists of 37 000 parent companies who control 200 000 foreign affiliates.

Within these TNCs there is an elite group. The largest 100 (which includes 11 UK firms) controls about one-third of the world stock of foreign direct invest-ment. In the early years of the 1990s US companies were the largest foreign investors, with UK companies being second highest. Surprisingly Japan slipped from being first in the 1980s to fifth in the early 1990s. The USA was the biggest recipient of foreign direct investment.

Clearly many major investment decisions are made despite all the problems involved in estimating the cost of capital, forecasting future returns, and the risks associated with exchange-rate movements and political uncertainties.

Investment decision making, particularly involving foreign investments, is a mixture of strategic decision making and detailed financial analysis. From a strategic point of view the company first has to decide whether or not it wishes to become multinational. Having decided it does, it has to decide in which parts of the world it wishes to operate.

The cash flows that can be returned to the parent company have to be discounted at the opportunity cost of capital of the parent company. The multi-national company does not have to invest its funds in any particular country. It will only be tempted to do so if the returns that it can earn in that country, after taking account of risk, are at least as high as those that it can earn elsewhere.

Risk is a complicating factor. Investing in a foreign country is one form of diversification. It is quite likely that there will be low levels of correlation between cash flows on home investments and those from overseas investments. Investing internationally is therefore one way of reducing risk relative to the overall expected return. The investing company needs to consider whether the particular overseas investment is in fact a good form of diversification. From a financial point of view the decision on whether or not to invest in a particular project in a foreign country is based on exactly the same theory and techniques as a home-country investment decision. The cash flows need to be forecast and discounted at the appropriate rate. However, there are certain complications. Cash flows with international aspects will be affected by such factors as move-ments in exchange rates, the local financial arrangements for the project, the tax position in the host and home country, and repatriation policies.

The foreign investment decision is a two-stage process. The first stage is to ascertain whether or not the cash flows in the host country justify the project – this is the cash flow generated in the currency of the host country. The second stage is to determine whether the cash flow that is returned to the home country (or elsewhere in the group) justifies the cash invested from the home country. If, for example, a UK company moves funds from the UK to a subsidiary in Kenya, is the cash flow returned to the UK in the form of dividends, management fees, etc., sufficient to justify the outflow?

This second stage, as described, is based on the company undertaking the investment seeing itself as a UK company. It is ultimately judging its performance in terms of its group accounts produced in pounds sterling in the UK and on the impact of these results on shareholders. It could be argued, however, that if a company is truly multinational, it would not see itself in terms of its performance summarized in the currency of one country. It could be argued that many multi-nationals now have shareholders in many countries of the world. Companies such as Philips have far more of their shareholders outside Holland, the country in which the parent company is registered, than inside that country. In some cases, therefore, the 'home country' concept may no longer be relevant.

Although legally a multinational is registered in one country and needs to produce its group accounts in the currency of that country and according to the rules of that country, it might also produce alternative group accounts in the currency and according to the rules of other countries in which its shares are quoted. From a management point of view the company might therefore not be trying to maximize its performance in the country in which it is registered. It could be judging its performance in terms of its worldwide position, with a portfolio of assets valued in different countries and different currencies.

The conventional technique for analysing foreign-country investment decisions is still the two-stage process, however.

21.9 MANAGING FOREIGN EXCHANGE RISK

All companies are exposed to business risk. The cash flows of all companies will depend on economy-wide effects such as economic growth, changing tastes and changes in technology. All companies are also exposed to financial risks which depend upon how the company is financed.

Multinational businesses are exposed to two further types of risk; foreign exchange risk and political risk. Foreign exchange risk can be divided between transaction risk, accounting risk and economic risk. We have already considered transaction risk in Chapter 20 (the actual exchange of one currency to another) and shall now move to the other two exchange risks.

Accounting (translation) risk

Accounting exposure arises not as a result of conversion of currencies but as a result of financial data denominated in one currency needing to be expressed in terms of another currency. Such translation of currencies occurs at the end of each accounting year when the accounts of all subsidiaries have to be expressed in the currency of the parent company in order to present the consolidated accounts of the group. The important question that arises is at what rate of exchange the accounts should be translated. There are a number of possibilities, one being the rate of exchange at the balance-sheet date, another the rate of exchange at the time that the asset was acquired or the liability incurred and a third being the rate of exchange mid-way through the trading year.

To illustrate the problem, let us say that on 31 December 19X8 a UK company acquired the net assets of a French company. The assets in France were worth FF 1 000 000; the rate of exchange at the time was £1 = FF 10 so that the British company acquired net assets which it consolidates in its 19X8 accounts as being worth £100 000. Assume no changes take place in the French company during 19X9. The exchange rate at the end of 19X9 is £1 = FF 12.5. To prepare the consolidated accounts for 19X9, translating at the current rate of exchange now gives net assets worth only £80 000. The UK company has suffered because the French franc has fallen in value against the pound. The fall in value of the assets results either in a charge to the profit-and-loss account of £20 000 or a charge to the reserves of the company of this amount; it is the result of a loss on foreign-currency translation.

The company has not made a transaction loss; no conversion of French francs to pounds has taken place. The company may or may not have the intention of selling its French assets, which are of as much worth in 19X9 within France as when they were acquired (subject to depreciation). Nevertheless in this case adopting a closing-rate method of translation results in a book loss occurring. It might be argued it is not a real (cash) loss, but the net effect of it in the accounts is the same as if it were.

Clearly companies need to be aware of their accounting exposure and to try to minimize its impact. It should be noted in the above example that if, in 19X9, the French assets had been translated into pounds sterling at the rate of exchange at the date they were acquired no translation loss would have occurred. If a company adopts such a policy it is using what is called the 'temporal method'. Which method of translation is recommended by the accounting profession?

The possible translation methods are as follows.

1   *Current–non-current method*: generally, this translates current assets and liabilities at the current rate (at the date of the balance sheet) and non-current assets and liabilities at applicable historical rates.
2   *Monetary–non-monetary method*: generally, this refers to the translation of monetary assets and liabilities at the current rate and non-monetary assets and liabilities at applicable historical rates.
3   *Temporal method*: assets, liabilities, revenues and expenses are translated at the rate of exchange ruling at the date on which the amount recorded in the financial statements was established. At the balance-sheet date, any assets or liabilities that are carried at current values are retranslated at the closing rate.
4   *Closing-rate method*: assets and liabilities denominated in foreign currencies are translated using the closing rate. Revenue items are translated using either an average or the closing rate of exchange for the period.
5   *Net investment*: the net investment that a company has in a foreign enterprise is its effective equity stake and comprises its proportion of such a foreign enterprise's net assets; in appropriate circumstances, intra-group loans and other deferred balances may be regarded as part of the effective equity stake.
6   *Closing-rate–net investment method*: this recognizes that the investment of a company is in the net worth of its foreign enterprise rather than as a direct investment in the individual assets and liabilities of that enterprise. The amounts in the balance sheet of the foreign enterprise should be translated into the reporting currency of the investing company using the closing rate, i.e. the rate at the balance-sheet date. Exchange differences will arise if this rate differs from that at the previous balance-sheet date or at the date of any subsequent capital injection (or reduction) and should be dealt with in the reserves. Revenue items should be translated at an average rate for the year or closing rate. Where an average rate is used which differs from the closing rate, the difference should also be dealt with in the reserves.

The accounting profession has struggled in an attempt to achieve some degree of standardization in the translation method to be used by companies.

The latest accounting view on the subject is that the closing-rate–net investment method should normally be used. The different methods adopted for translation do affect the level of accounting exposure. Most companies however would not hedge to cover accounting exposure. The danger being that such a policy could result in book losses turning into actual cash losses.

Economic (operating) exposure

The economic value of an asset, or collection of assets, is based on the present value (PV) of the future cash flows that such assets will generate. This approach was discussed in Chapter 3. A company is an asset; therefore in theory its value as a going concern is the PV of its future cash flows. However, for a multinational company the question arises of the cash flows in which currency? The owner of an overseas subsidiary will usually wish at some time to be able to convert the cash flows generated in the host-country currency into home-country or some other currency. If the subsidiary company is to be sold locally, taking the cash out of the country will involve an exchange. If it is sold to another foreign company, the sale price will need to be in a hard currency. Therefore the value of the future cash flows is not just influenced by business risks, but also by exchange-rate risks. The value of the business at any time depends upon the future cash flows and the expected future exchange rates.

The net present value NPV_0 of the foreign investment at time zero is given by

$$NPV_0 = \frac{CF_1 \times ER_1}{1+i} + \frac{CF_2 \times ER_2}{(1+i)^2} + \ldots + \frac{CF_N \times ER_N}{(1+i)^N}$$

where CF is the expected cash flow in the host country, i is the appropriate cost of capital and ER denotes the exchange rate between the appropriate currencies.

It is one thing to expect the future cash flows in the host-country currency to show good growth, but if this is counterbalanced by movement of the expected value of the host-country currency against the home-country currency (or other hard currencies) then the PV of the investment is not necessarily increasing. Economic exposure represents the potential loss in the total value of a business due to exchange-rate movements. It should be noted that accounting exposure is concerned with book values and economic exposure with market values.

The actual level of economic exposure depends on the polices pursued by the company. The more independent the subsidiary the less influence the exchange rate has on its actual cash flow. If all its sales and purchases are in the domestic currency, then the exchange rate has less influence than if there is much inter-company trade. If the foreign subsidiary is financed mainly by local borrowing, then the level of economic exposure will be less than if it is financed by parent-company loans. Repayments of local borrowing (which affects the annual domestic cash flow) are not affected by movements in exchange rates, but repayments of foreign borrowing are. Other factors that can affect the operating cash flows and hence the economic exposure of a subsidiary include the following.

1 The export component of sales and the responsiveness of export sales to changes in exchange rates: if the subsidiary invoices in the currency of buyers, it clearly has a different impact from invoicing in home-country currencies.
2 If a host country devalues it could affect the overall level of economic activity within the host country and so affect sales levels.

The ways in which a company can manage its operation to minimize the effect of economic exposure include the following.

1 With inter-company accounts, if a devaluation is expected, speed up payments out of the currency to be devalued and delay payments into the devalued currency.
2 Increase debts to third parties in the currency prone to downward valuation – stretch suppliers' terms of credit.
3 Reduce receivables from third parties in the currency prone to downward valuation – temporarily reduce sales.
4 If the local currency is expected to depreciate against the parent company's currency, the policy should be to rely on as little equity from the parent as possible and as much local borrowing as possible. Decisions on such factors will affect the level of economic exposure.
5 The management of economic exposure can be through financial markets as well as through the operating policies of the parent and subsidiary. For

example, the value of a foreign subsidiary can be covered in the forward exchange market and the money market as illustrated in Chapter 20 on the subject of managing foreign exchange risk. However, it is more complex to cover for economic exposure than transaction exposure.

If the parent forecasts certain levels of cash flow but is worried about the exchange rate, it can lock into existing exchange rates through the forward market – if, of course, such a market exists in the currency being considered. Alternatively, if it knows that it will be receiving local currency over time, if it is permitted, it can borrow in the local currency and immediately convert the borrowed funds into its own currency at the spot rate. In future it can repay the borrowed money out of the local cash flow that it receives.

The problem is uncertainty about the actual cash flows that it will receive. With transaction exposure the amounts to be paid and received are known. With economic exposure they are based on estimates. If the company is wrong in its measures of future cash flows it is converting paper profits and losses into real exchange gains or losses.

21.10 Internal hedging techniques

The external techniques for hedging against transaction risks were dealt with in Chapter 20 on foreign exchange markets. There are in addition a number of steps an MNC can itself take to reduce the risk of foreign exchange loss. These are techniques which do not involve using the foreign exchange markets, the money markets or financial derivatives. They are techniques internal to the company. They include the following.

Netting

This is the principal method of internal hedging. It reduces the number of transactions that a multinational company needs to make in the foreign exchange markets and so reduces risk. It requires the company to structure its business in such a way that cash is managed centrally. Central management is being used in this context to mean that foreign currency flows between subsidiaries or overseas branches are grouped together so that all opportunities are taken to offset inflows and outflows in the same currency.

There is bilateral netting where the flows between two subsidiaries are netted to just one amount that needs to pass from one to the other. There is multilateral netting, which is more complex, and which results in just a few net transfers of cash, rather than a large number of bilateral settlements.

Bilateral netting occurs when a pair of subsidiaries net out their own positions with each other. There is no attempt to introduce the net positions of other group companies. Consider a US parent company which has two subsidiaries, one in Germany and one in the UK that have trade flows between them (as illustrated in Figure 21.2). The German subsidiary will invoice the UK subsidiary in Deutschmarks for the equivalent of US$100 000 at the end of the month. At the same time, the UK subsidiary is billing the German subsidiary in pounds sterling for the equivalent of US$180 000. Through the netting process, the German subsidiary would only owe the UK subsidiary the equivalent of US$80 000.

As seen in the above example, netting has reduced the number and the amount of the cross-border transactions and the related fees and commissions. Bilateral netting is fairly straightforward to operate as long as the participants can decide on the currency denomination of the net remittance and on a reconciliation and settlement schedule. A centralized control system is not necessary in this form of hedging.

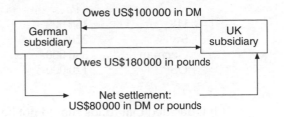

Figure 21.2
Bilateral netting

Multilateral netting, or inter-currency netting, can take place whenever affiliates both import from and export to companies within the same multinational company. All the payables are offset against all the receivables of the group, leaving the remaining net figures as the only items to be transferred (as illustrated in Figure 21.3). It reduces a series of cross-border fund flows to a bilateral flow between each subsidiary and the netting centre. In order to achieve successful implementation of the netting process, a netting centre is needed to co-ordinate participants' activities and to ensure that all subsidiaries are acting on the same predetermined schedule.

The calculation of the net flows (i.e. a summary of the first part of Figure 21.3) is as below (in US dollars):

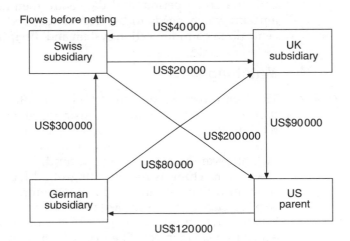

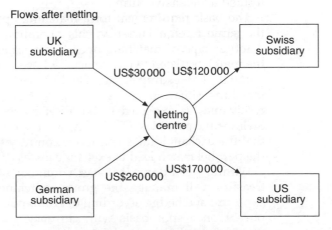

Figure 21.3
Multilateral netting

Amount of obligations offset:
(US$850 000 – US$290 000) = US$560 000 = 56%

Internal hedging techniques

	Pays	Receives	Net to/from centre
UK	130 000	100 000	−30 000
Swiss	220 000	340 000	+120 000
German	380 000	120 000	−260 000
US	120 000	290 000	+170 000
			0

If it is decided that funds should not be paid into a netting centre, an alternative approach is for one company to settle directly with another. The payment/receipts balances can be settled by just three transactions.

UK pays to Switzerland	$30 000
Germany pays to Switzerland	$90 000
Germany pays to USA	$170 000

Netting systems clearly reduce bank transfer charges and commissions. They can also assist a company in obtaining competitive foreign exchange quotes because of the centralized bargaining. They do not, however, reduce currency exposure up to the date at which the netting is performed.

An important aspect of a multilateral netting system is the collecting centrally of information. All subsidiaries must report all inter-company positions at the end of a given period, and the centre then advises the subsidiaries of the net amount which needs to be paid or received at a certain date. This requires a centralized communication system and discipline on the part of each subsidiary.

Matching

The terms 'netting' and 'matching' are often used interchangeably but in fact they are different. Netting, as illustrated above, refers to the netting out of *group* receipts and payments. It is typically used only for inter-company flows and as such is applicable only to the operations of a multinational company. In contrast, matching can be applied to both third-party and inter-company cash flows. In essence, matching is the offsetting of all receivables and payables by currency whether within a group or with other companies so that only the net exposure to each foreign currency is hedged externally or left exposed to exchange risk. Whether the company hedges the net position depends on its policy towards exposure management. The firm which seeks to maximize profit in the foreign exchange markets is termed an 'aggressive' firm: its counterpart which aims merely to minimize potential losses resulting from changed exchange rates is termed a 'defensive' firm.

The basic requirement for a matching operation is the two-way cash flow in the same foreign currency; this operation is regarded as 'natural' matching. Another type of matching operation is called 'parallel' matching; this involves the match between two currencies whose movements are expected to run closely parallel. For example, the Deutschmark and Swiss franc. In the 'parallel' matching situation, gains in one currency, say appreciation of Deutschmark receivables, is expected to be offset by losses in another, say appreciation of Swiss franc payables. Obviously, with parallel matching there is always the risk that the exchange rates will move contrary to expectations, so that both sides of the parallel match lead to exchange losses or gains.

Within a company that has a number of subsidiaries, typically, the central treasury will manage the group matching. The centre can identify the net exposure and hedge according to group policy. Individual group companies deal purely on a spot basis with currency gains and losses attributable to each subsidiary being booked into inter-company accounts and settled on, say, an annual basis.

Alternatively the central treasury can be a clearing centre which facilitates a reduction in currency conversions by the group either by having subsidiary cash flows pass through a common set of different currency accounts, or by assuming responsibility for all external currency cash flows.

Leading and lagging

Leading and lagging is the process of adjusting the timing of payments and receipts. 'Leading' refers to making payments early while 'lagging' involves delaying payment. This is a technique which can be used with cash flows internal to the group or external. It can easily be applied to intra-company transactions. In third-party trade, there is a clear conflict of interest between seller and buyer if flows are lagged.

Multilateral netting systems usually incorporate a facility to permit leading and lagging of inter-company payments. This allows for the possibility of group companies with cash surpluses helping reduce the need for short-term financing of fellow group companies which are cash-poor. Besides, inter-company leading and lagging can be used as part of either a risk-minimizing strategy, or an aggressive strategy to maximize expected exchange gains. In either case, a central treasury is usually required to ensure that the timing of inter-company settlements is effective from a group's point of view rather than a purely local one. The centre may also co-ordinate inter-company interest charges where lagging has caused additional costs at an operating unit.

There are many benefits of using the leading and lagging technique. For example, leading and lagging is a useful tool for shifting inter-company funds for the purpose of liquidity management. It also facilitates the use of netting and matching. It allows fine-tuning of group tax management in the way that it takes advantage of different tax rates in different countries. It means that if the currency of a creditor is expected to fall in value, lagging the payment will reduce the real cost.

Multicurrency reinvoicing centre

Foreign exchange exposure can be transferred from a sales subsidiary by a change of the inter-company billing arrangements. This can be accomplished by a replacement of a specific currency as the billing currency for inter-company transactions with the currencies, in which the individual sales subsidiaries bill their customers. Therefore, the sales subsidiaries are no longer involved in currency conversions. This is achieved by using a centre that receives one currency from the selling subsidiary and pays the manufacturing subsidiary in another currency. The centre is concerned with currency and with the transfer price.

The actual inter-company transfer prices can be in a base currency, usually the parent company's currency. But with billings to outside companies made in a variety of currencies, a centre is needed for the adjustment of the transfer prices in the individual currencies for significant exchange-rate movements and to ensure that all sales subsidiaries are supplied at essentially identical transfer prices. In most cases, the transfer price is arrived at by using a current exchange rate which may be the spot or a forward rate. The transfer prices are adjusted after a period of time.

Reinvoicing is a well-known and widely used technique for the centralization of currency exposures. Under reinvoicing, the manufacturing subsidiaries ship directly to the sales subsidiaries but bill to a separate entity, the reinvoicing company. The reinvoicing company bills the sales subsidiaries in turn (as illustrated in Figure 21.4). As a result, the currency-conversion exposure is now concentrated in the reinvoicing company. Usually the reinvoicing company operates in a low-tax location.

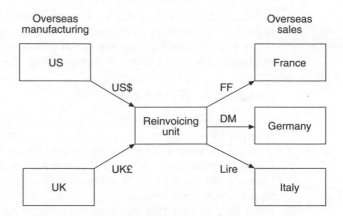

Figure 21.4
Reinvoicing

21.11 POLITICAL RISK

There are a number of ways in which the host government of a country can interfere with the operations of a company. These range from non-discriminatory interference to wealth deprivation.

1 Non-discriminatory interference is usually comparatively mild and might be aimed at all companies in a country, not just those that are foreign-owned. It would include interfering in transfer pricing arrangements and making the host-country currency not freely convertible.
2 Discriminatory interference is the next step up. It is aimed at foreign firms and includes insisting on joint ventures, with a certain percentage of the shares in the company to be held by nationals. It also includes special taxes on the profits of foreign-owned firms or on dividend and interest remittances.
3 Discriminatory sanctions are more serious than the previous level of interference. They are not outright nationalization or indigenization, but they make it so difficult for the multinational to operate profitably that it might decide to close down. The sanctions would include ending the right to remit profits.
4 Wealth deprivation is the takeover of the multinational, with or without compensation.

The multinational can take certain steps to prevent or minimize the effect of such interference. Management strategies can be divided between those taken prior to making the investment, the operating strategies and those to be followed after the event. One step in the management of such risks is to try to anticipate them. Forecasting political interference is part of any multinational company's investment planning exercise. This has to take place prior to the decision to move into a country, and must continue after moving in so as to be able to anticipate any changes.

Prior to undertaking the investment the company should negotiate to try to obtain the best terms possible from the host government. What terms can be obtained depend of course on the strength of the government and its political attitudes. Prior to investment the arrangements should be settled with regard to such items as remittance of dividends, management fees, transfer prices, access to host-country capital markets and provisions for local equity participation. Another possible pre-investment strategy might be planned disinvestment. This should make it clear to the host government how it will benefit from the investment in the short and long run. It might also be possible to obtain investment insurance.

The operating strategies to minimize political risk would cover such issues as local supply of goods and materials, the location of the investment, the control of transportation arrangements, the control of marketing, including brand names, methods of financing the subsidiaries using local banks and selling shares in the host-country, labour policy, employment, promotion and management contracts. Decisions can be taken on each of these issues which could increase or reduce the possibility of host-government interference.

21.12 INTERNATIONAL TAXATION

Taxation should not be relegated to one chapter in a book. Taxation affects all major decisions of a company:

- organizational structure;
- capital investment;
- sources of finance;
- management of cash;
- transfer pricing;
- calculation of profits.

Companies naturally pursue their own self-interest. They wish to minimize their tax bill. MNCs have more opportunities than domestic companies to be able to do so. Domestic taxation is complicated, international tax is even more difficult. There are many ways in which an MNC can organize its affairs so as to reduce its total tax bill. Before looking at such methods, we will briefly explain certain principles of international taxation.

Taxation of profits

A company is usually taxed in the country where it is established (registered). If the company is a subsidiary of a foreign company, then in addition to the host-country taxation, there *may* be additional taxes to pay in the home country of the parent company. The home country of the parent could tax the worldwide profits. If the host country is reluctant to see funds leave its country, it may levy a withholding tax (in addition to the profits tax) on dividends, interest and perhaps royalties sent out of the country.

The tax authorities in the home country of the parent will usually allow a credit for tax paid on profits earned in foreign countries. (This can be set against any tax the home country might charge against the foreign-subsidiary profits.) It may also delay (defer) charging home-country taxation until remittances are actually returned to the home country.

It should be appreciated that there are significant differences between the taxation policies of different countries; some host countries are keen to attract foreign companies and will have generous tax allowances to encourage inward direct investment. The extremes are tax havens, which may have zero profits tax and no withholding tax.

The policies of the home countries of multinationals can also vary. What is described above is the system of taxing companies on their total worldwide income (but possibly allowing tax credits and tax deferral). This is the tax system in the UK, the USA and Germany.

An alternative policy for the home countries of multinationals (one adopted in Belgium, the Netherlands, Italy and Australia) is only to tax profits earned in the home country by the parent. Profits earned by subsidiaries resident in foreign countries (even if remitted to the parent) are only taxed in the host country.

Tax neutrality

The UK principle, as explained above, is that an MNC is taxed in the home country of the parent on its worldwide income. A question that arises is: should the company be taxed on this worldwide income at the tax rate that would have been paid if all the income had been earned domestically? One can either have this so-called 'domestic' neutrality or what is called 'foreign' neutrality.

Foreign-tax neutrality means the profits are taxed at the rate that applies to the country in which the company earns the income (no additional home-country taxes being levied). Companies would usually prefer this approach as they argue that it means they compete on equal terms with the companies in countries in which they operate. The most usual approach in practice is domestic neutrality with concessions.

Double-taxation treaties

This is concerned with the taxation position on cross-border activities. If, for example, a payment, say dividends or interest, is made by a company in one country to a company in another country, the source-of-income country authorities may wish to tax the money before it leaves their country. The receiving country may also wish to fully tax the income received. This could result in the income transferred being taxed twice. To eliminate this, many countries enter into double-taxation agreements.

There are two ways in which the double-tax problem is overcome. One way is to adopt a version of the 'foreign neutrality' principle and the receiving country does not tax the income received (if it has already been taxed in the source country). The second approach is where the receiving country gives a credit against domestic tax for the amount of tax paid in the foreign country. A double-tax treaty between two countries can also lead to lower rates of withholding tax on payments between the two countries, than on payments between two countries with no treaty.

Branch versus subsidiary

Whether or not a commercial activity in a country is subject to local taxes is also an issue dealt with in double-taxation agreements. The usual practice is not to tax locally an enterprise unless it has established a permanent presence. The selling of goods or just providing services to local residents is not a form of permanent establishment. The setting up of a branch or subsidiary is a permanent establishment. The way in which a company is taxed in the countries in which it operates will affect how it organizes its foreign operations.

The tax treatment of a branch usually differs from that of a subsidiary. The profits of both will usually be taxed at the same rate, but the profits of the branch when remitted to the head office will not incur withholding tax. The payment of dividends of a subsidiary to its parent company will be subject to withholding tax.

Losses of a foreign subsidiary cannot usually be used to offset profits of a parent company.

If a foreign operation is expected to make losses for a number of years it could be advantageous to the MNC to set the activity up as a branch so that the negative earnings abroad may be used to offset profits at home. Both UK and US tax laws allow foreign-branch income to be consolidated in this way. If an MNC expects to earn income from its foreign activities which it intends not to repatriate, then there may be tax advantages in setting up a foreign subsidiary. As explained, unlike branches, foreign subsidiaries of UK and US parent companies do not pay taxes in their respective home countries until the income is repatriated.

Foreign-tax credits

Double taxation could arise if the host country and the home country both taxed the earnings of multinational companies at domestic rates of tax. To avoid this problem it is usual for the home country to allow its MNCs to claim the amount of tax paid in foreign countries as a credit against home-country tax.

Example 21.1

Rowington PLC has an operating subsidiary located in Turkey which pays dividends to the parent company in the UK. Suppose that corporate tax rates in Turkey are 50% and there Is a 10% withholding tax. The Turkish subsidiary earns 1000 million lira and the exchange rate is 50 lira equals £1 We will calculate the after-tax dividend (in pounds) received by Rowington.

Solution

		(*million*)
Before-tax earnings	Lira	1000
(50 lira = £1)		£20
Turkish corporation tax paid (50%)		£10
After-tax earnings		10
Withholding tax (10%)		1
After-tax dividend received		9
UK tax on Turkish profits (30%)		£6.60
Tax paid in Turkey		£11.00
Foreign-tax credit		
(used)		£6.6
(unused)		£4.4

In the UK foreign-tax credits must be taken source by source. This means that it would not be possible in the above example to use the £4.40 million credit to reduce tax on profits earned by a subsidiary in another country. In contrast, the USA allows unused credit to be pooled; it can also be carried back two years or carried forward five years. In the UK the treatment of credits is not so generous.

Tax deferral

Countries differ in the way their tax authorities treat the foreign earnings of their multinational companies. The differences include the way they treat tax deferral. This is a method for granting credit to the MNC for taxes paid to host-country tax authorities on foreign earnings.

The choice for the home country is basically between taxing foreign earnings when they are earned or when they are remitted to the home country. In the UK, the home-country MNCs are usually asked to pay UK tax only when the earnings are remitted to the UK in the form of dividends and interest. The same is the situation with US-based MNCs and the payment of US tax.

The same treatment applies to chargeable gains on the disposal of foreign assets. UK tax is only payable on the actual amounts received in the UK.

The MNC earns profits in a particular country: it pays tax on those profits in the host country. As mentioned above, with home-country tax neutrality, there may be additional taxes to pay in the parent country. However, the payment of these additional taxes may be delayed. The additional taxes will only have to be paid on foreign-source income remitted to the parent country.

This deferral is in fact only relevant if the taxation rates in the host country are less than those in the parent country. In the Rowington example above, more tax was paid in Turkey than needed to be paid in the UK. If the profits had not been repatriated, there would have been no advantage from tax deferral.

Tax-haven affiliates

As mentioned above, tax payment can be deferred on income earned until the time it is remitted to the parent country. Some tax will usually have been paid, of course, in the country where the profits were earned. It is any additional tax that is deferred. If the profits of the subsidiary are remitted to a tax-haven affiliate it will not be subject to additional parent-country tax. A typical company structure is therefore as shown in Figure 21.5.

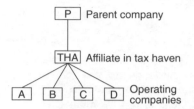

Figure 21.5

All transfers of funds, whether dividends, interest, royalties or management fees are channelled to the tax-haven affiliate. The additional parent-country tax can be delayed, perhaps postponed indefinitely, if the finance is first pooled in the tax-haven subsidiary, and then channelled to subsidiaries as and when needed.

Transfer pricing

Tax authorities do have rules to determine what is an acceptable transfer price. Companies are not completely free to set their own transfer prices simply with the object of reducing group tax bills. The rules are however not perfect and there is some disagreement between the tax authorities in different countries on what is acceptable. The rules tend to be based on accepting a transfer price based on what would be the market price in a deal between two independent companies at arm's length. Other factors looked at by some tax authorities include what would be a company's normal profit mark-up on items produced and sold to third parties.

Example 21.2

Let us suppose a parent company (P) has two subsidiaries one in a high-tax country (H) and the other in a low-tax country (L). The reporting currency of the group is dinars. The tax rates are as follows:

	P	H	L
Corporation tax	30%	50%	20%
Withholding fax	10%	10%	0%

Subsidiary L manufactures components and exports them to subsidiary H. The subsidiaries are involved in many other activities but for the purpose of this example we are only interested in the taxation impact of this inter-company trade. In one year L sells 1 000 000 units to H at a transfer price of D 20 per unit. L's cost per unit is equivalent to D 15. Subsidiary H undertakes certain work on the components and then sells them all to customers at a price equivalent to D 40 per unit. H's add-on costs are equivalent to D 10 per unit.

Both subsidiaries remit all their profits to the parent company at the end of each year. The tax authorities in the home country adopt a policy of domestic neutrality.

The earnings and tax position of the two subsidiaries is as below:

	L(000s)	H(000s)
Sales	20 000	40 000
Costs	15 000	30 000
Profits	5 000	10 000
Corporation tax	1 000	5 000
Dividend	4 000	5 000
Withholding tax	0	500
Dividend received by parent	4 000	4 500

The tax position of the parent company on transactions concerned with these two particular transfers is:

	L (000s)	H (000s)		L (000s)	H (000s)
Earnings	5000	10 000	Sales	25 000	40 000
Tax at domestic rates	1500	3 000	Costs	15 000	35 000
Maximum tax credits				10 000	5 000
available (paid in host country)	1000	5 500	Corporation tax	2 000	2 500
Tax credits used	1000	3 000		8 000	2 500
Tax paid in home country	500	0	Dividends	8 000	2 500
Total tax paid on earnings			Withholding tax	0	250
in home and host country	1500	5 500	Dividend received by parent	8 000	2 250

As can be seen, there is an unused possible tax credit from the subsidiary in the high-tax country.

If a different transfer price had been used the total tax bill of the group could have been reduced. We will now assume the transfer price of the components is D 25 per unit. All other costs remain the same.

The tax position of the two subsidiaries is now:

The tax position of the parent is:

	L (000s)	H (000s)
Earnings	10 000	5000
Tax at domestic rates	3 000	1500
Maximum tax credits available	2 000	2750
Tax credits used	2 000	1500
Tax paid in home country	1 000	0
Total tax paid	3 000	2750

The total tax bill of the group is now D 5750 as opposed to D 7000 under the previous transfer pricing arrangements.

The management of taxation

Having considered certain of the basics regarding international taxation we will now examine briefly some of the techniques and opportunities available to the MNC to help minimize its tax bill.

1 Establish cost centres (subsidiaries) in high-tax countries. These provide sufficient expenses to ensure that net taxable profits are not earned. Research and development centres should be set up in high-tax countries as opposed to low-tax countries.

2 Locate subsidiaries earning high profits in, or channel gains and other income through, countries with low taxes.

3 Locate a finance subsidiary in an offshore financial centre (tax haven). This issue will be dealt with separately below.

4 Adopt transfer pricing policies such that low profits are recorded as being incurred in high-tax countries and high profits in low-tax countries. An intermediary country can be used to purchase the goods from the producing country at a low price (near cost) and then to sell these at a high price to the ultimate destination. This is called 're-exporting'. Most of the profits are shown as being earned in the intermediary country, which is one chosen because of low taxes.

5 Take advantage of tax holidays, and other tax incentives on new investments offered by some countries.

6 Raise debt in countries with high tax rates in which the company is earning profits on other activities.

7 *Dividend mixer company*
This is a company set up in an offshore financial centre with the object of being able to influence the timing of, and source of, flows of dividends and interest to the parent company. The objective is to pay the lowest possible level of total tax. High rates of dividends can be channelled into the mixer company from high-tax-rate subsidiaries such that the tax

credits resulting in the home country compensate for the planned lower dividends received by the mixer company from subsidiaries in countries with low tax rates.

8 *Dividend cleaner company*

Dividend cleaner companies are another mechanism by which MNCs can manage tax liabilities in their home country. Dividend cleaning companies have the objective of maximizing the opportunities for double-tax relief from foreign subsidiaries before the tax charges on the income of the UK parent are determined. If cleaning companies did not exist there may be an insufficient UK tax charge to be covered by double-tax relief. This might result from the parent company incurring trading losses.

In some instances the double-tax relief of the dividend cleaning company may not be exactly comparable to the tax liability on the dividend income. In this case the cleaning company can transfer to the parent company the exact amount of group relief necessary to eliminate the tax charge without producing excess double-tax relief.

9 *Intermediate holding companies*

Dividends from foreign subsidiaries are sometimes channelled through intermediate holding companies who accumulate the funds. The intermediate company would retain dividends from subsidiaries in low-tax countries. The intermediate company would plan to take advantage of tax treaties in order to reduce withholding taxes. This form of tax planning is, however, subject to anti-avoidance tax legislation in both the UK and the USA.

10 *Co-ordination centres*

MNCs have been attracted by the tax-efficient features offered by certain countries to set up financial subsidiaries. Such features includes:

- favourable tax laws;
- no exchange controls;
- low capital taxes;
- good banking infrastructure;
- good tax treaty network.

In this context, Belgium, Luxembourg, the Netherlands and Switzerland have become popular with European MNCs for the location of financial subsidiaries. Belgium in particular has become very popular since major tax incentives were provided for MNCs which centred their co-ordination activities in Belgium. This legislation allows MNCs to establish centres designed to meet their own financial needs. Such centres are permitted to carry out a variety of financial and managerial services on a virtually tax-free basis.

11 *Currency management centres*

Given the complexity of the subject of foreign exchange dealings, most companies set up a currency management centre so that currency transactions can be controlled in ways which are tax-efficient. There are sometimes problems convincing tax authorities that such centres outside the normal operating territories are legitimate business ventures. The centres are established in favourable locations from a tax point of view.

12 *Fronting loans*

On occasions when a company wishes to move funds from a subsidiary in one country to a subsidiary in another, use may be made of an intermediary commercial bank. The government of the country to receive the inflow of funds may not regard a straight transfer from one subsidiary to another as an arm's-length transaction, and so not be willing to allow the interest to be paid on the loan as fully tax-deductible. There may alternatively be the possibility that the government of the country receiving the loan for political reasons will interfere to prevent the repayment of the inter-company loan.

A solution is for the subsidiary with the funds (say based in a tax haven) to deposit them in a bank, and to receive interest of say 7%. The bank then lends these funds to the subsidiary that needs them, charging say 8%. From the receiving country's point of view the funds are a loan from a bank, tax-deductible, therefore bringing down the cost of the debt after tax to say 6% (= 8%(1−t), where t = 25%). The group overall therefore receives interest of 7% on the funds (with no tax payable) and only pays 6%. The bank benefits. There is also less danger of political interference with the repayment of the loan to a large commercial bank.

13 *Insurance companies*

Many large multinational businesses have their own 'captive' insurance companies. There may be advantages in locating these in tax havens. The premiums paid may be tax-deductible in the country from where the payment is made, and the profits generated in the tax haven chargeable at low or zero rates.

Offshore financial centres (tax havens)

The name 'offshore financial centre' (OFC) is in fact a misnomer. The centre does not need to be off any shore. Two of the best-known OFCs are Luxembourg and Liechtenstein, which are both well away from any sea. Other centres are, however, islands, for example the Cayman Islands, Bermuda, the Isle of Man, the Channel Islands and Gibraltar.

OFCs are also known as tax havens for obvious reasons. Some have zero levels of corporation tax (Bahamas and the Cayman Islands), others very low levels of corporation tax (the Channel Islands 20%, and Hong Kong 16.5%). Most have zero levels of withholding tax, which is one of their particular attractions to MNCs. They can be used to collect and distribute dividends and interest without having tax deducted.

The demand to have OFCs established arises from the needs of companies, investors and politicians. The reasons include the following.

1 For companies to use as a base for financial subsidiaries: they can issue bonds from such centres, and pay interest around the world without having withholding tax deducted. They can be used as a centre for banking within a group of companies.

2. *Secrecy.* The money of investors and companies can be hidden away: it is very difficult for foreign authorities to find out who owns what. This secrecy is needed with transactions for illegal purposes such as capital flight, smuggling, fraud, money laundering and tax evasion.

3 Low rates of income tax, corporation tax and capital gains tax payable.

4 Used by investors to buy and sell shares – avoiding regulations, such as insider trading rules, and other security laws.

5 Used by governments to support undercover activities, such as supplying arms to freedom fighters (or rebels). Also for bribery purposes.

The reason why there is a 'supply' of OFCs is:

1 It is beneficial for the country that is the OFC, generating income, creating employment.

2 Countries differ in what is considered acceptable behaviour. What is criminal activity in one country might not be against the law in another. Secrecy is seen as a virtue in some countries and a cause for concern in other countries.

Conditions necessary for a country to be an OFC:

- secrecy and lack of disclosure requirements;
- low rates of taxation;
- absence of foreign exchange control;
- freedom from international regulations and agreements;
- international banking separated from local commercial banking;
- political stability;
- good communications system.

Money laundering

It has been estimated that approximately 20% of the money that is moved around the world is secret money. This can arise in the following ways.

1 Individuals place money in secret bank accounts to avoid tax or public criticism.
2 Companies and governments wish to have 'slush funds' that they can use to pay for certain services or assistance. They would rather not have such payments known about.
3 Criminal money that is the result of illegal activities. Fraud and drug dealing are well-known examples. Before money that is obtained from crime can be spent it needs to be laundered. That is, it needs to be made clean. This is necessary because if an individual was seen to be enjoying a very expensive life style, and there was no obvious way in which they obtained this money, they would arouse suspicion. The tax authorities would be interested in the source of the income, as would the police.

Businesses in which receipts are in a cash form, and in which the level of activity is not obvious are vehicles through which money to be laundered can be channelled. Many criminal organizations now employ accountants, lawyers and bankers who are experts on the subject of international finance. The money can be quickly moved around the world through different bank accounts, so that it is very difficult to establish how the money was initially earned.

The top criminals' organizations cannot spend all the money they generate, so they become investors in legitimate companies. Financial centres, such as London and Frankfurt, are centres where illegally acquired money is invested in equities and bonds of legitimate companies. Criminal groups are becoming stronger.

The criminal groups make use of nominee names, multiple bank accounts, back-to-back loans and cross guarantees. Very often the movement of funds gained from illegal activities involves cross-border transactions. Although the police authorities and other anti-crime organizations co-operate across borders there can be difficulties. For example, there are practices which are illegal in some countries but not in others, a case being insider dealing.

21.13 REFERENCES

1 UNCTAD (1994) *World Investment Report*, United Nations.

21.14 FURTHER READING

In Chapter 20 a number of books were listed in the further reading section. These are books on international financial management and so are relevant to this chapter. Other books and articles that are helpful are:

Euromoney (1992) *The 1992 Guide to Offshore Financial Centres*, Euromoney Publications, London.

Fatemi, A.F. (1984) Shareholder benefits from corporate international diversification, *Journal of Finance*, December.

Lee, C.K. and Kwok, C. (1988) Multinational corporations v. domestic corporations: international environmental factors and determinants of capital studies, *Journal of International Business Studies*, Summer.

21.15 PROBLEMS

1 Describe and discuss the advantages and disadvantages of the internal hedging techniques available to avoid foreign exchange exposure.

2 The degree of political risk experienced in foreign direct investment projects is determined solely by sovereign government action and is therefore impossible to predict. The best policy for the multinational company is to diversify its interests geographically and hope that the worst does not happen. Discuss.

3 Describe the main features of the Eurocurrency, Eurobond and Euroequity markets.

4 What factors might be important to the financial manager of a multinational company when deciding whether to borrow funds on the domestic bond market or the Eurocurrency or Eurobond markets.

5 A large British company is seeking to obtain 300 million US dollars for a two-year period. The finance director is pondering four alternatives.

(a) A $300m Eurobond issue at a fixed rate of interest of 6% p.a.

(b) A £200m bond issued in London at a fixed rate of 8% p.a. The principal would be exchanged into $300 in the foreign exchange market at the current spot rate of $1.50/£ and at the end of the two years exchanged back at the two-year forward rate and the proceeds used to help redeem the bond issue.

(c) A £200m bond issue at a fixed rate of 8% p.a. swapped into dollars. Under the terms of the swap, the £200m would be lent to the counterparty in exchange for $300m lent to the company. During the two-year term of the swap, the company would pay the counterparty 5% p.a. on the $300m and receive 7.5% p.a. on the £200m. The interest received by the company would be used to pay most of the interest on the bonds. At the end of the two years the company would repay $300m and receive £200m from the counterparty which it would use to redeem bonds.

(d) Seeking a quotation on the New York Stock Exchange, and selling to US investors sufficient equity share to raise the $300 million.

Required:

You are asked to explain to a financially unaware director the way in which each of the alternatives works commenting on the advantages and disadvantages of each of the methods. Discuss which alternative is likely to be the least expensive method and why. (You are *not* required to carry out detailed calculations).

6 In 1995 a French company plans to invest in Thailand to develop a local subsidiary. The company needs to borrow 20 million Thai baht. It can only borrow in Thailand at a fixed rate of interest of 10% per annum.

A Thai company that wishes to invest in France has offered to lend to the French company the required amount of baht funds at a fixed rate of 8%. In return the French company would be required to make available to the Thai company 5 million French francs at a floating rate of interest of LIBOR (on FF) plus 1%.

The swap deal would be for a three-year period. The current rate of exchange is 4 baht = 1 FF. The current LIBOR interest rate on the FF is 7%. The interest rates and exchange rates are not expected to change during the first year of the proposed swap deal.

In the second year of the swap, the French company expects the LIBOR rate on FF to fall by $\frac{1}{2}$% and the exchange rate to be 4.10 baht each to 1 FF.

In the third year is it thought the interest rate on the FF will fall by a further $\frac{1}{2}$% and the exchange rate to be 4.20 baht equal to 1 FF. In fact, there is a currency crisis in Thailand, and by the end of 1997 (the time for concluding the swap deal) the rate of exchange is 6 baht equal 1 FF.

Required:
(a) Show by means of boxes the expected cash flows between the companies.
(b) Taking into account the expected exchange-rate movements, is the proposed swap in the interests of the French company?
(c) What would be the risks to the French company if the Thai counterparty was to go into liquidation during the third year of the swap period?
(d) Taking into account the actual exchange rates would the deal be in the interests of the French company?

7 A UK company (Francis PLC) has a subsidiary in country XYZ. The subsidiary has been financed with £2 million of equity funds and £4 million of loan funds. The equity shares are all owned by the UK parent. One half of the loan finance has been provided by a local bank in XYZ, and the other half by a subsidiary of Francis PLC which is registered in the Cayman Islands.

In 1996 the subsidiary in XYZ made profits (after paying royalties of £250 000 to Francis PLC) before tax and interest of £1 million. The interest rate on all the loans is 10%. The corporation tax rate in XYZ is 20%, and there is a withholding tax which applies on royalties, interest and dividends of 10%. Royalties are tax-deductible in XYZ but are subject to withholding tax.

There is a double taxation agreement between the UK and XYZ, which reduces the withholding tax rate between the two countries to 5%.

The corporation tax rate in the UK is 33%. There is zero tax in the Cayman Islands. Francis PLC have a policy of paying a dividend (gross) equal to 50% of profits available for distribution (that is, after interest and corporation tax, but before withholding tax) and reinvesting the remaining funds in the host country.

Required:
(a) What is the total worldwide tax paid by Francis PLC?   (40% of the marks)
(b) How much tax is paid in each country?   (10% of the marks)
(c) How is the £1 million of profits divided between
   (i)   the different tax authorities
   (ii) banks; and
   (iii) Francis PLC and its subsidiaries?   (25% of the marks)

8 Debois SA, a French multinational company, has subsidiaries in the United Kingdom and Germany.

The UK subsidiary produces components that are transferred to Germany for final production.

The components are sold by the UK subsidiary to the German subsidiary for a unit price of 144 French francs, with annual sales of 125 000 units. Total production expenses are 80% of the sales price. The finished goods are sold in the German market for the equivalent of 350 French francs, yielding a taxable profit per unit in Germany of the equivalent to 70 French francs.

Tax rates are as follows:

	France	UK	Germany
Corporate tax on profits	33.3%	25%	40%
Withholding tax on dividends	10%	–	8%

Bilateral double tax treaties exist between each of the countries which allow credit for foreign tax paid against any domestic tax liability.

It is the policy of Debois to annually remit all profit from foreign subsidiaries to the parent company in the form of dividends.

Required:

(a) Illustrate how the tax liability of Debois SA might be reduced by a 20% increase in the transfer price between the UK and German subsidiaries.

(6 marks)

(b) Discuss briefly the possible practical problems of such a change in transfer price.

(4 marks)

(10 marks)

ACCA, Dec. 1995

22 MERGERS AND ACQUISITIONS

LEARNING OUTCOMES

By the end of this chapter, the reader will:

- understand the motives for one company purchasing another company, or merging with another company
- appreciate the tactics that can be adopted when seeking to acquire another company
- appreciate the defensive tactics that can be adopted by the target company
- be aware that not all parties involved benefit from the merger and acquisition process
- have been introduced to the concept of a strategic alliance

The valuation of a company which is an integral party of any merger or acquisition has already been discussed in Chapter 6.

22.1 INTRODUCTION

There is a great deal of interest in the subject of mergers and takeovers. It is an area of corporate finance that attracts much publicity. The media, including even the 'popular' press, give considerable coverage to the large takeover battles. The financial community, the investment bankers and others are involved with tactics, and receive large financial rewards for their own involvement whether their client companies win or lose. The managers and workers in the companies involved await the outcome of the bid with concern.

Academics and other researchers are fascinated by the subject, as there are so many questions about mergers and takeovers that remain unanswered. These questions include the following.

1   If the stock market is efficient, why is it that bidding companies are prepared to pay such a high premium above the pre-bid share price in order to obtain control?
2   Do mergers and takeovers lead to an increase in efficiency and profitability?
3   If mergers and takeovers do lead to gains, who is it that benefits from them: the shareholders, the managers, the workers in the acquiring company or the workers in the victim company?
4   Are there waves of mergers over time and, if so, why do they occur? What are they associated with?
5   What are the motives of those involved in mergers and takeovers? What are they hoping to achieve as a result of bringing companies together?

These and other questions are considered in this chapter. In Section 22.1 we con-

504   *Mergers and acquisitions*

sider the level of merger and takeover activity. The number of mergers appears to vary from one period to another. Why is this? In Sections 22.2 and 22.3 we examine the motives for mergers and takeovers. Why does one group of managers attempt to obtain control of the assets of another company? There are many reasons that can be put forward to justify a merger. Indeed, with every merger and takeover what appears to be a rational justification is advanced by those representing the bidding company. However, in contested takeover bids those representing the defending company put forward reasons why the acquisition would not be rational.

A merger or a takeover

In this chapter the terms 'merger' and 'takeover' are used interchangeably. This is because in many instances it is not clear whether one or the other is occurring. However, for certain purposes it is necessary to distinguish between the two forms of business combination.

When two or more companies come together under common ownership, this is referred to as a 'business combination'. Not all combinations are similar in nature. For business, legal and accounting purposes it is sometimes necessary to differentiate between the forms of combination.

At the extremes, it is easy to decide what is a merger and what is a takeover. When two companies of approximately equal size come together, with the shareholders and directors of the two companies supporting the idea of the combination and continuing to have an interest in the combined business, it is a merger. However, when a large company makes a cash bid for the shares of a smaller company, the directors of the small company advise their shareholders not to sell but the shares are sold anyway and neither the pre-bid shareholders nor the directors of the purchased company have any continuing interest in the enlarged business, it is clearly an acquisition or takeover.

In the first situation, what is known as 'merger accounting' is considered to be appropriate, and in the second situation the acquisition accounting method would be used. Unfortunately, few cases are as clear-cut as the two described.

With the merger accounting approach, the purchase of shares in one company by another is seen as the coming together of two businesses, the creation of a single group. The emphasis is on the continuity of ownership, the continuing interest in the business of both sets of shareholders. In the USA this is referred to as a 'pooling of interests'.

With the acquisition accounting approach one business is seen as having been purchased by the other just as if a set of assets and liabilities had been purchased, with the previous owners – the selling shareholders – giving up their interest in the business. This approach stresses the lack of continuity of ownership, with one group of shareholders ceasing to have an interest and the other group taking over their interests. This is a takeover.

The main differences resulting from the two accounting techniques arise over the treatment of (1) goodwill, (2) the value of the shares exchanged and (3) any pre-acquisition profits. Ignoring possible complications, the differences can be summarized as follows.

1 Acquisition: goodwill must be disclosed if acquired.
   Merger: as no real change in ownership occurs, the merger should produce consolidated accounts that do no more than combine the existing balance sheets, i.e. assets remain at the value at which they appear in the separate company accounts and goodwill is not recognized since none is effectively acquired.
2 Acquisition: shares issued to acquire another company are recorded at market value.

Merger:	shares issued to acquire another company earned prior to the acquisition are recorded at nominal value, i.e. no share premium is recognized.
3 Acquisition:	the undistributed profits of any acquired company earned prior to the acquisition are frozen and are not normally available for distribution by the group.
Merger:	the reserves of each company are merged, i.e. those that were distributable before the merger may be distributable after the merger.

The differences in the accounting treatment are therefore important and significant.

22.2 MERGER AND TAKEOVER ACTIVITY

Undoubtedly there are some periods in which there is more merger and takeover activity than in others. One takeover wave in the UK occurred in the 1960s, another in the early 1970s and another in the 1980s. There were similar waves in earlier periods.

What are the economic factors that explain the patterns? Why do these waves occur? One explanation for one of the booms, that of the 1960s, was that 'conglomerate' mergers became fashionable. One popular explanation for the late 1980s boom was that UK industry was preparing itself for the single European market in 1992, but a similar boom has occurred in the USA where the same motive would not apply. These are one-off explanations given to explain individual waves of activity.

There are a number of theories of mergers which attempt to offer a general explanation for these waves of activity. One of the most commonly cited theories is that mergers are associated with booms and slumps in the economy and in stock market prices. A number of studies have provided evidence that movements in economic activity, interest rates and securities prices are positively related to merger activity.

One basis for the theory is that at certain times shareholders have differing opinions as to the true value of a share because of imperfections in the information available and how it is assessed. These differences are greater at times of dramatic change such as rapid movements in share prices, changes in technology and changes in the relative price of energy. This is referred to as the 'economic disturbance theory of mergers' [1].

One recent study based on US data found a strong positive relationship between the level of what is known as Tobin's q and the level of merger activity. This would support the economic disturbance theory. Tobin's q will be considered more fully in the next section. It is a measure of the difference between the stock market value of a company and the replacement value of its assets. It indicates whether the company can be purchased at a bargain price.

The theories of merger waves being associated with periods of high economic performance remains unproven, and indeed the justification for the theory does not seem strong. The 1980s were a time of a sluggish economy and a depressed stock market, and yet of great takeover activity. The stock market collapse of 1987 did not halt activity. In the first quarter after the collapse takeovers were greater than in any quarter in 1987. In fact, when we go on to examine the motives for individual mergers, for example to remove inefficient management or to avoid bankruptcy, these reasons are as valid during times of poor economic performance as during boom periods.

Therefore there are no agreed reasons why each of the individual motives

Mergers and acquisitions

should lead many companies to act in a particular way during one period rather than another. There is much debate on these points but no agreed conclusions. For example, it has been argued that when the stock market booms, the price of some shares lags behind their true value, perhaps because of less financially aware managers, and these companies are good takeover targets. However, if the stock market is efficient this should not happen.

We still do not understand the economic forces underlying the pattern of merger activity. There is some support for the economic disturbance theory, with slumps as well as booms leading to activity. In fact, the reasons for the 'waves' may not be economic but behavioural. The 1990s have seen a modest level of merger and takeover activity.

It should be appreciated that not all mergers and acquisitions are contested. Often the companies involved are in agreement; the coming together is friendly.

The level of merger and takeover activity varies from country to country. In the UK and the USA, this so-called market for corporate control is very important. The stock markets in these two economies are very active, and if shareholders of a company are unhappy with that company's performance they will usually 'vote with their feet' by selling the shares they own. They walk away from the problem and leave it for new management to sort out. This is the 'external control' system of corporate governance.

In contrast, in Germany and Japan takeover battles fought out through the stock market are extremely rare. If a company is inefficient, the necessary corporate restructuring will be arranged quietly by the major shareholders of the companies involved. Usually the banks, the interlocking shareholders and inter-locking directors will come to an arrangement. It will be a quiet affair. The interested parties will vote with their voice, not just walk away.

The system discussed in this chapter relates to the situation in the UK and the USA.

Cross-border merger and acquisition

With the move to globalization in business, and the move to a single market in Europe there has been a big increase in cross-border takeover activity. The move towards larger trading blocks has meant that some of the barriers to cross-border acquisitions have been removed, but not all.

Barriers still include:

1 The method of corporate control. In Germany, the banks own shares, sit on supervisory boards, and control the proxy votes of many shareholders. It is difficult, therefore, for a takeover to succeed without bank support.
2 In some countries the principle of one share, one vote does not apply. The system exists where one shareholder, however many shares he or she owns, has a limit to the percentage of the total votes they can control. A shareholder may own 50% of the shares but only have 15% of the votes.
3 Bearer shares, which are very common on the Continent, mean that it is very difficult for the bidding company to contact existing shareholders. There is no list of registered shareholders that the target company has to make available to the bidding company. The message has to be passed through newspapers.
4 In some countries the employees of the target company have more say in the takeover situation than in the UK. In Germany employees are on super-visory boards, in France they can attend board meetings, and in the Netherlands their support for the takeover is required by law.
5 In some countries managers can defend the company against a takeover bid without consulting shareholders.

If the European Union is to create a single market some degree of harmonization on these and other matters will be required.

Studies have shown that cross-border acquisitions have a higher chance of being unsuccessful than acquisitions within a single country. Some studies have put the success rate in cross-border mergers as little more than 50:50. One reason for this relatively low success rate is that action taken in the period immediately following an acquisition is crucial to its success, and post-acquisition integration is more difficult with companies from different business cultures.

22.3 MOTIVES FOR INDIVIDUAL ACQUISITIONS

The first point that should be made is of course the obvious one that it is not a company that decides to merge with another or to attempt to take over another. It is the managers of the companies, the top directors, who make the decision. These decision makers should be acting in their shareholders' interests. In this section we shall look at situations in which a merger or takeover can benefit the shareholders. In Section 22.3 we shall consider the managers' own position in a merger situation, because this is not always identical with that of the shareholders.

One company, X, would wish to merge with or take over another company, Y, if it believes either that the two firms together are worth more than the value of the two firms apart or that it can purchase company Y at a price below the present value of its future cash flow in the hands of new management.

The first of these two explanations is referred to as 'synergy'. This is usually expressed by the relationship $2 + 2 = 5$. It refers to the combining of complementary resources, and implies that using the resources of the two firms together increases total value. The combined firms increase the potential for growth and profit. It makes possible the greater utilization of each firm's relative advantage. The financial theory of mergers and takeovers would indicate that a merger or takeover would be justified if

$$PV_{XY} = PV_X + PV_Y + gain$$

We shall now consider the economic theories and business situations that would indicate the situations in which gains from mergers and takeovers could occur.

Economies of scale

This topic is well covered in the literature. Economies of scale can arise in the production process, where larger machines produce at a lower cost per unit than smaller machines. They can arise in marketing, with advertising costs for example. They can arise in distribution, where fleets of vehicles and large warehouses can bring down the cost per unit of transport and storage. They can arise in finance where administrative costs per unit raised are less with large issues of finance than with small.

Internalization of transactions

This can occur in the case of vertical integration. Such integration can either be backwards with the acquisition of firms that supply raw materials or earlier stages of production, or forwards with the acquisition of firms nearer the selling of the product. Its importance is that it eliminates transaction costs when firms have to deal with each other at arm's length. It certainly reduces the uncertainty of supply and having to deal with a firm that may have considerable bargaining

Mergers and acquisitions

power in the short run. It may result in cost savings because dealings between divisions or companies within a group may be more efficient than dealings conducted at arm's length between two independent businesses. This has to be balanced with the possible extra costs resulting from lack of competition between suppliers.

Market power

The Office of Fair Trading, which is interested in mergers that might reduce competition, states that two-thirds of the acquisitions that they investigate involve horizontal integration. 'Horizontal' means that the firms concerned are in the same stage of the production process; a merger or takeover leads to control of a larger share of output in a particular market. It could lead to economies of scale with the new combination operating fewer and more efficient plants. However, the coming together of two such firms by definition increases concentration. This is attractive to the firms, as it has been shown that the higher the level of concentration in an industry, the greater is the level of profits. However, it reduces consumer choice; hence the interest of the Office of Fair Trading.

Entry into new markets and into new industries

Acquisitions often provide the quickest way of entry into new markets and new industries. Entry into areas where the expanding firm initially lacks the right know-how or, say, an adequate distribution system will be both risky and costly. Because growth through acquisition is rapid, it can provide almost immediately the necessary critical size for a firm to become an effective or even formidable competitor.

The single market place in the EU provides opportunities for companies to expand, but also creates threats to a company's market share as foreign competitors move in. This has led to a certain amount of so-called rationalization, and consequently to mergers and takeovers. It has been argued that it is necessary to increase the size of the organization to cope with the larger market.

Elimination of inefficient and misguided managements

Inefficient managements can exist for a limited period of time, but over the longer period, if the market is efficient, they will be identified and the market mechanism should ensure that they are replaced. It might not simply be that the firm is badly managed, rather that the interests of the managers are different from those of the shareholders. This is referred to as the 'agency problem'. Managers only owning a small percentage of shares can tend to pursue perquisites. The costs of these are passed on indirectly to shareholders. This can be seen as a misdirection of resources.

Takeovers serve as a control mechanism that limits the departure by managers from the maximization of their shareholders' wealth. If the managers of company Y are inefficient or neglect their shareholders' interests, then the managers of another company (say X) might well make a takeover bid for company Y. The managers of X may need to persuade their shareholders that if they managed the assets of company Y then returns would be greater than at present. Therefore it is worth company X offering a higher price than the current market price for the shares of Y. To avoid this possibility, with the probable loss of their jobs, the managers of company Y will need to look after their shareholders' interests and will need to utilize the assets efficiently.

Free cash flow and trapped equity

Jensen [2] has suggested that managers with cash flows in excess of that required to finance new investments within the firm will use them to finance acquisitions. If profitable organic growth opportunities (within the firm) are limited, then rather than return the surplus funds to the shareholders the managers would prefer to acquire other firms. In this way the managers keep control of the funds, whereas to return them to shareholders means that they lose control.

Another motive for using these 'surplus' funds for acquisition purposes might be based on shareholders' interests and not simply on a wish of managers to control larger corporate 'empires'. King [3] has shown that the tax system in the UK can influence the level of acquisitions. Two ways to provide benefits to the shareholders from the cash 'trapped in the company' are share re-purchases and acquisitions. Share re-purchases have been permitted in the UK since 1985. If capital gains taxes are less than income tax on dividend income, then the share-holder would prefer cash to be used to make acquisitions or to re-purchase shares, leading to gains in share prices rather than to receipt of the cash as dividends.

If money distributed to shareholders as dividend, rather than being reinvested, suffers an additional tax burden, then again it may be in the shareholders' interest for the funds to be used for investment. This is known as the 'trapped equity theory'. According to the theory, if free cash flow is used to purchase another company the stock market value of the shareholders' investment will increase more than their wealth would increase if the 'surplus' funds were to be returned to them. The evidence does not provide strong support for this model.

Undervalued shares?

It might be thought that the companies taken over are less efficient, i.e. those wasting valuable scarce resources. One difficulty in this approach is deciding in practice which firms are inefficient. Unfortunately, accounting profits are not necessarily good guides. One reason for an acquisition can arise when the stock market is underestimating the real value of a company. If the company is not too conscious of its stock market valuation, and its stock market price is low in relation to its potential, it is an ideal victim for a takeover bid. The purchaser may be of the opposite type: keenly conscious of its stock market valuation, which it is anxious to keep high, and always reporting to show the best short-term position. A merger or takeover between two such companies does not automatically result in real gains for the economy. The point being made is that the victims in takeovers and mergers are not necessarily the firms failing to make the best use of their resources. The victims could be firms using their assets to their best advantage, but their stock market price does not reflect the true value of the company, perhaps because of lack of knowledge.

A question that can be asked is: if the stock market is efficient, how can a company's share be undervalued? The definition of efficiency is that the stock market price fully reflects all available information. This was discussed in Chapter 8.

It has been found that the UK and US stock markets are to some extent efficient in that most prices reflect publicly available information. However, this does not mean that there are not undervalued companies. It has not been found that share prices reflect all privately available information. There are certain types of investors who can make excess profits through trading in the market. It has been shown that security analysts have superior information on companies, and if used properly this can give them above-average returns [4]. Again it has been shown that 'insiders' have superior knowledge and one company can have inside information about another.

It must be recognized that it is perfectly possible to find a company's shares correctly priced or even overpriced, with the current expectations of future returns, and for it still to be a good purchase for a takeover bidder. If the prospective purchaser can use the assets of the company, including the management, more profitably, then it may be prepared to purchase shares which in terms of present market knowledge are classed as overpriced. In bidding this price higher than might be expected, the purchasing company is showing a more optimistic view of the future, perhaps based on expectations of its own ability to manage the new subsidiary.

It can be argued that any company is worth purchasing if it can be obtained at a 'bargain' price. One indication of a 'bargain' can be obtained by comparing the price paid for the company with the value of the assets obtained. If the assets are to be continued in use in the combined business for the same purposes, then it is the replacement costs that give the relevant value; if the assets are to be sold by the combined business, then it is the realizable value.

Use of high price-to-earnings ratios – bootstrapping

This particular motive for acquiring other companies was of considerable importance during the conglomerate merger boom. If one company possesses a high stock-market rating relative to the other company, it is able to purchase on advantageous terms. The conglomerate companies were making use of their high stock-market ratings. As soon as their share price fell they were not in such a strong position to take over other companies.

The reason can be seen in the following simple example. If a potential acquisition is valued at £10000 and the present market price of the purchaser's shares is £5, then 2000 shares will have to be exchanged to take over the company. If the market price falls to £2.50, then 4000 shares will have to be transferred. It is obviously better for the existing shareholders of the purchasing firm to acquire the new assets by exchanging the smaller number of shares.

The key to the position of the shareholders lies in the earnings per share. The stock market attaches considerable importance to this variable. As can be seen in the following example, it is possible for a company to increase its earnings per share, not by the normal manufacturing, trading and selling cycle, but simply by purchasing companies. Assume that two companies, A and B, each have 1000 shares outstanding. The relevant financial details are as follows.

	Company A	Company B
Total earnings	£250	£250
Earnings per share	£0.25	£0.25
Share price	£4	£2.50
Price-to-earnings ratio	16:1	10:1

The reason that company A commands a higher price-to-earnings ratio than company B is because it is assumed to have greater growth prospects. Company A purchases company B. The market value of company B is £2500 (1000 shares at £2.50); 625 shares of company A will need to be offered in exchange. The position of company A after the purchase is as follows.

Total earnings	£500
Number of shares	1625
Earnings per share	£0.3077

The earnings per share have increased, purely because of the purchase of company B. If the stock market keeps the same price-to-earnings ratio for the company as it had before the purchase, the share price will be £4.92, showing a gain for the shareholders of company A. The wealth of the shareholders of company B will have increased. Before the merger they held 1000 shares priced at

£2.50 each, a value of £2500. After the merger they hold 625 shares priced at £4.92 each, a value of £3077. This is because they now hold shares in a company with higher growth prospects. This technique is sometimes known as 'bootstrapping'.

This example is an extreme case in which the stock market keeps the same price-to-earnings ratio for the company after the purchase as it had before. One justification for this course of action could be that the management of the purchasing firm is expected to use its abilities to achieve a similar growth rate on the assets of the purchased company as they are expected to achieve on their own assets.

Risk diversification

The rationale for conglomerate-type acquisitions and mergers is said to be diversification, which will lead to a more stable cash flow. Firms in different industries experience different levels of profitability and cash flow during the various periods of an economy's booms and slumps. Therefore bringing together firms in different industries, which is the result of conglomerate mergers and takeovers, could reduce the volatility of the combined cash flow. From a company's point of view this reduces risk.

It has been argued that the more stable earnings of the company appeal to lenders, leading to lower borrowing costs or even increased debt capacity.

The advantages to equity shareholders are less clear. If the shareholders want diversification they can achieve this through diversifying the investments in their own portfolio. The theory of portfolio management deals with investors reducing their own risks; they do not need companies to do it for them. This is certainly the case with other than small investors. In the context of the capital-asset pricing model covered in Chapter 11, diversification *per se* would not increase shareholder wealth or reduce risk because investors are assumed to hold fully diversified portfolios. However, as discussed below, managers could benefit from a reduction in the variability of a firm's cash flow. There is considerable disagreement in the literature on whether diversification by a company does reduce shareholders' risk.

The case for mergers and takeovers of the conglomerate type is far from clear. As a result of a generally poor performance by such groups over the last two decades, using diversification as an argument for justifying an acquisition has fallen from favour.

22.4 MANAGEMENT MOTIVES

In the traditional theory of mergers and takeovers discussed above it is assumed that one company (the bidding company) seeks to acquire the shares of another company (the target company). This is, of course, the technical position. However, it is not the shareholders of the bidding company that initiate the move and actually make the bid to purchase the shares of the target company. It is the managers, the directors of the bidding company, that are seeking to acquire the shares on their shareholders' behalf.

In other words, it is the managers of the bidding company who seek to appeal to the shareholders of the target company. They make an offer to the target company's shareholders, with or without the agreement of the target company's managers. Jensen and Ruback [5] refer to the takeover market as a market for corporate control in which alternative managerial teams compete for the rights to manage corporate resources. This is a shift from the traditional view. With this approach it is managers who are the primary activists, with shareholders playing a relatively passive role.

Of course, the shareholders have the final say. It is the target company's shareholders who, through their decision on whether or not to accept the offer, finally decide whether the takeover bid is successful. The bidding company's shareholders, although not consulted about individual bids, can decide whether on balance the managers are acting in their own interests or the shareholders' interests and, if they feel that it is necessary, can remove managers and directors.

The bidding company's managers cannot diverge too much from the shareholder-wealth maximization model, but they can and do take their own interests into account. One group who, on average, benefit from a successful takeover bid is the management team of the bidding firm. They finish up managing a larger business which gives them increased status and higher remuneration. One group who, on average, lose in a successful takeover is the management team of the victim firm. They therefore have a vested interest in fighting a takeover bid. If they act in their own interests they will contest the bid, whether or not it is in the interest of their own company's shareholders.

These points will be returned to later in this chapter. The point being made here is that managers' motives have to be taken into account when considering takeovers and mergers. It is not simply the division of gains between one group of shareholders and another.

One management motive might be survival (increased job security). Managers, unlike shareholders, cannot diversify to spread their risks. They are tied to one company. If that company is taken over, the managers have a high probability of losing their jobs. By acquiring other companies, the business that they operate becomes larger and so they themselves become less likely to be victims of takeovers. With conglomerate mergers, the risk diversification benefits the managers, increasing their security. However, as explained, the theory of portfolio analysis suggests that conglomerate mergers to reduce risk are not in the shareholders' interests.

We have already suggested that the private interests of managers can take precedence over the interests of their shareholders. For example, when managers of target firms decide to fight a takeover, they are not always doing so in the shareholders' interests. 'Golden parachute' contracts compensating managers who are displaced can be provided for in the event of a takeover. These are in their own interests, and not necessarily those of shareholders, as they may accept a bid rather than fight knowing that they will receive compensation if displaced.

Other management motives include:

- empire building;
- increased levels of remuneration, the level received being related to the size of company managed.

22.5 TAKEOVER TACTICS

The rules

The rules to be followed are both self-regulatory and statutory. First we shall consider the self-regulating rules of the City. These are detailed rules that have to be followed by both the bidding company and the target company at the time of a takeover bid. They are given in what is known as 'The City Code on Takeovers and Mergers'.

These rules were introduced to protect shareholders, and they have to be frequently modified as new bidding and defence practices are brought to light. For example, it became known after the Guinness–Argyll–Distillers takeover battle that the directors of Distillers, the target company, had agreed to cover the costs of a bid from Guinness, who were initially seen as a 'white knight', a rival bidder against the initial bid from Argyll. When this became known after the takeover battle, the Code was altered to prevent such 'poison pill' tactics happening again without the approval of the target-company shareholders. It was a poison pill because if Argyll had been successful it was something they would have had to swallow; they would have not only had to pay their own costs but also those of their rival bidder.

The Code does not have the force of law, but those who wish to operate through the securities market have to follow it. The Code is administered and enforced by the Panel on Takeovers and Mergers, a body representative of those using the securities markets. It applies to listed companies; it is also relevant to unlisted public companies but not to private companies. The Panel's role is to act as a referee in a takeover and merger situation and in particular to ensure that all shareholders are treated fairly.

We now turn to the legal rules which consist of some provisions in the Companies Act, the Fair Trading Act and the Monopolies and Mergers Act.

An Office of Fair Trading was established in 1973, with a Director of Fair Trading as its head. It is the Director's job to keep himself informed about prospective mergers and acquisitions and to advise the Secretary of State for Trade and Industry whether a proposed merger should be investigated by the Monopolies Commission. When a merger or acquisition is referred, the Commission have up to six months to conduct their investigation. They then report to the Secretary of State on whether or not they consider that the merger operates against the public interest. If they find that it *is* against the public interest, the Secretary of State can prohibit the merger or acquisition or can impose conditions that have to be met before it can go ahead.

In making a recommendation to the Secretary of State the Monopolies Commission does not have to find that the combined companies will be beneficial in order to give it their blessing; they only need to find that it does not operate against the public interest. In the Monopolies Commission report on the Scottish and Newcastle Breweries–Matthew Brown proposed merger it was stated: 'We discern no material advantages to the public interest arising from the proposed merger, but the question before us is whether the merger may be expected to operate against the public interest and in our view there are no sufficient grounds for such an expectation.'

Bidding tactics

Financial advisers

The services of an investment bank (merchant bank) are necessary. They may be used to help draw up a shortlist of target companies. Prior to this the acquisition objectives should have been settled; for example, is a niche business required or a company in a similar line of business? The bank will help arrange finance and advise on tactics.

It may be that a firm of accountants are also employed as advisers. They would help in valuing the target company. In large acquisitions the advisers might include stock brokers and public relations firms.

The purchase price

For an acquisition to be a success, it is necessary not to pay too high a price. The bidding company should have in mind a 'walk-away price'. Above this, the acquisition is not worthwhile. This price is based on the existing value plus the possible gains from synergy. It has to be remembered that there is a tendency to overestimate such gains.

The objective is to make an offer to the shareholders of the target company that is attractive, but at the least cost to the purchasing company. If the target company is listed on a stock market, a 'toe hold' may have already been made, some shares in the target company having been purchased by the investment banker or the bidding company.

Almost always the bidding firm does have to offer a premium: this is the difference between the value of the cash or securities being offered and the pre-merger market price of the target company. Empirical studies have shown that the size of the premium with the final offer can vary from 20% to over 100% of the pre-merger market price. The average premium with successful bids is in the region of 50%, although with contested takeover bids a premium of this level can be unsuccessful.

The Companies Act requires any person who acquires an interest of 5% or more of the voting share capital of a listed company to notify the company of that fact within five days of acquiring the interest. This disclosure requirement is necessary in order to enable a target company to know who it is who is buying its shares, and to give it advance notice of a possible takeover raid. These requirements became necessary in the 1960s and 1970s when there were a number of takeovers where the target company had been kept in ignorance of who it was behind significant changes in the ownership of its shares until it was too late for it to be able to act.

Market raids

Market raids arise when a person or company acts with such speed in buying the shares of a target company that the 'raider' has achieved their objective before they are required to notify the company of their acquisition. 'Dawn raids' are market raids that take place in the minutes or hours immediately after the stock market has opened.

What is unfair about such a market raid is that the high price is not being offered to all the shareholders of the target company. It is only the large institutional shareholders easily in touch with the brokers who can benefit from the early offer. By the time that the smaller shareholders, the private individuals, find out about the purchaser, the offer has closed. There is not equality in the treatment of shareholders.

In 1981 and 1982 the City Code was revised to strengthen the restrictions on acquisitions prior to the announcement of an offer. The rules now state that where 'any person acquires, whether by a series of transactions over a period of time or not, shares which [taken together with shares held or acquired by persons acting in concert with him or her] carry 30% or more of the voting rights of a company … such person shall extend the offer to any other holders of the voting shares'. This offer price must be not less than the highest price paid for the shares within the preceding 12 months. The offer must include a cash alternative.

In summary, if a person or persons acting in concert purchases 5% or more of the shares of a company they have to notify the company. They can continue to purchase shares in the market and are not required to make an offer for all the shares until their shareholding reaches 30%. When they do make an offer, if they have purchased 15% or more of shares within the offer period or within 12 months prior to the offer, then the offer price should be not less than the highest price paid for such shares during the offer period and within the 12 months prior to its commencement. A similar rule regarding paying the highest price applies if the offeror holds 30% or more of the voting rights at the time of making the bid.

Concert parties

A 'concert party' occurs where several persons act in concert to buy shares in a particular company. They do so in such a way that no one individual owns or has an interest in more than 5% and so individually becomes liable to notify the target company of this shareholding. The provision applies to all public companies whether or not their shares are listed on the Stock Exchange. The disclosure requirements extend to groups of persons acting together – in concert – who in aggregate have interests exceeding the 5% level. The City Code requires all persons with notifiable interests to disclose any relevant event not later than 12 noon on the dealing day following any such event.

The offer

When intending to make an offer, notice of the fact should in the first instance be communicated to the board of the company to be acquired or to its advisers. When this board receives notice that an offer is to be made, they must immediately inform the shareholders of their company by press notice, and following this they must send a copy of the notice or a circular dealing with the matter to each of the shareholders. The offer document should normally be posted within 28 days of the announcement of the terms of the offer. The acquiring company, therefore, first announces its intention to make an offer disclosing its terms and, then, within a certain number of days, posts the offer to each of the shareholders of the offeree company. The board of the offeree company must circulate its views on the offer to its shareholders as soon as possible after the dispatch of the offer document.

When the offer is announced, the terms of the offer and the identity of the offeror must be disclosed. The offeror must also disclose any existing shareholding that it has in the company that it wishes to acquire. It must also disclose any shareholding over which it has control or which is owned or controlled by any company or person acting in concert with the offeror.

An offer must initially be open for at least 21 days after the posting of the offer. If it is revised, it must be kept open for at least 14 days from the date of posting a notice of the revision of the offer. No offer shall become unconditional as to acceptances after the 60th day following the posting of the offer. After an offer has been declared unconditional as to acceptances, the offer must remain open for acceptances for not less than 14 days. After that date, the offer will have expired.

'Unconditional' means that the shareholders of the offeree company must now either 'take it or leave it': no better offer is to follow. The offer can only become unconditional when the offeror has acquired, or agreed to acquire by the close of the offer, shares carrying over 50% of the voting equity shares. Making the offer unconditional means in effect that the bidder has won: they have now obtained control of the offeree, and the shareholders who have not already sold to them should either do so within the next few days before the offer has expired or keep their shares and become minority shareholders in the company.

No offer which, if accepted in full, would result in the offeror having voting control of the company shall be made unless it is the condition of such an offer that it will not become unconditional unless the offeror has acquired or agreed to acquire shares carrying over 50% of the votes. After the offer has expired or it has become unconditional or it is revised, the offeror shall announce the position with respect to the offer, namely what percentage of acceptances have been received.

Failing to acquire all the shares

The usual takeover tactics are for the bidder to purchase some of the target company's shares in the market before making a formal offer. They then make an offer and hope to obtain acceptances in sufficient numbers to give them ownership of more than 50% of the shares. The offer must initially be open for at least 21 days after its posting, and the bidder is hoping to be able to announce within that 21 days that they own shares and have acceptances that together take them above the 50% figure. They then declare the offer unconditional. Prior to this position the offer to the target company's shareholders was conditional on the bidder obtaining this 50% ownership.

Once the offer is declared unconditional the target shareholders are not entitled to withdraw their acceptance; prior to this point they could have

Mergers and acquisitions

changed their minds. Similarly, if the offer period has lapsed and the acceptances received have not taken the bidding company's holdings over 50%, the bidding company does not have to take up what acceptances it has received. Usually, once the offer has been declared unconditional many of the target company's shareholders who had been unsure whether to accept, make up their minds and sell their shares to the bidding company at the offer price.

The takeover may be successful in securing for the purchaser a controlling interest in the target company but fail to obtain all the ordinary shares of the company. The shareholders of the purchased company who did not wish to sell their shares will hold a minority interest in the purchased company. This minority interest will be recognized in the consolidated accounts of the group.

The minority shareholders are entitled to receive dividends on their shares, and these will continue to have to be paid either in perpetuity or until the holders eventually sell their shares to the holding company.

Where a takeover takes place and the shares of one company are being exchanged for the shares of another company, it is possible under certain conditions to buy out any dissenting minority of the shareholders of the selling company. If, within four months of making the offer, nine-tenths in value of the shares whose transfer is involved, which means that any shares already held at the date of making the offer are excluded, have been acquired, then the purchasing company can give notice to any dissenting shareholders that it wishes to acquire their shares. The purchasing company is then entitled to acquire those shares under the terms on which the other shares had been transferred.

Defence against a takeover bid

The directors of a company that is the subject of a takeover bid should act in the best interests of their shareholders. The City Code on Takeovers and Mergers specifies certain general principles that must be observed. The Code does not apply to private companies although they are wise to follow what is in it. The board should normally seek competent independent advice when they receive a bid. The directors should disregard their own personal interest in the offer and in advising their shareholders act in the interests of all the shareholders.

If the directors decide to fight the takeover there are a number of tactics open to them. However, they must carefully consider their motives for recommending the rejection and put all the facts to the shareholders necessary for them to make up their minds: such facts must be accurately and fairly presented and be available to the shareholders early enough to enable them to make a decision in good time.

Information must not be given to some shareholders that is not available to all shareholders.

If the directors of the offeree company decide to fight a bid that appears to be financially attractive to their shareholders then they should try to convince their shareholders of the truth of either of the following.

1 The current market price of the offeror's shares is unjustifiably high and will not be sustained, which could happen if there was expected to be heavy selling of the shares allocated to shareholders of the offeree company.
2 The price of the offeree's shares is too low in relation to the real value and earning power of the assets that the offeror company is trying to acquire.

If the directors decide on course 2, then assets need to be revalued and possibly even sold and profit forecasts prepared to support this line of defence. In addition, there may be promises of higher future dividends and management changes to improve efficiency and profitability.

A well-managed defensive campaign would include aggressive publicity on behalf of the company. Investors could be told of any good research ideas within the company and of the management potential, or merely made more aware of the name of the company and any of its achievements. An announcement might be made about a proposed increase in dividend payments.

We shall now consider some of the more glamorous defensive tactics that have been employed. It should be appreciated, however, that although it might be possible to fight off a bid from an unwelcome suitor, it does not mean the company will necessarily be able to maintain its independence. Sometimes the defence technique employed means finding a more acceptable partner. Sometimes as a result of the methods adopted in the defence the company makes itself vulnerable to another acquirer.

White knights

One defensive tactic that has been used with success is for the directors of the offeree company to offer their company to a more friendly outside interest, i.e. a defensive merger. The friendly acquirer is referred to as a 'white knight'. It is a tactic to be adopted only in the last resort, for it means that the company is being taken over, but the directors decide they would rather work within one group than another. This tactic is acceptable to the City Code, provided that certain rules are observed. Any information, including particulars of shareholders, given to a preferred suitor should, on request, be furnished equally and as promptly to a less welcome but bona fide potential offeror. Of course, in addition, the directors must always ensure that they are acting in the interests of their shareholders as a whole, and not acting in the interests of their own personal future or out of spite.

Referral to the Monopolies Commission

It is generally believed that if a target company can have the takeover bid referred to the Monopolies Commission it either means that the bid immediately dies, as the predator will withdraw it, or there will be a delay, possibly of up to six months, while the Commission listens to all the arguments.

Poison pills

Reference has already been made to poison pills in the section on takeover rules. This refers to the case of an acquirer finding itself having to pay the costs of a rival bidder. With this approach a company takes steps before a takeover has been made to make itself less attractive to a potential bidder. One such method is for existing shareholders to be given rights to buy in future loan stock or preference shares. If a bid is made for the company before the date by which the rights have to be exercised, the terms of the arrangement are that the rights are to be automatically converted into ordinary shares. Of course, these new shares have to be purchased by the bidder. This adds to the cost of the acquisition.

Crown jewels

The tactic of selling off certain highly valued assets of the company subject to a bid is referred to as 'selling the crown jewels'. The intention is that the target company without the crown jewels will be less attractive to the bidding company. This tactic is more common in the USA than in the UK, where Rule 38 of the City Code makes it clear that once the board of the offeree company believes that an offer is imminent this defence is not feasible. However, the offeree is allowed to state that if the bid fails an asset will be sold in the future.

The latter tactic can mean that the offeree shareholders are less likely to sell their shares to the bidder. A variation on this approach is that, once the company knows it is being bid for, it purchases assets which it knows that the bidder will not want.

Golden parachutes

Another defence is the golden parachute. This is a policy of introducing attractive termination packages for the senior executives of the offeree company. It clearly makes defeat in the takeover less painful for the victim company's executives, but it also makes it more expensive for the bidding company to make the acquisition. These termination payments have to be made when the acquiring company takes over. The City Code makes clear that details of service contracts have to be made known in any documents sent to shareholders of the companies involved, including any details of amendments within the last six months.

Producing a revised profit forecast

A classic defensive technique is to produce profit forecasts that indicate that the future will be very much better than investors in the market place had been expecting. If these forecasts are accepted by the market as realistic, it will naturally force up the price of the target company's shares and make the offer price relatively less attractive. It is of course one thing to make a forecast and quite another to achieve the results. How these higher profit figures are to be achieved could be the result of improved efficiency, a management shake-up or changed methods of accounting.

Pac-Man strategy

This is a defensive tactic that has often been used in the USA and occasionally in the UK. It involves the target company trying to take over the bidding company. The name is based on the famous computer game in which the object being chased turns the tables on the pursuer.

Greenmail and arbitrageurs

Arbitrageurs are investors who speculate on takeovers and mergers. They know that if a company is to be the subject of a takeover bid the price of its shares will increase dramatically. They therefore purchase shares of companies that they expect to be the subject of a takeover bid. When the bid materializes the shares will rise in value and they can sell at a profit. This would seem to be an interesting but not controversial type of stock market activity. The arbitrageur is taking a risk; if the company is the subject of a bid, the arbitrageur gains.

Unfortunately in the late 1980s the activities of a number of arbitrageurs became discredited. The leading player in the USA was Ivan Boesky who, it turned out, was reducing his risks by buying information from merchant bankers on which companies were to be the subject of a bid. He was obtaining information illegally and acting before the offer was publicly announced. What he was doing was disclosed, and he was tried and sent to jail.

Arbitrageurs when acting legally can have an important influence on the outcome of a bid. The block of shares that they hold in a company which is the subject of the bid can take on a crucial importance. If they sell to the predator the bid can succeed; if they hold or sell to someone other than the predator the bid can fail. Hence, we have the expression 'greenmail', where 'green' refers to the colour of the US dollar. They can try to obtain 'rewards' from the bidding company in return for their support, or alternatively 'rewards' from the company that is the object of the bid for not selling. A question arises as to whether such tactics by the arbitrageurs are legitimate.

Other tactics

Other defensive tactics include encouraging a company's own pension funds to purchase shares in the company and introducing employee share-option schemes. These approaches are based on the idea that existing employees and their representatives are not likely to sell to a potential acquirer but to remain loyal to their existing employer.

Employee share-option plans (ESOPs) have been used as a means of placing shares in friendly hands. There are considerable tax advantages with such schemes in the USA and less so in the UK, but nevertheless the defence has been used in the UK.

The way in which the tactic works is for the company concerned to borrow funds from a bank, insurance company or other financial institution. The proceeds of the loan are used to buy the company's own shares, which are then put in a trust for eventual purchase by the employees. The shares purchased are in fact used as a security for the loan. As the employees contribute to the ESOP the money collected is used to repay the loan. The shares under the scheme are allocated to employees. The result is that the shares are placed in friendly hands.

22.6 FINANCING ACQUISITIONS

The popularity of the alternative methods of financing an acquisition varies from period to period. When stock market prices are high, share-for-share exchanges are popular. When stock market prices are low, cash becomes more popular.

In fact, in the UK there is a high proportion of mixed bids, with only half of all bids being either all equity or all cash. These mixed bids can be partly explained by the fact that many bids provide for a cash alternative to the equity offer. Cash tends to be used more than equity in bids that are contested or are being opposed by the managers of the target firm. Evidence has also been found that cash tends to be used in high-value acquisitions. Underwriters are particularly important in cash bids, helping with the financing arrangement if the bidder is short of cash.

Methods of payment

Cash offers

An offer is made to purchase the shares of the target company for cash. The acquiring company may, prior to the bid, have been purchasing up to 30% of the target company's shares on the stock market as and when they become available. Finally, it offers to buy the remainder of the shares at a specified price. As previously explained, the same offer must be made to all the target company's shareholders; it is a breach of the City Code to offer a higher price to one group of shareholders than is available to another group.

A cash offer has two advantages from the point of view of the target company's shareholders.

1 The price that they will receive is obvious. It is not like a share-for-share offer, where the movement in the market price will alter their wealth. A share-for-share offer increases the number of shares in the purchasing company, and the effect on the share price of the increase in the supply of shares on the market price is uncertain.

2 A cash purchase increases the liquidity of the selling shareholder who is then in a position to alter his or her investment portfolio to meet any changing opportunities. If a shareholder receives shares, until steps are taken to sell these they will not be in a position to take advantage of other opportunities.

A disadvantage to individual shareholders in receiving cash is that if the price that they receive on sale is in excess of the price paid in purchasing the shares, they may be liable to capital gains tax. This would not be the case if they received shares in exchange. The receipt of cash brings the share transaction to an end, and so the tax assessment can be made. The exchange of one share for another does not bring the transaction to an end; capital gains tax does not arise until the exchanged share is sold.

If the individual shareholder receives cash for his or her shares then they are subject to capital gains tax on the increase in the amount that they receive for the share above the price that they originally paid.

The taxation position is a critical factor in determining whether a shareholder in a takeover bid situation will accept a cash payment or will want a share exchange deal. A cash payment may embarrass an individual shareholder with a large capital gains tax bill. He or she would prefer a share-for-share exchange. However, a cash payment gives institutional investors the opportunity to reinvest their funds in any area they see as suitable. They could be attracted by a cash offer.

From the point of view of the bidding company's shareholders a cash offer has a number of advantages.

1 It represents a quick, easily understood, approach when resistance is expected. If it is reasonably priced it stands a fair chance of being successful.
2 A straight cash offer will not affect the equity of the bidding company. It is often important for the bidding company's shareholders that their control over their company is not diminished. However, the gearing position of the bidding company is almost certainly going to alter unless the takeover can be financed out of existing cash funds.

Borrowing to obtain cash

Of course, with an acquisition of any size it is unlikely that a company will have enough cash available to be able to pay fully for the purchase by this method. It could also be unable to offer a cash alternative to a share price offer or able to rely on its own cash. In such situations the purchasing company will need to borrow or at least obtain a standby line of credit. To be able to do this depends to some extent on its pre-bid level of gearing. Does the purchasing company have enough borrowing capacity? Are its bankers and advisers willing to bring together a group of backers to guarantee that loans will be available if the bid is successful and if the selling shareholders choose the cash alternative that is offered to them?

In the 1980s leveraged takeovers became relatively common. These are discussed elsewhere in this chapter. They involve the purchasing company borrowing and obtaining much higher levels of gearing than are usually thought acceptable. The cash raised from the borrowing is used to finance the purchase. Usually the intention is to reduce the gearing levels to an acceptable level as quickly as possible following the acquisition. This can be achieved by selling off some of the assets acquired.

There are, however, dangers in using borrowed funds to finance an acquisition. If after the purchase interest rates rise, so will the cost of borrowed funds. There could be a further problem with higher interest rates leading to lower levels of economic activity.

One major takeover battle was for the purchase of the well-known RJR Nabisco, the US food and tobacco group, which was eventually sold by its shareholders for $25 billion to a private firm, Kohlberg, Kraves and Roberts (KKR), which was almost unknown outside financial circles but was a pioneer in arranging leveraged buy-outs. It might be asked how a little-known private firm can finance such an acquisition. The answer is that it was backed by large international investing institutions who were prepared to lend it cash to finance the purchase of Nabisco shares. Therefore a comparatively small company, with only a small amount of equity, was able to purchase a huge company through high levels of borrowing. This is an extreme example of a leveraged buy-out.

Why are (or were) banks prepared to lend large sums to a business with little equity backing? They do so because the loans are secured by the assets of the company that is to be purchased. If need be some of the assets of the acquired company can be sold to pay off the borrowing. This practice is called 'asset stripping'.

Vendor placing and vendor rights

For a merger (as opposed to an acquisition) to take place, the shares in one company have to be exchanged for the shares in the other company. Sometimes, however, the shareholders in the company to be purchased do not want shares in the acquiring company; they want cash. This should mean that a merger is not possible, although an acquisition is.

The wording of the Accounting Standard on the subject provided a loophole: 'Merger accounting is considered to be an appropriate method of accounting when two groups of shareholders continue, or are in a position to continue, their shareholding as before but on a combined basis.'

The words 'or are in a position to' permitted a technique to develop whereby the selling shareholders (the vendors) could receive cash for their shares, but still be in a position to continue their shareholding as before. This is made possible by vendor placing and vendor rights. A share-for-share exchange takes place between the shareholders of the company being purchased and those of the acquiring company, but arrangements are made for the shares received by the vendor to be placed with institutional investors, if this is what the vendor wants. The shareholders in the company being acquired are therefore in a position to receive cash in payment for their shares in the acquired company. The scheme is usually set up by the acquiring company's merchant bank, which arranges for the shares to be placed with a third party.

Vendor rights are a variation on vendor placing. With vendor placing the shares received by those selling off their business are placed, usually with institutional shareholders. This means that the shares of the acquiring company can become widely dispersed. With vendor rights, if the shareholders of the target company do not want to retain the shares that they receive in consideration, then the acquiring company will again arrange through its brokers to have them placed. With this approach, however, the shares will first be offered to other shareholders of the acquiring company, who will have a right to buy them before they are placed with institutions. From the point of view of the acquiring company's shareholders, it is like a rights issue. But with vendor rights, the existing shareholders pay out cash not to the acquiring company but rather to those who were once shareholders of the company that has been purchased.

Share-for-share exchanges

One advantage of a share-for-share exchange has already been discussed, namely the effect of the relatively high price-to-earnings ratio of the bidding company on the earnings of the target company. Two other advantages of a share-for-share exchange, from the point of view of the shareholders of the target company, are as follows.

1 Capital gains tax is delayed.
2 The shareholders will still have a financial interest in the fortunes of the company that they have sold. They will still be able to share in any profits that are earned. They will normally have lost control of the company, but if they considered their original company a worthwhile investment and are not disillusioned with the managers of the purchasing company, they can still expect a satisfactory return.

The disadvantages to the purchasing company of an exchange of shares are as follows.

1 Equity shares are being issued, and this is a comparatively expensive form of capital.
2 Share exchange may reduce the gearing of the group company at the time of purchase. Whether it does so or not depends on the gearing of the acquired company. It may be possible to use the asset base acquired to increase the amount of borrowing, but this cannot be done immediately; it will take time.
3 The effect on the share price of the increase in the number of shares of the

purchasing company is uncertain. If the share price falls or is expected to fall, this would have to be taken into account by the purchasing company in deciding whether the acquisition is advantageous to its own shareholders.

4   A share-for-share exchange deal causes a dilution in the power of the bidding company's original shareholders. Thus for the takeover bid to be popular with the bidding company's shareholders there needs to be clear evidence that the bid is for the long-term benefit of the company. The dilution of the equity will in some cases cause the bidding company's share price to fall. This is partly because, by offering its shares to others, there is a likelihood that soon after the acquisition or merger has been completed many of the bidding company's shares may come onto the market for sale.

Perhaps one of the main advantages of share-for-share exchanges to the bidding company is that the initial cost of this method, from the point of view of cash flow, is comparatively small as no money passes to the shareholders of the company being taken over, although in the long run dividends have to be paid out to these additional shareholders. In the long run equity is the most expensive form of capital.

Debentures, loan stock and preference shares

Very few acquisitions are today financed by the issue of debentures, loan stock or preference shares. The main problems with loan stock and debentures for the offeror are that, first, there is a difficulty in knowing at what rate to fix the interest payment to attract the shareholders of the target company. Secondly, at times of high interest rates, issuing a fixed-interest stock can be an expensive long-term commitment which in later years, if interest rates fall, will be unnecessarily onerous on the company.

Floating-rate loan stock is occasionally offered to the offeree shareholders, but it can be difficult to entice them to accept such a security. The shareholders would have the disadvantage of indefinite returns without the advantages of their stock's being marketable or having any voting power and so having influence in the way that the company is run.

Convertible loan stock is sometimes used in acquisitions. This gives the offeree the chance to have fixed-interest payments for a given period and on the expiry of this period to decide whether to receive full ordinary shares in the bidding company. To the bidding company convertibles postpone the diluting of the equity.

The main advantage to the bidding company of using loan stock is that, unlike dividend payments, all interest payments made are tax-deductible. If the offeror firm can persuade the target company's shareholders to accept loan stock for their shares then this would be a very satisfactory method of payment. The offeror does not have to offer any equity shares and, with the loans not having to be repaid until a date well in the future, has a much longer period of time to collect the finance together to pay for the takeover bid. During the period of life of the loan stock, the successful bidder will have the time to build up reserves or a sinking fund to be used for the redemption of the stock. Hopefully, the increased profits of the new larger organization will be the major contributor in the build-up of the reserve fund.

Earn-outs

This is one way of making it easier for the acquiring firm to pay for the acquired firm. The payment is satisfied in part by an initial payment and in part by subsequent payments that are dependent upon the future profit levels of the acquired business.

Such arrangements were particularly popular in the late 1980s. Saatchi & Saatchi made extensive use of them when acquiring other advertising companies.

The percentage of the total purchase price to be paid at the time of acquisition, and the target profit levels that need to be achieved are a matter of negotiation between the parties.

The advantages of this approach to financing an acquisition are as follows.

- It reduces the initial financial outlay.
- The total profits of the new subsidiary earned after acquisition can be added to those of the parent company even though the total purchase price has not been paid. This helps the profit-to-asset (capital-employed) ratios.
- An earn-out encourages the management team (who own shares) of the acquired company to continue with enthusiasm. The overall purchase price received depends on future performance. In the advertising industry profitability depends very much on the performance of individuals. An acquisition is not the purchase of assets but of the skills of individuals. The same occurs in business where intellectual capital is important.
- It reduces the risks of the acquiring firm. They are less likely to be paying more than the purchased company is worth, because the price is limited by future performance.

Such earn-out agreements can be very complicated. The agreement has to consider all possible issues that can arise in order to avoid future problems. The formula for determining profit has to be agreed. Usually the total consideration is subject to a 'cap', an upper limit. This is necessary to protect the purchaser. Usually the earn-out period is between three and five years. This is not too long to expect key individuals to remain in the acquired firm.

Junk bonds

In the USA junk bonds have been issued to enable smaller companies to purchase larger companies. The smaller company uses the bonds to raise cash in the market place. The cash is used to purchase the larger company. As a result of issuing these bonds, the acquiring company finishes up with a very high level of gearing. It often plans to sell off some of the assets that it has acquired to repay the cash that it has borrowed.

In fact, the junk bond market in the USA became discredited in 1988. The leading investment banker in the US junk bond market, Drexel Burnham and Lambert, got into considerable trouble. In 1988 they agreed to pay the US government $650 million to avoid criminal and racketeering charges. In the settlement, the bank admitted insider dealing, stock manipulation, parking of bonds and shares in outside accounts to conceal true ownership and keeping false records.

22.7 FACTORS INFLUENCING SUCCESS OR FAILURE

There is somewhat of a paradox. There are in theory many good reasons to justify mergers and acquisitions. These would indicate a high percentage of acquisitions should be successful. The empirical evidence is, however, that a surprisingly high percentage of acquisitions do not succeed. Why should this be so?

One reason could be that the motives for a large number of acquisitions are management-based and so the results of the companies coming together do not necessarily benefit the shareholders of the acquiring firms.

Undoubtedly there are lessons to be learned from past mergers and acquisitions which indicate key issues in determining success. These include the following.

1 It is dangerous to purchase a company whose size is so large that if the acquired company fails it will financially destroy the acquiring company.
2 Following the acquisition, action has to be taken quickly to achieve tight financial control of the purchased firm. There should be a pre-planned integration programme, with the vision of what is to be achieved communicated to the staff of the acquired business.
3 The acquiring company needs management with multiple skills who can work with the management of the acquired firm. The interface should be well planned.
4 Following the acquisition it is necessary to have a mix of local and parent-company management who are tolerant of the possibly different management styles. This is particularly important with cross-border acquisitions.
5 There is a danger if the acquiring company tries to take over or merge with too many companies within a period of time.
6 The incentives and benefits to the staff of the acquired company should be improved.

To conclude, merger and acquisitions can be seen as part of the normal investment decision-making process of a company. There should be pre- and post-acquisition planning. The logical steps in the process are:

strategic objectives → search and screening of potential companies
to acquire → strategic evaluation → financial evaluation →
negotiation → agreement → integration

The rational view of mergers and acquisitions is that of the efficient, well-managed company taking over the less-efficient, less well-managed company, for the benefit of the shareholders. Unfortunately this is not always the reality.

22.8 THE RESULTS - WHO WINS?

Of course, whether a merger or acquisition is a success or not depends on the circumstances of each case. It is one thing to have the conditions for synergy to arise; it is quite another to manage the enlarged organization to deliver the extra returns.

All mergers and acquisitions are portrayed at the time they take place as being good for the shareholders involved and for the economy in general. Presumably the directors involved would not be proposing the new acquisition if they did not believe it to be beneficial to them. It is surprising therefore that studies show that on average, mergers and acquisitions do not result in higher profits or greater efficiency. It is one thing to talk of synergy and economies of scale, it is another thing to deliver.

A large amount of research has been undertaken in the attempt to prove or disprove the existence of economies of scale. Theoretically there are economies of production, marketing, research and finance. Economies should mean that the larger the organization, the lower are the unit costs and the greater the proportional returns. The reasons put forward to justify many mergers can be interpreted as attempts to obtain increased economies of scale. However, there is no automatic reason why economies should emerge when two companies are brought together. There may be possible advantages from large-scale operation, but this does not mean that all large organizations can achieve them.

Synergy does not automatically arise. The success of the merger or takeover depends upon the management's ability to take advantage of opportunities to realize the potential economies. The type of acquisition is one factor determining the success or failure of an acquisition. Research into post-merger performance emphasizes the fact that success depends on planning and management. Profits are not produced by machinery, buildings or products. It is people who give life to these otherwise dormant assets. The key to the success of a merger or takeover turns out to be the amount of thought and planning that has gone into it and the ability of the people involved.

Diversification typically leads to basic changes in the nature of a firm's management problems. The firm may move into product areas where the research, design and production technologies may be quite new, and where the marketing, financial and economic problems involved may differ significantly from those encountered previously. Therefore, diversification often brings on substantial extra costs and financial risks, and for that reason should not be undertaken unless the firm has carefully analysed the motives for diversification and proceeds only after it has carefully reviewed opportunities.

As has been mentioned several times in this chapter, there are a number of motives for a merger. There are the motives based on the concept of shareholder wealth maximization and motives based on managerial goals. Consequently, if a company is taken over because the directors of the acquiring company wish to run a particular prestigious enterprise, with a high public profile, it does not mean that the shareholders of the acquiring company will necessarily benefit.

We shall consider the evidence as to who in fact does gain from mergers and acquisitions. The interested parties, any one or more of which could gain (or lose), are as follows: the economy – a social gain; shareholders of the bidding firm; shareholders of the target firm; directors of the bidding firm; directors of the target firm; employees of the two firms; the financial institutions involved in the acquisition.

The position of each of these interest groups will now be considered.

The economy – a social gain

There have been numerous studies of mergers and takeovers in the UK which attempt to ascertain their economic impact. As long ago as 1969 the Monopolies Commission concluded that, on the evidence that they had seen, the effect of mergers and takeovers on the economy was at best neutral [6].

Other studies show that mergers and takeovers seldom live up to the expectations expressed at the time that the companies come together. The true motives for mergers are often to be found outside economics, and yet the statements made at the time of a merger or takeover usually seek to justify it in economic terms. Firth [7] found that the gains to some parties in the transaction were equally offset by the losses of the others. A similar conclusion was reached in a very detailed study by Cowling *et al.* [8]. These researchers attempted to determine whether the increased efficiency resulting from the economies of scale and improved management compensated for the consumer welfare loss resulting from the increased concentration. They saw the issue as one of cost–benefit analysis: comparison of the costs in the form of increased monopoly power with the gains in the form of increased efficiency. The only way to attempt such analysis is through detailed case studies, and consequently they investigated a large number of cases of acquisitions in the engineering and other manufacturing industries. They concluded that it is difficult to sustain the view that merger is a necessary or sufficient condition for efficiency gains. In many cases efficiency has not improved above the increase that could have been expected if the firms had not merged.

Although the results show that overall the economy does not gain from merger and takeover activity, this does not discourage managers of individual companies from engaging in such activity. There are at least two reasons that can explain this:

1 The results show that on average there are no gains. But, of course, some acquisitions are successful. The managers of a company believe that the acquisition in which they are engaged will be one of those that is successful.
2 Although an individual merger or takeover may not benefit the economy,

there are parties involved in the acquisition who do benefit. It might be the shareholders of one of the companies involved or the managers of one of the companies involved.

Shareholders

The bidding firms almost always have to offer a premium to the shareholders of the victim firm. This clearly leads to a gain to the shareholders of the target firm. Indeed, the empirical evidence on this fact is quite consistent. The price of the target shares usually rises dramatically even on the basis of rumours of an intended bid. Mandelker [9] examined a number of mergers in the USA and found that large gains were made, in terms of share-price increases, during the eight-month period up to the announcement date of the acquisition. The shareholders of the victim firm gained on average 18% over this period, and the shareholders of the bidding firm gained 3.5%.

The numerous US studies on this subject have been summarized by Jensen and Ruback [10]. They show average above-normal percentage share-price gains of 30% to the target shareholders associated with a successful takeover bid, whereas the gains to the bidding-company shareholders are only 4%. The calculation of the above-normal price changes is the result of adjustments made to the actual price change that occurred in order to be able to eliminate the effects of market-wide price changes. The authors differentiated between takeovers and mergers, with the latter being defined as where negotiations take place between the two sets of directors before going to a vote of target shareholders for approval. Jensen and Ruback's results, which come from analysing the numerous studies on the subject, are shown in Tables 22.1 and 22.2.

Clearly, one group that gains from a successful takeover bid is the victim shareholders, as these are the target shareholders in the acquisitions that are successful. The tables illustrate a dilemma for the directors of the target company. If they fight the takeover bid successfully, they are not benefiting their own shareholders. It may benefit the directors to remain independent, but it would not seem to benefit their shareholders. Clearly, they should try to obtain the best possible price for their shareholders, and this might mean recommending rejection of the first bid, with the hope that the bidding firm will come back with an improved offer. They have to be careful, however, that they act in their shareholders' interests and not their own. To recommend to their shareholders that they accept the first bid might help their own employment prospects, but not their shareholders' wealth. To put up some fight, but eventually lose, will benefit their shareholders, but not them.

Table 22.1 *Abnormal percentage share-price change associated with successful company acquisitions*

	Target shareholders (%)	Bidder's shareholders (%)
Takeovers	30	4
Mergers	20	0

Table 22.2 *Abnormal percentage share-price change associated with unsuccessful takeover bids*

	Target shareholders (%)	Bidder's shareholders (%)
Takeovers	−3	−1
Mergers	−3	−5

Overall, even though the shareholders of the bidding firm on average experience little if any gains in share price resulting from the merger or acquisition, the overall impact is an increase in the wealth of shareholders. In the typical acquisition, the total losses to the bidding firm's shareholders are less than the gains to the target firm's shareholders.

It has to be remembered that many big institutional shareholders own shares in both the acquiring firm and the victim firm. They may therefore be happy to lose on the shares in the acquiring firm and take gains on shares in the victim firm. The gains on the one outweigh the losses on the other.

It is perhaps not surprising that in percentage terms target-company shareholders do better than bidding-company shareholders. Apart from the obvious point of having to pitch the offer above current market value, on average bidders tend to be larger than targets. Hence benefits of bidders have to be shared between more shareholders with a larger capital base. If a company valued at, say, £100 million takes over a company valued at £10 million, creating synergy of £6 million, and the target is acquired for £13 million, a gain of 30% is made by target shareholders. However, if the acquiring company's share price reflects the expected net benefits, a gain of only 3% will be shown.

Directors of the bidding firm

It seems to be generally agreed that the directors of an acquiring company gain from a successful acquisition policy. They receive increased status and power from running a larger business, and there is evidence that at the same time they receive increased financial rewards. The level of executive remuneration is linked to company size.

There are financial incentives to managers who have little or no ownership interest in a company to pursue rapid growth, possibly at the expense of profitability. This could explain the desire to grow through acquisition rather than through organic growth.

Directors of the victim firm

There is a need for research on this topic. The folklore of the subject is that the directors of the victim company lose. They are likely to be dismissed from their jobs, either because they are judged to be inefficient or because they have fought the acquisition and so cost the bidding firm a lot of money. This is the overall impression, but of course there are exceptions. A number of managing directors of larger firms have come into those firms as a result of being a director of a victim firm. Also directors of the victim company usually own shares and options and so will gain from the premium offered above the pre-bid share price.

Employees

Again, more research is needed. Often, however, a number of the employees of the victim firm will lose. Following the takeover certain parts of the victim firm might well be closed down with resulting redundancies. Sometimes assurances are given during a takeover battle that redundancies will not follow the acquisition.

However, if the situation is looked at when the excitement of the battle is over it will often be found that, despite the assurances, redundancies have followed. In fact, in many cases, it is the employees of the target firm who are anxious to fight the takeover bid, as they realize that they have much to lose. But it must be recognized that in order for a merger or takeover to be a financial success it may be necessary to create redundancies. There could be duplication of functions and processes within the combined business. It could be that the victim firm had more employees than was necessary, and it was this inefficiency that had made it a takeover target.

Financial institutions

One group who certainly benefit from takeovers and mergers are the financial institutions – the merchant bankers, the financial public relations firms and other City institutions involved in the negotiations and any resulting battles. These professionals have to be used both by the bidding firm and the target firm. Their expertise is considerable, and there is no hope of being successful either in bidding or in defending unless good advice is obtained. Of course, the fees of these professionals have to be paid whether or not their advice leads to success.

A company's merchant banker is involved with mergers and takeovers in a number of ways.

1 Merger broking: they can advise companies on likely target companies. They have lists of companies who wish to be purchased and they will help to find suitable target companies to purchase if a company wishing to expand is looking for opportunities to diversify.
2 They can help to plan an acquisition, giving advice on the value of the company and the 'best' tactics to be followed either with an agreed merger or a takeover bid.
3 Defence: they will advise target companies on the 'best' ways to resist a takeover bid.
4 Merchant banks buy and sell shares of companies as part of their normal activities. However, they are not supposed to buy and sell shares of companies which they are advising clients to buy. There is an interesting question as to how far they, and/or other banks with which they are involved, should go in purchasing their clients' shares to support the price during the bid.

A merchant bank is not just expected to give advice; often it is expected to assist with the provision of finance. If they are advising on a defence that involves a financial restructuring, they could be expected to make loans and organize other banks to make loans to increase the level of gearing. If they are working with the bidding company, again they could be expected to make loans available, this time to provide the cash to purchase the shares.

In every takeover battle one group of advisers wins and another group loses. One banker might be advising a bidding firm in one takeover battle and advising a target firm in another. They all win some and lose some. The costs of a takeover battle are considerable and have to be paid by the companies involved. The more spectacular battles involve large amounts of advertising expenditure and costs of preparing and circulating many circulars. Undoubtedly financial institutions gain from a lively takeover and merger scene.

In general therefore we have identified three groups who gain from mergers and takeovers and two groups who lose. The winners in successful acquisitions are the victim shareholders, the bidding directors and the financial institutions. The losers are the directors and employees of the victim firms. The position of society and the bidding-company shareholders seems on balance to be neutral – with some acquisitions they win, and with others they lose. Of course, these are generalizations, but they do give some clue as to why the motives involved in mergers and takeovers are so complex.

Companies can of course work together without merging or without one acquiring another. A strategic alliance is an arrangement between two or more companies for their mutual benefit. An alliance might be formed in order to exploit new markets, to share new ideas or technology or to cut costs of production or research. The alliance could result in a joint venture or companies becoming associates. An alliance falls short of one company becoming a subsidiary of the other; it is an alternative to a merger or acquisition.

Such alliances have become popular amongst medium-sized firms. The firms may wish to enter into global markets but the costs of doing so are too great for each individual firm. They have also proved useful in overcoming political barriers when governments restrict foreign ownership in certain activities to a certain level. A local partner is found for the joint venture.

The terms of the alliance will need to be negotiated and will vary from case to case. The issues to be considered include:

- how much each party is to invest in the joint venture, and the form the investment will take;
- the balance of risk and reward for the parties: how will profits be shared? what happens if there is a loss?;
- the roles and responsibilities of each party;
- the mechanism for developing future policy, and for the taking advantage of future opportunities;
- the mechanism for dealing with disputes.

Alliances between companies in different countries can be particularly complex and the taxation issues need to be considered, as do the possible differences in management style. Cultural differences can be important and lead to future difficulties if not properly understood.

Companies working together can result in any one of the following:

1 a subsidiary company;
2 a joint venture;
3 a strategic alliance;
4 a strategic minority stake. This is an agreement to purchase and maintain a minority shareholding in another company, which it is thought will be useful. The benefits could be future business passing between the two companies or an exchange of technology.

  Honda had a minority shareholding in the Rover Car Company, before Rover was sold to BMW. Honda were happy with a strategic minority stake in Rover, which resulted in an exchange of technology and shared production. For strategic reasons Honda did not want such a link with BMW, and so sold their shareholding when the majority holding in Rover was sold by British Aerospace to the German car manufacturer.

Economic interest groups (EIGs)

One form of strategic alliance that has been encouraged by the European Union is an EIG. This is a form of business venture similar to a partnership. Two or more firms agree to work together for a particular purpose.

The situations in which it might be advantageous to form such a group include:

- to combine research and development activities;

- to form a joint selling or distribution network;
- to tender for a major public-works contract.

The first official EIG came into operation in 1989, although there is a history of such groups existing in Europe before this date. These European EIGs are designed to benefit the smaller-sized firms. The EIG itself must not employ more than 500 people, although of course the member companies forming the partnership can be bigger than this.

The profits of the EIG are divided between the participating firms according to an agreed formula. The members act collectively in making decisions.

22.10 REFERENCES

1 Marris, R. (1964) *The Economic Theory of Managerial Capitalism*, Macmillan, London.
   Gort, M. (1969) An economic disturbance theory of mergers, *Quarterly Journal of Economics*, November.
2 Jensen, M.C. (1986) Agency costs of free cash flow, corporate finance and takeovers, *American Economic Review, Papers and Proceedings*, May, 323–9.
3 King, M. (1989) Takeover activity in the UK, in *Mergers and Merger Policy* (eds J. Fairburn and J. Kay), Oxford University Press, Oxford.
4 Dimson, E. and Marsh, P. (1984) An analysis of brokers' and analysts' unpublished forecasts of UK stock returns, *Journal of Finance*, **39**(5): 1257–92, December.
   Elton, E., Gruber, M. and KIeindorfer, P. A close look at the implications of the stable Paretian hypotheses, *Review of Economics and Statistics*, **57**(2): 231–5, May.
5 Jensen, M.C. and Ruback, R.S. (1983) The market for corporate control, the scientific evidence, *Journal of Financial Economics*, April.
6 Monopolies and Mergers Commission (1969) *Report on the Proposed Merger of Unilever Ltd and Allied Breweries Ltd*, HMSO, London.
   Monopolies and Mergers Commission (1969) *Report on the Proposed Acquisition of De La Rue Ltd by the Rank Organisation*, HMSO, London.
7 Firth, M. (1980) Takeovers, shareholders' returns and the theory of the firm, *Quarterly Journal of Economics*, March.
8 Cowling, K., Stoneman, P. and Cubbin, J. (1980) *Mergers and Economic Performance*, Cambridge University Press, Cambridge.
9 Mandelker, G. Risk and return: the case of merging firms, *Journal of Financial Economics*, **1**: 303–35.
10 Jensen, M.C. and Ruback, R.S. – see [5].

22.11 FURTHER READING

Cooke, T.E. (1988) *International Mergers and Acquisitions*, Basil Blackwell, Oxford.
Fairburn, J. and King, J.A. (eds) (1989) *Mergers and Merger Policy*, Oxford University Press, Oxford.

An interesting article summarizing the takeover activity in the UK is:

Bank of England Quarterly (1989) Takeover activity in the 1980s, **29**(1).

A special edition of the *Journal of Financial Economics*, April 1983 dealt with many aspects of mergers and takeovers, and included the review article by M.C.

Jensen and R.S. Ruback entitled: The market for corporate control, the scientific evidence.

Other significant publications include:

Bannock, G. (1990) The takeover boom: an international and historic perspective, Hume Occasional Paper 15, The David Hume Institute.

Dodd, P. The market for corporate control: a review of the evidence, in *The Revolution in Corporate Finance* (ed. J.M. Stern and D.H. Chew), Blackwell, Oxford.

Franks, J.R., Harris, R.S. and Mayer, C. (1988) Means of payment in takeovers: results for the UK and US. In *Corporate Takeovers: Causes and Consequences* (ed. M.J. Avernack), University of Chicago Press, Chicago.

Glaister, K.W. and Buckley, P. (1994) UK international joint ventures: an analysis of patterns of activity and distribution, *British Journal of Management*, **5**: 33–51.

Gregory, A. (1997) An examination of the long run performance of UK acquiring firms, *Journal of Business Finance and Accounting*, September, 971–1002.

Jarillo, J. Carlos and Stevenson, H.H. (1991) Cooperative strategies, the payoffs and pitfalls, *Long Range Planning*, **24**(1): 64–70.

Kay, J. (1993) *Foundation of Corporate Success*, Oxford University Press, Oxford, chs 3 and 10.

Lei, D. (1993) Offensive and defensive uses of alliances, *Long Range Planning*, **26**(4): 32–41.

Lev. B. (1986) Observations on the merger phenomenon, in *The Revolution in Corporate Finance* (ed. J.M. Stern and D.H. Chew), Blackwell, Oxford.

Mitchell, M. and Lehn, K. (1990) Do bad bidders become good targets? *Journal of Political Economy*, **2**.

Sudarsanam, P.S. (1995) *The Essence of Mergers and Acquisitions*, Prentice-Hall.

Wheaton, J.B. (1993) EEA and EC competition law: application to joint ventures, IIR Conference, Helsinki.

Zahra, S. and Elhagrasey, G. (1994) Strategic management of international joint ventures, *European Management Journal*, **12**(1): 83–93.

22.12 PROBLEMS

1 Your company is subject to an unexpected takeover bid by a rival company. Your board of directors proposes to reject the bid, but believes that increased bids might follow.

   Discuss the policies that your company might adopt to defend itself against the takeover bid(s), and comment upon the significance of the City Code on Takeovers and Mergers in this process.

ACCA

2 The Uni-Tours PLC is in the service sector and is considering merger to achieve more favourable growth and profit opportunities. After an extensive search of a large number of companies, it narrowed the candidates to a company in the same sector, Poly-Travellers PLC. As the treasurer of Uni-Tours you are investigating the possible acquisition of Poly-Travellers. You have the following basic data to start from:

	Uni-Tours PLC	Poly-Travellers PLC
Earnings per share	£5.00	£1.50
Dividend per share	£3.00	£0.80
Share price	£90.00	£20.00
Number of shares	1 000 000	600 000

Further investigations lead you to estimate that investors currently expect a steady compound growth of about 6% each year in Poly-Travellers' earnings and dividends. Under Uni-Tours' control this growth should increase to about 8% each year, without any additional capital investment and without any change in the riskiness of operations.

Required:
(a) Compute the increase in value resulting from the merger.   (5 marks)
(b) What are the gains or losses likely to be to the shareholders in the two companies, assuming Uni-Tours pays £25 in cash for each share in Poly-Travellers.   (3 marks)
(c) What will be the gains or losses if Uni-Tours offers one of its shares for every three shares of Poly-Travellers.   (5 marks)
(d) Calculate the gains or losses on the assumption that the market does not expect Poly-Travellers' increased growth rate to materialize. Discuss the theoretical and empirical implications of (d) with respect to (a), (b) and (c) above.   (10 marks)

3 Killisick PLC wishes to acquire Holbeck PLC. The directors of Killisick are trying to justify the acquisition to the shareholders of both companies on the grounds that it will increase the wealth of all shareholders.

The supporting financial evidence produced by Killisick's directors is summarized below:

	£000	
	Killisick	*Holbeck*
Operating profit	12 400	5800
Interest payable	4 431	2200
Profit before tax	7 969	3600
Tax	2 789	1260
Earnings available to ordinary shareholders	5 180	2340
Earnings per share (pre-acquisition)	14.80 pence	29.25 pence
Market price per share (pre-acquisition)	222 pence	322 pence
Estimated market price (post-acquisition)	240 pence	
Estimated equivalent value of one old Holbeck share (post-acquisition)		360 pence

Payment is to be made with Killisick ordinary shares, at an exchange ratio of 3 Killisick shares for every 2 Holbeck shares.

Required:
(a) Show how the directors of Killisick produced their estimates of post-acquisition value and, if you do not agree with these estimates, produce revised estimates of post-acquisition values.

All calculations must be shown. State clearly any assumptions that you make.   (10 marks)
(b) If the acquisition is contested by Holbeck PLC, using Killisick's estimates of its post-acquisition market price calculate the maximum price that Klllisick could offer without reducing the wealth of its shareholders.   (3 marks)
(c) The board of directors of Holbeck PLC later informally indicate that they are prepared to accept a 2 for 1 share offer.

Further information regarding the effect of the acquistion on Killisick is given below:
  (i) The acquisition will result in an increase in the total pre-acquisition after-tax operating cash flows of £2.75 million per year indefinitely.
  (ii) Rationalization will allow machinery with a realizable value of £7.2 million to be disposed of at the end of the next year.
  (iii) Redundancy payments will total £3.5 million immediately and £8.4 million at the end of the next year

(iv) Killisick's cost of capital is estimated to be 14%.

All values are after any appropriate taxation. Assume that the pre-acquisition market values of Killisick and Holbeck shares have not changed.

Required:

Recommend, using your own estimates of post-acquisition values, whether Killisick should be prepared to make a 2 for 1 offer for the shares of Holbeck. (6 marks)

(d) Assuming no increase in the total post-acquisition earnings, assess whether this acquisition is likely to have any effect on the value of debt and equity of Killisick PLC. (6 marks)

(25 marks)

ACCA

4 The directors of Compro PLC and Vendo PLC consider that a merger of the two companies would be beneficial. The proposed merger would involve the issue of new ordinary shares in Compro PLC which would be given in exchange for the existing ordinary shares of Vendo PLC. The directors are now concerned with the question of the ratio in which new shares of Compro PLC should be offered for shares of Vendo PLC.

Both companies are totally equity-financed and you have the following information about the ordinary shares currently in issue:

	Number of shares in issue (millions)	*Current share price*
Compro	600	£5.00
Vendo	300	£4.00

The cost of equity of both companies is 20% and it is expected to remain the same after the merger. It is expected that the merger will generate post-tax cost savings of £40 million in the first year and that the level of these post-tax cost savings will rise at 10% per annum thereafter in perpetuity. Additionally, the immediate sale of assets rendered redundant by the merger is expected to realize post-tax proceeds of £200 million which will be invested to produce a return equal to the current cost of capital.

You may treat the post-tax cost savings as though they result in annual cash inflows commencing one year after the merger.

Required:

(a) What should be the ratio of new shares in Compro PLC issued in exchange for existing shares in Vendo PLC in order that all of the benefits of the merger will accrue to:
   (i) the pre-merger shareholders of Compro PLC; or
   (ii) the pre-merger shareholders of Vendo PLC? (12 marks)

(b) What other factors will influence the level at which the directors of Compro PLC pitch their bid for Vendo PLC, assuming they act solely in the interests of their shareholders? (3 marks)

(c) Discuss what other motives might be involved in the decision to merge or acquire companies, addressing in particular:
   (i) the role of diversification;
   (ii) the observation that shareholders of acquirer companies tend to lose as a result of takeovers;
   (iii) the implications for corporate governance. (10 marks)

(25 marks)

ICAEW, June 1993

23 COMPANY RESTRUCTURING, REFINANCING AND LIQUIDATION

LEARNING OUTCOMES

By the end of this chapter the reader should:

- understand the different forms of restructuring companies that have been popular in recent years
- appreciate the needs for such restructuring
- be able to propose ways in which a management buy-out can be financed
- be able to identify the factors that lead to company failure
- understand the differences between insolvency and liquidation, and appreciate the different methods of liquidating a company

23.1 INTRODUCTION

In the previous chapter we considered a number of aspects of mergers and acquisitions. In fact, mergers and acquisitions are only one form of company restructuring. They are usually the aspect of company change that makes the headlines. However, during the 1980s and 1990s another trend has been in evidence, namely a move towards demerger or divestment. This came about partly as a result of a greater emphasis in the strategic planning processes within companies on concentrating on 'core' business activities. By 'divestment' or, to give it yet another name, 'divestiture' is meant the sale of a subsidiary, division or product line by one business to another.

We give below a number of forms of company restructuring, and in this chapter we shall examine the motives and methods behind divestment and other methods of introducing change.

1   expansion:
    (a)   mergers;
    (b)   takeovers/acquisitions;
    (c)   joint ventures;

2   divestment:
    (a)   sell-offs;
    (b)   liquidation;
    (c)   spin-offs;
    (d)   management buy-outs;

3   other forms of change:
    (a)   going private;
    (b)   buy-ins;

(c)   increasing the amount of borrowing;
(d)   share re-purchases;
(e)   premium buybacks;
(f)   reverse takeovers.

Unfortunately, yet another form of divestment occurs in some companies: namely, liquidation. Due to changes in the economic situation and due to mismanagement some companies are forced out of existence.

We will briefly consider the causes of failure, and then consider what can happen to companies when they get into financial difficulties.

23.2 DIVESTMENT

The reasons given by companies to justify a restructuring exercise include the following.

The sum of the parts of a business is worth more than the whole

The individual parts of a business can be worth more than the whole when the shares of a company are selling at a price below their potential value. Some of the assets of the company are worth more than is appreciated, or some could be put to better use. Selling off a part or parts of the business brings in cash, and the resulting increase in company wealth is greater than any fall in share value resulting from an expected reduction in future cash flow. This is sometimes expressed as $5 - 1 = 5$.

Selling off parts of the business can be seen as similar to 'asset stripping', although this term is usually reserved for describing the practice of selling unwanted parts of a business following an acquisition. Divestment can occur whether or not a company has been engaged in takeover activity.

But why should the sum of the parts of a business be greater than the whole? It is sometimes claimed that the financial community does not always understand the true nature and structure of certain companies. For example, a company can be classified as a manufacturing business when some of its activities are in merchandising or mining. Investors and their advisers believe that a certain share price is appropriate based on the classification of a company in one industry; this can result in an undervaluation. If the company sells off its non-core interest and obtains a true value for it, the sale results in the recognition and revaluation of a previously undervalued asset. The result is that the value of the company after the sale, which is the cash collected plus the true value of the core business, can be greater than the value of the company before the sale.

It can be argued that some assets may be worth more in the hands of one set of managers than in the hands of another set. The buyers of the assets in a divestment situation see themselves as being able to make better use of them than the seller can. Therefore they are worth more to the buyer than to the seller. Thus the buyer offers a higher value than that based on their future cash flow in existing hands. In this situation the market is correctly valuing the assets in existing hands before the sell-off – it just values them more highly in the hands of a different set of managers.

Selling off unwanted parts

During the 1970s many conglomerates sold off assets they had acquired that were unprofitable to them. However, the sell-off spree of the 1980s and 1990s is different. Disillusion with the concept of conglomerates developed from both a company-management and a financial-community point of view. Rather than simply dumping the bad parts, companies started to spin off and scale down healthy businesses to concentrate on what they could do best. In a number of cases these divestments have been accomplished by means of management buy-outs or spin-offs.

At times of considerable change in the economy, constraints put on management become more explicit. The lack of time available to manage and the level of uncertainty can lead to diversified companies facing extreme difficulties in keeping up with market trends. The result has been a move towards the creation of more independent decision-making units in order to obtain better and quicker decisions.

A situation developed in which large conglomerates were seen as being risky and also less efficient from a management point of view. The increasingly competitive environment forced companies to take a long hard look at the group structure. A company was not likely to be profitable, i.e. not likely to be competitive, in all its markets. More specialization was therefore seen as desirable.

Divestment as a crisis response

In a relatively stable environment the organization structure of the firm and its accompanying control systems may be able to absorb incremental development and associated problems. In a turbulent and uncertain environment where, at the extreme, survival is threatened, a quantum change in the organization may be required.

Rapid and uncertain environmental change may break down the traditional affinities between product areas within an organization, so that the original synergistic benefits from integration or conglomerate risk-spreading no longer apply. It may thus become difficult to control across these integrated processes. Integration in different markets may now be required, or alternatively different markets may now need to be entered for effective conglomerate risk-spreading. Ownership mobility provided by divestment helps to overcome the barriers.

Where crisis involves financial problems further control issues arise. A parent facing a severe financial constraint is limited in its ability to operate an internal capital market. Not only may the company be unable to act as 'lender of last resort' to its divisions/subsidiaries, but it may not be able to finance worthwhile projects. In extreme cases, the company's survival itself may be threatened – either by bankruptcy or by an unwelcome takeover bid. Hence crisis conditions may lead to divestment.

Under conditions of capital rationing some units may be designated as 'cash cows' and deliberately starved of investment funds whilst being 'milked' to finance priority developments elsewhere. This treatment is likely to impair operating efficiency and innovation in the division concerned, the more so where the 'cash cow' division is supporting divisions with crisis performance problems. Divestment may be necessary to rescue its long-run performance. For the divesting parent the lump-sum proceeds of sale may better help restructuring.

23.3 SELL-OFF

A sell-off is the sale of part of the original company to a third party. Assets are sold to the third party, most probably another company, and cash is usually received in exchange. A company may take this course of action under the following circumstances.

1 It is short of cash.
2 It has carried out a strategic planning exercise and has decided that it wishes to concentrate its management efforts on certain parts of its business and not on other parts. It wishes to restructure.

3 It wishes to protect the rest of the firm from takeover by selling a desirable area of its activities that it knows is attractive to the bidder. It is selling the crown jewels in order to make itself less of a target.

4 It has a loss-making activity; by removing the loss from the consolidated accounts, it will improve the year's profit performance.

Sell-offs are likely to involve the less profitable and more peripheral business units of a multi-product firm and also to be related to the profitability of the parent. This is consistent with the view that the sale of divisions/subsidiaries can ease control problems (by reducing complexity as peripheral units are sold off) and that divestment represents a plausible response to financial difficulties.

Sell-offs should be undertaken as an investment decision by management. If management are interested in wealth creation, such a decision should have a positive effect on total net present value (NPV) and accordingly this should provide a signal to investors which results in an upward movement in the share price.

Sell-offs can occur because of a strategic decision to change the emphasis of the business. An interesting example of such a sell-off was the 1997 sale by ICI of its majority shareholding in its Australian subsidiary. This was the result of a change in its strategy: it wished to 'refocus' the company on higher-margin speciality chemical products. It planned to use the money raised from the sale to purchase another speciality chemical business. The sale of its Australian shares was to be either to a single buyer or a public offering.

Liquidation

Liquidation is the most extreme form of divestment: the sell-off of the entire business. The owners might decide to close the whole business down, sell off the assets piecemeal and use the funds raised to pay off creditors. The situation being referred to is a voluntary dissolution, not a compulsory liquidation.

When part of the business is sold off, the funds received are reinvested in the firm or used to pay off borrowings, but this is not the case with a liquidation. This step would be taken if a firm was worth more 'dead than alive'. This situation could arise if for some reason the current organizational structure was not leading to the best use being made of the firm's assets and the business was no longer seen as a viable concern. It would arise if the current owners lost interest in the business. Although such a voluntary liquidation might be in the shareholders' interests it is not necessarily in the managers' interests. Of course, with owner–managers there could be goal congruence. A voluntary liquidation involves making a decision to sell off all the assets of the business rather than spinning them off or selling them off as individual parts.

23.4 SPIN-OFF (DEMERGER)

With a spin-off there is no change in ownership of assets. A new company is created and the shares in the new company are owned by the shareholders of the company making the distribution of the assets. The result is to create two or more companies whereas previously there was one. Each company now owns some of the assets of the former single company. The shareholders own the same proportion of shares in the new company as in the original company. The assets are transferred to the new company and not sold. The new company will usually have different management from that of the continuing company. Over time the new company might well develop different policies from those of the continuing company. As a separate entity it might in time even be sold independently of the original continuing company. From a shareholders' point of view the spin-off is similar to a scrip dividend (stock dividend). The shareholders are given new shares, in this case in a new company.

An extreme version of the spin-off is where the original company is split up into a number of separate companies. The entire original company is broken up, in which case there are a number of spin-offs. The original company ceases to exist.

There are three main methods of achieving a spin-off, or what is sometimes called a 'listed demerger'. The simplest is a 'dividend in kind'. This means that shares in the subsidiary to be disposed of are distributed to company shareholders as a non-cash dividend.

There are two ways of handling this 'dividend in kind'. If the shares in the company being demerged are distributed directly to the shareholders, it is treated as a sale for tax purposes and tax may have to be paid. An alternative version is for the shares in the company being disposed of to be distributed to a newly formed company. It is this newly formed company that distributes its shares to shareholders. This second approach delays the payment of tax.

An alternative demerger method is through a 'scheme of arrangement'. This requires a court order. The third approach is through a 'scheme of reconstruction'. This arises when two or more new companies are established. The original company is liquidated. The liquidator distributes the assets of the old company to the new companies. The shares in the new companies are distributed to the shareholders of the old company. This is clearly much more of a demerger than a spin-off. Everything is in fact, in this case, being 'spun off'.

The spin-off, with its separation of management but continuation of shareholders, usually results in a positive response from the stock market. The reasons put forward to explain this response include the following.

1 The changes result in a clearer management structure. The managers of the activity that has been separated are expected by the market to do a better job with the assets than was done by management in the larger group. The assets are worth more in the hands of the new management than in the hands of the previous management. It is thought that there will be an improvement in efficiency.
2 The change could result in making it easier in the future for a merger or takeover of the spun-off part to take place.
3 It is a way of protecting the crown jewels from a predator.
4 It allows the market to see the true value of a business that was hidden within the larger conglomerate structure. This refers back to the discussion of sell-offs. If there are hidden assets whose potential is not appreciated, they need not be sold off; they could be placed in a separate company.
5 It avoids offending regulatory agencies. In the past this reason has been more relevant in the USA than in the UK, but as a result of privatization in the UK and the resulting need for regulatory agencies it could become more significant in the future. With business activities separated, price increases might be allowed in some activities but not in others.
6 Shareholders may benefit from an increase in the opportunity set as they are able to adjust the proportions of their investment in the demerged entities.
7 Shareholders may benefit at the expense of bondholders where equity in the spun-off company is distributed solely to shareholders of the parent corporation, leaving the bondholders with no claim on the assets of the new entity.

A number of studies have reported significant positive abnormal returns, which were particularly pronounced in larger spin-offs. It has not been found that this results from a transfer of wealth from bondholders. The available evidence on spin-offs appears to support the view that shareholders' gains are attributable to an improvement in the efficiency of the new structural arrangements.

The UK buy-out/buy-in market began to develop in the early 1980s. By 1989 the annual investment in these activities exceeded £7.5 billion. The market then declined (1993, £2.5 billion) because a number of high-priced, highly leveraged deals ran into difficulties. High prices had been paid to buy-out companies and then when the economy showed a downturn, the companies had difficulty meeting their high interest payments. The buy-in/buy-out market recovered in 1995 and 1996.

Management buy-outs vary greatly in scale and method. They can be defined as a transaction through which the management of a business acquires a substantial stake in, and frequently effective control of, the business which it formerly managed. The buy-out team may consist of only one individual or a whole team of directors and employees, together with external associates. In some management buy-outs some equity ownership is offered to employees below the level of top management. In rare cases the offer is to all employees. An example of this latter approach was that of the National Freight Consortium. This was the sale of a publicly owned company to the management and employees. It was privatization. It was hoped that an equity involvement by all employees would increase motivation. In the majority of cases, however, it is just the top group of managers who are involved in the equity purchase.

It will become clear below that management buy-outs take place under all sorts of circumstances and that consequently every buy-out is different. For example, there are seller-motivated buy-outs in which the selling company decides that the financial and management resources spent on a peripheral activity are not sensible. They require a greater involvement than the group is willing to commit to its non-core activity.

Alternatively, the management of a division may feel that they are isolated from the group's main decision-making process, thereby feeling frustrated in their abilities to obtain sufficient funds. This is an example of what becomes a buyer-motivated buy-out. With this situation the buyer has the advantage of buying a business which is already in existence. It does not have to move up through a learning-curve process. This cuts down starting costs and running-in times.

The reasons behind a seller-motivated management buy-out are similar to those listed earlier in the chapter as reasons for divestment:

1 sale of a subsidiary giving financial problems;
2 sale of a subsidiary that does not fit in with the new strategic plan for the group;
3 sale of unwanted parts to raise cash to fund an acquisition;
4 in a family-controlled business the owners might be happy to sell to the managers as it avoids publicity and should result in a speedy sale, and they may feel that they are helping to preserve the jobs of staff who have been loyal to them.

One aspect of a management buy-out that has concerned some people is the use of inside information. Nobody knows more about the business being bought than the managers themselves; they know its potential and also its weaknesses. They probably know more about the business than the directors of the main company that is making the sale. Therefore the managers are in a good position to be able to buy at an 'advantageous' price. If they do so, it is the shareholders of the selling company that lose.

In fact, managers of a subsidiary are sometimes in a position where they can produce reports that will make a management buy-out more likely and on terms favourable to the buyers. It is the managers who can 'create' the impression that they want to give by controlling the information released. Clearly the group (the parent company) should have a good internal control system so that they always know the 'true' position, but this is not always the case. Wright and Coyne [1] have found that in some cases manipulation of figures has taken place in order to affect the buy-out price.

The market for corporate control was referred to in Chapter 22 on mergers and takeovers. The management buy-out is also a part of this corporate control system. If the managers and directors at group level do not perform to the satisfaction of shareholders, they can be threatened from outside the company. If they do not meet the expectation of interest groups within the company they can be threatened from within.

The buy-out allows incumbent managers to exploit informational asymmetries in entering a transaction which will give them a substantial equity stake. Once they have committed themselves to the deal, the investment would be expected to act as a powerful incentive towards maximizing the value of the new entity. This pressure may be further strengthened by the bonding of the newly independent management team to their financiers, since any deviation from agreed financial targets could lead to loan default and failure. The buy-out restores to the managers of the newly formed independent business the threat of the bankruptcy sanction which is arguably absent where a corporate head-quarters can act as 'lender of last resort'.

The funding of a management buy-out can be very complicated. Venture capitalists are usually needed to assist with the provision of the equity funds. They usually finish up holding a certain percentage of the equity in the new business for what they hope will be a relatively short period of time. To begin with they might have to purchase a larger proportion of the equity than the management carrying out the buy-out. It is their hope, however, that they will be able to sell these shares at a healthy profit in, say, three to five years' time. That length of time could elapse before the company can be launched on the stock market or the managers can accumulate enough finance themselves to be able to buy the shares of the venture capitalist or the company is successful enough for other investors to be interested in purchasing the shares. These are the possible exit routes for the venture capitalists.

The finance to acquire the assets from the selling company will come from a mixture of debt and equity. Usually relatively high levels of debt finance are required. Hence buy-outs are sometimes called 'leveraged buy-outs'. In a normal management buy-out gearing (leverage) levels of 5:1 may be necessary, but in leveraged buy-outs the level can rise to 20:1 (this is the ratio of debt to equity). Ratios of 10:1 are quite common. To support the resulting high levels of interest payments requires an extremely strong cash flow and the capacity to move quickly to create a market for the sale of the company's shares.

The use of leveraged buy-out techniques has paved the way for many new entrepreneurial efforts. Because only a small proportion of equity finance is required, leveraged buy-outs make it much easier for managers plus possible outside investors to try to run a business on their own. In a leveraged management buy-out it may not be possible to raise all the finance required from the equity investment and the secured debt is usually taken up by a leading bank. Hence mezzanine finance, or as it is sometimes called 'strip' finance, is required, as are specialist advisers.

A bank that specializes in buy-outs is usually needed to put a suitable financial package together. The buy-out specialist will purchase some of the equity. It will also arrange the loans required. The buy-out specialist could well initially control the board of directors. It would of course leave the day-to-day running of the company to the managers, but it would be involved in setting strategic plans and long-range goals.

There are many banks who will assist with the raising of finance to fund a management buy-out. Possible sources include the following:

1 the leading High Street banks;
2 dedicated buy-out funds – many merchant (investment) bankers have set up subsidiaries specifically to deal with such situations;
3 venture capital companies.

It is always possible, but difficult, for the managers wishing to buy a business to avoid heavy borrowing. They could try to arrange a deferred purchase scheme, i.e. to purchase the assets slowly over time. Another approach is a sale and lease-back: acquire the assets, sell them quickly and use the money raised to pay for the purchase.

Mezzanine finance

Mezzanine finance can be considered as a source of funds ranking between equity shares and the secured debt of a company. It is more risky than secured debt, but less risky than equity. It offers higher expected returns than senior debt issues but lower returns than equity. It comes in many different forms. It could be debt to which a warrant is attached which only becomes convertible if and when the company is floated on the stock market. If the company issuing such mezzanine finance were liquidated, the securities issued would rank for repayment below other forms of debt finance. A major bank might well provide the senior debt that could be secured against assets. After this the debt structure might include

B notes These are notes, in which the company promises to repay the money advanced, in one single 'bullet' payment, possibly as far as eight years ahead. The notes may or may not be secured.
C notes These are similar to the above but with even longer-maturity profiles.
High-yield bonds These are publicly traded bonds that offer high interest rates. The high rates are to compensate for the risks involved in holding them. They are a form of 'junk bond'.
Asset-based finance This involves securing borrowings against debtors and inventory. It also includes entering leasing contracts to enable plant and machinery to be used.

Example 23.1

It is easier to arrange a leveraged buy-out for a company with cash flows that are expected to show a relatively stable growth over time. This example illustrates the point and shows how a leveraged buy-out can work.

The new company purchases net assets of £1 million, half of which are depreciable. The fixed assets have a life of ten years. The company finances the purchase with £100 000 equity and £900 000 of debt finance. Its earnings before interest and tax (EBIT) in the first year is £200 000 and is expected to grow at 20% per annum. It pays corporation tax at a rate of 25%. Interest on the debt is at 15% per annum.

Profit-and-loss account (£000)

	Years				
	1	2	3	4	5
EBIT	200	240	288	346	415
Interest paid	135	125	111	92	63
	65	115	177	254	352
Tax payable	16	29	44	64	88
Earnings available	49	86	133	190	264
Sources and uses of funds					
Earnings	49	86	133	190	264
Depreciation	50	50	50	50	50
	99	136	183	240	314
Repayment of loans	70	90	130	190	270
Dividends	10	12	15	20	25
Increase in working capital	19	34	38	30	19
	99	136	183	240	314

Balance sheet

	Opening	1	2	3	4	5
				Years		
Equity	100	139	213	331	501	740
Debt	900	830	740	610	420	150
	1000	969	953	941	921	890
Assets	1000	1000	950	900	850	800
Less depreciation		50	50	50	50	50
		950	900	850	800	750
Working capital/ opening balance/ increase during year			19	53	91	121
		19	34	38	30	19
	1000	969	953	941	921	890

The resulting profit-and-loss account, sources and application of funds statement and balance sheet are shown above.

Basically what is happening is that the company, which is highly profitable, is using the funds generated each year to pay off the loans. It is only paying a small percentage of the funds earned to shareholders as dividends. The shareholders will in time receive their rewards in terms of capital gains. The funds retained in the business each year are not quite adequate to cover the loss in value of the fixed assets, and hence the total value of the assets slowly declines over the five years. The equity increases each year by the earnings available for distribution less the actual dividends paid. The year 1 figure is the initial equity of £100 000 plus the £49 000 profits, less the £10 000 dividend payment. A major change is that at the beginning of the period only 10% of the assets belonged to the shareholders, but at the end of the five years 83% of the assets belong to them. In book terms the value of the equity investment has increased sevenfold over the period. It is this increase that will lead to substantial capital gains for the original investors, i.e. the managers and any venture-capital company that backed them.

The expression 'mezzanine finance' also includes preference shares and convertible loans, as well as less well-known forms of finance such as vendor notes with an equity 'kicker'.

23.6 BUY-IN

In a buy-in a group of managers who have, or who believe that they have, the necessary skills to run a particular type of business look around for such a business to purchase. They hope to find a company that has considerable potential but that has not been run to its full advantage, perhaps because of poor existing management. Having found a suitable company they will then work with a financier, usually a venture capitalist, to put together a deal to buy the target business from its existing shareholders. The target could be the whole of the company, or just a part of it. They will make an offer to either the managers or the existing owners of the business, and hope that the target company will be prepared to sell off part of its business or that the shareholders will sell off the whole of the business.

It is the opposite of a buy-out, in which existing managers of a business attempt to buy the assets that they already manage. In a buy-in a group of outside managers attempt to take control of the target assets from the existing owners and to take over management from existing managers. With a buy-in, unlike a management buy-out, there is no advantage of insider knowledge.

The financial backer – the venture capitalist – is crucial in such buy-ins. Usually the managers who are planning to run the business have limited resources of their own and so high levels of borrowing or mezzanine finance are required. In a number of buy-ins it is in fact the venture capitalist who initiates the deal. A financial institution might notice that the managers of a business are not making the best use of opportunities and so they seek a team of managers whom they would be willing to support to run the business.

With this a small group of individuals, who might include existing shareholders and/or managers with or without institutional support, between them purchase all the shares of a public company. The small group end the public status of the company. It could result in the shares of a company no longer being dealt in on a stock exchange and so no longer being subject to whatever regulations applied. This type of restructuring is quite common in the USA.

On occasions a group of existing shareholders in the company purchase the shares of all the other shareholders. They would do this because the small group involved prefer private company status. An example of this occurred in the UK with the Virgin Company. Richard Branson, the founder of the company, built it up and then launched it as a public company. He later decided to revert to private company status and did so by buying back shares from the public and financial institutions.

The reasons for going private include the following.

1 The administrative burden and costs of meeting listing requirements are reduced.
2 The independence of a company that is financially attractive and vulnerable to a takeover bid is protected.
3 A company that is having financial problems that would result in a falling share price, with whatever that may bring about, is protected.
4 Agency costs are reduced; the small group of shareholders are more likely to be close to the managers than in a public company and there should be greater goal congruence.
5 The owner/manager does not wish to maximize short-term performance.

It has been found that existing shareholders benefit from a 'going private' buy-out situation. Their shares are purchased and this could well result in a capital gain. The reward situation is similar to that of shareholders in a company takeover: the vendor shareholders show gains. However, as mentioned above, in a normal management buy-out situation, the sale price can sometimes benefit the purchasers who have inside information and opportunity to control information to affect the purchase price.

It might be difficult for the small group to fund the acquisition, so that the assistance of a venture-capital company or another third party might be required. If a large proportion of borrowed funds are required, it resembles a leveraged buy-out. If the management of the original company are involved in the group making the acquisition it is a form of management buy-out, with the buy-out being for the whole of the assets of the selling company.

Leveraged management buy-outs do, however, differ from going private in a number of ways. One of the key differences is that third-party equity participation is usually necessary in the buy-out. Another difference is the amount of borrowing required. A going private deal usually does not need so much outside finance.

23.8 SHARE RE-PURCHASE

Since the Companies Act 1981, it has been possible for companies in the UK to re-purchase their own shares. This is a form of capital restructuring. For a company to do this it is necessary for its articles of association to give it the right to do so. There must be approval by the shareholders for a general power to buy in the market or specific approval for an off-market purchase. Own shares purchased by a UK company must be cancelled; there is no provision for them to be held for subsequent resale, as there is in the USA.

GEC was one of the first UK quoted companies to obtain and use this power. In the accounts for the year ended 31 March 1985, the Directors' Report gave a summary of the transactions in which 73 million shares of 5p each (nominal value £3.6 million) were purchased for £156 million.

A company may wish to re-purchase its shares in the following circumstances.

1 It has cash available and, rather than paying it out to shareholders as dividends, it purchases some of its shares in the market place. The continuing shareholders should benefit as the share price should rise. The total supply of the company's shares has fallen and there is no reason to believe that the total demand for the shares will have changed.

2 A major shareholder may wish to dispose of his or her shares and the shareholders agree that the company should use its funds to buy these shares and cancel them.

Although the possibility of re-purchase is comparatively new in the UK, it has existed for a long time in the USA. It has been seen in that country as an alternative to paying a dividend. It has been discussed in this book in Chapter 14 in connection with dividend policy. In theory, if the capital market is efficient and there are no commission and taxation problems, the company and the shareholders should be indifferent between a dividend payment and a share re-purchase.

One result of the re-purchase is an increase in earnings per share, and it is sometimes suggested that this will benefit the shareholders because it leads to an increase in share price. However, if the company had retained the cash and reinvested, this should have led to an increase in earnings, and so in share price, and if it had paid the cash out as a dividend a shareholder could have invested the cash to increase his or her returns.

23.9 REVERSE TAKEOVER

Reverse takeover occurs when one company X takes over another company Y that is larger than itself. If the purchase was paid for just in shares, the situation would finish up with the original shareholders of Y owning more shares in the amalgamated company than the original shareholders of X. The shareholders of X would finish up with a minority interest in their 'own' company. This situation can be avoided if some of the payment is in the form of cash. X could raise the cash through a rights issue or by borrowing.

An attempt at a reverse takeover occurred in the UK when the Australian brewing company Elders IXL attempted to take over the much larger UK company Allied-Lyons. Elders planned to finance the acquisition by borrowing from a consortium of banks. The bid was eventually withdrawn.

One result of a reverse takeover financed by borrowing is to raise dramatically the level of gearing of the company making the bid. It becomes like a leveraged buy-out. The banks funding the acquisition need to be assured that the acquirer will be able to service the debt taken on.

A reverse takeover bid requires the agreement of the shareholders of the bidding firm. This technique can be used in situations where a private company wishes to go public. It needs to be organized such that it is the public company X, the smaller company, that takes over the larger private company Y. X would issue its shares to the shareholders of Y. The original shareholders of Y will now be the majority shareholders in a public company. The public company, which may or may not have a listing, will be much larger following this reverse takeover.

23.10 ASSET SWAPS

These arise when one company swaps some of its assets for assets in another company. Such swaps often arise in cross-border deals. A British company may have a certain asset (say a factory) in the UK it does not want. It may be looking for a factory in France. If it can find a French company that wishes to dispose of a factory in France and to obtain one in the UK then a deal can be struck.

An example arose in the case of the British company Powergen. The company was required to dispose of certain generating plant in the UK. The disposal was necessary because of an arrangement it had come to with the Regulator of the electricity industry. Rather than sell the generating plant to a purchaser, and so obtain cash, Powergen preferred to swap the assets for assets in another country.

Another example for a different reason occurred in 1995 when Tarmac and Wimpey, two big companies in the UK construction industry, swapped assets worth £600 million. Wimpey exchanged its building, quarrying and engineering subsidiaries in exchange for Tarmacs UK housebuilding operations. The reason given for the swap was that neither company had sufficient cash to be able to invest what they thought was needed in all the types of business they were running. They each decided to focus on core activities.

23.11 BUSINESS FAILURE

The earlier sections in this chapter were concerned with positive aspect of restructuring.We now turn to negative reasons for change. There can be many different reasons why a company might encounter financial difficulties and fail. There is evidence that the percentage of companies that fail in any year is highly correlated with macro-economic factors, such as changes in interest rates and changes in the level of economic activity. Other significant factors outside the firm's control can be changes in technology and changes in consumer demands. Changes in technology mean that the firm's production methods become obsolete, and changes in consumers' tastes and habits mean that the demand for the product or service produced quickly disappears.

The main reason, however, why a particular business fails is inadequate management. It can be argued that even if there are changes in macro-economic factors, in technology or in consumer habits a management that thinks ahead should have been ready for these events. They should have been able to anticipate these changes. A management with a strategy, with a plan, should be sufficiently diversified to be able to withstand all but the most dramatic crises.

The sequence of events leading to the typical failure can be summarized as follows:

1 Bad management leads to:
2 Poor management information (including poor accounting information) leads to:
3 Mistakes, including one of the following
   (a) not responding to change in the market place, in technology or in society;
   (b) overtrading – rapid expansion;
   (c) the launch of a big project or making a large acquisition – either the growth is too much for the management to handle or the timing is wrong;
   (d) allowing financial gearing to rise – poor financial structure;
   (e) overdependence on a small number of customers or suppliers.

Company restructuring, refinancing and liquidation

Difficulties resulting from one of these policies leads to:

4 Financial ratios deteriorating and/or creative accounting techniques being utilized.

We will briefly look at each of these 'stages'.

Bad management

There is some agreement in the literature on the management characteristics which can be dangerous and result in bad decisions. We list some of these characteristics below. It is not being suggested that all companies that experience one or more of these characteristics will fail. All that is being pointed out is that in a high proportion of companies that do fail there is one or more of these characteristics present. There are, for example, companies that are successful and have been successful for a long time that are dominated by one individual. This is not being denied. But there are also a high proportion of firms that fail that are dominated by one person.

Worrying characteristics

1 one-man (or one-woman) rule;
2 combined position of chairman of board of directors and chief executive of the company;
3 unbalanced board of directors;
4 unbalanced top-management team;
5 lack of depth in management team;
6 weak finance function in the company;
7 a board of directors with too few independent non-executive directors.

Most of these items are self-explanatory. The Cadbury Report on Corporate Governance commented on a number of the same issues. They had been discussed in the literature of corporation failure for a long time. The Cadbury Report was more concerned with the abuse of power; that is, the top management team acting in their own interests rather than in the interests of their shareholders. It is intriguing that the same factors which can lead to an abuse of power can also lead to business failure.

Inadequate management information systems

It is important that a company's decision makers have certain up-to-date information on such items as turnover, cash flow, rate of gross profits and levels of creditors and borrowing. When failed companies are analysed after the event it is often found that:

- they have poor management-accounting data, therefore lack of information of true costs;
- there is poor budgetary control;
- there are inadequate cash-flow forecasts;
- the decision makers are not aware of the true value of the assets;
- there is poor control of working capital.

Mistakes

The weakness in management combined with poor information leads to mistakes. Certain of the more common are mentioned above. Other mistakes include:

- badly directed research and development programmes;
- inappropriate diversification.

On the subject of an acquisition or capital expansion programme that is too large, Sir Kenneth Cork, a leading UK liquidator, has expressed the opinion that a company should not undertake an investment which if it fails could not be written off and the company still remain a viable business. 'Too large' is of course a function of the size of the company. All that is being suggested is that a company 'should not bite off more than it can chew'. There is a danger that some management teams that have done well during a boom period think they can achieve anything. This tempts them into undertaking big projects relative to their size or into making a major acquisition. It only requires a small change in the macro-economic situation to prove that the management team has its limitations.

Financial accounts

It is only some time after management mistakes have been made that this will become apparent from the published accounting numbers. The annual report and accounts is mainly a historical document. Through the use of techniques for smoothing accounting profits and losses and through creative accounting techniques, recognition of the actual financial position of a company may be delayed. Directors in companies that have something to hide will adopt a policy involving the 'management of earnings disclosure'. In the end, of course, the true position will become apparent.

It is precisely because of this time lag between a company's getting into financial difficulties and it being possible to detect this from annual accounts that superficial financial ratio analysis is of limited use. There are, of course, many models based on financial ratios that are used in practice to identify companies in financial difficulties. (These are discussed in Chapter 2.)

The point being made in this section is that anybody interested in the credit standing of a company or in valuing the company's shares needs to look for the symptoms and possible causes of failure in a company. These are of course subjective but it does not mean they can be ignored. It is dangerous to wait until the financial problem can be identified objectively through the annual reports of accounts.

Small-company failure

The rate of failure is very much a function of company size, and the length of time the company has been in existence. Of all companies which fail, between 50% and 60% are of the newly formed small company category. Clearly not all newly formed companies fail, but the success rate is comparatively small. It is said that venture capital companies, when assessing which companies to support with finance, work on the principle that on average only two out of ten companies achieve any considerable success. A further four out of ten survive but do not really grow. The remaining four out of the ten fail. To the professional investor the problem is identifying which of the ten will succeed and which will fail.

Much of this failure is due to poor management. A study by the 3i [2] concluded that most small business start-ups were

- under-capitalized,
- undergeared,
- burdened with the wrong mix of short- and long-term debt,
- ignorant of sources of finance open to them and
- ignorant of the real need for adequate cash planning and financial control.

As indicated above management failures may well be reflected in many ways, e.g. in lack of financial control and financial records. Managers are conscientious but too often they are too optimistic and financially inept. They have little idea

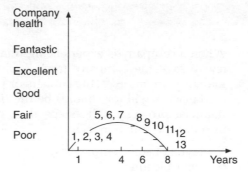

Figure 23.1

of the finance their businesses needed, either the amount or the appropriate type.

Argenti [3] distinguishes three paths to company failure. One path is that applicable to a newly formed small company. The second path relates to a dynamic company, the company which starts small and grows quickly. The third path relates to an established company. In this section we shall concentrate on the first path.

Argenti's research indicates that the maximum life for the small companies that follow his first path to failure is eight years. The path is illustrated in Figure 23.1. Over the life-span of these companies, certain pointers to their eventual failure, certain indicators, can be identified. Clearly not all these points apply to a particular company that fails, although Argenti does believe that points 1–5 appear in all that do fail. In fairness it must be said that some of the points that suggest future failure can also be found in some small companies that are successful.

Argenti's paths to failure are an attempt to put into sequence what he feels are the characteristics present in most company failures. These patterns are subjective, but they indicate points that should be looked for in trying to identify at an early stage those companies that may experience failure or financial distress.

The key to the numbered points on the path to type-one failure is as follows.

1 Launch of the company: the founder is the manager and he or she knows little about business in general, only about the goods or services that are to be offered by the company.
2 No accounting information is available within the business, no budget, no cash flow plans, no costing system – in fact, no financial yardsticks at all.
3 The company obtains a bank loan or acquires equipment on a hire-purchase or lease scheme. The result is high gearing from the start.
4 A large project is launched, usually with an overestimate of the sales revenues and an underestimate of the costs.
5 At this point it becomes obvious that the proprietor was too optimistic.
6 Cash flows are probably bad; financial ratios also look poor.
7 Creative accounting is begun because the proprietor needs more money from the bank.
8 The proprietor begins to succumb to stress; non-financial indications of failure appear.
9 A normal business hazard, such as a large bad debt or an economic downturn occurs.
10 The proprietor takes panic action such as cutting prices to increase sales. This leads to overtrading.
11 Further loans are obtained. At this point the liabilities exceed the assets.
12 Profit is not enough to service the loans.
13 The receiver is called in.

When a company is experiencing financial difficulties steps need to be taken to try to save the company from liquidation. The steps can be initiated by the managers themselves, the bankers or possibly the shareholders.

Managers will (or should) be the first to be aware that a company is having financial problems. The steps they can initially take which it is hoped will improve the situation include:

- layoff of some employees;
- plant closure;
- sale of assets;
- reduction of expenditure on research and development;
- begin to negotiate with banks for either extra finance and/or rescheduling of existing debts.

The banks may become aware of a company's difficulties as a result of increasing borrowing requirements or they may become aware that a company is near to breaking its borrowing covenants. The banks should be monitoring the company's cash-flow position. Shareholders may become aware of difficulties as a result of falling profits, of boardroom disputes, of creative accounting techniques being adopted. The shareholders (the legal owners) could well be the last to know of the financial problems.

The first step in the UK in saving a company is a 'standstill agreement'. This means that the company's bank or bankers agree to continue to provide banking facilities for a period of time in order to allow the company to work out proposals for the future. Standstill agreements are usually short: usually only a month or two is allowed.

There has been much ill-feeling over this matter. It has been argued that the banks in the UK have been too quick to close down the smaller company. It is argued that the larger the company, the bigger the debts, the more likely it is that banks will give a company time in which to be saved.

Once a standstill agreement has been agreed upon, it is usual to appoint a firm of accountants to provide a view on the future prospects of the company. Hopefully a rescue plan is proposed. This plan will be concerned with operational matters, such as ceasing to trade in certain areas, and with financial matters.

The financial plan will have to take into account the interests of shareholders, bondholders, banks, managers and creditors. All could well have conflicting views as to whether, and how, the company should be saved.

The lenders, whether bondholders or banks, might well be reluctant to invest any further money, but might well have to put up with the restructuring of the existing loans. The restructuring could involve

- extension of the period before the loan is repaid;
- agreement to defer the payment of interest on the debt;
- agreement to roll up interest into future periods;
- the swapping of debt for an equity stake in the company.

The giving up of debt in return for an equity stake by banks was once uncommon in the UK, but it has now become more widespread. It had for a long time been a common practice in continental Europe. British banks have argued that they are there as lenders, not as investors. They see debt swaps only as a last-resort solution.

In a restructuring the interests of ordinary and preference shareholders need to be considered. In fact, their position is usually very weak. They are usually unwilling to invest new money in a company in a poor financial condition.

A high-profile company that needed to restructure was Laura Ashley. In 1989 the company had high debts and trading conditions were very poor. The company was using a multiple currency option facility to enable it to borrow short-term up to a certain level. The agreement contained a gearing covenant. The level of gearing was approaching the limit. It should be appreciated that the banks are in a position to monitor the level of gearing of a company at any time; they require regular cash-flow information to be supplied by the company as a condition of a loan.

Managers of Laura Ashley had a meeting with the bankers. The company wanted additional short-term lines of credit. They were worried that the need for short-term facilities would exceed the limits. It was reported in the press that some banks wanted to withdraw previously agreed commitments. They were worried Laura Ashley would default.

The company complained that they had paid 'commitment fees for years and when the funds were needed they were not there' – the commitment fee being payable to provide for a line of credit as and when needed.

The banks eventually agreed (in 1990) to make more short-term finance available, but it was reported that the terms were 'excessively punitive'. The company also had high fees to pay to lawyers, accountants and bankers for arranging the refinancing. To obtain a long-term financial solution to its problems the company in the end did a deal with a Japanese company who paid cash for shares in the company.

23.13 INSOLVENCY/LIQUIDATION

One hopes that as a result of the study of how to manage the financial affairs of a business the reader of this book will never experience his or her own business becoming insolvent. One hopes that the closest the reader will come to a business liquidation is that of a company supplying goods or services moving into the hands of a receiver or of a debtor becoming bankrupt or being liquidated. It has to be appreciated, however, that sometimes the reason companies are liquidated is through little fault of their own. Changes in patterns of trade, in technology, in government economic policy, or as a result of political actions can all lead to a company's becoming insolvent.

We will briefly explain the meaning of the terms involved in this, the ultimate form of business reorganization. Insolvency arises when a business or an individual does not have enough assets to cover the debts. Insolvency, of course, differs from being illiquid. In the latter case a company merely does not have the cash available to pay its debts; it does not mean that if the company realized its fixed assets or sold its inventory it would not have the cash it needs.

Insolvency does not necessarily lead to liquidation. There are a number of actions that can be taken that will avoid the ultimate end of the business. Insolvency is a fact. Either the company has enough assets to cover its debts or it does not. It is the responsibility of the directors of a company to know whether or not a company is insolvent. There are very heavy fines that directors (executive and non-executive) may have to pay if they allow a company to continue trading when it is insolvent. For them to do so is known as 'wrongful trading'. It is no excuse that they did not know the company was insolvent – it is their job to know.

When a company announces it is insolvent, or it fails to pay a debt on time, there are a number of procedures the banks and creditors involved with the company and the courts can follow. We list below five of these procedures in which the court or creditors or bankers are involved:

1 company voluntary arrangement (CVA);
2 administrations;
3 receivership (administrative receiverships);
4 creditors' voluntary liquidations;
5 compulsory liquidations.

Most insolvencies result in the company going into administration. A CVA is the second most common outcome. The third most common is receivership, followed by creditors' voluntary liquidation.

With a company voluntary arrangement, the creditors ask the court to appoint an insolvency practitioner to be an administrator with the task of attempting to rescue the company. The company management work with the administrator in an attempt to save the business – the company management and the administrator jointly run the business. Such arrangements have had mixed success and on occasions they can be unworkable.

Administration

This is a procedure designed to allow a business to continue while plans are developed either to rescue the business or to attempt to maximize its asset value. Its aim is to give a business time to breathe. It is not necessarily beneficial for a company to cease trading the moment it becomes insolvent. It might be possible to rescue the company, or to improve the value of the assets of the business prior to disposal.

For a company to go into administration, it is necessary to obtain permission from a court. Either the representatives of the company that is insolvent or creditors of that company can seek from the court an administrative order. The court, before granting such an order, will wish to see some evidence that allowing administration now could lead to greater benefits than proceeding immediately to liquidation.

If the court grants an administrative order, the day-to-day running of the company is put in the hands of an administrator who is appointed by the court. While the administrator is running the company the creditors cannot take steps to recover assets or to interfere with the running of the business. This means that administrations are not always popular with banks and other creditors. The banks and creditors are concerned because the administration process can be costly and time-consuming, and does not necessarily rescue the business or lead to an improvement in the value of the assets of the business.

Receiverships

These are officially called 'administrative receiverships'. With this process a receiver is appointed by a bank or another institution which has lent to the insolvent company and which has a fixed charge, a floating charge or a debenture over a substantial part of the company's assets. A major difference between a receivership and an administration is that with a receivership it is a lending institution or institutions that make the appointment of the person to run the affairs of the insolvent company whereas with an administration it is the court that makes the appointment. The receiver is often seen by the insolvent company as simply a debt collector for the banks and other lending institutions, whereas the administrator is seen as a person trying to save the company in a restructured form.

Technically, the receiver acts in the best interests of all creditors, not just of the institutions that made the appointment. They frequently keep a business running for a period after their appointment in order to make it easier to find a buyer for the whole business. They do not necessarily sell off the individual assets in order to obtain funds to pay off the major creditors. The Society of Practitioners of Insolvency estimate that receivers in fact manage to save 45% of insolvent companies in their care.

Banks prefer receiverships to administrations, because with the latter process they are not in a position to interfere with the administrator while he or she is trying to save the business. With a receivership it is the banks who appoint the person to run the business. If and when a receiver finds it not possible to find a buyer for the business a liquidator is appointed to take over and the assets are sold, and what cash is realized is distributed to creditors.

It is sometimes claimed in the UK that when a company is experiencing financial difficulties banks frequently call in a receiver far too quickly. It is claimed that if the banks were to give a company a little more time to solve its problems the company could be saved.

Creditors' voluntary liquidations

This is a procedure for winding up insolvent businesses. It involves selling off a company's assets and distributing what cash is available. With a creditors' voluntary liquidation the shareholders of the company, on realizing that the company is insolvent, appoint a liquidator. This is followed by a creditors' meeting at which the person proposed by the shareholders as a liquidator will be confirmed or another liquidator appointed. The liquidator is expected to act in the best interest of all creditors.

The appointment of a liquidator almost always means the end for a company; it almost always means the company ceases trading.

Compulsory liquidation

This is a form of liquidation in which an individual creditor can take steps that will lead to the winding up of a company. Compulsory liquidation is the last step of a creditor or group of creditors who cannot obtain the co-operation of the management and shareholders of a company when there are debts unpaid. The creditors petition the court for a winding-up order.

This procedure differs from creditors' voluntary liquidation, in that with the voluntary process the company shareholders agree to go into liquidation. With the compulsory process the company's wishes do not matter. If the court is satisfied that a creditor is owed money and that the company is insolvent, it will order that the company be wound up.

Members' (shareholders') voluntary liquidation

This is a winding-up process initiated by a company. It differs from the five methods mentioned above in that it occurs, not when a company is insolvent, but when a company is in a position to pay its debts in full. The members, that is the shareholders, wish to have the company's assets turned into cash, to have the creditors paid and for the balance to be returned to them, They wish to cash in their investments. They may wish to do this when they believe the company has fulfilled the objectives set when it was formed, or because they no longer wish to be involved in the business venture.

Practices within the European Union

Since the time the European Economic Community was formed attempts have been made to harmonize the insolvency laws of the different states. None of the attempts has been successful, the main reason being that the results one country wishes to achieve from its insolvency laws differ from the results another country wishes to achieve. For example, the French put greater weight in their insolvency laws to protecting the rights of the employees of the insolvent company than do the British. The pecking order in which the different types of creditor of the company are repaid varies from one country to another.

The attitude towards an undischarged bankrupt also varies from country to country. The term 'bankruptcy' of course applies to individuals. In the UK a person who is bankrupt is nearly always automatically discharged two or three years after being declared bankrupt. When the person is discharged from bankruptcy this means that any unpaid balance of debts is written off. The person involved can then enter into another business venture. This is not the case in most other countries in the European Union, where the practice is that a person remains bankrupt until able to pay fully the outstanding debts. The British seem keen to give a person another chance even though the bankrupt person may have large amounts of outstanding debts. Unfortunately, it is not uncommon for an individual having been given another chance to fail yet again with a new list of creditors unable to be paid.

The differences in insolvency and bankruptcy laws within the European Union are so far apart that it will be a long time before any degree of harmonization can be achieved.

USA Chapter 11

There has been much criticism of the banks in the UK for allegedly withdrawing financial support too quickly from companies in financial difficulties. The result is that the company goes into receivership. The argument is that if the bank that had lent money to the company continued to provide support the company would survive. For the bank the decision on whether to continue support or to appoint a receiver is often finely balanced. The bank has to decide whether if it allows the company to continue to trade it could result in even greater future losses for the bank and the other creditors of the company. The bank can argue that their primary responsibility is to their own shareholders, and not in attempting to preserve jobs and maintain levels of employment.

Critics of the UK banks point enviously to the system that exists in the USA. Chapter 11 of the US Bankruptcy Code is geared more to assisting a company to survive than to protecting the creditors. If a company in the USA in financial difficulties applies to the courts for protection under Chapter 11, it is given time in which to try to solve its financial problems. The company is given the time in which to work with its creditors in an attempt to come up with a rescue package. Usually this means the business is restructured – it is reconstructed. Perhaps parts of the business will be sold, perhaps the debt repayments will be retimed. The creditors are prevented from moving in quickly and closing the business down. The company is given breathing space.

This US procedure has had some spectacular successes, but its critics claim it is expensive to administer, and is only successful with larger companies. It is claimed that not more than 12% of Chapter 11 cases result in a successful reorganization. The management of a company in difficulties in the UK would not surprisingly favour US Chapter 11-type legislation, as it gives them an opportunity to continue to control the business, which would not happen in receivership. It keeps the company out of the hands of the banks at least for some time.

23.14 REFERENCES

1 Wright, M. and Coyne, J. (1985) *Management Buyouts in British Industry*, Croom-Helm, London.
2 3i (1994) *The Changing Face of Management Buy-ins*, 3i Group, London.
3 Argenti, J. (1976) *Corporate Collapse: the Causes and Symptoms*, McGraw-Hill, London.

23.15 FURTHER READING

For a selection of interesting articles on the subject see:

Deangelo, H., Deangelo, L. and Rice, E. (1986) Going private: a study of the effects of changes in corporate ownership structure, in *The Revolution in Corporate Finance*, (ed. J.M. Stern and D.H. Chew), Blackwell, Oxford.

Franks, J.R. and Harris, R.S. (1989) Shareholder wealth effects of corporate takeovers: the UK experience 1955–1985, *Journal of Financial Economics*, **23**.

Jensen, M.C. (1989) Eclipse of the public corporation, *Harvard Business Review*, Sept./Oct.

Rybczynski, T. (1989) Corporate restructuring, *National Westminster Bank Quarterly Review*, August.

Wright, M. (1986) Demergers, in *Divestment and Strategic Change*, (ed. J. Coyne and M. Wright), Philip Allan.

Wright, M., Chiplin, B. and Thompson, S. (1993) The market for corporate control, divestments and buyouts, in *European Mergers and Merger Policy*, (ed. M. Bishop and J. Kay) Oxford University Press, Oxford.

Wright, M., Robbie, K. and Thompson, S. (1989) On the finance and accounting implications of management buyouts, *British Accounting Review*, September.

Wright, M., Thompson, S., Chiplin, B. and Robbie, K. (1991) *Buy-ins and Buy-outs*, Graham & Trotman.

23.16 PROBLEMS

1 Management buy-outs have become popular in UK industry since 1980, and accountants play a part in appraising the viability of such schemes.
   (a) State what you understand by the term 'management buy-out', and outline three situations in which such an operation might be attempted. (11 marks)
   (b) As an accountant advising a management buy-out team, set out the main matters covered by your reports:
      (i) to the members of the team;
      (ii) to a financial institution which is requested to provide capital for the venture. (14 marks)

ACCA

2 (a) In recent years there has been a large increase in the number of management buy-outs, often when a company is in financial distress. What are the possible financial advantages to the seller of a management buy-out relative to a liquidation?
   (b) Five managers of Leivers Ltd are discussing the possibility of a management buy-out on the part of the company that they work for. The buy-out would require a total of £700 000, of which £525 000 would comprise the purchase cost and £175 000 funds for a small expansion in activity, and for working capital. The managers believe that they could jointly provide £70 000.

(i) Discuss possible sources of finance that the managers might use to raise the required funds.

(ii) What are likely to be the major factors that a potential supplier of finance will consider before deciding whether to offer finance? What type of security or other conditions might providers of finance specify?

ACCA

3 A large retail store decides to spin off one of its subsidiaries that produces shop fittings. You are one of the directors of this subsidiary and with other colleagues you decide that you would like to acquire it. Between you it is possible to produce £500 000 of capital, but the parent company hopes to obtain £5 million from the sale. The current level of earnings of the subsidiary before tax is £300 000. The corporation tax rate is 30%. Put together a financial proposal to purchase the subsidiary that might appeal to financial backers and to the parent company.

4 It has been argued that leveraged buy-outs are self-limiting, short-term organizations, which are likely to produce significant adverse effects on corporate investment. To what extent do you agree or disagree with this view?

5 Analyse the case for requiring the parties to a merger to show that it would produce positive benefits before allowing it to proceed. To what extent do you consider that 'divestment deals' may have a positive role to play in allowing the market for corporate control to function?

6 The senior management of the plastics division of Kram PLC is planning a 'leveraged' buy-out of the division. The division will become an unlisted public limited company after the buy-out. Recent financial details of the division are summarized below:

Plastics division: Summarized profit-and-loss account for:

	Last year £000	Two years ago £000
Turnover	8500	8100
Earnings before interest and tax	946	958
Interest[1]	520	466
Attributable taxation[2]	206	187
Earnings after tax	220	305

Plastics division: Summarized balance sheet as at the end of:

	Last year £000	Last year £000	Two years ago £000	Two years ago £000
Land and buildings[3]		880		840
Plant and machinery (net)		1336		1440
		2216		2280
Stock	1830		1440	
Debtors	1160		940	
Bank	40	3030	87	2467
Less:				
Creditors	720		680	
Attributable taxation	206		187	
Bank overdraft	320	(1246)	–	(867)
		4000		3880
Financed by:[4]				
Equity		2800		2720
Debt		1200		1160
		4000		3880

Notes

[1] This represents an annual payment to the group for the total amount of long-term finance provided, plus interest on the bank overdraft. The cost of the long-term finance provided by the group is based upon the group's weighted-average cost of capital of 12% per year.

[2] The division is charged taxation by the group according to the percentage of group earnings before interest and tax that are generated by the plastics division.

[3] The land and buildings are estimated to have a market value 30% higher than the book value.

[4] Financing is based upon the same proportions as the book value of the group's equity and debt. The group has provided all external financing for the division, with the exception of the bank overdraft.

The managers of the plastics division have been told that the division may be purchased for the cash sum of £5 million. The bank overdraft would be repaid by the group prior to any purchase and there would be no outstanding long-term liabilities or tax liability at the time of purchase.

The managers would contribute a total of £500 000 in return for 500 000 £1 ordinary shares. Grow-Venture PLC would provide the other £4.5 million, £400 000 in ordinary shares, £1.5 million in fixed-rate bonds at a fixed annual interest rate of 13%, £1 million in subordinated debt at an annual interest rate of 14% and the remainder in 9% convertible loan stock. Conversion is at the rate of 50 shares for every £100 loan stock, and may occur at any time after six years.

A condition imposed by Grow-Venture is that the £1.5 million 13% debt and the £1 million 14% debt are both repaid by a series of equal annual payments (including interest and principal) over five years.

Grow-Venture plans to dispose of its shareholdings (but not convertible loan stock) in a little over five years' time when it is hoped that the company will be listed on the USM with a market value of equity at least as great as the book value of equity at that time.

Corporate tax is payable at the rate of 35% in the year that profit is earned. No further capital issues are planned, nor major purchases or disposals of fixed assets during the next five years. Annual dividends are expected to be 20% of available earnings for the foreseeable future, and the division's cost of equity is estimated to be 22% per year. The average price–earnings ratio of small listed companies in the plastics industry is 14.1:1.

Earnings before interest and tax are expected to increase by 8% per year.

Required:

(a) Estimate the minimum annual compound percentage increase in the book value of its equity holding that Grow-Venture PLC hopes for over a five-year period. State clearly any assumptions that you make. (10 marks)

(b) Explain what is meant by a 'leveraged' (geared) management buy-out and estimate how gearing is expected to alter during the first five years after the management buy-out. (6 marks)

(c) Discuss, showing any relevant calculations whether you think that the price of the buy-out of £5 million is a fair price, too high or too low.

(9 marks)

(25 marks)

ACCA, June 1990

7 A group of managers in the textile subsidiary of Grocas PLC are considering a management buy-out of the subsidiary. They are proposing to bid £6 million pounds for the subsidiary, and can raise £1 million pounds in equity between them. Advise the managers on the key factors that they must consider in order for the buy-out to succeed.

Table 1 *Future value of £1 after n years at 100r% compound interest: (1 + r)n*

Years n	Discount rate as percentage (100r)					
	1	2	3	4	5	6
1	1.0100	1.0200	1.0300	1.0400	1.0500	1.0600
2	1.0201	1.0404	1.0609	1.0816	1.1025	1.1236
3	1.0303	1.0612	1.0927	1.1249	1.1576	1.1910
4	1.0406	1.0824	1.1255	1.1699	1.2155	1.2625
5	1.0510	1.1041	1.1593	1.2167	1.2763	1.3382
6	1.0615	1.1262	1.1941	1.2653	1.3401	1.4185
7	1.0721	1.1487	1.2299	1.3159	1.4071	1.5036
8	1.0829	1.1717	1.2668	1.3686	1.4775	1.5938
9	1.0937	1.1951	1.3048	1.4233	1.5513	1.6895
10	1.1046	1.2190	1.3439	1.4802	1.6289	1.7908
11	1.1157	1.2434	1.3842	1.5395	1.7103	1.8983
12	1.1268	1.2682	1.4258	1.6010	1.7959	2.0122
13	1.1381	1.2936	1.4685	1.6651	1.8856	2.1329
14	1.1495	1.3195	1.5126	1.7317	1.9799	2.2609
15	1.1610	1.3459	1.5580	1.8009	2.0789	2.3966
16	1.1726	1.3728	1.6047	1.8730	2.1829	2.5404
17	1.1843	1.4002	1.6528	1.9479	2.2920	2.6928
18	1.1961	1.4282	1.7024	2.0258	2.4066	2.8543
19	1.2081	1.4568	1.7535	2.1068	2.5270	3.0256
20	1.2202	1.4859	1.8061	2.1911	2.6533	3.2071
21	1.2324	1.5157	1.8603	2.2788	2.7860	3.3996
22	1.2447	1.5460	1.9161	2.3699	2.9253	3.6035
23	1.2572	1.5769	1.9736	2.4647	3.0715	3.8197
24	1.2697	1.6084	2.0328	2.5633	3.2251	4.0489
25	1.2824	1.6406	2.0938	2.6658	3.3864	4.2919
26	1.2953	1.6734	2.1566	2.7725	3.5557	4.5494
27	1.3082	1.7069	2.2213	2.8834	3.7335	4.8223
28	1.3213	1.7410	2.2879	2.9987	3.9201	5.1117
29	1.3345	1.7758	2.3566	3.1187	4.1161	5.4184
30	1.3478	1.8114	2.4273	3.2434	4.3219	5.7435

n	7	8	9	10	11	12
1	1.0700	1.0800	1.0900	1.1000	1.1100	1.1200
2	1.1449	1.1664	1.1881	1.2100	1.2321	1.2544
3	1.2250	1.2597	1.2950	1.3310	1.3676	1.4049
4	1.3108	1.3605	1.4116	1.4641	1.5181	1.5735
5	1.4026	1.4693	1.5386	1.6105	1.6851	1.7623
6	1.5007	1.5869	1.6771	1.7716	1.8704	1.9738
7	1.6058	1.7138	1.8280	1.9487	2.0762	2.2107
8	1.7182	1.8509	1.9926	2.1436	2.3045	2.4760
9	1.8385	1.9990	2.1719	2.3579	2.5580	2.7731
10	1.9672	2.1589	2.3674	2.5937	2.8394	3.1058
11	2.1049	2.3316	2.5804	2.8531	3.1518	3.4785
12	2.2522	2.5182	2.8127	3.1384	3.4985	3.8960
13	2.4098	2.7196	3.0658	3.4523	3.8833	4.3635
14	2.5785	2.9372	3.3417	3.7975	4.3104	4.8871
15	2.7590	3.1722	3.6425	4.1772	4.7846	5.4736
16	2.9522	3.4259	3.9703	4.5950	5.3109	6.1304
17	3.1588	3.7000	4.3276	5.0545	5.8951	6.8660
18	3.3799	3.9960	4.7171	5.5599	6.5436	7.6900
19	3.6165	4.3157	5.1417	6.1159	7.2633	8.6128
20	3.8697	4.6610	5.6044	6.7275	8.0623	9.6463
21	4.1406	5.0338	6.1088	7.4002	8.9492	10.8038
22	4.4304	5.4365	6.6586	8.1403	9.9336	12.1003
23	4.7405	5.8715	7.2579	8.9543	11.0263	13.5523
24	5.0724	6.3412	7.9111	9.8497	12.2392	15.1786
25	5.4274	6.8485	8.6231	10.8347	13.5855	17.0001
26	5.8074	7.3964	9.3992	11.9182	15.0799	19.0401
27	6.2139	7.9881	10.2451	13.1100	16.7386	21.3249
28	6.6488	8.6271	11.1671	14.4210	18.5799	23.8839
29	7.1143	9.3173	12.1722	15.8631	20.6237	26.7499
30	7.6123	10.0627	13.2677	17.4494	22.8923	29.9599

n	13	14	15	16	17	18
1	1.1300	1.1400	1.1500	1.1600	1.1700	1.1800
2	1.2769	1.2996	1.3225	1.3456	1.3689	1.3924
3	1.4429	1.4815	1.5209	1.5609	1.6016	1.6430
4	1.6305	1.6890	1.7490	1.8106	1.8739	1.9388
5	1.8424	1.9254	2.0114	2.1003	2.1924	2.2878
6	2.0820	2.1950	2.3131	2.4364	2.5652	2.6996
7	2.3526	2.5023	2.6600	2.8262	3.0012	3.1855
8	2.6584	2.8526	3.0590	3.2784	3.5115	3.7589
9	3.0040	3.2519	3.5179	3.8030	4.1084	4.4355
10	3.3946	3.7072	4.0456	4.4114	4.8068	5.2338
11	3.8359	4.2262	4.6524	5.1173	5.6240	6.1759
12	4.3345	4.8179	5.3502	5.9360	6.5801	7.2876
13	4.8980	5.4924	6.1528	6.8858	7.6987	8.5994
14	5.5348	6.2613	7.0757	7.9875	9.0075	10.1472
15	6.2543	7.1379	8.1371	9.2655	10.5387	11.9737
16	7.0673	8.1372	9.3576	10.7480	12.3303	14.1290
17	7.9861	9.2765	10.7613	12.4677	14.4265	16.6722
18	9.0243	10.5752	12.3755	14.4625	16.8790	19.6733
19	10.1974	12.0557	14.2318	16.7765	19.7484	23.2144
20	11.5231	13.7435	16.3665	19.4608	23.1056	27.3930
21	13.0211	15.6676	18.8215	22.5745	27.0335	32.3238
22	14.7138	17.8610	21.6447	26.1864	31.6293	38.1421
23	16.6266	20.3616	24.8915	30.3762	37.0062	45.0076
24	18.7881	23.2122	28.6252	35.2364	43.2973	53.1090
25	21.2305	26.4619	32.9189	40.8742	50.6578	62.6686
26	23.9905	30.1666	37.8568	47.4141	59.2696	73.9490
27	27.1093	34.3899	43.5353	55.0004	69.3455	87.2598
28	30.6335	39.2045	50.0656	63.8004	81.1342	102.9666
29	34.6158	44.6931	57.5755	74.0085	94.9270	121.5005
30	39.1159	50.9502	66.2118	85.8499	111.0646	143.3706

n	19	20	21	.22	23	24
1	1.1900	1.2000	1.2100	1.2200	1.2300	1.2400
2	1.4161	1.4400	1.4641	1.4884	1.5129	1.5376
3	1.6852	1.7280	1.7716	1.8158	1.8609	1.9066
4	2.0053	2.0736	2.1436	2.2153	2.2889	2.3642
5	2.3864	2.4883	2.5937	2.7027	2.8153	2.9316
6	2.8398	2.9860	3.1384	3.2973	3.4628	3.6352
7	3.3793	3.5832	3.7975	4.0227	4.2593	4.5077
8	4.0214	4.2998	4.5950	4.9077	5.2389	5.5895
9	4.7854	5.1598	5.5599	5.9874	6.4439	6.9310
10	5.6947	6.1917	6.7275	7.3046	7.9259	8.5944
11	6.7767	7.4301	8.1403	8.9116	9.7489	10.6571
12	8.0642	8.9161	9.8497	10.8722	11.9912	13.2148
13	9.5964	10.6993	11.9182	13.2641	14.7491	16.3863
14	11.4198	12.8392	14.4210	16.1822	18.1414	20.3191
15	13.5895	15.4070	17.4494	19.7423	22.3140	25.1956
16	16.1715	18.4884	21.1138	24.0856	27.4462	31.2426
17	19.2441	22.1861	25.5477	29.3844	33.7588	38.7408
18	22.9005	26.6233	30.9127	35.8490	41.5233	48.0386
19	27.2516	31.9480	37.4043	43.7358	51.0737	59.5679
20	32.4294	38.3376	45.2593	53.3576	62.8206	73.8641
21	38.5910	46.0051	54.7637	65.0963	77.2694	91.5915
22	45.9233	55.2061	66.2641	79.4175	95.0413	113.5735
23	54.6487	66.2474	80.1795	96.8894	116.9008	140.8311
24	65.0320	79.4968	97.0172	118.2050	143.7880	174.6306
25	77.3881	95.3962	117.3908	144.2101	176.8592	216.5420
26	92.0918	114.4754	142.0429	175.9363	217.5368	268.5121
27	109.5892	137.3705	171.8719	214.6423	267.5703	332.9549
28	130.4112	164.8447	207.9650	261.8636	329.1115	412.8641
29	155.1893	197.8136	251.6377	319.4736	404.8072	511.9515
30	184.6753	237.3763	304.4816	389.7578	497.9128	634.8198

n	25	26	27	28	29	30
1	1.2500	1.2600	1.2700	1.2800	1.2900	1.3000
2	1.5625	1.5876	1.6129	1.6384	1.6641	1.6900
3	1.9531	2.0004	2.0484	2.0972	2.1467	2.1970
4	2.4414	2.5205	2.6014	2.6844	2.7692	2.8561
5	3.0518	3.1758	3.3038	3.4360	3.5723	3.7129
6	3.8147	4.0015	4.1959	4.3980	4.6083	4.8268
7	4.7684	5.0419	5.3288	5.6295	5.9447	6.2749
8	5.9605	6.3528	6.7675	7.2058	7.6686	8.1573
9	7.4506	8.0045	8.5948	9.2234	9.8925	10.6045
10	9.3132	10.0857	10.9153	11.8059	12.7614	13.7858
11	11.6415	12.7080	13.8625	15.1116	16.4622	17.9216
12	14.5519	16.0120	17.6053	19.3428	21.2362	23.2981
13	18.1899	20.1752	22.3588	24.7588	27.3947	30.2875
14	22.7374	25.4207	28.3957	31.6913	35.3391	39.3738
15	28.4217	32.0301	36.0625	40.5648	45.5875	51.1859
16	35.5271	40.3579	45.7994	51.9230	58.8079	66.5417
17	44.4089	50.8510	58.1652	66.4614	75.8621	86.5042
18	55.5111	64.0722	73.8698	85.0706	97.8622	112.4554
19	69.3889	80.7310	93.8147	108.8904	126.2422	146.1920
20	86.7362	101.7211	119.1446	139.3796	162.8524	190.0496
21	108.4202	128.1685	151.3136	178.4059	210.0796	247.0645
22	135.5253	161.4924	192.1683	228.3596	271.0027	321.1838
23	169.4066	203.4804	244.0538	292.3003	349.5934	417.5390
24	211.7582	256.3853	309.9483	374.1444	450.9756	542.8007
25	264.6978	323.0454	393.6343	478.9048	581.7585	705.6409
26	330.8722	407.0372	499.9156	612.9981	750.4684	917.3332
27	413.5903	512.8669	634.8928	784.6376	968.1042	1192.5331
28	516.9878	646.2123	806.3138	1004.3361	1248.8545	1550.2931
29	646.2347	814.2275	1024.0186	1285.5503	1611.0222	2015.3810
30	807.7935	1025.9266	1300.5037	1645.5043	2078.2188	2619.9951

Table 2 *Present value of £1 due after n years at 100r% compound interest: $(1 + r)^{-n}$*

Years n	Discount rate as percentage (100r)									
	1	2	3	4	5	6	7	8	9	10
1	0.9901	0.9804	0.9709	0.9615	0.9524	0.9434	0.9346	0.9259	0.9174	0.9091
2	0.9803	0.9612	0.9426	0.9246	0.9070	0.8900	0.8734	0.8573	0.8417	0.8264
3	0.9706	0.9423	0.9151	0.8890	0.8638	0.8396	0.8163	0.7938	0.7722	0.7513
4	0.9610	0.9238	0.8885	0.8548	0.8227	0.7921	0.7629	0.7350	0.7084	0.6830
5	0.9515	0.9057	0.8626	0.8219	0.7835	0.7473	0.7130	0.6806	0.6499	0.6209
6	0.9420	0.8880	0.8375	0.7903	0.7462	0.7050	0.6663	0.6302	0.5963	0.5645
7	0.9327	0.8706	0.8131	0.7599	0.7107	0.6651	0.6227	0.5835	0.5470	0.5132
8	0.9235	0.8535	0.7894	0.7307	0.6768	0.6274	0.5820	0.5403	0.5019	0.4665
9	0.9143	0.8368	0.7664	0.7026	0.6446	0.5919	0.5439	0.5002	0.4604	0.4241
10	0.9053	0.8203	0.7441	0.6756	0.6139	0.5584	0.5083	0.4632	0.4224	0.3855
11	0.8963	0.8043	0.7224	0.6496	0.5847	0.5268	0.4751	0.4289	0.3875	0.3505
12	0.8874	0.7885	0.7014	0.6246	0.5568	0.4970	0.4440	0.3971	0.3555	0.3186
13	0.8787	0.7730	0.6810	0.6006	0.5303	0.4688	0.4150	0.3677	0.3262	0.2897
14	0.8700	0.7579	0.6611	0.5775	0.5051	0.4423	0.3878	0.3405	0.2992	0.2633
15	0.8613	0.7430	0.6419	0.5553	0.4810	0.4173	0.3624	0.3152	0.2745	0.2394
16	0.8528	0.7284	0.6232	0.5339	0.4581	0.3936	0.3387	0.2919	0.2519	0.2176
17	0.8444	0.7142	0.6050	0.5134	0.4363	0.3714	0.3166	0.2703	0.2311	0.1978
18	0.8360	0.7002	0.5874	0.4936	0.4155	0.3503	0.2959	0.2502	0.2120	0.1799
19	0.8277	0.6864	0.5703	0.4746	0.3957	0.3305	0.2765	0.2317	0.1945	0.1635
20	0.8195	0.6730	0.5537	0.4564	0.3769	0.3118	0.2584	0.2145	0.1784	0.1486
21	0.8114	0.6598	&.5375	0.4388	0.3589	0.2942	0.2415	0.1987	0.1637	0.1351
22	0.8034	0.6468	0.5219	0.4220	0.3418	0.2775	0.2257	0.1839	0.1502	0.1228
23	0.7954	0.6342	0.5067	0.4057	0.3256	0.2618	0.2109	0.1703	0.1378	0.1117
24	0.7876	0.6217	0.4919	0.3901	0.3101	0.2470	0.1971	0.1577	0.1264	0.1015
25	0.7798	0.6095	0.4776	0.3751	0.2953	0.2330	0.1842	0.1460	0.1160	0.0923
26	0.7720	0.5976	0.4637	0.3607	0.2812	0.2198	0.1722	0.1352	0.1064	0.0839
27	0.7644	0.5859	0.4502	0.3468	0.2678	0.2074	0.1609	0.1252	0.0976	0.0763
28	0.7568	0.5744	0.4371	0.3335	0.2551	0.1956	0.1504	0.1159	0.0895	0.0693
29	0.7493	0.5631	0.4243	0.3207	0.2429	0.1846	0.1406	0.1073	0.0822	0.0630
30	0.7419	0.5521	0.4120	0.3083	0.2314	0.1741	0.1314	0.0994	0.0754	0.0573

n	11	12	13	14	15	16	17	18	19	20
1	0.9009	0.8929	0.8850	0.8772	0.8696	0.8621	0.8547	0.8475	0.8403	0.8333
2	0.8116	0.7972	0.7831	0.7695	0.7561	0.7432	0.7305	0.7182	0.7062	0.6944
3	0.7312	0.7118	0.6931	0.6750	0.6575	0.6407	0.6244	0.6086	0.5934	0.5787
4	0.6587	0.6355	0.6133	0.5921	0.5718	0.5523	0.5337	0.5158	0.4987	0.4823
5	0.5935	0.5674	0.5428	0.5194	0.4972	0.4761	0.4561	0.4371	0.4190	0.4019
6	0.5346	0.5066	0.4803	0.4556	0.4323	0.4104	0.3898	0.3704	0.3521	0.3349
7	0.4817	0.4523	0.4251	0.3996	0.3759	0.3538	0.3332	0.3139	0.2959	0.2791
8	0.4339	0.4039	0.3762	0.3506	0.3269	0.3050	0.2848	0.2660	0.2487	0.2326
9	0.3909	0.3606	0.3329	0.3075	0.2843	0.2630	0.2434	0.2255	0.2090	0.1938
10	0.3522	0.3220	0.2946	0.2697	0.2472	0.2267	0.2080	0.1911	0.1756	0.1615
11	0.3173	0.2875	0.2607	0.2366	0.2149	0.1954	0.1778	0.1619	0.1476	0.1346
12	0.2858	0.2567	0.2307	0.2076	0.1869	0.1685	0.1520	0.1372	0.1240	0.1122
13	0.2575	0.2292	0.2042	0.1821	0.1625	0.1452	0.1299	0.1163	0.1042	0.0935
14	0.2320	0.2046	0.1807	0.1597	0.1413	0.1252	0.1110	0.0985	0.0876	0.0779
15	0.2090	0.1827	0.1599	0.1401	0.1229	0.1079	0.0949	0.0835	0.0736	0.0649
16	0.1883	0.1631	0.1415	0.1229	0.1069	0.0930	0.0811	0.0708	0.0618	0.0541
17	0.1696	0.1456	0.1252	0.1078	0.0929	0.0802	0.0693	0.0600	0.0520	0.0451
18	0.1528	0.1300	0.1108	0.0946	0.0808	0.0691	0.0592	0.0508	0.0437	0.0376
19	0.1377	0.1161	0.0981	0.0829	0.0703	0.0596	0.0506	0.0431	0.0367	0.0313
20	0.1240	0.1037	0.0868	0.0728	0.0611	0.0514	0.0433	0.0365	0.0308	0.0261
21	0.1117	0.0926	0.0768	0.0638	0.0531	0.0443	0.0370	0.0309	0.0259	0.0217
22	0.1007	0.0826	0.0680	0.0560	0.0462	0.0382	0.0316	0.0262	0.0218	0.0181
23	0.0907	0.0738	0.0601	0.0491	0.0402	0.0329	0.0270	0.0222	0.0183	0.0151
24	0.0817	0.0659	0.0532	0.0431	0.0349	0.0284	0.0231	0.0188	0.0154	0.0126
25	0.0736	0.0588	0.0471	0.0378	0.0304	0.0245	0.0197	0.0160	0.0129	0.0105
26	0.0663	0.0525	0.0417	0.0331	0.0264	0.0211	0.0169	0.0135	0.0109	0.0087
27	0.0597	0.0469	0.0369	0.0291	0.0230	0.0182	0.0144	0.0115	0.0091	0.0073
28	0.0538	0.0419	0.0326	0.0255	0.0200	0.0157	0.0123	0.0097	0.0077	0.0061
29	0.0485	0.0374	0.0289	0.0224	0.0174	0.0135	0.0105	0.0082	0.0064	0.0051
30	0.0437	0.0334	0.0256	0.0196	0.0151	0.0116	0.0090	0.0070	0.0054	0.0042

n	21	22	23	24	25	26	27	28	29	30
1	0.8264	0.8197	0.8130	0.8065	0.8000	0.7937	0.7874	0.7813	0.7752	0.7692
2	0.6830	0.6719	0.6610	0.6504	0.6400	0.6299	0.6200	0.6104	0.6009	0.5917
3	0.5645	0.5507	0.5374	0.5245	0.5120	0.4999	0.4882	0.4768	0.4658	0.4552
4	0.4665	0.4514	0.4369	0.4230	0.4096	0.3968	0.3844	0.3725	0.3611	0.3501
5	0.3855	0.3700	0.3552	0.3411	0.3277	0.3149	0.3027	0.2910	0.2799	0.2693
6	0.3186	0.3033	0.2888	0.2751	0.2621	0.2499	0.2383	0.2274	0.2170	0.2072
7	0.2633	0.2486	0.2348	0.2218	0.2097	0.1983	0.1877	0.1776	0.1682	0.1594
8	0.2176	0.2038	0.1909	0.1789	0.1678	0.1574	0.1478	0.1388	0.1304	0.1226
9	0.1799	0.1670	0.1552	0.1443	0.1342	0.1249	0.1164	0.1084	0.1011	0.0943
10	0.1486	0.1369	0.1262	0.1164	0.1074	0.0992	0.0916	0.0847	0.0784	0.0725
11	0.1228	0.1122	0.1026	0.0938	0.0859	0.0787	0.0721	0.0662	0.0607	0.0558
12	0.1015	0.0920	0.0834	0.0757	0.0687	0.0625	0.0568	0.0517	0.0471	0.0429
13	0.0839	0.0754	0.0678	0.0610	0.0550	0.0496	0.0447	0.0404	0.0365	0.0330
14	0.0693	0.0618	0.0551	0.0492	0.0440	0.0393	0.0352	0.0316	0.0283	0.0254
15	0.0573	0.0507	0.0448	0.0397	0.0352	0.0312	0.0277	0.0247	0.0219	0.0195
16	0.0474	0.0415	0.0364	0.0320	0.0281	0.0248	0.0218	0.0193	0.0170	0.0150
17	0.0391	0.0340	0.0296	0.0258	0.0225	0.0197	0.0172	0.0150	0.0132	0.0116
18	0.0323	0.0279	0.0241	0.0208	0.0180	0.0156	0.0135	0.0118	0.0102	0.0089
19	0.0267	0.0229	0.0196	0.0168	0.0144	0.0124	0.0107	0.0092	0.0079	0.0068
20	0.0221	0.0187	0.0159	0.0135	0.0115	0.0098	0.0084	0.0072	0.0061	0.0053
21	0.0183	0.0154	0.0129	0.0109	0.0092	0.0078	0.0066	0.0056	0.0048	0.0040
22	0.0151	0.0126	0.0105	0.0088	0.0074	0.0062	0.0052	0.0044	0.0037	0.0031
23	0.0125	0.0103	0.0086	0.0071	0.0059	0.0049	0.0041	0.0034	0.0029	0.0024
24	0.0103	0.0085	0.0070	0.0057	0.0047	0.0039	0.0032	0.0027	0.0022	0.0018
25	0.0085	0.0069	0.0057	0.0046	0.0038	0.0031	0.0025	0.0021	0.0017	0.0014
26	0.0070	0.0057	0.0046	0.0037	0.0030	0.0025	0.0020	0.0016	0.0013	0.0011
27	0.0058	0.0047	0.0037	0.0030	0.0024	0.0019	0.0016	0.0013	0.0010	0.0008
28	0.0048	0.0038	0.0030	0.0024	0.0019	0.0015	0.0012	0.0010	0.0008	0.0006
29	0.0040	0.0031	0.0025	0.0020	0.0015	0.0012	0.0010	0.0008	0.0006	0.0005
30	0.0033	0.0026	0.0020	0.0016	0.0012	0.0010	0.0008	0.0006	0.0005	0.0004

Table 3 *Present value of an immediate annuity of £1 for n years at 100r% compound interest:* $\dfrac{1-(1+r)^{-n}}{r}$

Years n	Discount rate as percentage (100r)									
	1	2	3	4	5	6	7	8	9	10
1	0.9901	0.9804	0.9709	0.9615	0.9524	0.9434	0.9346	0.9259	0.9174	0.9091
2	1.9704	1.9416	1.9135	1.8861	1.8594	1.8334	1.8080	1.7833	1.7591	1.7355
3	2.9410	2.8839	2.8286	2.7751	2.7232	2.6730	2.6243	2.5771	2.5313	2.4869
4	3.9020	3.8077	3.7171	3.6299	3.5460	3.4651	3.3872	3.3121	3.2397	3.1699
5	4.8534	4.7135	4.5797	4.4518	4.3295	4.2124	4.1002	3.9927	3.8897	3.7908
6	5.7955	5.6014	5.4172	5.2421	5.0757	4.9173	4.7665	4.6229	4.4859	4.3553
7	6.7282	6.4720	6.2303	6.0021	5.7864	5.5824	5.3893	5.2064	5.0330	4.8684
8	7.6517	7.3255	7.0197	6.7327	6.4632	6.2098	5.9713	5.7466	5.5348	5.3349
9	8.5660	8.1622	7.7861	7.4353	7.1078	6.8017	6.5152	6.2469	5.9952	5.7590
10	9.4713	8.9826	8.5302	8.1109	7.7217	7.3601	7.0236	6.7101	6.4177	6.1446
11	10.3676	9.7868	9.2526	8.7605	8.3064	7.8869	7.4987	7.1390	6.8052	6.4951
12	11.2551	10.5753	9.9540	9.3851	8.8633	8.3838	7.9427	7.5361	7.1607	6.8137
13	12.1337	11.3484	10.6350	9.9856	9.3936	8.8527	8.3577	7.9038	7.4869	7.1034
14	13.0037	12.1062	11.2961	10.5631	9.8986	9.2950	8.7455	8.2442	7.7862	7.3667
15	13.8651	12.8493	11.9379	11.1184	10.3797	9.7122	9.1079	8.5595	8.0607	7.6061
16	14.7179	13.5777	12.5611	11.6523	10.8378	10.1059	9.4466	8.8514	8.3126	7.8237
17	15.5623	14.2919	13.1661	12.1657	11.2741	10.4773	9.7632	9.1216	8.5436	8.0216
18	16.3983	14.9920	13.7535	12.6593	11.6896	10.8276	10.0591	9.3719	8.7556	8.2014
19	17.2260	15.6785	14.3238	13.1339	12.0853	11.1581	10.3356	9.6036	8.9501	8.3649
20	18.0456	16.3514	14.8775	13.5903	12.4622	11.4699	10.5940	9.8181	9.1285	8.5136
21	18.8570	17.0112	15.4150	14.0292	12.8212	11.7641	10.8355	10.0168	9.2922	8.6487
22	19.6604	17.6580	15.9369	14.4511	13.1630	12.0416	11.0612	10.2007	9.4424	8.7715
23	20.4558	18.2922	16.4436	14.8568	13.4886	12.3034	11.2722	10.3711	9.5802	8.8832
24	21.2434	18.9139	16.9355	15.2470	13.7986	12.5504	11.4693	10.5288	9.7066	8.9847
25	22.0232	19.5235	17.4131	15.6221	14.0939	12.7834	11.6536	10.6748	9.8226	9.0770
26	22.7952	20.1210	17.8768	15.9828	14.3752	13.0032	11.8258	10.8100	9.9290	9.1609
27	23.5596	20.7069	18.3270	16.3296	14.6430	13.2105	11.9867	10.9352	10.0266	9.2372
28	24.3164	21.2813	18.7641	16.6631	14.8981	13.4062	12.1371	11.0511	10.1161	9.3066
29	25.0658	21.8444	19.1885	16.9837	15.1411	13.5907	12.2777	11.1584	10.1983	9.3696
30	25.8077	22.3965	19.6004	17.2920	15.3725	13.7648	12.4090	11.2578	10.2737	9.4269

n	11	12	13	14	15	16	17	18	19	20
1	0.9009	0.8929	0.8850	0.8772	0.8696	0.8621	0.8547	0.8475	0.8403	0.8333
2	1.7125	1.6901	1.6681	1.6467	1.6257	1.6052	1.5852	1.5656	1.5465	1.5278
3	2.4437	2.4018	2.3612	2.3216	2.2832	2.2459	2.2096	2.1743	2.1399	2.1065
4	3.1024	3.0373	2.9745	2.9137	2.8550	2.7982	2.7432	2.6901	2.6386	2.5887
5	3.6959	3.6048	3.5172	3.4331	3.3522	3.2743	3.1993	3.1272	3.0576	2.9906
6	4.2305	4.1114	3.9975	3.8887	3.7845	3.6847	3.5892	3.4976	3.4098	3.3255
7	4.7122	4.5638	4.4226	4.2883	4.1604	4.0386	3.9224	3.8115	3.7057	3.6046
8	5.1461	4.9676	4.7988	4.6389	4.4873:	4.3436	4.2072	4.0776	3.9544	3.8372
9	5.5370	5.3282	5.1317	4.9464	4.7716	4.6065	4.4506	4.3030	4.1633	4.0310
10	5.8892	5.6502	5.4262	5.2161	5.0188	4.8332	4.6586	4.4941	4.3389	4.1925
11	6.2065	5.9377	5.6869	5.4527	5.2337	5.0286	4.8364	4.6560	4.4865	4.3271
12	6.4924	6.1944	5.9176	5.6603	5.4206	5.1971	4.9884	4.7932	4.6105	4.4392
13	6.7499	6.4235	6.1218	5.8424	5.5831	5.3423	5.1183	4.9095	4.7147	4.5327
14	6.9819	6.6282	6.3025	6.0021	5.7245	5.4675	5.2293	5.0081	4.8023	4.6106
15	7.1909	6.8109	6.4624	6.1422	5.8474	5.5755	5.3242	5.0916	4.8759	4.6755
16	7.3792	6.9740	6.6039	6.2651	5.9542	5.6685	5.4053	5.1624	4.9377	4.7296
17	7.5488	7.1196	6.7291	6.3729	6.0472	5.7487	5.4746	5.2223	4.9897	4.7746
18	7.7016	7.2497	6.8399	6.4674	6.1280	5.8178	5.5339	5.2732	5.0333	4.8122
19	7.8393	7.3658	6.9380	6.5504	6.1982	5.8775	5.5845	5.3162	5.0700	4.8435
20	7.9633	7.4694	7.0248	6.6231	6.2593	5.9288	5.6278	5.3527	5.1009	4.8696
21	8.0751	7.5620	7.1016	6.6870	6.3125	5.9731	5.6648	5.3837	5.1268	4.8913
22	8.1757	7.6446	7.1695	6.7429	6.3587	6.0113	5.6964	5.4099	5.1486	4.9094
23	8.2664	7.7184	7.2297	6.7921	6.3988	6.0442	5.7234	5.4321	5.1668	4.9245
24	8.3481	7.7843	7.2829	6.8351	6.4338	6.0726	5.7465	5.4509	5.1822	4.9371
25	8.4217	7.8431	7.3300	6.8729	6.4641	6.0971	5.7662	5.4669	5.1951	4.9476
26	8.4881	7.8957	7.3717	6.9061	6.4906	6.1182	5.7831	5.4804	5.2060	4.9563
27	8.5478	7.9426	7.4086	6.9352	6.5135	6.1364	5.7975	5.4919	5.2151	4.9636
28	8.6016	7.9844	7.4412	6.9607	6.5335	6.1520	5.8099	5.5016	5.2228	4.9697
29	8.6501	8.0218	7.4701	6.9830	6.5509	6.1656	5.8204	5.5098	5.2292	4.9747
30	8.6938	8.0552	7.4957	7.0027	6.5660	6.1772	5.8294	5.5168	5.2347	4.9789

n	21	22	23	24	25	26	27	28	29	30
1	0.8264	0.8197	0.8130	0.8065	0.8000	0.7937	0.7874	0.7813	0.7752	0.7692
2	1.5095	1.4915	1.4740	1.4568	1.4400	1.4235	1.4074	1.3916	1.3761	1.3609
3	2.0739	2.0422	2.0114	1.9813	1.9520	1.9234	1.8956	1.8684	1.8420	1.8161
4	2.5404	2.4936	2.4483	2.4043	2.3616	2.3202	2.2800	2.2410	2.2031	2.1662
5	2.9260	2.8636	2.8035	2.7454	2.6893	2.6351	2.5827	2.5320	2.4830	2.4356
6	3.2446	3.1669	3.0923	3.0205	2.9514	2.8850	2.8210	2.7594	2.7000	2.6427
7	3.5079	3.4155	3.3270	3.2423	3.1611	3.0833	3.0087	2.9370	2.8682	2.8021
8	3.7256	3.6193	3.5179	3.4212	3.3289	3.2407	3.1564	3.0758	2.9986	2.9247
9	3.9054	3.7863	3.6731	3.5655	3.4631	3.3657	3.2728	3.1842	3.0997	3.0190
10	4.0541	3.9232	3.7993	3.6819	3.5705	3.4648	3.3644	3.2689	3.1781	3.0915
11	4.1769	4.0354	3.9018	3.7757	3.6564	3.5435	3.4365	3.3351	3.2388	3.1473
12	4.2784	4.1274	3.9852	3.8514	3.7251	3.6059	3.4933	3.3868	3.2859	3.1903
13	4.3624	4.2028	4.0530	3.9124	3.7801	3.6555	3.5381	3.4272	3.3224	3.2233
14	4.4317	4.2646	4.1082	3.9616	3.8241	3.6949	3.5733	3.4587	3.3507	3.2487
15	4.4890	4.3152	4.1530	4.0013	3.8593	3.7261	3.6010	3.4834	3.3726	3.2682
16	4.5364	4.3567	4.1894	4.0333	3.8874	3.7509	3.6228	3.5026	3.3896	3.2832
17	4.5755	4.3908	4.2190	4.0591	3.9099	3.7705	3.6400	3.5177	3.4028	3.2948
18	4.6079	4.4187	4.2431	4.0799	3.9279	3.7861	3.6536	3.5294	3.4130	3.3037
19	4.6346	4.4415	4.2627	4.0967	3.9424	3.7985	3.6642	3.5386	3.4210	3.3105
20	4.6567	4.4603	4.2786	4.1103	3.9539	3.8083	3.6726	3.5458	3.4271	3.3158
21	4.6750	4.4756	4.2916	4.1212	3.9631	3.8161	3.6792	3.5514	3.4319	3.3198
22	4.6900	4.4882	4.3021	4.1300	3.9705	3.8223	3.6844	3.5558	3.4356	3.3230
23	4.7025	4.4985	4.3106	4.1371	3.9764	3.8273	3.6885	3.5592	3.4384	3.3254
24	4.7128	4.5070	4.3176	4.1428	3.9811	3.8312	3.6918	3.5619	3.4406	3.3272
25	4.7213	4.5139	4.3232	4.1474	3.9849	3.8342	3.6943	3.5640	3.4423	3.3286
26	4.7284	4.5196	4.3278	4.1511	3.9879	3.8367	3.6963	3.5656	3.4437	3.3297
27	4.7342	4.5243	4.3316	4.1542	3.9903	3.8387	3.6979	3.5669	3.4447	3.3305
28	4.7390	4.5281	4.3346	4.1566	3.9923	3.8402	3.6991	3.5679	3.4455	3.3312
29	4.7430	4.5312	4.3371	4.1585	3.9938	3.8414	3.7001	3.5687	3.4461	3.3317
30	4.7463	4.5338	4.3391	4.1601	3.9950	3.8424	3.7009	3.5693	3.4466	3.3321

Table 4 *Future value of an annuity of £1 for n years at 100r% compound interest:* $\dfrac{(1 + r)^n - 1}{r}$

Years n	Discount rate as percentage (100r)					
	1	2	3	4	5	6
1	1.0000	1.0000	1.0000	1.0000	1.0000	1.0000
2	2.0100	2.0200	2.0300	2.0400	2.0500	2.0600
3	3.0301	3.0604	3.0909	3.1216	3.1525	3.1836
4	4.0604	4.1216	4.1836	4.2465	4.3101	4.3746
5	5.1010	5.2040	5.3091	5.4163	5.5256	5.6371
6	6.1520	6.3081	6.4684	6.6330	6.8019	6.9753
7	7.2135	7.4343	7.6625	7.8983	8.1420	8.3938
8	8.2857	8.5830	8.8923	9.2142	9.5491	9.8975
9	9.3685	9.7546	10.1591	10.5828	11.0266	11.4913
10	10.4622	10.9497	11.4639	12.0061	12.5779	13.1808
11	11.5668	12.1687	12.8078	13.4864	14.2068	14.9716
12	12.6825	13.4121	14.1920	15.0258	15.9171	16.8699
13	13.8093	14.6803	15.6178	16.6268	17.7130	18.8821
14	14.9474	15.9739	17.0863	18.2919	19.5986	21.0151
15	16.0969	17.2934	18.5989	20.0236	21.5786	23.2760
16	17.2579	18.6393	20.1569	21.8245	23.6575	25.6725
17	18.4304	20.0121	21.7616	23.6975	25.8404	28.2129
18	19.6147	21.4123	23.4144	25.6454	28.1324	30.9057
19	20.8109	22.8406	25.1169	27.6712	30.5390	33.7600
20	22.0190	24.2974	26.8704	29.7781	33.0660	36.7856
21	23.2392	25.7833	28.6765	31.9692	35.7192	39.9927
22	24.4716	27.2990	30.5368	34.2480	38.5052	43.3923
23	25.7163	28.8450	32.4529	36.6179	41.4305	46.9958
24	26.9735	30.4219	34.4265	39.0826	44.5020	50.8156
25	28.2432	32.0303	36.4593	41.6459	47.7271	54.8645
26	29.5256	33.6709	38.5530	44.3117	51.1135	59.1564
27	30.8209	35.3443	40.7096	47.0842	54.6691	63.7058
28	32.1291	37.0512	42.9309	49.9676	58.4026	68.5281
29	33.4504	38.7922	45.2188	52.9663	62.3227	73.6398
30	34.7849	40.5681	47.5754	56.0849	66.4388	79.0582

n	7	8	9	10	11	12
1	1.0000	1.0000	1.0000	1.0000	1.0000	1.0000
2	2.0700	2.0800	2.0900	2.1000	2.1100	2.1200
3	3.2149	3.2464	3.2781	3.3100	3.3421	3.3744
4	4.4399	4.5061	4.5731	4.6410	4.7097	4.7793
5	5.7507	5.8666	5.9847	6.1051	6.2278	6.3528
6	7.1533	7.3359	7.5233	7.7156	7.9129	8.1152
7	8.6540	8.9228	9.2004	9.4872	9.7833	10.0890
8	10.2598	10.6366	11.0285	11.4359	11.8594	12.2997
9	11.9780	12.4876	13.0210	13.5795	14.1640	14.7757
10	13.8164	14.4866	15.1929	15.9374	16.7220	17.5487
11	15.7836	16.6455	17.5603	18.5312	19.5614	20.6546
12	17.8885	18.9771	20.1407	21.3843	22.7132	24.1331
13	20.1406	21.4953	22.9534	24.5227	26.2116	28.0291
14	22.5505	24.2149	26.0192	27.9750	30.0949	32.3926
15	25.1290	27.1521	29.3609	31.7725	34.4054	37.2797
16	27.8881	30.3243	33.0034	35.9497	39.1899	42.7533
17	30.8402	33.7502	36.9737	40.5447	44.5008	48.8837
18	33.9990	37.4502	41.3013	45.5992	50.3959	55.7497
19	37.3790	41.4463	46.0185	51.1591	56.9395	63.4397
20	40.9955	45.7620	51.1601	57.2750	64.2028	72.0524
21	44.8652	50.4229	56.7645	64.0025	72.2651	81.6987
22	49.0057	55.4568	62.8733	71.4027	81.2143	92.5026
23	53.4361	60.8933	69.5319	79.5430	91.1479	104.6029
24	58.1767	66.7648	76.7898	88.4973	102.1741	118.1552
25	63.2490	73.1059	84.7009	98.3471	114.4133	133.3339
26	68.6765	79.9544	93.3240	109.1818	127.9988	150.3339
27	74.4838	87.3508	102.7231	121.0999	143.0786	169.3740
28	80.6977	95.3388	112.9682	134.2099	159.8173	190.6989
29	87.3465	103.9659	124.1354	148.6309	178.3972	214.5827
30	94.4608	113.2832	136.3075	164.4940	199.0209	241.3327

n	13	14	15	16	17	18
1	1.0000	1.0000	1.0000	1.0000	1.0000	1.0000
2	2.1300	2.1400	2.1500	2.1600	2.1700	2.1800
3	3.4069	3.4396	3.4725	3.5056	3.5389	3.5724
4	4.8498	4.9211	4.9934	5.0665	5.1405	5.2154
5	6.4803	6.6101	6.7424	6.8771	7.0144	7.1542
6	8.3227	8.5355	8.7537	8.9775	9.2068	9.4420
7	10.4047	10.7305	11.0668	11.4139	11.7720	12.1415
8	12.7573	13.2328	13.7268	14.2401	14.7733	15.3270
9	15.4157	16.0853	16.7858	17.5185	18.2847	19.0859
10	18.4197	19.3373	20.3037	21.3215	22.3931	23.5213
11	21.8143	23.0445	24.3493	25.7329	27.1999	28.7551
12	25.6502	27.2707	29.0017	30.8502	32.8239	34.9311
13	29.9847	32.0887	34.3519	36.7862	39.4040	42.2187
14	34.8827	37.5811	40.5047	43.6720	47.1027	50.8180
15	40.4175	43.8424	47.5804	51.6595	56.1101	60.9653
16	46.6717	50.9804	55.7175	60.9250	66.6488	72.9390
17	53.7391	59.1176	65.0751	71.6730	78.9791	87.0680
18	61.7251	68.3941	75.8364	84.1407	93.4056	103.7403
19	70.7494	78.9692	88.2118'	98.6032	110.2846	123.4135
20	80.9468	91.0249	102.4436	115.3797	130.0329	146.6280
21	92.4699	104.7684	118.8101	134.8405	153.1385	174.0210
22	105.4910	120.4360	137.6316	157.4150	180.1721	206.3448
23	120.2048	138.2970	159.2764	183.6014	211.8013	244.4868
24	136.8315	158.6586	184.1678	213.9776	248.8076	289.4945
25	155.6196	181.8708	212.7930	249.2140	292.1048	342.6035
26	176.8501	208.3327	245.7120	290.0883	342.7627	405.2721
27	200.8406	238.4993	283.5688	337.5024	402.0323	479.2211
28	227.9499	272.8892	327.1041	392.5027	471.3778	566.4808
29	258.5834	312.0937	377.1697	456.3032	552.5120	669.4474
30	293.1992	356.7868	434.7451	530.3117	647.4391	790.9479

n	19	20	21	22	23	24
1	1.0000	1.0000	1.0000	1.0000	1.0000	1.0000
2	2.1900	2.2000	2.2100	2.2200	2.2300	2.2400
3	3.6061	3.6400	3.6741	3.7084	3.7429	3.7776
4	5.2913	5.3680	5.4457	5.5242	5.6038	5.6842
5	7.2966	7.4416	7.5892	7.7396	7.8926	8.0484
6	9.6830	9.9299	10.1830	10.4423	10.7079	10.9801
7	12.5227	12.9159	13.3214	13.7396	14.1708	14.6153
8	15.9020	16.4991	17.1189	17.7623	18.4300	19.1229
9	19.9234	20.7989	21.7139	22.6700	23.6689	24.7125
10	24.7089	25.9587	27.2738	28.6574	30.1128	31.6434
11	30.4035	32.1504	34.0013	35.9620	38.0388	40.2379
12	37.1802	39.5805	42.1416	44.8737	47.7877	50.8950
13	45.2445	48.4966	51.9913	55.7459	59.7788	64.1097
14	54.8409	59.1959	63.9095	69.0100	74.5280	80.4961
15	66.2607	72.0351	78.3305	85.1922	92.6694	100.8151
16	79.8502	87.4421	95.7799	104.9345	114.9834	126.0108
17	96.0217	105.9305	116.8937	129.0201	142.4295	157.2533
18	115.2659	128.1167	142.4413	158.4045	176.1883	195.9942
19	138.1664	154.7400	173.3540	194.2535	217.7116	244.0327
20	165.4180	186.6880	210.7583	237.9893	268.7853	303.6006
21	197.8474	225.0256	256.0176	291.3469	331.6059	377.4648
22	236.4384	271.0307	310.7813	356.4432	408.8753	469.0563
23	282.3618	326.2368	377.0454	435.8607	503.9166	582.6298
24	337.0105	392.4842	457.2249	532.7501	620.8174	723.4609
25	402.0424	471.9810	554.2421	650.9551	764.6054	898.0916
26	479.4305	567.3773	671.6329	795.1652	941.4646	1114.6335
27	571.5223	681.8527	813.6759	971.1016	1159.0015	1383.1456
28	681.1116	819.2233	985.5478	1185.7439	1426.5718	1716.1005
29	811.5228	984.0679	1193.5128	1447.6075	1755.6833	2128.9646
30	966.7121	1181.8815	1445.1505	1767.0812	2160.4905	2640.9160

n	25	26	27	28	29	30
1	1.0000	1.0000	1.0000	1.0000	1.0000	1.0000
2	2.2500	2.2600	2.2700	2.2800	2.2900	2.3000
3	3.8125	3.8476	3.8829	3.9184	3.9541	3.9900
4	5.7656	5.8480	5.9313	6.0156	6.1008	6.1870
5	8.2070	8.3684	8.5327	8.6999	8.8700	9.0431
6	11.2588	11.5442	11.8366	12.1359	12.4423	12.7560
7	15.0735	15.5458	16.0324	16.5339	17.0506	17.5828
8	19.8419	20.5876	21.3612	22.1634	22.9953	23.8577
9	25.8023	26.9404	28.1287	29.3692	30.6639	32.0150
10	33.2529	34.9449	36.7235	38.5926	40.5564	42.6195
11	42.5661	45.0306	47.6388	50.3985	53.3178	56.4053
12	54.2077	57.7386	61.5013	65.5100	69.7800	74.3270
13	68.7596	73.7506	79.1066	84.8529	91.0161	97.6250
14	86.9495	93.9258	101.4654	109.6117	118.4108	127.9125
15	109.6868	119.3465	129.8611	141.3029	153.7500	167.2863
16	138.1085	151.3766	165.9236	181.8677	199.3374	218.4722
17	173.6357	191.7345	211.7230	233.7907	258.1453	285.0139
18	218.0446	242.5855	269.8882	300.2521	334.0074	371.5180
19	273.5557	306.6577	343.7580	385.3227	431.8696	483.9734
20	342.9447	387.3887	437.5726	494.2130	558.1118	630.1654
21	429.6808	489.1097	556.7172	633.5927	720.9641	820.2150
22	538.1011	617.2783	708.0309	811.9986	931.0437	1067.2795
23	673.6263	778.7706	900.1992	1040.3583	1202.0464	1388.4634
24	843.0329	982.2510	1144.2529	1332.6586	1551.6399	1806.0024
25	1054.7911	1238.6362	1454.2013	1706.8029	2002.6154	2348.8030
26	1319.4889	1561.6816	1847.8356	2185.7078	2584.3738	3054.4441
27	1650.3611	1968.7189	2347.7512	2798.7058	3334.8423	3971.7771
28	2063.9514	2481.5857	2982.6440	3583.3435	4302.9463	5164.3105
29	2580.9392	3127.7981	3788.9580	4587.6797	5551.8008	6714.6035
30	3227.1738	3942.0254	4812.9766	5873.2300	7162.8232	8729.9844

Table 5 *Sinking fund of £1 for n years at 100r% compound interest:* $\dfrac{r}{(1+r)^n - 1}$

Years n	Discount rate as percentage (100r)									
	1	2	3	4	5	6	7	8	9	10
1	1.0000	1.0000	1.0000	1.0000	1.0000	1.0000	1.0000	1.0000	1.0000	1.0000
2	0.4975	0.4950	0.4926	0.4902	0.4878	0.4854	0.4831	0.4808	0.4785	0.4762
3	0.3300	0.3268	0.3235	0.3203	0.3172	0.3141	0.3111	0.3080	0.3051	0.3021
4	0.2463	0.2426	0.2390	0.2355	0.2320	0.2286	0.2252	0.2219	0.2187	0.2155
5	0.1960	0.1922	0.1884	0.1846	0.1810	0.1774	0.1739	0.1705	0.1671	0.1638
6	0.1625	0.1585	0.1546	0.1508	0.1470	0.1434	0.1398	0.1363	0.1329	0.1296
7	0.1386	0.1345	0.1305	0.1266	0.1228	0.1191	0.1156	0.1121	0.1087	0.1054
8	0.1207	0.1165	0.1125	0.1085	0.1047	0.1010	0.0975	0.0940	0.0907	0.0874
9	0.1067	0.1025	0.0984	0.0945	0.0907	0.0870	0.0835	0.0801	0.0768	0.0736
10	0.0956	0.0913	0.0872	0.0833	0.0795	0.0759	0.0724	0.0690	0.0658	0.0627
11	0.0865	0.0822	0.0781	0.0741	0.0704	0.0668	0.0634	0.0601	0.0569	0.0540
12	0.0788	0.0746	0.0705	0.0666	0.0628	0.0593	0.0559	0.0527	0.0497	0.0468
13	0.0724	0.0681	0.0640	0.0601	0.0565	0.0530	0.0497	0.0465	0.0436	0.0408
14	0.0669	0.0626	0.0585	0.0547	0.0510	0.0476	0.0443	0.0413	0.0384	0.0357
15	0.0621	0.0578	0.0538	0.0499	0.0463	0.0430	0.0398	0.0368	0.0341	0.0315
16	0.0579	0.0537	0.0496	0.0458	0.0423	0.0390	0.0359	0.0330	0.0303	0.0278
17	0.0543	0.0500	0'.0460	0.0422	0.0387	0.0354	0.0324	0.0296	0.0270	0.0247
18	0.0510	0.0467	0.0427	0.0390	0.0355	0.0324	0.0294	0.0267	0.0242	0.0219
19	0.0481	0.0438	0.0398	0.0361	0.0327	0.0296	0.0268	0.0241	0.0217	0.0195
20	0.0454	0.0412	0.0372	0.0336	0.0302	0.0272	0.0244	0.0219	0.0195	0.0175
21	0.0430	0.0388	0.0349	0.0313	0.0280	0.0250	0.0223	0.0198	0.0176	0.0156
22	0.0409	0.0366	0.0327	0.0292	0.0260	0.0230	0.0204	0.0180	0.0159	0.0140
23	0.0389	0.0347	0.0308	0.0273	0.0241	0.0213	0.0187	0.0164	0.0144	0.0126
24	0.0371	0.0329	0.0290	0.0256	0.0225	0.0197	0.0172	0.0150	0.0130	0.0113
25	0.0354	0.0312	0.0274	0.0240	0.0210	0.0182	0.0158	0.0137	0.0118	0.0102
26	0.0339	0.0297	0.0259	0.0226	0.0196	0.0169	0.0146	0.0125	0.0107	0.0092
27	0.0324	0.0283	0.0246	0.0212	0.0183	0.0157	0.0134	0.0114	0.0097	0.0083
28	0.0311	0.0270	0.0233	0.0200	0.0171	0.0146	0.0124	0.0105	0.0089	0.0075
29	0.0299	0.0258	0.0221	0.0189	0.0160	0.0136	0.0114	0.0096	0.0081	0.0067
30	0.0287,	0.0246	0.0210	0.0178	0.0151	0.0126	0.0106	0.0088	0.0073	0.0061

n	11	12	13	14	15	16	17	18	19	20
1	1.0000	1.0000	1.0000	1.0000	1.0000	1.0000	1.0000	1.0000	1.0000	1.0000
2	0.4739	0.4717	0.4695	0.4673	0.4651	0.4630	0.4608	0.4587	0.4566	0.4545
3	0.2992	0.2963	0.2935	0.2907	0.2880	0.2853	0.2826	0.2799	0.2773	0.2747
4	0.2123	0.2092	0.2062	0.2032	0.2003	0.1974	0.1945	0.1917	0.1890	0.1863
5	0.1606	0.1574	0.1543	0.1513	0.1483	0.1454	0.1426	0.1398	0.1371	0.1344
6	0.1264	0.1232	0.1202	0.1172	0.1142	0.1114	0.1086	0.1059	0.1033	0.1007
7	0.1022	0.0991	0.0961	0.0932	0.0904	0.0876	0.0849	0.0824	0.0799	0.0774
8	0.0843	0.0813	0.0784	0.0756	0.0729	0.0702	0.0677	0.0652	0.0629	0.0606
9	0.0706	0.0677	0.0649	0.0622	0.0596	0.0571	0.0547	0.0524	0.0502	0.0481
10	0.0598	0.0570	0.0543	0.0517	0.0493	0.0469	0.0447	0.0425	0.0405	0.0385
11	0.0511	0.0484	0.0458	0.0434	0.0411	0.0309	0.0368	0.0348	0.0329	0.0311
12	0.0440	0.0414	0.0390	0.0367	0.0345	0.0324	0.0305	0.0286	0.0269	0.0253
13	0.0382	0.0357	0.0334	0.0312	0.0291	0.0272	0.0254	0.0237	0.0221	0.0206
14	0.0332	0.0309	0.0287	0.0266	0.0247	0.0229	0.0212	0.0197	0.0182	0.0169
15	0.0291	0.0268	0.0247	0.0228	0.0210	0.0194	0.0178	0.0164	0.0151	0.0139
16	0.0255	0.0234	0.0214	0.0196	0.0179	0.0164	0.0150	0.0137	0.0125	0.0114
17	0.0225	0.0205	0.0186	0.0169	0.0154	0.0140	0.0127	0.0115	0.0104	0.0094
18	0.0198	0.0179	0.0162	0.0146	0.0132	0.0119	0.0107	0.0096	0.0087	0.0078
19	0.0176	0.0158	0.0141	0.0127	0.0113	0.0101	0.0091	0.0081	0.0072	0.0065
20	0.0156	0.0139	0.0124	0.0110	0.0098	0.0087	0.0077	0.0068	0.0060	0.0054
21	0.0138	0.0122	0.0108	0.0095	0.0084	0.0074	0.0065	0.0057	0.0051	0.0044
22	0.0123	0.0108	0.0095	0.0083	0.0073	0.0064	0.0056	0.0048	0.0042	0.0037
23	0.0110	0.0096	0.0083	0.0072	0.0063	0.0054	0.0047	0.0041	0.0035	0.0031
24	0.0098	0.0085	0.0073	0.0063	0.0054	0.0047	0.0040	0.0035	0.0030	0.0025
25	0.0087	0.0075	0.0064	0.0055	0.0047	0.0040	0.0034	0.0029	0.0025	0.0021
26	0.0078	0.0067	0.0057	0.0048	0.0041	0.0034	0.0029	0.0025	0.0021	0.0018
27	0.0070	0.0059	0.0050	0.0042	0.0035	0.0030	0.0025	0.0021	0.0017	0.0015
28	0.0063	0.0052	0.0044	0.0037	0.0031	0.0025	0.0021	0.0018	0.0015	0.0012
29	0.0056	0.0047	0.0039	0.0032	0.0027	0.0022	0.0018	0.0015	0.0012	0.0010
30	0.0050	0.0041	0.0034	0.0028	0.0023	0.0019	0.0015	0.0013	0.0010	0.0008

n	21	22	23	24	25	26	27	28	29	30
1	1.0000	1.0000	1.0000	1.0000	1.0000	1.0000	1.0000	1.0000	1.0000	1.0000
2	0.4525	0.4505	0.4484	0.4464	0.4444	0.4425	0.4405	0.4386	0.4367	0.4348
3	0.2722	0.2697	0.2672	0.2647	0.2623	0.2599	0.2575	0.2552	0.2529	0.2506
4	0.1836	0.1810	0.1785	0.1759	0.1734	0.1710	0.1686	0.1662	0.1639	0.1616
5	0.1318	0.1292	0.1267	0.1242	0.1218	0.1195	0.1172	0.1149	0.1127	0.1106
6	0.0982	0.0958	0.0934	0.0911	0.0888	0.0866	0.0845	0.0824	0.0804	0.0784
7	0.0751	0.0728	0.0706	0.0684	0.0663	0.0643	0.0624	0.0605	0.0586	0.0569
8	0.0584	0.0563	0.0543	0.0523	0.0504	0.0486	0.0468	0.0451	0.0435	0.0419
9	0.0461	0.0441	0.0422	0.0405	0.0388	0.0371	0.0356	0.0340	0.0326	0.0312
10	0.0367	0.0349	0.0332	0.0316	0.0301	0.0286	0.0272	0.0259	0.0247	0.0235
11	0.0294	0.0278	0.0263	0.0249	0.0235	0.0222	0.0210	0.0198	0.0188	0.0177
12	0.0237	0.0223	0.0209	0.0196	0.0184	0.0173	0.0163	0.0153	0.0143	0.0135
13	0.0192	0.0179	0.0167	0.0156	0.0145	0.0136	0.0126	0.0118	0.0110	0.0102
14	0.0156	0.0145	0.0134	0.0124	0.0115	0.0106	0.0099	0.0091	0.0084	0.0078
15	0.0128	0.0117	0.0108	0.0099	0.0091	0.0084	0.0077	0.0071	0.0065	0.0060
16	0.0104	0.0095	0.0087	0.0079	0.0072	0.0066	0.0060	0.0055	0.0050	0.0046
17	0.0086	0.0078	0.0070	0.0064	0.0058	0.0052	0.0047	0.0043	0.0039	0.0035
18	0.0070	0.0063	0.0057	0.0051	0.0046	0.0041	0.0037	0.0033	0.0030	0.0027
19	0.0058	0.0051	0.0046	0.0041	0.0037	0.0033	0.0029	0.0026	0.0023	0.0021
20	0.0047	0.0042	0.0037	0.0033	0.0029	0.0026	0.0023	0.0020	0.0018	0.0016
21	0.0039	0.0034	0.0030	0.0026	0.0023	0.0020	0.0018	0.0016	0.0014	0.0012
22	0.0032	0.0028	0.0024	0.0021	0.0019	0.0016	0.0014	0.0012	0.0011	0.0009
23	0.0027	0.0023	0.0020	0.0017	0.0015	0.0013	0.0011	0.0010	0.0008	0.0007
24	0.0022	0.0019	0.0016	0.0014	0.0012	0.0010	0.0009	0.0008	0.0006	0.0006
25	0.0018	0.0015	0.0013	0.0011	0.0009	0.0008	0.0007	0.0006	0.0005	0.0004
26	0.0015	0.0013	0.0011	0.0009	0.0008	0.0006	0.0005	0.0005	0.0004	0.0003
27	0.0012	0.0010	0.0009	0.0007	0.0006	0.0005	0.0004	0.0004	0.0003	0.0003
28	0.0010	0.0008	0.0007	0.0006	0.0005	0.0004	0.0003	0.0003	0.0002	0.0002
29	0.0008	0.0007	0.0006	0.0005	0.0004	0.0003	0.0003	0.0002	0.0002	0.0001
30	0.0007	0.0006	0.0005	0.0004	0.0003	0.0003	0.0002	0.0002	0.0001	0.0001

Table 6 *Annual equivalent annuity of £1 over n years at 100r% compound interest:* $\dfrac{r}{1-(1+r)^{-n}}$

Years n	Discount rate as percentage (100r)									
	1	2	3	4	5	6	7	8	9	10
1	1.0100	1.0200	1.0300	1.0400	1.0500	1.0600	1.0100	1.0800	1.0900	1.1000
2	0.5075	0.5150	0.5226	0.5302	0.5378	0.5454	0.5531	0.5608	0.5685	0.5762
3	0.3400	0.3468	0.3535	0.3603	0.3672	0.3741	0.3811	0.3880	0.3951	0.4021
4	0.2563	0.2626	0.2690	0.2755	0.2820	0.2886	0.2952	0.3019	0.3087	0.3155
5	0.2060	0.2122	0.2184	0.2246	0.2310	0.2374	0.2439	0.2505	0.2571	0.2638
6	0.1725	0.1785	0.1846	0.1908	0.1970	0.2034	0.2098	0.2163	0.2229	0.2296
7	0.1486	0.1545	0.1605	0.1666	0.1728	0.1791	0.1856	0.1921	0.1987	0.2054
8	0.1307	0.1365	0.1425	0.1485	0.1547	0.1610	0.1675	0.1740	0.1807	0.1874
9	0.1167	0.1225	0.1284	0.1345	0.1407	0.1470	0.1535	0.1601	0.1668	0.1736
10	0.1056	0.1113	0.1172	0.1233	0.1295	0.1359	0.1424	0.1490	0.1558	0.1627
11	0.0965	0.1022	0.1081	0.1141	0.1204	0.1268	0.1334	0.1401	0.1469	0.1540
12	0.0888	0.0946	0.1005	0.1066	0.1128	0.1193	0.1259	0.1327	0.1397	0.1468
13	0.0824	0.0881	0.0940	0.1001	0.1065	0.1130	0.1197	0.1265	0.1336	0.1408
14	0.0769	0.0826	0.0885	0.0947	0.1010	0.1076	0.1143	0.1213	0.1284	0.1357
15	0.0721	0.0778	0.0838	0.0899	0.0963	0.1030	0.1098	0.1168	0.1241	0.1315
16	0.0679	0.0737	0.0796	0.0858	0.0923	0.0990	0.1059	0.1130	0.1203	0.1278
17	0.0643	0.0700	0.0760	0.0822	0.0887	0.0954	0.1024	0.1096	0.1170	0.1247
18	0.0610	0.0667	0.0727	0.0790	0.0855	0.0924	0.0994	0.1067	0.1142	0.1219
19	0.0581	0.0638	0.0698	0.0761	0.0827	0.0896	0.0968	0.1041	0.1117	0.1195
20	0.0554	0.0612	0.0672	0.0736	0.0802	0.0872	0.0944	0.1019	0.1095	0.1175
21	0.0530	0.0588	0.0649	0.0713	0.0780	0.0850	0.0923	0.0998	0.1076	0.1156
22	0.0509	0.0566	0.0627	0.0692	0.0760	0.0830	0.0904	0.0980	0.1059	0.1140
23	0.0489	0.0547	0.0608	0.0673	0.0741	0.0813	0.0887	0.0964	0.1044	0.1126
24	0.0471	0.0529	0.0590	0.0656	0.0725	0.0797	0.0872	0.0950	0.1030	0.1113
25	0.0454	0.0512	0.0574	0.0640	0.0710	0.0782	0.0858	0.0937	0.1018	0.1102
26	0.0439	0.0497	0.0559	0.0626	0.0696	0.0769	0.0846	0.0925	0.1007	0.1092
27	0.0424	0.0483	0.0546	0.0612	0.0683	0.0757	0.0834	0.0914	0.0997	0.1083
28	0.0411	0.0470	0.0533	0.0600	0.0671	0.0746	0.0824	0.0905	0.0989	0.1075
29	0.0399	0.0458	0.0521	0.0589	0.0660	0.0736	0.0814	0.0896	0.0981	0.1067
30	0.0387	0.0446	0.0510	0.0578	0.0651	0.0726	0.08'06	0.0888	0.0973	0.1061

n	11	12	13	14	15	16	17	18	19	20
1	1.1100	1.1200	1.1300	1.1400	1.1500	1.1600	1.1700	1.1800	1.1900	1.2000
2	0.5839	0.5917	0.5995	0.6073	0.6151	0.6230	0.6308	0.6387	0.6466	0.6545
3	0.4092	0.4163	0.4235	0.4307	0.4380	0.4453	0.4526	0.4599	0.4673	0.4747
4	0.3223	0.3292	0.3362	0.3432	0.3503	0.3574	0.3645	0.3717	0.3790	0.3863
5	0.2706	0.2774	0.2843	0.2913	0.2983	0.3054	0.3126	0.3198	0.3271	0.3344
6	0.2364	0.2432	0.2502	0.2572	0.2642	0.2714	0.2786	0.2859	0.2933	0.3007
7	0.2122	0.2191	0.2261	0.2332	0.2404	0.2476	0.2549	0.2624	0.2699	0.2774
8	0.1943	0.2013	0.2084	0.2156	0.2229	0.2302	0.2377	0.2452	0.2529	0.2606
9	0.1806	0.1877	0.1949	0.2022	0.2096	0.2171	0.2247	0.2324	0.2402	0.2481
10	0.1698	0.1770	0.1843	0.1917	0.1993	0.2069	0.2147	0.2225	0.2305	0.2385
11	0.1611	0.1684	0.1758	0.1834	0.1911	0.1989	0.2068	0.2148	0.2229	0.2311
12	0.1540	0.1614	0.1690	0.1767	0.1845	0.1924	0.2005	0.2086	0.2169	0.2253
13	0.1482	0.1557	0.1634	0.1712	0.1791	0.1872	0.1954	0.2037	0.2121	0.2206
14	0.1432	0.1509	0.1587	0.1666	0.1747	0.1829	0.1912	0.1997	0.2082	0.2169
15	0.1391	0.1468	0.1547	0.1628	0.1710	0.1794	0.1078	0.1964	0.2051	0.2139
16	0.1355	0.1434	0.1514	0.1596	0.1679	0.1764	0.1850	0.1937	0.2025	0.2114
17	0.1325	0.1405	0.1486	0.1569	0.1654	0.1740	0.1827	0.1915	0.2004	0.2094
18	0.1298	0.1379	0.1462	0.1546	0.1632	0.1719	0.1807	0.1896	0.1987	0.2078
19	0.1276	0.1358	0.1441	0.1527	0.1613	0.1701	0.1791	0.1881	0.1972	0.2065
20	0.1256	0.1339	0.1424	0.1510	0.1598	0.1687	0.1777	0.1868	0.1960	0.2054
21	0.1238	0.1322	0.1408	0.1495	0.1584	0.1674	0.1765	0.1857	0.1951	0.2044
22	0.1223	0.1308	0.1395	0.1483	0.1573	0.1664	0.1756	0.1848	0.1942	0.2037
23	0.1210	0.1296	0.1383	0.1472	0.1563	0.1654	0.1747	0.1841	0.1935	0.2031
24	0.1198	0.1285	0.1373	0.1463	0.1554	0.1647	0.1740	0.1835	0.1930	0.2025
25	0.1187	0.1275	0.1364	0.1455	0.1547	0.1640	0.1734	0.1829	0.1925	0.2021
26	0.1178	0.1267	0.1357	0.1448	0.1541	0.1634	0.1729	0.1825	0.1921	0.2018
27	0.1170	0.1259	0.1350	0.1442	0.1535	0.1630	0.1725	0.1821	0.1917	0.2015
28	0.1163	0.1252	0.1344	0.1437	0.1531	0.1625	0.1721	0.1818	0.1915	0.2012
29	0.1156	0.1247	0.1339	0.1432	0.1527	0.1622	0.1718	0.1815	0.1912	0.2010
30	0.1150	0.1241	0.1334	0.1428	0.1523	0.1619	0.1715	0.1813	0.1910	0.2008

n	21	22	23	24	25	26	72	28	29	30
1	1.2100	1.2200	1.2300	1.2400	1.2500	1.2600	1.2700	1.2800	1.2900	1.3000
2	0.6625	0.6705	0.6784	0.6864	0.6944	0.7025	0.7105	0.7186	0.7267	0.7348
3	0.4822	0.4897	0.4972	0.5047	0.5123	0.5199	0.5275	0.5352	0.5429	0.5506
4	0.3936	0.4010	0.4085	0.4159	0.4234	0.4310	0.4386	0.4462	0.4539	0.4616
5	0.3418	0.3492	0.3567	0.3642	0.3718	0.3795	0.3872	0.3949	0.4027	0.4106
6	0.3082	0.3158	0.3234	0.3311	0.3388	0.3466	0.3545	0.3624	0.3704	0.3784
7	0.2851	0.2928	0.3006	0.3084	0.3163	0.3243	0.3324	0.3405	0.3486	0.3569
8	0.2684	0.2763	0.2843	0.2923	0.3004	0.3086	0.3168	0.3251	0.3335	0.3419
9	0.2561	0.2641	0.2722	0.2805	0.2888	0.2971	0.3056	0.3140	0.3226	0.3312
10	0.2467	0.2549	0.2632	0.2716	0.2801	0.2886	0.2972	0.3059	0.3147	0.3235
11	0.2394	0.2478	0.2563	0.2649	0.2735	0.2822	0.2910	0.2998	0.3088	0.3177
12	0.2337	0.2423	0.2509	0.2596	0.2684	0.2773	0.2863	0.2953	0.3043	0.3135
13	0.2292	0.2379	0.2467	0.2556	0.2645	0.2736	0.2826	0.2918	0.3010	0.3102
14	0.2256	0.2345	0.2434	0.2524	0.2615	0.2706	0.2799	0.2891	0.2984	0.3078
15	0.2228	0.2317	0.2408	0.2499	0.2591	0.2684	0.2777	0.2871	0.2965	0.3060
16	0.2204	0.2295	0.2387	0.2479	0.2572	0.2666	0.2760	0.2855	0.2950	0.3046
17	0.2186	0.2278	0.2370	0.2464	0.2558	0.2652	0.2747	0.2843	0.2939	0.3035
18	0.2170	0.2263	0.2357	0.2451	0.2546	0.2641	0.2737	0.2833	0.2930	0.3027
19	0.2158	0.2251	0.2346	0.2441	0.2537	0.2633	0.2729	0.2826	0.2923	0.3021
20	0.2147	0.2242	0.2337	0.2433	0.2529	0.2626	0.2723	0.2820	0.2918	0.3016
21	0.2139	0.2234	0.2330	0.2426	0.2523	0.2620	0.2718	0.2816	0.2914	0.3012
22	0.2132	0.2228	0.2324	0.2421	0.2519	0.2616	0.2714	0.2812	0.2911	0.3009
23	0.2127	0.2223	0.2320	0.2417	0.2515	0.2613	0.2711	0.2810	0.2908	0.3007
24	0.2122	0.2219	0.2316	0.2414	0.2512	0.2610	0.2709	0.2808	0.2906	0.3006
25	0.2118	0.2215	0.2313	0.2411	0.2509	0.2608	0.2707	0.2806	0.2905	0.3004
26	0.2115	0.2213	0.2311	0.2409	0.2508	0.2606	0.2705	0.2805	0.2904	0.3003
27	0.2112	0.2210	0.2309	0.2407	0.2506	0.2605	0.2704	0.2804	0.2903	0.3003
28	0.2110	0.2208	0.2307	0.2406	0.2505	0.2604	0.2703	0.2803	0.2902	0.3002
29	0.2108	0.2207	0.2306	0.2405	0.2504	0.2603	0.2703	0.2802	0.2902	0.3001
30	0.2107	0.2206	0.2305	0.2404	0.2503	0.2603	0.2702	0.2802	0.2901	0.3001

SOLUTIONS TO PROBLEMS

No solutions provided for this chapter.

2 FINANCE AND ACCOUNTING

Solutions to problems

Problem answer 1

(a)

	£000s		£000s
Equity	35	Fixed assets	92
R/E	65		
	100		
		Inventory	60
LT debt	40	A/R	30
Creditors	60	Cash	18
	200		200
Sales	300	Profit after interest and tax	20

(b)

Retained earnings	£12 million
∴ Dividends	£12 million
Total earnings	£24 million
E per share	£4
∴ Total number of shares	6 million
Book value of assets per share	£40
∴ Total value of assets	£240 million

$$\text{Debt} - \text{assets ratio} = \frac{120}{240} = 0.5$$

If given book value per share is taken as based on net assets (net of liabilities)

then ratio $= \dfrac{120}{120 + 240} = 0.33$

Problem answer 3

	Co. X	Co. Y

(i) *Current ratio*

$$\frac{CA}{CL} \qquad \frac{40}{10} = 4 \text{ to } 1 \qquad \frac{22}{11} = 2 \text{ to } 1$$

(assume loans long-term)

(ii) *Gearing ratios*

$$\frac{\text{Total debt}}{\text{total assets}} \qquad \frac{30}{120} = 0.25 \qquad \frac{61}{121} = 0.50$$

(iii) *Profitability*

$$\frac{\text{Profit after tax}}{\text{shareholders' funds}} \qquad \frac{8.1}{90} = 9\% \qquad \frac{7.2}{60} = 12\%$$

(iv) E per S (excluding extraordinary items)

$$\frac{£8100}{50\,000} = £0.16 \qquad \frac{£7200}{50\,000} = £0.14$$

(v) P/E ratios (if extraordinary items excluded)

$$\frac{£3.24}{£0.16} = 20.3 \text{ to } 1 \qquad \frac{£2.16}{£0.14} = 15.4 \text{ to } 1$$

One reason why the market might attach a lower P/E ratio to Company Y is because of the extraordinary loss shown in the 1988 accounts. Another usually important reason is that Y is a slower-growth Company than X.

3 INVESTMENT APPRAISAL

Solutions to problems

Problem answer 1

The net present value of the specified cash flow is:

$$\text{NPV} = -400 + \frac{500}{(1.12)} - \frac{100}{(1.12)^2} + \frac{700}{(1.12)^3}$$

Using a calculator, the result correct to two decimal places is:

$$\text{NPV} = 464.96$$

A possible layout for the workings would be:

Year	Cash flow	Present value factor: 12%	Present value at: 12%
0	−400	1.0000	−400.00
1	500	0.8929	446.43
2	−100	0.7972	−79.72
3	700	0.7118	498.25
		Net present value:	464.96

Using the values in a four figure table of discount factors, the result is:

$$NPV = -400 + 500(0.8929) - 100(0.7972) + 700(0.7118) = 464.99$$

The negligible difference in the two results is due to rounding in the table values.

Problem answer 2

With the data provided, the present value workings are as shown in the following table:

Year	Receipt (outlay)	Present value factor: 10%	20%	Present value at: 10%	20%
0	−500	1.0000	1.0000	−500.00	−500.00
1	100	0.9091	0.8333	90.91	83.33
2	150	0.8264	0.6944	123.97	104.17
3	250	0.7513	0.5787	187.83	144.68
4	200	0.6830	0.4823	136.60	96.45
5	150	0.6209	0.4019	93.14	60.28
			Net present value:	132.45	−11.09

So the net present value is positive at 10%, indicating acceptance of the project, but is negative at 20% and rejection would be implied on the basis of the net present value criterion at this rate of discount.

Problem answer 3

The net terminal value of the investment is obtained by using the equation:

$$NTV = \sum_{t=1}^{n} R_t(1+r)^{n-t} - K(1+r)^n$$

where R_t is the return in year t, K is the initial outlay, n is the number of years for which the project runs and where the discount rate is $100r\%$.

So in this case the formula is evaluated for $n = 3$ $r = 0.12$ and with the given cash flow. The calculations can be laid out in tabular form as follows:

t	R_t	$(1.12)^{3-t}$	$R_t(1.12)^{3-t}$
0	−400	1.4049	−561.97
1	500	1.2544	627.20
2	−100	1.1200	−112.00
3	700	1.0000	700.00
			NTV = 653.23

The net terminal value of 653.23 obtained in Table 4.2 can be checked for consistency with the net present value result of Problem 1. Since:

$$NTV = NPV(1 + r)^n$$

then in this case:

$$464.96(1.12)^3 = 653.24 = NTV$$

where the trivial difference of 0.01 is due to rounding.

Problem answer 6

(a) The net present values of the three projects at the two rates of discount are as follows:

	NPV(10%)	NPV(25%)
Project A	27.60	13.60
Project B	35.37	8.00
Project C	44.63	4.80

So that at 10% project C should be selected, while at 25% project A should be chosen.

(b) The IRR figures can be found by discounting at estimated rates and interpolation, or by direct solution since only quadratic expressions are involved. Thus, for instance, to find the yield of project A in a similar fashion to the previous question we should solve:

$$60R^2 - 60R - 40 = 0$$

which solves for:

$$R = \frac{60 \pm \sqrt{(3600 + 9600)}}{120}$$

for which the positive root gives $R = 1.4574$ corresponding to an IRR of 45.74%. Using interpolation to estimate the IRR for project B, the NPV of B at 30% is 0.71 and at 31% it is -0.66, so the interpolated result is:

$$\text{IRR} \approx 30 + \left[\frac{0.71}{1.37}\right]\% = 30.52\%$$

which is correct to two decimal places. By either exact calculation or linear interpolation the yield for project C emerges as 27.18%.

(c) Applying the incremental yield method to the choice between B and C gives the cash flow:

$$\text{C} - \text{B:} \quad -80 \quad 80 \quad 20$$

as the incremental project. Since the yield on this incremental project is 20.71%, the extra funds required to finance the more expensive project C are well used when the interest rate is only 10%.

Problem answer 8

With an interest rate of $100r\%$ and over a period of n years, the present value of an annuity of £1 is given by the formula:

$$\frac{1 - (1 + r)^{-n}}{r}$$

In the present case, substituting for $r = 0.1$ and $n = 6$ gives the result to four decimal places:

$$\frac{1 - (1 + 0.1)^{-6}}{0.1} = 4.3553$$

So with the annuity at £100 per annum, the required answer is:

$$4.3553(100) = £435.5261 \approx £435.53$$

which result to two decimal places also follows from the use of the four figure tables of annuity factors.

Problem answer 9

The present value of a perpetuity of £1 discounted at $100r\%$ compound is given by:

572

$$\frac{1}{r}$$

So with a perpetuity of £200 and a discount rate of 4%, the required result will be:

$$200\frac{1}{0.04} = 5000$$

Problem answer 10

Purchase of the security would produce a cash flow as follows:

$t = 0$	$t = 1$	$t = 2$	$t = 3$	$t = 4$	$t = 5$
-1200	150	150	150	150	$(150 + 1500)$

Using the table values in this case, with an initial estimate for the yield to maturity of 15%, the following present values are produced:

Interest:	$150(3.3522) =$	502.8300
Lump Sum:	$1500(0.4972) =$	745.8000
		1248.6300

So the yield is greater than 15%. Trying 16% next:

Interest:	$150 (3.2743) =$	491.1450
Lump Sum:	$1500 (0.4761) =$	714.1500
		1205.2950

So 16% is a little too low, though it clearly is the whole number part of the result. Trying 17%:

Interest:	$150 (3.1993) =$	479.8950
Lump Sum:	$1500 (0.4561) =$	684.1500
		1164.0450

So that by linear interpolation, the yield to maturity is estimated as:

$$16 + \left[\frac{1205.295 - 1200}{1205.295 - 1164.045}\right]\% = 16.13\%$$

Exact calculation shows this to be accurate to two decimal places.

Problem answer 11

The relevant formula here is that for the future value of an annuity. With an interest rate of $100r\%$ and over a period of n years, the present value of an annuity of £1 is given by:

$$\frac{(1+r)^n - 1}{r}$$

In the present case, substituting for $r = 0.1$ and $n = 10$ gives the result to four decimal places:

$$\frac{(1+0.1)^{10} - 1}{0.1} = 15.9374$$

So with the annuity at £700 per annum, the required answer is:

$$15.9374 (700) = 11156.1972 \approx £11156.20$$

the result to two decimal places using four figure tables is £11156.18.

Problem answer 12

The relevant formula in this case is that for a *sinking fund*. The amount required to be set aside annually at an interest rate of $100r\%$ to give £1 after n years is:

$$\frac{r}{(1+r)^n - 1}$$

So if £5 000 000 is required at the end of nine years at 15% the annual sum to be set aside is:

$$\frac{5\,000\,000(0.15)}{(1.15)^9 - 1} = 297\,870$$

Use of four figure tables of sinking fund values would give the less precise answer as:

$$£5\,000\,000\ (0.0596) = £298\,000$$

which would be acceptable for all practical purposes.

Problem answer 14

Calculating exactly, the net present value of the cash flow at a 15% rate of discount is:

Year	Cash flow	Present value factor: 15%	Present value at: 15%
0	1200	1.0000	1200.00
1	350	0.8696	304.35
2	500	0.7561	378.07
		Net present value:	1882.42

From the formula, the annual equivalent annuity factor for two years at a discount rate of 15% is:

$$\text{Annual Equivalent Annuity} = \frac{r}{1-(1+r)^{-n}}$$

$$= \frac{0.15}{1-(1.15)^{-2}}$$

$$= 0.61511628$$

The annual annuity equivalent to the cash flow is found by multiplying the NPV value by the annual equivalent annuity factor. The exact result to two decimal places is 1157.91.

Using table values, the present value works out at 1882.41 and with a four figure annual equivalent annuity factor of 0.6151, the result is an annual annuity equivalent to the cash flow of:

$$1882.41\ (0.6151) = 1157.87$$

where the trivial difference of 0.04 is due to rounding in the table values.

Problem answer 16

Calculations for possible cycle lengths can be laid out as follows:

Cycle length	Net cash flow $t = 0$	$t = 1$	$t = 2$	$t = 3$	$t = 4$	NPV	AE Fac	AE Ann
1 yr	5000	−2000				3214	1.12000	3600
2 yr	5000	1400	−200			6091	0.59170	3604
3 yr	5000	1400	1800	1200		8539	0.41635	3555
4 yr	5000	1400	1800	2000	1600	10125	0.32923	3334

So a four year cycle length is optimal since with an annual equivalent annuity of 3334 it produces the lowest AE annuity figure.

Problem answer 17

The 'make' decision would produce the flow of costs:

$t = 0$	$t = 1$	$t = 2$	$t = 3$	$t = 4$
1 000 000	1 300 000	1 400 000	1 700 000	1 800 000

Whereas the 'buy' decision would give the costs:

$t = 0$	$t = 1$	$t = 2$	$t = 3$	$t = 4$
0	1 700 000	1 700 000	2 200 000	2 200 000

The decision can be made by evaluating the difference between the two streams. The gain from make over buy is:

$t = 0$	$t = 1$	$t = 2$	$t = 3$	$t = 4$
−1 000 000	400 000	300 000	500 000	400 000

and if this cash flow has a positive present value, the make decision is indicated. The discount rate is 15% at which the present value of the gains from making over buying is £132 128 so the product should be made in house. This NPV figure is, of course, the difference between the present value of the costs associated with buying (£5 468 098) and the present value of costs associated with manufacture (£5 335 970).

4 RATIONING, UNCERTAINTY AND CORPORATE STRATEGY

Solutions to problems

Problem answer 1

(a) First determine the net present value of each investment. Then obtain the NPV/outlay ratio. The results obtained are as follows:

	Investment				
	1	2	3	4	5
NPV	203.31	55.25	95.39	126.78	68.62
NPV/outlay	.0847	.0276	.0530	.1057	.1372

Now rank the projects by size of NPV/outlay ratio, and work down the list until the budget is exhausted. The outcome is:

Investment	Ratio	Σ outlay	Σ NPV
5	.1372	500	68.62
4	.1057	1700	195.40
1	.0847	4100	398.71
3 (1/9)	.0530	4300	409.31

So the maximum NPV achievable under these conditions is £409.31.

(b) If all projects were repeatable it would be possible to place all funds in investment 5 (i.e. take 8.6 units of this investment instead of one unit), the achievable NPV would then have been £590.13.

(c) The rate of return on the marginal project (no. 3 in this case) is 16.88%.

(d) The overall yield on the £4300 invested is 15.01%.

(e) The actual cash flow of the optimal investment programme is given as Σcash flow in the following table:

	Investment				
5	4	1	3(1/9)	ΣCash flow	t
−500	−1200	−2400	−200	−4300	0
150	350	1500	55.55	2055.55	1
150	350	1500	55.55	2055.55	2
150	350	0	55.55	555.55	3
150	350	0	55.55	555.55	4
150	350	0	55.55	555.55	5

This pattern, with the larger returns occurring earlier on, would be regarded as acceptable in most circumstances.

Problem answer 2

(a) Letting x_j represent the percentage of overall funds invested in the jth company and with F as overall yield, with the given constraints the problem is to maximize:

$$F = 16x_1 + 12x_2 + 8x_3 + 10x_4 + 7x_5 + 15x_6 + 13x_7$$

subject to:

$$
\begin{aligned}
x_1 + x_2 + x_3 + x_4 + x_5 + x_6 + x_7 &= 100 \\
x_1 + x_2 &\le 45 \\
x_3 + x_4 + x_5 &\le 45 \\
x_6 + x_7 &\le 45 \\
x_3 + x_4 + x_5 &\ge 20 \\
x_1 &\le 25 \\
x_2 &\le 25 \\
x_3 &\le 25 \\
x_4 &\le 25 \\
x_5 &\le 25 \\
x_6 &\le 25 \\
x_7 &\le 25
\end{aligned}
$$

with $x_j \ge 0$ for all j.

Were it not for the restrictions, all funds would be placed in agricultural share no. 1 ($x_1 = 100$), giving an overall yield of 16%. But the maximum allowable level of x_1 is 25. The next most attractive investment is x_6 which is also set at 25.

Manufacturing must receive at least 20% of the total funds, so before working further through the list set $x_4 = 20$. The next best investment after x_1 and x_6 is x_7 which is set at 20 due to the sectoral investment constraint of 45%. Just 10% of total funds now remain, so that these are placed in x_2.

(b) Overall yield can be worked out as follows:

(1) Share	(2) Weight	(3) Yield	(4) (2) × (3)
x_1	25	16	400
x_6	25	15	375
x_4	20	10	200
x_7	20	13	260
x_2	10	12	120
			$\Sigma = 1355$

so the overall yield achieved is thus 13.55%.

(c) Removal of the manufacturing minimum requirement produces the following results:

$$x_1 = 25 \quad x_6 = 25 \quad x_7 = 20 \quad x_2 = 20 \quad x_4 = 10$$
$$\text{overall yield} = 13.75\%$$

The only improvement that this relaxation allows is the increase of investment in x_2 from 10% to 20% (due to the sectoral limit of 45%) so that 10% remains in manufacturing share x_4.

(d) This tightened restriction means that x_7 must be reduced to 15% which allows an increase in x_2 to 15%. The full results are:

$$x_1 = 25 \quad x_6 = 25 \quad x_7 = 15 \quad x_2 = 15 \quad x_4 = 20$$
$$\text{overall yield} = 13.50\%.$$

so the net effect on overall yield is small.

Problem answer 3

(a) The payback calculations are as follows:

Year	Cash flow A	ΣCash flow A	Cash flow B	ΣCash flow B
0	−100	−100	−100	−100
1	5	−95	55	−45
2	15	−80	25	−20
3	25	−55	10	−10
4	55	0	5	−5
5	25	25	10	5
6	15	40	35	40
7	5	45	45	85

So project A pays back in four years, while project B takes five years to recover its outlay. If payback was the only criterion, project A would be selected.

(b) The present value workings are:

Year	Discount factor	A	PV(A)	B	PV(B)
0	1.0000	−100	−100.0000	−100	−100.0000
1	0.9091	5	4.5455	55	4.5455
2	0.8264	15	12.3967	25	12.3967
3	0.7513	25	18.7829	10	18.7829
4	0.6830	55	37.5657	5	37.5657
5	0.6209	25	15.5230	10	15.5230
6	0.5645	15	8.4671	35	8.4671
7	0.5132	5	2.5658	45	2.5658
			−0.1533		30.6473

So project B would be selected on the basis of net present value. In the table, note that the values shown in the PV(A) and PV(B) columns are correct to four decimal places rather than being the product of the rounded discount factors and the cash flow components. Differences with the use of table values are, of course, trivial.

(c) Payback period did not take into account the big returns from project B in the later years. It also did not, in this case, give weight to the fact that B has paid back 55% of the outlay after one year and 80% after two years.

For project A the corresponding figures are 5% and 20%. If the cash flow for the first four years of project A was reversed to 55, 25, 15, no account would be taken of this by payback period. Finally, note that the yield on project A is 9.95%, whilst the yield on project B is 19.87%.

Problem answer 4

(a) With the five year horizon, the present value calculations are:

Year	Discount factor	Cash flow	Present value
0	1.0000	−3000	−3000.0000
1	0.9091	1650	1500.0000
2	0.8264	750	619.8347
3	0.7513	300	225.3944
4	0.6830	150	102.4520
5	0.6209	300	186.2764
			−366.0424

so that a project would be rejected by the finite horizon method with a five year horizon.

(b) Using a seven year time horizon the present value calculations are:

Year	Discount factor	Cash flow	Present value
0	1.0000	3000	3000.0000
1	0.9091	1650	1500.0000
2	0.8264	750	619.8347
3	0.7513	300	225.3944
4	0.6830	150	102.4520
5	0.6209	300	186.2764
6	0.5645	1050	592.6976
7	0.5132	1350	692.7635
			919.4187

So the project would be accepted under the finite horizon method if a seven year horizon is used.

(c) Use of a horizon of length such that there is likely to be an upsurge in post horizon returns is not an appropriate use of the method, so a five year horizon should not be employed in a case such as this.

Problem answer 6

Risk premia of five and ten percentage points on a base of 10% mean discounting at 15% and 20% respectively. The present value workings are as follows:

Time	Cash Flow	PV 10%	PV 15%	PV 20%
0	−500.00	−500.00	−500.00	−500.00
1	200.00	181.82	173.91	166.67
2	250.00	206.61	189.04	173.61
3	300.00	225.39	197.25	173.61
4	350.00	239.05	200.11	168.79
		352.88	260.32	182.68

so the effect of a risk premium of five percentage points is a reduction of net present value from 352.88 to 260.32, a drop of 26.23%. The ten percentage-point risk premium reduces the NPV figure by 48.23%.

5 EQUITY CAPITAL AND IT VALUATION

Solutions to problems

Problem answer 9

(a)
$$\text{Ex-right price} = P_\text{p}\left(\frac{N_0}{N}\right) + P_\text{N}\left(\frac{N_n}{N}\right)$$

$$= £5\left(\frac{4}{5}\right) + £4\left(\frac{1}{5}\right)$$

$$= £4.80$$

$$\text{Value of one right} = £4.80 - £4.00$$
$$= £0.80$$

(b) $\dfrac{P_\text{p}N_0 + P_\text{n}N_\text{n}(Y_n/Y_0)}{N} = £5.066$

$$\text{Value of one right} = £5.066 - £4.00$$
$$= £1.066$$

Problem answer 10

(a)
$$\left[\frac{4}{5} \times 173\text{p}\right] + \left[\frac{1}{5} \times 140\text{p}\right]$$

$$= 166.4\text{p}$$

The reason why the actual price is higher than the theoretical price could be:
  (i) The rights issue conveys a message of confidence in the future. New information is released to the market at the time of the rights issue.
  (ii) The company is no longer overgeared.
(b) If the existing shareholders do not subscribe to the rights issue, they will be reducing their wealth.

An investor who owns 1000 shares before the issue has wealth of £1730. If he or she does not exercise the rights, the wealth becomes £1710.

If investors exercise the rights, they own 1250 shares, worth £2137.50, and the additional cost has been (250 × 140p) £350. This is a net wealth of £1787.5.

Whether this increase of £77.50 is worthwhile depends ultimately on the cost of borrowing. The investor will be receiving dividends on an extra 250 shares and paying interest on £350. Interest would have to be very high to make the investment not worthwhile.
(c) If an issue is not underwritten, if the existing shareholders are not interested in exercising the rights, and potential investors are not interested in purchasing the rights, then no new finance is available to the company. If the issue is underwritten, the company receives the required funds.

Paying an underwriter is like paying the writer of an option. You know what the cost will be. You may or may not wish to exercise the agreement. If events turn out badly you will. If they turn out well you will not. To value the agreement we need to have details of the probability of the rights being taken up by investors.

(d) A rights issue pleases existing shareholders. It means the percentage of the company's shares they own need not be reduced. A private placement does reduce the relative holdings of existing shareholders and therefore their influence.

A private placement is probably less expensive from an administrative point of view. There are fewer people to contact.

(e) The longer-term fixed interest rate debt means the company does not need continually to approach the bank or money market to renew its borrowings. This reduces risk.

6 EQUITY VALUATION

Solutions to problems

Problem answer 5

(a) *Dividend growth model.*
Manu's cost of equity:

$$i = \frac{D_1}{350} + g$$

$$D^1 = \frac{600(1.08)}{4000} = 16.2\text{p}$$

$$i = \frac{16.2}{350} + 8\% = 12.63\%$$

Europa's cost of equity:
$i = 12.63 \times 1.2 = 15.6\%$

$$D_1 = \frac{200(1.1)}{2160}$$

$$P = \frac{D_1}{i - g}$$

$$= \frac{10.185}{0.1516 - 0.10} = 197.4\text{p}$$

(b) *P/E ratio*
(P/E) Manu = £3.50 : £0.35 = 10:1
(EPS) Eur = 500/2160 = 23.15p
∴ Price per share Eur = 23.15 × 10 = 231.5p

(c) *Asset value per share*

Land and buildings	2000
Plant and machinery	2800
Current assets	1876
	6676
Less: Current liabilities	1600
	5076
Less: Debt	
Total equity	£5.076 million
Asset value per share	$\frac{5076}{2160} = 235\text{p}$

Solutions to problems

Problem answer 8

8(a) (i) Funds available for dividend initially are £1.4 million. £0.70 per share on 2 million shares. This would decline to £0.9 million if funds were retained to finance the investment, leaving a dividend of £0.45 per share to be paid. The *ex div.* price becomes £4.20 − £0.45 = £3.75, to which must be added the increase in value arising on the project; this is:

$$\frac{120\,000}{0.20} - 500\,000 = £100\,000 \text{ or 5p per share}$$

∴ Ex div. price will be £3.75 + 5p = £3.80.

(ii) A rights issue at £2.50 to raise £500 000 would require the issue of 200 000 shares.

(b) Adoption of the investment increases firm value by:

$$\frac{120\,000}{0.20} - 500\,000 = £100\,000$$

The *ex div.* price should rise to £3.55, and this is the price new shares should be issued at if existing shareholders are to get the benefit of the profitable project.

$$\text{Number of shares to be issued} = \frac{500\,000}{3.55} = 140\,845$$

$$\text{Dividend per share in one year's time} = \frac{1\,400\,000 + 120\,000}{2\,140\,845}$$

$$= 71\text{p}$$

The new shareholders will receive a return of $71/355 \times 100 = 20\%$, which is the return expected from investment in the shares.

(c) The gain made by present shareholders will be the same in each case under the assumptions made in the question. Value of firm increases by £100 000.

(d) Use of retained earnings provides funds without the expenses involved in making new issues, be they rights or to the general public. In addition, there will be no losses in taxes paid by shareholders who may then be called upon to subscribe for further shares. The question assumes perfect knowledge and markets; however, in reality a decrease in dividend could lead to a fall in share price. Even though this might only by temporary, shareholders seeking to boost cash available for consumption through sale of shares could lose.

A rights issue is a good way of issuing new equity, in that the risk of equity dilution is avoided. However, issue costs including underwriting will be incurred and this will make it more expensive than retentions. Underwriting could be avoided by making a deep discount issue.

The problem with a public issue would be in fixing the issue price. In the question the price had to be £3.55 (above expected *ex div.* price) to avoid any dilution of existing shareholders' interests. In reality, it would not be possible to fix a price at this level and the normal expectation would be to make an offer of shares at a small discount, which would mean some dilution of existing shareholders' interests. Issue costs would probably be greater than with a rights issue and underwriting would be unavoidable in this case.

Solutions to problems

Problem answer 6

6(b) Day 1 total value of each firm is:

A £1 × 2 million = £2 million

B £2 × 5 million = £10 million

B is making an offer of £3 million for A which appears to be worth only £2 million – this will reduce the value of B by £1 million to £9 million or £1.80 per share.

  When it is known that the takeover will result in savings, the total value of B will rise by the amount of the savings to £10.6 million, which is £2.12 per share.

(i) If the market is semi-strong form efficient, the market will react only when the information becomes public knowledge; this will produce the following values per share:

		Value per share	
		A	B
Day 2	No new information	£1.00	£2.00
Day 4	Takeover bid announced. B appears to be paying £3 million for assets worth £2 million	£1.50	£1.80
Day 10	Information available which revises the market value of B	£1.50	£2.12

(ii) If the market is strong form efficient, all information is reflected in share price, even if it is not publicly available information. This will mean that on day 2, when the management of B decide to offer £1.50 for A, the share prices will then react to reflect the full impact of the bid on both shares (the *process* by which this is assumed to be carried out is difficult to specify precisely). This will give the following share prices:

		Value per share	
		A	B
Day 2	Full impact of decision to bid and make savings reflected in share price	£1.50	£2.12
Day 4	Public announcement of bid (i.e. information of which the market is aware and therefore has no new information content)	£1.50	£2.12
Day 10	Public announcement of savings to be derived from bid (i.e. further information of which the market is aware and therefore has no new information content)	£1.50	£2.12

Problem 11

Scenario 1

The market overreacts to the good news about the successful research programme. This is evidence of inefficiency, although there is evidence that this

is how the market does behave on some occasions following the announcement of good news. After overreaction the price returns to its 'true' value.
Scenario 2
This is how an efficient market would be expected to behave.
Scenario 3
This is evidence of an inefficient market. It should react quickly.

Solutions to problems

Problem answer 2

(a) £463.20 = £1000 × 0.4632 Present value
Factor at 8% for 10 years
Answer = 8%

(b)
$$v = \frac{£1000}{(1.12)^4} = £1000 \times \frac{1}{(1.12)^4} = £624.60$$

Problem answer 8

(a)
$$\text{Value} = \frac{120}{(1.08)} + \frac{120}{(1.08)^2} \ldots + \frac{1120}{(1.08)^8}$$
$$= (120 \times 5.7466) + (1000 \times 0.5403)$$
$$= £1230$$

(b)
$$\text{Value} = \frac{120}{(1.14)} \ldots + \frac{1120}{(1.14)^8}$$
$$= (120 \times 4.6389) + (1000 \times 0.3506)$$
$$= £907$$

Problem answer 11

(a)
$$1 + {}_0R_1 = \frac{100.}{94.34}$$

$${}_0R_1 = 6\%$$

$$(1 + {}_0R_2)^2 = \frac{100.}{87.34}$$

$${}_0R_2 = 7\%$$

$$(1 + {}_0R_3)^3 = \frac{100.}{79.38}$$

$${}_0R_3 = 8\%$$

$$(1 + {}_0R_4)^4 = \frac{100.}{73.50}$$

$${}_0R_4 = 8\%$$

(b)

$$1+_1F_2 = \frac{(1+_0R_2)^2}{1+_0R_1}$$

$$_1F_2 = \frac{(1.07)^2}{1.06} - 1$$

$$= 8\%$$

$$1+_2F_3 = \frac{(1+_0R_3)^3}{(1+_0R_2)^2}$$

$$_2F_3 = \frac{(1.08)^3}{(1.07)^2} - 1$$

$$= 10\%$$

$$1+_3F_4 = \frac{(1+_0R_4)^4}{(1+_0R_3)^3}$$

$$_3F_4 = \frac{(1.08)^4}{(1.08)^3} - 1$$

$$= 8\%$$

(c) Price of Bond C two years from now is expected to be $79.38(1.07)^2 = \$90.88$
Price of Bond D two years from now is expected to be $73.50(1.07)^2 = \$84.15$

Problem answer 13

(a) Stock A
Estimated market price at year three:

	PVF at 14%	£
Interest £30	4.288	128.64
Principal £100	0.400	40.00
		£168.64

Current market price:

			PVF at 13%	£
Cash flows –	1	30	0.885	26.55
	2	30	0.783	23.49
	3	198.64	0.693	137.66
				£187.70

Stock B
Current market price = £100 × 0.712 = £71.2

Stock C

	Cash flows			Present values			
				12%		13%	
			PVF	PV	PVF	PV
Year 0	−99	= −99.00	1.000	−99.000	1.000	−99.000
1	5 × 1.10 =	5.50	0.893	4.912	0.885	4.868
2	5 × 1.18 =	5.90	0.797	4.702	0.783	4.620
3	105 × 1.23 =	129.15	0.712	91.955	0.693	89.501
				2.569		−0.011

Yield, in money terms, on stock C is slightly under 13%.

Interest received at years 1 and 2 will be reinvested until year 3; the appropriate factors are:

Year 1: $(1.1)^2 = 1.21$
Year 2: $(1.09)^1 = 1.09$

Year	Stock A Cash flow (£)	Stock A Final value (£)	Stock B Cash flow (£)	Stock B Final value (£)	Stock C Cash flow (£)	Stock C Final value (£)
1	30	36.30	–	–	5.5	6.655
2	30	32.70	–	–	5.9	6.431
3	198.64	198.64	100	100	129.15	129.150
		267.64		100.00		142.236

	Stock A	Stock B	Stock C
Final value	267.64	100.0	142.236
Initial investment	187.70	71.2	99.000
Final value per £ of initial investment	1.426	1.404	1.437
Equivalent annual yield after reinvestment	12.55%	12%	12.84%

Hence stock C should be chosen.

(b) The other factors to which consideration should be given include:

1 Taxation. The potentially differing tax treatment between stocks and between interest and capital gain (or loss) elements of the gross return may alter the relative desirability of each stock.

2 Risk of default.

3 Uncertainty surrounding reinvestment rates at year one and two.

4 Uncertainty surrounding seven-year interest rates likely to exist at time 3. A small change here could have a significant impact on the year three value of stock A and hence on the choice now between stock A, B and C.

5 Uncertainty surrounding future inflation rates.

6 The expected return and risk of other available investments.

10 RISK AND RETURN

Solutions to problems

Problem answer 1

$$\text{Return} = \frac{12 + 235 - 250}{250} \times \frac{100}{1}$$
$$= -1.2\%$$

Problem answer 2

The two-year return would be:

$$\text{Return} = \frac{55 + 548 - 520}{520} \times 100$$
$$= 16\%$$

Problem answer 3

	Probability	Outcome (%)	Product (%)
Rapid expansion	0.3	10	3
Moderate growth	0.4	5	2
Recession	0.3	2	0.6
		Expected return	5.6
		Standard deviation	7.1

Problem answer 4

(a) $\bar{R}_{AB} = 0.24$ (24%), $\sigma^2_{AB} = 0.0632$
(b) $\bar{R}_{AB} = 0.24$ (24%), $\sigma^2_{AB} = 0.06224$
(c) The lower correlation, the less will be the variance of the resulting portfolio. Maximum and minimum values range from +1 to −1.

Problem answer 5

(a) $\bar{R}_V = 20\%$, $\sigma^2_V = 540$, $\sigma_V = 23.2$
(b) $\bar{R}_Z = 10\%$, $\sigma^2_V = 0$, $\sigma_Z = 0$
(c) $Co_V(R_V, R_Z) = 0$, $\rho_{VZ} = 0$
(d) $\bar{R}_{VZ} = 15\%$, $\sigma_{VZ} = 11.6$

Problem answer 6

The answer in both cases is no; the expected return on a portfolio is the sum of the expected returns weighted by proportion invested of all the individual securities. Thus from any given set of securities the maximum portfolio return would be obtained by investing 100% in the maximum-yielding security and the minimum portfolio return would be obtained by investing 100% in the minimum-yielding security.

Problem answer 7

(a) $\bar{R}_A = 0.25\ (16) + 0.50\ (12) + 0.25\ (8) = 12\%$
$\bar{R}_B = 6\%$
$\bar{R}_C = 14\%$
$\sigma_A = 2.83\%$
$\sigma_B = 1.41\%$
$\sigma_C = 4.24\%$
(b) $cov_{AB} = -4$
$cor_{AB} = -1$
$cov_{BC} = -6$
$cor_{BC} = -1$
$cov_{AC} = 12$
$cor_{AC} = +1$
(c) $\bar{R}_{AB} = 9\%$
$\sigma_{AB} = 0.71\%$
$\bar{R}_{BC} = 10\%$
$\sigma_{BC} = 1.41\%$
$\bar{R}_{AC} = 13\%$
$\sigma_{AC} = 3.53\%$
$\bar{R}_{ABC} = 10.67\%$
$\sigma_{ABC} = 2.55\%$

Problem answer 8

In a well-diversified portfolio the covariance and hence correlation between securities will be the important factor. In a large portfolio the individual unique risk can be diversified away, leaving the risk contributed by the covariance terms.

Problem answer 9

If the distribution of returns is a normal distribution, then standard deviation will be a satisfactory measure of risk as there is equal likelihood of above- or below-average returns. However, if the distribution is skewed, then standard deviation would not be such a satisfactory measure; in these circumstances, the semi-variance which only considers returns below the mean could be used. However, because it is difficult to use the latter in the context of portfolios, it is more usual to use standard deviations in portfolio analysis.

Problem answer 10

(a) *Month*   *Return %*

Month	D	E
2	−0.024	0.088
3	0.017	0.145
4	0.017	0.029
5	0.016	0.125
6	0.032	0.062
7	0	0.070

(b) $\bar{R}_D = 0.0097$
$\sigma_D = 0.0177$
$\bar{R}_E = 0.0865$
$\sigma_E = 0.0389$

(c) $cor_{DE} = -0.045$

(d) $\bar{R}_{DE} = 0.0481$
$\sigma_{DE} = 0.021$

Problem answer 11

(a) (i) 100% Wye
$\bar{R} = 10\%, \sigma = 20\%$

(ii) 100% Zee
$\bar{R} = 12\%\ \sigma = 25\%$

(iii) 50% Wye, 50% Zee,
$\bar{R} = 0.5\ (10) + 0.5\ (12) = 11\%$
$\sigma = \sqrt{[(0.5)^2\ (0.20)^2}$
$+ (0.5)^2\ (0.25)^2$
$+ 2(0.5)\ (0.5)\ (0.5)\ (0.2)\ (0.25)]$
$\sigma = 0.1953\ (19.53\%)$

(iv) 25% Wye, 75% Zee,
$\bar{R} = 0.25\ (10) + 0.75\ (12) = 11.5\%$
$\sigma = \sqrt{[(0.25)^2\ (0.20)^2 + (0.75)^2\ (0.25)^2}$
$+ 2(0.25)\ (0.75)\ (0.5)\ (0.2)\ (0.25)]$
$\sigma = 0.2169\ (21.69\%)$

(v) 75% Wye, 25% Zee,
$\bar{R} = 0.75\ (10) + 0.25\ (12) = 10.5\%$
$\sigma = \sqrt{[(0.75)^2\ (0.20)^2}$
$+ (0.25)^2\ (0.25)^2$
$+ 2(0.75)\ (0.25)\ (0.5)\ (0.2)\ (0.25)]$
$\sigma = 0.1892\ (18.92\%)$

Solutions to problems

Problem answer 1

Systematic risk is that risk which affects all securities to a greater or lesser degree through their relationship with the market. It is market risk which cannot be diversified away and is measured by beta in the CAPM framework. *Unsystematic risk*, also called specific, unique or idiosyncratic risk, is risk peculiar to that particular security. It is diversifiable, in that unexpected pieces of good or bad news relating to specific securities can be expected to cancel out each other; however, market factors will tend to affect all securities.

Problem answer 2

(a) False. (b) False. (c) False. (d) False.

Problem answer 3

(a) If the portfolio is efficient and fully diversified, this will be the case. But if all unsystematic risk has not been diversified away, total risk will have to be considered.

(b) Total risk comprising both unsystematic *and* systematic risk would need to be considered by such an investor.

(c) A cautious investor should ensure that all unnecessary risk has been diversified away and will therefore hold a portfolio where unsystematic risk has been eliminated and only market or systematic risk remains. In these circumstances, the level of systematic risk will be the appropriate measure of risk.

(d) In theory it would be possible to have a security with a negative beta, in which case the expected return would be lower than the risk-free return because of the negative risk premium. Although in practice it may be difficult (impossible?) to identify such an asset, it is feasible to consider its existence.

(e) We can definitely rule this out. There are many assets/securities with betas of less than one which will have required returns lower than that required from the market.

Problem answer 4

If A with a beta of 0.5 has a risk premium of 4%, then B will have a risk premium of $1.75 \times \frac{4}{0.5} = 14\%$. As the expected return of B is 20% the risk-free rate must be 6% and the expected market return 14%.

The return required from betas given are:

Security	Beta	Return	
1	2.00	22	Overpriced
2	0.75	12	Underpriced
3	1.25	16	Overpriced
4	−0.25	4	Underpriced
5	3.25	32	Overpriced

Problem answer 5

First of all, compute risk-free rate, market return and risk premium using data given.

Comparing A and C: we find the market risk premium is 8%. Using any of the securities, this gives a risk-free rate of 6% and a market return of 14%. Or use simultaneous equations.

(a) Current beta $= 0.1 (0.2) + 0.1 (0.8) + 0.1 (1.2) + 0.2 (1.6) + 0.5 (0)$
$$= 0.54$$
Expected return $= 0.1 (7.6) + 0.1 (12.4) + 0.1 (15.6) + 0.2 (18.8) + 0.5 (6)$
$$= 10.32 \text{ (or could use beta calculated)}$$

(b) $12 = 0.1 (7.6) + 0.1 (12.4) + 0.1 (15.6) + 0.2 (18.8) + x (6) + (0.5 - x) 14$
$x = 0.21$, i.e. 21% in risk-free asset, 29% in market portfolio

(c) $12 = x (6) + (1 - x) 14$
$x = 0.25$, i.e. 25% in risk-free asset, 75% in market portfolio

(d) It measures market/systematic risk, which represents risk which cannot be diversified away by holding a portfolio. It can be used in risk management by investors.

Solutions to problems

Problem answer 1
(a) Food:
$$\beta_A = 0.9 \left(\frac{10}{14} \right) = 0.64$$

Chemicals:
$$\beta_A = 1.2 \left(\frac{10}{12.5} \right) = 0.96$$

Tools:
$$\beta_A = 1.4 \left(\frac{10}{15} \right) = 0.93$$

(b) Average assets beta $= 0.5(0.64) + 0.3(0.96) + 0.2(0.93)$
$$= 0.794$$

$$\beta_E = \beta_A \frac{(12.5)}{10}$$
$$= 0.99$$

(c) Food $= 10 + 0.64 (18 - 10)$
$\qquad\quad = 15.12\%$
Chemicals $= 17.68\%$
Tools $\quad = 17.44\%$

(d) This will depend on how reliable are the betas which have been calculated for each company, and how similar each of the companies is in terms of activities to the division of the company.

Problem answer 2
(a) Use of the cost of debt as the discount rate when appraising risky projects is not supportable; the main reasons include:

1 Raising debt finance increases gearing, which will cause the cost of equity to rise. Hence the true marginal cost of debt is the cost of debt itself, plus the effect that debt will have on the cost of equity.

2 Debt has a lower cost than equity due to its lower level of risk. It is inappropriate to use a debt-related cost which is a required return for a low-risk investment by a lender to appraise a higher-risk project. Risk and return should be related. (Alternatively, all future risky cash flows can be reduced to a certainty equivalent and this is discounted at a risk-free rate.)

Retained earnings have a real opportunity cost and are not 'free'. By utilizing retained earnings in a project the opportunities to invest those funds outside the firm, or to return them to shareholders, are forgone. These forgone opportunities should be attributed to retained earnings as its cost.

The weighted average cost of capital (WACC) reflects the market-required return for the overall risk of the firm. When the risk of a project is the same as the overall risk of the firm, then the use of WACC to appraise that project is reasonable. Hence when Victoria operated only one division, it is likely that WACC was a correct discount rate as most projects were probably of similar risk characteristics. However, even in these circumstances, projects of abnormal risk characteristics should not have been appraised with WACC.

With several divisions of unequal risk, Victoria's WACC will reflect the overall – or composite – risk of the whole firm and this rate will not necessarily relate to the expected return for any one division. The rate will not then be generally suitable for use as the discount rate in investment appraisal.

(b) Theoretically the discount rate, or required return, should be related to the risk of each project (or all future cash flows reduced to a certainty equivalent and all projects discounted at a risk-free rate), risk in this case being determined by the relationship of a project's returns to the market's return – i.e. the systematic or beta risk. Total risk is not a good measure as much total risk can be reduced in a well-diversified portfolio.

Hence Victoria should determine a discount rate for each of the three divisions based on the level of systematic risk in that division. Each division's discount rate is likely to be different from WACC, but WACC will equal the weighted average of divisional rates. Within each division a further adjustment may be needed for projects not representative of the division's average risk.

Victoria may apply this concept subjectively by adjusting WACC for each division according to perceptions of risk differences between divisions – a positive risk premium being added to WACC in order to obtain the luxury goods division discount rate and a reduction from WACC for the low-risk food retailing division, further adjustments being made for unusual projects.

Alternatively, Victoria could apply a capital asset pricing model approach and obtain representative betas for firms engaged in each of the three industries in which Victoria is now operating. These betas may then be applied in the CAPM formula to obtain a divisional discount rate suitable for normal projects within each division.

Obviously adjustments may be required to ungear observed betas and for differences in operational gearing, as well as the adjustment required for projects with risks different from the divisional average.

Problem answer 3

(a) Ungear industry group equity beta:

$$\beta_A = 1.32\left(\frac{10}{12}\right) = 1.1$$

$$\overline{R}_A = 12 + 1.1(9) = 21.9\%$$

(b)
$$\beta_E = 1.1\left(\frac{13}{10}\right) = 1.43$$

$$\overline{R}_E = 12 + 1.43(9) = 24.87\%$$

Problem answer 4

(a) C and D

(b) Project required returns should be calculated using CAPM:
$$\overline{R}_A = 8 + 0.5\,(7) = 11.5\%$$
$$\overline{R}_B = 13.6\%$$

$\bar{R}_C = 16.4\%$
$\bar{R}_D = 19.2\%$
Therefore A and C should be accepted, B and D rejected.
(c) Using cost of capital A would be incorrectly rejected, whilst D would be incorrectly accepted.

Problem answer 5

(a) $\bar{R}_E = 8 + 1.5\,(10) = 23\%$

(b) $\beta_A = 1.5\left(\dfrac{6}{10}\right) = 0.9$

(c) $\bar{R}_A = 8 + 0.9\,(10) = 17\%$
(d) 17%
(e) Yes

$$\beta_E = 0.9\left(\dfrac{10}{9}\right) = 1$$

(f) 17%
(g) $\bar{R} = 8 + 12\,(10) = 20\%$

Problem answer 6

(a) If no economies or synergies were to arise, then the value of the combined organizations would simply be the sum of the individual values. First, calculate required returns on equity using CAPM:

$\bar{R}_A = \bar{R}_f + (\bar{R}_m - \bar{R}_f)\beta_A$
$\quad = 7.5 + (13.8 - 7.5)\,1.85$
$\quad = 19.155\%$
$\bar{R}_B = 7.5 + (13.8 - 7.5)\,0.68$
$\quad = 11.784\%$

$$V_{A+B} = \frac{48.5}{0.19155} + \frac{37.8}{0.11784}$$

$$= 253.20 + 320.77$$
$$= £573.97 \text{ million}$$

(b) Systematic risk of combined firm is value of weighted average of constituent betas:

$$\beta_{A+B} = \beta_A\left(\frac{V_A}{V_{A+B}}\right) + \beta_B\left(\frac{V_B}{V_{A+B}}\right)$$

$$= 1.85\left(\frac{253.20}{573.97}\right) + 0.68\left(\frac{320.77}{573.97}\right)$$

$$= 0.82 + 0.38$$

$$= 1.20$$

$\bar{R}_{A+B} = 7.5 + (13.8 - 7.5)1.20$
$\quad = 15.16\%$

or:

$$\bar{R}_{A+B} = \frac{86.3}{573.97} \times 100 = 15.04\%$$

(difference in rounding betas)
Value of combined firm with synergy:

$$\frac{48.5 + 37.8 + 3.85}{0.1504} = £599.40 \text{ million}$$

(c) If there are no scale economies or synergies arising on a merger, then the value of the combined organization will simply be the sum of the values of the merging firms. The risk of the combination will reflect the value-weighted risks of the merging firms. It is only if synergies or economies arise as in (b) that value is increased. In the context of CAPM, mergers *per se* would not benefit shareholders. No additional benefits of diversification arise as shareholders themselves can undertake all necessary diversification and indeed, in a CAPM world, are assumed to have done so.

13 CAPITAL STRUCTURE

Solutions to problems

Problem answer 1

(a) ABC PLC:

$$\text{Return on equity} = \frac{100\,000}{700\,000} \times 100 = 14.29\%$$

$$= \text{WACC (all equity)}$$

XYZ PLC:

$$\text{Return on debt} = \frac{32\,000}{400\,000} \times 100 = 8\%$$

$$\text{Return on equity} = \frac{100\,000 - 32\,000}{400\,000} \times 100 = 17\%$$

$$\text{WACC} = 8\% \times \frac{400\,000}{800\,000} + 17\% \times \frac{400\,000}{800\,000}$$

$$= 4\% + 8.5\%$$

$$= 12.5\%$$

The total value of XYZ exceeds that of ABC, despite the operating cash flows of both companies being equal and of the same risk class. In an MM world the value of both companies should be the same and therefore the ordinary shares of XYZ and ABC must be misvalued – i.e. ABC shares undervalued, XYZ overvalued.

(b) As a holder of 4% of XYZ's share capital, the strategy should be to sell at market value, take on personal borrowing to make financial risk the same as faced by shareholders in XYZ and invest the total in ABC shares:

4% of XYZ shares would sell for:	16 000
Personal borrowing at 8%	16 000
Invested in ABC shares	£32 000
Income from ABC shares:	
$\dfrac{30\,000}{700\,000} \times 100\,000$	4 571
Less: Interest on personal borrowings: $16\,000 \times 8\%$	1 280
	3 291
Previous income from XYZ shares: $16\,000 \times 17\%$	2 720
Gain from arbitrage	£571

Problem answer 2

(a) As both companies have the same total earnings and business risk in a Modigliani and Miller (MM) world, they should have the same total value. As the markets for ABC ordinary shares and XYZ debentures are in equilibrium, the market for XYZ ordinary shares is not in equilibrium and the shares undervalued. XYZ equity should be valued at £1 600 000.

Holders of shares in ABC could increase their income by selling and investing the proceeds in XYZ shares and debt. XYZ shareholders would be advised to maintain their holdings until arbitrage activities increase the value of their holdings.

(b) Mr Money should sell his shares in ABC PLC for £4000. This should then be invested:

$$\frac{12}{32} \times 4000 = 1500 \text{ ordinary shares}$$

$$\frac{20}{32} \times 4000 = \frac{2500}{\underline{£4000}} \text{ debt}$$

Income:
Before = £400

$$\text{After} = \frac{2}{12} \times 1500 + \frac{16}{200} \times 2500 = £450$$

Gain from arbitrage = £50

(c) The return on ABC equity:

$$\frac{360}{3600} \times 100 = 10\%$$

The return on XYZ debt:

$$\frac{160}{2000} \times 100 = 8\%$$

Return on XYZ equity should be:

$$\frac{200}{1600} \times 100 = 12.5\%$$

i.e.

$$12.5 = 10 + (10 - 8)\frac{2\,000\,000}{1\,600\,000}$$

$$= 10 + 2.5$$

$$= 12.5\%$$

Problem answer 3

(a) The company is likely to benefit from restructuring its capital if its weighted average cost of capital falls.

(b) Alpha's equity and Beta's debentures are assumed to be in equilibrium and therefore values and returns can be accepted as correct:

$$\text{Return on Alpha equity} = \frac{45\,000}{600\,000} \times 100 = 7.5\%$$

$$\text{Return on Beta debentures} = \frac{27\,200}{340\,000} \times 100 = 8.0\%$$

MM, with tax, have shown that the value of a geared firm is equal to value of a firm ungeared plus the present value of the interest tax shield. In this case:

Value of Beta	$= 600\,000 + (340\,000 \times 0.50) = £770\,000$
As value of Beta	$=$ Value of equity + value of debt
As value of debt	$= £340\,000$
Equilibrium value of equity	$= £430\,000$

The cost of the company's debt may be estimated from the redemption yield of the existing debentures.

If the company does not pay corporate taxes this may be found by solving the equation.

$$80 = \frac{5}{1+r} + \frac{5}{(1+r)^2} + \frac{5}{(1+r)^3} + \ldots + \frac{105}{(1+r)^{10}}$$

As the nominal yield is 5% per year, and, based on December 1987, there are 10 years to redemption, then £20 gain over 10 years will give more than an extra 2% per year in addition to the nominal yield.

If, therefore the equation r is solved using 8%:

$$80 = \frac{5}{(1+0.08)} + \frac{5}{(1+0.08)^2} + \ldots + \frac{105}{(1+0.08)^{10}}$$

	£
The present value of an annuity of £5 for 10 years at 8% is £5 $\times$ 6.71	$= 33.55$
The present value of £100 in 10 years' time at 8% is £100 $\times$ 0.463	$= \underline{46.30}$
	$\underline{79.85}$

This is approximately equal to £80. Therefore, the company's cost of debt is estimated to be 8% per annum.

If the company pays corporate tax the cost of debt may be estimated by:

$$80 = \frac{5(1-0.35)}{1+r} + \frac{5(1-0.35)}{(1+r)^2} + \ldots + \frac{5(1-0.35)}{(1+r)^{10}} + \frac{100}{(1+r)^{10}}$$

At 6%	£
The present value of an annuity of £3.25 for 10 years is £3.25 $\times$ 7.360	$= 23.92$
The present value of £100 in 10 years' time is £100 $\times$ 0.558	$= \underline{55.80}$
	$\underline{79.72}$

The after-tax cost of debt is approximately 6%.

Both of these estimates of the cost of debt are only approximations, as the latter does not take account of the time lag caused by the payment of most corporate taxes in arrears.

The cost of the company's equity may be estimated using the capital asset pricing model:

$$E(R_e) = R_F + [E(R_M - R_F]\beta e$$
$$E(R_e) = 5.5\% + (15\% - 5.5\%)\,1.24 = 17.28\%$$

The present cost of capital may be found by taking a weighted average, based on market values, of the cost of debt and equity.

(i) If the company pays tax at 35%:

	Market value (£000)	Proportion	Cost	Weighted cost
Debt	7 500	0.1997	6%	1.20
Equity	30 060	0.8003	17.28%	13.83
	37 560	1.0000		15.03%

(ii) If the company does not expect to pay corporate tax:

	Market value (£000)	Proportion	Cost	Weighted cost
Debt	7 500	0.1997	8%	1.60
Equity	30 060	0.8003	17.28%	13.83
	37 560	1.0000		15.43%

With the revised capital structure:

(i) If tax is paid at 35%:

	Market value (£000)[1]	Proportion	Cost	Weighted cost
Debt	12 500	0.3328	6%	2.00
Equity	25 060	0.6672	17.28%	11.53
	37 560	1.0000		13.53%

[1] Assuming that £5 million value shares can be bought at 167p per share.

(ii) If the company does not expect to pay corporate taxes:

	Market value (£000)	Proportion	Cost	Weighted cost
Debt	12 500	0.3328	8%	2.66
Equity	25 060	0.6672	17.28%	11.53
	37 560	1.0000		14.19%

On the basis of this information it is likely to be beneficial to Rickery PLC to restructure its capital as the cost of capital is expected to fall whether or not the company pays tax.

(b) The proposed change in capital structure considerably increases the gearing and the financial risk of the company. An increase in financial risk will normally result in an increase in the return required by shareholders and higher gearing is likely to increase risk and the return required by the providers of corporate debt. A higher cost of equity and debt will change the market values of equity and debt.

Most theories of capital structure suggest that an increase in gearing will lead to a change in the value of equity, and often debt for the reasons given below.

In a world without taxation Modigliani and Miller argued that as gearing increases the cost of equity rises, the cost of debt remains constant (except at extreme levels of gearing) and the overall cost of capital remains constant. The overall value of the company remains unchanged but the value of equity will fall.

In a world with corporate taxes Modigliani and Miller argue that the cost of equity will rise, the cost of debt will remain constant, but the overall cost of capital will fall due to the benefit of the tax shield on debt interest payments. Once again, the market value of equity will fall.

The traditional theory argues that both the cost of equity and debt will rise as gearing increases, which results in either a reduction or increase in the overall cost of capital (depending on the level of gearing of the company), and a change in the value of both equity and debt. For example, the use of more debt will increase the risk to shareholders and lead to a fall in share price, but the expected return on equity normally increases with the use of debt, which tends to increase share price. The overall effect could be either a rise or fall in share price.

When bankruptcy costs, agency costs and other costs of high gearing are also considered, the likelihood of a change in the value of equity and debt becomes even greater as gearing increases.

The finance director is, therefore, likely to be wrong in his belief that the market price of the company's existing shares and debentures will not change. The value of existing equity could either increase or decrease; the value of existing debt is likely to decrease if new debt, at a higher price, is issued by the company.

Problem answer 4

(a) *Dividend valuation model*

Cost of equity may be estimated using

$$K_e = \frac{D_1}{P} + g$$

Dividend per share is

$$\frac{£2\,140\,000}{10\,000\,000} = 21.4p$$

Given an 11% growth rate, D_1 is 21.4 (1 + 0.11) = 23.75p

$$K_e = \frac{23.75}{321} + 0.11 = 0.184 \text{ or } 18.4\%$$

Cost of debt (K_d), as corporate debt is assumed to be risk-free, is 12%, the Treasury Bill yield.

The after-tax cost is 12 (1 − 0.35) = 7.8%.

The weighted average cost of capital (WACC) is the cost of debt after tax × proportion of debt financing + cost of equity × proportion of equity financing.

$$\text{WACC} = 7.8\% \times \frac{1}{3} + 18.4\% \times \frac{2}{3} = 14.87\%$$

(b) *The capital asset pricing model*

Cost of equity may be estimated using

$$E(r_e) = r_f + [E(r_m) - r_f]\beta_e$$

$$\beta_e = \frac{\sigma e \rho em}{\sigma m}$$

where ρem is the correlation coefficient between total company returns and total market returns.

$$\beta_e = 20\% \times \frac{0.7}{10\%} = 1.4$$

$$E(r_e) = 12\% + (16\% - 12\%)1.4 = 17.6\%$$

$$K_d = 7.8\% \text{ as in part (a)}$$

$$WACC = 7.8\% \times \frac{1}{3} + 17.6\% \times \frac{2}{3} = 14.33\%$$

If the stock market is in equilibrium, and the inputs into the models are correctly specified (i.e. the dividend valuation model reflects only systematic risk), then the cost of equity K_e from the dividend valuation model should approximately equal the expected return on equity $E(r_e)$ of the CAPM.

Problem answer 5

(a) As Berlan has constant earnings which are all distributed as dividends, the cost of equity may be estimated as:

$$K_e = \frac{D}{V}$$

where D = annual dividend and V = ex div market value.
Earnings available to be paid as dividends are:

	£000
Earnings before interest and tax	15 000
Interest (£23.697m at 16%)	3 792
	11 208
Taxation (35%)	3 923
Available as dividend	7 285

The ex div market value is 50 million shares at 80p per share, or £40m.

$$\text{Therefore } K_e = \frac{7\,285}{40\,000} = 18.21\%$$

The cost of debt may be estimated by equating the current market price of debt to the discounted payments that the company must make on the debt until its redemption.

$$105.5 = \frac{16(1-0.35)}{1+K_d} + \frac{16(1-0.35)}{(1+K_d)^2} + \frac{16(1-0.35)}{(1+K_d)^3} + \frac{100}{(1+K_d)^3}$$

By trial and error:

	Discount rate 8%	£	10%	£
£10.40 for 3 years	2.577	26.80	2.487	25.86
£100 in 3 years' time	0.794	79.40	0.751	75.10
		106.20		100.96
		105.50		105.50
NPV		0.70		(4.54)

By linear interpolation:

$$K_d = 8\% + \frac{0.70}{0.70 + 4.54} \times 2\% = 8.27\%$$

The market value of debt is £23.697m × 1.055 = £25m

$$WACC = 18.21\% \times \frac{40}{65} + 8.27\% \times \frac{25}{65} = 14.39\%$$

(b) (i) According to Modigliani and Miller, the market value of a geared company is the market value if all equity is financed plus the present value of tax relief on debt interest.

$$V_g = V_{ug} + Dt$$
$$V_g^g = £32.5m + £5m \times 0.35 = £34.25m$$

The overall value increases by £1.75m.

(ii) The market value of equity is the total market value less the market value of debt.

$$E = V_g - D$$
$$E = £34.25m - £5m = £29.25m$$

Earnings before interest and tax are

$$£32.5m \times 0.18 \times \frac{100}{65} = £9m$$

	£000
EBIT	9000
Interest (£5m at 13%)	650
	8350
Tax (35%)	2922
Available as dividend	5428

$$K_e = \frac{5428}{29\,250} = 18.56\%$$

Alternatively, using $K_{eg} = K_{eug} + (K_{eug} - K_d)\dfrac{D}{E}(1-t)$

$$K_e = 18\% + (18\% - 13\%)\frac{5(1-0.35)}{29.25} = 18.56\%$$

The cost of equity has increased by 0.56%, reflecting the introduction of financial risk.

(iii)
$$\text{WACC} = 18.56\% \times \frac{29.25}{34.25} + 13(1-0.35)\frac{5}{34.25} = 17.08\%$$

or, using $\text{WACC} = K_u\left(1 - \dfrac{D_t}{D+E}\right) =$

$$18\%\left(1 - \frac{5(0.35)}{34.25}\right) = 17.08\%$$

(*Note:* K_u is the overall cost of capital for an ungeared company, which is the same as the cost of equity for an ungeared company.)

The weighted average cost of capital has fallen by 0.92%, reflecting the benefits of tax relief on interest payments.

(c) The traditional theory of capital structure suggests that each company has an optimal capital structure (level of financial gearing) that it should try to achieve in order to minimize its costs of capital and, in an efficient market, to maximize its market value. The theory reflects what is believed by some managers, analysts and academics to be the relationship between the cost of capital and financial gearing. It suggests a non-linear relationship between the cost of equity and gearing (the required return of equity rises at an increasing rate with gearing), which is not consistent with the capital asset pricing model. It is an intuitive theory which is not backed up by a rigorous empirical model, as is Modigliani and Miller's work.

The theory might be useful in that it draws managers' attention to the fact that an optimal capital structure (or range of structures) might exist for a company (but does not directly show what this is) and that the financing decision might have a significant effect on the company's value.

Modigliani and Miller's (MM) theory in a world with corporate tax implies that the optimal capital structure will be almost 100% debt. The proposal of a capital structure almost entirely of debt is unlikely to be accepted by corporate financial managers. MM's model has been criticized for a number of reasons:

(i) Assumptions: Some of MM's major assumptions are unrealistic, for example:
   (1) Individuals can borrow at the same interest rate as companies, and this rate remains constant at all levels of gearing.
   (2) Individuals are willing to substitute personal gearing (by individual borrowing) for corporate gearing.
   (3) Information is freely available and no transactions costs exist.
   (4) No bankruptcy costs exist.

(ii) It ignores possible costs associated with high gearing. Such costs include:
   (1) Bankruptcy costs – The direct and indirect costs associated with corporate failure which would not occur if the company does not fail. As gearing (and interest payments) increases, the probability of bankruptcy increases, as does the expected cost of bankruptcy.
   (2) Agency costs – Agency costs arise because of the constraints (e.g. restrictive covenants) that suppliers of finance (the principals) might impose on managers (the agents) in order to protect the principals' interests. At high levels of gearing more constraints are likely to be imposed.
   (3) Tax exhaustion – Debt finance is attractive because of the tax relief on interest payments. This tax relief is only available if a company has enough tax liability on its earnings to utilize the tax relief. The higher the gearing level, *ceteris paribus*, the more tax relief is available and the greater the chance of tax exhaustion where there is insufficient liability to utilize available relief. A company's use of non-debt corporate tax shields, especially capital allowances on investment, will also affect the likelihood of tax exhaustion.
   (4) Debt capacity – As security must be provided on many types of debt, a company's financial gearing may be limited by its ability to offer acceptable security to the providers of debt finance.

Such factors will offset the benefits of tax relief on interest payments and might, at some level of gearing, outweigh such benefits. At this point the minimum cost of capital will be achieved. At higher levels of gearing the cost of capital will rise.

Miller in a later article argues that in a world with both personal and corporate taxes the choice of capital structure does not affect the market value of the firm. However, this too ignores bankruptcy costs and other costs of high gearing, suggested above.

Modigliani and Miller's theory advocating almost 100% debt is of little practical value to managers. However, if bankruptcy costs and the other above-mentioned factors are considered in conjunction with the basic theory, a company might be able to identify the approximate level of gearing that minimizes the cost of capital and maximizes market value.

Problem answer 6

(a) The current cost of capital may be estimated by using the weighted average of the cost of equity and the cost of debt.

$$K_d = \frac{10}{125} = 8\%$$

If this is taken as the risk-free rate, then, using CAPM:

$K_e = 8\% + (13\% - 8\%)\,1.2 = 14\%$

The market value of equity is:

60 million shares $\times$ 320p = £192m

The market value of debt is:

$£40m \times 1.25 = \dfrac{£50m}{£242m}$

The cost of capital is:

$14\% \times \dfrac{192}{242} + 8\%(1 - 0.33)\dfrac{50}{242} = 12.21\%$

Alternatively β_e ungeared $= 1.2 \times \dfrac{192}{192 + 50(1 - 0.33)} = 1.0217$

$K_{eu} = 8\% + (13\% - 8\%)\,1.0217 = 13.1085\%$

$K_o = 13.1085\%\left(1 - \dfrac{50 \times 0.33}{242}\right) = 12.21\%$

(b) (i) The impact of the tax reduction is to increase the NPV of operating cash flows by £1.5m, but the value of the company will also decrease due to less tax relief on interest payments.
According to MM:

$$V_L = V_u + Dt$$

The tax change will cause the value of Dt to fall from £50m $\times$ 0.33 = £16.5m, to £50m $\times$ 0.30 = £15m, a decrease in value of £1.5m (assuming no change in the market value of debt).
The value of equity will increase overall by £13.5m to £205.50m or an expected price per share of approximately 343p.

(ii) The new cost of equity may be estimated by ungearing the existing equity beta and regearing it, taking into account the new capital structure and tax rate.

Ungearing

β_e ungeared $= 1.2 \times \dfrac{E}{E + D(1 - t)} = 1.2 \times \dfrac{192}{192 + 50(1 - 0.33)} = 1.0217$

Regearing

β geared $= 1.0217 \times \dfrac{E + D(1 - t)}{E} = 1.0217 \times \dfrac{205.5 + 50(1 - 0.3)}{205.5} = 1.196$

K_e geared $= 8\% + (13\% - 8\%)\,1.196 = 13.98\%$

$\text{WACC} = 13.98\% \times \dfrac{205.5}{255.5} + 8\%(1 - 0.3)\dfrac{50}{255.5} = 12.34\%$

or alternatively $K_o = 13.1085\%\left(1 - \dfrac{50 \times 0.3}{255.5}\right) = 12.34\%$

(c) There is negligible difference between the old and new cost of capital. The tax change produces an increase in the value of equity and hence in the proportion of equity in the capital structure. As the company is not as highly geared, the financial risk for shareholders is reduced, and the equity beta and cost of equity fall slightly. However, as there is less debt in the capital structure, which is a relatively cheap form of finance (given the tax relief on debt), the overall weighted average cost marginally increases.

(d) (i) Practical limitations are mainly related to the assumptions implicit in the analysis.

   (1) Corporate debt is risk-free. In practice there will be a risk premium on corporate debt for default and other risks.

   (2) The cost and market price of debt do not change as a result of the tax change. There is likely to be a small change in both of these factors.

   (3) Only corporate taxes are relevant. Personal taxes are likely to influence the investor's required rate of return and hence the cost of capital of the company.

   (4) The analysis ignores the possible effects of bankruptcy costs, agency costs, tax exhaustion and debt capacity on the determination of the cost of capital.

   (5) Modigliani and Miller's model relies on restrictive assumptions including: personal and corporate gearing are perfect substitutes, transactions costs do not exist, individuals and companies can borrow at the risk-free rate, the cost of debt does not increase as gearing increases and earnings before interest and tax are constant. None of these assumptions are realistic.

   (ii) Accurate cost of capital estimates will lead to more accurate estimates of investment NPVs, and decisions as to what capital structure a company should adopt. However, none of the methods of calculating the cost of capital result in total accuracy; there will always be some margin of error.

   The cost of capital is *not* the most important influence on an investment decision. Investment decisions are normally much more sensitive to changes in the cash flows from sales, materials costs, labour costs etc., than to the cost of capital Strategic, political and other non-financial factors might also be of much greater importance than the cost of capital.

14 DISTRIBUTION POLICY

Solutions to problems

Problem answer 4

(a) Before the Board's decision the value of shares would have been:

$$V_0 = \frac{D_1}{r-g} = \frac{0.20(1+0.06)}{0.08-0.06} = £10.60$$

After the Board's decision the value of shares becomes:

$$\frac{\left(\dfrac{0.25}{0.08-0.07}\right)}{(1+0.08)^3} = \frac{25}{(1.08)^3} = £19.84$$

(b) Under the assumption made, shares could be sold at the end of the next three years to yield £200 (approximately), as follows:

	Y_1	Y_2	Y_3
Sell 10 shares @ £21.43 =	£214.3		
Sell 9 shares @ £23.15		£208.35	
Sell 8 shares @ £25.00			£200
27			

At this point, 973 shares valued at £25 = £24 325 held.
If no project, 1000 shares valued at £12.625 = £12 625

Problem answer 5

(a) The main points include:

1 Legal requirements.

2 Restrictions contained in loan agreements: many loan agreements contain clauses placing limitations on dividends; failure to comply with these restrictive covenants may entitle the lender to demand immediate repayment of the loan.

3 Liquidity: apart from legal constraints on liquidity, the firm should consider its desired level of liquidity required to facilitate its expected operations and not to jeopardize these with over-generous dividend payments.

4 Investment and financing opportunities: if external finance is not available, or available only after incurring significant transaction costs, then the payment of dividends may mean forgoing worthwhile investment opportunities. Note that if alternative forms of finance are readily obtainable, then dividend policy should not have any significant effect on investment policy.

5 Taxation: differences in the taxation of dividend income and capital gains (less in the the UK than before) may alter the relative desirability of dividends and retained earnings. Most taxation systems tend to tax dividends more heavily than retained earnings for the standard-rate taxpayer and this would suggest that dividend payments should be kept low. However, for tax-exempt shareholders this bias does not exist.

In the UK the imputation system tends to treat dividends more favourably than, identically to or less favourably than retained earnings depending upon the marginal tax rate of the shareholders. Hence the marginal tax rates of the firm's clientele of shareholders can be an important consideration in determining dividend policy.

Reaction of the market to:

(i) dividend levels; and

(ii) changes in dividends levels.

Dividends may be considered to have an informational content and to be considered by the market not as mere cash flows, but also as signals, from the company concerning future prospects. The main body of opinion tends to suggest that changes in dividend levels are considered more important than absolute levels of dividends – such changes being perceived as direct indications of future prosperity. These opinions are used to support arguments for dividend stability. Unfortunately, the empirical evidence is difficult to interpret and does not convincingly support, or disprove, these frequently expressed assertions.

The views expressed by Haaste's Board appear to support some of the main schools of through concerning dividends:

Comment 1: supports the idea that dividend levels and especially stability of dividends are important. This would suggest that the payment of a dividend should be perceived as a constraint to be satisfied by the firm rather than as an objective.

Comment 2: is easy to prove to be correct when analysed within the context of a perfect market without discriminatory taxes. With 'real-world' discriminatory taxes and transaction costs, the theoretical conclusions are unlikely to be universally correct;

Comment 3: perceives dividends as a residual, to be paid when the firm has run out of worthwhile investment opportunities. This view implies that these opportunities would not be undertaken if a dividend is paid and therefore external financing is either not available or expensive.

(b) The implications of the proposed changes to reduce retained earnings and increase dividends will include:

Corporate financial management

1 Managers no longer have access to the considerable sums of finance previously retained and which it was possible to utilize without *formal* justification.

2 The majority of funds required for expansion will need to be obtained externally and justified to investors and lenders. This may produce greater efficiency in the use of capital and encourage more formal financial planning.

3 More frequent recourse to finance providers may mean more importance is attributed to shareholder and lender satisfaction.

4 It will probably produce pressure for earnings to be based on current cost profits rather than historic cost figures.

Shareholders

1 More positive involvement with decisions concerning reinvestment (or consumption, see below) of dividends. Large retained earnings are, effectively, passive reinvestments by shareholders in their firm.

2 Unless the personal taxation system is altered, the enforced payment of dividends could reduce shareholder wealth.

Financial system and financial institutions

1 The increased mobility of funds may result in funds being more speedily channelled to the more productive sectors of industry.

2 The organization of financial institutions will need to develop to enable funds to be channelled from shareholders to industry without excessive transaction costs.

3 The increased dividends paid may result in some (probably small, personal) shareholders increasing their consumption rather than reinvesting dividends. This could, in the short term, reduce the total amount of funds available for productive investment.

Solutions to problems

Problem answer 1
Appropriate amounts are as below:

	Supermarket	Heavy MFG	Hotel	Bank
Equity	257	251	370	10 992
Loans	100	250	500	7 000
Short-term borrowing	357	501	870	17 992

Notes:
Supermarket – already has high level of liabilities (short term); Hotel – long-term loans secured against land and buildings; Banks – most of liabilities are short-term; arise in connection with normal banking activities such as receiving deposits.

Problem answer 2

(a) Business risk is the variability in earnings before interest and tax (EBIT) associated with a company's normal operations. It is the riskiness of the company's operations without regard to how the company is financed. Business risk is an important matter to consider when deciding the appropriate capital structure for a company.

Business risk varies considerably between industries, and even between companies within the same industry, and may alter significantly over time as consumer tastes and technology change. It depends upon both macro-economic and microeconomic factors (e.g. the state of the economy, government actions and controls, competitors' actions, labour relations, fires and accidents) which will influence a company's demand, sales price, cost and ability to alter the sales price when costs change.

(b) The business risk of a company is partially the result of factors that are specific to that company and partially the result of factors affecting the whole market. The company-specific business risk (unsystematic risk) may be eliminated by diversification. Well-diversified shareholders will not bear this unsystematic risk, but will still have to bear the market-related risk (which forms the systematic risk in an ungeared company). Part of business risk will therefore be relevant to an investor owning a well-diversified portfolio.

(c) (i) *Degree of operating gearing* (DOG)

DOG at a given level of turnover is:

$$\frac{\text{Turnover} - \text{variable costs}}{\text{profit before interest and tax}}$$

At the start of the current financial year

$$\text{DOG} = \frac{3381 - 2193}{462} = 2.57$$

assuming that variable costs comprise wages and salaries, raw materials and direct selling expenses. (In reality, these are not all likely to vary directly with turnover.)

A 2.57 DOG may be interpreted as meaning that a 1% change in sales will lead to a 2.57% change in profit before interest and tax (in the same direction).

At the end of the financial year, the expected profit and loss account, assuming no price changes except those stated, is:

	£000	£000
Turnover (15% increase)		3888
Operating expenses		
Wages and salaries (1220 × 0.80 × 1.15)	1122	
Raw materials (15% increase)	1004	
Direct selling expenses (15% increase)	115	
General administration (no increase)	346	
Other fixed costs	465	3052
Profit before interest and tax		836

Therefore expected DOG at the end of the year is:

$$\frac{3888 - 2241}{836} = 1.97$$

The degree of operating gearing is expected to fall.

If a high percentage of a company's total costs are fixed, that company will have a high degree of operating gearing. If other factors are held constant, the higher the operating gearing, the higher will be the business risk of a company. In this case, other factors have not been held constant; the unit variable cost of wages and salaries and also the level of fixed costs are expected to change. The overall result is a lower DOG at the sales level of £3 888 000.

Financial gearing
Financial gearing may be defined in several ways. Here the definition of $\dfrac{\text{Medium - and long - term debt}}{\text{shareholders' equity}}$ is used, although other definitions

such as $\dfrac{\text{Total debt}}{\text{shareholders' equity}}$ or $\dfrac{\text{Total debt}}{\text{total assets}}$ are acceptable.

At the start of the year, financial gearing (using book values) is

$$\frac{570}{1510} = 37.7\%.$$

At the end of the year, profit before interest and tax has been estimated to be £836 000.

	£000
Profit before interest and tax	836
Interest[1]	207
Profit before tax	629
Tax	252
Profit available to ordinary shareholders	377
Estimated dividend	189
Retained earnings	188

Note:
[1] Assuming that interest of 84 will still be payable next year. Estimated financial gearing:

$$\frac{570 + 820}{1510 + 188} = 81.8\%.$$

The expected financial gearing (by this measure) more than doubles by the end of the year. The higher the level of financial gearing, the higher the financial risk placed on the ordinary shareholders.

(ii) (1) If turnover increases by 15%, the expected profit available to ordinary shareholders is £377 000. There are 3 200 000 issued ordinary shares, resulting in an expected earnings per share of 11.78p.

The earnings per share at the start of the year is:

$$\frac{£227\,000}{3\,200\,000} = 7.09\text{p per share}$$

Because of the financial and operating gearing effects, earnings per share are expected to increase by 66%

(2) If turnover falls by 10%

	£000	£000
Turnover		3043
Operating expenses		
Wages and salaries (1220 × 0.90 × 0.80)	878	
Raw materials (10% fall)	786	
Direct selling expenses (10% fall)	90	
General administration (no change)	346	
Other fixed costs (85 increase)	465	
		2565
Profit before interest and tax		478
Interest		207
Profit before tax		271
Tax		108
Profit available to ordinary shareholders		163

The estimated earnings per share is

$$\frac{163}{3200} = 5.09\text{p}$$

This is 28% lower than the current earnings per share.
The changes in the operating and financial gearing have increased the risk for the shareholders.

Problem answer 3

		Days	Days
(a) Days raw materials	1000 − (3000/365)	122	
Less credit taken	600 − (3000/365)	73	49
Days WIP	600 − (5000/365)		44
Days	1200 − (5000/365)		88
Finished goods			
Debtors 20 000 − (8000/365)			91
			272

		£
WC at target		
RM	3000 × 20/365	164
WIP	500 × 12/365	164
Finished goods	5000 × 45/365	616
Credit granted	8000 × 40/365	877
		1821
Less: credit taken	3000 × 60/365	493
		1328

New WC £1 328 000
Old WC £4 200 000
Reductions £2 872 000
@ 7% £201 040 p.a. saving

Stock levels should *not* increase proportionately with sales. RM and finished goods stock appear to be (but increase in days RM stock when related to purchases), WIP has increased significantly and requires urgent attention. Are there production hold-ups with the large increase in turnover?

Debtors increased more than sales. Credit management policy should be reviewed unless the increase in debtors was a deliberate marketing device to stimulate sales.

The extra working capital needs could adversely affect cash flow. This may be resulting in a slowing down of payment to creditors which might affect future credit terms offered from suppliers. Unless extending the payment period is unlikely to result in adverse action by suppliers, the company should consider paying more promptly.

(b) No solution is given here as the appropriate answer can be found in the relevant chapter of the textbook.

16 INTRODUCTION TO DERIVATIVES AND OPTIONS THEORY

No answers given for this chapter.

17 CASH AND INTEREST RATE MANAGEMENT

Solutions to problems

Problem answer 1

(a) The question does not give us the sales and cost figures for the earlier period, but we are told to assume they are the same as for the last months of 1995.

The March cash collected

March sales (50%)	=	6
February sales (25%)	=	3
January sales (25%)	=	5
		14

The *March* payment for purchases relates to the April sales figure. The goods to be sold in April are purchased three months in advance; that is January. They are paid for two months after purchase, which is March. The amount is 60% of the April sales, i.e. (60% × 20).

(b–d) No solution is given here as the appropriate answer can be found in the relevant chapter of the textbook.

	Estimate cash flows				
	Opening cash balance	Cash collected	Payment for purchases	Overheads + tax	Closing balance
J	20	25	−7.2	−10	27.8
F		23	−7.2	−10	22.0
M		14	−12.0	−10	14.0
A		16	−19.2	−30	−19.2
M		24	−60	−10	−65.2
J		63	−96	−10	−108.2
J		113	−60	−10	−65.2
A		115	−28.8	−10	−22.2
S		89	−7.2	−10	59.6
O		43	−7.2	−10	85.4
N		21	−28.8	−10	67.6
D		30	−12.0	−10	75.6

Problem answer 2

(a) A steady level of production and sales throughout the years is assumed. Sales are estimated to be

$$85\,500 \times £50 = £4\,275\,000$$

Sales at $2\frac{1}{2}\%$ discount are

$$85\,500 \times 0.4 \times £48.75 = £1\,667\,250$$

Sales at full price are

$$85\,500 \times 0.6 \times £50 = £2\,565\,000$$

Debtors £
Average credit granted on discount sales

$£1\,667\,250 \times \dfrac{2}{52} =$ 64 125

Average credit granted on full-price sales

$£2\,565\,000 \times \dfrac{10}{52} =$ 493 259

 557 394

Stock

Raw materials $85\,500 \times £15.51\ \dfrac{4}{52} =$ 102 008

Work in progress (assuming that when production commences, all necessary materials are issued to the production process, and that work in progress and finished goods are valued at the direct costs of production):

 Materials $85\,500 \times £15.51 \times \dfrac{4}{52} =$ 102 008

 Wages $85\,500 \times £17.35 \times \dfrac{2}{52} =$ 57 005

 Energy $85\,500 \times\ £4.95 \times \dfrac{2}{52} =$ 16 278

Finished goods:

Materials	$85\,500 \times £15.51 \times \dfrac{8}{52} =$	204 016
Wages	$85\,500 \times £17.35 \times \dfrac{8}{52} =$	228 219
Energy	$85\,500 \times £4.95 \times \dfrac{8}{52} =$	65 112
Total cost of stock		774 696

Creditors £

Raw materials	$85\,500 \times £15.51 \times \dfrac{8}{52} =$	204 016
Wages	$85\,500 \times £17.35 \times \dfrac{1}{52} =$	28 527
Energy	$85\,500 \times £4.95 \times \dfrac{13}{52} =$	105 806
Salaries	$£264\,000 \times \dfrac{4}{52} =$	20 308
Overheads	$£92\,000 \times \dfrac{6}{52} =$	10 615
		369 272

Working capital required for debtors and stock less the benefit from creditors is:

$$£557\,394 + £774\,696 - £369\,272 = £962\,818$$

The present overdraft facility is:

$$\frac{£118\,000}{0.11} = £1\,072\,727$$

This facility is therefore adequate to finance the net requirements of debtors, stock and creditors, as long as production and sales are constant. If, as is likely, fluctuations exist in production and sales levels during the year, the facility might be inadequate. This will also depend upon the timing of cash generated from profits, some of which might be available for working capital purposes.

Whether or not the overdraft facility is large enough to finance *all* working capital requirements during the year depends upon the net effect of both the above working capital items and other cash flows within the company, including other working capital items such as cash, marketable securities, tax payable and dividends payable.

There are inadequate data to establish the total working capital needs for the next year.

Problem answer 3

(1) If LIBOR remains at 10% for the whole year:

Manling: Pays fixed rate interest of 12%
Pays floating rate at LIBOR + $1\frac{1}{2}$%
Receives fixed-rate interest of $11\frac{5}{8}$%
The net cost is LIBOR + $1\frac{7}{8}$%

The current cost of fixed-rate debt is:

		£
£14m × 12% less tax relief at 35% =		1 092 000

The cost under the swap is:

£14m × $11\frac{7}{8}$% less tax relief at 35% =	1 080 625
Plus the arrangement fee £20 000 less tax relief =	13 000
Total costs	1 093 625

If LIBOR remains at 10% the swap would not be beneficial to Manling.

(2) If LIBOR falls to 9% after six months the cost for the year is:

	£
£14m × $11\frac{7}{8}$% × 0.5 × 0.65 =	540 312
£14m × $10\frac{7}{8}$% × 0.5 × 0.65 =	494 813
	1 035 125
Plus arrangement fee	13 000
	1 048 125

The swap would then be beneficial

	Manling	Other Company	Differential
Fixed rate	12%	$11\frac{3}{4}$%	$\frac{1}{4}$%
Floating rate	LIBOR + 2%	LIBOR + $1\frac{1}{8}$%	$\frac{7}{8}$%

As the differentials are not the same, an interest rate swap offers arbitrage gains totalling $\frac{7}{8}$% − $\frac{1}{4}$% = $\frac{5}{8}$%. If this gain is equally shared each company benefits by $\frac{5}{16}$%. Manling currently gains $\frac{1}{8}$% from the swap (the market cost of LIBOR + 2% less the net cost if the swap occurs of LIBOR + $1\frac{7}{8}$%).

The terms of the swap could be varied as follows (other terms are possible):

Manling: Pays fixed rate interest of 12% (as at present)
Pays floating rate interest of LIBOR + $1\frac{5}{16}$% (i.e. $1\frac{1}{2}$% − $\frac{3}{16}$%)
Receives fixed-rate interest of $11\frac{5}{8}$% (as at present)
The net cost is LIBOR + $1\frac{11}{16}$% (a benefit of $\frac{5}{16}$% relative to issuing floating rate debt at LIBOR + 2%)

The other company:` Pays floating rate interest of LIBOR + $1\frac{1}{8}$% (as at present)
Pays fixed-rate interest $11\frac{5}{8}$%
Receives floating rate interest of LIBOR + $1\frac{5}{16}$%
The net cost is $11\frac{7}{16}$% (a benefit of $\frac{5}{16}$% relative to issuing fixed-rate debt).

The total cost to Manling of using these new terms is:

£14m × $11\frac{11}{16}$% × 0.65 =	1 063 562
Plus arrangement fee	13 000
	1 076 562

This is a saving of £15 438 relative to not undertaking the swap.

18 MANAGEMENT OF DEBTORS AND INVENTORY

Solutions to problems

Problem answer 1
(a) 100 × (5/95) × (365/25) = 76.9%
(b) 152.0%
(c) 75.3%

Problem answer 2

(a) (i) Increased sales   1200 units per month

Extra sales	£14 400
Extra direct costs	12 960
	1 440

Interest cost of extra credit: £12 960 $\times$ 11% $\times \frac{1}{2}$
It should extend the credit period.

(ii)

Sales (11 200 units)	£134 400
Direct Costs	120 960
Contribution	13 440

Interest cost on extra credit: £12 960 $\times$ 11% $\times \frac{1}{2}$ = £11 088
It should extend the credit period.

(b) Bad debts and other costs should be considered. By lengthening the period of credit given, the company will be attracting a different class of customer.

Problem answer 3

Assumptions: (i) That invoices for goods sold are sent out at the end of each month and invoices for goods purchases are received at the end of each month. (ii) That an inventory of 50 days is equal to $\frac{1}{7}$ of annual sales.

Cash inflows at present:

£100 000	sales per month
1 000	bad debts
£99 000	cash collected

With the change:

£110 000	sales per month
2 200	bad debts
£107 800	cash collected

Cash flow now:	1	2	3	4	5	6
			Months			
Collected	0	0	99	99	99	99
Paid out	0	−70	−70	−70	−70	−70
Inventory	0	−171.4				
Net	0	−241.4	29	29	29	29

Cash flow with change:	1	2	3	4	5	6
			Months			
Collected	0	0	0	107.8	107.8	107.8
Paid out	0	−77	−77	−77	−77	−77
Inventory	0	−188.6				
Net		−256.6	−77	30.8	30.8	30.8

Difference resulting from change:						
	0	−24.2	−106	+1.8	+1.8	+1.8

The increase in cash flows of £1800 per month can be assumed to continue into perpetuity. With a cost of capital of 12% per annum (i.e. approximately 1% per month) the present value of £1800 per month is £1800/0.01 = £180 000. This is the present value in month 4. To achieve this means a net cash outflow of £24 200 in month 2 and £106 000 in month 3. The returns are greater than the cost. The new sales policy seems worth adopting.

Problem answer 4

(a) Benefit to Comfylot will be measured by the incremental effects of the proposed changes, initially during the next year. Domestic sales are £11.2m in total, £8.96m on credit. Export sales are £4.8m, £4.08m on credit (net of the 15% initial deposit).

	Incremental effects	
	£	£
Administration: Savings	85 000	
Factor cost – credit sales of £8.96m × 1.5%	(134 400)	
		(49 400)

Financing:
Existing cost:

$$£8.96m \times \frac{57}{365} \times 15\% \qquad 209\,885$$

Cost with factor:

$$£8.96m \times \frac{57}{365} \times 0.8 \times 15.5\% \qquad (173\,505)$$

$$£8.96m \times \frac{57}{365} \times 0.2 \times 15\% \qquad (41\,977)$$

		(5 597)
Redundancy payment		(15 000)
Saving in bad debts (as the factor is non-recourse)		
£8.96 × 0.75%		67 200
		(2 797)

Although the incremental effect of using the factor appears to be unfavourable, the redundancy payment is a one-off cost which would not be repeated in future years. If the other net savings are maintained after year one, the use of the factor is likely to result in savings of approximately £12 200 per year.

Problem answer 5

(a) The economic order quantity is given by the square root rule as:

$$EOQ = \left[\frac{2(400)(2500)}{8} \right]^{\frac{1}{2}} = 500$$

(b) The optimum number of replenishments is the annual demand divided by the economic order quantity:

$$\frac{A}{EOQ} = \frac{2500}{500} = 5$$

On the basis of a full 365 day year, five re-orders per annum corresponds to a cycle length of 73 days.

(c) The lowest possible level of annual inventory costs, C^*, (corresponding to the use of the EOQ) is given by:

$$C^* = (2AC_o iC_m)^{\frac{1}{2}}$$

which in this case will be:

$$C^* = (2(2500)\,(400)8)^{\frac{1}{2}} = £4000$$

Problem answer 6

(a) The economic order quantity given by the square root rule is:

$$EOQ = \left[\frac{2(75)(1000)}{6} \right]^{\frac{1}{2}} = 158.11$$

(b) The EOQ value of 158.11 means that the number of cycles per annum will be:

$$\frac{A}{EOQ} = \frac{2500}{158.11} = 6.32$$

that is, there will be a rate of 6.32 orders per annum. Minimum total costs are:

$$C^* = (2(75)\,(1000)6)^{\frac{1}{2}} = £948.68$$

(c) With only five re-orders allowed each year, the re-order size would be 200. Putting this value into the cost expression gives:

$$C = 6\frac{200}{2} + 75\frac{1000}{200} = 600 + 375 = 975$$

The absolute maximum that the company would be prepared to pay to escape this condition is the full saving it would achieve by being allowed to use its EOQ. This is:

$$975 - 948.68 = £26.32$$

Problem answer 7

(a) The best size of cash investment, q^*, is given by the square root formula as:

$$q^* = \left[\frac{2AC_0}{iCm} \right]^{\frac{1}{2}}$$

so in this case:

$$q^* = \left[\frac{2(25)(250\,000)}{0.125} \right]^{\frac{1}{2}} = 10\,000$$

which value means that the number of investments that should be made per annum is:

$$\frac{250\,000}{10\,000} = 25$$

(b) With the alternative scheme, the optimal size of investment is:

$$q^* = \left[\frac{2(100)(250\,000)}{0.125} \right]^{\frac{1}{2}} = 20\,000$$

in which case the investments should be made at the rate of 12.5 per annum.

(c) The company will prefer whichever scheme produces the lower overall costs. In the case of the original scheme, the costs will be:

$$C = 0.125\frac{10\,000}{2} + 25\frac{250\,000}{10\,000} + 0.01(250\,000) = 3750$$

In the case of the revised scheme, the best value of costs achievable would be:

$$C = 0.125\frac{20\,000}{2} + 100\frac{250\,000}{20\,000} + 0.0075(250\,000) = 4375$$

so that the original arrangement is preferable and would be selected by the firm.

Solutions to problems

Problem answer 1

(a) (i)

	£000s
Current average debtors: £7.2m $\times \dfrac{90}{360}$ =	1800
New average debtors: £7.2m $\times \dfrac{70}{360}$ =	1400
Funds improvement caused by factoring	£400
Cost of factoring:	
Factoring services: $1\frac{1}{2}$% $\times$ £7.2m	108
Less: Savings	60
	£48
Effective annual cost: $\dfrac{£48}{£400} \times 100\%$ =	12%

(ii) (a)

	£000s	£000s
Funds advanced		
Gross funds advanced: 80% $\times$ £7.2m $\times \dfrac{90}{360}$ =		1440
Less: Commission		
$2\frac{1}{2}$% $\times$ £1.440m =	36	
Interest:		
1.25% $\times$ £1.440m $\times$ 3 =	54	90
Funds improvement caused by factoring		£1350
Total annual cost of factoring		
Factoring services – net cost	48	
Commission: $2\frac{1}{2}$% $\times$ 0.8 $\times$ £7.2m =	144	
Interest: 15% $\times$ £1.44m =	216	
Total annual cost	£408	
Effective annual cost: $\dfrac{£408}{£1350} \times 100\%$ =	30.2%	

(ii) (b)

	£000s	£000s
Funds advanced		
Advance from factor		
Gross funds advanced:		
80% $\times$ £7.2m $\times \dfrac{60}{360}$ =		960
Less: Commission		
$2\frac{1}{2}$% $\times$ £0.96m =	24	
Interest:		
1.25% $\times$ £0.96m $\times$ 2 =	24	48
Funds advanced		912

Improvement in average debtors
Current average debtors:

$$£7.2m \times \frac{90}{360} = \qquad\qquad 1800$$

New average debtors:

$$£7.2m \times \frac{60}{360} \qquad\qquad 1200$$

Improvement in average debtors	600
Improvement caused by factoring	£1512

Total annual cost of factoring

Factoring services – net cost	48
Commission:	
$2\frac{1}{2}\% \times 0.8 \times £7.2m =$	144
Interest: $15\% \times £0.96m =$	144
Total annual cost	£336

$$\text{Effective annual cost: } \frac{£336}{£1512} \times 100\% = \qquad 22.2\%$$

(b)   £000s

Current average debtors:

$$£7.2m \times \frac{90}{360} = \qquad\qquad 1800$$

Revised average debtors:

$$£7.2m \times \frac{80}{360} \qquad\qquad 1600$$

Funds improvement	£200

$$\text{Effective annual cost of improvement } \frac{£30}{£200} \times 100\% = \qquad 15\%$$

Hence, as the incremental cost of this internal improvement exceeds the cost of factoring-based finance (calculated in (a) (i)), factoring is the cheaper of the two sources of finance and both are less expensive than borrowing.

	Internal improvement (1) £000s	Factoring-based improvement (2) £000s	Factoring less internal (2) − (1) £000s
Finance improvement	200	400	200
Cost	30	48	18

$$\text{Incremental annual cost: } \frac{£18}{£200} \times 100\% = 9\%$$

This may be seen more clearly by examining the incremental costs of the factoring-based benefit compared with this internal improvement:

Therefore, if Beaver is in need of additional funds, the factoring agreement is the best of the three sources considered.

However, having entered into the factoring agreement, and obtained the benefit of the factor reducing the collection period to 70 days, no further funds should be obtained from the factor as the implicit interest rate always exceeds the 16% borrowing rate. For each £100 gross borrowed the costs are at least:

Interest	£15 per annum
Commission	£2.5
Total	£17.5
Funds provided: £100 − £17.5 =	£82.5

Effective cost: $\dfrac{£17.5}{£82.5} \times 100\% =$ 21.2%

However, this percentage cost will increase with short borrowings as the $2\frac{1}{2}\%$ commission is a fixed charge irrespective of length of borrowing.

Should Beaver require further finance, it should be borrowed at 16% rather than obtained from the factor.

Problem answer 2

(a) *Cost option 1*
Interest £200 000 × 18% × $\frac{1}{2}$ = £18 000

Cost option 2
With discount of 2% the monthly payments equal £100 000. Therefore stop paying for supplies of September and October within 30 days. This makes £200 000 available by end-October.

The result is that for each of the six months in which payments are delayed, an extra payment of £2041 has to be made (the discount forgone). This extra payment has an opportunity cost, either cost of extra money borrowed or interest missed. Assume the cost of such opportunities is 18% per annum (i.e. $1\frac{1}{2}\%$ per month).

The total cost of this policy can be calculated using the terminal value of an annuity table. For six periods it equals £12 715 (i.e. £2041 × 6.2300).

Cost option 3

Basic advance		£225 000
Less: Fee	£6000	
Interest	£2700	8 700
Net advance		£216 300

Interest equals 1.25% per month on amount advanced.

Therefore £219 000 (after fee) equals 101.25%. 100% equals £216 300. The difference £2700 is the interest charge.

The cost of this policy is:

Fee		£6000
Interest		2700
		8700
Less: Administration saving		−4000
Interest at 1% (on balance)		
(£16 300 + £4000)		−200
		£4500 per month

This is the most expensive of the three alternatives.

(b)

					In £000s			
	Sep	Oct	Nov	Dec	Jan	Feb	Mar	Apr
Investment	−200							
Advanced (net)	+216	+216	+216	+216	+216	+216	+217	+216
Balance on sale		+75	+75	+75	+75	+75	+75	+75
Sales (August)	+300							

(c) No solution is given here as the appropriate answer can be found in the relevant chapter of the textbook.

Problem answer 6

The rationale for the salesman's statement is difficult to understand, particularly the treatment of the initial outlay for the lease. There would seem to be no theoretical support for the calculation of benefits and an appraisal should be made using DCF techniques.

No reference is made to taxation, so an appraisal will first be made assuming no tax implications are involved.

PV of purchase costs = £120 000

$$\text{PV of leasing costs} = 12\,000 + \sum_{t=1}^{5} \frac{24\,000}{(1+r)^t}$$

(using borrowing rate to discount at 4%)
$$= 12\,000 + 24\,000\,(4.4518) = 12\,000 + 106\,843 = \text{£}118\,843$$

$\therefore$ Leasing appears preferable to purchase.

$$\text{NPV of project} = -118\,843 + \sum_{t=1}^{5} \frac{30\,000}{(1+r)^t}$$

(using risk-adjusted rate to discount at 10%)
$$= -118\,000 + 30\,000\,(3.7908) = -118\,000 + 113\,724 = -\text{£}5119$$

On this basis the project should not be undertaken.

Now assume that first-year allowances of 100% are available and corporation tax rate is 50%. Further assume that tax benefits/liabilities are lagged by one year.

NPV of purchasing and operating machine:

$$NPV = -120\,000 - \frac{120\,000 \times 0.50}{(1+0.10)} + \sum_{t=1}^{5} \frac{30\,000}{(1+0.10)^t} - \sum_{t=2}^{6} \frac{30\,000 \times 0.50}{(1+0.10)^t}$$

$$= -120\,000 - 60\,000(0.9091) + 30\,000(3.7908) - 15\,000(3.4462)$$

$$= -120\,000 - 54\,546 + 113\,724 - 51\,693$$

$$= -3423$$

Project funded by purchase does not seem profitable in this case.

Now compare purchase with leasing:

$$NPV = +120\,000 - \frac{120\,000 \times 0.50}{(1+0.04)} - 12\,000 - \sum_{t=1}^{5} \frac{24\,000}{(1+0.04)^t}$$

$$+ \frac{12\,000 \times 0.50}{(1+0.04)} + \sum_{t=2}^{6} \frac{24\,000 \times 0.50}{(1+0.04)^t}$$

$$= +120\,000 - 60\,000(0.9615) - 12\,000 - 24\,000(4.4518)$$

$$+ 6000(0.9615) + 12\,000(4.2806)$$

$$= +120\,000 - 57\,690 - 12\,000 - 106\,843 + 5769 + 51\,367$$

$$= +603$$

Leasing would therefore improve the position, but by only £603. Again, project should not be undertaken.

Solutions to problems

Problem answer 7

(a) *Spot* is the rate of exchange appropriate to an immediate exchange of one currency for another.

Three months is the rate that can be agreed for an exchange that will take place in three months' time.

(b) £/$

	1.5015	1.5025
+	3	6
	1.5018	1.5031	1 month
	1.5015	1.5025
	13	17	3 months
	1.5028	1.5042

$/Yen

	231.87	231.97
−	0.63	−0.59
	231.24	231.38	1 month
	231.87	231.97
−	1.85	−1.80
	230.02	230.17	3 months

(c) (i) 231.87 yen
   (ii) 9.3690 DKr
   (iii) 1.5042 $ = £1
   (iv) 231.25 yen
   (v) $1 = DKr 9.3920

(d) (i) $1.5020 = £1

$$\$1 = \frac{£1}{1.502} = £0.666$$

$$\$1 = 231.92 \text{ yen}$$

$$\therefore £0.666 = 231.92 \text{ yen}$$

$$£1 = \frac{231.92}{0.666} = 348.23 \text{ yen}$$

(ii) $1.5025 = £1

$$\$1 = \frac{1}{1.5025} = \$0.665$$

$$\$1 = 9.3722 \text{ DKr}$$

$$\therefore £0.665 = 9.3722 \text{ DKr}$$

$$£1 = \frac{9.3722}{0.665} = 14.094 \text{ DKr}$$

(e)

$$\frac{i_A - i_B}{1 + iB} = \frac{F_0 - S_0}{S_0}$$

$$\frac{[x - 0.12]}{1.12} \times \frac{3}{12} = \frac{1.5035 - 1.5020}{1.5020} = +0.0009986$$

x = approximately 0.125 (i.e. $12\frac{1}{2}$%)

Spot and forward prices taken at mid-point. UK = country B.

If the US interest rate was $15\frac{1}{2}$% rather than $12\frac{1}{2}$%, the policy would be to sell immediately sterling and buy dollars, and invest dollars in the USA.

At the same time as entering the spot transaction, one could agree a three-month forward deal to sell dollars and buy sterling.

Problem answer 9

(a) DM is trading at a discount
$ is trading at a premium

$$\frac{1.7593 - 1.7483}{1.7483} \times 100 = 0.63\% \text{ per quarter}$$

∴ Annual premium on the dollar = $0.63\% \times \dfrac{12}{3} = (2.52\%)$

Differential between interest rates:

$$\frac{(R_G - R_s)}{1 + R_s} \times 100 = 2.8\%$$

Where R_G and R_S are German and US nominal interest rates.
$R_G = 5.8\%$ per annum; $R_S = 3\%$ per annum.
For simplicity we divide these interest rates by four to get the quarterly rates.

$$R_G = \left[\frac{5.8}{4} = 1.45\%\right] \frac{0.0145 - 0.0075}{1.0075} * 100 = 0.695\%$$

$$R_s = \left[\frac{3}{4} = 0.75\%\right]$$

Interest rate parity theorem would enable investors to check whether there is any room for arbitrage.

In this case the premium is not equal to the differential interest rates:

(b) (i) Investors would borrow dollars and invest in deutschmarks.
1 Borrow $10 000 000 after three months: 10 000 000 × 1.0075 = $10 075 000.
2 Sell dollars in the spot market for DM: 10 000 000 × 1.74830 = 17 483 000 DM.
3 Invest in deutschmarks for three months: 17 483 000 × 1.0145 = 17 736 504.
4 Sell investment forward for $s: $\dfrac{17\,736\,504}{1.7593} = 10\,081\,569$.

Riskless profit from arbitrage = 10 081 569 − 10 075 000 = $6569.

Problem answer 10

(i) There are at least five possible policies that Runswick might adopt:
1 *Take no action.* In this case, the company is accepting the foreign exchange risk and will have to buy Swiss francs at the prevailing spot rate on the foreign exchange market in three months' time. This rate may be favourable or unfavourable.
2 *Forward foreign exchange market cover.* This involves buying Swiss francs at a known price for delivery at a fixed date in the future. In this case, the contract of 54 000 Swiss francs may be covered by buying Swiss francs three months forward at an exchange rate of 2.925 SF/£ (i.e. 2.970 − 0.045): the cost will be:

$$\frac{54\,000}{2.925} = £18\,462$$

If the Swiss franc does not strengthen as much as was expected in forward rate, the company will have made an opportunity loss. If the

Swiss franc strengthens more than was expected, the company will make an opportunity gain.

3 *Lead payment.* As the Swiss franc is strengthening relative to the pound, it might be beneficial to make an early payment for the goods rather than take the risk of having to pay a greater number of pounds on the due date.

If a lead payment is made now the costs will be:

$$\frac{54\,000}{2.97} = £18\,182$$

But this will have to be borrowed to permit payment to be made. The overall cost over three months, including interest payments, will be:

$$£18\,182 + [£18\,182 \times 12\% \times \frac{3}{12}] = £18\,727$$

4 *Money market cover.* This involves borrowing in one country, converting the funds borrowed at the spot rate into the currency in which payment is due, and investing it in the second country. The total proceeds will then be used to make payment for the goods. In this case:

Borrow £18 002 for three months at 12%
Convert to Swiss francs at 2.97 SF/£ = 53 466 SF
Invest 53 466 SF for three months at 4%. To receive a total of 54 000 SF at the end of three months. Use this to make payment for the goods. The total costs is:

$$£18\,002 + [£18\,002 \times 12\% \times \frac{3}{12}] = £18\,542$$

5 *Cover via a financial futures contract.* The process is similar to the forward market cover, except that contracts are less flexible, being only available in a fixed size for specific dates. Additionally, transactions require the provision of margins, which will add to the overall cost.

If the company takes any action to protect itself against the foreign exchange risk, it is recommended that the forward foreign exchange market cover is chosen, as this is the lowest-cost alternative.

(ii) The cost of the goods if the discount is taken will be 52 650 SF.

Forward market cover:

$$\frac{52\,650}{2.945} = £17\,878$$

Borrow £17 878 for two months at 12%, giving a total cost of £18 235.

Lead payment:

$$\frac{52\,650}{2.97} = £17\,727$$

Borrowing costs for three months:

$$£17\,727 \times 12\% \times \frac{3}{12} = £532$$

Overall is £17 727 + £532 = £18 259
Money market cover
Borrow £17 668.4 for 3 months at 12%
Convert spot to SF at 2.97 = 52 475 SF

Invest for 1 month at 4%, yielding a total of 52 650 SF
Use this to make payment for the goods
The total cost is:

$$£17\,668.4 + [£17\,668.4 \times 12\% \times \frac{3}{12}] = £18\,198$$

If the discount is offered, it is worthwhile for Runswick to take the discount. Money market cover is now the recommended alternative, with a total cost of £18 198.

Problem answer 11

(a) No solution is given here as the appropriate answer can be found in the relevant chapter of the textbook.

(b) Any belief about future spot exchange rate by the company's treasurer is a personal viewpoint and, if acted upon, could leave the company exposed to foreign exchange risk. If the company is worried about foreign exposure it should hedge the risk using options, forward contracts or other techniques no matter what the treasurer personally believes that future spot rate will be.

   If the company acts upon the treasurer's forecasts it will need to sell sterling for dollars, i.e. *buy* put options on sterling. £1 625 000 will require 130 contracts.

   (i) $1.8950 − $1.8970/£. The relevant future spot rate for selling pounds for dollars is $1.8950/£. If the future spot rate is $1.8950, the company would receive $3 079 375 using the spot market. The pound is expected to weaken relative to the dollar. September options are available at exercise prices of $1.90, $1.95, $2.0. At all of these prices the option will be exercised.

At $1.90, receipts are 1.625m × $1.90 =	$3 087 500
Less option costs of 1.625m × 0.42 cents =	6 825
Net	$3 080 675
At $1.95	
Receipts 1.625m × $1.95	$3 168 750
Option cost 1.625m × 4.15 cents	67 438
Net	$3 101 312
At $2.00	
Receipts 1.625m × $2.00	$3 250 000
Option cost 1.625 × 9.40 cents	152 750
Net	$3 097 250

   All three options result in higher expected dollar receipts than using the spot market in three months (excluding any further transactions costs). Selection of the $1.95 exercise price would give the highest expected receipts.

   (ii) $2.0240 − $2.0260/£. If the spot rate for buying dollars in three months' time is $2.0240/£ then, if purchased, the options would not be exercised as using the spot rate in three months would give a higher dollar receipt than any of the available option exercise prices. Therefore, the company would not purchase currency options.

   It must be stressed that this would leave the company exposed to foreign exchange risk, as the spot rate in three months' time could be very different to the rate forecast by the treasurer.

Solutions to problems

Problem answer 6

(a) Initial Flow

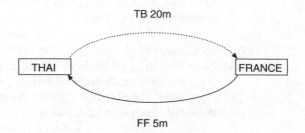

(b) Annual

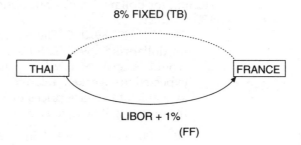

(c) Final

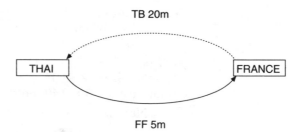

Year 1	French Co. Pays	
	$8\% \times \text{TB } 20\text{m} = \dfrac{1.6\,\text{TB}}{4}$	= FF 0.4m
	French Co. Receives	
	$(7\% + 1\%) \times \text{FF } 5$	= FF 0.4m
Year 2	French Co. Pays	
	1.6 m TB ÷ 4.10	= FF 0.3902m
	French Co. Receives	
	$(6\tfrac{1}{2}\% + 1\%) \times \text{FF } 5$	= FF 0.3750m
	Loss	FF 0.0152m

Year 3	French Co. Pays			
	1.6m TB ÷ 4.20		= FF 0.3809m	
	French Co. Receives			
	(6% + 1%) × FF 5		= FF 0.3500m	
	Loss		FF 0.0309m	
Repayment	French Co. Pays			
	20m TB ÷ 4.20		= 4.760m	
	French Co. Receives		= FF 5.000m	
	Gain		0.240m	

Problem answer 7

(a) Total world wide tax

XYZ		£164 500	
UK		97 000	
			£261 500

(b) Taxation in XYZ

Profit		1 000 000	
less interest		400 000	
		600 000	
Corp. tax (20%)		120 000	
		480 000	
Retain		240 000	
Dividends		240 000	
Withholding tax on payments to UK			
Dividends		240 000	
Royalties		250 000	
		490 000	
at 5%			24 500
Withholding tax to Caymans			
Interest		200 000	
at 10%			20 000
Taxation in Cayman Islands			
Interest received (net)		180 000	
No further tax			
Taxation in UK			
Royalties		250 000	
Dividends (gross)			
	240 000		
	60 000	300 000	
		550 000	
Tax at 33%		181 500	
Less tax credit			
Corp. tax	60 000		
Withholding	24 500		
		84 500	
UK tax to pay		£ 97 000	

(c) Summary

Retained in XYZ subsidiary			240 000
Tax paid XYZ		164 500	
UK		97 000	

Banks in XYZ – interest	261 500
	200 000
Cayman Island subsidiary	180 000
UK parent [240 000 − 24 500 − 97 000 + 250 000]	368 500
Profits and Royalties	£1 250 000

Solutions to problems

Problem answer 3

(a) The answer to this question depends heavily on what assumptions are made.

The current price/earnings (P/E) ratios of Killisick and Holbeck are:

Killisick $\dfrac{222}{14.80} = 15{:}1$

Holbeck $\dfrac{322}{29.25} = 11{:}1$

Assuming that no synergy occurs, and that the earnings available to ordinary shareholders after the acquisition is the sum of the pre-acquisition earnings for the two companies, post-acquisition earnings total £7.52 million:

Killisick has £5.18m ÷ £0.148 = 35m shares;
Holbeck has £2.34m ÷ £0.2925 = 8 m shares.

At an exchange ratio of three for two Killisick will need to issue 12m new shares.

Killisick's directors have assumed that the post-acquisition P/E ratio will be the same as Killisick's pre-acquisition P/E ratio 15:1.

The post-acquisition earnings per share =

$$\frac{£7.52m}{47m \text{ shares}} = 16p$$

The estimated post-acquisition market price of Killisick shares is 16p × 15 = 240p.

One old Holbeck share will be exchanged for 1.5 Killisick shares, giving an estimated value per old Holbeck share of:

$$240p \times 1.5 = 360p$$

Killisick's directors are engaging in what is sometimes referred to as bootstrapping the earnings per share. If no synergy occurs (including synergy through the improved management of Holbeck's assets) and if Holbeck's current share price is not undervalued in an inefficient market, it is very unlikely that the market will hold the P/E ratio of Killisick constant at 15:1. In the absence of any reasons for shareholders' wealth to increase or decrease in a reasonably efficient market, it is likely that the post-acquisition P/E ratio would be the weighted average of the two pre-acquisition P/E ratios at approximately 14:1.

If there is no change in the total market value post-acquisition, the total value will be:

Killisick 35m shares at 222p = £77 700 000
Holbeck 8m shares at 322p = £25 760 000
£103 460 000

The value will be split $\frac{35}{47}$ to existing Killisick shareholders:

= £77 044 681 or 220p per share

(or the total post-acquisition value divided by the total number of shares £103.46m ÷ 47m = 220p)

and $\frac{12}{47}$ to existing Holbeck shareholders = £26 415 319 or 330p per share.

Holbeck's shareholders experience a slight increase in wealth because the share exchange ratio of three for two is more favourable than the ratio of the companies' market prices:

$$(322 \div 222 = 1.45 \text{ for } 1 \text{ or } 2.9 \text{ for } 2).$$

This gain is at the expense of Killisick's shareholders. As Killisick is paying more than the current market value for Holbeck, the wealth of its shareholders will fall.

If any change in expected shareholder wealth occurs because of the acquisition, or if the market is not efficient, different estimated values will result.

(b) Using Killisick's estimate of its post-acquisition market price, the total post-acquisition value of the company will be:

47m × 240p	= £112.8m
Killisick's pre-acquisition value (found earlier)	= £77.7m
Gain from acquisition	= £35.1m

A total of £35.1m (in cash or the equivalent of this sum in shares or other forms of payment) could be offered without reducing the total wealth of Killisick's shareholders.

(c) A two for one share offer would value one Holbeck share at 444p or the company at £35.52m.

The current market value of Holbeck is:

$$322p \times 8m = £25.76m$$

If a two for one share offer is to be acceptable to Killisick, the expected present value of the effects of the new information must exceed £9.76m (£35.52m − £25.76m).

After tax, operating cash flows are expected to increase by £2.75m per year indefinitely. The present value to infinity of these cash flows is £2.75m/0.14 = £19.64m.

Alternatively, the present value might be calculated for a finite number of years, for example, ten years: the present value would be £2.75m × 5.216 = £14.344m.

The present value of the revenue from the sale of machinery is:

$$£7.2m \times 0.877 = £6.31m$$

The present value of redundancy cost is:

$$(£3.5m + £8.4m) \times 0.877 = (£10.87m)$$

The expected present value of the effects of the new information is:

$$£19.64m + £6.31m - £10.87m = £15.8m$$

This is in excess of the required present value of £9.76m (even if the ten-year period for operating cash flows is used). On the basis of these data, Killisick should be prepared to make a two for one offer for the shares of Holbeck.

(d) As long as the earnings streams of the two companies are not perfectly positively correlated, the riskiness of the combined earnings stream will be reduced, and the post-acquisition company will be less likely to default on its debts. This could be important, in this case, as both Killisick and Holbeck have large amounts of interest payable and therefore large amounts of debt. As the probability of default is lower, debt is less risky than it was before the acquisition and its value to the lenders of debt increases. This will probably lead to a fall in the cost of new debt for the company.

If the total post-acquisition value is unchanged and the value of debt rises, the value of equity must experience a corresponding decrease. Existing holders of debt are likely to gain at the expense of shareholders.

The shareholders may avoid some of these theoretical losses if the acquisition is partly financed by debt or additional debt is issued and used, where permitted, to repurchase equity – in both cases, making use of the increased debt capacity of the company caused by the greater earnings stability.

A well-diversified shareholder, interested only in systematic risk, will not place a higher value on the company's shares because Killisick is now a more diversified company.

Problem answer 4

(a) The first step required is to calculate the total value of the business following the merger; this requires an estimate to be made of the benefits of the merger.

The cost savings will be £40m in the first year, rising at a rate of 10% in perpetuity. We know the cost of capital is 20%. Therefore the PV of this future income stream equals:

$$\frac{£40m}{0.20 - 0.10} = £400m$$

This formula should be recognized as that used to value an equity share using the constant growth in dividend model.

The sale of surplus assets will realize £200m. This will be invested to earn a return (20%) equal to the cost of capital (20%). Its PV is therefore £200m.

The total market value post merger equals £4800m.

	No. of shares (millions)	Share price £	Market value £m
Compro PLC	600	5	3000
Vendo PLC	300	4	1200
Total market value pre-merger			4200
Benefits of merger			600
Total market value post-merger			4800

(i) Assume all benefits accrue to Compro shareholders. The benefits equal £600m. The existing market value of Compro shares equals £3000m. This is an increase of 20%.

∴ Share price increases post-merger by 20% to £6.

Therefore three existing shares in Vendo (worth £12) should be exchanged for two new shares in Compro (worth £12).

(ii) Benefits accrue to Vendo shareholders: Benefits £600m. Existing value £1200m. Total value £1800m.

The new shares offered to Vendo will have to be equal in value to £1800m. The price of Vendo shares will remain at £5.

Therefore 360m shares will need to be issued.

$$\left[\frac{1800}{5} = 360\right]$$

There are 300m existing shares. Therefore 3.6 new shares will need to be exchanged for every three existing shares.

(b) Other factors will included:
(i) the motives of the directors of Vendo;
(ii) the possibility of a rival bid.

(c) See issues discussed in textbook.

INDEX

Index